A

B O O K

The Philip E. Lilienthal imprint
honors special books
in commemoration of a man whose work
at the University of California Press from 1954 to 1979
was marked by dedication to young authors
and to high standards in the field of Asian Studies.
Friends, family, authors, and foundations have together
endowed the Lilienthal Fund, which enables the Press
to publish under this imprint selected books
in a way that reflects the taste and judgment
of a great and beloved author.

The publisher gratefully acknowledges the generous contribution to this book provided by the Philip E. Lilienthal Asian Studies Endowment, which is supported by a major gift from Sally Lilienthal.

A TRANSLUCENT MIRROR

A TRANSLUCENT MIRROR

History and Identity in Qing Imperial Ideology

PAMELA KYLE CROSSLEY

UNIVERSITY OF CALIFORNIA PRESS

BERKELEY   LOS ANGELES   LONDON

University of California Press
Berkeley and Los Angeles, California

University of California Press, Ltd.
London, England

First paperback printing 2002

Library of Congress Cataloging-in-Publication Data

Crossley, Pamela Kyle.
A translucent mirror : history and identity in Qing imperial ideology /
Pamela Kyle Crossley.
   p.   cm.
"The Philip E. Lilienthal Asian studies imprint."
Includes bibliographical references and index.
ISBN 0-520-23424-3 (pbk. : alk. paper)
1. China—Politics and government—Ch'ing dynasty, 1644–1912.
2. Nationalism—China. I. Title. II. Title: History and identity in
Qing imperial ideology.
DS754.17.C76   1999
951'.03—dc21   99-11002
                                            CIP

Manufactured in the United States of America

09 08 07 06 05 04 03 02
10 9 8 7 6 5 4 3 2 1

To the authors and editors of
Eminent Chinese of the Ch'ing Period

萬物一原

Fang Chao-ying	Tu Lien-chê
Hiromu Momose	Earl Swisher
George Kennedy	Li Man-kuei
Teng Ssu-yü	Rufus O. Suter
Yang Ju-chin	Dean R. Wickes
Tomoo Numata	L. Carrington Goodrich
M. Jean Gates	Knight Biggerstaff
S. K. Chang	Wang Chung-min
John King Fairbank	E. S. Larsen
Wu Kwang Tsing	Paul Yap Teh-lu
Tsêng Hsien-san	Feng Chia-shêng
Y. M. Chin	Tsêng Mien
Ch'i Ssu-ho	Walter Fuchs
C. H. Ts'ui	Shunzo Sakamaki
Meribeth Cameron	Hellmut Wilhelm
Alfred Kühn	Michael J. Hagerty
Wang Ch'ang-ping	William R. Leete
Cyrus H. Peake	A. V. Marakueff
Jen Tai	Thomas C. La Fargue
William J. Hail	Nancy Lee Swann
Homer H. Dubs	C. Martin Wilbur
Eduard Erkes	Arthur W. Hummel
Han Shou-hsüan	John C. Ferguson
Roswell S. Britton	A. K'ai-ming Ch'iu
Gussie Esther Gaskill	Hu Shih
Marybelle Bouchard	

Contents

Maps

Acknowledgments

This book is the culmination of a long-term project begun in 1983, interrupted in 1993, and resumed in 1995. It is consequently difficult for the acknowledgments not to read as a sort of prose *vita*. I have done my best to avoid that while trying to do some justice to the following.

Jonathan Spence's *Ts'ao Yin and the K'ang-hsi Emperor* first posed for me, during my years as an undergraduate, many of the questions of sympathy, abstraction, personality, and identity that underlie this study, and over the long term the author's guidance and intellectual companionship have made the content of this book what it is. As I have previously acknowledged, an overheard conversation involving John E. Wills Jr. in 1982 inspired me to examine the Tong lineages closely enough to open up many of the questions that underpin this study. Professor Wills has in many more deliberate ways supported this project over its protracted life, and I have consistently benefited from the attention he has paid to the intermediate forms it has assumed.

Of those whose guidance and encouragement have come in more conventional but no less influential forms are those who shaped my earliest interests in Qing history: Lillian M. Li, Jonathan D. Spence, Yü Ying-shih, Joseph Francis Fletcher Jr., Susan Naquin, Beatrice S. Bartlett, Evelyn Sakakida Rawski, and Benjamin Elman. As professionals and as friends, all provided the challenge and support that generated this study. In subsequent years I have thrived on criticism and encouragement, both generously ladled, from William T. Rowe, Morris Rossabi, R. Kent Guy, Dru Gladney, Gene R. Garthwaite, Dale F. Eickelman, Nicola di Cosmo, Frank Dikötter, and Richard von Glahn, the last of whom read and commented on the manuscript for the Press. At many points, whether in response to presentations of parts of this work, to my inquiries, or to an impulse to be helpful, I have received important comment, readings or suggestions from Sarah Allan, Harold Baker (and the participants of SEELANGS), Cheryl Boettcher, Peter Bol, Dorothy Borei, Cynthia Brokaw, Colin G. Calloway, Chia Ning, Annping Chin, Jerry Dennerline, Ruth Dunnell, Carter Eckart, Mark Elliott, Michael Ermarth, Carl Estabrook, Jack Dull, Robert Fogelin, Philippe Forêt, Gao Xiang, Shalom Goldman, Samuel Martin Grupper, Stephen Harrell, Chang Hao, Martin Heijdra, Laura Hess, James Hevia, Roland Higgins, Robert Hillenbrand, R. Po-chia Hsia, Hsiung Pingchen, Max Ko-wu Huang, Kam Tak-sing, Kang Le, Hsin-i Kao, Richard Kremer, Philip A. Kuhn, Lai Hui-min, Li Hongbin, Li Hsüeh-chih, Beatrice Forbes Manz, Victor Mair, Eugenio Menegon, David O. Morgan, Marysa Navarro, Peter Perdue, Gertraude [Roth] Li, Benjamin I. Schwartz, Helen Siu, Nathan Sivin, Justin Stearns, Donald Sutton, Lynn Struve, Frederick E. Wakeman Jr., Joanna Waley-Cohen, Arthur Waldron, Wang Peihuan, Wang Zhonghan, Ellen Widmer, Mi-chu Wiens, R. Bin Wong, Wong Young-tsu, Phillip Woodruff, Alexander Woodside, Yan Chongnian, Robin Yates, and Angela Zito.

Charles Tuttle Wood and Susan Reynolds have both gone far out of their way to scrutinize the form and content of earlier drafts of this work. As model professionals and as critics of my writing they have afforded me the rare stimulation of complementary virtues. I hope that both will see some good from their labors in these pages, paragraphs, sentences, and words. The book's present form is a direct product of their intervention, and despite its persisting faults it is vastly evolved over its preceding forms.

The completion of this, as with other work done in the same period, would have been impossible without the support of Gail Vernazza, friends and colleagues at Dartmouth, and those I should refer to as P.N., G.B. and G.L.

I am grateful to the institutions who invited me to share parts of this study and advanced the specifics of its expression: The Association for Asian Studies (1981, 1984, 1988, 1989, 1990, 1991, 1993, 1994, 1996, 1997), the American Historical Association (1982, 1991, 1997), and the American Ethnological Society (1991). Also, in chronological order beginning in 1984: the China-Japan Program, Cornell University; "Workshop on Wen and Wu" at Department of East Asian Languages and Civilizations, Harvard University; Southern California China Seminar at the University of California, Los Angeles; American Council of Learned Societies conference on "Education and Society in Late Imperial China"; Institute for Qing Historical Studies (Qingshi yanjiu suo), National Peoples' University (Renmin Daxue), Peking; Naval and Military History Circle, Whitney Humanities Center, Yale University; "Four Anniversaries" China Conference, Annapolis; Department of East Asian Languages and Cultures, Columbia University; Jackson School of International Studies, University of Washington; Premodern China Seminar, Harvard University; Mansfield Freeman Center for East Asian Studies, Wesleyan University; Program in Asian Studies, State University of New York; East Asian Languages and Civilizations Department, Harvard University; Modern China Seminar, Columbia University; Faculty Seminar, Department of History, New York University; Faculty Seminar, Department of History, Johns Hopkins University; Faculty Seminar in Race and Ethnicity, University of Texas, Austin; the Asia Program, Woodrow Wilson International Center for Scholars, Washington, D.C. (1991 and 1992); Department of History, Princeton University; Faculty Seminar on Race and Science, University of Pennsylvania; "Continuing Relevance of Traditional Chinese Institutions and Values in Modern China," Conference at the East-West Center, Honolulu; School for East Asian Studies, University of Sheffield; "China's Margins" Conference at Dartmouth College; Contemporary China Institute, School of Oriental and African Studies, University of London; Centre for Chinese Studies, Oxford; "Inventing the Past and Imagining the Future: The Construction of 'Nationhood' in Late Qing China, 1895–1912," Institute for Modern History (Chin-tai shih so), Academia Sinica (Chung-yang yen-chiu yüan), Taipei; New England China Seminar, Harvard University; Revisions Seminar at Dartmouth College sponsored by the Pat and John Rosenwald '52, Tuck '53 Research Professorship.

The research has also been facilitated by the professionalism and courtesies of the staffs of Sterling Memorial Library, Yale University; the National Palace Museum Archives (Ku-kung po-wu yüan), Nankang, Taiwan; the Wasson Collection, Cornell University; Baker Library, Dartmouth College; the Harvard-Yenching Library, Harvard University; the Bibliothèque Nationale, Paris; Gest Oriental Library, Princeton University; Library of Congress; Library of the Arthur M. Sackler Museum of Asian Art; and the Number One Historical Archives (Diyi lishi dang'an), National Palace Museum (Gugong bowu guan), Peking; federated libraries of the Academia Sinica (Chung-yang yen-chiu yüan), Nankang, Taiwan.

It is also my honor to bring to the reader's attention the financial sponsors of this work over the years, not only in gratitude but in some despair at the number of sources included here but no longer available to scholars: For my period at Yale (where the ideas underlying this study first became of interest to me): Yale University Fellowship, National Defense Foreign Languages Fellowship, the Arthur F. Wright Memorial Fellowship, the Yale Council for East Asian Studies and the Concilium for International and

Area Studies, the Mrs. Giles Whiting Fellowship. And in subsequent years: American Council of Learned Societies, Mellon Fellowship in Chinese Studies; Committee for Scholarly Communication with the People's Republic of China (National Academy of Sciences); Mary Ingraham Bunting Institute of Radcliffe College; Wang Institute Fellowship in Chinese Studies; Junior Faculty Fellowship at Dartmouth College; Marion and Jasper Whiting Foundation; Woodrow Wilson International Center for Scholars; Senior Faculty Fellowship at Dartmouth College; John Simon Guggenheim Memorial Foundation; and the Pat and John Rosenwald Research Professorship at Dartmouth College.

Final thanks go to the editorial staff at the University of California Press, especially Sue Heinemann. Sheila Levine, whose extraordinary patience with the longevity of this project has only been rewarded by my wheedling to publish all this accumulation of acknowledgments, has been both shrewd and good, both indulgent and firm—she is the sine qua non of *A Translucent Mirror*.

Friends in diverse places, some mentioned above in other capacities and some unnamed, have provided more inspiration than they can know or I can express here. As always, I claim all stubbornly persisting errors of fact, interpretation, or judgment.

Introduction

For some time the sources of modern "national" and "ethnic" identities have appeared to lie in concepts of community, solidarity, and common interest that have taken various forms over the centuries and in the past hundred years have been newly refined by print and digital media, as well as by the recession of imperialism. This appearance cannot be entirely deceptive, particularly with respect to the nineteenth and twentieth centuries, when many peoples indeed imagined themselves into communities, to abuse Benedict Anderson's phrase. The explanation has an appealing versatility, in that it can be and has been imposed upon an infinite variety of national histories. Yet no matter how well the paradigm works in describing the processes by which communitarian concepts become propagated as national identities, the substance of any particular national narrative remains elusive. The cultural bits out of which such identities have been cobbled have vastly divergent origins, and the bits themselves are not theoretically neutral or interchangeable. That being the case, the historian wonders to what extent the variety of idols available to nationalist movements in the modern era represents continuing authority of earlier times. For some nations presently existing, those "earlier times" were centuries of government by empires of conquest, whose rulerships had need of constructing categories of affiliation that would correspond to multiple, simultaneously expressed codes of legitimacy in the rulership. The Qing empire (1636–1912) had a rulership that functioned in this way, and the historical result was a legacy of historical identities that exerted distinctive influence not only upon the particulars of national and ethnic concepts emerging in the nineteenth century, but upon the fundamental concepts of identity.

During the Qing, ideas about the ruler and ideas about the ruled changed each other. Seventeenth-century expressions of the relationship of the khan Nurgaci (r. 1616–26)[1] to peoples under his dominion differed fundamentally from concepts of subordination to the first Qing emperor, Hung Taiji (r. 1627–35, 1636–43). In the eighteenth century, particularly under the Qianlong (1736–95) emperor Hongli, the ideological relationship between the ruler and the ruled completed another turn. It gained not only new complexities but new purchase on the indoctrination of aspiring officials and literate elites outside of government as the motors of conquest slowed, then rooted into pillars of civil rule. The substance of these changes may, for purposes of introduction, be crudely simplified to this paradigm: Under the khanship created by Nurgaci, a symbolic code of master to slave (these terms used after some consideration and explained in Chapters 2 and 3) was amended to a highly differentiated system of cultural and moral identities under the Qing emperorship of the later seventeenth century. In the eighteenth century, the burden of the emperorship to impersonate its diverse peoples was a primary theme in the representations—historical, literary, ideological, architectural, and personal—of universal rule. Increasingly abstract court expression of undelimited rulership required circumscription of its interior domains, so that criteria of identity were necessarily embedded in this ideology.

To readers with a general interest, the above statements may appear self-evident. To specialists, they may appear sententious and problematic. What follows immediately is unfair to every scholar working on the Qing period and the many disciplines its history encompasses; all aim to deviate from the common narrative at some significant point. Nevertheless, in the field

1. This name is more frequently written Nurhaci or Nurhachi. The names Nurgaci and Hung Taiji are extremely rare in Manchu documents; they are, however, amply attested in contemporary Chinese and Korean records. The names were well known in the early seventeenth century, but for reasons of protocol (if this can include spiritual considerations) are expunged from the imperial records. Both names, in the forms known in Manchu, occur only in the "old" Manchu script, which did not distinguish between certain consonants and vowels that the reformed script had after 1632. This means that as written the name could have been pronounced as "Nurgachi," "Nurghachi," "Nurhachi," or "Nur'achi." I have chosen to follow the known orthography, though it seems to me that authors are perfectly justified in writing the name however they imagine it might have been pronounced. In the case of Hung Taiji, there is also a choice of following Chinese romanization, so that Hong Taiji or Hongtaiji both are reasonable. Huang Taiji however is not, since it is based on a mistaken Chinese interpretation of the name. See also Chapter 3, nn 81, 82, 83.

of Qing history certain basics are accepted. The empire is considered to have been founded by, or controlled by, or given a certain political and cultural cast by, the Manchus in the early seventeenth century. Before the institutionalization of the name "Manchu," the majority population of the Qing predecessor state—the Jin, usually called the Later Jin—were the "Jurchens," whose name was attested in Chinese characters over the better part of the period from about 800 to 1636. Jurchens officially became Manchus in 1635. Apart from the Jurchens/Manchus, the Qing court recruited some Mongols and conquered China, taking the Ming capital of Peking in 1644. By that time the Qing had enlisted or impressed many Chinese who joined the Qing military organization, the Eight Banners, as "Chinese" bannermen. The Eight Banners led the assault at Peking in 1644 and during the ensuing forty years consolidated Qing control over central and southern China. The Qing rulers of the later seventeenth and early eighteenth century—foremost among them the brilliant and enduring Kangxi emperor (r. 1661–1722)—remade the court to bring it into harmony with established Chinese values, giving it stability and legitimacy that it could not gain by conquest alone. In the eighteenth century, the Qing reached its height of political control (over Manchuria, Mongolia, Chinese Turkestan, Tibet, and China, as well as the states recognizing Qing superiority in the system of court visitation, sometimes called the "tributary system"); of economic power (ensnaring Europe in an unbalanced trade relationship based on Qing exports of tea, porcelain, silk, and other goods); and of military expansion (with ongoing campaigns in Southeast Asia as well as suppression of disaffected groups—whether "ethnically" or socially defined—within the empire). This golden age was represented in the rule of the Qianlong emperor, the most "Confucian," "sinified," or simply grandest of the Qing rulers. After his abdication in 1796 and death in 1799, the empire went into a "decline," during which it became vulnerable to the expansionist, colonialist, and imperialist actions of Europe, the United States, and eventually Japan.

The most evident point of departure in the present book from this usual understanding of Qing origins and conquest is that the monolithic identities of "Manchu," "Mongol," and "Chinese" (Han) are not regarded as fundamentals, sources, or building blocks of the emergent order. In my view these identities are ideological productions of the process of imperial centralization before 1800. The dependence of the growing imperial institution upon the abstraction, elision, and incorporation of local ideologies of rulership favored the construction and broadcast—in imperial publishing,

Qing Empire Boundaries in the Qianlong Period, 1736–95

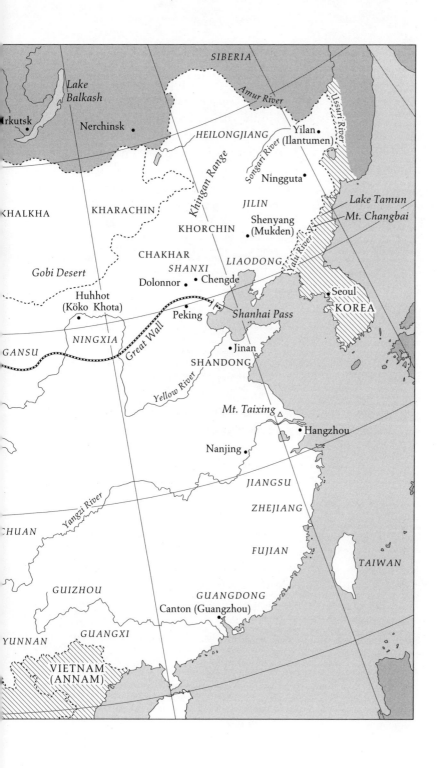

architecture, ritual, and personal representation—of what are here called "constituencies" but are usually reified as "peoples," "ethnic groups," and what were once called "races." If the precedence of these identities is removed as a motivation, other aspects of the usual narrative must also be re-examined. This particularly applies to the characterization of the Kangxi court as striving to present a "Chinese" or "Confucian" face to overcome antipathy of Chinese elites to the Manchu rulers, and to the greatness of the Qianlong era as being best understood as a zenith point in the power and influence of "Chinese" culture, or a Chinese "world order." In contrast to the more common treatment of the various peoples of the Qing empire, this work proposes that the process by which historicized identities were produced is obscured when the antiquity of those identities is accepted.

Since 1983 I have published some general ideas about the relationship of theoretically universal (culturally null) emperorship to idealized codifications of identity.[2] What remains is to attempt a more detailed account of the means of and, if possible, reasons for these synchronies of conquest, imperial ideation, and the erection of criteria of identity. The general story has many parallels in other work done on eighteenth-century China—as examples, P.-E. Will's *Bureaucracy and Famine in Eighteenth-Century China* (Stanford, 1990) and P. A. Kuhn's *Soulstealers* (Harvard, 1990), though many other works could be cited—which suggest that government elites were impatient with social, cultural, and political phenomena that were ambiguously positioned in relation to the umbrella of state influence or jurisdiction. But I have also become aware that subplots of the imperial narrative under the Qing had their cognates in other early modern empires, a reminder of the degree to which many supposed new things of the nineteenth and twentieth centuries may be seen equally well as reflexes against or revenants of the ideological legacies of the Eurasian empires.

The emphasis on continuities with the early modern period, however, should not be construed as a general proposition that remote phenomena of the medieval or ancient period are the sources of imperial expression in the early Qing. Although many elements of imperial speech or ritual will be noted as having antecedents distant in time or space from the Qing, this is not taken in any sense as explaining their uses, potency, or meaning in the period dealt with in this study.[3] In the same way, the discussion here will

2. See Crossley, "The Tong in Two Worlds"; idem, "*Manzhou yuanliu kao* and the Formalization of the Manchu Heritage"; idem, "An Introduction to the Qing Foundation Myth"; idem, *Orphan Warriors*; idem, "The Rulerships of China: A Review Article"; and idem, *The Manchus*, 112–30.

3. This should be particularly noted with respect to the word "emperor." The

often note parallels with other early modern empires. But this book has no ambition to be a comparative work, nor is observation of parallel phenomena intended to suggest explanations for those parallels. Finally, my arguments appear to me rather strictly limited to Qing imperial ideology (as ✗✗ manifested through several media), and its relationship to concepts of identity, with no obvious import for a reinterpretation of all aspects of Qing history. "Identity" is ambiguous itself, since there are many kinds of identities, some relating to nationality, some to religion, some to gender, some to class, and so on. Though to modern observers these may seem separate phenomena, there is no reason to assume that they represent separate historical processes (a point nicely represented in the eighteenth-century catalog of Qing tribute peoples, in which male and female costumes are almost without exception represented as distinct emblems of identification).[4] Moreover, none of these species of identity would conform to "identity" in the context of the Qing empire in the seventeenth and eighteenth centuries. First, the identities dealt with are predecessors of "national" or "ethnic" identities, and not in themselves demonstrably national or ethnic;[5] second—as historians of those other sorts of identities have commented many times—by the end of the imperial period national and ethnic forms of identity occluded in public discourse every other sort of identity one could hypothesize. Ironically this book has been organized around categories of identity whose realities it is obliged to discredit; historical argument has little

---

first uses of the word (*imperator*) for a single individual with supreme secular authority and unique supernatural approval are probably to be found in the reign of Augustus (27 BCE–14 CE). But invocation of this word here on the basis of sound parallels and continuities is not meant to suggest that Roman emperors were the source for emperorship in eastern Eurasia or that peculiarities of either the Roman or the Chinese institutions are unimportant.

4. *Huang Qing zhigongtu,* see Chapter 6. The relationship between sexualizing and "orientalizing" processes is a familiar one in modern scholarship, noted as early as Edward Said's *Orientalism,* but for a study more relevant to this discussion, see Rey Chow, *Woman and Chinese Modernity,* esp. 3–33; Millward, "A Uyghur Muslim"; Dikötter, *Sex, Culture, and Modernity in China,* esp. 8–13; and Dorothy Ko's study of the coinciding markings of gender and Manchu "ethnicity" in "The Body as Attire: The Shifting Meanings of Footbinding in Seventeenth-Century China," *Journal of Women's History* 8, no. 4 (Winter 1997).

5. The phenomena relating to constituency construction with which I am dealing here do not appear to me to be the same as, but seem to predate and to have stimulated, what Dru Gladney has in the contemporary context called "overly structured identities" (see "Relational Alterity," 466–68, though this has been in one form or another the subject of a vast literature in cultural anthropology). See also Crossley, "Thinking about Ethnicity in Early Modern China" and the Postscript to this book.

choice but to acknowledge contemporary assumptions as beginnings and to tell every story backward.

More limitations should be noted. There is not much here about emperorship (or rulership) as a political factor, or about society, or about Qing history generally. Choices that had to be made regarding coverage of the period of Qing rule before 1800 aggravate these difficulties. Those periods best covered by earlier scholarship—the Kangxi (1661–1722) and Yongzheng (1723–35)—have been slighted to make room for earlier and later times.[6] I have treated some of the social and ideological mechanisms of identity in the nineteenth and early twentieth centuries in *Orphan Warriors*, and I have avoided extensive repetition in order to look at their sources. Many topics and the narratives of some individuals are broken up among two or more chapters. This has been necessary to allow the content of the book to be anchored by the two poles of rulership and of identity. I have intended that they will reflect each other in the chapter structures, and as a consequence some narrative sequences are refracted in the interests of the overall arguments. I hope that the annotation may help clarify any confusion resulting from this choice. Readers will also find that some central Qing subjects—for example, the Eight Banners (*jakūn gūsa*) and the garrisons;[7] the "tributary system;"[8] administration of the Mongol territories;[9] histo-

---

6. On the Kangxi period see Spence, *Ts'ao Yin and the K'ang-hsi Emperor;* idem, *Emperor of China: Self-Portrait of K'ang-hsi;* Kessler, *K'ang-hsi and the Consolidation of Ch'ing Rule;* on the Yongzheng period see Pei Huang, *Autocracy at Work,* and Silas Wu, *Passage to Power;* Zelin, *The Magistrate's Tael,* and Beatrice S. Bartlett, *Monarchs and Ministers* are two classic studies of the imperial administration in the Yongzheng and Qianlong eras. There are in addition many excellent specialized studies of court policy making in the early eighteenth century in particular.

7. The foundation modern study is Meng Sen, "Baqi zhidu kao" (1936), and there has been important research on individual banner or garrison histories by Ch'en Wen-shih, Okada Hidehiro, Liu Chia-chü, and others. For more general studies see Sudō, "Shinchō ni okeru Manshū chūbō no toku shusei ni kansuru ichi kō satsu"; Wu Wei-ping, "The Development and Decline of the Eight Banners" (Ph.D. diss., University of Pennsylvania, 1969); Im, *The Rise and Decline of the Eight-Banner Garrisons in the Ch'ing Period (1644–1911);* Wang Zhonghan, ed., *Manzu shi yanjiu ji;* Deng, *Qingdai baqi zidi;* Crossley, *Orphan Warriors;* and forthcoming work by Mark C. Elliott and Edward J. M. Rhoads.

8. Pelliot, "'Le Sseu-yi-kouan et le Houei-t'ong-kouan'"; Fairbank, ed., *The Chinese World Order;* Wills, *Pepper, Guns, and Parleys;* Crossley, "Structure and Symbol in the Role of the Ming-Qing Foreign Translation Bureaus"; Chia, "The Lifan Yüan in the Early Ch'ing Dynasty"; Hevia, *Cherishing Men from Afar;* Howland, *Borders of Chinese Civilization,* esp. 11–18; Wills, "Maritime China from Wang Chih to Shih Lang," esp. 204–10.

9. The best short introduction to Mongol social history is Fletcher, "The Mon-

ries of the many Muslim groups who lived within the Qing borders,[10] the peoples of the Southwest[11]—receive truncated or even eccentric treatment. Fortunately, these subjects have been studied in other works and I have had the luxury of dealing with them only where they touch upon my subject.

IDEOLOGY, RULERSHIP, AND HISTORY

The Qing emperorships took in information, gave it associative forms, and sent it back out again. No agency performing these acts starts from scratch. Ideally one could isolate each moment in the transformation and dissemination of ideas, but since this is impossible it falls to the reader to remember that none of the Qing reign periods was static in this regard, and so much less the Qing era as a whole. The dynamism of the court's constant reworkings of its historical knowledge can only be suggested. The activity in its entirety—the taking in and putting out—is regarded as "ideological," a matter explored below. What is found herein is necessarily a circumstantial case, since an ideology that announced its presence and its intentions would not be an ideology. The subject cannot be seen, heard, counted, or in any satisfactory way verified, but only inferred from the shapings of language, ceremony, political structures, and educational processes. I have keenly experienced the doubts that enter into the study of such a problem, but I believe that the preponderance of evidence affirms a genealogizing historical idiom under the middle and late Qing, linked to the universalization of the emperorship in the eighteenth century. Present theory on the past has been adamant that "history" does not exist outside its sources, which appears to me to be an insistence that historical study can-

gols: Ecological and Social Perspectives," though it focuses almost exclusively on the imperial period from Chinggis to Möngke. For general histories see also Morgan, *The Mongols;* Grousset, *The Empire of the Steppes;* Jagchid and Hyer, *Mongolia's Culture and Society;* and for the imperial period most recently, Allsen, *Mongol Imperialism;* Togan, *Flexibility and Limitations.* For the Qing period, Bawden, *The Modern History of Mongolia;* Bergholz, *The Partition of the Steppe;* Chia, "The Lifan Yüan in the Early Ch'ing Dynasty"; Fletcher, "Ch'ing Inner Asia, c.1800"; Crossley, "Making Mongols." In Chinese, perhaps the clearest and most comprehensive single volume is Zhao Yuntian, *Qingdai Menggu zhengzhi zhidu.*

10. See particularly Rossabi, "Muslim and Central Asian Revolts"; Fletcher, "Ch'ing Inner Asia, c.1800"; Lipman, *Familiar Strangers;* Gladney, *Muslim Chinese,* esp. 36–63; Millward, *Beyond the Pass.*

11. For background see Herman, "Empire in the Southwest."

not be other than an extension of the study of ideology. But the processes by which those sources are produced, are given their conceptual contours, and become matrices for the production of further documentation are often left in the abstract.[12] This study can forgo a prolonged rumination on the relationship of ideology to power, since in the instance of an imperial ideology that relationship is clear. More central are the tension between the imperial order of the eighteenth century and its own ideological past and the trace of this tension in historical sources, whether ceremonial, legal, literary, or architectural in nature.

rulership Though that still leaves a bit to be said about ideology as a theoretical consideration, I will first describe the originator of historical production: rulership. The ruler as a person is important (more important, in some instances, than one would grant at first thought), but rulership here includes all instruments that extend the governing personality of the ruler—spiritual, ritual, political, economic, and cultural.[13] Rulership may, as I have written elsewhere, be seen as an ensemble of instruments playing the dynamic role, or the ascribed dynamic role, in the governing process. It orchestrated not only the ruler himself but also the nearer circles of his lineage; the rituals he performed; the offices that managed his education, health, sexual activity, wardrobe, properties, and daily schedule; the secretariats that functioned as extensions of his hearing in the form of intelligence gathering and expedited reports or proposals; the editorial boards that functioned as extensions of his speech in the generation of military commands, civil edicts, and imperial prefaces to reprinted or newly commissioned literary works. In many instances I will refer to the inmost ranks of the ensemble as "the court," which is what most writers on Qing history have meant in employ-

---

12. Often, but not always. China studies has for some time concretely explored the relationship between historical construction and the generation of literary categories. This was given large expression in the "Four Treasuries" project of the eighteenth century, but its roots date at least to the Tang—depending on definition, perhaps much earlier—in the attempts of scholars to codify the historical revelation of culture as the evolution of literary genres. On this, see Bol, *"This Culture of Ours;"* Wilson, *Genealogy of the Way;* and Elman, *Classicism, Politics, and Kinship.*

13. "Rulership" is the grammatical equivalent of "monarchy," which is both an idea and a set of institutions. See Crossley, "The Rulerships of China." My use of rulership is partly inspired by Perry Anderson's use of "monarchy" in *Lineages of the Absolutist State.* For comparative discussions of Chinese rulership (theory and practice), primarily before the Qing, see Chan Hok-lam, *Legitimation in Imperial China;* Ames, *The Art of Rulership;* Rule, "Traditional Kingship in China"; Taylor, "Rulership in Late Imperial Chinese Orthodoxy"; and Woodside, "Emperors and the Chinese Political System."

ing the term.[14] By viewing the rulership as these orchestrated parts, one sketches out both the possibilities for consonance among them, and also the possibilities for dissonance. In the case of the Qing empire, this rulership was definitively an emperorship: a mechanism of governance over a domain in parts.[15] The Qing emperorship was in its expression what I have called "simultaneous" (in Chinese *hebi*, in Manchu *kamcime*).[16] That is, its edicts, its diaries, and its monuments were deliberately designed as imperial utterances in more than one language (at a minimum Manchu and Chinese; very commonly Manchu, Chinese, and Mongolian; and after the middle eighteenth century frequently in Manchu, Chinese, Mongolian, Tibetan, and the Arabic script of many Central Asian Muslims that is often called "Uigur"), as simultaneous expression of imperial intentions in multiple cultural frames.[17] The simultaneity was not a mere matter of practicality.

14. I believe this is generally consistent with Rawksi's definition (*The Last Emperors*, 8), though lineage infrastructure of the court is far more important to her study than to this one. This leaves aside for the moment the important exception of Bartlett's *Monarchs and Ministers*, which for good reasons distinguishes between an "inner" and an "outer" court in the differentiation of bureaucratic functions during the eighteenth century. There is some antecedent to this in Chinese political writing, especially during the late Ming when reform parties from the Donglin to the Kuangshe (see Chapter 1) proposed that the "outer" court (its lecturers, middle bureaucrats, and censors) strive against the "inner court" (primarily the eunuchs) in order to eradicate corruption and restore the moral equilibrium of the emperor. I do not believe that either use is incompatible with my proposed use here of the single word "court."

15. I have tried not to use the word "dynasty" when I am referring to an order that clearly compares to what in European history would be an "empire." A dynasty is merely the collection (often familial) of people who form the main source of action (the "dynamo") in any order—be it extremely local or extremely vast, bureaucratic or royal, legal or criminal, artistic or economic. The inner branches of the Aisin Gioro lineage are clearly a dynasty within the Qing empire, and there are many examples of successive dynasties within single empires.

16. The meaning is quite different from what George Marcus has used in discussing ethnography, which relates to the modern phenomena of "nested," "hierarchical," "dialogic," and "relational" identities (all different, but similar). As I hope this study will suggest, such identities may well have existed—virtually necessarily existed—in eighteenth-century China but were not an important part of the historicizing process by which the "constituencies" were institutionalized. See also Gladney, "Relational Alterity," 466.

17. For a study very much in the interpretive frame of this study see Waley-Cohen, "Commemorating War in Eighteenth-Century China," in which are described the stelae of the Shishang si, the memorial temple that once stood in the Fragrant Hills west of Peking and at Chengde (Rehe), inscribed with Manchu and Chinese, and in instances with Mongolian and Tibetan also; Uigur script is found in the Peking environs. There were also local monuments celebrating putative Qing victories in the Jinchuan ward, the conquest of Xinjiang, and campaigns in Guilin

Each formally written language used represented a distinct aesthetic sensibility and a distinct ethical code. In the case of each language the emperor claimed both, as both the enunciator and the object of those sensibilities and those codes. The separate grammars must, in the end, have the same meaning—the righteousness of the emperorship. Or, to use the wheel metaphor that was common among those emperorships in the eighteenth century, the separate spokes must lead to a single hub. An aesthetic and ethical vector leading away from that hub was no less than a literal as well as a metaphorical vehicle for revolution.

This simultaneity in the Qing emperorship resembled a fashion of expression used in many earlier empires of Eurasia—as far back, at least, as the Achaemenids, but most famously the Mongol Great Khans.[18] I do not mean that land empires before the early modern period were precursors of or interchangeable with the Qing empire. On the contrary, the workings of the Qing appear to me meaningfully early modern—obviating the secular/ sacred dichotomies of earlier political authority, establishing a transcendence over culture that would be the foundation of a new universalism. Nevertheless, the Qing construction of earlier empires, particularly the Tang (618–907), the Jin (1121–1234), and the Yuan (Mongol, 1272–1368), became important elements in the imperial ideologies of the seventeenth and eighteenth centuries. Certainly, elements of simultaneous expression do appear in medieval, and possibly in ancient times, and the Qing were one of those empires inheriting, elaborating on, and employing such practices, even if the context of that employment yielded an effect distinct from what can be observed in earlier periods. As a political and cultural mechanism, imperial simultaneity seems precisely captured in the word "persona," as a visage through which the voice is projected, and I will use the word in that sense. To ignore this quality of Qing emperorship risks misconstruction of the context in which Qing historical sources were formed.

persona

Faulty characterization of the mode of expression of Qing rulership, however, is not as hazardous as the assumption that "racial" or "ethnic" condi-

---

and Lhasa. I wish to distinguish the form of imperial expression being described here from utilitarian multilingual inscriptions, which are found in much earlier inscriptions in Western Asia and the Mediterranean, and in China to commemorate local religious communities from the eighth century.

18. References throughout this book to the "Mongol" empire and to "Mongol" political traditions are made only in the context of the retrospective understanding of these items, particularly in the earlier Qing period. It will be impossible to note in every case where that retrospective departs from facts knowable in the Qing period or known today.

tions can explain change in the early modern period. Such ideas continue to inspire attempts by earlier scholars to resolve Qing political culture as either more "Chinese" or more "Manchu."[19] Among the more influential was Franz Michael, who in *The Origin of Manchu Rule in China*[20] wished to defeat a notion made fashionable by Karl Wittfogel[21] that Manchu rule had definitively "alien" origins. On the basis of work done in Michael's generation (and derived from Chinese scholars of the early nationalist period), the Qing was seen as a "sinicized" regime, in which issues relating to difference—whether earlier or later in the Qing period—were often dismissed as contrived or frivolous. Until rather recently the term "sinicization" was regarded as unproblematic by historians of China, though I have argued elsewhere[22] that the concept's lack of specificity muddles issues of cause and effect and inhibits questioning of a series of received notions about how and why the Chinese language, Chinese customs, and social structures have spread to various parts of East Asia. "Assimilation" and "acculturation" are not as words or concepts denied to historians of China. This being the case, "sinicization" has no purpose other than as a vessel for a set of ideological impositions describing assimilation and acculturation as having causes and meanings with relation to China that are somehow special.[23] As an idea in the intellectual history of studies of China, "sinicization" remains interesting and important; as a theorem in contemporary discourse, it represents only a tangle of undemonstrable but sentimentally charged explanations for cultural change in East Asia. This book dwells at some length on the transformationalist ideas of the Yongzheng emperor's "Great Righteousness Resolving Confusion" of 1730, but transformationalism of the sort described here is not an early form of sinicization discourse. The ideology of the Yongzheng emperor and his predecessors was focused on moral

19. See also Crossley, *Orphan Warriors*, 224–27.
20. First published as *The Origin of Manchu Rule in China: Frontier and Bureaucracy as Interacting Forces in the Chinese Empire*, by Johns Hopkins University Press, 1942, and reissued by Octagon Books in 1965.
21. Wittfogel and Feng Chia-shêng, *History of Chinese Society*, "Introduction."
22. "Thinking about Ethnicity" and *Orphan Warriors*.
23. For a diatribe on this see Ho Ping-ti, "In Defense of Sinicization," which argues that since assimilation and acculturation have happened in China and its environs in historical times, "sinicization" is proven. Not much of the current critique of sinicization is addressed by the essay. "Sinicization" is simultaneously a characterization of and an explanation for cultural change, and accepting it entails accepting an ideology of historical causation to which Ho subscribes (attributing it to weaknesses in non-Chinese cultures, strengths in Chinese culture, and the "magnanimous spirit" of the ancient Chinese). The facts would license others to dissent.

transformation of populations through systemic exposure to Civilization; "sinicization," in contrast, can sometimes be triggered by facts no more profound than adoption of the Chinese language.

Impatience with the tautologies and historical thinness of the sinicization hypotheses later led to interpretations of the Qing as more "Manchu."[24] The politics of the eighteenth-century court have for some time been construed in terms of imputed racial allegiances and tensions. In the same vein, there have also been attempts to ascribe the Chinese defeat in the Opium War (1839–42) to preexisting "racial" conflicts in Chinese society.[25] It is important to establish a threshold for what a "racial" phenomenon is.[26] The proposition that racial differences caused things to happen in the Qing period assumes that such differences existed before the Qing state did. Through history some groups distinguish themselves from others, and there is frequent hostility between groups. Neither phenomenon appears to me to be racial. Even comment in the historical record on physical differences between groups would not qualify. Further, the attribution of physical differences to genealogical affiliations, or in modern times to some mechanism of heritability, would not yet be racial. But the explicit attribution of a fixed moral or cultural character, based on ancestral affiliations, and making individuals or groups unassimilable, or untransformable, would certainly satisfy my criteria of "racial." Indeed, in this light racism and racial thinking must always be theories of the future. In any event, "race" is nothing more in this study than a phenomenon of social, cultural, and intellectual history.[27]

24. Most recently and specifically Rawski, *The Last Emperors.* Bartlett, *Monarchs and Ministers,* stresses the political importance of the Grand Council in the eighteenth century, its domination by Manchus, and the Qianlong emperor's "preference" for Manchus, while being based in part upon Manchu documents. See also Hevia, *Cherishing Men from Afar,* 29–49.

25. On racial politics as a prelude to the Opium War see, most recently, Polachek, *The Inner Opium War.* On the ascribed role of racial conflict in the Qing loss in the Opium War see Crossley, *Orphan Warriors,* 259 n 127, and Elliott, "Bannermen and Townsmen."

26. For fuller argument see Crossley, "Thinking about Ethnicity," and the Postscript to this book. See also Sollors, *Beyond Ethnicity.* On China particularly see Dikötter, *The Discourse of Race in Modern China.*

27. It appears that one cannot be too clear about this. A previous short study by me ("Thinking about Ethnicity in Early Modern China") that as its title suggests was devoted to discursive contradictions in extant writing on "sinicization" (*hanhua*) has been taken by several writers to be commentary on assimilation and acculturation as historical processes, and at least one writer has been concerned that I have "conflated" race and ethnicity. In the essay at issue and elsewhere I have ad-

There is an implied comparison in claiming a "racial" product of eighteenth-century Qing imperial ideology, as there is in the proposition that ideology is present in the behavior of the Qing court. As used in this book, "ideology" has a basic and perhaps unsophisticated meaning. My referent is to the watershed discussions of "impressions" and the "association of *ideology* ideas" by David Hume. Some of Hume's discussion was derived from John *Humean* Locke, but it appears to me that Hume's skepticism regarding language in particular is the direct ancestor of modern discussion of ideological issues. Destutt de Tracy assigned the term "ideology" to the associative process (and "sensations" to "impressions") Hume had defined, a helpful addition. Succeeding scholars, from Kant to Todorov, who have explored the impact of social and political ideology upon individuals or societies have contributed many grace notes and specific insights into the workings of ideology, but without varying much from the basic discursive notions of Hume. Certainly, Hume's comment on identity fully covers the theoretical ground, such as it is, of the present study: " . . . all the nice and subtle questions *D* concerning personal identity can never possibly be decided, and are to be *per Hume* regarded rather as grammatical than as philosophical difficulties. Identity depends on the relations of ideas; and these relations produce identity, by means of that easy transition they occasion."[28] The early modern phenomenon of the imposition of historical identity through the process of imperial centralization has as its enduring analyst an early modern writer. Of course Hume's "identity" is essentially the problem of the differentiation of the experiencing self from what surrounds it, and not, as in many modern discussions of identity, the positioning of any self relative to social or cultural structures. But contemporary theory on ideology and identity is not consistently informed by this distinction (or cannot demonstrate a factual distinction between the processes of individuation as understood by thinkers well into the twentieth century and the processes of solidarity with which it is now associated). In any event Hume's "identity" problem is much closer to the facts of the Qing case than a twentieth-century theoretical imposition could be. A more serious objection, it seems to me, is that

---

dressed such a conflation as a property of scholarly discourse. For clarity I would repeat that I do not acknowledge race as a historical phenomenon but do confirm the existence of and importance of racial discourses in many societies at many times. And I believe that assimilation and acculturation occur, even if they are not distinguished in received discourse on "sinicization." But for alternative views of my view, see Brown, "Becoming Chinese," 42–44, and Shepherd, *Statecraft and Political Economy on the Taiwan Frontier*, 521.

28. *A Treatise of Human Nature*, Book I:321.

my use of Hume is specious; he intended his view of identity to apply to Europeans, certainly to exclude all peoples of Asia and Africa, due to his belief that morally informed cultural advance (that is, history) was the exclusive property of European peoples. Nevertheless, a part of Hume's philosophy has continued to animate modern theory on identity, memory, sentiment, and interpretation.[29] With respect to the role of emperorship particularly, Talcott Parsons pointed out that while the intake and output of ideological content could certainly affect collectivities on a national or international scale, it was also a property of "sub-collectivities," even down to a sub-collectivity of "one." In the case of the Qing emperorship, it is probably not necessary to rely upon that "one," but allowing the emperorship to be understood as an ideological "sub-collectivity" is useful and allows entry to the ideological life of the eighteenth-century Qing state.

Still, the means by which one orders one's sensation of the past (or of remains of the past) as an objectified phenomenon is not well explained by this. Herman Ooms commented upon the relationship of the contemporary historians to their subjects, "In structuring the case they want to make, they often play out one historical personality against another, one Zeitgeist against another."[30] Though Ooms continues with his reasons for disapproving of this, he is surely correct that it "often" happens, and it has affected not only historians of the present attempting to construct the past but past historians attempting to construct pasts of their own. I share Ooms' conviction[31] that the historian's task is to understand the meaning of writings in the context of their original suspension between contemporaneous

29. Goldberg, in *Racist Culture*, makes the important point that in eighteenth-century Europe racism and rationalism were indispensable to each other. In my reading this is a comment not only on content, but on function: Racism was the necessary underpinning to subject-object relations between European empires and their non-European victims, and at the same time offered an elusive hope of reintegrating the disintegrating cosmologies on which Peter Burke has made comment with respect to the public presentation of Louis XIV (see below). As I suggest elsewhere, these general observations have considerable use in understanding the Qing world of the eighteenth century, too. And, *mutatis mutandis*, one has a slight fear that Goldberg, like some other authors, has mistaken the product for the method: Presenting eighteenth-century European thought as more or less monolithic in its views and argumentation leaves unanswered the question of whether that homogeneity is not largely a result of the choice made by those of a subsequent era to enshrine such works as the "classics," the representatives, the epitome of the previous age.

30. *Tokugawa Ideology*, 6.

31. "It is the task of the historian, then, to locate those particulars that are plausible subsidiaries for the meaning that is already located in the text" (*Tokugawa Ideology*, 11).

writers and readers—for though writers may anticipate the existence of future readers, they cannot foresee those readers' language. This study, in turn, shares Ooms' goal of placing texts and individuals within the larger frame of changing rulership. I hope this discussion will provide a reminder that "historicism" is not a problem whose fundamental conceptual mechanics are limited to the "West." Edward Said commented on this in 1978 and in 1985, to the effect that historicizing premised on a concept of time and change leading toward the triumph of Western rationalism (of which historicizing itself is a part) and the perceived deviance of other cultures were constructs from which historians had not freed themselves (and to which putative "new" historicists adhered in spite of their protestations). Partly under the inspiration of Said's own suggestions but more as a result of over-credulous adaptation of his writings, Said's ideas have been transmitted as the tenet that only the imperializing West historicized in this self-referential way and deformed the epistemological field for large masses of humanity. The nineteenth and twentieth centuries certainly have been affected by European and American historicisms to a degree that earlier cultural centers had not achieved. But there is reason to be skeptical that historicism is peculiarly "Western" or that historicizing by other orders had a parochial or ephemeral impact.[32] Indeed, the sort of historicizing

32. I am equally skeptical of the narrowness of Derrida's idea of "logocentrism" as a peculiar idol of European thought and as the unique self-referential quotient in the "West's" myths of rationality, superiority, and centrality. I should think that scholars of the Islamic empires would find the notion of logocentrism (except in the smallest and most technical sense) as absent from the historical theory and cultural legitimation of other traditions rather troubling. In Central Asian empires and empires based in China, a logocentrism is impossible to distill from early and enduring political expression (and this is literally true of *dao*, which means "utterance," "expression," "channel," and, best known, "way"). Post-imperial China is more problematic, though tempting: Levenson was being, I think, metaphorical but nevertheless serious in describing Maoist China as "a Word for the world, beginning with all its Bolivias." (*Revolution and Cosmopolitanism*, 25). One could possibly re-Westernize Derrida's logocentrism by insisting on an unexceptional noumenal or ideal derivation, but again, this would be easily challenged by any close examination of the origins of political and cultural ideology in China. As for the association of rationalism and imperialism, the parallels in early modern Chinese thought are also strong, and only a determined narrowness would seem capable of denying comparison to Derrida's "Reason." The theory's internal contradictions have been noted by Robert C. Young (see *White Mythologies*, 9–11; 63–68), but without reference to whether truly comparable dialectical critiques cannot be found in other imperial or post-imperial cultures. On the question of very late discourses on historicism and nationalism in India and China see also Duara, *Rescuing History from the Nation*.

done by Chinese of the very early twentieth century, in which even the near past was alienated—orientalized—as "tradition," was one of the phenomena of great interest to Joseph Levenson.[33] Nevertheless, the second part of Said's observation is certainly relevant to this study: Historicism and imperialism must certainly go together, and this appears to me to be demonstrable in many case studies, even without reference to European imperialism or the massive propagating effects of nineteenth- and twentieth-century technologies.

The emperorship before 1800, then, was author of many of the sources by which the seventeenth and early eighteenth centuries can be known. Placing the emperorship as author of texts requires some notes on epistemology, ideology, and identity. For some readers it will be enough to say that the Qing emperorship, like all governing regimes, was eager to affirm its legitimacy, displace coercion with persuasion whenever possible, and maintain its hegemony over instruments of violence in its domains. This may explain why all governments need ideology but does not explain why all government ideologies—or even all imperial ideologies—are not the same. With respect to ideology in the Qing, many aspects of this book complement the only long study in English of the Qianlong emperor, Harold Kahn's *Monarchy in the Emperor's Eyes* (1971).[34] Kahn focuses on historical construction and imperial ideology ("self-image") as both the subjects and the objects of that construction. Given the prodigious literary agenda of the Qianlong period, the role of history in creating personae within the emperorship is perhaps an obvious focus of inquiry. But where Kahn finds the Qing emperors to have been indifferent in their accomplishments in the study of conventional philosophical works, I find the emperors to have been indifferent to the philosophy itself. Where Kahn describes the emperors cultivating a conventionalized imperial demeanor based on abstractions from Chinese history, I describe the crafting and use of a China-oriented imperial persona in relation to progressive historicization of a "Chinese" identity and attempt to place this process alongside a series of other pro-

33. Levenson's first publication of the "Confucian"/"Modern" argument in book form was in the 1958 edition of *Confucian China and Its Modern Fate*, later restructured, augmented, and revised, leading to *Modern China and Its Confucian Past: The Problem of Intellectual Continuity* in 1964. The original book was enlarged again into a "trilogy" and published in 1968 by the University of California Press.

34. Kahn has supplemented his characterization of the Qianlong reign with his study of the Qianlong love of display, "A Matter of Taste." See also Chun-shu Chang's short study of imperial presentation in "Emperorship in Eighteenth-Century China."

cesses that were equally fundamental to Qing rule. Where Kahn finds little ideological import in the wide range of Buddhist imagery, cultic initiations, and shamanic[35] activities of the emperors, I view them as indispensable to the coherence of imperial authority and the graduated refinement of certain constituencies within the realm. There are nevertheless points where the ground relating to ideological aspects of the Qing emperorship has been well covered by Kahn's work, and I have found little cause to revisit them.

Ideology in historical writing works backward and forward. As suggested above, the instruments of ideological propagation author views or reviews of earlier periods and also shape the narrative language(s) of succeeding

35. For background on shamanism and Tibetan Buddhism (which can be difficult to differentiate) at the Qing court, see Rawski, *The Last Emperors*, 231–63. Studies such as S. M. Shirokogoroff's and Ling Chunsheng's on early-twentieth-century people of Heilongjiang must be used with great care, though Shirokogoroff's work, in particular, often remains the only source used by those studying Tungusic or particularly Manchu shamanism (see for instance Siikala and Hoppál, *Studies on Shamanism*, 13–40). This is not to forget that Shirokogoroff placed Manchu shamanism, particularly, so firmly in the center of shamanic studies that it remains a pole around which much theoretical discussion of shamanism rotates; indeed the recent enthusiasm for international release of shaman documentaries has drawn heavily on the work of the Nationalities Institute of the Chinese Academy of Social Sciences, which since the 1950s has accumulated film of ostensibly "Manchu" (this can sometimes subsume Evenk, Hezhe [Gold], Oronchon, and other Northeastern peoples) shamanic behaviors (for discussion of some aspects of the work see Siikala and Hoppál, *Studies on Shamanism*, 191–96). Fu Yuguang and Meng Huiying's *Manzu samanjiao yanjiu* is a valuable synthesis of their own and previous fieldwork on shamanic survivals in the Northeast, Mongolia, and some parts of China, but its historical perspective cannot transcend the limitations of available information on earlier periods. The Qianlong court commissioned and published a review of imperial ritual liturgies and objects, very many of them shamanic in origin or application; see *Manju wecere metere kooli bithe*, later *Manzhou jishen jitian dianli*. For the Qing Manchus, there are specific indications that some lineages retained their patron spirits—the Šumuru clan, for instance, had venerated and continued to venerate a sable spirit. But in Liaoning in the early twentieth century, household shrines to the magpie spirit were common. See Mo Dongyin, *Manzu shi luncong*, 178–79. In light of consolidation of Qing imperial influence over the shamanic practices and folklores of Northeastern peoples, Humphrey comments (after discussion of Daur myths): "The imperial dynasty had recourse to the periphery in its attempt to define its identity and reaffirm its power. The people on the frontier, too, people who were not even Manchus, had at least one shamanic idiom of self-definition that spanned the distance between the village and the capital city in metaphors of effortless travel and self-transformation. It is a mistake to suppose that the practice of shamanism in face-to-face social groups limits its concerns to the local or restricts imagination" ("Shamanic Practices and the State in Northern Asia," 223). See also Chapter 4.

times. Indeed it is a desideratum of ideology to control the distinction between past and present, sometimes bleeding the evident ideas of one into
the other, sometimes creating new thresholds between "then" and "now."
In the case of the Qing, my attempt to see these aspects of the imperial ideology in motion is predicated upon a distinction between the evidence of
early documents and the imposed narrative that reached full form in the
Qianlong period. The problem is how to see the seventeenth century before
the eighteenth century—or, how to distinguish the presence of the eighteenth century atop the remains of the seventeenth century. By virtue of
its extraordinary expressive capacities the Qianlong court obscured much
of what it inherited from the ideologies of the Qing courts that preceded it,
though a surprising amount of earlier ideology can still be traced. It is justified to say, though it is puzzling to understand, that historians of the Qing
still have not broken the spell of the eighteenth century in interpreting the
origins of and early history of the empire. This phenomenon is more pronounced for American and European scholars, who work when they can
from published documents that were either written or last revised during
the Qianlong period. Historians from China and some from other parts of
Asia have slightly readier access to what pre-Qianlong "originals" exist. Yet
there are other reasons for the discrepancy. The following example might
at first glance appear a trivial diversion to European or American readers,
but to many Chinese and Russians today, as well as peoples without national states in Northeast Asia, its implications are burning.

Two places in the Northeast[36] have similar names: Ninggūda in present-
day Liaoning province of China and Ningguta[37] in Jilin province. In the early
seventeenth century these two places had nothing whatever to do with each
other. Ninggūda was a small settlement, once the home of the ancestors of
Nurgaci, near the borders of Ming (1368–1644) territory. Ningguta was an
isolated region of hunting, pelting, gathering, and trade in modern Jilin
province. When writing their history in the later seventeenth century, the
Qing began to suggest an identity between these two places, by the handy
device of using the Chinese characters for Ningguta to make reference to

36. The region now called "the Northeast" (*dongbei*) in Chinese encompasses
the provinces of Liaoning, Jilin, and Heilongjiang, including the Korean Autono-
mous District (*Yanbian chaoxianzu zizhi zhou*) and the UNESCO preserve at Changbaishan. Westerners have traditionally called part of the region "Manchuria."

37. This romanization is based upon the convention of *Mambun rōtō* (see *Tianming* [hereafter *TM*] 10:8:23 and elsewhere). Ninguta, which is often used by
modern geographers (perhaps to avoid the confusion being discussed here) I would
consider correct by convention.

Nurgaci's ancestors, the "six princes" of Ninggūda (who had neither been remotely like princes nor lived remotely near Ningguta).[38] How many people were deceived by this is irrelevant, since the purpose was not to falsify, but to create what I refer to as "a consistency of figuration"—in this instance, that Qing origins lay in the bosom of the traditional Northeast. In happy fulfillment of the intentions of the eighteenth-century Qing court, modern American and European scholars do indeed get themselves confused about Ninggūda and Ningguta.[39]

But the distinction between Ninggūda and Ningguta is not trivial in Russia and China, where one of the immediate concerns of the Qing court in promoting an identification of the two places remains a thorny issue. Russian scholars (led primarily by Georgii Vasil'evich Melikhov)[40] and Chinese scholars (led primarily by Ji Ping)[41] have debated the matter in the context of historical claims to the general region of the Amur River. Ji and

38. *Ningguta beile*, from *Manzhou shilu*. This term is interesting on several levels. It was a linguistic impossibility that it was ever actually applied to Nurgaci's ancestors. The place name, Ninggūda, was derived from the Jurchen terms *ninggū*, "six," and *da*, "headman." In the invented title for these progenitors, *da* has been retained (transmuted into *ta* to accommodate the Chinese characters for Ningguta) but is followed by the nonsensical repeating word *beile*, a grander term (see Chapter 3). The six headmen became not the inspiration for a place name but the "princes" of the place itself. Thus the later seventeenth century both upgraded Nurgaci's predecessors and suggested that they originated very far from their actual locality.

39. Hummel et al., *Eminent Chinese of the Ch'ing Period* (hereafter *ECCP*), spells the place near Liaodong as "Ningguta" and identifies it accurately in the account of Hōhōri (291) but with the same spelling refers to Ningguta in Jilin in the account of Kanggūri (410); two more references to Ningguta are correct. Wakeman's index refers only to a "Ningguta," the correct Chinese pinyin transcription for the characters used to transcribe the Jilin place-name. Like the index, the citations for this "Ningguta" unwittingly treat the two places as if they are one. Thus, 47 n 58 apparently intends to state that Hūlan Hada (see Chapter 3) was another name for "Ningguta" (not literally correct, but the two places were very close if Ninggūda is in fact intended). The next reference (370 n 163) to "Ningguta" is as the place of exile of Hong Chengchou—this is indeed Ningguta, the place in Jilin. Next comes "Ningguta," mysteriously removed to Heilongjiang, as the place where women seized in the conquest of Nanjing were seen during the Kangxi years as aged and abused captives. Finally "Ningguta" comes back again (1000 n 28) as the place in Jilin to which Zhang Jinyan was exiled. So far as I can see, the first mention of Ningguta in Jilin in the Manchu annals occurs for 1626, when some "military guard people" (*tuwakiyara coohai niyalma*, later the normal Manchu term for "garrison") were sent there (*TM* 10:2:18).

40. Melikhov's studies on the subject have been drawn together in *Man'chzhury na Severo-Vostoke*. See also Chapter 4, n 46.

41. The responses were primarily published in the journal *Lishi yanjiu*, in 1974 and 1975. In addition to those authored by Ji Ping, there are additional contributions by Shi Youxin, Liang Xiao, You Shengwu, and others. In those days *Lishi yan-*

others argue that because the Qing imperial lineage were originally part of the cultural population that had lived in the Amur region for thousands of years and because they created a unified rule over China and the Northeast, this is legitimately Chinese territory. Melikhov and others replied that Jilin and Heilongjiang (from the upper bend of the Amur[42] to the northern border of Korea, including the Qing sacred mountain of Changbai) were not the ancestral territory of the Qing but were merely constructed as such in imperial documents of the seventeenth and eighteenth centuries; that the peoples of the area acknowledged suzerainty to the Romanovs before the Qing, expressed in their payment of tax or tribute in the middle seventeenth century; and that the area was only superficially controlled by Qing troops after violent campaigns of conquest in the later seventeenth century.

Boundary marking, nominalizing, historicizing, and valorizing are now frequently cited as the capacities of "centers," "hegemons," and other power orders. In this book these faculties are more specifically related to imperial expression in the earlier Qing period.[43] The "Ningguta" problem is an example not only of the ways in which historical facts relating to boundary marking may appear trivial or momentous from the various perspectives of historians today but also of the importance of attempting to disentangle successive layers of historical authority in the Qing record. In theory few readers should object to this, though in practice disentangling present from past habits of thought and expression is doomed never to be perfectly realized. Yet without the attempt knowledge that before the later seventeenth century was not really obscure would remain obscured today, and our ability either to discern the workings of eighteenth-century imperial ideology or to guess its motives would be obstructed. There is no need here to ascribe comprehensive, minute, or subtle manipulation to the Qianlong court. What is important is the manifest alteration in expression (from which the historian deduces an outlook) of the rulership in this period.[44] The

alteration
_in_
expression
of the R/S.
_C/L_

---

jiu contributions were occasionally written by committee and published under pseudonyms.

42. In modern China this is the name of both a province and a river. To avoid confusion I use the name "Amur" for the river and "Heilongjiang" for the province.

43. I find my theoretical views here consonant with those reviewed very clearly in Hay, "Introduction," esp. 6–23, in Hay, ed., *Boundaries in China.*

44. My understanding of the irrelevance of intentions in this particular respect agrees with Peter Burke's (*The Fabrication of Louis XIV,* 49): "Whether or not there was a master-plan for the presentation of the king in the age of Mazarin, such a project can certainly be documented in the period which followed."

eighteenth-century changes required recasting of the history of the rise of the Qing state, of the conquest of China, and of the origins of legitimacy for the Qing empire. Disparities between public discourse and ritual, on the one hand, and covert institutions—historical, ritual, religious, and familial—on the other, produced a tendency in the eighteenth century to use the cultural authority of the court to taxonomize culture, space, and time.

The incongruities between seventeenth- and eighteenth-century evidentiary layers have inspired the title for this work. From the perspective of the Qianlong court, history might be seen as a translucent mirror, in which was reflected not only the bright present but the darkened past behind it. The metaphor of "mirror" as historical narrative having a didactic, morally informative, or partisan import was widespread throughout Eurasia, from ancient to early modern times. "Mirrors" in this sense could also be rulers, who in life or retrospectively were regarded as providing instruction for their successors. Much of this meaning of the historically instructive mirror was captured in Tang Taizong's[45] comments, "One may use bronze as a mirror to straighten one's clothes and cap; antiquity as a mirror to understand the rise and fall of states; a man as a mirror to correct one's judgment."[46] We should not be too ready to associate the mirror with reflection of oneself, though modern academic theory predisposes us to see all as our own projection and to regard self-narrative as the only authentic enterprise. In earlier uses, "mirror"—whether the historical narrative, the model ruler from the past, or the tool used to inspect one's own image—was associated with words for looking, and especially for "light." The ability to capture light as an emanation from its supreme, original source was probably behind the magical properties attributed to mirror surfaces in early times. It is the image of light, more than self-reflection, that best applies to Qing use of "mirror": light as knowledge and intelligence (also the meaning of *sems*, the central cultic theme of the Qianlong emperor's personal religion), light as time, light as the matrix of all image and sensation. The historical mirrors intended to idealize rulership were, one expects, intended to be opaque; their sources, motives, and means were obscured, the more brilliantly to reflect the subject at hand. In this book I hope that the

45. Li Shimin (r. 627–49), second emperor of the Tang but the architect of its expansion and consolidation, especially in Central Asia. As will be discussed in Chapter 5, Tang Taizong was a special focus of ideological attention in the Qing period.

46. Quoted in Wechsler, *Mirror to the Son of Heaven*, frontispiece, from Taizong's eulogy to Wei Zheng.

back layers may be exposed (if by necessity dimly) and the images made translucent as a result.

This brings us to a point of approaching a theory of Qing documentation. I have said that the emperorship is best thought of as a loose but viable organism, or an orchestra, or a sub-collectivity, but it remains to suggest how that entity communicated its ideology to its contemporary audience and its successors. One might additionally provide a sense of the impact, if any, of that ideology upon the society or societies exposed to it, but that is a task which, with a few important exceptions, I have placed almost entirely outside this study. Still one is obliged, by common sense and all common theory, to examine the process of documentation, and here I would like to switch metaphors. The sub-collectivity of emperorship becomes a single object: a star, generating heat and light. It exists within a gravitational field, though whether the field is produced by the mass, or the mass by the field, is irresolvable and in its deepest elements imponderable. I have found it useful to think of documentation not in terms of "official" or "unofficial"[47] but in terms of a "main sequence" and an "off-sequence." The first of these terms will be recognized as lifted from the field of astronomy, where it is used to describe a star of mass sufficient to attain generation of a high rate of heat and light.[48] One might in this respect think of stars as born in nebulosity, then either aborting because of insufficient mass or beginning the consumption of internal resources that incorporates them into the main sequence. Finally they die either in diminution, cooling, and darkness or in explosion.

By the "main sequence" in Qing historical ideology I mean materials that have been used to contribute to the central ideas of the eighteenth-

47. This was the dichotomy suggested by Kahn in his approach to historical narrative in the eighteenth and nineteenth centuries (*Monarchy in the Emperor's Eyes*, 37–64), in which the court, the bureaucratic sphere, and a "private" space are demarcated and the content of some historians' writings associated with their placement in one of these implied categories. This works well enough for histories generated under the direct surveillance of the court but does not account for the fact that many "private" histories subscribed to the imperial model, while imperial works over the course of time were affected by changes in the ideological outlook of the court. The documentary model I discuss below makes a much weaker connection between the historian's personal geography with relation to the court and the outlook of his writings.

48. Astronomers amateur or professional will readily recognize that my "star" incorporates the dynamics of a proto-star (as described before the use of the Hubble space telescope) and conflates variations on main-sequence types. Such is metaphor.

main sequence -
11
sequence

century universal emperorship (the stable generation of the ideological force behind state documentation), and by "off-sequence" I mean materials that either did not lend themselves to such purposes or have been neglected for some other reason (aborted because of insufficient mass). The notion of a main sequence and an off-sequence in materials that either have been generated by the court or have come under court control (including private writings that for some reason adopt elements of the court narrative) may have a general applicability to many kinds of historical documentation. In the same way, there is a gravity in the formation of a heavy, or "orthodox," narrative that curves the perception and organization of new information and experience.[49] What is important here is not truth or falsehood but the process, to the extent it can be made visible, by which accretions in the main sequence have contributed to a powerful documentary basis for the imperial vantage, which in turn has controlled the generation of further documentation. The mode of translation from a dominating organization of sensation to the molding of language, history, and affiliation is what is under review.

In the present work, these thoughts have been brought to bear upon several forms of imperial documentation, including but not limited to the annals (*shilu*) of the reigns from Nurgaci [50] through his great-great-grandson Yinzhen (the Yongzheng emperor), the late eighteenth-century compendia "An Account of the Founding of the Qing Empire" (*Daicing gurunni fukjin*

---

49. The primary sustained English-language discussion of "orthodoxy" in the Qing context is the volume edited by Kwang-ching Liu, *Orthodoxy in Late Imperial China*. The authors offer several meanings of "orthodoxy," but Liu's "Introduction" to the volume is surely most persuasive in describing orthodoxy as socially and politically applied ideas that are both "accepted" and "enforced." Liu's discussion here captures the process by which principles of interpretation are shaped and reshaped by persisting pressure by the center(s) of governance upon institutions of education, accreditation, publication, adjudication, and intimidation. Liu associates the Chinese term *lijiao* ("right and correct teaching") with orthodoxy, which does seem to me about the closest we can come (but for a different view see Chen Chiyun, in the same volume). Liu's definition has the important virtue of allowing ideology to be distinguished from orthodoxy.

50. The annals of the Nurgaci period were collated, edited, and revised in both Manchu and Chinese under the Hung Taiji court, resulting in their first printing as *Qing Taizu wuhuangdi shilu*, December 11, 1636; they were revised again for the Kangxi printing, *Qing Taizu gao huangdi shilu*, 1686. In the Qianlong period, they were reprinted twice: in 1740 and in 1781 as *Manzhou shilu tu*, *Taizu shilu tu* (with illustrations by Meng Yingzhao, a bannerman who later served as a magistrate in Anhui). The 1636 edition was reproduced under the auspices of the Japanese-sponsored Manchukuo publications office in 1932.

doro neihe bodogon i bithe, [Huang Qing] Kaiguo fanglue),[51] "General History of the Eight Banners" (*Jakūn gūsai tongjy bithe, Baqi tongzhi*), "Collected Genealogies of the Eight-Banner and Manchu Lineages" (*Manjusai mukūn hala be uheri ejehe bithe, Baqi manzhou shizu tongpu*),[52] "Researches in the Origins of the Manchus" (*Manzhou yuanliu kao*), "Rituals for the Manchu Worship of the Spirits and of Heaven" (*Manju wecere metere kooli bithe, Manzhou jishen jitian dianli*),[53] "Biographies of the Twice-Serving Ministers" (*Erchen zhuan*), and the twentieth-century composition "Draft History of the Qing" (*Qingshi gao*), derived from these sources. In total these works present a self-referential and in an ideological sense coherent imperial narrative, not very surprising since in their present form they were issued by or are directly derived from works issued by the Imperial Historiographical Office (*Guo shi guan*). A parallel sort of government production is represented by the maps, dictionaries, language primers, and encyclopedias drawn partly from the accretion of materials and published compendia of the "Translators' Bureaux" (*siyi guan*) and related offices that continually reworked the imperial "knowledge" of certain peoples foreign to the empire, living at its borders, and at the internal interstices where "Confucian" or "Chinese" culture was seen as not having completed its work by the beginning of the nineteenth century.[54] But they are supplemented by some private writings, among them [Aisin Gioro] Zhaolian's "Miscellaneous Notes from the Xiao Pavilion" (*Xiaoting zalu*), the large collation "Overview of the Unconfirmed Histories of the Qing Dynasty" (*Qingchao yeshi daguan*), and [Suwan Gūwalgiya] Jinliang's extensive series of historical essays, some based on his access to early Manchu documents in Shenyang.[55]

51. Commissioned in 1774, completed in 1786, and printed in 1789. See *ECCP*, 685, and Chapter 6. In 1926 the annotated translation into German by Erich Hauer was published; hereafter *KF*.

52. Commissioned in 1739, completed in 1745, revised in 1747; hereafter *BMST*. Since the Manchu and Chinese titles do not have quite the same meanings, and since the genealogies are not exclusively Manchu, it is difficult to know how to title this work in English. At any rate I like this better than the more cumbersome title used in *Orphan Warriors*, 21, 37.

53. The Manchu original of 1747 was not commissioned in Chinese translation until thirty years later. It is extensively discussed in Zito, *Of Body and Brush*.

54. A source that will be used here is "Illustrated Tributaries of the Qing Empire" (*Huang Qing zhigongtu*), published by the court in 1805, based on the *Zhigongtu* ("illustrations of tributaries") of 1790. This was an illustrated companion to geographical works and was so classified by the *Siku quanshu* compilers.

55. Zhaolian (1780–1833) was a descendant of Nurgaci through Daišan (see Chapter 3) and thus a collateral kinsman of the imperial lineage. *Xiaoting zalu*

There is a large pool of off-sequence materials (this can be discerned better in retrospect), which allow the formation of the main sequence to be more visible. These encompass the works of the Ming ethnographers based in the Northeast (most of these works were suppressed by the Qianlong literary encyclopedia—the "Four Treasuries" [*Siku quanshu*]);[56] the annals of the Yi court in Korea (*Yijo sillok*);[57] the records left by Korean travelers of the sixteenth and seventeenth centuries, including the famous report of Shin Chung-il;[58] private Qing writings, as those of the nineteenth-century

---

(hereafter *XZ*) was evidently completed and privately circulated in 1814 or 1815, and Zhaolian appears to have continued to add notes to a sequel (*xulu*) until about 1825. The work was not published until about 1875, when it was brought out in an edition from the printing house of Yihuan (then Prince Chun), and soon afterward a similar edition was published by the newspaper *Shunbao* in Shanghai.

56. The "Four Treasuries" is a reference both to the process and to the result of literary review, censorship, and republication that occupied the greater part of the Qianlong reign. In imitation of several earlier emperors in China (and quite possibly of emperors elsewhere in Eurasia), the Qianlong emperor established a parallel bureaucracy that would work on new histories—including the uncompleted history of the Ming empire; histories of the Qing conquest in the various regions of China, Taiwan, Mongolia, and Central Asia; and origin histories of the imperial constituencies—as well as review "all" existing literature, using "evidentiary" (see Chapter 6, n 15) techniques to discriminate between the authentic and the false, establishing criteria for good literature and bad literature, and finding treasonous writing. The encyclopedia of literature, when produced, was housed in seven imperial libraries built in China and the Northeast to house it. The best-known recent study is Guy, *The Emperor's Four Treasuries;* see also Goodrich, *The Literary Inquisition of Ch'ien-lung;* Elman, *From Philosophy to Philology,* 65–66; Wu Che-fu, *Siku quanshu xuanxiu zhi yanjiu.* For the "Four Treasuries" in the lives of the bannermen, see Crossley, *Orphan Warriors,* 123–24.

57. The annals of the Yi period in Korea have been issued in several forms, with both Japanese and Chinese annotation. The entire series, edited by Yi I-hwa, has been reissued in paper by Yogang Ch'ulp'ansa (Seoul, 1991–93), after original publication by Minjok kojŏn yŏn'guso in Pyongyang (1975–91). The series for Sunjo taewang through Sunjong (that is, volumes 373–400) are relevant to the early Qing state and its antecedents.

58. Shin's report has been briefly summarized by Giovanni Stary, "Die Struktur der Ersten Residenz des Mandschukhans Nurgaci." The manuscript was discovered in 1938 by Yi Yinsong and the next year was reproduced in *Xingjing er dao hezi jiu lao cheng,* a publication of the Manzhouguo daxue (Manchukuo University) in Mukden. It afterwards was published under the title *Kŏnju jichŏng dorok,* in Korea. In 1977 a new, corrected, and partially restored edition by Xu Huanpu was published (in *jiantizi*). It appears that the original manuscript was lost long ago, but the text was entered into the *Yijo sillok* (*Senjo reign*). A well-known but less widely consulted account is that of Shin's rough contemporary Yi Minhwan, whose account of Hetu Ala and its environs was submitted to the Yi court in 1619–20. An introduction, translation, and annotation is found in di Cosmo, "Nuove fonti sulla formazione dello stato mancese."

bannerman Sayingge, which preserve independent historical traditions; and probably other sources yet undiscovered. The Manchu materials, particularly the annals normally called "Manchu Old-Script Archives" (*Mambun rōtō*[59] and "Written Laws in Manchu" [*Manju i yargiyan kooli*]) are, to my mind, the superheated protoplasm of the Qing ideological body. They are in some ways ideologically symmetrical (unvoiced) but contain the inchoate expression of the khanal political personality, which not everyone in the empire was intended to hear. These are the most problematical documents, since they are close to the sources but all revised afterward. It would be nice to find, as one can in the case of "Written Laws of the Manchus," surviving originals with the emendations actually on the page. But these visible moments in the historicizing process are rare.

More often the transitions in imperial ideology are only suggested by the condition of extant documents and documentation about the documents. This study is heavily invested in examining the change from and the persisting tensions between the ideology of the first Qing emperorship (of the Hung Taiji through Yongzheng periods) and a second Qing emperorship under the Qianlong emperor, Hongli. It is built upon a periodization that distinguishes an early phase in state-building and identity demarcation under Nurgaci and the first reign of Hung Taiji. Paucity of surviving documentation is the superficial criterion for this, but what is of deeper interest is the relative scarcity of documents actually produced, and the minimal development of the institutions needed to produce them. A second phase is characterized as that dominated by conquest and occupation from the second Hung Taiji reign to the middle eighteenth century. In this period, not only did the capacities of the state for documentation of present and past expand very rapidly, but so did the articulation of what will be called a "transformationalist" ideology of identity. In the third phase of Qing emperorship, the progress of conquest was halted for various reasons, and at roughly the same time the ideology of the court turned sharply from a transformationalist one to another, accepting essentialist identities throughout the empire and an exclusive universal identity for the emperor. That universalist, self-referencing Qianlong emperorship was not to endure. Its expressive energies declined very rapidly after Hongli's death in 1799 (at which time he was no longer emperor in name), and its institutions mutated somewhat in the early nineteenth century. But this imperial style did not come to an end until the 1860s, in the late stages of the Taiping War

59. See also Fletcher, "Manchu Sources"; Crossley and Rawski, "Profile."

(1850–64). It was replaced by the series of archly particularist, fastidiously "Confucian"[60] regencies and aristocratic alliances that carried on the Qing imperial name and some of its symbolism until 1912.[61] This last period is of little interest in the present study, since its ideological bases were alienated from that of its predecessors and, for many reasons relating to the attenuated structure and function of the emperorship, the later Qing court neither aspired to nor attained a coherence of view and authority over documentation comparable to its predecessors. It is noted in the Postscript, however, that the enemies of this particularist, post-Taiping emperorship positioned themselves well within the universalizing imperial idioms of the seventeenth and eighteenth centuries.

CONQUEST AND THE BLESSING OF THE PAST

In recent writing on the Qing period, it has become normal to mute the ✓ characterization of the empire as a conquest regime. The reasons are various, and may all be laudable. For instance, in Japanese scholarship of some generations ago, the Qing was often classed with other empires in China— the Liao, Jin, and Yuan particularly—as a "conquest dynasty" (*seifu ōchō*). This corresponded, with too much ease, to the Chinese (and English-language) category of "non-Han" (*fei han*) "dynasties" (an improvement on the former description as "barbarian" dynasties). The resulting monolithic assumption that there were "Chinese" dynasties that were somehow not conquest dynasties, contrasted to "conquest" dynasties, all of which had

60. Since this is not an intellectual history, I do not feel obliged to define "Confucianism." This is as well, since from the perspective of the history of thought there is no such thing. From the perspective of political ideology and rhetoric, however, "Confucianism," "Confucius," "neo-Confucianism," and so on are all identifiable objects. After this Introduction, I will not put words connected to "Confucianism" in scare quotes, but the reader may mentally insert them. There is further comment in Chapter 5 on the exploitation of selected terms and exegetical practices in creation of a state rhetoric that I term, as I think a few others do, "imperial Confucianism." The general idea was to convey, through some public media, that the legitimacy of any empire was based upon its commitment to modeling state relations on those of the (prescriptive) household, by stabilizing society through the enforcement of a (natural, just, wise) hierarchy, and demanding that all in the polity conduct themselves according to the moral requirements assigned to their statuses.

61. Wright, *The Last Stand of Chinese Conservatism*; Bastide, "Official Conceptions of Imperial Authority at the End of the Qing Dynasty"; Onogawa, *Shimmatsu siji shisō kenyū*; Dikötter, *The Discourse of Race in Modern China* (esp. 61–163); and forthcoming work by Edward J. M. Rhoads and Peter Zarrow.

been perpetrated by foreign (barbarian, non-Han, alien) dynasties, was not credible. All empires in China, from that of the Qin in 221 BCE, are manifestly conquest empires, regardless of the origins of the ruling house. A related objection was against the constant focus on the "Manchus" as conquerors. It was a very old obsession, first established in Europe by the seventeenth-century histories (really journalistic accounts) of Martini and Bouvet, and was a subject of intense propagandizing by Chinese nationalists at the beginning of the twentieth century (see Postscript). This, too, came to be regarded as a distasteful subject for scholarly discourse, particularly after the rise of the policy of "nationalities unity" (*minzu tuanjie*) in the People's Republic of China, which discouraged any reference to historical conflicts between peoples construed as "Chinese" and those alien peoples who could be connected with a living "minority nationality" (*shaoshu minzu*). Since the Manchus as a people could not be conquerors, the Qing empire ("Manchu dynasty") could not be treated as a conquest empire. In modern fulfillment of the famous logic problem posed in the *Gongsun longzi* (" . . . a white horse is not a horse . . . "), a Manchu conquest was not a conquest.

Two difficulties have resulted. The first is that the received association of "Manchu" with conquest has been expunged rather than qualified, and the second is that the history of the Qing tends not to be written in its rather obvious context of conquest and occupation. On the first issue, it has long been established that the Qing forces between the time of the conquest of north China to the completion of Qing control of south China contained only a small proportion of "Manchus" (itself a complex matter of definition, as discussed in Chapters 2, 4, and 6). The conquest was effected by a diverse group of people, the overwhelming majority of whom would by any definition simply be called Chinese men—most of whom had lately been serving in the Ming armies or militia. Their leaders were largely, but not exclusively, Qing bannermen, and of the bannermen a (declining) portion were registered as "Manchu." The conquest, then, was primarily a phenomenon of Chinese fighting Chinese. One might argue, on consideration of modern as contrasted to early modern writing, that characterizing the conquest as "Manchu" is a reference not to the combatants in the field, but to the empire itself—or, to make a rare precision, its ruling family. The Aisin Gioro were certainly as "Manchu" as anybody was, and they continued an ostensibly Manchu style of rule in some aspects of their regime for centuries. But a person, or a family, is not an empire. As suggested above, nominalizing the Qing empire as "Manchu" is an error, and here the error has again been costly to historical inquiry. For though the Qing conquest was not a Manchu conquest, it was indeed a conquest.

Conquest regimes have particular ideological needs. Whether conquest is by the Qing empire in China, or by the British empire in South Africa, or by the United States of America over the middle width of the North American continent, its dynamics impose at least two imperatives. The first is that distinctions of identity between conquerors and the conquered must be plastic, subject to arbitrary alteration by the state as its needs change and its local mission metamorphoses from conquest to occupation to governance (should that sequence be completed). Second, the arbitrary alteration of identities must be legitimated by an axiomatic assertion that lines of identity—or "difference"—are in fact natural. The state does not invent them but discovers them and proceeds from that discovery to the enforcement of distinctions, whether that requires it to engage in war, in the inequitable distribution of privilege and resources, or in segregation of groups within territorial, economic, or cultural limits. It will be observed that the first of these two needs is strategic and the second ideological. Moreover, the second is, in its central meaning, a direct contradiction of the first, which is only a reflection of the latter's ideological character. But the conflict between the ideology of identity in a conquest regime and the facts of conquest dynamics is not enough to explain its particulars (which become more particular as one examines any case history). If one could assume that the ideologies of identity under conquest regimes were unexceptionally "racial," then one could draw upon points made above and suppose that conquest regimes are in need of ostensibly natural lines of identity in order to give an aspect of futurity to their enterprises; the end of conquest would be mandated only by the end of nature, or "the world"—as it happens, this is indeed where the Qing drew the limits of their moral authority. But looking, again, at the back layers and not the reflections from the mirror (that is, at the past of the event and not its future), one finds a possibly more compelling scenario. Conditions of the early modern period had created cultures all over Eurasia, Africa, and the Americas in which economic livelihoods, religions, languages, and in many cases gene pools were distributed according to the common routes of commerce, war, and pilgrimage and mixed as the flow of goods and people determined. Many of these cultures existed in environments of exclusively local political organization. Over the course of the past five hundred years, virtually all these areas came under the control of one empire or another. In this process, identities in these regions were aggressively clarified by the dynamics of conquest and the administrative practices of occupation. Very often, this produces a glamorization of genealogy, both as a genre of social or political documentation and as a metaphor.[62] The reason, I think, is not that genealogies show the depth or breadth of ancestry (which is surely the same for everybody). Rather, in imperial settings association with a written (or better, published) genealogy means that an individual's antecedents (real or fictive) have been clarified, subjected to the processes of regularization that are generally connected to some status (whether land owning or military command or access to bureaucratic office) that the court endorses. Genealogy is a sign that the individual's social identity has been objectified through the imperial documentary process; and empires have a way of persuading their subjects that objectification is an honor.

This process was so profound that at present we hardly have words to describe pre-imperial societies without recourse to distortions such as "hybrid,"[63] or "transfrontier" (since the dynamics of empire tended to promote such societies at its margins).[64] Such words, suggesting a crossing of two or more distinct layers of cultural or political orientations, may well apply to milieux at the end of imperial or colonial processes; what one wishes to avoid is confusion of these conditions with pre-imperial or un-imperial life. The need to discriminate between conquerors and conquered—and to translate individuals and groups across these lines as necessary—was fundamental. The ideological matrices for this were cultural and in some cases constructedly racial. These particular forms occur again and again in the facilitation of identity between the center of empire and its local agents of conquest and occupation. The first reason, I would suggest, was the in-

62. There is a distinct but related phenomenon of genealogical discourses in reaction to imperially imposed identity and status. Dru Gladney has characterized this in one instance as "nomadic nostalgia" (see "Relational Alterity," 461–66). These reactions seem to come after and in complex reaction to the "glamorization" I am suggesting here, even though oral genealogies have a revered place in many of the cultures of Central and Inner Asia.

63. A similar idea is called by Akhbar Abbas "hyphenation" (a precursor to a "postcultural" condition); see *Hong Kong: Culture and the Politics of Disappearance* (Minneapolis: University of Minnesota Press, 1997). But see Robert C. Young's particular objections to the ubiquity of "hybrid" in *Colonial Desire* and Dru Gladney's more general one in "Relational Alterity." In a different vein see the insightful discussion of "hybridity" in the work of John King Fairbank by Barlow, "Colonialism's Career in Postwar China Studies," 386–94, which if generalized would point to several possible routes of escape for contemporary scholarship out of the slough of hybridity.

64. See Wakeman, *The Great Enterprise*, 44 n, where he explains his adaptation of the term from the work of Philip Curtin.

escapable need to maintain subject-object relations between the imperial regime and its zones of conquest and occupation. This need was inescapable because in every instance the empires of this period were themselves the products of undistilled societies in which construction and relative place-ment of identities had been a necessary precondition to emergence of a con-quest state; to fail to establish the state's prerogative in the imposition of clarified, if fictive, identities would prevent the distillation of subject and object roles that made possible the basic elements of organization, language, hierarchy, aggression, allegiance, and submission. So far we have only got as far as "alterity"—the usefulness of identifying the Other for purposes of identifying Oneself, of justifying One's action upon the Other, and plac-ing Oneself within an aggrandizing political, cultural, or gender schema. Modern readers do not need to be told about alterity any more. Indeed it is not much use in understanding empires (in which the problem is not Other but Others), unless we go further to make distinctions between emperor-ships and other forms of conquest rule. As will be suggested in the Post-script, the conquest ideology works in markedly different ways in post-imperial environments than it did under emperorship. But across early modern Eurasia, one finds imperial ideology tending toward a universality of representation that depended not upon all-as-one (as many modern re-publican ideologies have done) but upon one-as-all, that "one" being the emperor. I have called it concentric in its political cosmology and simulta-neous in its expression.

Perhaps the most stimulating study (or suggestion of what could have been accomplished in a major study) of the role of conquest in the devel-opment of Qing emperorship has been that of Joseph F. Fletcher, Jr. (1934–84).[65] Until shortly before his death Fletcher was working on the problem of monarchical development in the post-Mongol regimes of Eurasia. Those empires with a connection to the Mongol political tradition—Fletcher con-centrated on the Qing and the Ottomans—had experienced progressive

---

65. For Fletcher's best-known work published in his lifetime, see "China and Central Asia, 1368–1884," "Ch'ing Inner Asia c. 1800," and "The Mongols: Eco-logical and Social Perspectives." Much of Fletcher's work remained in manuscript at the time of his death and has since been revised by other authors for publication. See particularly that revised, reshaped, and edited by Beatrice Manz, *Studies on Chinese and Islamic Inner Asia* (Aldershot, U.K.: Variorum, 1995), which for the first time presents in complete form Fletcher's remarkable discoveries on the con-nections among the religious cultures of West Asia and China in the eighteenth and nineteenth centuries. See also "A Bibliography of Published and Unpublished Work" printed in the issue of *Late Imperial China* dedicated to Fletcher—vol. 6, no. 2 (December 1985).

formalization in accession to rulership and gradual institutionalization of the personal power of the ruler himself. At the threshold from legitimation by a group of political peers to individual transcendent rule dependent only upon an ascribed relationship to conquering predecessors, Fletcher marked the transition from "khan" to "emperor."[66] This, in my view, corresponds to the (possibly prolonged) ideological moment discussed by other writers, at which the rulership becomes self-legitimating by rooting itself in its own constructed past rather than in contemporary mechanisms of political affirmation. In proposing a meaningful comparison between the Qing and Ottoman regimes, Fletcher was noting that in each case elements of rulership evidently transmitted from Mongol khanship had generated conflicts in institutional development. His tendency was to associate collegial rule with a conquest posture and institutionalized monarchical power with the adapted political technologies of the conquered traditions. The evolution of new, centralized, bureaucratized orders from the interplay of these two was, for Fletcher, virtually ineluctible. In his brief study of the seventeenth-century Ottomans and the Qing, he described the development of the state from one in which the khan, as a war leader, was recognized only after prolonged power struggles and attendant instability to one in which a single ruler could obviate the succession struggle through his control of the bureaucracy, the military, the aristocracy, and the instruments of dynastic domination. Whatever the factual support for Fletcher's view—which is now regarded very skeptically by Ottoman historians[67] and used so simplistically by some Qing historians that it invites skepticism there too—it is certainly the case that the process of transition from more corporate to more personal rule was much on the minds of Qing court historians, who did their best to create a retrospective imperial heritage for the Jin and Qing states, and expected this to address the strains in the political culture posed by ongoing centralization of imperial power in the earlier eighteenth century.

Emperorship must understand itself as a complete history, with interior origins, impulses, and ends. In its narrative (which must be repeatedly revised), it tends to far predate the empire it rules (indeed emperors tend to be heralded as reincarnations of "past" conquerors and simultaneous rulers,

66. Fletcher, "Turco-Mongolian Tradition in the Ottoman Empire," 251. See also Crossley, "The Rulerships of China," 1473–74.
67. Verbal criticisms are common, but for a written critique of Fletcher's larger idea and the Ottoman case, see Heywood, "'Turco-Mongolian Kingship?'" By contrast, see the Fletcher-inspired interpretation of medieval Inner Asian Turkic/early Mongolian political history in Togan, *Flexibility and Limitations*, 109–11.

whether Solomon, Ašoka, Alexander, Caesar, Constantine, Clovis, or Tang Taizong) and clearly points toward future incarnations in future empires.[68] Thus alongside of (or woven among) the prosaic bureaucratic annals and detailed narratives of episodes in linear time there exists imperial non-time (another simultaneity) of the "once-and-future" emperor—a concept that was a comfortable parallel to the personal religious concepts of the Qianlong emperor. A cogent discussion of this conflation is offered in Peter Burke's *The Fabrication of Louis XIV*, where the author contrasts imperial time, or "medallic time," to "the time of events." [69] Yet the imperial narrative is not limited to the looping of one imperial image into another. Emperorships also generate a progressive history of their own—cognate to Louis' "l'histoire du roi" [70]—that is not a national history, but the punctuated epic of the ruler's (or the dynasty's) progress as a purposive, universal conqueror.[71] Whether and under what circumstances those aspiring to lead "national" republics have appropriated these imperial narratives and agenda has been one of the great dramas of the late nineteenth and twentieth centuries.[72]

68. For discussion of this in the founding of the Safavid empire in Iran, see Garthwaite, *The Persians.*

69. Burke, *The Fabrication of Louis XIV,* 3.

70. Burke, *The Fabrication of Louis XIV,* 6–13.

71. Resistance to this time dominance could take many forms. The problem of time-rebels, of the sort represented by Lü Liuliang, will come up at various points in this book. They certainly had a concern with time discipline as a marker of legitimacy, and on the implications of this see the discussion in Hay, "The Suspension of Dynastic Time." With regard to China, and to the Qing in particular, the theoretical aspects of this become a bit confused. Hay invokes, for instance, Ricoeur's notion of an "axial moment"—that event in relation to which all other events are marked (172)—and suggests that 1644 worked as this time/space marker for writers, artists, loyalists, and so on who wished to express loyalty to the Ming by perpetuating the Ming calendar (that is, 1644 is purported to be the axial moment they flaunt). As will be suggested in Chapters 2 and 6, the Qianlong court occasionally used 1644—that is, the Great Wall—as a marker, but this was indeed occasional. Earlier markers had been 1618 (the "Seven Great Grievances" and establishment of the Jin dynasty name for Nurgaci's khanate), 1634 (the incorporation of the Chakhar khanate into the Jin rulership), 1636 (initiation of the Qing empire), and later markers would arise. This floating axial moment does not seem to fulfill Ricoeur's criteria, and indeed there is no single axial moment in Chinese history before the twentieth century; the most an eremite could achieve in time rebellion was loyalty to the last emperor of the former dynasty (the exact practice followed by Qing loyalists after demise of that empire). The only axial moment known by me to be observed by a people considering themselves Chinese is in Taiwan, the Republic of China, where secular time still begins with outbreak of the Republican revolution of 1911.

72. For a related discussion see Duara, *Rescuing History,* 17–50.

During the seventeenth and eighteenth centuries, the Qing emperorship was required to revise both its simultaneous components and its imperial narrative. Some of the changes were gradual, and all had some kind of antecedents in previous decades. But there came a strong shift with the consolidation of the rule of the Qianlong emperor, particularly from the 1740s on. Qing tolerance of the complexities and ambiguities that underlay the identities of the original conquest elite had been challenged by the uprising of the Three Feudatories in the 1670s, by the changes in cultural practice and regional affinity of the conquest forces, and by the ambitions of the court itself as it moved closer to domination not only of China but also of Mongolia, Central Asia, and Tibet. The test of the early Qing imperial ideology of cultural (and moral) transformation through imperial leadership came with the inquisition against Zeng Jing in 1730, which was remarkable not only for its subtle handling by the Yongzheng emperor but the vigorous rejection of that verdict by the yet unenthroned Hongli (soon to be the Qianlong emperor) soon after his father's death in 1735. Ultimately, the regionalist, particularist, transformationalist character of the original regime gave way before the universalist and idealist developments of the Qianlong (1736–95) era, with profound resonances for the terms of identity that would pertain in modern China and other parts of eastern Asia.

IMPERIAL UNIVERSALISM AND CIRCUMSCRIPTION OF IDENTITY

"Universalism" is sometimes used in a very hazy sense, to indicate that people of one belief assume that all other people think or should think the way they do. This appears to be what a majority of writers mean by "Confucian universalism"—that is, that "Confucians" assumed their moral system was applicable everywhere, and should be everywhere applied. In the same sense there is "Western" universalism (everybody will be happy being rational) or "American universalism" (everybody should be democratic and capitalistic). It is not clear what universalism might be contrasted to. Presumably every philosophical system is universalist, in that most have cosmological underpinnings and none known to me assume the existence of sectors corresponding to human societies in which their principles do not apply. Even relativism, which one is often instructed to contrast to universalism, is universalistic, since everything everywhere is relative. If universalism is taken to mean, then, the assumption that there are no discontinuities in the fabric of reality (that is, to coincide with a "rationalist," "objectivist," or "scientific" view of causes and effects in the world), and that truths discovered in the shadows of Ayer's Rock are by induction also truths at the juncture of Twelfth Street and Sixth Avenue, then it is still faithful to the meaning of "universe"—all things turning one way.

These reductionist comments are meant only half in jest; they have helped me to see how attempts to better define the workings of universalist philosophies or ideologies illuminate some aspects of the problem, but not all. One can use universalism in slightly more effective ways. This was done by Joseph Levenson, who contrasted the universalism of "traditional" Confucian thought to the particularism of nationalist thought. Levenson was dealing with a specific form of late Qing Confucianism based upon a universalistic historical paradigm: Civilization and its values bringing humane, orderly, creative existence to all people, largely through the medium of Chinese political transformation and subsequent world leadership. Slightly more will be said on Levenson's interpretation in the Postscript to this work, but the point here is that by contrasting the capacity to have a universalist conviction to the fragmented, particularistic, self-preserving, self-alienating wariness of nationalism, he built his famous contrast of *tianxia* ("world") to *guojia* ("the nation"). What had been "benevolent" or "righteous" or "filial" actions in the earlier ideology became "Chinese" specialisms. Not everything in political philosophy or even personal ideology, Levenson showed, was universalist.[73]

With reference to Qing emperorship, universalism can be used effectively by building a slightly different context. It is common for a reference to Chinese, or Confucian, universalism to be followed by some allusion to *tianxia*.[74] I find the equation in English writing of *tianxia* with "universe" misleading, and instead translate it as "world."[75] World is not the same as universe. Indeed, world can be not only distinguished from universe, but opposed to it: Universes, like the early modern emperorships, can contain worlds, and thus the finite, local, consistent qualities of a world contrast to

---

73. Some scholars of the Song period in particular would claim that this transition occurred earlier, but in that case the meaning is not as Levenson proposed; his discussion marked a threshold between "modernity" and "nationalism" to coincide with the ideation of "tradition," as an idol of nationalist thought.

74. For meditation on this from another perspective see Duara, "Knowledge and Power in the Discourse of Modernity," 70.

75. "World" here is used with a consciousness of the parallel meanings of the English word (*wer-eald, woruld*), the Chinese *tianxia* and its Manchu cognate *abka fejergi*, and the Tibetan *nödchöd* (part of the Qianlong emperor's personal understanding), all of which denote the human plane, as contrasted to the divine, in which time and form exist (or, in Buddhist references, give the illusion of existence).

the infinitely heterogeneous qualities of a universe. It is relevant to a discussion of the Qianlong emperor to note that many expansive religions, including branches of Zoroastrianism, Buddhism, Christianity, and Islam, with which the Qing had contact, could be said to distinguish between a "world" of the present in which their doctrines prevailed and an undelimited "universe" of the future in which there were no competing truths; a universalist ruler's mandate could parallel the teleology of such a religion, should he engage in mutual legitimation with it (as indeed the Ottomans ruled the Muslim world as sultans and caliphs, contained within the more universalist personae by which they ruled non-Muslims). By the Qianlong period, it is evident that the emperorship had assumed a style of expression that claimed the capacity to contain worlds. A frequently invoked metaphor for the position of the emperorship with respect to these worlds was the wheel, in which spokes beginning in unique places all met at a single hub. And a common feature of such imperial expression, across Eurasia, was the tendency to miniaturize, whether in encyclopedias, zoos, gardens, or curiosity cabinets. The abstract as well as concrete aspects of this will be discussed in Chapter 5. At this point it must be connected to an overt value of the early modern era, the universal man, a source for secular aspects of the universal ruler and the universal emperor. As an individual, the universal man had aspired to all art and science, and the universal ruler had patronized all, and the universal emperor had expressed all. The European idiom of the universal man was woven into the representations of the Qing emperors, primarily through the contributions of Jesuits from Joachim Bouvet to Giuseppe Castiglione. But Qing universalist representation had another source, in the transcendent pose retrospectively attributed to rulers in late medieval Central Asia and to the Great Khans of the Mongol empire; having constructed such a legacy, the Qing lay a direct claim to it.

Joseph Fletcher's interest in the ways in which the attributed universalism of the Great Khans had animated Qing political culture had some parallels in the earlier work of Michael Cherniavsky (1920–73),[76] who was also interested in the ways in which khanal traditions had informed the po-

---

76. The early part of Cherniavsky's career was dedicated to the study of the political culture and traditional institutions of rule. The theme was introduced in his 1952 doctoral thesis at Berkeley, "The Concept of the Prince in Medieval Russia, 1300–1500," and continued in his seminal article "Khan or Basileus," first published in 1959 and reprinted several times thereafter. *Tsar and People: Studies in Russian Myths*, first published by Yale in 1961 and republished by Random House in 1969 and 1971, was the last extended study by Cherniavsky on this theme, which has been little pursued since.

litical development of Eurasian land empires. Cherniavsky's case study was Romanov Russia, and his understanding of a "khan" was different from Fletcher's. For Cherniavsky, a "khan" was a proprietor, who ruled his state as his possession, standing above law and above custom. It was a resonating khanal image in Russian political tradition that permitted the transformation of the state under Peter the Great from a theocratic princedom to a secular empire. Where Fletcher had seen the khan transformed into emperor, Cherniavsky saw the competition within the early modern Russian rulership between the person of the "khan" and that of the "king" (*basileus*). The khan triumphed,[77] resulting in a new order of rule, the Petrine emperorship.

Despite differences, there remains this similarity between Cherniavsky and Fletcher: Both observed the fashion in which progressive centralization of power in land-based, early modern Eurasian empires with khanal pedigrees resulted in differentiation and transcendence of monarchy over other cultural authorities of the realm. Each noted the self-conscious transformation of the ruler into an emperor—in the Ottoman and the Russian cases, the word *imperator*[78] signaled the change. The qualities of emperorship were consistent with a developing myth of self-generation and self-sufficiency. In the Ottoman case, this was reflected in the choice of the monarchical title *pādishāh*, the reference to the self-legitimating rulership of the Il-khans as contrasted to the *sultān*, who had been endorsed by the caliph.[79] The title, when referring to a leader who sought no legitima-

77. Cherniavsky, "Khan or Basileus," 459–76. See also the remarks on Cherniavsky's work by Grupper, "The Manchu Imperial Cult of the Early Ch'ing Dynasty," 4, 28.

78. In Turkish, *imparator*, in Russian, *gosudar' imperator*. In both cases, the literal referent of the title was the Byzantine emperorship (which based its mandate upon a retrospective construction of the Roman empire as created by God to end the chaos of the political fragmentation of mankind). Mehmet II adopted it after his conquest of Constantinople in 1453, and Peter adopted it during his campaigns to wrest the city from the Ottomans. Louis XIV, though not directly engaged in the struggle for Constantinople, from afar appropriated the mantle of the Byzantine universal emperors: he reproduced work of Byzantine historians and adapted terminology of universal emperorship ("monarque de l'univers," "universe" here equated with the Byzantine *oikumene*); Burke, *The Fabrication of Louis XIV*, 184. Though the Qing knew little of and cared nothing about the furor over the loss and imagined reconquest of Constantinople, they were aware of some "medallic" elements in the European imperial narrative and managed to incorporate a reference to *ceasar*, in their cult of Geser of Ling. See Chapter 5.

79. The Seljuks, whose empire preceded that of the Il-khans in Iran, had used the title *sultān* and depended upon the Abbāsid caliphs for legitimation. The Mongols, however, had killed the last caliph of Baghdad in 1258 and the local Mongol

tion external to the group he led, was known among Turkic-speaking peoples of Central Asia before the Mongols, and after the Mongols became even more widely used; the Yongle (r. 1403–24) emperor, who of all the Ming rulers most starkly emulated the Mongol Great Khans, had used it (*Dāyming pādishāh*) in claiming simultaneous, secular supremacy in both China and Central Asia.[80] In the case of Peter the Great, the capacity of self-legitimation elevated him over his Romanov predecessors by lessening the legitimating function of the clergy. He acted the role not of a prince of the church but of a living, self-contained god (a pose adopted earlier, and for the same reason, by the Byzantine emperors from whom Peter and the Ottomans adapted their title).[81] And typically the emperorships posited an intuitive connection between themselves and their subjects which cut out not

---

regime of the Il-khans set about legitimating themselves with the title *pādīshāh*, the "ultimate, supreme" kings, a practice later continued by the Ottomans (who retained function as *sultāns*). For a succinct discussion see also Gibb and Bowen, *Islamic Society and the West*, vol. 1, *Islamic Society in the Eighteenth Century*, 33–35.

80. See the quotation of the Yongle emperor's letter to Shahrukh (addressed as a limited-domain *sultān*) in 1418 in Fletcher, "China and Central Asia," 212–13.

81. Early rulerships came before the ideologically self-contained emperorships of the period under discussion here, and so the distinctions between sacred and secular realms were more clear and functioned in ways that do not appear to have been duplicated in later eras (with respect to material treated in this book, the distinction might be made between the carefully dichotomous formulations—*khoghar ghosun*—of the medieval "White History" [*Chaghan teüke*] of the Mongols and the universalist [in S. M. Grupper's phrase, "absolutist"] ideology of the late Ming and Qing period Mahākāla cult of the *čakravartin*). In Chapter 5, the secular/sacred distinction codified in the "White History" is characterized as "Tibetan" (as contrasted to Central Asian) and contrasted to the later ideology of the Qing. The antecedents of sacred accoutrements were there in medieval legitimation ideologies to be extracted by their successors, and the Byzantine system (though having its own antecedents in Rome and elsewhere) was the direct source of important imagery for the Romanov and Ottoman courts. Moreover, Mango's description (*Byzantium*, 219) of the forbidden precincts of the Byzantine emperors will sound familiar to those contemplating the Qing, Ottoman, and Mugal periods particularly: "His palace was likewise sacred, a *domus divina*, and surrounded by a protective zone of 'apartness' (*nam imperio magna ab universis secreta debentur*). When he appeared in public, this was done through a medium of ceremonial which was a reflection of the harmonious working of the universe and was itself synonymous with order (*taxis*). His subjects communicated with him by means of acclamations which were rhythmical and repetitive as in the divine liturgy, and when received in audience prostrated themselves on the ground" (for graphic discussion of the reflection of these ideas in Ottoman imperial architecture, see Necipoglu, *Architecture, Ceremonial, and Power*). According to scholars as early as Ostrogorsky, performance of the *proskynesis*, the prostration (Chinese *ketou*, Manchu *hengkilembi*) was introduced to Europe from Persia by Alexander the Great (Mango, *Byzantium*, 192–93).

only intermediary religious and ethical but also bureaucratic agents. The Byzantine concept of *philanthropia* (which has a parallel in the Chinese imperial concept of *ren*) adapted by the Ottomans characterized this imperial "love of man": the peculiar, original insight of the emperor into the feelings, needs, and desires of people (that is, subjects). In the development of this ideology of imperial self-generation, the Ottomans, the Qing, and the Romanovs all found affirmation in self-referential poses. "The source of his power," Cherniavsky noted of Peter, "lay in itself, in its ability to conquer, rather than in any unique quality or myth of Russia."[82]

The narrative and moral autarchies achieved by these emperorships were associated with a marked abstraction in the ways they expressed or projected themselves. This was partly manifested in archetypal representations of the rulers, as in the formulaic portraits of the Ottoman and Qing emperors where dress and pose are prescribed by the imperial status of the subject and not by individuality. But the emperorship tended toward liberation from the limitations of a single cultural affiliation. The Ottomans distanced themselves from an exclusive identification with the Turks by using Arabic and Persian as the languages of the court.[83] Louis had his epigrams in Latin rather than any vernacular, and—probably in conscious imitation of Louis' model—Peter insisted that inscriptions referring to him as emperor should be in Latin rather than Greek or Russian. The point here is not so much the proximate causes of these language policies, but the consistency of their effects. Secularization under the Ottomans and under Peter removed from them the particularizations of religion (and subordination to clerical injunctions), while making more abstract and unbounded the innovative capacities of the emperorship. In the case of the Petrine emperorship particularly, the abstraction became so extreme that, as Cherniavsky observed, "a German woman could fill the position."[84]

This ideological transcendence of the emperorship allowed the state wide latitude in the manipulation and representation of cultures, even as the

82. Cherniavsky, *Tsar and People*, 89.
83. The Ottomans used many languages, including—in the period after conquest of Anatolia—Greek. In the early fifteenth century Mehmet I, usually described as motivated by Turkic enthusiasms (certainly expressed in his historical projects) and a kind of Muslim piety, banned Byzantine influences from the court. But despite a strategic reorientation of the empire toward Central Asia in the rest of the century, neither Mehmet nor his successors installed Turkish as an official language. In accord with the traditions established by the Seljuks (and continued in modified form under the Il-khans), Arabic remained the language of religion and law, Persian the medium for some administrative functions and of the arts.
84. Cherniavsky, *Tsar and People*, 91.

rulership itself was freed of cultural limitations. In Peter's case this was accomplished by retaining some archaic images having powerful cultural resonance. Thus, despite his imperiality and divinity, Peter could claim that within his enlarged self there still dwelt the traditional sentimentality of the Father of the Orthodox Church. Similarly, the Ottoman *pādishāh* and self-styled emperor would claim the dual traditional functions of *sultān* and *khalīfa,* both distinct and resident within his larger imperial self. These concentric personae were indispensable to the functioning of imperial institutions in early modern times and were frequently imitated by local power holders seeking the new cachet of the emperorships. The self-description by Selīm II is only a slightly overdone version of such sobriquet bouquets: " . . . we who are the Caliph of God Most High in this world, far and wide; the proof of the verse 'and what profits man abides in the earth'; the Solomon of Splendor, the Alexander of eminence; haloed in victory, Fārīdūn triumphant; slayer of the wicked and the infidel, guardian of the noble and the pious; the warrior in the Path, the defender of the Faith; the champion, the conqueror; the lion, son and grandson of the lion; standard-bearer of justice and righteousness, Sultān Selīm Shāh."[85] These conventional epithets were not metaphorical descriptions of the imperial roles. They were the literal enumeration of the imperial presences.

In these processes of ideological abstraction and cultural refraction, the Qing empire evinced the tendencies toward self-legitimation and ideological self-generation that paralleled the Ottoman and Romanov orders. In the seventeenth and eighteenth centuries the state underwent a transformation from a khanal to an imperial regime. Like the Ottomans and Romanovs, the Qing emperors retained their earlier monarchical structures, including a regional tradition of khanship, within their imperial selves. Weber noted, and historians have since commented, that the Qing rulership (as contrasted to the Tang, one supposes) did not experience the overt struggle against politically entrenched religious authorities, nor was society under the Qing rent by cultural realignments in the way that Europe was in the early modern period. It is true there was no "Confucian" clergy or pope, no alternative establishment (before the nineteenth century) around which dissidents could rally or whose ancient authority they could invoke. But Qing rulership had its moral enemies, who were sometimes louder and sometimes softer, and like early modern dissenters elsewhere looked to an authoritative past of their own making for language and for legitimation. To rein-

---

85. McNeill and Waldman, *The Islamic World,* 338–39.

voke the analogy used above, they were simply—for a time—outshone by
the court, which until the nineteenth century had the raw power and the
ideological resources to isolate, mutate, or obliterate (singly or in series, as
necessary) its interrogators. A rhetoric of identities emerged from these
struggles.

removing the opposition—classic model

An imperial narrative required the establishment of histories for the
values upon which the emperorship, in different periods, depended. In his
own study of the Qianlong ideology Kahn, quoting Bagehot, has suggested
one means by which definition of imperial status mirrored the definition of
common status. Elevating the emperor created value for and strongly suggested the reality of undifferentiated "equality" in his subjects (an observation that in fact works much better for the state under Nurgaci than for
the Qianlong era).[86] Cherniavsky suggested something similar, but for the
realm of historical identity, not political status. Each imperial persona derived its animation from, and remained dependent for its meaning on, a delimited audience. In this observation is found the point of contact between
ideological abstraction in the emperorship and the foundations of early
modern national identities. "By the eighteenth century the myth of the
ruler had acquired sufficient complexity, a sufficient number of different aspects, facets, and possible interpretations to perform the function of myth:
to allow individuals and groups to express, with ever-growing variety, their
personal and collective problems and aspirations within its framework."[87]
In the Romanov emperorship the church could see reflected the traditional
image of the pious prince, and the serfs could see the enduring patriarchal
figure. The gentry found in Peter a concept of the archetypal Russian. For
Cherniavsky, a "myth" of the people was a necessary corollary to the
"myth" of the ruler. The emperorship's abstraction made increasingly ideal
the identities whose expectations were putatively cast upon it. Under Peter,
the land of the Rus became the abstract Russia, and Peter extended the archetypal national entity in his innovative reference to himself as "Father of
the Fatherland" (*Otets Otechestva*).[88] Mythicizing that worked similarly,
but with a different content, is remarkable throughout the histories generated by the post-conquest Qing courts.

the common status.

moving to myth

abstraction leads to unity

Such myths were a necessary but not sufficient mechanism for the empire building in which the Qing were intensely engaged during the seventeenth and eighteenth centuries. The process required changes in the ways

86. *Monarchy in the Emperor's Eyes*, 8 n 1.
87. Cherniavsky, *Tsar and People*, 95.
88. Cherniavsky, *Tsar and People*, 80–81, 93, 99.

emperorship saw, named, ranked, and narrated its parts. New identities could be created, encouraged, or affirmed by these processes, others could be ignored, diminished, or disappeared. I call the constructed audiences to which the multiple imperial personae addressed themselves "constituencies." One could also think of these as "peoples," but there is the hazard that some readers could be led to believe that there was always a reliable historical or cultural content in these constructions. As will be underscored later, each imperial persona had of necessity to address itself to a constituency. Nominalization and historicization of these constituencies were primary functions of the conquest emperorship. In fact imperial expression tended to demand increasing rigidity in the recognition and assignment of ostensibly special qualities to the constituencies. Cultural components of simultaneous rulership were not chosen at random. The Qing, like their Eurasian predecessors and contemporaries, employed diverse idioms intended to represent the relationship between distinct and finite cultural spheres—not always strictly geographical and rarely relating to the real life of anybody—and the imperial elements as they were imbricated in the process of conquest. Those peoples, rulers, cultures, or rhetorical systems that had been instrumental in the conquest were represented, while many other cultures under Qing rule were ignored. The Qianlong era was marked by greater idealization and stereotyping of the constituencies and decreasing tolerance for those that displayed no external, conspicuous (or conspicuously representable) systematic differences from others.

Early modern emperorships needed to be able to legitimate or delegitimate certain criteria of identity. Some constituencies had to be laden with codified distinctions to become objects to which the emperorship addressed itself, and to function as presences in the imperial narrative; those less amenable to such representation were liable to be shrunken or obliterated. Since action in this respect was related in important ways to the motives of the emperorship itself, one should find examples of identity groups who did not survive the formative era of some imperial institutions. A case of this type is offered in the Chinese-martial bannermen (*hanjun baqi*),[89] who are examined in Part I. Among recent studies with a striking parallel to the problem of the Chinese-martial is Benzion Netanyahu's *The Origins of the Inquisition in Fifteenth-Century Spain*, which describes the "New Christians" as pressured by racializing criteria championed by the emerging emperorship of Ferdinand and Isabella. Netanyahu puts aside the narrative

89. For explanation of this term please see Chapter 2, n 23.

that had characterized victims of the Inquisition as Jews who had resisted forced conversion to Christianity by privately adhering to Jewish beliefs and practices.[90] Instead, using sources from the Jewish community, Netanyahu concludes that those persecuted in the Inquisition were largely not Jews who had superficially yielded to the demand for conversion. He considers the targets of the Inquisition to have been Christians descended from Spanish Jews—Conversos, Marranos, New Christians, none to be understood in the sense of "crypto-Jews," "Judaizers," or "heretics."[91] Netanyahu links the elimination of the New Christians to the necessity for the emperorship to patronize urban elites who combined anti-Semitism with economic rivalries against the New Christians. In reifying the racial axioms behind the Inquisition, the new emperorship positioned itself as a champion of orthodoxy, the protector of the peace in the cities that had experienced turmoil at the hands of discontented merchants, and inventor of a Spanish identity, consummated in the emperorship itself as the joining of Aragon and Castile, and precipitating—among other upheavals—the expulsion of the Jews in 1492.[92] Netanyahu's is an extended study of the destruction of an identity group by the imperial process, and many others could be examined.[93]

The eradication of Chinese-martial identity was far less violent, dramatic, and sudden than that visited upon Netanyahu's "New Christians" of Spain. But it shares with that story the features of an existing cultural group being newly bisected by superimposed genealogical affiliations—as the New Christians were required by the emperorship to be resolved as either Jews or Christians (Spaniards), so the mass of the Chinese-martial were eventually required to be resolved as either "Manchu" or "Han." Perhaps more profound, the crushing of these identities under the prow of advancing emperorship was repeated by historians who until recently con-

---

90. The New Christians in Amsterdam are treated in Miriam Bodian, *Hebrews of the Portuguese Nation: Conversos and Community in Early Modern Amsterdam* (Bloomington: Indiana University Press, 1997).

91. Netanyahu, *The Origins of the Inquisition in Fifteenth-Century Spain*, xvii.

92. Netanyahu, *Origins of the Inquisition*, 925–1094.

93. Spain during the Christian reconquest, culminating in the empire of Ferdinand and Isabella, is rich in cases for studying the relationship of changes in the rulership to concepts of identity. There are grounds for seeing the Spanish empire in its continental phase as the vanguard Eurasian agent for the processes of conquest, genealogization, and racialization. See also L. P. Harvey's *Islamic Spain, 1250–1500*, which in my reading is not so much a history of the period as a study of the transformation of Muslim communities into "minorities" with progressive extension of the Christian political realm. On an ideological legacy of imperial Spain see also Chapter 5 of this book.

tinued to interpret these ages of change and cultural destruction in the static vocabulary of identity that had been a leading instrument of the destruction in the first place. The Chinese-martial have not, perhaps, needed to be discovered anew. But their history and cultural identity may need to be characterized anew. In many ways, the demise of Chinese-martial identity (that is, imposition of an undifferentiated "Chinese" identity) that occupies the early part of this book was a function of the construction of "Manchu" and "Mongol" identities. The Qing court observed a distinction between the Liaodongese and the more recently incorporated populations of north China until the end of the seventeenth century, and in the middle of the eighteenth century dismantled the distinction for reasons that are well reflected in the changing imperial ideology. The result was a constructed, monolithic identity for "Chinese" (Han) under the later Qing empire.[94] Parallel processes were imposed upon Manchus, Mongols, and other peoples subject to invention as imperial constituencies. I have discussed the history of Manchu identity and more particularly its later shaping by the emergence of Chinese nationalism in my earlier work *Orphan Warriors*, and I have no wish to repeat material I treated there. The Mongol story, to the extent that it too has felt the effects of Qing imperial evolution, figures in the present discussion, though readers are advised that a great part of

---

94. There can be confusion, as many scholars have recently noted, in the use of the word "Chinese"—for instance, in the twentieth century one can be a "Chinese" (*Zhongguo ren*) without being a "Han." This is fairly easy for modern readers to understand and does not seem to require belaboring. But though this distinction would be transparent to most people now alive in China, it would have been difficult even two generations ago, and at the beginning of the twentieth century most people in China (and, indeed, elsewhere) would have found it nonsensical. The Qing emperors regularly distinguished in their Chinese writing between the "people(s) in China" and "Han" people. One of the central texts cited in this book, the Yongzheng emperor's *Dayi juemi lu*, uses the phrase "people(s) of China" (*zhongguo zhi ren*) rather than "Chinese people" (*zhongguo ren*). See also remarks on the Manchu word *nikan* in Chapter 2. One presumes that this phrasing was inspired by Manchu and its own antecedents, which much more frequently than Chinese used the genitive case to identify people "of" a certain territory (*Ming i niyalma*). This is like, but not the same as, the distinction we would now make between "Chinese" and "Han." In this book I follow a convention established by my co-authors and me in our "Introduction" to a forthcoming volume on ethnicity issues in the early Qing. "Chinese" is freely used to refer to the cultural style associated with the general region of China, and *han* to suggest a distinction based upon ostensibly genealogical criteria. For precision I have sometimes referred to "Ming Chinese," meaning the cultural complex (and those perceived to be subsumed under it) formed under and associated with the Ming empire.

early modern and modern Mongol history lies outside the perimeters of the history of Qing imperial ideology and can be followed in works with a more general historical view.

Though in the eighteenth century the Qing emperorship was mythically self-legitimating, earlier Qing rulership had not been so self-sufficient. Its *early Q* sources of political rhetoric were partly derived from peoples of Liaodong and Jilin who were enticed or coerced into subscribing to Nurgaci's leadership. Earliest of these were portions of the Jianzhou Jurchens who for some time had been led by Nurgaci's family, and close behind were the Chinese-speaking populations of Liaodong and western Jilin. Later were added portions of the Kharachin and Khorchin federations and the hunting peoples of upper Jilin and Heilongjiang. As the Nurgaci regime grew and eventually assumed the form of a khanate in 1616, it acquired a complex and not always orderly intertwining of political cultures. Under Nurgaci's successor Hung Taiji, the state attempted to view more systematically the simultaneous codes it commanded. The culmination of this early ordering process was the proclamation of the first Qing emperorship, in 1636—a prophylactic against, but not an antidote to, the profound disordering of patterns of loyalty and identity that would result from the conquest of China. This instance is a reminder that emperorships in conquest are required to create constituencies, if only to stabilize affiliations in highly destabilizing circumstances.

There is nothing new about the starting point—fungible identities in seventeenth-century Liaodong and Jilin—of this story. Owen Lattimore was able to guess that the region prior to the Ming-Qing transition was a "reservoir" in which the fluid elements of Chinese, Mongol, Korean, and native cultures swirled in response to political and economic currents.[95] From this he speculated that the Jurchens *cum* Manchus must have been cultural "chameleons," blending alternately with the Mongols, the Chinese, or the Koreans as advantage dictated. Historical work since Lattimore's time has elaborated his description of the cultural character of Liaodong and Jilin in the sixteenth and seventeenth centuries. What has not been done, however, is an examination of the interaction of those processes with the evolution of rulership. I read Lattimore's "chameleon" description of the Jurchens

95. See *Inner Asian Frontiers of China,* first issued by the National Geographic Society in 1940 and reprinted as late as 1988 (with an introduction by Alastair Lamb) by Oxford University Press. A similar idea is developed for medieval China in Eberhard, *Conquerors and Rulers,* esp. 5–11.

as an attempt—like "transfrontier," or "creole"—to give name to what is not readily named in our present vocabulary. Again following the cues of the eighteenth century, modern writers on the seventeenth century have demonstrated a very limited ability to describe seventeenth-century identities that appear to us to be ambiguous, complex, or difficult to place. The reading back of modern "racial" (now referred to, with little further qualification, as "ethnic")[96] identities to times when they did not apply is ubiquitous. A frequently invoked object of such discussion in the very late Qing is the bannerman Duanfang (1861–1911), a loyalist martyr in the 1911–12 revolution. His family, who were registered with the Tokoro lineage, claimed to have been Chinese, surnamed[97] Tao, who moved in the Wanli period (1573–1620) from Zhejiang province on the China coast to Liaodong, a largely sinophone area just outside the Great Wall, north of the Shanhai Pass. On the basis of this, Duanfang's *Eminent Chinese of the Ch'ing Period* biographer Hiromu Momose notes that, in spite of his Manchu registration, his subject was "not a full-blooded Manchu."[98] In earlier Qing times stories like that of the Tao/Tokoro lineage were not rare and were not regarded as compromising Manchu status. The idea that "blood" had anything at all to do with being a Manchu arises from a reading back of later Qing racial taxonomies to a time and place in which they did not yet exist. Unfortunately this is not a quaint, discarded notion of earlier scholarship, but continues to animate some current writing on Qing history.[99]

96. Crossley, "Thinking about Ethnicity."

97. Throughout this book I have used "surnamed" for the Chinese verb *xing*.

98. *ECCP,* 780. For more comment on the possible significance of this case for understanding "Manchu" and "Han" relations at the end of the Qing period, see forthcoming work by Edward J. M. Rhoads.

99. See, for example, the strangely two-dimensional discussion of the "ethnicity" of inhabitants of Daoyi, Liaoning, in James Lee and Cameron Campbell, *Fate and Fortune,* 7. The problem, as stated, is that eighteenth-century immigrants to the Daoyi military farm were "considered" by the Qing court as being "ethnically Han" but to outside civilians were considered "Manchu," and their descendants at present all consider themselves "Han." Since in fact the Qing court did not "consider" anybody to be "ethnically" anything, what is evidently being said here is that the eighteenth-century Qing court was aware of transferring companies of Chinese-martial bannermen, all or most of whom had genealogies tracing their ancestors to northern China, to Daoyi—or it might merely mean the bannermen in question were all registered *hanjun,* which would be a distinct matter. Civilians often abridged the identities of all bannermen to *qiren,* which in the nineteenth century could indeed be equated in casual speech to "Manchu" (which was uncommonly used). I hope that this book will make clear (as has already been argued in "The Qianlong Retrospect on the Chinese-martial Banners") that these were nor-

The ascribed "betweenness" of the Chinese-martial has captured the imagination of the field for some time. In *Ts'ao Yin and the K'ang-hsi Emperor* (1966), Jonathan Spence explored the culture of the family Cao. They had a legendary but uncertifiable origin in Shandong and had lived for generations in Liaodong province. The process of state-building in the early seventeenth century that resulted in the rise of the Qing empire brought the Cao into the Manchu fold, as "bondservants," or bound household managers, of the Qing imperial line. Spence was unwilling to portray the Cao as fully Chinese, but attributed their cultural character to generations of intimate contact with the Qing court. As a consequence the family— progenitors of the best-known Qing novelist, Cao Zhan (Xueqin, c. 1715– 63)—were, in Spence's words, "balanced between" the culture of China and the culture of the Manchus.[100] "Balanced between" evidently recalled itself to Frederic Wakeman as he worked on the central analytical passage of *The Great Enterprise* (1985). Wakeman invoked Spence's discussion of the Cao family as a prelude to his discussion of an entire class of bureaucrats (the "twice-serving officials," *erchen*, who began their careers in the Ming and continued under the Qing).[101] Many of them, Wakeman recognized, had actually come to China with the Qing, but he described that portion as "transfrontiersmen," or putative Chinese who had gone eastward from the Great Wall into Ming Liaodong, become caught up in the wars of Nurgaci and Hung Taiji to unify the Northeast, and returned to China with the new regime. They were, in Wakeman's text, the "Chinese" bannermen, the representatives of the Chinese population among the Eight Banners. They lived, like Spence's Cao family, "between."

Since the time that Spence published *Ts'ao Yin*, our general ways of talking about culture have changed surprisingly little. I would not expect myself to be alone in objecting to the idea that any culture is properly described as a balance, mixture, or amalgam of two or more others. The culture of which the Cao were exemplars was not in its own context "between," or "hybrid." It was a coherent one with a history and a discrete geographical contour. It may, however, have been without a future. Qing rhetoric of the

---

mal and predictable arrangements for the earlier empire and had nothing to do with "ethnicity" and not much to do with identity.

100. Spence, *Ts'ao Yin and the K'ang-hsi Emperor*, 53. There are some parallels here to Wittfogel's characterization of the Han of lineages of the Liao period as representing a "third culture" (that is, neither Kitan nor "Chinese"); see Wittfogel and Feng, "Introduction" to *History of Chinese Society*.

101. *The Great Enterprise*, 1016 n 62. See also Chapters 2 and 6 of this book.

late seventeenth and eighteenth centuries was inexorably eroding the historical context from which the Cao and many other families emerged. In the lifetime of Cao Zhan, the Qianlong court distilled the regional cultures of Liaodong into what it conceived as two categorical and contrasting realms, one "Chinese," one "Manchu." Thus "balanced between" reflects not a demonstrable amalgam of two antecedent cultures but the imposition of retrospective incoherence upon what in its own time was a coherent—though not homogeneous—cultural milieu. What is likely to appear to many modern readers as nameless (and in need of naming) can be shown to have been unnamed (and in need of having that process described). Obscuring the terminology of the seventeenth century by calling this group "Han" or "Chinese" bannermen is like editing the word "water" from our language and permitting only "hydrogen" and "oxygen" to be used.[102]

The writers identified here as conceptual sources of this study have insisted that the generation and the reception of the ideologies of universal emperorship were facilitated by larger social, political, and cultural changes. In my view, none of these approaches to imperial universalism in the early modern period excludes the others, and none is peculiarly applicable to only the empires on which these authors have focused. Fletcher associated the emergence of emperorship in the Qing and Ottoman contexts with the transition from conquest to stable regimes. Cherniavsky saw the invention of the Petrine rulership as marking the secularization of the state in Russia, a line of argument not inconsistent with Netanyahu's understanding of the foundation of the emperorship of Ferdinand and Isabella. Peter Burke's explanation of the meaning of the universalism of Louis XIV's representations is complex, and not precise in all its particulars. In general he argues that a local (European) epistemological reordering was in process and cen-

---

102. Discussion along these lines was nearly opened up by Lawrence Kessler, whose work on the institutional history of Chinese-martial civil officials is fundamental. In *K'ang-hsi and the Consolidation of Ch'ing Rule*, 117–18, Kessler warned against reading Fairbank's ideas of the Qing as a Manchu-Chinese "dyarchy" back before the nineteenth century, because so many officials who might otherwise be considered "Chinese" were actually "Chinese bannermen." But the discussion was truncated by Kessler's following definition of "Chinese bannermen" as "those Chinese politically allied with and controlled by Manchus." Thus, every "Chinese bannerman" being exposed as an element in Manchu political control, the early period becomes for Kessler more "Manchu" than "dyarchic." Bartlett, however, proposes a Manchu-Chinese dyarchy at the highest level of bureaucratic government for the early eighteenth century; see *Monarchs and Ministers*, 33–37, and elsewhere. Allowing for differences in definition and period, these views are not incompatible; where they contrast to the approach of this book is in permitting assumed "ethnic" phenomena to control their characterization of large expanses of Qing history.

trally featured a dissipation of the habits of "organic analogy" that had been characteristic of earlier times.[103] Concepts of cause and effect displaced theories of correspondence (in astrology and numerology, medicine, and historical thinking). This was accompanied, as historians of literature, philosophy, and science have already pointed out, by an awareness of and a theory of metaphor; reality and its representation could now be divorced—"disenchanted" in Weber's phrase—and "magic" excised from the practice of rulership. In Burke's explanation, the diminution of the influence of religious establishments and even of folk religion enhanced the centrality of emperorship. The comment underscores the irony of the way the early modern emperorship schematicized its relation to the "world." Emperorship contained worlds, and worlds comprised emperorship.

In this scenario, the ideology of universal emperorship was an attempt to encompass and on an idealized plane reintegrate the apparently disintegrating systems of culture, society, and politics of the early modern world. If the cosmos were a machine—as it was often allegorized—then emperorship would remain its pivot, its axle, its point of orientation and integration. The rulers could accommodate both the irrational (as in Louis' healing touch) and the rational, as they became the patrons of universities, encyclopedias, and philosophers.[104] The urge to control was paramount, and the universal capacity to nurture knowledge through education, publishing, libraries, and international communications was also the power to suppress it (as when Louis forbade the teaching of the dangerously dichotomous Descartes). Readers with even a cursory acquaintance with the Qing empire of the eighteenth century will see the potential points of comparison. I should like to make them clearer and to connect them to ideations of identity rooted (though not flowering) in the eighteenth century and influencing the political development of China and related territories in the nineteenth and twentieth centuries. To the extent possible, I have tried to avoid analyzing these topics as mere preludes to "nationalism." But I cannot expect to have been wholly successful, nor can I expect the reader not to remember that na-

[margin annotation: not merely preludes to nationism]

---

103. The same theme has been invoked by Antony D. Smith to examine the rise of early modern nationalism (without special reference to rulership) in *The Ethnic Revival*, 87–104, and by David Theo Goldberg to help explain the institutionalization of racial concepts (see *Racist Culture*).

104. Burke, *The Fabrication of Louis XIV*, 127–29. There are strong parallels here to Dumont's discussion of "traditional" hierarchies (which would include imperial systems) as capable of accommodating contradictions and a lack of limitations in ways that "modern" forms of political and social organization (being border-oriented rather than center-oriented) are unable to do (*Essays on Individualism*).

tionalism, whatever one may mean by that, is the next chapter of the story. There are several problems interwoven. One, already thrown profoundly into doubt by the work of Frank Dikötter and others, is the extent to which racism and nationalism could actually be distinguished from each other in radical speech in eastern Asia at the turn of this century. This depends on definitions to a great extent, but also on being able to guess what people meant in the seventeenth and eighteenth centuries, as contrasted to what people in the nineteenth century said they meant. In the Postscript I have chosen two of the most over-researched and over-written writers of the very early twentieth century, Liang Qichao and Zhang Binglin, and related selected elements in their ideas to the substance and the effects of Qing ideology. What is remarkable with each man is that he recognized that affirming the manifest tendency of humans to form groups did nothing to explain or justify racism or nationalism; for that, sources much nearer were necessary, and the historical narratives generated by the Qianlong court were indispensable. Even closer to the center of this work, each man recognized (and was in a minority in his own time for it) that the transition from an empire with an emperor to an empire without an emperor would be historic, overwhelmingly complex, and likely to end in one form or another of disaster. Their proposed solutions were different, though each showed himself strongly subject to the imperial ideologies of the eighteenth century.

PART I
THE GREAT WALL

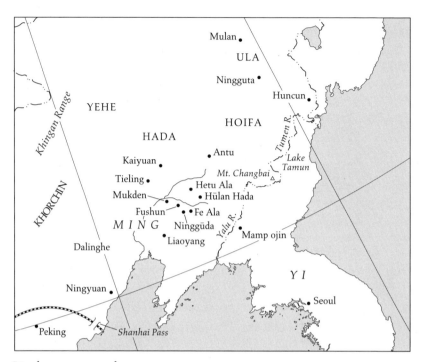

Liaodong, seventeenth century

W HEN IN THE LATE-EIGHTEENTH-CENTURY QIANLONG EM-
peror ommissioned "Biographies of Twice-Serving Officials"
(*Erchen zhuan*) and demanded a reconsideration of generals and officials
who had deserted the Ming to serve the Qing during the seventeenth-
century conquest, he allowed the Great Wall of China to mark a moral
boundary derived from a newly adopted vision of identity. Natives of China
proper—*guannei*, inside the Shanhai Pass in the Great Wall—were condemned for being faithless to the Ming, which had nurtured them when
young and granted them their examination degrees. But those who originated outside the Great Wall—*guanwai*—in the Northeast were implied to
be in a special position. Moreover, a group of long-established lineages from
the eastern trading towns of Liaodong were given distinct status within this
special category. The ancestor state of the Qing had been a regional regime,
claiming dominion over all those native to that region, regardless of their
family cultures. By imperial logic, the Liaodongese (even those who had
served as Ming officials) were not as culpable as those who originated in
China proper and later submitted to the Qing.

At the time the Qianlong emperor passed this historical judgment, the
historical source for it was obscured. The khanate from which the Qing
empire was formed took root at the eastern edge of Liaodong, at the heart
of a world dominated by Ming soldiers and Jurchen traders. Its early divisions were cultural, distinguishing the khan's sphere from that of the Chinese. From the perspective of the inhabitants of the Jurchen territories, the
"Chinese" (whom they called Nikan) were those who behaved as Chinese.
Boundaries between groups were frequently crossed from one generation
to the next, as populations moved in and out of the territories claimed by
the Ming. Jurchen lands received a steady influx of Chinese-speaking farmers and soldiers; the towns of western Liaodong received a steady influx
of Jurchen traders and mercenaries. Household cultures were complicated,
with affinities and alliances often scattered from northern China in the west
into the Jurchen territories of Nurgan in the east. Lineages with these regional characteristics, crossing the Liaodong-Nurgan frontier, were the pillars of the khanates of Nurgaci and Hung Taiji. Foremost among such lineages were the Tong of Fushun, a Liaodong garrison town at the nexus of
these cultural and political lines.

A pun current at the Qing court of the late seventeenth century was *Tong
banchao*. It meant "the Tong who fill up half the court," a fair description
of the numerous people of this name serving in very high military and bureaucratic office. It also meant "the Tong who are half the court," a reference to the fact that Empress Xiaokang, the mother of the Kangxi emperor

Xuanye, was born a Tong. The people indicated by the phrase *Tong banchao* belonged to several lineages that claimed Fushun as their ancestral home. In the early seventeenth century some of their members had been distinguished for their service to the faltering Ming regime. But others, such as Tong Yangzhen and Tong Yangxing, had in the same period become followers of Nurgaci, where they joined a well-established and politically significant sinophone population whom the Jurchens referred to as Nikan. To the early Qing state the Nikans who had lived outside the Great Wall—and consequently played a role in the creation of the empire—were different from those who lived inside the Great Wall and after 1644 occupied primarily the status of conquered people. Between 1618 and 1645 most of the Tong of Fushun came to be registered in the Chinese-martial banners. By special order, the Kangxi emperor transferred selected groups of the family to the Manchu banners in 1688; they were thereafter considered to be Manchus, past and future. The more general (though never total) transformation of this population into Manchus did not occur until 1741, by order of the Qianlong emperor. These administrative actions were accompanied by a plain ideological position adopted by the Qianlong court that the Chinese-martial banners were not to be distinguished from the Han civilian population in cultural or genealogical provenance. His well-displayed utterances on these matters became the foundation for a historical ideology subsuming Chinese-martial under "Han" identity that guided not only Qing imperial documentation thereafter but historical works, both state and private, on related topics up to the present.

The story of the Tong lineages of Fushun illuminates the seventeenth-century struggle to control and impose terms of identity on a specific population. The late Ming military official Tong Bunian was caught in the Ming conception of identity (and guilt) as defined by contours of descent. The regimes of Nurgaci and Hung Taiji of necessity repudiated this concept in their period of state-building. Instead, they marked identity by cultural and political function. In this spectrum the Nikans stood out sharply, and their history in the making of the state was recognized. But changing criteria of identity altered the political condition of the Nikans in the later view of the Qing court, and by the eighteenth century their history had been overwritten with new criteria of genealogy that obliterated much, though not all, of the historical consciousness that had driven Qing imperial and cultural ideology up to that time.

1   Trial by Identity

The Ming empire (1368–1644) was perpetually engaged in a struggle against various peoples along its northern borders. By the early seventeenth century, an elaborate set of ideas justified by allusion to ancient selected philosophical and historical texts was repeatedly invoked by the Ming court to legitimate itself in opposition to outsiders, and to justify both open warfare with and hostile border policies against unruly peoples of the north. In philosophical circles emerging materialism was often compatible with state rhetoric on the question of civilization and identity, so that issues of descent, environment, and immutable moral character combined both to make Chinese affiliations at the borders more rigid and to discredit the barbarians' political and economic organization. As a competitor with the Ming for the domination of the Liaodong region in particular, the Jianzhou Jurchen regime fostered an entirely different view of affiliation. Identity was subordination. Neither ancestors nor place of origin could override a sincere, unselfish wish to serve the Jianzhou ruler. These rival ideologies were in manifest conflict during the wars between the Ming and the Jin/Qing in the earlier seventeenth century. They also met in exquisitely precise debate over the fate of Tong Bunian and the history of the "lineage" with which he became associated.

In Ming official geography the region just outside the Great Wall, east of Shanhai Pass and north of western Korea, was Liaodong. By Qing times the Fengtian prefectural administration would subsume most of the area. But the name Liaoyang, which was also the name of a town within the district, remained common, and harked back to the administrative geography of the Jurchen Jin empire (1121–1234). Seventeenth- and eighteenth-century documents refer to the area inconsistently as Liaodong or Liaoyang. It lay within a roughly semicircular network of barriers and guard stations that marked the Ming boundary in Northeast Asia. Directly north was the territory of the Haixi, who thrived at the interface of multiple economic and cultural spheres.[1] Northeast and east of Liaodong was the vast territory called "Nurgan," where Jurchens with complex relationships to the Ming court in China and the Yi in Korea dominated a rich trade in raw goods. "Liaodong" and "Nurgan" were not only geographical entities; they respectively marked political and cultural territories that before the Qing conquest of China were critical to definition of the rulership and its constituencies. After the conquest, the shadows of "Liaodong" and "Nurgan" would continue to vex Qing attempts to define the imperial lineage, its following, and the shape and style of its dominion.

A DISCOURSE ON ANCESTRY

The town of Fushun (Manchu Fušun), just inside the Ming military pale, was the primary licensed center for trade with Nurgan.[2] In the early seventeenth century Tong Bunian, whose courtesy name (*hao*) was Babai and whose literary style (*zi*) was Guanlan, was registered at Fushun. His father, Tong Yangzhi, had been a Ming military officer posted to Kaiyuan in Liaodong. The year of Bunian's birth is not clear, but he received the Ming national examination degree (*jinshi*) in 1616, and the average age of receiving the national degree in the late imperial period appears to have been about thirty-four. His success in the examinations suggests that his family was wealthy enough to raise him to be exclusively devoted to his studies. They also had the means to support him during his travels to Shenyang,

---

1. For background see Rossabi, *The Jurchens in the Yüan and Ming;* Robert Lee, *The Manchurian Frontier in Ch'ing History.*

2. Seventeenth-century Ming gazetteers identify Nurgan as the territories occupied by the Haixi, Jianzhou, and "wild" Jurchens (the latter group subsuming the Nivkhs, Ulch, Golds, Nanni, Evenks, Orochons, Giliaks, and other groups of Northeastern Asia), which indicates undelimited territories northeast of Liaodong and north of Korea. The Wanli period (1588–1620) writer Ma Wensheng, however, considered Nurgan to be a rather discrete area one month's travel north of the Songari River, in Heilongjiang ("Fu'an Dong Yi kao," 2). This is in accord with the earlier specification of Nurgan as the immediate vicinity of the Yongning temple. The site was by the fifteenth century inhabited by Giliaks but had a century earlier been a penal colony established under the Yuan empire. See Grupper, "The Manchu Imperial Cult," 37. Generalization of the name may be been connected with the patenting of a Ming "garrison" (see below) with the Nurgan name and the tendency of such garrisons to mutate in size and location.

where he would have had to take the provincial degree (*juren*), and subsequently the Ming capital (then Peking), where he would have had to stay for weeks, or more likely months, to complete the sittings leading ultimately to the palace examinations (*dianke*). After succeeding in the examination, Bunian returned to Fushun briefly to await his first appointment. He married a woman of another Fushun family, surnamed Chen, and may have started planning his house in the town of Liaoyang, a grander and more central locality than Fushun. In 1618 his assignment came, and the next year he took up duties first as magistrate of Nanpi, Zhili, and then as the magistrate of Hejian, Zhili, near Peking. So far as is known, these successive, prestigious posts occasioned Bunian's only prolonged residence outside of Liaodong. It may have been during the period of his magistracy in Zhili that his only son, Tong Guoqi, was born at the house in Liaoyang.

In 1621 Tong Bunian was returned to his native terrain, with critical and dangerous responsibilities. He was called to serve under Xiong Tingbi (1569–1625),[3] the Ming military intendant of Liaodong. In 1618 warfare had broken out in Liaodong between the Ming and the Jianzhou Jurchens. The Jianzhou chieftain Nurgaci had announced himself khan and formed a regime announcing itself as "Jin," the name of the former Jurchen empire in the region four hundred years before. Now, Nurgaci had captured Fushun. The town's entire population, including many of the collateral members of Bunian's lineage, had been taken into the Nurgan territories.[4]

Xiong Tingbi hoped that the recruitment of Tong Bunian would help break the downward spiral of Ming defenses in Liaodong. Xiong had been stationed in Liaodong on and off since 1608. Early in his exposure to the region he had expressed alarm at the amassing of wealth and armaments by the Jianzhou. Local Jurchen groups had all federated themselves to some degree with the Ming court. They entered into the schedule of visits to Peking to make ritual obeisance to the Ming emperor and in return were given titles, stipends, and trading rights across the Ming border. Ming records give the arrangement the easily discerned fiction of a "garrison" (*weisuo*) system and identify the federations—which were in fact liable to change their location in accord with certain political, economic, or belligerent events—as military establishments, with their headmen recorded as officials.[5] A certain amount of abuse of the system was to be expected from

3. *ECCP*, 308.
4. *Qing shilu*, "Taizu wuhuangdi" 1:12.
5. See Yang Yang et al., "Mingdai liuren zai Dongbei." On Jurchen commerce with Liaodong see also Serruys, *Sino-Jürched Relations in the Yung-lo Period;* Ross-

the Jurchen. Xiong felt that the political scales had tilted too far in favor of local magnates, including but not limited to leaders of Jurchen groups in the Liaodong vicinity. He also noted the ways in which the Jurchens were amassing agricultural laborers for themselves—largely by kidnapping farmers living in border regions. Xiong attempted to impress upon the court that loyalties among the prisoners might be far more flexible than Ming officials assumed:

> Formerly the bandits were poor and hungry, and in winter and spring, when the grass was dry, their horses were as thin as sticks, and therefore we had some respite in those seasons. Recently, however, their prisoners have built shelters to live in. A great chieftain may have several thousand prisoners and émigrés; a small one, a thousand. They make the laborers cultivate the land, and hand over grain and fodder, so that both men and horses are fed, and they can move against us at any time. Corrupt Ming border officials force the hungry populace into the vanguard of their armies so that anger and resentment have become extreme: by force of circumstances these oppressed farmers leave us and join the rebels. Once I overheard residents of the borders say, "We used to be afraid that the Jurchens would kill us." But now I hear them say, "The Jurchens build houses to let us live in; they provide clothes and food to support us; from the yearly harvest they take only a sack of millet and a few bales of hay, and there are no other taxes to annoy us; and besides, among the prisoners previously captured we have relatives and friends who will look after us. Rather than die of hunger and starvation and becoming empty-bellied wraiths, or die by the sword and become headless ghosts, we would rather throw in our lot with the Jurchens. This way we may be able to save our lives." These are ominous words coming up in conversation and recently more often than before.[6]

In this one brief passage Xiong not only encapsulated a fundamental aspect of Liaodong society but also foreshadowed the struggle for allegiance in which the Ming and Jin would be fiercely engulfed.

Xiong's stridency then had struck his court audience as unreasonable, and he was extracted from his post to serve as an education inspector in Nanjing. But the capture of Fushun by Nurgaci in 1618 and a series of defeats visited upon Ming commanders in its aftermath had brought forth, in

abi, *The Jurchens in the Yuan and Ming;* Deng Shaohan, "Shilun Ming yu Hou Jin zhanzheng de yuanyin ji qi xingzhi"; and Yang Yulian, "Mingdai houqi Liaodong mashi yu Nuzhen zu de xingqi."

6. Adapted from Serruys, "Two Remarkable Women in Mongolia," in *The Mongols and Ming China,* 8:244–45. See also his citations to the work of Wada Sei.

some quarters, positive comment regarding Xiong Tingbi's earlier performance in Liaodong. His political enemies responded aggressively to the
new favor of Xiong. They put him on the line in Liaodong, tasking him to
correct what a decade of inaction had spawned.[7] Xiong was aggressive in
pursuit of his duties, and equally aggressive in his denunciation of the court
party. By 1621 he was demoted once more from his command. Xiong was,
in effect, sharing responsibility with the Liaodong military governor, Wang
Huazhen (d. 1632),[8] whom he deemed a fool and a liar, when Tong Bunian
reported to his native region for service. Nurgaci's forces were increasing
exponentially and already controlled the former Ming provincial capital at
Shenyang. Failure now to suppress the Jin would lead to indictment, tor-
ture, imprisonment, and very likely death for Xiong Tingbi. But he found
the Liaodong population indifferent to the complexities of Peking factional
quarrels. Nor were they galvanizing themselves in support of the Ming effort against Nurgaci. Xiong gambled on bringing Tong Bunian into the upper rungs of the military effort in Liaodong—specifically as the "intendant"
(*jianshi*) of the regional defense force, the Laijian Army—as a catalyst for
the local spirit, using Bunian's Liaodong associations and the prestige of the
Tong lineage in Fushun to garner support in the region for the Ming cause.[9]
Failure would mean that Liaodong would fall to the control of the Jianzhou,
and, of more immediate concern, Xiong Tingbi would be headed for the execution yard.

However, what Xiong saw as the hope of Tong Bunian was regarded by
others as a threat. It was suspected by some at the Ming court that the
Laijian intendant was not promoted merely because he was a native of
Liaodong, but because he was actually a Jurchen. "Someone," memorial-
ized Liu Zongzhou (1578–1645) at the time of Bunian's appointment, "who
is one of a subject people and who is not personally loyal to us has nevertheless been promoted from magistrate to military intendant. It is Tong
Bunian."[10] Xiong Tingbi managed to ward off Bunian's detractors until
March 1622, when the Ming forces suffered their disastrous defeat at
Guangning. The rout had been a brilliant display of regionalist polemiciz-
ing on the part of Nurgaci and his representatives, who had persuaded mer-

7. See also Woodruff, "Foreign Policy and Frontier Affairs along the Northeastern Frontier of the Ming Dynasty."

8. *ECCP*, 823.

9. *Ming shi* 241.9b. *ECCP*, 792. Mou Ranxun, "Mingmo xiyang dapao you Ming
ru hou Jin kaolue," part 2, in *Mingbao yuekan* (October 1982): 89, quotes remarks
by Zhang Haoming from *Liangchao congxin lu, juan* 9, *Tianqi* 6:10.

10. Mou, "Mingmo xiyang dapao you Ming ru hou Jin kaolue," 89.

cenaries, mostly Mongols, defending the town for the Ming to desert their posts. Indeed the Ming troops, in mass, had streamed through Shanhai Pass and back inside the Great Wall. Xiong Tingbi's small force had mutinied and withdrawn in the wake of the collapse of Guangning; he and Tong Bunian had had no choice but to follow. On reaching the inner side of the Great Wall at Shanhai Pass, Xiong, Wang, and Tong were arrested by Ming officers and remanded to Peking for trial. Xiong and Wang were tried for desertion. Death verdicts were swift, but execution was delayed by the intervention of their political allies. Xiong Tingbi was decapitated on September 27, 1625. His head was piked over a city gate until 1629, when his eldest son was allowed to bury it and the court granted Xiong the posthumous title of Xiangmin ("an end to grieving").[11] Wang Huazhen was executed in 1632.

Tong Bunian was tried separately from but simultaneously with Xiong and Wang in 1622. Unlike Xiong and Wang, Tong was charged not with desertion but with sedition. In April 1622 one Du Xu, a convicted traitor, claimed in his confession that Bunian had secretly communicated with Li Yongfang, a former Ming commander in Fushun who was now in the service of Nurgaci.[12] An intense investigation that at one point caused the torturing to death of two witnesses failed to turn up any evidence that Bunian had aided the enemy, and for three years he remained in prison while his case was debated. The prosecutors acknowledged that criminal acts had not been proved. But proof was irrelevant; the acts could have occurred without leaving any evidence. They further acknowledged that it was perfectly possible that Bunian had never yet communicated with the enemy. But the act was irrelevant, too, for Tong Bunian could be demonstrated to have treason in his ancestry, and innocence was no defense. His kinsmen, Tong Yangxing (d. 1632) and Tong Yangzhen (d. 1621), had gone over to Nurgaci's side and were taking the lead in the supply and command of enemy artillery units. Zhang Haoming, secretary of the Board of War, wrote, "Yesterday I discovered some information about Tong Yangzhen, to the effect that Tong Bunian's great-grandfather was the grandfather of Tong Yangzhen. How can there be any doubt that the traitor Tong Yangxing is

11. This was the same posthumous name given in 1489 to Li Bing, who perished in similar circumstances: Li had been dispatched to Liaodong to suppress the uprising of Cungšan (son of Nurgaci's ancestor Möngke Temür), as a punishment for having criticized the court. See Goodrich and Fang, *Dictionary of Ming Biography* (hereafter *DMB*), 495; also the account in *KF* 1:9b.

12. Mou, "Mingmo xiyang dapao you Ming ru hou Jin kaolue," 89. For Li Yongfang see *ECCP,* 499. For Nurgaci's communications with Li see Chapters 3 and 4.

also a close relative [of Tong Bunian]?"[13] Gu Dazhang (1576–1625), who conducted the investigation into the charges of Tong Bunian's communication with the enemy, did not discover any proof of guilt; he nevertheless recommended banishment on the basis of the suspect's family connections.[14] Qian Qianyi (1582–1664) reasoned, "First of all, [Tong Bunian] is of the same lineage as Tong Yangzhen, and should therefore be treated identically under the law. It is not necessary to wait for him to commit treason. Second, he has the same surname as the Jianzhou and is not merely Yangzhen's kinsman. Yang Dongming [1548–1624] has submitted a memorial saying Bunian is in fact a Jianzhou and each year worships at the tomb of the Jin emperor Shizong."[15]

In prison Bunian wrote his testament of innocence, "Record of Prisoned Rage" (*Yufen lu*), in which he averred his loyalty to the Ming and denied the significance of the association of the Tong surname with Nurgan: "Tong is such a common surname," he argued, "that you cannot claim that all who use it are related." He described the centuries of loyal service given the Ming by his lineage. His cousins who had recently gone over to the Jurchen camp, he showed, only shared an ancestor with him four generations in the past. "In the twenty garrisons of Liaodong, no fewer than twenty-five families are surnamed Tong. They are not all one lineage. There is a Tong family [in China] in Northern Zhili, also, and in Shandong, and in the Yangzi Delta region. With generations of military and civil achievements before me, why is suspicion directed only at me? It has all been done on the basis of flimsy reports, saying that the children and wives of Tong Yangxing and Li Yongfang are all called [by the status of] sons-in-law [of Nurgaci], that's all there is to it."[16] Accepting the persuasiveness of genealogical affiliation, Tong provided his own narrative—to be discussed below—of ancestral

[margin note:] Tong a common name—

---

13. Mou, "Mingmo xiyang dapao you Ming ru hou Jin kaolue," 89.

14. *Ming shi*, 241, as above. For more on the tension between Gu and Xiong, see Chen Ding, *Donglin liezhuan* 3:18a–23b.

15. Zhu Xizu, *Hou Jin guohan xingshi kao*, 49. Zhu's text originally read, "Li Dongming has submitted a memorial. . . . " I have assumed Li Dongming to be a mistake for Yang Dongming. The charge of being a Jurchen is repeated in very similar words in the deposition of Gu Dazhang. The Jurchen Jin emperor Shizong (r. 1161–89) was entombed at Fangshan, now part of greater Peking. Meng Sen, in his "Jianwen xunguo shi kao" (1936, published in *Ming Qing shilun zhu jikan*, 1961), 2, relates a very affecting description of the ruins there. The potency of this charge can perhaps be conveyed by the fact that in 1629, when he made his first invasion of the Peking environs, Hung Taiji did indeed perform a prostration before Shizong's tomb. See Chapter 4.

16. Zhu Xizu, *Hou Jin guohan*, 49, quoting the *Yufen lu*, "Appendix 1." On the ennoblement of new recruits as *efu* (royal sons-in-law) see Chapter 3 and 4.

identity with the Ming. He asserted that the report of his prostration before the tombs of the Jin ancestors was a calumny. He was loyal.

These arguments were without effect. In April 1625 Bunian was ordered to hang himself in prison.[17] His wife Chen-shi left Liaodong to settle with her relatives in Zhejiang province and took her young son, Guoqi, along.

The trial of Tong Bunian took place at the friction point between two volatile spheres in late Ming China: dangerously deteriorating political management of the northern borders and increasingly deadly political rivalries at court. The most proximate political context was what is often referred to as the "persecution" of the Donglin faction by the eunuchs who established themselves close to the emperor in the late Wanli period (roughly the second decade of the seventeenth century). The Donglin group was one of several reform parties that began among the provincial literati. Most were openly critical of the scholars who had aligned themselves with the thought of Wang Yangming (1472–1529). They denounced Wang's philosophy for having promoted a kind of crypto-Buddhism among aspiring bureaucrats, advisors, and local leaders, who in this view became so detached from practical matters that the instruments of government had been allowed to fall into ruin.[18] Amid the crumbling political structure, eunuchs had gained roaming rights and now corrupted the government with their influence over the emperor and their control of policy. The reform groups—including the Donglin—committed themselves to purging their own ranks of the idealism and distraction of the Wang Yangming influence and to dislodging the corrupt elements from the Ming imperial government. They pursued these ends through the discussion and instruction in their affiliated academies, while working their high political connections to gain the ear of the emperor and a foothold for themselves at court. They had some success in this, particularly after 1620. The reformists were as canny and ruthless in the pursuit of their political goals as were their enemies, and the result was that the 1620s was a period of especially intense political intrigue in Peking. The timing of the alterations in power balances was critical to the fates of Xiong Tingbi and Tong Bunian, in particular. Xiong's task in defending Liaodong was complicated by the fact that he had, through his connections with the Donglin, incurred the wrath of court officials. In the view of the Donglin sympathizers, and probably of Xiong himself, the court party led by Feng Quan (1595–1672) were using the Liaodong crisis as a

17. [Ming] Xizong shilu 12:21:24.
18. Onogawa credits reform groups with beginning the critical studies of the Qing period. See Shimmatsu seiji shisō kenkyū, 99–101.

political purgative against the Donglin supporters.[19] Feng, who with his father had been cashiered in 1619 for miscarriage of their duties in the defense of Liaodong, assiduously worked to curry favor with the eunuch Wei
Zhongxian (1568–1627) and to recover some of his standing at court. The
military reverses that directly caused the arrests of Xiong and Tong coincided with a fall from power of prominent Donglin political leaders, leaving the two of them at the mercy of the Wei Zhongxian faction—and particularly of Feng Quan, who made himself the leading prosecutor of Xiong
Tingbi.

Donglin sympathizers attempted to save Xiong but distanced themselves
from Tong Bunian (perhaps supposing that by directing blame at Tong,
Xiong might be reprieved). Tong's accusers Qian Qianyi and Gu Dazhang,
for instance, were both prominent Donglin activists, and Gu was ultimately
martyred for his beliefs. Whatever the "facts" of Tong's case, his death in
prison was most likely a product of the confluence of the Donglin's enemies
targeting the Liaodong military command and the Donglin activists looking for sacrificial victims to save their more prominent and more familiar
colleagues. But this does not fully explain the choice of Tong for this role.
Both factions were evidently attracted by the ease with which Tong could
be implicated in and ultimately convicted of sedition, despite a complete
lack of evidence that he had committed any seditious act. He became a mag-
net for these accusations because the Donglin reformers, quite as much as
the Wei Zhongxian faction, were deeply immersed in a cosmological discourse that virtually compelled the conclusion that Tong was by nature
treasonous (or would inevitably become treasonous). The charges against
Tong were emphatically not the sort that might be associated with notions
of collective responsibility as they are frequently met in Chinese law; he
was not punished for the sins of his relatives or putative relatives, but was
ascribed an affective profile—complete with an ineluctably seditious future—on the basis of evidence relating to his ancestry. Neither Tong Bunian himself nor any of his accusers dissented from the assumption that

19. *ECCP*, 240–41. Feng must have been good at pleasing other sponsors, too,
for he escaped the general purge of the Wei faction that followed the Wanli's emperor's death. When the Qing invasion force under Dorgon reached Peking in 1644,
Feng rushed to join the new regime and was rewarded with posts both in the Hong-
wen yuan and the Board of Appointments (*libu*). Though Feng was good at avoid-
ing political pitfalls in his lifetime, he could not avoid the judgment of the Qianlong
emperor's history. As noted below (Chapters 2 and 5), he was condemned in the
"Biographies of Twice-Serving Ministers" and post-posthumously stripped of his
posthumous honor.

genealogy determined sympathy; Tong merely disputed the interpretation of his own genealogy. The unanimity of the disputants on this point is remarkable when it is remembered that the late Ming period knew a variety of discourses of descent, morality, and identity. There is in fact in Chinese writing of the late sixteenth and earlier seventeenth centuries a wide variety of assertions and inferences relating to the interplay of culture, geography, economics, and politics among peoples in all parts of the empire and at its borders.[20] But among court-oriented literati (including Tong Bunian), and particularly those officials with no ambitions as philosophers of great originality, those philosophical elements that had a happy congruence to the rhetoric of Ming emperorship predominated.

Establishing the moral invalidity of the Yuan empire (1280–1368) of the Mongols in China and the concomitant legitimating of the Ming had been the first agendum of those, like Song Lian and Fang Xiaoru, who were prominent in the formation of the new empire's political rhetoric.[21] The Ming court was eager to nurture and guide this strain of thought and expression, whose forceful combination of righteous indignation against the political pretensions of non-Chinese peoples, rather loose theory of kinship for all Chinese, and characterization of the Ming emperorship as the avatar of Chinese virtue imbued court speech with new vigor. The moral realm of the Ming emperor extended equally to Chinese who left the immediate geographical confines of the Ming empire; this was vividly demonstrated when Zheng He's marines virtually obliterated a community of ancestral Chinese on Sumatra who refused to acknowledge submission to the Yongle emperor in 1407. As late as the early 1620s, when powerful leaders in Mongolia and the Northeast were openly defying Ming pretentions to rule their

---

20. Examples include Xiao Daheng, Mao Ruizheng, Zheng Xiao, Ye Xianggao (1562–1627), and Ma Wensheng, who despite great differences in political outlook were among those writers of the time (most of whom had served as officials in some capacity) who wrote closely descriptive accounts of life in the border territories and gave informed analyses of political organizations, where they were to be found. Of the writers in this vein, Xiao Daheng is best known; he was repeatedly quoted by Bawden (*Modern History of Mongolia*), is very extensively quoted and analyzed by Serruys ("Pei-lou Fong-sou"), and his best-known work, *Beilu fengsu*, is available in several reprints (perhaps most accessible the Guangwen shuju facsimile, Taipei, 1972). As will be noted in the Postscript, these writers were generally neglected in favor of Wang and other philosophers of difference in the nineteenth-century revival of "nationalist" or "loyalist" writers of the seventeenth century.

21. Song Lian and Fang Xiaoru (*Hou zhengtong lun*). Fang, it should be noted, opposed employment of centralizing instruments that in his time were firmly associated with "Legalism" and was as critical of the authoritarian Wang Mang as he was of the Mongols. See also Fincher, "China as a Race, Culture, and Nation."

areas, the need was still felt to formulate and propagate arguments for Ming
military domination of the borders. Connected to this was the necessity to
construe Chinese identity in genealogical (that is, stable) terms, since Chinese settlement of the border areas was fundamental to justification of considering border areas part of the Chinese world. That world at the death of
the Wanli emperor in 1620 was one in which the struggle for identity and
sovereignty was rhetorically strenuous and physically perilous.

In this thinking there is a template of ethnological theory that connected
cultural, historical, and moral identity in a kind of magic circle. The historical record could be used to determine the ancestors of any contemporary
people, and on the basis of that their moral character in the present could
be assessed. These premises were used to argue not only the permanence
of Chinese association but also its obverse: despite imitation of Chinese imperial dress and ritual, despite any degree of apparent outward transformation, the inward quality of barbarians cannot change. Ancestry, in Ming
ideology, was identity; attempts to obscure this equation were stratagems
of illegitimate barbarian dynasties, who hoped to recruit Chinese traitors
into their regimes. Many writers of the period could be invoked to capture
this influential complex of ideas, but it is perhaps most illuminating to cite
Wang Fuzhi (1619–92), to whom this study will return in Chapter 5. Wang,
who was not born until the very late Ming and was still a young man at the
time of the Qing conquest of north China, was heir to two generations of
scholars developing what is often called the "materialist" critique, which
repudiated the "idealism" of Wang Yangming and his followers. The slight
anachronism of citing Wang in this context appears justified for the sake of
clarity; Wang, after all, thought that philosophy can only be understood in
retrospect: "At the time one speaks, no one understands one. In setting forth
what I have understood, I am also trying to advise future generations."[22]

Wang accepted the axiom that the fundamental difference between civilized people and barbaric people is moral. This came down to a consistent
code of evidence: Civilized people are those who respect their elders and
their dead ancestors; who read and write; who record history and take lessons from it; who use orderly methods of communication (whether in
script, in ritual, or in music) to negotiate relationships among people, as
well as between people and Heaven; who form states and allow themselves
to be governed by law and reason (a criterion that would become central to
the argument of the Yongzheng emperor of the Qing in the early eighteenth

22. McMorran, *The Passionate Realist*, 162, from *Huangshu houxu* 1b.

century). Barbaric people are those who are controlled by greed and lust; who take no notice of the past; who do not know or respect ancestors (and thus marry chaotically among the lineages and the generations) or divine forces; who cannot maintain stable states and do not care for law. The immediate sources of these differences, Wang explained, were environmental: Civilized people—the people of the "central country" (*zhongguo*), inheritors of the traditions of the Hua and Xia—were born in one place (China), and were shaped by its moderate temperatures, its fertile lands, abundant waters and edifying scenery. Barbaric peoples were from elsewhere— parched or steamy or frigid or scrabbly lands where the patterned life necessary to the development of agriculture, orderly families, literature, philosophy, and political arts was limited or impossible. Wang had also a more cosmological explanation, to which we will return in a later chapter.

Wang, like many seventeenth-century thinkers, used a broad genealogical schema to undergird his taxonomy of moral identities: "When the families of things became clearly defined and the lines of demarcation among them were fixed, each was established in its own position and all living things were contained within their own protective barriers. . . . Conflicts could thus be avoided."[23] As he commented in his "Writings Bound for the Fire" (*Huang shu*), material law (which Wang hoped would gain ascendancy over the subjective remnants of the influence of "idealistic" philosophy) required that demarcations based upon a learned perception of differences between circumstantial similarities and essential differences be observed, with humans distinguished from objects, and Chinese distinguished from barbarians. Wang explicitly denied that superficial biological dissimilarities were markers of identity. Man had in common with beasts his composition by *yin* and *yang* elements, also his necessity to eat and breathe; but man was not an animal. It was not such superficial physical similarities between Chinese and barbarians that were definitive, but their irreducible moral differences.[24] The state that neglects enforcement of these barriers violates natural principle (*tianwei*) and allows chaos, moral disorder, and injustice to reign. Though the state, Wang admitted, plays a conscious role in the

23. From *Du tongjian lun.* There is a concise introduction to Wang's thought on the relationship between civilization and barbarism, with quotations and citations to critical original passages, in Ji, *Wang Chuanshan xueshu luncong*, 148–54. See also McMorran, "Wang Fu-chih and His Political Thought"; Wiens, "Anti-Manchu Thought during the Ch'ing"; Black, *Man and Nature in the Thought of Wang Fu-chih.*

24. *Huang shu* 24 (*juan*).

ability of its agents to perceive these differences and to maintain boundaries, the differences themselves might be called "material" and inherent.

This insistence on a material basis for distinct cultural and moral identities may suggest that Wang considered these differences to be essential, and immune to change by time or circumstance. Here a qualification is in order.[25] Wang and others assumed the phenomenal and noumenal worlds to be of one continuous moral substance. Civilization was morality, but so was illness, hunger, or the tendency of things to fall downward when released. Additionally, these philosophers were working within the context of a reaction against late Ming philosophical fashion, which was alleged to have weakened the political culture by encouraging intellectuals to focus excessively upon their own inner lives and perceptions to the neglect of the factual investigation of history, economics, linguistics, medicine, and in some cases mathematics. For these new critics, the phenomenal world was comprehensive, and metaphysics was only a species of moral knowledge equally gained through inquiries into history and the present.

Frequently Wang Fuzhi and others claimed the authority of the "Spring and Autumn Annals" (*Chunqiu*) or "Writings of Zuo" (*Zuo zhuan*) for their discussion of boundaries between barbarians and Chinese. But the vocabulary of the classical texts, in which social or cultural groups were delineated by terms of classification claiming no inherited, immutable character *[classical vocab displaced]* (*lei, chun*) had been displaced by a new vocabulary of fictive kinship (*zu, lun*). The shift was important because for the first time it introduced a causality of distinctions. Early formulations had depended upon a description of cultural differences to mark lines between peoples.[26] Such differences produced secondary differences in thought and feeling, but no theory was offered to explain how differences of circumstance were caused. The new vocabulary, however, suggested that inherent differences descended from one generation to the next—and from one people to its heirs—with-

---

25. Notwithstanding Dikötter's admonition: "The delusive myth of a Chinese antiquity that abandoned racial standards in favour of a concept of cultural universalism in which all barbarians could ultimately participate has understandably attracted some modern scholars . . . " (*The Discourse of Race in Modern China*, 3). It is indeed desirable that modern scholars abjure an attraction of their own to this "myth" but not that they ignore the fact that it is in some texts and exercised its own attraction over certain empires and their scholastic supporters.

26. There is the famous exchange in *Zuo zhuan* 14, for instance, in which a leader of the Qiang group of the Rong people sums up his differences from the Chinese (Hua) as differences of food, dress, customs of exchange, and language.

out being immediately affected by environment.[27] Biology, food, and climate having produced the distinctions between Chinese and barbarian, Wang reasoned, the distinctions cannot be abrogated, any more than a family tree can be negotiated. This association of genealogy with identity became nearly unexceptional in Ming literati circles of the early seventeenth century. In the prosecution of Tong Bunian, no individual ever dissented from this basic principle, including Tong Bunian himself, who consistently and energetically pursued his defense by writing and annotating an exhaustive genealogy.

The history of Fushun, Tong's ancestral town, was itself a monument to the hopelessness of saving Tong Bunian by arguing an impeccable Chinese ancestry for him. The settlement has previously been described as typical of the "transfrontier" environment that communicated Chinese cultural and political influence to Northeast Asia in Ming times. This characterization of Fushun was fundamental to Tong Bunian's defense, was suggested by "Record of Prisoned Rage," was perpetuated by his son Tong Guoqi in the later seventeenth century, and would become of ideological significance to the eighteenth-century court. However, contemporary documentation (mostly from Ming government records, but also some private histories) suggests another cultural history for Fushun, one perilous to Tong Bunian: Fushun was among the westernmost and southernmost of urban settlements in Liaodong that Jurchen immigration had helped create. The Qing court would later acknowledge Fushun as a major source of the regime's organizational and ideological resources; unstated in the imperial literature is the fact that Fushun was the key to the fortune amassed by Nurgaci's ancestors, upon which his own career was built.

During the early seventeenth century Fushun was one of the smaller of a network of Ming garrisons and fortifications in eastern Liaodong that marked the western boundaries of the Jurchen territories. Unlike its sister towns to the north and west—Kaiyuan (Manchu Keyen) and Tieling (Manchu Cilin)—Fushun had not been a town before the coming of the garrison.[28] Under the Ming, Fushun's livelihood was exclusively and inex-

27. See also Hsiung, "Shiqi shiji Zhongguo zhengzhi sixiang zhong fei chuan-tong chengfen de fenxi," 14–15; 30–31.

28. The Fushun environs have been a fruitful archaeological resource for the study of ancient and medieval Northeastern cultures. See Ikeuchi Hiroshi, *Man Son shi kenkyū* (1949), 161–76, and Miyake Shunjo, *Tohoku Ajia kokugaku no kenkyū* (1949): 403–69 passim. It shared with the rest of the region a history of settlement by the Puyŏ, a Tungusic people who inhabited present-day Liaoning and Jilin sometime in the late centuries BCE, and later control by the Parhae (Bohai), who had oc-

tricably bound to trading and defense. As Kaiyuan to the north was the portal of Liaodong trade with Haixi,[29] and Guangshun Gate with Hada, Fushun was the point of contact with Jianzhou to the east; all were consequently targets for Jurchen settlement, and Liaodong was dotted with Jurchen communities. The exact date of the founding of Fushun is unclear, but its purpose was to house the soldiers who managed the Fushun Gate (Fushun guan), the "Gate of Firm Pacification," the physical interface with Jianzhou. The town was originally a camp (*zuo*) under the jurisdiction of the Liaodong Central Garrison.[30] Its walls were reported to have been about one mile (three *li*) in circumference, and just outside the town walls lay the camp of the chiliarch (*qianhu*), the military granaries, and the drill field.[31] Also outside the city walls were the markets, which were filled with the pearls, ginseng, pelts, pine seeds, falcons, dogs, and other precious items brought from the Jurchen territories to be exchanged for the silk, cash, or finished goods offered by the residents of Fushun. After 1464 Fushun became an official horse market.[32] It also received semiprocessed goods; the Jianzhou had invented a new way of curing ginseng (*orhoda*),[33] and the Hoifa of northern Liaodong and Jilin had taken their name from their process of dyeing cloth.[34] The chiefs of the federations, who enjoyed a large portion of the wealth generated by Jurchen trade and industries, were in the habit of stopping in the towns of Fushun, Tieling, Kaiyuan, Guangshun, and elsewhere to spend their money. Fushun was frequently visited by the Jianzhou band led by Giocangga of the Jianzhou (Nurgaci's grandfather) in the 1570s and very early 1580s. Records preserve notice of Nurgaci's own visit to Fushun in the company of his grandfather as early as 1578,[35] and the settle-

cupied the area from the eighth to the tenth centuries and were, like the Jurchens, descendants of the Mohe. The Jurchen Jin empire had made the area north and east of the site of Fushun the heart of its administration.

29. For discussion and citations from *Ming shilu* on the Haixi and Kaiyuan, see Zhu Chengru, "Qing ru guan qian hou Liao Shen diqu de Man (Nuzhen) Han renkou jiaoliu," 74–75.

30. *Liaodong zhi* 2:4b.

31. *Liaodong zhi* 2:15b.

32. Yang Yulian, "Mingdai houqi de Liaodong mashi yu Nuzhenzu de xingqi," 29.

33. Jurchen *or-ho da* (Jin, *Nuzhen wen cidian*, 154, meaning "root of the grass").

34. *Hoifan*, "A dye made from the leaves and stems of the wild tea plant *wence moo*," verb infinitive *hoifalambi*, "to dye black with a concoction of the leaves and stems" of the same plant (Norman, *A Concise Manchu–English Lexicon*, 133–34, from *Qingwen Zonghui*).

35. Yang Yulian, "Mingdai houqi de Liaodong mashi," 30, cites a Fushun tax document of 1578. Nurgaci was at this time nineteen or twenty years old and had

ments of the Giocangga lineage were located in an area directly accessible to Fushun by river travel.

Fourteenth-century Jurchen traders visited the Liaodong towns continually and frequently settled there; others were part of the "garrison" arrangement in Liaodong who had been permitted (many were actually enticed) to defend some of the towns, either under Chinese or acculturated Jurchen commanders. Jurchen and Mongolian-speaking soldiers willing to work for hire for the Ming had been brought from the Ilantumen (Sanxing) region of Nurgan to settle at Kaiyuan, inside the Ming boundaries. In time some of the descendants of those soldiers had also become traders and followed the paths of commerce into the towns of Tieling, Fushun, Guangning, Liaoyang City, Ningyuan, and Shenyang. They had settled, married the townspeople, taken to speaking Chinese, entered the urban and even the official occupations. The ubiquity of Jurchens in the late sixteenth century in Liaodong was commented upon by the Korean official Shin Chung-il, who pointed out to the Yi court in 1596, "I had gone only a few paces outside the Shanhai Pass before I began encountering Jurchens."[36]

Fushun was in the fateful position of affording accommodation, refreshment, and entertainment to Jurchen embassies passing from Nurgan to Peking. Jurchen "tribute" missions to the Ming capital were actually expeditions for imposing upon the hospitality of the Ming court and its eunuch managers, collecting bribes in goods and cash to ensure another year of amicability, and wringing high prices for their horses.[37] The chieftains and their attendants may have told the Fushun townsmen of their strategies for maximizing their advantages in the legalized extortion that constituted the Ming "tributary" system with the Jurchens and the Mongols. Putative tributaries were accustomed to write the court in advance notifying it of their desires, specifying such and such a title (inevitably accompanied, it was understood, by a cash payment), so many bolts of silk, and certain items of clothing. Jurchen chieftains delighted in swelling their embassies with petty retainers and relatives; more than one headman had brought along his

----

just concluded his first marriage, to Hahana Jacin, of the Tunggiya lineage of Jilin. See Chapter 3.

36. Shin, *Kŏnju jichŏng dorok,* hereafter *KJD,* 38.

37. Ma Wensheng, writing in the Wanli period, complained of the Jianzhou Jurchen's abuse of the tributary system: "The barbarians did not number more than several thousand, though it was normal for them to send a hundred on an embassy" ("Fu'an Dong Yi kao," 2). The Jurchen's pattern of exploitation of the system resembled that of the Mongols, who sometimes sent thousands on an embassy designed to accommodate a hundred.

mother to personally collect her booty.[38] The results were further drain on the strained resources of the Ming empire and, at the same time, a boon to Fushun. Giocangga and his son Taksi came through more than once on embassies to Peking. Nurgaci led at least one large tribute embassy, reaching Fushun in the late spring on the way to a June 1 imperial audience in 1590. Jurchen resentments of the Ming military presence in the Northeast may have been commonly voiced already among the Jurchens passing through Fushun. Nurgaci claimed in 1618 that his grievances against the Ming were to be traced to the 1580s, and Korean emissaries to Nurgaci's territories in the 1590s heard his detailed complaints of abuse of Jurchen economic and political rights by Ming officials in Liaodong. It is reasonable to suppose that what became Nurgaci's famous "grievances" (see Chapter 3) were in some forms not unfamiliar to the Fushun public at the end of the sixteenth century.

In the eyes of the leading families of Jianzhou the Ming officials were arrogant. They pretended to military hegemony in the Northeast, when in fact they maintained their dominion in Liaodong at Jurchen sufferance. So long as the trade upon which Jurchen wealth depended continued, the Ming officials, unbearable as they were, would be borne. But interference with Jurchen economic enterprises, whether hunting, fishing, gathering, farming, mining, pearl curing, or ginseng reduction, would mean war. There was no question of the Jurchens not being ready to fight. Low-grade warfare was frequent among the Jurchen villages, as they competed for control over agricultural lands, hunting grounds, and mineral deposits. Danger drove increasing numbers of Jurchens into the relative, if temporary, safety of Liaodong.[39] Nor were the disorders isolated in Nurgan; raids into central Liaodong, as far as Liaoyang, by Nurgan-based marauders were common in the 1570s and 1580s. But the chance of outright battle against the Ming was not great in the late sixteenth century. Indeed the dominant leaders of the time—Wanggoo of the Jianzhou Right Garrison, Wan of Hada, Yangginu of Yehe, and the Jianzhou Left Garrison leaders Soocangga and Giocangga—were all known to have bargained with the Ming in efforts to reduce or subvert the powers of their Jurchen rivals. As hostilities intensified between the Ming and the Jianzhou Jurchens in the very late sixteenth and

38. The custom of having family members, including wives and mothers, present at the distribution of booty or the rendering of tribute continued through the Nurgaci period. Typical is *MR TM* 10 [1625]:1:2, which describes a gifting ceremony of the new year by the Taizi River.

39. Zhu Chengru, "Qing ru guan qian," 76.

early seventeenth centuries, the Fushunese confronted two distinct hazards: impoverishment from the loss of trade and physical peril from the hazards of war. Whatever the duration or ultimate outcome of a large conflict, a Jurchen onslaught against Fushun was a certainty, and it would mean death or slavery for a considerable portion of the population.

Fushun and the other towns of Liaodong were to become major sources of Qing political and economic capacity, though the legacy of these towns proved fragile in the rehistoricizing of the eighteenth century. Sinophone but acquainted with Jurchen, giving evidence of diverse religious influences,[40] commercial but possessed of a small literate elite, populated primarily or secondarily by westerly influxes of Jurchen immigrants, dependent on continuing close ties to the Jurchen federations through their markets and hostels, these towns, when captured by Nurgaci between 1618 and 1625, provided the material and social base for the creation of a state. As backdrop to an elaborate genealogical defense, Fushun was not promising for Tong Bunian.

POLITICAL NAMES IN NURGAN

Qian Qianyi had sought to damn Tong Bunian with the remark that "he has the same surname as the Jianzhou." By "Jianzhou" Qian meant to indicate the powerful Jurchen federation based in the nearby Tunggiya valley, as well as the lineage of its leader Nurgaci.[41] The use of the Tong sur-

---

40. The evident Jesuit influences upon the Tong family will be discussed below. One should also note the observation of Susan Naquin, discussing the participation of bannermen in the pilgrimages to Miaofeng shan, as part of the veneration of the "Jade Woman," *Bixia yuanjun*, that shrines to the deity were well attested in seventeenth-century Liaodong. The Bixia cult is suggestive of many continuities between the town cultures of seventeenth-century Liaodong and garrison cultures of the early and middle Qing period. See "The Peking Pilgrimage to Miao-feng Shan," 371, where Naquin cites *Fengtian tongzhi* (1934) 93.18 and 93.32.

41. The origins and meaning of the name Jianzhou are unclear. Xu Zhongshu, on the basis of the Xin Tang shu, thought it might be derived from a regional name of Parhae, possibly in the vicinity of the origins of the Songari and Hun Rivers, between present-day Jilin City and Mt. Changbai ("Mingchu Jianzhou nuzhen ju di qian tu kao," 163). Xu disagreed with the opinion of Japanese scholars that the name "Jianzhou" had been carried north to Ilantumen with the migrating Jurchens; instead he thought that the Yuan records placed Jianzhou on the Suifen River, near the present border with Korea. On the basis of Ming and Yi records, Xu outlined the patenting of and subdivision of the Jianzhou "garrison" (*wei*) in the fifteenth century.

name by Nurgaci and his ancestors was well known in China and Korea, so well known that the Nurgan territories were often called "Tong Nurgan" in recognition of the influence there of the Jianzhou federations. The first reference to Tong as a surname survives from the fifth-century Northern Wei empire of the Xianbei. It was the name of Tong Wan, a literary figure, and of Tong Shou, a general; both were natives of Liaodong.[42] In Zheng Qiao's twelfth-century catalog of surnames, Tong occurs only as part of a complex of names common among the peoples of the north.[43] By the first years of the fifteenth century, it was established among the Jurchens of Jilin, particularly the lineage of Möngke Temür, who used it when intro- ✓ ducing himself to the Yi court of Korea with other Jurchen headmen of federations recently migrated from the north. In Liaodong, the Tong name was limited to the family descended from Tong Dali and hailing from Fushun, later dispersed (as Tong Bunian noted) throughout Liaodong and northern China. But in the Jurchen territories of Nurgan, the name "Tong" was part of a complex interplay of historical geography and political affiliation, shaped by the massive southward and westward migrations of the Jurchens in the thirteenth and fourteenth centuries, then by the northward migrations of the fifteenth.

Following the fall of the Jurchen Jin empire in the thirteenth century, the Yuan empire of the Mongols organized the Jurchens who remained in the Northeast into the Kaiyuan "circuit" (*lu*), subordinate to Liaoyang province.[44] The Kaiyuan circuit was the geopolitical ancestor of the Nurgan territories. It encompassed modern Yilan (medieval Ilantumen) in Heilongjiang province, which was at the time a region inhabited by three great Jurchen federations, recorded in the Yuan history as the Wodolian, Huligai, and Taowen.[45] The Ming at first followed closely the outline of Yuan administration in the Northeast. The intention of both was to make the geographical conformation of Northeast administration correspond to cultural contours: Liaodong came to connote the territory dominated by Jurchen and Chinese immigrants, and Nurgan indicated the native lands to the east and north. Ilantumen was translated into Chinese as Sanwan and the "garrison" was established in 1388. The Jurchens struggled among themselves for trading monopolies in the border towns and prizes from the Ming. In the early 1420s the town of Kaiyuan was disrupted by an upris-

---

42. Zhu Xizu, *Hou Jin guohan*, 49, quotes the *Bei Yan lu*.
43. *Tong shi* 25:1a–2b.
44. *Yuan shi* 59:3.
45. *Yuan shi* 59:4.

ing of Jurchens (apparently Jianzhou), who when dispersed by Ming troops set upon Maolian Jurchens (probably Uriangkha remnants), driving them out of the territory. But Jurchen power in Liaodong and at its peripheries was jeopardized when troops under the Oyirod commanders Toghto-bukha and Alacu invaded Liaodong at the time of the Oyirod siege of Peking in 1449. By the fifteenth century the remaining federations had all but dissolved in the migrations from Ilantumen toward the Nurgan territories of the east, into southern Jilin, into Liaodong, and into Korea.

This was the second, and lesser, of the Jurchen migrations to northern Korea. The connections—sometimes friendly and sometimes hostile—between the Jurchens and Korea were old. People calling themselves Jurchens were settled as far south as Hamhŭng in north central Korea at the beginning of the twelfth century. The Yi court from its inception in 1392 had considered some Jurchen headmen as useful allies, and it honored the Jurchen Li Douran (Yi Tu-ran), who had become a loyal attendant of Yi Sŏng-gye, the founder of the Yi dynasty.[46] Shortly after their southerly migration in the 1380s (following the fall of the Yuan, and Ming attempts to impose some control on the Kaiyuan/Nurgan territories), the surviving Wodolian—who would later be known as the Odori,[47] or Jianzhou—sought an alliance with the Yi lineage who were struggling to establish a dynastic government to displace that of the Koryŏ. Of the three Jurchen headmen presenting themselves at the new Yi court, Möngke Temür,[48] using the lineage name

46. T'aejo (r. 1392–98) of the Yi dynasty. On the orthodox narrative of Korean-Jurchen relations in the Yi ideology see Peter H. Lee, *Songs of Flying Dragons*, 154–55; for the reflection of Yi Tu-ran's part in the conquests, 209–10; 236.

47. Odori (Wodoli, Wodolian) is also a name of obscure origin. Informants to the Yi court explained that Odori, Hurka, and Tuowen were "towns" (*sŏng, cheng*) in Ilantumen. They were more likely federations, though each might well have had a principle settlement (Xu Zhongshu, "Mingchu Jianzhou nuzhen ju di qian tu kao," 166). On the basis of the geographical entries in the Yuan history, Xu guessed that Odori might originally have been in Jilin, even close to the Sarhū River and in the vicinity of the Pozhujiang (Tunggiya). If so, the ancestors of Nurgaci spent centuries in the same locality, which is not in agreement with the account, partially confirmed in Yi records, of a large migration led by Möngke Temür's younger brother Fanca from northern Korea (where Qing tradition insists Odori was located) to the Tunggiya valley in the early fifteenth century. There are problems with Xu's theory, first of which is that it seems to read backward from the records of the Ming, where several localities or federation names associated at that time with Jilin are mentioned together.

48. This is Menggetiemur of the Ming records, Mengtemu of the Qing. For a biography of Möngke Temür in English see *DMB*, 1065–66. In Chinese, see *Qingshi gao* 222:4b–5a (1977 edition, 9116–9117, appendix to Ahacu biography). Möngke Temür is mentioned frequently in the *Yijo sillok* for the reigns of T'aejong

Tong, came as head of the Odori; Ahacu (using the lineage name Gurun) came as head of the Hurka, and Burhu (using the lineage name Gao) came as head of the Udika (Woji). Of Burhu little more is heard, possibly because he represented a group of very loosely organized Jurchens who soon became objects of the mercenary incursions by the followers of Möngke Temür and Ahacu.

Not later than the early years of the fifteenth century, Möngke Temür led his Odori followers south of the Tumen, into the territory of Omohoi in the northern Korean peninsula.[49] The Yi rise in Korea had included intense military campaigns to drive Jurchens not allied with the new order northward toward the Yalu (in Korean, Amnok) River and ultimately beyond it. Part of the motivation may have been to establish Yi sovereignty in the north of the peninsula. By commissioning the Jurchen "garrisons" in the early fourteenth century, the Ming had taken advantage of the territorial haziness of the Jurchen federations to make a latent claim on lands south of the Yalu. Möngke Temür and Ahacu were among the powerful Jurchen leaders who threw in their lot with the Yi government, wiping up pockets of unassimilated Jurchen settlement. Both these headmen were seeking Ming as well as Yi recognition, and it came in the Yongle period, probably in 1411 with creation of a Jianzhou garrison.[50] At the time of its creation command seems to have rested with Ahacu's son, Šigiyanu (Chinese, Shijianu). Ahacu had been awarded the name Li Sicheng by the Chinese; Šigiyanu, in his relations with the Ming, was known as Li Xianzhong.[51] During his long leadership over the Odori (eastern Jianzhou) Jurchens,

---

(1401–18) and Sejong (1418–50); see chapters 5–19. References to Jurchens in the *Yijo sillok* have been collected in Wang Zhonghan, ed., *Chaoxian "Lichao shilu" zhong de nüzhen shiliao xuanpian* (September 1979); see esp. 1–48.

49. Womuhe of the Ming records, Emouhui of the Qing *shilu*. This place remained Möngke Temür's base in the ensuing years, but he was occasionally forced to abandon it temporarily because of pressure from wildmen, Koreans, and Mongols. Some of these withdrawals are mentioned in *DMB*, 1066.

50. The basic materials on the founding of garrisons in Nurgan are now represented in the *Mingshi* (1739) 90:9b–13b, "Nurgan dusi." Serruys, *Sino-Jürched Relations*, 73ff., has culled a chronology of garrison registration from the *Yonglu shilu* which provides the closest dates available.

51. The most coherent work on the Lis of the Jianzhou garrison probably remains Wu Han, "Guanyu Dongbai shi shang yiwei guaijie de xin shiliao" in *Yenching Journal of Chinese Studies (Yanjing xuebao)* 17 (1931), see esp. 60–62. The assertion of the *Qingshi gao*, 222:1a, that Ahacu was given the name Li Chengnian is at variance with known Ming records and probably an error. See also Kyoto index, 23–25.

Möngke Temür succeeded in nearly monopolizing Jurchen trade with the Koreans, which set the stage for shattering of the power of the Li federation in the Pozhu valley. (The Pozhu is a northeasterly tributary of the Hun River that flowed north of the Yalu toward Liaodong through present-day Jilin province of China.)[52] From the time of their arrival at Huncun the Odori Jurchens carved out a military and commercial domain of their own, mostly under the pretext of battling the "wildmen."[53] Later Šigiyanu's son Li Manzhu succeeded to leadership of the Jianzhou federation in Pozhu. During the deep rivalry between Möngke Temür's federation and Ahacu's, political allegiances came to be signaled by the names "Tong" (for those associated with Möngke Temür and the Odori) and "Li" (for those associated with the Ahacu lineage and the Hurka federation).

Following the patenting of the original Jianzhou garrison, Šigiyanu and his Li-surnamed affiliates seem to have enjoyed some favor from the Ming court and were frequent visitors to Peking. But in the 1420s he began encountering political and economic difficulties from the "Tong" Jianzhou in the east. Möngke Temür overshadowed Šigiyanu in the eyes of the Yi border authorities, and the Li Jianzhou eventually found themselves cut out of the trade with the Koreans. At the same time Möngke Temür began suing in Peking for a command of his own. Shortly after Šigiyanu's death in 1426 Möngke Temür was made "general commander" (*dudu qianshi*) of the Jianzhou garrison in a rather grand ceremony at the Ming court that included the bestowal of a good deal of wealth, mostly in the form of paper money, upon Möngke Temür and his entourage—one of whose mother, née Tong, had come along to collect her packet of bills in person. Two months later Li Manzhu, the son of Šigiyanu, was given a less prestigious title within the garrison. By 1428 a "left"—that is, east—garrison had been created for Möngke Temür and most ranks filled by men using the surname Tong.[54] Money-collecting embassies from the Jianzhou Left Garrison to

[margin note: Tong Connection]

52. This is clearly visible in *Qingdai yitong ditu* (1966), a photo reprint of the 1760 imperial map collation, p. 103, lattitude 42–43, longitude 10–11.

53. *Woji* [*niyalma*], Jurchen *udi-e* [*nialma*], "forest [dwellers]," the term for the people the Ming and Yi called "wildmen" (Chinese *yeren*, Korean *ya'in*), and, on occasion, used to mean "Jurchens" generally. The Jurchen word evidently had a glottal or fricative before the generative *e*, which was reflected in the Ming and Yi transcriptions of *wudiha* and *udika*, respectively. The Woji included the ancestors of the present Nivkhs, Ulchs, Nanays, Giliaks, Oronchons, Evenks, and other peoples of Northeast Asia.

54. See, for instance, Kyoto index, 30ff.

*1430's   Möngke Temür – against Ahacu
— gains ground – both w/ th Yi &
th Ming*

the Ming court were continuous; the Li's were being cut off at Peking just as they had been pushed out of the Korean commerce. In 1429 Li Manzhu asked to be appointed a bodyguard-in-residence at Peking; the request was denied. The next year he came to Peking to complain of Möngke Temür's monopolization of the Korean trade. The year after that his mother came to court to plead his case. Nothing seems to have helped. Li Manzhu evidently continued to try to battle for a foothold in Korea, but Yi forces contained him at the Pozhu in 1434. Meanwhile Möngke Temür and his younger brother Fanca continued to rise in the estimation of the Ming court, and in 1432 the former was given the title of "General of the Right [that is, westerly garrison]" (*you dudu*). The following year, Möngke Temür and his son Agu were killed in Omohoi, apparently while fighting Qixing/Nadan Hala (seven-surnames) "wildmen."[55] Fanca withdrew north across the Tumen River, possibly under pressure from Yi forces or possibly because of a rebellion among the Odori. He set his sights upon the Pozhu valley, where Li Manzhu was based.[56] It was probably in 1436 that Fanca and his people arrived. There ensued a power struggle that resulted in the permanent subordination of Li Manzhu and his descendants within the Jianzhou federation.[57] After the breaking of Li power, the Pozhu valley became known as Tunggiya—in Chinese Tongjia, "the Tong home"—and the Pozhu River became the Tongjiajiang. Shortly thereafter the "garrison"

55. Kyoto index, p. 54, to Ming *shilu*, "Xuande 9," second month, "gengshen" (fourteenth day). It may be that Möngke Temur's younger brother, name unknown, was also killed in the incident; *KF* and this chapter's note 47. His killers are recorded in the *Qingshi gao* 222:4 as Qixing *yeren*. Ming and Yi records frequently write the name of this group as "seven star" (*qixing*), but the *Huang Qing zhigong tu* describes them in Chinese and in Manchu as the more likely "seven surnames" (*ilan nadan, qixing*). The circumstances suggest that at this time Möngke Temür was in the employ of the Yi court. It is equally possible, however, that the Ming report obscures the fact that Möngke Temür was actually killed while fighting Yi troops. In this period Korean forces were pushing Jurchens out of Omohoi; the deaths of Möngke Temür and Agu coincide with the routing of Li Manzhu from his southern base and his containment north of the Yalu by the Koreans.

56. Li was forced to abandon it several times; on Li's fortunes and misfortunes see Rossabi, *The Jurchens in the Yüan and Ming*, 41–42, and Wu Han, "Guanyu Dongbei shi shang yiwei guaijie xin shiliao," passim. This is about 225 miles (about 160 kilometers) as the crow flies. In fact the group probably followed the Tumen west to Tianchi, then the Yalu at least as far as present-day Linjiang, at the eastern Tunggiya perimeter. The trek could hardly have been less than 550 kilometers (about 340 miles).

57. If Shin Chung-il was correctly informed, Fanca or Cungšan may even have appropriated Li's own homestead. See Chapter 3.

was split once again, into a "left camp" (*zuo suo*) for Möngke Temür's son Cungšan[58] and a "right camp" (*you suo*) to be retained by Fanca. The two groups soon moved farther west, to a hill site at the Liaodong perimeter.

Möngke Temür is reported to have used the surname "Tong."[59] He certainly had no wish to disguise his lineage name, which was known and frequently recorded. Nor does it appear to be the case that Möngke Temür or his fellow Tong intended anyone to think that they had a "Chinese" surname. He may have declined to even indicate which Chinese character was intended, since scribes wrote the name variously and developed their own regional conventions for standardizing it. It is possible, as Mitamura Taisuke has speculated, that Tong—meaning, in some transcriptions, "with" or "same"—was a sort of nickname applied to Möngke Temür's lineage because they were of Hurka origin and wished to play upon the fact that the Hurkas had supplied consorts to the imperial Wanyan / Wanggiya lineage of the Jin Jurchens.[60] What is certain is that the connection of the epithet "Tong" with the lineage of Möngke Temür was not an eccentricity or an innovation. It was already established among the Jurchens who had settled in north China after the fall of the Jurchen Jin empire, and Tao Zongyi noted in his "Records of a Rest from Plowing" (*Zhuogeng lu*) in the thirteenth century that Tong was the surname used by those descended from

58. "Dongshan" in *Qingshi gao* (222, passim); "Chongshan" in the *Qing shilu*. Zhu Xizu, *Hou Jin guohan*, 36, speculated that the name and others of Möngke Temür's descendants were inspired by the Tong surname they used. This is possible, but it should also be noted that Cungšan was a common Jurchen name.

59. For a sampling of citations see Zhu Xizu, *Hou Jin guohan*, 34ff. On the use of the surname among his descendants up to Nurgaci see Ch'en Chieh-hsien *Qingshi zab* (Taipei, 1977), 2: 155–56. The use of the Tong surname by the lineage has been discussed by Mitamura, *Shinchō zenshi no kenkyū*, 99–103. The name is completely unacknowledged by Qing records but is confirmed in abundance by Ming and Yi records. Interestingly, the Qing accounts come close referring to it. KF 1.9a describes the beginnings of the Jianzhou garrison in the Yongle period and says that the garrison commanders and their sons "all received surnames and personal names in recognition of their service." Immediately below (9b) is provided a sketchy account of the deaths of a Jianzhou commander, his younger brother, and his son while fighting the "seven-surname wildmen" (*Qixing yeren*), who then "escaped to Korea." This can be nothing other than an account of the deaths of Möngke Temür, his younger brother, and his son Agu in Omohoi in 1434—but with no names for the principals, dates, or other specifics. Möngke Temür, of course, has already appeared in the work as the mythical Emperor Zhaozu, source of Nurgaci's political authority, and associating him in this instance with facts may have been seen as contrary to the spirit of the text.

60. Mitamura, *Shinchō zenshi*, 99–101.

the Jurchen lineage whose name was written with the characters "Jiagu."[61] In Möngke Temür's time the lineage name was what would now be pronounced as "Jiawen" or "Juewen"; in the lexicographical section (*guoyu jie*)[62] of the Jin imperial history the Jiagu lineage name was glossed "Kalegu"; and in Qing times it would be standardized as "Gioro."[63]

In the eighteenth century the geographical origins of the earliest Manchu constituency, which the Qianlong court attempted retrospectively to construct, were key to the cultural ambiguities of Liaodong. Onomastics became an essential ideological tool of those in service to the Qing court as it attempted to refine and redefine the names associated with the regime's own sources. The "Collected Genealogies of the Eight-Banner and Manchu Lineages" of 1745 established a maxim in its remark that Manchu lineage names were "place names" (*diming*). This apparent law has created a great deal of confusion regarding a distinction between some names that are assumed to be old, or genuine, and others that are new, or somehow considered artificial.[64] In the latter category are those evidently based upon Chinese surnames and the addition of the Chinese word for family, *jia*.[65] Names formed in this way were numerous among the Qing Manchus, and include Magiya (Ma jia), Gaogiya (Gao jia), Janggiya (Zhang jia), Joogiya (Zhao jia), Ligiya (Li jia), and Tunggiya (Tong jia). In many instances these names were adopted by Chinese-martial bannermen wishing to transpose their own Chinese surnames into ostensibly Manchu lineage names, and these instances clearly are exceptions to the stated rule that Manchu lineage names are place names. But a majority of names in this category cannot be accounted for as altered Chinese surnames. Moreover, some of the names which would appear to be derived from Chinese surnames are not new Manchu names but old Jurchen ones, and it is possible that they include

61. *Zhuogeng lu* 1: "Shizu zhi." Jin Qizong (*Nuzhen wen cidian,* 79) has reconstructed this as Jurchen Gia-gu.

62. This has been omitted from the Guofang edition of the *Jinshi,* where a text almost identical to Tao Zongyi's has been substituted. But it is still present in the Zhonghua reprint of the Qianlong edition (following *juan* 116).

63. For citations and a discussion of their phonological significance see Zhu, *Hou Jin guohan,* 25–26.

64. This distinction is in the imperial prefaces, and I myself mistakenly followed it in 1983; see "'Historical and Magic Unity.'"

65. Qing records in Chinese do not acknowledge this etymology in Jurchen or Manchu lineage names. *KF,* for instance, transliterates *giya* in Manchu lineage names as the word for "happy, auspicious." *BMST* uses that character or the word for "pillar." In no case is the character for "family, household" used.

the Gūwalgiya (Guan jia) and its branches, as well as the Wanggiya/ Wanyan (Wang jia),[66] who were the ruling lineage of the Jurchen Jin empire in the twelfth century.

Nevertheless, the assertion of the "Collected Genealogies of the Eight-Banner and Manchu Lineages" that Manchu surnames are place names is a clue to the social history of the Liaodong and southern Jilin environs. Jurchen/Manchu lineages (to be discussed in Chapter 3) were not eternal entities but were constantly formed and re-formed through the social and economic processes of life in the Jurchen territories. Because of social and economic importance of these lineages, nomenclature changed as circumstances required. Many Jurchen lineages took up the practice of using surnames. Settlers moving into a new region might cause a valley, river, or settlement to be called after their own surnames. The presence of settlers having Chinese or Korean surnames and the attachment of these names to places within the Jurchen territories is well attested, for instance, in Shin Chung-il's record of his visit to Nurgaci's homestead in 1596.[67] Jurchens who moved to the region later and formed new lineage groups would call themselves after the name of the place where they lived, or the name of the closest place. If it was the village of the Ma family, the Jurchens might thereafter be called the Magiya lineage. The problem of degenerating and regenerating lineages among the Jurchens is connected to the alienation of individuals from lineage affiliations, whether through migration, urbanization, or enslavement. This was a long-standing social phenomenon in Northeastern Asia, referred to under the term *baišin* as early as the composition of the "Secret History of the Mongols."[68] Qing genealogical

66. Jin Qizong (*Nuzhen wen cidian*, 82, 132) reconstructs this as Jurchen Won (g)ien.

67. See as examples Wangjia (Shin *KJD*, 11), Huangjia (12), or Wang Zhi Chuan (*KJD*, 13).

68. *Baišin niyalma* could be a corruption of Chinese *baixing*, "the hundred names." *Baišin* was a venerable institution in Inner Asia. The term was known among the Mongols of the thirteenth century and occurs in "Secret History of the Mongols" (on this work see Chapter 6). Though the meaning of *baišin* in Qing registries is clear—individuals without lineage affiliation—the etymology seems more ambiguous to me now than it did in 1989 ("Qianlong Retrospect"). The borrowing is more likely via Mongolian than directly from Chinese and may be connected to a similar word, *bayising*, which in the sixteenth century was both the name for a town (Chinese Bansheng, "wooden places" near Guihua) and a term for a house of wood, brick, or rammed earth. Rozycki, however, thinks the Mongolian term was of Persian origin, in which case the Chinese may have been a false etymology (*Mongol Elements in Manchu*, 23). These dwellings were characteristic of the sort of community where agricultural servants of the Mongols and later the

records preserve a portrait of a social category with this name made up of people of indeterminate descent.[69] Shunzhi (1644–61) era revisions of earlier records call these individuals *baishen ren,* "individuals of blank status," a transposition of Manchu *baišin niyalma,* and their vulnerable identities were powerfully affected by the state-building processes overseen by Nurgaci and Hung Taiji.

The conquest of the Pozhu valley by Jurchens using the Tong surname became the determining factor in the identification of the Tunggiya lineage of the Qing period. According to the "Collected Genealogies of the Eight-Banner and Manchu Lineages," the Tunggiya originated at Maca.[70] Detailed maps of the Qianlong period show Maca as an easterly tributary of the Tunggiya-ula, "Tunggiya River," which had earlier been the Pozhu River. The Tunggiya of the fifteenth or early sixteenth century were a new lineage, formed in the Tunggiya valley by Bahu Teksin.[71] This could not have happened before the arrival of Fanca and the changing of the name of the valley in the middle fifteenth century. In Bahu Teksin's time, ancestors of Tong Bunian were already well established in eastern Liaodong, and especially at Fushun. Though Qing scholarship would later insist upon an identification of the Tunggiya lineage of Nurgan with the Tong families of Fushun, the political geography of the Pozhu/Tunggiya valley demonstrates the impossibility of this identification (for which there is no evidence at all apart from that manufactured by the Qing court in the later seventeenth century).

The general vicinity of Tunggiya remained the Jianzhou base until the early seventeenth century, when central Liaodong was conquered and occupied. At the time that Nurgaci gained control of the federation—a century and a half after Fanca had occupied the sometime Pozhu River valley

[margin handwritten note: Fanca— brother of Mongke Timur]

Jurchens lived, and it is certainly possible that the name for the type of settlement became the term for the people living there (see Serruys, *The Mongols and Ming China,* 8:240–41). Chinese *baixing* (hundred names), *bansheng* (wooden structures), or Persian could be the source for the Jurchen word, by way of Mongolian. This is not to rule out the possibility of two words ("individuals of blank status" and "communities with wooden structures") with distinct etymologies.

69. For early citations of *baišin* in the seventeenth century see Chen Jiahua, "Qingchu baishen ren xi."

70. *BMST* 19:1a. All of *juan* 19 and much of *juan* 20 is devoted to the Tunggiya lineage. Almost without exception, those hailing from Tunggiya proper were enrolled in the Manchu Plain White Banner. They are the lineage of Nikan Wailan (19:18a), on whom see Chapter 3.

71. *BMST* 19:1a–b. No date is given for the formation of the *mukūn.* See also Mitamura, *Shinchō zenshi,* 72.

and it had been renamed Tunggiya—the Tong surname was an emblem of the hegemony of the Jianzhou federation and of the lineage of Möngke Temür. It was not a lineage name proper but more like an alliance name. When Shin Chung-il visited Nurgaci's settlement at Fe Ala in 1596, he found that not only the entire lineage of Nurgaci used the Tong surname, but it was also used by close political associates—including Yangguri, Hōhōri, and Hurgan, who would later be among the founders of the "eight great families" (*ba dajia*) of the Qing—and those like Cinggiha and Hurgan's father Hūlagū, who had married into Nurgaci's family. Of the thirty-eight headmen appearing in Shin's account, thirty used the Tong surname, five used the Li surname, two used Wang, and one had the Korean surname of Kim. Nurgaci himself used the Tong surname in his youth as a mark of identity and political affiliations meaningful to both the Ming and the Yi courts.

THE LIAODONGESE

Tong Bunian did not dispute the authority of genealogy in matters of identity and loyalty, and he assumed the importance of family narrative in the manifestation of loyalty or treason. In "Record of Prisoned Rage" he provided nine generations of Chinese names for his ancestors and described them as circuit traders who had taken an early role in the establishment of Ming military and commercial hegemony in Liaodong. He never suggested that his ancestors may have come from anywhere but northern China. He pointed to his forebears, who had participated in the earliest Ming actions in Liaodong: "Our founding ancestor served as an infantryman [*xiaoqi*] during the northern campaigns of Hongwu 16 [1383]; in 21 [1388] he was sent to post notices in the Tieling garrison and also did so in Korea, where he was promoted to office [*zongqi*]. Because of his service in the suppression of the Nurgan wildmen he was appointed centuriarch [*baihu*], was reassigned to the right camp [*you suo*] of the Sanwan garrison in 28 (1395) and killed wildmen in the Hūlawun region. He was originally married to a woman surnamed Wang."[72]

[handwritten margin note: T.B.'s lineage]

72. From the genealogical appendix, in eight *juan*, which Tong Guoqi attached to his father Bunian's *Yufen lu* (issued in 1654); see 1:2a. It was quoted at length by Zhu Xizu, *Hou Jin guohan*, 46, 49–50. The Hūlawun River region was apparently in southern Heilongjiang, and a Ming-period Jurchen citation for a phrase very similar to the one used by Tong Bunian here has been found by Jin Qizong: *He-lu-un ula udi-e nialma*, "forest people of the He-lu-un River" (see *Nuzhen wen cidian*, 139).

The career that Tong Bunian sketched for his "founding ancestor" Tong Dali in the genealogy he appended to the "Record of Prisoned Rage" is like that of a Jurchen soldier, or mercenary, in the ranks of the Ming occupation forces in Liaodong. Indeed the date of his recruitment, 1383, is very close to the time of a remark preserved in the Chinese annals indicating that Ming military recruitment for service in Liaodong was surging among Jurchens and Koreans.[73] The perambulations attributed to Tong Dali in his career as a Ming soldier correspond neatly with the movements of the Sanwan garrison, first established at Ilantumen and moved to Kaiyuan in 1395, after a series of defeats in their attempts to pacify "wildmen" at the Korean border. Tong Dali's ranks were all the normal ranks of the Northeastern garrison system. In these particulars his career was typical of the "capitulated" (*guifu*) Jurchens. It closely paralleled, for instance, that of one Tong Dalaha who also received centuriarch (*baihu*) rank, campaigned against wildmen along the Yalu River, and married into the "Wang" family—Wang (Wanyan, Wanggiya) being in various forms a surname as common among Jurchen descendants as it was among Chinese descendants in the region.[74]

The evidence, then, suggests that Tong Dali was one of the Jurchens from the Sanwan garrison who were permitted by the Ming government to settle in Liaodong. He was a rather early adherent to the Ming cause, serving in their army even before the formal registration of the Sanwan garrison at Ilantumen, and may have inspired sufficient trust to have been among the many Jurchens asked to serve as intermediaries between the court and the federation leaders; his "posting notices" (*zhanggua*) in Tieling and in Korea may have been references to such activities.[75] The lavish title with which he is supposed to have been honored, "General Who Stabi-

73. Zhu Chengru, 74, from *Ming Taizu shilu*, 167 (Hongwu 15).

74. Scraps of information on Tongdalaha / Tong Dalaha are found in *Ming shilu*, "Xuande 6," sixth month, *kuichou* (twenty-first day). *Mindai manmōshiryō, Manshu hen* (1954), 48. He is not the same person as Tong Dali. Mitamura Taisuke (*Shinchō zenshi*, 72) provides a reconstruction of Tongdalaha's genealogy, based on Ming records. In contrast to Mitamura's reconstructed genealogy, Zhu Xizu (*Hou Jin guohan*, 44–45) suggests that Tong Dalaha was of the same lineage as Ahacu and that Dalaha was the father of Tong Dali, for which there is no convincing evidence. Zhu attributes to Naitō Torajirō the hypothesis that Tong Dalaha was the same person as Darhan Tumet, the son of Bahu Teksin; this is posited on the false testimony of the *BMST* (see next chapter), appears to be linguistically adventurous, and is in addition a chronological improbability.

75. Relaying information from the Ming government in Peking to the Nurgan tribes and back again was a profession for many Jurchens. Morris Rossabi touches on this several times; see *The Jurchens in the Yüan and Ming*, esp. 27. See also Serruys, *Sino-Jürched Relations*, 50–51.

lizes the Nation" (*zhenguo jiangjun*), was also characteristic of Ming treatment of their tenuous allies in the Northeast.[76] A branch of the family probably arrived in Fushun by the middle or later fifteenth century. According to local tradition,[77] an ancestor named Darhaci brought the family there. "On account of trade" he had moved first from Liaoyang to Kaiyuan and then from Kaiyuan to Fushun. If Darhaci used a Chinese name, it may have been any of several provided in Tong Bunian's genealogy for the descendants of Dali's son, Tong Jing. Darhaci was evidently one of those Jurchens of the area, on good terms with Ming trade officials, who made an ample living through the sale of ginseng, horses, pelts, and luxury foodstuffs.[78]

By the later sixteenth century the Tong of Fushun were one of the most prominent, largest, and wealthiest collection of lineages in the region. Their stability in Fushun was remarkable. Tong Bunian had emphasized the ancestral distance between himself and Tong Yangxing and Tong Yangzhen—the two who caused him so much trouble by joining Nurgaci's military efforts after the taking of Fushun in 1618—by pointing out that they shared a single ancestor with him no closer than four generations in the past. Yet they were all raised in Fushun, and as a group they may have exemplified Fushun's literate elite. Bunian possibly shared with his distant cousins a knowledge of Christianity and perhaps the skills—cannon manufacture and deployment—with which it was associated. Certainly Yangzhen and Yangxing were familiar with military arts introduced by the Jesuits, and Tong Bunian's son Guoqi would later distinguish himself as a friend of the Jesuits in Fujian, Zhejiang, and Peking.[79] Numerous and influential as they were, the Tong lineage was not the only lineage of easterly origin who were leaders in seventeenth-century Liaodong. Among the better known of such families were the Cui—or Ch'oe—family,[80] the Shi family of Guangning, and the Li, or Yi, lineages of Tieling. The latter were descendants of immigrants to northern Liaodong from a region south of the Yalu River. As mentioned above, northern Korea, including Omohoi, had been a heavily Jur-

76. This was a common honorific for higher ranks in the *dusi* system; see for instance one Zhang Wang, cited in *Nurgan Yongningsi beiji*, "Appendix," 2.

77. See *Liaodong zhi*, "Shizu" (1537) 1.2a.

78. See Deng, "Shilun Ming yu Hou Jin zhanzheng de yuanyin ji qi xingzhi," esp. 12–13.

79. On the Jesuit associations of the Kangxi emperor's uncle Tong Guowei see also Yang Zhen, *Kangxi huangdi yijia*, 361–63.

80. The surname used by this family was probably of Korean inspiration. Those interested in them might begin with Huang Weihan's *Heishui xianmin zhuan, juan* 16–24.

chen area for hundreds of years before the later fourteenth century, when the government of Yi Korea began campaigns to drive them north. Like the Ming, the Yi used a combination of military occupation and agricultural colonization to secure the region. Many Jurchens joined the Yi garrisons established in the vicinity of the Yalu, and others entered trade, frequently assuming Korean surnames. Li Chengliang's ancestor Li Yingni (or Yi Yŏng-nok) may have been a contemporary of Tong Dali and Möngke Temür.[81] He left his home in northern Korea and entered Liaodong, where he became a scribe in the Tieling garrison. That is, like Tong Dali he entered the Ming military at a time when the large numbers of Jurchen and Korean recruits were noted and took up a role resembling Tong Dali's. Given the demography of northern Korea in Li Yingni's time, the probability that he was of Jurchen descent, and followed a career path similar to Tong Dali's (either opportunistically or under pressure from Korean incursions) is greater than that he was a "Korean" who abandoned agriculture or trade to undertake an illegal trek to Liaodong.

These are not the only similarities between the Li lineages of Tieling and the Tong lineages of Fushun. Li Yingni's descendant (and Li Chengliang's son) Li Rubo (1553–1621), like Tong Bunian, was a Ming military official and died a reported suicide in prison (after Nurgaci's victory at Sarhū); his brother Li Ruzhen (d. 1631) was imprisoned the same year for refusing to aid in the defense of Tieling.[82] Following the conquest of Tieling, Rubo's nephews Li Zunzu and Li Sizheng joined their distant relative Li Yongfang (who had refused to defend Fushun) at Nurgaci's side and encouraged others of the lineage to defect from the Ming. Fang Chao-ying commented with reference to the Li of Tieling, "Contrary to customs, these men not only did not avenge the deaths of their forebears but served the Manchus vigorously and rose to be high officials."[83] Indeed, like the Tong of Fushun and the Shi of Guangning, the Li of Tieling became prominent in the occupation government in China, were ennobled by the Qing court, and frequently took "Manchu" names and wives. For reasons to be discussed below, the histories of such families were strongly overwritten in the later seventeenth century and in the eighteenth century, so that a precise estimate of the size of this cultural stratum is difficult to achieve. Nevertheless, the Tong, Li,

[handwritten marginalia: the Li family]

81. *ECCP* places him "five generations" before Li Chengliang.

82. Rubo had succeeded his brother Li Rumei as brigade-general in Liaodong in 1618, but was arrested with his superior Yang Hao after the Ming attempt to attack Hetu Ala, which resulted in the disastrous rout at Sarhū. Rubo committed suicide in prison very shortly afterward.

83. *ECCP*, 451.

Cui, and Shi are prominent examples of the contemporary cultural complexities of late Ming Liaodong and of the sources of Qing state-building.

Ming fear of subversion by Nurgaci in the Northeast was profound. If they were not aware themselves of Nurgaci's talent for converting to his cause those who had migrated and even been forcibly taken to his territories from Liaodong, they were provided with plentiful information from Koreans who were better informed of Nurgaci's world than they. In the early 1620s reports from Liaodong of the activities of Nurgaci's spies—who could have been ancestral Chinese, Jurchens, Mongols, or any one of these passing for any of the others—in Liaodong were continuous.[84] The common people of Liaodong were, as Xiong Tingbi had noted, apparently insufficiently interested in whether they were ruled by the Ming or by Nurgaci to actively support the Ming defense effort, and military officers were increasingly found to be undependable in their responsibilities. That minority of real or imagined subversives—including Li Rubo, Li Ruzhen, and Tong Bunian—who could be seized and brought to trial were not adequate as examples to deter new deserters. The larger number who—following the examples of Li Yongfang, Tong Yangxing, and Tong Yangzhen—arrived at Nurgaci's camp not only avoided the Ming prosecutors but were reported to live literally as princes in Nurgaci's realm. Liaodong, having suffered for generations under the exactions and mismanagement of Ming eunuchs and officials, had social and cultural complexities that Nurgaci strummed shrewdly, but to which the Ming court was tone-deaf. The result was that the Jin conquest of Liaodong (though not its governance) was easier than perhaps even Nurgaci had expected, and the Ming were left to blame spies, witches, and traitors for the precipitous deterioration of their rule in the Northeast.

84. Yan, *Nurhachi zhuan*, 126–28, provides documentation.

2   The Character of Loyalty

The posthumous titles Qing emperors bestowed upon prominent men were soft ground for ideological traces. The Kangxi and Yongzheng emperors employed a variety of terms connoting "righteousness" (*yi*), "courage" (*yong*), "determination" (*zhi*), and, above all, "erudition" (*wen*). But in the eighteenth century, the Qianlong emperor Hongli awarded with unusual frequency one character for which he had a rather comprehensive philosophy: *zhong*, "loyalty."[1] In the historical revisionism of the later eighteenth century the Qianlong commitment to loyalty became so abstract that Ming loyalists who had opposed the Qing onslaught were enshrined, while those who had deserted the Ming to join the Qing were in varying degrees condemned. When viewed through the lens of Ming philosophies of identity and loyalty, the cultural layering of Liaodong (where after 1618 Nurgaci was confederalizing the population through more or less coercive means) had had fatal consequences for Tong Bunian. When viewed through the lens of Qianlong idealism, it had fatal consequences for the culture in which Tong Bunian was raised.

Nurgaci's khanate, in contrast to the Ming empire, made its primary distinctions culturally and geographically. It discriminated between those who lived in the east, participated in Jurchen lineages and Jurchen livelihoods, and spoke Jurchen, on the one hand, and those who lived in the

---

1. Abe Takeo, "Shinchō to ka i shishō," where, most specific to the present discussion, it is shown that the epithet *zhong*, "loyal," became the most frequent *shi* only during the Qianlong period, displacing *wen*, "cultured," which had been most common in earlier eras. See also Fisher, "Lü Liu-liang and the Tseng Ching Case," 180–85. The term figured in the posthumous names granted Tong Yangzhen (Zhonglie) and Tong Guogang (Zhongyong).

89

west, in towns or in farming villages, and spoke primarily Chinese, on the other. The Jianzhou Jurchens called the latter group Nikan, whether their ancestors were Chinese, Korean, or Jurchen. Later the term would be redefined by the Qing court, and with every redefinition would come a reimagining of the history of seventeenth-century Liaodong and of the Qing rise. Though the population of whom the Tong of Fushun were exemplary had been indispensable to early Qing state-building, their cultural representation became difficult after the conquest of north China. As the westward boundaries of Qing ambition crept to and beyond the Great Wall, the conquest state found itself increasingly challenged by the problems of constructing and enforcing identities. The continuing paradox was how to stabilize the identities of conqueror and conquered without creating legal, political, or ideological obstacles to continued incorporation of imperial servitors. One result, to be examined here, was the introduction of new narrative and new language relating to the Chinese-martial banners,[2] the general effect of which was to simplify, genealogize, and ultimately racialize Chinese-martial identity, in the service of forging a history of "Chinese" devotion to the Qing.

THE EARLY NIKAN SPECTRUM

The problem of loyalty is often viewed from the late Qing perspective, when the idea that the Chinese-martial were Ming Chinese who had chosen to support the Qing had become fundamental to the imperial narrative. The well-known "one in ten thousand" aphorism used by Zhang Zhidong (1837–1909) to position the Chinese-martial within the Chinese population as a whole in his introduction to "Writings from the Eight Banners" (*Baqi wenjing*)[3] was typical; indeed the late-nineteenth-century imperial regulations (*Guangxu huidian*) had given court imprimatur to the usage "Han Eight Banners" (*han baqi*) for the first time. The source for this sweeping characterization was the Qianlong emperor, who had announced flatly in the middle eighteenth century that "the Chinese-martial originally are ✓

---

2. For general background on the *hanjun* banners see Meng Sen, "Baqi zhidu kaoshi"; Liu Chia-chü, "The Creation of the Chinese Banners in the Early Ch'ing"; and Chao Ch'i-na [Zhao Qina], "Qingchu baqi hanjun yanjiu."

3. 1902. The collection was edited by [Aisin Gioro] Shengyu (1850–1900) and in 60 *juan* presented the writings of 197 bannermen from various periods. Zhang, a close friend of Shengyu, paid for the posthumous publication of the work and wrote an introduction to it. See *ECCP*, 649.

all Han" (*Hanjun zhi chu ben xi han ren*).[4] The emperor clearly intended his audience to ignore—if they knew—how complex the identity of the Han/Nikan had been in the early Qing. The court was at pains to disseminate the newly straightened view of Chinese-martial origins and enlisted, among others, the eighteenth-century writer Shen Qiyuan: "The Chinese who surrendered first were called the *hanjun;* they called the *hanjun* to distinguish them from the Chinese who had not yet surrendered."[5] But before the Qianlong period, histories of the banners and of the Chinese-martial in particular had still attempted to convey the complexity of the issue, while grappling with a narrowing vocabulary of identity that barely allowed even the administrative divisions of the early Nikan populations to be described. Thus Jin Dechun—himself a Chinese-martial bannerman— evoked the fading tints of early Nikan diversity when he wrote in 1715, "The inhabitants of the Liao valley who were descendants of the former Ming guard commanders, the Chinese soldiers and officers who had surrendered and those who were captured in raids were separately put under the Chinese-martial."[6] In fact, the guard commanders were in many cases not of Chinese descent, or even avowedly Chinese in their own time, and so the "separately" in this sentence is important.

The Tong and other families of Liaodong who had joined Nurgaci in the late sixteenth or early seventeenth century were consistently marked as "Nikan" by the Jurchen-speaking majority. The Jurchen word *nikan* (plural *nikasa*) was evidently based upon the Chinese word *han*.[7] Though from the eighteenth century on the presumption would grow that the term indicated Chinese or descendants of Chinese in Liaodong, it was understood in the seventeenth century to indicate simply the sedentary sinophone population of Liaodong, regardless of ancestry. *Han* had functioned this way in the political terminology of the Kitan Liao (*hanersi*), Jurchen Jin (*han*), and

4. Guan Tianting, "Qingdai huangshi shizu ji xuexi," 61. It is not an inviolable rule that all nineteenth-century writers adhered to the Qianlong historical doctrine on the Chinese-martial banners. Sayingge, for instance, in "Independent Record of Jilin" (*Jilin waiji*, 1827), the first narrative of Jilin province, is steadfast in asserting both that Nikan immigrants to Jilin assimilated with the local populations and that in the formation of the banners the Manchu divisions absorbed both Nikan and "old Mongol" populations (see 35–37).

5. From *Huangchao jingshi wenbian*, cited in Liu Chia-chü, "The Creation of the Chinese Banners," 63.

6. From *Qijun zhi*, 2, cited in Liu Chia-chü, "The Creation of the Chinese Banners," 62–63.

7. It has possible parallels in Jurchen *nindzu*, from Chinese *zhu* (cited in Jin, *Nuzhen wen cidian*, 139).

Mongol Yuan (*han, kidad*) empires. In those periods the population of northern China, Liaodong, and parts of Mongolia had been settled by successive groups of Chinese, Turkic, Kitan, Jurchen, or Mongol descent who had come to share a cultural style based on agriculture, on speaking Chinese, and on at least some familiarity with Chinese family structure and ritual. Similarly, *nikan* for the Jianzhou Jurchens were people who lived in the Chinese style (or what was understood to be the Chinese style), whether their ancestors, near or remote, had actually been Ming Chinese, Jurchens, Turks, Mongols, or Koreans. Some indirect but colorful evidence that *nikan* was regarded by the sixteenth- and seventeenth-century Jurchens as a "type"—possibly in some instances a comic type—and not as a genealogical group is provided by the fact that Nikan was a common name among Jurchens (one of Nurgaci's own grandsons was called by it) and remained so well into the eighteenth century.[8] Though it was not a property of the word *nikan* to entail Chinese ancestry in anyone so denoted, those living within the boundaries of Ming China were the primary subset of the *nikan*. Indeed it was incumbent upon seventeenth-century Jurchen to qualify the word *nikan* to specify its meaning, and this was consistently done: *nikan i gurun*, the "country of the Nikans," was Ming China. But *nikan* could be a place—for example, "east of Nikan" (*nikan i dergi*) meant Nurgan (which as a cultural distinction excluded Liaodong). Until the middle seventeenth century, the Qing court would continue to qualify *nikan* to create references to certain populations in Liaodong.

From the earliest days of Nurgaci's regime, there were Nikans in his entourage, and given the history of Chinese immigration to Liaodong and beyond it is reasonable to suppose that there were also Nikans in the service of Giocangga and Taksi and of Wan of Hada (who is treated in the next chapter of this book). Integration of peoples of diverse geographical origins or cultural backgrounds through the estates of nobles was a tradition of the region, well described in records as early as the Liao, and clearly continued among Nurgaci's followers until the very early seventeenth century. In 1596, during a visit to Fe Ala, Shin Chung-il encountered many men (presumably indentured) with Chinese or Korean[9] names managing the properties of Nurgaci, Šurgaci, or their followers. He also met Fushunese spe-

---

8. Solgo (Solho), "Korean," was also a common name, and in modern times Shirokogoroff found "Russian" (Locan). For the same practice among the Khorchins note the individual Kitat Taiji "Chinese prince," or ("Prince Chinese") *TM* 10:3:7.

9. Since both are represented with Chinese characters, it is impossible to distinguish them in his account.

cifically (for instance, Tong Yangcai), among Nurgaci's entourage. It was Shin who provided details on the family history of the man he knew as "Kim Ado," the "Adun" of the Manchu annals.[10] In 1594, when difficulties over murders south of the Yalu had arisen, Adun of Giyamuhu led the Jianzhou troops south to talk peace. His father, called by the Jurchens Jeocangga, had originally been from Liaodong, but while in Jianzhou service had spent time in Korea and had readily "assimilated Korean ways" (that is, become useful to the Korean authorities). In recognition of this the Yi court had awarded Jeocangga the name Kim Ki-song and the stipend of a minor official. Adun himself had been stationed at Nurgaci's successive headquarters eight or nine years by the time Shin saw him at Fe Ala in 1596, "and because his father submitted [to Nurgaci] this is his native land, and he will not come away."[11] Adun never did go away, and served Nurgaci long into the Later Jin era.

The range of conditions for Nikans under the Nurgaci and Hung Taiji regimes is well known. It may be described as economically insecure, vulnerable to arbitrary punishment or abuse by powerful Jurchens, and perpetually distrusted by those who controlled the state after 1616.[12] The large group called bondservants (*boo-i aha*) included a majority of apparent Nikan provenance and a minority of Jurchen. Bondservants were organized into companies and registered with the Chinese-martial banners during the Hung Taiji years, but their later status was not confused with that of the regular Chinese-martial bannermen and their attachment to the Imperial Household Department (*neiwu fu*) rather than the Board of Military Affairs (*binbgbu*) was considered a more accurate representation of their relationship to the court. Before the war in Liaodong there were few institutional expressions of differential legal statuses between Jianzhou Jurchens and the good number of people among them who were different. Social stratification remained important. Primary was the difference between slaves and commoners, the former category containing a majority of individuals who had originally been Nikan or of the unaffiliated condition of

10. *Adun* is a word in Jurchen/Manchu, meaning a "herd" (borrowed from Mongolian *adughun*) usually of horses (it occurs in the name for the imperial stud, Adun be kalara yamun). It would be rash to assume that Adun acquired his name from some association with herds or horse breeding, but it is certainly possible.

11. Shin Chung-il, *KJD*. Yi Minhwan later met Adun at Hetu Ala, probably in 1619. See di Cosmo, "Nuove fonti," 148.

12. The basic work in English on the *nikan* population in this period is Roth [Li], "The Manchu-Chinese Relationship." See also Guo Chengkang, "Shixi Qing wangchao ruguan qian dui hanzu de zhengce."

the *baišin*. Servile status was normally determined at conclusion of a military confrontation, when the losing forces would be divided into the captured, destined for slavery, and the capitulated, in most cases destined to become agricultural workers or bureaucratic functionaries with limited freedom. Kidnapped populations were used as the needs of the moment demanded.[13]

The rapid evolution of the social and legal definitions of Nikan groups after 1616 marked a watershed both for the non-Jurchen Northeastern natives living under Jurchen control and for the new state itself. Establishment of the Nurgaci khanate in 1616 fostered a more institutionalized status for the Nikan population and for the military service sector that would emerge from it. Nevertheless, there is little evidence that the status of the Nikans merited special comment until 1619, a year after Nurgaci's forces seized Fushun and transported its population to Jin territory. This was the time at which Nurgaci is supposed to have uttered his famous phrase demarcating the original, Liaodongese Nikan military servitors (who would later be called the *tai nikan*) from those incorporated later: "Judge them on the same basis as the Manchus."[14] It was to the Nurgaci period in Jurchen state formation that the motto "there was originally no principle for discrimination" (*yuan wu er shi zhi li*)[15] referred. This would later, thanks to the Qianlong court's folding of Chinese-martial identity onto Chinese, become a cliché for the court's ostensible impartiality in treatment of Manchus

13. An, "Shun Kang Yong sanchao baqi ding'e qianxi," 102. On servitude among the Jurchens see Wei Qingyuan et al., *Qingdai nupei zhidu*; for an introduction to early Qing institutions see Spence, *Ts'ao Yin and the K'ang-hsi Emperor*, 7–22; Torbert, *The Ch'ing Imperial Household Department*, 53–59; Roth [Li], "The Manchu-Chinese Relationship," 10–15. A very useful technical discussion of the Chinese terms related to Banner servitude is included in Fu Kedong, "Baqi huji zhidu chucao."

14. See Roth [Li], "The Rise of the Early Manchu State," 30; also Wakeman, *The Great Enterprise*, 45. This was in the aftermath of Nurgaci's successful defense of Sarhū against Ming forces in 1619, a major step in his development of a credible political and military presence in the province. On periodization of Northeastern campaigns see Li Zhiting, "Ming Qing zhanzheng yu Qingchu lishi fazhan shi." As always, attributions to Nurgaci must be handled tentatively, since they were subject to liberal emendation, "clarification," and beautification during Hung Taiji's reign. In the present instance the word "Manchu" is a self-evident interpolation from the following reign.

15. Literally, "originally no principle for having two perceptions" (from *Qing shilu, Shizu chao*, 44). For Qianlong use of the Manchu counterpart of the convention *daci acu tuwaha be akū* see Meadows, *Translations from the Manchu with the Original Texts*, Manchu: 14a.

and Chinese[16]—despite the fact that the original remark was intended to underscore the difference between Nikans and Ming Chinese. Prominent lineages of the Chinese-martial would later trace their ancestry to the Liaodong and neighboring populations who were integrated with Nurgaci's forces in these early years of the khanate.

From the beginnings of Nikan involvement with the Jurchen regimes of Nurgan, there was an important distinction between those assuming military roles and those going into civil labor servitude. A considerable and identifiable portion of the male Nikan population functioned as Nurgaci's bodyguards and as his troops in time of battle. The black banners of the Nikans were spotted by Shin Chung-il in 1596.[17] Sometime after the founding of the khanate in 1616 Nikan soldiers, still flying their black flags, appear to have been referred to as "cherished soldiers," *ujen cooha*.[18] In 1637 the *ujen cooha* unit, still represented under a black banner, was split into two; in 1639 the two became four; and in 1642 the eight Chinese-martial, or *hanjun*, banners flying the colors of the previously commissioned Manchu and Mongol Banners were created. The emergence of a professional military sector of the Nikans was one product of a larger development in the expansion of the state's capacity to create and enforce status rules, while

16. See also Kessler, *K'ang-hsi and the Consolidation of Ch'ing Rule*, 117.

17. *KJD* citation; also *Yijo sillok* (Senjo) 29:1. Flags in five colors were ubiquitous in eastern Asia from at least Han times, when the imperial armies used yellow to mark the location of the emperor (or his representative), and the five traditional colors of the directions (green for east, white for south, red for west, and black for north) in order to orient soldiers on the field of battle and improve the precision of orders issued in combat. The practice was diffused throughout Northeast Asia, possibly via the Northern Wei empire. Its use by the time of the Kitans was ambiguous: In the long painting by Li Tang (1049–1130) depicting the scenes from Han history of the return of Cai Wenji from the "Barbarians" the colored flags are very clearly seen, and they may (if the picture is reversed) still represent the cardinal directions (the group is evidently riding south). Historically these barbarians were Xiongnu, but Li has not surprisingly depicted them as very specifically Kitan. This painting has recently been the object of an extended study by Irene Leung (see "Conflicts of Loyalty in Twelfth-Century China"). The flags occur in clutch, which suggests that they may more importantly represent the divisions (or "wings") of the Liao military organization. The association with "banners" cannot predate the Ming, who established these military units (perhaps derived from the decimal divisions of the Mongol armies), and from whom Nurgaci seems to have adapted the idea of "banners" and "bannermen." The evidence seems clear that he originally used five flags, in the traditional manner, and continued to use the black flag—but now for the *ujen cooha*—after the initial founding of four banners in 1601.

18. Yi Minhwan reported the five colors of banners (that is, including black) at Hetu Ala in 1619 (di Cosmo, "Nuove fonti," 148).

Nikan
ᠵᡠᠴᡳᠩ

simultaneously fretting the Nikans with new distinctions of rank. By the end of Nurgaci's khanate in 1626, the identification of Nikan with literate, civil, bureaucratic functionaries, distinct from the bannermen of the "various" peoples, was overt.[19] The military segment of the Nikan population, on the other hand, had a special role as the pivot upon which Nurgaci's earliest rhetoric of khanal solicitude turned. "Cherished soldiers" (*ujen cooha*),[20] which is used in the "First Edition of the General History of the Eight Banners" (*Baqi tongzhi* [*chuji*] [1739]) and "Imperially Commissioned General History of the Eight Banners" ([*Qinding*] *Baqi tongzhi* [1799]) for the pre-conquest companies, was probably the more formal designation (to the extent this makes sense in the very early period) for this group. In Hung Taiji times, there was a shift (which is very hard to date precisely, because of the continual revision of documents) from this semantically general term to ones of much greater specificity. At some point, probably in the later 1620s, the term "Nikan armies" (*nikan cooha*) was

19. See also Chapter 4, n 3.

20. The exact date of the introduction of this term and its precise meaning are unresolved. I have myself changed my idea about the meaning of this term, as well as its linguistic, social, and ideological affinities. Liu Chia-chü proposed that the term might mean that the soldiers in question were armored and sent ahead of the invading Jurchens / Manchus as "cannon fodder" (see "The Creation of the Chinese Banners," 60). The practice of driving captives ahead of the invading army was traditional and attested, but given the high value placed on armor, it hardly seems that such protection would be lavished on those treated this way, and as a consequence this does not appear a strong possibility for the origin of the term. *Ujen* might mean "heavy" in the sense of laboring under a burden, like a pack animal or like a team of men attempting to drag, position, and operate a cannon—and the Jurchens first acquired their cannons at Fushun. I have previously suggested that it might, alternatively, mean "slow," in the sense of unmounted soldiers, carrying their own provisions; Jurchens ("free men") rode and had their provisions carried by slaves.

Having studied Jin Qizong's citations from Jurchen and thought anew about related words in Manchu, and having considered the context from which the term *ujen cooha* emerged, I now have a different understanding of it. Jurchen *udzə*, like Manchu *ujen*, meant both "heavy" and "important, emphasized, serious, valuable, respected." Jin (100–101) cites two verbs, evidently variants of each other, *udzə bimei* and *udzubimai*, both meaning "to respect." They are reflected in Manchu *ujelembi*, whose meanings Norman (*A Concise Manchu–English Lexicon*, 292), cites as "1. to be heavy, 2. to act respectfully, to treat respectfully, 3. to be serious, to act in a serious manner, 4. to act generously, 5. to value highly." The root of these words is also related to Jurchen *udzu-dzi-ru*, "to nourish, cherish, raise," reflected in Manchu *ujimbi*, which has the same meaning. This puts these words in extreme intimacy with Nurgaci's usual description of himself as "raising, nourishing, cherishing" (*ujire, ujikini*, etc.) the "various nations" (*geren gurun*). This interpretation has been previously presented in Crossley, *The Manchus*, 203–5, and for further elaboration, see Chapter 4 of this book.

used, at least informally. Extant (revised) records use it in reference to the populations of Guangning (1622) and those incorporated after.

Since *nikan cooha* appears to be the Manchu equivalent of the Chinese term "Han armies" (*hanjun*), modern historians often take the two as interchangeable. There are no textual grounds for equating the terms before 1642.[21] *Hanjun* was one of the terms that were critical in Hung Taiji's programs appropriated from the (Jurchen) Jin imperial history, which Hung Taiji had ordered translated into Manchu and which he was reported to read avidly. When North China had been conquered by the Jurchen Jin in the twelfth century, "Han armies" (*hanjun*) was a term used for the Chinese (that is, Han, as described in earlier pages) who were incorporated into the military (*mouke-minggan*) system.[22] The normal Chinese term for the Chinese-martial Eight Banners from their inception in 1642 to the later eighteenth century was never *hanjun,* or even *han baqi,* but *hanjun baqi.*[23]

[handwritten margin note: nikan cooha = hanjun *]*

---

21. There are many studies of Chinese-martial banners in particular: perhaps the clearest remains Liu Chia-chü, "The Creation of the Chinese Banners."

22. *Jinshi* 44:1–4. On the *mouke-minggan,* see Tao Jingshen, *The Jurchens in Twelfth-Century China,* 11–12.

23. In the Jin history *hanjun* meant the "army of the Han (i.e., north China) people." In the Eight Banners, however, *hanjun* is an adjective, used to describe either a Chinese-martial division of the Eight Banners (*hanjun baqi*) or Chinese-martial bannermen associated with that division (*hanjun qiren*). It was not used in the Qing official records to mean "Han army" and aside from some idiosyncratic instances it has no grammatical equivalent in the appellations for the Manchu and Mongol Banners (there is no *manjun* or *mengjun*); its equivalents are simply *manzhou* (*manzhou baqi*) and *menggu* (*menggu baqi*). This book argues the value of distinguishing the *hanjun* from what in the middle seventeenth century was readily identifiable as the "Chinese" population, and it is useful to have a word to aid in making that distinction. "Chinese-martial," a substantive noun (like secretary[ies]-general, court[s]-martial, etc.) that lends itself to the adjectival uses of *hanjun* itself has seemed to me to suggest the grammatical functions, the meaning, and the flavor of *hanjun.* Though Martial Chinese would be equally good and grammatically interchangeable, it would not preserve the word order of the original, which is merely a nicety. Only the grammatical peculiarities of the English word "Chinese" prevents Chinese-martial from changing its form with respect to adjective/noun or singular/plural usage. If there is a value beyond convenience in this translation, it is the opportunity to dispel the notion that *hanjun,* in its Qing form, is a noun meaning "Han army" or "Chinese army," when, despite its form, it is an adjective meaning "martial Chinese"—that is, Chinese-martial. It also, importantly, avoids the imputed raciality which the term *han* had strongly accrued by the end of the Qing period.

Lest I be accused of inconsistency here, readers should be aware that I do not endorse the mystifying term "Chinese martials," which occurs in the published version of an essay authored by me and appearing in Elman and Woodside, eds., *Education and Society in Late Imperial China, 1600–1900.* I am at a loss to account

Because *hanjun* was adopted, evidently during the Hung Taiji period, to represent the Manchu term *ujen cooha* in some records, there was introduced an apparent identification of the Chinese-martial with the population of China proper. That identification would in future times leave the Chinese-martial open to ascriptive loyalties, functions, and judgments founded not upon the circumstances of their formation as an administrative entity but upon the priorities of the post-conquest state. Moreover, there is no seventeenth-century evidence known to me which would indicate that this was ever a reference to people of any ascribed racial identity. As late as the eighteenth century, as the Qing court became increasingly intent upon ge-
√ nealogizing identities within the Eight Banners, the term still was not cognate to phrases for Chinese civilians (*hanren, hanmin, minren*). In Nurgaci and early Hung Taiji times, the Nikans who were in professional service to the state (*nikan hafan*, plural *hafasa, hanguan*) had been distinguished from the common subject population (*irgen nikan*, plural *nikasa, hanmin*), and all were in turn distinguished from bondservants, serfs, and slaves.

Formalization of the Chinese-martial banners during the 1640s closed a period of prolonged political ambiguity in Nikan status. The delay in creating the Nikans as a legally distinct group had perpetuated the discretionary advantage of Jurchens in socioeconomic relations (as in the cohabitation interlude examined in Chapter 4), and a single legal identity for all Nikans was not forthcoming. In this early process of definition certain people of Chinese descent were excluded, primarily on the grounds of their manifest cultural orientation (irrespective of ancestry), from being registered as Chinese-martial. Chinese immigrants—the majority of them deserters from Ming military forces—had been trickling into Jilin and Heilongjiang steadily during the Ming period, and many took up life among the Jurchens. Such individuals participated in the attack upon Fushun in 1618, and into the early post-conquest period many were still recognized as *baišin*. But they became, after 1635, part of the Manchu population, not the Chinese-martial. In sharp contrast, the Chinese-martial incorporated between 1618 and 1643 had been living not in Nurgan but in Liaodong, or at least within the territory claimed and defended by the Ming. Conversely, in Hung Taiji's time it was understood, and later reigns preserved the knowledge, that the Mongol Banners and the Chinese-martial Banners encompassed the descendants of Jurchens, though those descendants were not

either for the grammatical or the lexical logic behind the editorial interference in this particular instance.

in the middle seventeenth century considered "Manchu" on the strength of that.[24] The populations of the Liaodong towns, with their mixed heritages, were an important target for Nurgaci's persistent claims of being the successor of the imperial Jurchens who had ruled the Northeast and North China in the thirteenth century. The Ming court noted the interactions of the great Liaodong lineages with each other and with Nurgaci. In 1622, for instance, when building their case against Tong Bunian, prosecutors cited the curious relationship of the Tieling Li lineages with Nurgaci and the pending trial of Li Rubo for sedition: "General Li's family have lived for generations in Liaodong," the testimony noted suspiciously, "His ancestor [Li Chengliang] and several of his sons cultivated the thief, Nurgaci."[25] The Ming bureaucratic elite regarded the appeal as potent enough in itself to possibly transform the loyalties of those within the Ming jurisdiction who were of even remote Jurchen descent, which is one of the lessons of the ordeals and deaths of Tong Bunian and Li Rubo.

CONQUEST AND DISTINCTIONS

Abduction of human beings was a common element of life in the Jurchen territories long before the war in Liaodong. The Nurgaci khanate, like its predecessor order the Jianzhou confederacy, was a booty state that depended heavily upon traffic in human beings for its stability and growth. Noblemen — or, those who were ennobled in the process of affiliating themselves with Nurgaci's regime — were given proprietary rights over places, things, animals, and people. The campaigns of Jurchen unification under Nurgaci in Nurgan had depended strongly upon control of conquered populations through enslavement. As the Later Jin forces moved westward, toward the Great Wall and finally inside it, mass incorporation of settled populations and their transfer into the control of Later Jin political leaders were necessary for agricultural support of the growing Jin population, for the professionalization of the state and the military, and for the maintenance of political power by the lineage that would eventually be called "Aisin Gioro." Abduction seemed not to predispose the owner toward one sort of rela-

---

24. Fu Kedong and Chen Jiahua, on the basis of their reading of *Baqi manzhou shizu tongpu*, count lineal descendants of at least thirteen identified Jurchens among the registrants in the early Mongol Banners. See "Baqi zhidu," 31.

25. "Cultivate" here (*qu*) is a verb usually applied to the raising of livestock. Cited in Yan, *Nurhachi zhuan*, 19, in connection with the role of Li Chengliang in Liaodong, from *Liao chou* [Memorials on Liaodong], "Ti Xiong shi yushu du xu."

tionship or another with his property. Some remained individuated objects to be employed in the fields, or the workshops, or battles as the owner pleased. Others became trusted followers, advisors, or even part of the family. In the last decade of his life, as he conquered and attempted to govern Liaodong, Nurgaci faced a special problem in the use and control of men who knew how to do the few things he could not do: speak foreign languages, and, most troubling, write.

The taking of Fushun in 1618 was characteristic of the mass kidnappings that made the growth of the Jianzhou regime and its successor, the Jin khanate, possible. After the conquest the population was divided according to levels of education and property. The less educated and less propertied were liable to be distributed among members of Nurgaci's family or other noblemen, where they might become agricultural workers, miners, or artisans in the households and workshops. The educated were likely to be brought into the command ranks of the military, which had been the fate of Tong Yangzhen and Tong Yangxing. Yet Fushun was not of outstanding scale in the overall human pillage that built the Jin and early Qing states. The Qing annals cite Hung Taiji, in particular, as keenly attentive to the effectiveness of his raiding parties (see Chapter 3). After a sweep through Yongping in 1643 he is quoted as demanding to know the harvest, commenting, "One is not happy enough when merely taking goods, one is only satisfied when one takes people." [26] Hung Taiji enjoyed a double delight in kidnapping, because it weakened an opponent while bringing new skills into the Jin or Qing organization. These points had been appreciated by Nurgaci, too, but he had had much smaller ambitions for his state and a much more limited appreciation of the importance of educated Nikans for his enterprises.

For years Nurgaci had been employing interlocutors (Chinese *tongshi*, Manchu *tungse*), who could most likely read at least a bit, to handle his affairs in Liaodong and in Korea. Shin Chung-il met some of them in 1596, including a man from Fushun, who was at that moment attempting to carry Nurgaci's grievances to the Liaodong authorities. Part of the agreement Nurgaci proposed with the Yi would have permitted interlocutors to act as overseers in the capture and return of people and livestock crossing the borders between the Jianzhou and the Yi territories. Literate men — or at a minimum men who could translate verbally between Jurchen or Mon-

---

26. Zhu Chengru, "Qing ru guan qian," 79, from *Donghua lu Tiancong*, 5. See also Chapter 4.

golian and Chinese or Korean—were still hard to find and to incorporate into his entourage. Anecdotal evidence suggests that Nurgaci was fond of some of his interlocutors and may even have trusted them. In retaliation for Nurgaci's destruction of watchtowers in Liaodong, Ming spies waylaid one Kanggūri, acting as Nurgaci's interlocutor, and beat him. Nurgaci was outraged and gave Kanggūri 500 ounces of silver (a fortune) "to ease his mind." The incident recalled itself in 1618 when Nurgaci complained that on a much later mission Kanggūri and Fanggina had been bound and forced to watch their entourage killed as they attempted to press Nurgaci's claims for economic independence with the Liaodong authorities.[27] Kanggūri and Fanggina were among those Nikan interlocutors for whom Nurgaci may have had a special regard. Among this group was Onoi (originally Gong Zhenglu, or Zhengliu, of Shaoxing, Zhejiang), whom Shin Chung-il considered semi-literate. Though Shin did not know it, the relationship between Nurgaci and Onoi was solid and already of some duration. Onoi was one of those tens of thousands of individuals kidnapped during Jianzhou raids into Liaodong in the 1580s. His family had offered 10,000 taels of silver (not an inconsiderable sum even to Nurgaci) for his return, but the Manchu annals claim that both Nurgaci and Onoi refused the ransom. Instead, Nurgaci gave Onoi a house, wives, and slaves and employed him as tutor to his sons (evidently Nurgaci's estimate of Onoi's skills was more favorable than Shin's).[28]

Highly literate men were a different matter; the idea of them being able to write what were purportedly his own meanings and orders, particularly in languages Nurgaci did not know, seemed to incite anxiety. Though Chinese literati (of Liaodong, primarily) are best remembered as the objects of Nurgaci's suspicion and contempt,[29] it hardly appears that he had a higher

27. This is not Kanggūri of *ECCP,* 409–10, who did not join Nurgaci until 1610, when the Woji of Ningguta were subordinated to Nurgaci.

28. The identification of Onoi is Yan Chongnian's, based upon very convincing parallels in the Korean reports of Nurgaci's scribe (see *Nurhachi zhuan,* 40). According to Korean intelligence entered into the *Yijo sillok* (*Sonjo* 28:12:*kuimao* and 33:7:*xuwu*), a certain Gong Zhenglu or Zhengliu migrated to Liaodong from Zhejiang and shortly afterward was kidnapped by the Jianzhou. It is possible (though not certain) that this was the same Onoi, a third-class *iogi* (*yuji,* "major") of Jakūta, whose ruling of not guilty of insubordination is recorded in the judicial judgments of 1627 (*TM* 11:5).

29. Such pronouncements are preserved primarily in the *Mambun rōtō.* See two very different and very important studies of Nurgaci by Yan Chongnian (*Nurhachi zhuan,* 249–57) and Deng Shaohan (*Nurhachi ping zhuan,* 310–16). See also

opinion of men who were learned in Mongolian, or in the Manchu script he caused to be created in 1599. There are many recorded remarks made by him and by Hung Taiji on the opportunism, inconstancy, and ambition of such men (very many of whom, the records do not remind the reader, were brought involuntarily into Nurgaci's or Hung Taiji's service). Nurgaci, who knew little Chinese (though he may have had some ability in Mongolian), was faced with a problem of control. As his organization became more complex, he became more dependent upon these individuals for keeping track of his wealth, committing his intentions for conduct of civil and military affairs to writing, and communicating with both his allies and his enemies (many of whom, by the late 1580s, were sending letters of submission from remote localities rather than endure the approach of Nurgaci's forces). The matter of lawmaking could be extremely intimate—as when, in 1626, Nurgaci used the Nikan scribe Tuša to announce that those spending the night with women in the khan's house and fornicating with wetnurses of the khan's sons would be summarily executed.[30]

Despite his intensifying reliance upon these groups, Nurgaci had not the temperament, the skills, or the time to oversee their activities himself. They were a constant threat to his power and his personal safety, since a single disloyal act by one of them could lead to disaster. His solution to the problem seems to have been to institutionalize both state suspicion of these early literati and a permanent terror on their part of the state. Their functions and the circumscriptions on their activities were soon encoded in law as well as in custom. By the Hung Taiji period they had assumed an identity based on their skills. Certainly by the time that he conquered Liaodong, Nurgaci had a far more impersonal and hostile view of the unknown literati of that region. His attitude of the time, one strongly woven into the administrative and legal terminology of the Hung Taiji records afterward, was that literate men were tools. They were to be used (and this is frankly conveyed in the Chinese documents by the verb *yong* and Manchu documents by forms of *baitalambi*). This had a rhetorical background in Chinese historiography that the Qing would later co-opt, since the histories of the Liao, Jin, and Yuan empires employed the verb liberally in relation to literate men from the Chinese regions who assumed professional functions in the early (conquest) regimes. When, under Hung Taiji, this function be-

---

Wakeman, *The Great Enterprise*, 71, 73, and Roth [Li], "The Rise of the Early Manchu State," 64, 85–86.

30. *TM* 10:6:29.

came an identity, it would be represented in the population class of the *baitangga*—tools of conquest.[31]

During the campaigns for western Liaodong in particular, the definition and manipulation of the status of Nikan servitors, whether of old families or newly submitted groups, were cornerstones of strengthening monarchical rule. Fundamentally the new policies represented an assault by the khanate upon the traditional Jurchen elite domination of the service classes. This was consistent with policies designed to extend increasing central control over social and economic spheres once ruled by the nobility and to force the Jurchen elite to redistribute a large portion of its wealth to Nikan capitulators, who were normally under Hung Taiji's personal protection. His government further increased the facility with which it could isolate and objectify Nikan status with the creation of the Civil Departments (*wenguan*) in 1629. A civil professional role was expanded for the Nikans, and new state faculties for the documentation and routinization of status were established. In the case of the military Nikans, the changes after Hung Taiji's reforms were sweeping. After 1636 the rapidity of changes in the classification and legal status of the Nikans was related to acceleration of the westward conquest. Consecutive Qing incorporations of the central and southwestern Liaodong populations defined to a great extent the character and the internal hierarchies of the pre-conquest Chinese-martial. Post-conquest typology would divide the Chinese-martial of pre-conquest times (*conglong ruguan*, those who "followed the dragon into the Pass") into two separate groups: The *tai nikan* (of whom the Fushun Nikan were a subgroup) or the Nikan population of eastern and central Liaodong, most of whom were incorporated between 1618 and 1629; and the *fu xi baitangga*, "functionaries of the Western conquest," those of western Liaodong, northern Zhili, Shandong, and Shanxi provinces who joined forces with Hung Taiji after he began his assault upon northern China in 1629 and who came to prominence during the westward campaigns but before the fall of Jinzhou in 1643.

The first group (the *tai nikan*) were generally individuals incorporated and rising to prominence during the struggle for Liaodong. Li Yongfang, Tong Yangxing, and Tong Yangzhen, for instance, were among the Fushun residents who entered Nurgaci's service in the aftermath of their town's fall in 1618—indeed Li Yongfang, who had been charged by the Ming govern-

---

31. Literally *baitangga* means "being useful (for a particular task)," but it normally denotes a minion, inferior, a stooge or a flunky.

ment with defense of the town, surrendered it to Nurgaci without a fight. Li was then made governor of the population resettled from Fushun, and Tong Yangxing soon became the commander of the military force drawn from that population, who numbered among their traits some familiarity with the *hongyi pao*, the cannons that had been cast for the Ming by the Jesuits.[32] They were later joined by the brothers (all claiming to be Jurchen descendants) Shi Tingzhu (1599–1661), Shi Guozhu, and Shi Tianzhu of Guangning. *Tai nikan* such as the Tong of Fushun and the Shi of Guangning dominated the command structure of the earliest Nikan armies. Tong Yangxing, for example, remained chief commander (*amba janggin*) of the *ujen cooha* forces until his death in 1631; he was succeeded by Ma Guangyuan (d. 1663) of Yongping and Shi Tingzhu of Guangning consecutively, the latter of whom became commander (*ejen, dutong*) of the first Chinese-martial banners at the time of their creation in 1642.[33] Of the second group (*fu xi baitangga*), Fan Wencheng (1597–1666) and Ning Wanwo (d. 1665), who was a bondservant of (Aisin Gioro) Sahaliyan until 1629 and only then began to be prominent in the western campaigns, were examples. Those surrendering after 1629 in Zhili were frequently registered in the banners instead of as "cherished soldiers."[34] This suggests that the state under Hung Taiji was at first reluctant to mix the earlier and later populations who would be known as "those who followed the Dragon into the Pass." A comprehensive Chinese-martial identity uniting all Liaodong and northern Zhili populations and reintegrating those of bondservant status was not firmly established until 1642, when the eight Chinese-martial banners were commissioned. And the administrative unification of the disparate Chinese-martial populations would not have an ideological representation until the end of the century. By the Kangxi period (1662–1722) the Qing court had developed the convention of referring to the Liaodongese who had par-

32. See Mou Ranxun, "Mingmo xiyang dapao you Ming ru Hou Jin kaolue," 89ff.

33. Also prominent among the early Chinese-martial commanders were Zu Zirun, Liu Zhiyuan, Wu Shoujin, Jin Li, Tong Tulai, Shi Tingzhu, Bayan, and Li Guohan. See *Qing shilu, Taizong chao* 61.7a. See also Chapter 6.

34. Examples include Zu Kefa, Zhang Cunren, Zhu Shikai, Lang Zhaozhu, Qiang Gaozao, and others, all discussed in Du Jiaji, "Qingdai baqi lingshu wenti kaocha." The units called "Heavenly Protected Army" (Tianyu bing) and "Heavenly Assisted Army" (Tianzhu bing) were adjuncts of the Nikan military force based upon the previously organized Ming military units brought into Hung Taiji's campaign by Kong Youde (d. 1652) and Shang Kexi (1604–76), respectively. See also Liu Chia-chü, "The Creation of the Chinese Banners," 62, and Wakeman, *The Great Enterprise*, 200.

ticipated in the campaigns of conquest—both in Liaodong and in north China—as "those who made a contribution in former times" (*jiu you gong xun*), often contracted to "old men" (*jiu ren*).[35] By this the court meant the amalgamated *tai nikan* and *fuxi baitangga* populations. The once vivid differences between these two groups, preserved in Qing political terminology until the last years of Hung Taiji's rule, paled after the conquest of north China. Now the differences between the *tai nikan* of Fushun, for instance, and the *fuxi baitangga* of Ningyuan appeared inconsequential in comparison to the differences between both groups and the population within the Great Wall. The "old men" were conquerors, which in the early Kangxi political culture attached them to the Manchus.

The roles of the Chinese-martial in the conquest have been carefully and convincingly narrated by several writers. Some served in full-time military positions, indistinguishable in their career paths from registered Manchus. Others were indispensable in establishing the occupation governments in the provinces. The years between 1644 and 1685, as the conquest in China was virtually completed, might have marked a period of unity for the Chinese-martial and the Manchus, when the historical identity of the former could have been institutionalized. But several factors intervened. One was the vigor with which the Shunzhi (1644–61) and Kangxi (1662–1722) courts employed (before their Chinese constituency within the Great Wall) the rhetoric of rulers in the Chinese style, complete with a conceit of Chinese ministers (*chen*—which originally meant "servant" but over two millennia had come to mean an aide, minister, assistant, or other sort of civil functionary) advising the government of morally enlightened monarchs. Another was the rapid cultural changes among the Manchu bannermen, some of whom showed a tendency to acculturate to the local populations they were policing, even before the conquest of China was complete. A third was the war usually called the "Three Feudatories Rebellion" (*san fan zhi luan*), in which the court faced the impossibility of

---

35. See An, "Shun Kang Yong sanchao baqi ding'e qianxi," 102. There may have been an indirect reflection here of the Mongolian phrase *ütegü boghol*, "those who have been in our service since olden times," which occurs in the "Secret History" with specific reference to domestic slaves of the imperial lineage—by analogy, closest to the bondservants of Qing times (on the phrase in the "Secret History," Togan, *Flexibility and Limitations*, 116 n 280, cites work of Gerhard Doerfer). But it is an analogy only: the term, like *baišin*, may have been absorbed from Mongol political vocabulary, and for the Qing as for the Mongols the notion of "free" was comparatively irrelevant, but the Qing reference was not to bondservants exclusively.

continuing with the Chinese-martial on the terms that had been established during the previous century.

During the Shunzhi (1644–61) years, appointments were shuffled so that surrendering Ming Chinese who had been temporarily appointed to the posts were supplanted by Chinese-martial. In this way, natives of the pre-conquest Qing order in Liaodong were given control over consolidating the conquest in China. The court rested more easily knowing that the occupation was not in the hands of those considered Ming deserters, and the political effects of using men who spoke Chinese in these posts were considerable. Some leaders of the Manchu banners were unhappy over this policy, and later the policy would change. But before administrative politics discredited the Chinese-martial leadership in the provinces, the apostasy of the three southern military governors occurred. The Three Feudatories (*fan*) as they stood in 1673 were the survivors of the slightly larger number of military governorships (*zongdu*) established throughout China in the first decade of conquest. These military governments of the south had been given extraordinary powers to conquer, police, and tax the southern regions of Yunnan, Guizhou, Guangdong, Guangxi, and Fujian. All were regimes of Nikan lineages (specifically *fuxi baitangga*) who had joined the Qing in the later, westward campaigns of Hung Taiji.[36] The most powerful of them was Wu Sangui (1612–78),[37] the ruler of Yunnan and Guizhou. Wu was a native of Liaodong, whose father, Wu Xiang, was reprimanded by the Ming court in the 1630s for his reluctance to join the fight against Nurgaci. Later, Wu Xiang was induced to enlist in the Ming effort under the command of Kong Youde, and Wu Sangui—then aged twenty-five— followed his father into Ming service by 1637. Sangui rose very rapidly in the ranks, and by 1640 was commander of the troops defending the shrinking Ming portion of Liaodong. Wu Xiang had by this time gone into retirement in Peking.

In April 1644 Peking fell to the rebel forces of Li Zicheng, and the last Ming emperor to be enthroned in Peking committed suicide. Sangui received a delayed summons from the Ming emperor to relieve Peking from

---

36. Geng Zhongming (*erchen* 1c—see Chapter 6), a native of Gaizhou, Liaodong, fought well against Ming resisters of the Qing invasion of China but committed suicide in disgrace in 1649 after fugitive slaves were discovered among his troops. Jingzhong, registered in the Chinese-martial Plain Yellow Banner, had inherited his father Jimao's rank as the satrap of Fujian when he joined the Three Feudatories revolt in 1674.

37. *ECCP*, 877–80.

the rebel onslaught, but before he could arrive he learned that the city had already fallen and that both his father and his concubine were in Li Zicheng's hands. Li decided to send his forces to Shanhai Pass, where Wu was stationed, and in May 1644 Wu was presented with the choice of surrendering to Li Zicheng or joining forces with the Qing leader Dorgon, who was positioned just outside the Great Wall. He chose Dorgon. Li Zicheng's forces were defeated at the Shanhai Pass and forced back to Peking, where he made a point of killing Wu's father before the combined armies of Dorgon and Wu Sangui could retake the capital. In June the Qing occupied Peking and installed the child Fulin, eldest son of the late Hung Taiji, as the Shunzhi emperor. Both the forces of the remnant Ming court in Nanjing and the Qing bid for Wu's services, and the Qing won again. His son Wu Yingxiong was given a sister of the young emperor Fulin as wife, and the Kangxi emperor made Wu an imperial prince. Wu Sangui drew his extraordinary civil and military powers in the southwest from his destruction of Ming resistance in Yunnan and Burma in 1661, when the Ming pretender was executed. His mission in the southwest accomplished, Wu showed no signs of remitting his special political or economic rights. In fact his activities resembled the early campaigns of Nurgaci to monopolize control over economic resources (in Wu's case, salt, gold, copper, ginseng, and rhubarb) and to dominate local political relations (the bureaucracies of Yunnan and neighboring provinces, as well as Tibetan settlements east of Lhasa). The Board of Revenue complained to the Kangxi court of the enormous subsidies provided to Wu's troops, and the emperor hinted that Wu might, in view of his age (he was in his middle fifties), retire. In 1667 Wu announced he would retire, but an orchestrated clamor from the bureaucrats of his domains moved the Qing court to reject his offer. Uneasiness over Wu's growing power and anxiety over his subsidies continued at Peking.

In 1673 another of the Chinese-martial military rulers of the south, Shang Kexi, was deposed by his own son, and requested that the Kangxi emperor allow him to abdicate and return to Liaodong to live out his last years. Shang Kexi, the emperor realized, proposed to make his governorship into a hereditary kingdom (which had already been attempted by another Chinese-martial military governor, Geng Jimao). Over the apprehensions of many of his court advisors, the emperor abolished the Shang military governorship and ordered its armies dismantled. Wu Sangui understood the court's action as a declaration of war against the southern governors. In late December of 1673 he announced Yunnan to be the independent state of Zhou and went on the offensive in Guizhou and Hunan. He appealed for support of Ming loyalists, including Wang Fuzhi, who did not see anything Ming-like in Wu's regime and denied it his allegiance. Wu also approached the Dalai Lama, who equivocated in his response (see Chapter 4). Wu's northeastern background showed itself rather vividly in his proposal to the emperor that they should agree to put China into Wu's hands and Liaodong under control of the Qing (an inversion of Nurgaci's suggestion to the Ming that they should let him have Liaodong and be happy with China inside the Great Wall). The emperor rejected the proposal and had Wu's son Wu Yingxiong—also son-in-law of the late Shunzhi emperor—executed. Wu attempted to march north toward Peking, but Qing troops had already been positioned to stop him. By 1679 the Qing forces had broken the will of Wu's supporters. Wu Sangui, stockaded in the fastnesses of Yunnan, died that year. He was succeeded as emperor of the Zhou dynasty by his grandson Wu Shifan, who effectively ended the civil war by committing suicide in 1681.

The Kangxi court attended to the ideological as well as the strategic issues raised by the Three Feudatories Rebellion. The court's relationship to the Chinese-martial, particularly the "old men," had to this point been a minor variation on the simplest forms of political affiliation in the Northeast. In terms of the "inner" (*dorgi*) and "outer" (*tulergi*) dichotomies of which the Qing were fond, the Chinese-martial, together with the Manchus and the Mongol bannermen, were "inner." Chinese civilians were "outer."[38] The Three Feudatories Rebellion coincided with other developments of the conquest and occupation to make the Kangxi court dissatisfied with the few distinctions between the political identities of the Chinese-martial and those of other bannermen. The utility of the occupation governments they were overseeing in the provinces was declining, their trustworthiness was in some cases in question, and the ability of the state to create specialized programs for the education and maintenance of Manchus (both major policy issues in the 1680s)[39] was hampered by the question of whether Chinese-martial were "Manchus" or not. Between the suppression of the Three Feudatories Rebellion and the end of the seventeenth century, the court took its first major steps to genealogize the Chinese-martial as "Chinese"—with a few critical exceptions—and simulta-

---

38. This was dramatically illustrated in Tong Guowei's performance of the Grand Sacrifice (including the Sacrifice to Heaven) in 1684–85 (when he was still Chinese-martial) and 1694–95; see also Rawski, *The Last Emperors*, 216.

39. See also Crossley, "Manchu Education."

neously to diminish the political stature of the Chinese-martial in the provincial governments.

The Tong lineages of Fushun figured centrally in these developments. After the fall of Fushun in 1618, Tong Yangzhen and Tong Yangxing became prominent figures in Nurgaci's armies. They joined generations of Fushunese, some of them members of the Tong lineages who had submitted to Nurgaci as early as two decades before.[40] Tong Yangxing was an original commander of the "cherished soldiers" battalion.[41] Tong Yangzhen, a former Ming military officer, served with distinction in Nurgaci's siege of Liaoyang in 1621 and died the same year attempting to suppress one of the frequent incursions of Mao Wenlong.[42] Tong Yangzhen's son Tulai (who used this Manchu name in preference to his Chinese name, Shengnian) was commander of the Chinese-martial Plain Blue Banner in 1642 and became one of the most distinguished soldiers of the Shunzhi years.[43] Tulai's daughter became consort to the Shunzhi emperor Fulin and in 1654 gave birth to Xuanye, later to be the Kangxi emperor; she was then elevated to the title of Zheng Gong [huanghou].[44] Her brothers Tong Guogang (d. 1690) and Tong Guowei (d. 1719), both of whom were addressed as "maternal

40. See also Chapter 3. It should be mentioned here that Okada Hidehiro, "How Hong Taiji Came to the Throne," 250–51, speculated that Nurgaci married a woman of the Tong lineage, Hahana Jacin, as early as 1577. She was the daughter of Tabun Bayan of Tunggiya. I believe that Okada is in error in concluding that the Tunggiya were kinsmen of the Tong of Fushun (see Chapter 1), an error based on the deliberate falsehood discussed in the present chapter and institutionalized in the imperial literature of the eighteenth century. The first known marriage of the Qing imperial lineage with the Tong of Fushun occurred in 1653, when the Shunzhi emperor married Xiaokang (Zheng Gong), the daughter of Tong Tulai. See below.

41. For biographies of Yangxing see *ECCP*, 797–98, and *Qingshi gao* (1928), 237:1a.

42. After the accession of the Yongzheng emperor, Yangzhen's personal name was written Yangzheng. See also *ECCP*, 797, and *Guochao qixian leizheng* 331:4a. Mao Wenlong was a Ming general in Liaodong who continued a kind of guerrilla warfare there after the capture of the region by Later Jin troops. See *ECCP*, 567–68.

43. See *ECCP*, 794–96.

44. The discussion in Kessler, *K'ang-hsi and the Consolidation of Ch'ing Rule*, 53–54, on the meaning of Zheng Gong's Tong connections for the K'ang-hsi emperor and his court is characteristic of the way this subject is normally discussed. "K'ang-hsi," we are told, "was less than half-Manchu ethnically." The "Mongol" ancestors of his maternal grandmother are discussed, then the "half-Chinese" ancestry of his mother. The emperor's bloodlines are then expressed in fractions. "K'ang-hsi's ancestry shows that even early in the dynasty Manchu and Chinese blood was mixing—and in the highest places. Politically, however, the young K'ang-hsi could not be considered anything but a Manchu prince."

uncle"[45] by the emperor and his court, realized outstanding military careers in the campaigns against the Dzunghars when Qing military ambitions turned toward Central Asia (see Chapter 6).[46]

Ironically, Tong Bunian's son, Tong Guoqi (d. 1685), was also an important figure in the Qing conquest of China, though he had been separated from his native regions, and from other Tong lineages, at an early age. At the time of Tong Bunian's death in 1625 his household had already left Shenyang and passed inside the Great Wall. They settled first in Wuchang, Hubei, and in 1623 moved to Nanjing, then to Zhejiang province, where Tong Guoqi grew up. When Zhejiang was captured by the Qing in 1645, the conquerors registered Tong Guoqi and his family as Chinese-martial of the Plain Blue Banner; there they joined the legions of Tong who had under one circumstance or another submitted to Nurgaci twenty, thirty, and forty years before. Guoqi served as a quartermaster under Ma Shiying in the conquest of Zhejiang and Jiangsu. He was later governor of Fujian and there personally managed a campaign to persuade Zheng Zhilong and Zheng Chenggong to withdraw from Fujian, finally forcing Zheng Chenggong off the mainland in 1664. Thereafter Guoqi had an outstanding career in the conquest regime and was known as one of the most competent, compassionate, and open-minded civil officials of the new order—so compassionate, in fact, that he seriously strained his relationship with the Shunzhi court over the treatment of the widow of a convicted official.

Guoqi was also known as a Catholic sympathizer, and he is reported to have been baptized by Felicianus Pacheco at Nanjing in 1674. His affiliation with the Catholic church seems to have long preceded his baptism, since he was credited with building a chapel in Hangzhou during his period as governor of Zhejiang. His wife's family may have influenced his religious interests; evidently she was baptized, with the name Agatha, years before Tong Guoqi himself. In 1663 he and his friend Xu Zhizhe were denounced by Yang Guangxian, then leading his anti-Christian campaign. The court ordered an investigation of possible sedition, but it was prosecuted with little interest; as late as 1668 Giulio Aleni (1582–1649)[47] and Ferdinand Verbiest were submitting petitions to the court on behalf of Tong and Xu,

---

45. Chinese *jiujiu*, though it is probable that Manchu *nakcu* was also used. On the relationship between the emperor and his uncles see Yang Zhen, *Kangxi huangdi yijia*, 351–69.

46. For Guogang see *Qingshi gao* 293:1a (adapted in the *Qingshi* [1961], 3996). For Guowei see *ECCP*, 795–96; *Qingshi gao* 287:1a.

47. On Aleni's life and his involvement in Jesuit developments in the late Ming and Qing periods see Menegon, "A Different Country, the Same Heaven," and "Je-

and sometime thereafter the investigation was concluded. The verdict was evidently not only favorable but beneficial. Within a short period Tong Guoqi had made a large bequest for the restoration of the Nantang and the Dongtang cathedrals in Peking, and it was claimed that 3,000 converts were added to the Peking congregations in 1669 alone. Historians interested in Catholicism in early modern China have characterized Tong Guoqi's contribution to the restorations as being on behalf of empress Zheng Gong.[48] If this was so, it was the closest Tong Guoqi came to a political association with the imperial Tong lineage descended from Tong Yangxing. There is no credible evidence that Tong Guoqi enjoyed intimate relations with these lofty aristocrats. And if the imperial uncles Tong Guogang and Tong Guowei were secret Catholics (the evidence is primarily the piety of their sister, empress Zheng Gong), this was the effect not of their acquaintance with Tong Guoqi but possibly of the Fushun heritage of which both the Tong Yangxing and the Tong Bunian lineages partook.

Tong Guoqi never lost interest in rectifying his father Bunian's case, and repeatedly returned to the genealogical documentation to argue that his father had lived and died a loyal Ming official, a victim of the corruption of the Ming bureaucracy. In 1654 he wrote an introduction to and published Bunian's "Record of Prisoned Rage." An augmented genealogy appended to the edition showed Guoqi himself as a tenth-generation descendant of Tong Dali and the cousins Tong Yangzhen and Tong Yangxing as descendants in the ninth generation. But just as in his own time Tong Bunian had found his genealogical conclusions inimical to the state agenda of the Ming, so Tong Guoqi found that his private attempt to continue Bunian's argument for a Ming identity was coming into ironic conflict with a new wave of genealogizing encouraged by the Qing—with the result that the Tong of

---

suits, Franciscans, and Dominicans in Fujian." Menegon is also author of the full-length Aleni biography *Un solo Cielo* (Brescia: Grafo Edizioni, 1994).

48. For the Catholic version of Tong Guoqi's background see Fang Hao, *Zhongguo tianzhujiao shi renwu zhuan*, 48–50. He describes Guoqi as a younger brother of the empress dowager Zheng Gong and a nephew of Tong Tulai. It is argued that Guoqi and many members of the Tong lineage in Peking after the conquest were Catholics but unable to acknowledge their faith because of their membership in the imperial family. This amalgamation of the various Tong lineages was vainly protested by Tong Bunian. It defies explanation because of the ease with which the lineages can be distinguished on the basis of readily available records but is frequently seen in Chinese scholarship and has its reflection in Western writing too. See, for example, Wakeman's rendition of the history of "the" Tong lineage (*The Great Enterprise*, 1017 n 63), where Tong Guoqi's grandfather Tong Yangzhi is erased from history and replaced by Tong Yangxing.

Fushun were favored to be construed not as urban Jurchens of Liaodong but as rustic Manchus of Nurgan. In 1688, after Tong Guoqi's death, the state formally reinvented the lineage of Tong Yangzhen and Tong Yangxing. That summer Tong Guogang publicly requested of his nephew, the Kangxi emperor, that the Tong be taken from the Chinese-martial banners and enrolled in the Manchu. He claimed that his family hailed from Tunggiya—that is, that the Tong of Fushun were originally of the Tunggiya lineage of Jilin. The request of Tong Guogang was accompanied by a similar one from Hūwašan (Huashan),[49] the third son of Shi Tingzhu of Guangning.[50] "Although we are considered Chinese-martial," Hūwašan wrote, "we are really Manchu."[51]

Hūwašan, producing a genealogy, claimed that he was descended from the Suwan Gūwalgiya lineage—the lineage of Fiongdon (1569–1620), one of the most socially prominent lineages in the empire.[52] He cited a great-great-grandfather with the Mongolian-Manchu name Bukha, great-grandfather Arsungga, grandfather Sihan, all of whom had been born and raised (he claimed) among the lineage, somewhere within the Jianzhou territories. Sihan, however, had moved to Guangning in Liaodong and, Hūwašan claimed, had expressed his regrets about it on his deathbed to his sons Shi Tingzhu (Hūwašan's father), Shi Tianzhu, and Shi Guozhu. Later, Shi Tingzhu became commander of the "cherished soldier" units, and thus, Hūwašan explained, he found himself in the position of being mistaken for a Chinese-martial. The Tong brothers had a similar story. Their ancestors had lived in Tunggiya, in the Jianzhou territories, until an ancestor had happened to settle within the Ming pale shortly before the conquest. Their grandfather Tong Yangzhen had been a "cherished soldier," and now they were mistaken for Chinese-martial.

Hūwašan's claim may have been partly true. His ancestors might indeed have been from a branch of the numerous Gūwalgiya lineages, whose members had settled in many parts of Liaodong by the seventeenth cen-

49. This name was not uncommon among Manchus of the Qing period and meant "Buddhist monk," from Mongolian *khuoshang*, from Chinese *hezang*, the origin of which is not known. See also Rozycki, *Mongol Elements in Manchu*, 114–5.

50. Hūwašan's biography is found in *Qingshi gao* 256.6a (appended to biography of Hazhan). See also Spence, *Ts'ao Yin and the K'ang-hsi Emperor*, 104.

51. Cited in the resulting order for transfer, see *Qing shilu, Shengzu renhuandi* 135.2a–b (Kangxi 27:4:2 [*kuimao*], i.e., May 1, 1688).

52. On the Suwan Gūwalgiya lineage—of Oboi, Furdan (1683–1753), Wenxiang (1818–76), and Ronglu (1836–1903)—see Crossley, *Orphan Warriors*, especially Chapter 2.

tury.[53] His petition has the additional authenticity of showing three brothers adopting a patronymic, a long-standing practice of Nurgan Jurchens that was frequently the object of imperial criticism when practiced by the Manchus of the Qing period. In its entirety, however, the petition was false. The Suwan lineage of Fiongdon was well documented to as early as 1588 and on the basis of oral tradition could be accounted for to the fourteenth century; not a single one of the individuals mentioned in the Hūwašan petition can be found in the generations of the Suwan lineage of the Gūwalgiya. In any event, the Suwan Gūwalgiya were not originally settled in the Jianzhou territory; they traveled from upper Jilin to join Nurgaci's camp in 1588. As for the Tong brothers, their claims were false. More important, they were impossible on their face. They had no connection with the small and lately formed Tunggiya lineage of Nurgan. In fact their genealogy had already been well publicized by their distant cousin Tong Guoqi and showed their ancestors established in Fushun before the Tunggiya lineage was founded. Notwithstanding the obvious fabrications of the Tong and Shi claims, the requests were granted by the emperor, though in both cases it was noted that their relatives in the Chinese-martial banners were so numerous that only the lines immediate to the petitioners could be removed to the Manchu rolls. Tong Guogang, Tong Guowei, Hūwašan, and their children were admitted to the prestigious Manchu Bordered Yellow Banner.[54]

The significance of this episode can be discerned from the implied ideological proposition of the petition of Hūwašan, Tong Guogang, and Tong Guowei. The Eight Banners had long been instruments of the state,[55] and all criteria related to banner affiliation were demonstrably functions of state fiat. From the time of Nurgaci to the time of this petition, identities could be and frequently were metamorphosed by edict. Now those created Chinese-martial by the state were informing the state that it had erred in doing so. The implication was that in enrolling these lineages in the Chi-

53. A list of Liaodong settlements where Gūwalgiya clansmen settled during Ming times is included under the Suwan Gūwalgiya entry in *BMST* 1.1a. See also Mitamura Taisuke, "Manshu shizoku seiritsu no kenkyū," 70, and Liu Xiamin, "Qing kaiguo chu zhengfu zhu bu jiangyu kao," 129; Crossley, *Orphan Warriors*, Chapter 2.

54. The edict is quoted in *Qing shilu*, "Shengzu renhuangdi" 135:2a–2b, Kangxi 27:4:2 (*kuimao*)—i.e., May 1, 1688. Guogang was then a *neidachen*. The fiction established in this case was institutionalized in *BMST* and on the basis of that has become the account generally credited in *ECCP* and most secondary works dealing with the period of the founding of the Qing state.

55. The banners were institutions of the Jianzhou Jurchens under Nurgaci and were later used to give form to the first state (Chapter 3).

nese-martial banners some objective but previously unidentified principle in the assignment of identity had been violated. That principle was the sole foundation of the argument, and it was genealogy. The premise of Hūwašan and Tong Guogang was that genealogies had been the original criteria upon which Manchus had been distinguished from the Chinese-martial. This was manifestly not so; had it been, the Chinese-martial banners could never have existed. It was also demonstrably untrue, since the records of the banner genealogy office indicated that at the time of Nurgaci's wars of unification in the Northeast, lineage affiliations had been rather arbitrarily altered or invented as a means of facilitating the creation of banner companies.[56] But the Kangxi court in 1688 legitimated the notion that Manchu and Chinese-martial identities could be bounded by proof of blood-ties to "Manchu" or "Chinese ancestors." Indeed, the Hūwašan-Tong petition was scripted to herald a change—over the long term—in the grammar of identity.

The resolution adhered to the fundamental interests of the Kangxi period. The court declined to reidentify the vast majority of the population having newly documented Jurchen descent as Manchu on the grounds that it would be logistically awkward. But the response of the court to the petitions of the Tong Guogang and Shi Hūwašan lineages gave credit to an ideological construction of identities as determined by genealogy—an exclusively ideological proposition, since the identities established in this decision were produced by imperial edict. Equally important, the decision strongly illuminates the early Qing understanding of Chinese-martial identity and the ways that identity was being transformed by the changing political and ideological interests of the court. The precise qualities the petitioners of 1688 hoped to have "corrected" by imperial decree had been the defining historical characteristics of the Chinese-martial as a group. Implied or demonstrable Jurchen descent and regional association with the territory north and east of Liaodong were now to be associated with "Manchus" (as anticipated in the genealogical indictment of Tong Bunian by the Ming court). The fiat placed the Tong and the Shi within the Nurgaci territories at the turn of the seventeenth century and gave them no important cultural connection with Ming Liaodong. At the same time it gave them genealogical proof of Manchu bloodlines. Thus the false genealogy of the Tong lineage was in agreement with both the older criteria of "Jurchen" identity and the newly emerging criteria of Manchu identity. The novel reliance

56. See the *précis* (*fanlie*) of *BMST* 1.a.

upon bloodlines tended to erase the ambiguities that were now seen to afflict the social histories of the Northeasterners who had composed the original Chinese-martial.

The distinctness of the change is more evident when the decision is placed in context. Amendments of status were not infrequent. Individual cases were normally handled as the business of banner company captains, who managed them at a relatively low (and ideologically inaudible) bureaucratic level. In the case of the family of the novelist Cao Zhan (Cao Xueqin), for instance, the family's antecedents are registered as both Manchu and as Chinese-martial, possibly as a result of alterations in the family's status because of a conviction of Cao Fu, Zhan's putative father, for embezzlement.[57] Much modern scholarship on this question contains a suggestion that identities in the Kangxi era could have fundamental realities transcending the facts of banner registration, a proposition of historically "real" identities legitimated in the Tong-Shi petition of 1688. But the Tong-Hūwašan petition was staged at a level to be conspicuous in court annals and subsequent revisions precisely because of its novelty.

It is not mysterious that Chinese-martial bannermen should hope to claim the theoretically indifferent but in actuality more desirable status of Manchus (that desirability being ostentatiously highlighted by the petition itself). What the motives of the Kangxi court might have been in fostering such a petition in 1688 is a question less transparent, but critical. The obvious but probably not the most significant factor in the court's posture toward the petition is that the Tong brothers were the maternal uncles of the Kangxi emperor Xuanye, who may have had strong personal sentiments in seeking a rectification of his own background in the rectification of theirs.[58]

57. The family has long been known to have been registered as bondservants in the Manchu Plain White Banner, which under Hung Taiji was brought under control of the Imperial Household Department. For summaries of this small part of the genealogical disquisition on the Cao lineages, see Feng Qiyong, *Cao Xueqin jia shi; Honglou meng wenwu tulu*; Zhang Shucai, "Zai tan Cao Fu zui zhi yuanyin ji Cao jia qi jie" and "Xin faxian de you guan Cao Xueqin jiashi de dang'an"; and Xu Duanmen, "Dongyuan jilin Xiyuan yin."

58. This is unsatisfactory on several grounds. First, it assumes that there were large numbers of significant people who in 1688 thought the Tong of Fushun were actually of "Chinese" background, which ignores the fact that the entire purpose of the petition of 1688 was to rewrite a family history that was already very well known. Second, the high profile given this case and the obvious falseness of the Tong brothers' claims would have worked against, not for, the motives implied by this explanation. Third, it is not clear that the Kangxi emperor would not have made do with a "Chinese" grandmother, had this become an issue. Manchus were not and were not yet claiming to be a group that was "full-blooded" in our terms, and par-

But there were other, more immediate and more palpable considerations. Forty-four years after the conquest of Peking—and exactly seventy years after the taking of Fushun—thoroughgoing changes in the composition and character of the Chinese-martial had occurred, in tandem with a perceptible alteration in their relations with the Manchus. The motive of the court was to advance an accommodation of the contradictions in the past and future of the Chinese-martial population that fulfilled the needs of conquest ideology as discussed in the Introduction to this book. The Chinese-martial, as a novel symbol for the "Chinese" population, was brought across the line between conquered and conqueror, and in harmony with the axiom that a natural identity was being discovered, not invented. Manchu identity, which was becoming of some concern to the court, would be politically stabilized through the introduction of the same genealogical criteria. In a single stroke the court introduced a crucial instrument in its campaign to create persuasive concepts of loyalty for the Chinese population in general and for its literati class in particular.

PERSONIFICATIONS OF FIDELITY

The Chinese-martial were precisely poised between the contradictions of the ideologies of loyalty developing in the Kangxi period. Their culture had been a major resource for the early Qing state, which had been able to use regionalist polemic and strategic applications of force to co-opt the educated and propertied elite of parts of Liaodong. After the conquest of China, however, the court lost some interest in the regional culture that had made its early state-building possible, and moved gradually toward a subsuming of Chinese-martial identity under the undifferentiated category of *han* or "Chinese." This demanded a revising of the past of the Chinese-martial, since their history was in many ways a standing refutation of the genealogical thinking that had begun to receive the court's encouragement. The

---

tial Chinese descent might have given a literalness to his fitness to rule the Chinese that might have been appealing, if handled acutely. Fourth, this explanation does not account for the free ride given Hūwašan, who was no relation to the Kangxi emperor and who could easily have been dissuaded from joining in (contrariwise, Hūwašan himself was insufficient to obscure the emperor's personal motives in granting the petition of the Tongs). Sixth, if this were a real attempt to deceive rather than to symbolize, one would expect slightly more interest to be shown in suppressing the evidence that disproves part or all of the claims made by Hūwašan and the Tongs in the petition.

cases of the Shi and Tong lineages recommended themselves to the court not only because of the prominence of the petitioners (and their closeness to the emperor personally) but also because they were able to offer special evidence of the affective meaning of their genealogical "facts." Their ancestors, though urban and sinophone (like Tong Bunian), were reported to have harbored a devotion to their homeland and its recently risen khan, Nurgaci. By 1688 the Nurgaci annals, first revised in the Hung Taiji period, already included Nurgaci's statement of affinity with the Liaodong population: "The people of the Liaodong garrisons (*wei*) were originally the same people as ourselves."[59] It was important that there should be an answer from the Liaodongese. The story of Hūwašan's Shi family of Guangning supplied what is represented as a deathbed statement of affinity with the Nurgan Jurchens, ascribed to Sihan, who had been raised in the Jurchen lands but later settled in Ming territory in the earlier seventeenth century: "Despite the fact that I have temporarily come to the Chinese territories, my heart wends constantly toward home, and I have lost none of my memories of my youth. Now my illness is grave, and it is apparent that I will not be able to live out my original hope of returning; you brothers must expend your efforts to realize my desires, take every challenge, and establish every merit to return to our home."[60] In the aftermath of the Three Feudatories Rebellion, the retroactive logic of this testimony was comforting: Those with love of the homelands were real Manchus; those who considered loyalties negotiable or disposable were something else.

In the same way that the "cherished soldiers" had been demarcated from the non-military portions of the Nikan populations of the very early seventeenth century, the Chinese-martial were posited as the military population drawn from the "Chinese" during the conquest of China. As the conquest progressed, enrollment in the Chinese-martial banners became more exclusive as there were many (hundreds of thousands) more joiners than

---

59. *MR Taizu*, juan 20. Zhu Chengru, "Qing ru guan qian," 74. I do not see this quotation as requiring an interpretation to the effect that Nurgaci considered the Jurchens as Chinese or the Chinese as Jurchens; he appears rather to be commenting upon the cultural and economic spectrum that extended across eastern Liaodong to western Jilin.

60. See Chen Wan, "Shi Tingzhu shiyi yu jiapu jikao," 33, from *Baqi tongzhi* 296 (1739). The factuality of this testimony is beside the point here, but in connection it might be mentioned that Sihan's statement is not unlike a statement attributed to (Kim) Adun by Shin Chung-il, who had no political motivation in reporting it. See Chapter 3.

could possibly be accommodated in the Eight Banners. The Green Standard armies were created to organize the larger number of apostates from the Ming armies and militias. For newcomers, appointment to the Chinese-martial banners was a rare honor after 1645, a situation that did not displease the court.[61] The political advantages of having more applicants to the banners than could be admitted were plain. Less obvious, from the modern point of view, was the logistical imperative for halting further growth in the size of the Chinese-martial banners. On the eve of the Qing conquest of north China it appears that 164 of 592 banner companies may have been Chinese-martial companies; they may have represented as much as 40 percent of the conquest force in 1644. The bulk of these companies had been created after the long-promised but much-delayed defection of Zu Dashou (d. 1656) in 1642.[62] This was followed closely by the re-formation of the two "cherished soldier" banners into eight Chinese-martial banners, in the course of which the number of companies may have doubled from 50 to 100. Thus in the three years before the invasion of China in 1644 the number of Chinese-martial companies continued to surge while growth in the number of Manchu and Mongol companies may have been negligible.[63] Figures for 1649 show that all categories of Chinese-martial now accounted

61. For a history of the Green Standard armies, see Luo Ergang, *Luying bingzhi*. His account of the motivations for the founding of the Green Standard armies (1–6) is based, I think, upon a misconstruction of the numerical balance within the banners between Manchus and Chinese-martial.

62. *Diyilishi* 18 provides a list of those surrendering at Dalinghe, on the basis of *MR TC* 8:2:8. Zu Kefa was given the daughter of Boba as a wife, and she brought along her own slave. Sons of the surrendering generals were given separate rewards of their own (a sort of peremptory nativization, one imagines, since they then became heirs of the khan rather than of their own fathers).

63. These figures are based on independent revisions of the number of banner companies that appear to have been in existence in 1644 and earlier. See Li Xinda, "Ru Guan qian de baqi bingshu wenti," and Guo Chengkang, "Qingchu niulu de shumu." Knowing the number of companies in existence would not fix the number of individual soldiers the Qing had at their disposal, since the earliest Jurchen/Manchu and Mongol companies were created on the basis of lineage units, few of which appear to have conformed closely to a regulation population size (despite the promulgated number of 300 men per company), and some of which seem to have been quite small. This analysis has been developed by Zhou Yuanlian; see "Guanyu baqi zhidu de jige wenti." The evidence leads one to suppose that Chinese-martial companies may have been populous in comparison to their Mongol and some of their Manchu counterparts. Guo proposes that Chinese-martial companies in the years just prior to 1644 may have numbered 100 out of 500 and increased during 1643 and 1644 to more than 160 out of 500; Li's figures for 1644 are as given in the text above. For further comment on the population figures of the banners see Roth [Li], "The Manchu-Chinese Relationship," 35 n 2.

for over 75 percent of the banner force. Ten years later, Chinese-martial may have outnumbered the Manchu and Mongol bannermen by as many as four or five to one, though they were still only a small proportion of the actual total of Ming deserters.[64] This ballooning of the Chinese-martial enrollments created a security question for the conquest regime, combining the old issues of dependence upon the cultural particulars of the Chinese-martial with the new danger of their being a numerical majority within the conquest forces. In the later 1640s fewer adherents were incorporated into the Chinese-martial banners as it became clear to the Qing that it was no longer a meaningful, necessary, or, for the state, logistically advantageous regular reward for surrender. By 1667 the Chinese-martial portion of the banner forces had fallen to under 70 percent, and would continue to decline under the pressure of state policies thereafter.[65]

Exclusiveness of Chinese-martial status in the first decade of the conquest was connected to the fact that the Chinese-martial were a charter group within the conquest elite. The Liaodong–northeastern Zhili (*conglong ruguan*) populations were a charter group within this charter group, distinguished from the "Peking Chinese" (*Beijing hanren*—those who defected at the conquest of Peking in the summer of 1644 or in the months immediately following, many of whom had not only formerly served the Ming but had also had bureaucratic posts under the short-lived Shun regime of Li Zecheng) and from the "surrenderers with land" (*daidi touchong*—those among the provincial landowners who traded their land rights to the garrisons for incorporation). As a group even the newly in-

64. Secondary works have established the number of adherents during Dodo's march through Jiangnan at something under 240,000 by the conquest of Nanjing; the campaign against Li Zicheng may have attracted as many as 100,000, and it seems to me conservative to posit a total number of former Ming adherents at 500,000 to 600,000 for the campaigns of conquest. The bannermen of 1644, on the other hand, probably numbered perhaps 120,000 to 150,000. See also Dennerline, *The Chia-ting Loyalists*, 66, and Wakeman, *The Great Enterprise*, 306, 791.

65. An Shuangcheng, "Shun Kang Yong sanchao baqi ding'e qianxi," 101–2. An presents this series of percentages for the composition of the conquest banners in the following three years—1649: Manchus 15.95, Mongols 8.3, Chinese-martial 75.75; 1667: Manchus 22.12, Mongols 8.84, Chinese-martial 69.04; 1723: Manchus 23.4, Mongols 8.9, Chinese-martial 67.7. An further notes that information for 1720 indicates that of the 68.94 percent of the banner population accounted for by the Chinese-martial, the following percentages can be assigned to the subgroupings: the pre-conquest Chinese-martial (*tai nikan* and *fuxi baitangga*) together with uncategorized Chinese-martial 29.5 percent, the bondservants (*booi aha nikan*) 34.48 percent, and the eunuchs, *Beijing hanren*, and *daidi touchong* 4.68 percent. The records are likely not complete, and so the percentages are overly precise, but the general picture is clear.

corporated Chinese-martial were not confused with the subject civilian Chinese, or *hanmin*. One of the legal distinctions still enjoyed by the "old men" of Liaodong was the right to return to their native region to live. Those who applied to do so were normally permitted to relocate during the Shunzhi period, and those who wished to farm in Liaodong received fresh allotments of land. Chinese, on the other hand, were legally forbidden in this period to pass outside the Great Wall.[66]

Chinese-martial skills in the Chinese language (this was, after all, one of their defining traits) made the court disposed to use Chinese-martial bannermen to best advantage in bureaucratic appointments in the early conquest period, and the numerical predominance of Chinese-martial in bureaucratic appointments during the early post-conquest period reflects not only their political utility but also the numbers of the bloated Chinese-martial banners.[67] The quotas for banner studentships and garrison appointments, which usually maintained an innocuous-looking 1:1 ratio for Manchus and Chinese-martial, were not generous in a situation where the Manchu:Chinese-martial ratio was possibly as low as 1:4; they were, nevertheless, a defensible expression of "parity" between "Manchus" and "Chinese," and contortedly consistent with Nurgaci's early dictum that "no distinctions" be made among his peoples. Chinese-martial commoners sent out to the provincial garrisons often found that in cramped urban situations no living space had been provided for them within the walls of the garrisons; where agricultural land was sparse, they were given no pastures for their horses and truncated burial grounds. In many cases Chinese-martial companies were introduced into garrisons only years after the garrisons had been established, when local pecking orders as well as land and housing allocations had already been fixed.[68] Where there was plenty, in other

---

66. Zhu Chengru, from *Qingchao wenxian tongkao*, 1.

67. The predominance of *hanjun* officials in regional posts in the early post-conquest period was established by Kessler, "Ethnic Composition of Provincial Leadership during the Ch'ing Dynasty."

68. An exception was the garrison at Canton, which remained exclusively Chinese-martial until the eighteenth century and, also in contrast with most other garrisons, was unwalled. The reasons for this and the origins of the Chinese-martial bannermen based there are rather unclear (see Im, *The Rise and Decline of the Eight-Banner Garrisons*, 19). Studies of garrison life, as distinct from institutional studies of the Eight Banners, are still few. The records of the *Baqi tongzhi*, revised in 1799, do not cover the nineteenth century. There are two well-known and accessible garrison gazetteers, *Zhu Yue baqi zhi* (1884) for Canton and *Hangzhou baqi zhufan ying zhilue* (1893) for the Hangzhou-Zhapu system. See also Im, *The Rise and Decline of the Eight-Banner Garrisons*; Chai Yü-shu, *Qingdai Xinjiang zhu-*

words, the common Chinese-martial might enjoy their ostensible quota. Where there was dearth—the more usual case—the military commissioners often pled the ability of the Chinese-martial to fend better for themselves in Chinese society as reasons for tightening their provisions. But whatever tensions might have been created by provincial-level discriminations against common Chinese-martial bannermen, they remained bound to the Eight Banners by privileges, financial dependence, and common symbols of identity.

What the Chinese-martial view of themselves was in the first thirty or forty years after the conquest is a difficulty. Conditions did nothing to encourage expressions of sympathy with the Chinese, and demonstrations of allegiance with the Manchus would have been meaningless before the outbreak of the Three Feudatories Rebellion in 1673. By the later seventeenth century, however, the Chinese-martial had begun to acquire the hallmarks of second-rate status within the banners, apace with their graduated official submergence with the subject Chinese population. The court was receiving complaints from Manchu banner officials who felt that the Chinese-martial were given unjust preference in the appointment process. Within some garrisons, continued enrollment of Chinese-martial households had become an issue, since those who had been marginalized in the original settlement process were most likely to violate garrison regulations regarding livelihood, travel, and marriage to the subject population. More significant, in the decades since the conquest there had been rapid differentiation of cultural development within the Chinese-martial as a group, though this differentiation as a pattern can hardly be distinguished from that seen among the Manchus in the same period. Many fell away from military training and spoke local Chinese as a native language. Some Chinese-martial had intermarried frequently, even exclusively, with Manchus; others had married only within the Chinese-martial; and some had undoubtedly done as many Manchus had done and illegally intermarried with the civilian population. Some had petitioned to be educated in Manchu and pursued military careers;[69] others had been educated in Chinese and taken the civilian examinations. Some used Manchu names, without surnames; others used Chinese names. Many lineages alternated naming styles from generation to generation, or in a single generation might display different patterns. Tong Yangzhen's son, originally named Tong Shengnian, took the

---

fang bingzhi de yanjiu; Crossley, "The Sian Garrison" and *Orphan Warriors,* esp. Chapter 3; and forthcoming work by Mark C. Elliott.

69. On this and the following points see also Deng, *Qingdai baqi zidi,* 27–40.

Manchu name of (Tong) Tulai. Tong Yangzhen's grandsons had the Chinese names Tong Guogang and Tong Guowei (the Kangxi emperor's petitioning uncles). Among his great-grandsons are found the Chinese names Tong Jiefu and Tong Qingfu and the Manchu names Sunggayan, Orondai, Fahai, and Lungkodo.[70] Shi Tingzhu's first three sons were called by the Manchu names Jormen, Jorgero, and Hūwašan (our petitioner), while his next three sons were Shi Lin, Shi Zhen, and Shi Jing; among his grandsons were Wenying and Wenbing, and among his great-grandsons, Fudari. Among the sons of Li Yongfang were both Bayan and Li Shuaitai; among his descendants in succeeding generations were Li Yuanliang (fourth generation), Li Shiyao (fifth generation), Yuxiu, Yuwen, and Yuji (sixth generation).[71]

By the time of the suppression of the Three Feudatories Rebellion, the political and cultural complexities of the Chinese-martial bannermen tolerated the imposition of nearly any generalization that might be officially promulgated. For the Kangxi court, the fact that the Hūwašan and Tong histories were representative only of the small but venerable Liaodong core—the *tai nikan*—of the early Chinese-martial was inconvenient. By acquiescing in their request the emperor had endorsed (more properly in this context, invented) the principle of the congruence of ancestry and loyalty for those with some "proof," if only symbolic, of Manchu ancestors. But this did not entirely cover the trauma of the Three Feudatories Rebellion. The perfidy of Wu and his collaborators—untrustworthy Liaodongese—had been only one side of the story. The other side had been that portion of the Chinese-martial, whether from within or without the Great Wall, who had martyred themselves for another principle, equally valuable to the post-conquest state: that of fidelity beyond ancestry.

The suppression of the Three Feudatories had been led by banner troops under the command of minor Aisin Gioro princes—among them Nurgaci's grandson Cani, great-grandson Jangtai, and Šurgaci's grandson Šangšan. None distinguished themselves, and in fact the serious military work was done by the Chinese-martial governors and commanders who were managing the occupation governments neighboring the Three Feudatories.

70. Lungkodo (d. 1728), the third son of Tong Guowei, was registered in the Manchu Bordered Yellow Banner and was both a cousin and a brother-in-law of the Kangxi emperor, who nevertheless called him "uncle" (*jiujiu, nakcu*) in imitation of his favorite term for Tong Guowei and Tong Guogang. Like his distant relative Tong Bunian, Lungkodo also came to grief over a genealogy, though it happened to be a copy of the records (*yudie*) of the imperial Aisin Gioro lineage, found in his home and condemned by the Yongzheng emperor as seditious.

71. On Li Shiyao and Yuji, see Crossley, *Orphan* Warriors, 249 n 100.

Among the best known is Cai Yurong (1633–99),[72] who had a complex career in the conquest and occupation periods and was a founder of a distinguished Qing lineage that included the poet Cai Wan (wife of Gao Qizhuo). Cai's father was a native of western Liaodong who surrendered to Hung Taiji with Zu Dashou in 1641. At the time Cai Yurong was less than ten years old, and spent virtually his entire life as a member of the banner elite (enrolled, like his father, in the Chinese-martial Plain White). In the Three Feudatories Rebellion he provided sound service to the court, preventing the incursion of Wu Sangui into the provinces of Hunan and Hubei. Still, the court demanded more of him than he delivered; more than once in the war against Wu Sangui, Cai was excoriated by the court for his deficiencies, lashed with fines and demotions, but told to keep at his post and prove himself. He did this and at the conclusion of the war was rewarded with civil governorship over the territories Wu had ruled. But Cai was also anxious to show the court that he had taken seriously the distinction it had impressed upon him between claims and achievements. Like many commanders who were eager to highlight themselves in narratives of successful campaigns, he wrote a conquest history but prefaced it with the pointed comments, "The difference between accomplishment and reputation is whether, regardless of obstacles, commoners and ministers exhaust thought and action solely to return Beauty [*mei*] to the emperor."[73] That difference between accomplishment and reputation—between claims and realities—had, Cai suggested, exposed the distinctions among the bannermen, and particularly the Chinese-martial bannermen; some were unswerving servitors of the court, and some were opportunists. Cai wished to place himself among the loyal, and—despite some missteps in his later career—he and his family were never viewed by the Qing court as anything other than staunch members of the banner elite.

Still, Cai had not paid the ultimate price for his loyalty. He would live many years after the Three Feudatories Rebellion and was not the sort of towering figure on whom dramatic and even romantic ideals of loyalty and sacrifice could be hung. The two great stories were those of Fan Wencheng's son, Fan Chengmo (1624–76) and Ma Xiongzhen (1634–77). Fan, then serving as governor-general of Zhejiang and Fujian, was murdered by the rebel Geng Jingzhong in October 1676 when he refused to join the Three Feudatories' cause. Ma, the governor of Guangxi, was killed by Wu

---

72. *ECCP*, 734–36.
73. From *Nanping jilue*, 222, quoting Hu Yin.

Shizong, a grandson of Wu Sangui, eleven months later for the same reason. The Kangxi emperor ennobled Fan's and Ma's survivors and encouraged literary lionization of the two heroes. They became, as Frederic Wakeman has pointed out, the personal paradigms of loyalty to the new state.

The Fan lineage was ostentatiously rehistoricized in this process. The court elevated them to the status of a "chief lineage" among the "old men," which did not accord entirely with the way the term had been used before that time. Characterization of the Fan as "old men" of the conquest depended upon a peculiar retelling of the story of Chengmo's father, Fan Wencheng, a retelling accomplished in stages beginning in the Hung Taiji years and ripe for plucking in the aftermath of the Three Feudatories Rebellion. It appears that Fan Wencheng was among the population abducted from Fushun in 1618. The earliest records did not mention him among the servitors of the Later Jin rulers until Hung Taiji's initiation of campaigns in western Liaodong and the undoing of Yuan Chonghuan in 1629, in which Fan played a very useful role. Properly, Fan Wencheng's status was that of a "functionary in the Western conquests" (*fu xi baitangga*). He was twenty-one years old when abducted. Unlike his elders Li Yongfang, Tong Yangzhen, and Tong Yangxing, he did not become a highly visible military official and may not even have had military status at the time. During Nurgaci's life Fan Wencheng was not someone who attracted the khan's trust, let alone accolades. Indeed Fan's abduction occurred in the context of Nurgaci's growing dislike of literate men, particularly from Liaodong. The annals of the period were frank about the process of abducting and impressing such individuals as Fan Wencheng into service (*de gong*). In a typical utterance, Nurgaci lectured an assembly of the educated Nikans: "We took you and we nourished you" (*de er yu zhi*).[74]

Beginning with the Shunzhi era revisions of the annals, however, terminology was changed to indicate a sort of spontaneous allegiance on the part of the educated Nikans of Liaodong and in return a warm welcome accorded them by the khan. This might be connected with the "Chinese" enthusiasms for which the Shunzhi emperor was frequently criticized by the Manchu banner elite. But it was also the period, in the first years of the conquest of China, when the dividing line between conquerors and the conquered was under special stress. Unlike the new empire under Hung Taiji,

---

74. Chinese *de* is equivalent to Manchu *bahambi*, which usually occurs in the texts as *bahafi* ("having taken"). Compare also *nikan be muse jing ujimbi*, TM 10:10:3.

the Shunzhi court and after were not satisfied with explaining the conquest in terms of righteous coercion, backed by Heaven. Qing rule was to have a history of mutual attraction, and trust, between the court and Chinese elites. A detailed passage on Nurgaci's response to Fan Wencheng's appearance at his court was concocted in the early post-conquest period and inserted into the annals. Its imagery is instructive. Soon after the fall of Fushun (the new version explained) Fan Wencheng was brought to Nur- *h* gaci's headquarters. Nurgaci admired the Nikan's demeanor and only then *hisdn'cd* learned of Fan's ancestral connections to the Song official Fan Zhongyan (989–1052), with whose story Nurgaci is depicted as being casually familiar. The khan was delighted and said to the gathered nobles (out of Fan's hearing, evidently), "This is the descendant of a famous minister [*chen*], and you are to greet him most cordially." Fan Wencheng had been promoted from a flunky to a statesman.[75] It was only a step further to suggest, as the annals indeed do, that Fan Wencheng and his colleagues had the whole idea of conquering China and cajoled the Jin khans into pursuing this "great enterprise." It is not surprising that the emperor acclaimed Fan Chengmo as comparable in "ministerial fidelity" only to Wen Tianxiang (1236–83) of the Song period.[76]

The reinvention of Fan Wencheng shares with the martyrography of his son Fan Chengmo the intertwining tropes of genealogized Chinese identity and enlightened, voluntary loyalty to the Qing forces of conquest. Loyalty as such was not the issue. All Manchus and Mongols articulated their relationship to the Qing emperors through the language of slaves and masters that was evident in the Nurgaci era rendition of the taking of the Nikans. This political notion of the "slave" existed independent of the many social forms of slavery attested in Qing history.[77] When generalized as a political conceit for affiliation and followership in the Qing, it was invariably accompanied by an intensely affective political vocabulary (as contrasted to the relatively impersonal, moral vocabulary of Chinese political thought), and it leveled all followers to the general status of "slave": some were

75. Details of the revision of the capitulation of Fan Wencheng have been published by Zhang Yuxing, "Fan Wencheng gui Qing kaobian."

76. Wakeman, *The Great Enterprise*, 1115–27, after the funerary ode by Li Yu (1611–80). Wen had been one of the last and greatest Song holdouts against the Mongols and was the conventional personification of loyalism in Ming times; the Qing would later promote the Yue Fei cult (see also Fisher, "Lü Liu-liang"), which would result in Wen's lesser status as a loyalist icon.

77. This point is elaborated on in *Orphan Warriors*, 15–17.

grander slaves than others, but all found their point of political orientation in their personal subjection to the ruler.

Both the English "loyalty" and the Chinese *zhong*, which are most often used to translate *jurgan*, omit or obscure the connotations of the master-slave relationship. *Tondo*, "loyalty" (or perhaps more appropriately *comitatus*),[78] is also rendered *zhong* in Chinese, but has its roots in the hunting or warring collective, not in slavery. The Manchu word most frequently used during the Qing for "loyalty," *jurgan*,[79] was explicitly a reference to the obedience and self-sacrifice owed a master by a slave, and there is no evidence that the Qing ever regarded this ideal as less compelling than the Confucian ideals of service that they were equally able to exploit. But this virtue of the Nurgaci era was not the virtue being imputed to the Fan lineage of the conquest period. What was at issue was the establishment of a taxonomy of loyalties that would congress with the emerging taxonomies of genealogy and culture. In strictest policy the Chinese-martial bannermen were, like all bannermen, slaves of the emperor, and they called themselves so (*nucai*) in communications with the court. In the later seventeenth century, however, the court's political priorities clearly dictated that not *jurgan*, the slave virtue, but *zhong*, the ministerial value, should be the guiding ideal of loyalty for at least a portion of the Chinese-martial bannermen. Recasting of the incorporation of Fan Wencheng and other Liaodong Nikans was essential to the construction of a mythic model of Chinese loyalty to the Qing emperors. The Chinese served the emperors not as loving, childlike slaves but as Confucian erudites, true both to their past and to the empire of which China was, after 1644, the strategic foundation.

78. *Mambun rōtō* gives *sei*, "uprightness, correctness, honesty" for *tondo*. *Jurgan* was a Qing Manchu borrowing from Mongolian *jirugh-a*, which meant, as *jurlgan* literally does, a line, straightness, rectitude, duty, discipline, devotion. This accords with many glosses of the late seventeenth and eighteenth centuries translating *jurgan* as loyalty, rectitude of standards of behavior. In the sense of upright, righteousness, or rectitude it comes semantically close to Chinese words for uprightness, honesty, and government (*zheng, zheng*), which have been associated with possible translations making the same connections in European languages: corregio, regime, regimen, regimentation, and so on. The translations of *Mambun rōtō*, however, have chosen "righteousness" (*gi*) for *jurgan*. When *jurgan* changed its meaning in the eighteenth century, it became part of the bureaucratic lexicon of ethics and of administration; these uses were virtually unknown to the early Qing and in all cases displaced earlier Chinese loan-words. On the translations of *jurgan* and other words that were used in Manchu translations of the classics, see Hess, "The Manchu Exegesis of the *Lünyü*," 410–11.

79. See also Crossley, *Orphan Warriors*, Chapter 1.

Much has been written of the need on the part of the Qing emperors to present themselves as Confucian rulers, which is only to say that they were at pains to present the image of a benevolent monarch open to the guidance of and in return receiving the loyal dedication of a morally cultivated ministerial class as the primary construction of relationships between the emperor and the government (which became the central theme of the Yongzheng emperor's "Great Righteousness Resolving Confusion"). Less has been written regarding the necessity of creating models of Confucian devotion to those Confucian monarchs or the resulting transformation of the historical status of the late-seventeenth-century Chinese-martial bannermen. The deaths of Fan Chengmo and Ma Xiongzhen were grisly dramas that offered comfort to a Qing court uncertain of the steadfastness of the Chinese-martial adherents (as it was occasionally unsure of Manchus, too). In and of themselves, however, their stories of the heroic loyalty to the dynasty to whom their fathers had been early adherents were not sufficient for the needs of a court that had been straining to establish and control persuasive images of fidelity to an alien regime. The fact was that Ma and Fan, as Liaodongese, had been the conquerors, not the conquered. What was needed was to dehistoricize the Chinese-martial, to create a myth of monolithic "Chinese" identity for the Chinese-martial banners and to transfix it with the martyrdoms of these Chinese-martial loyalists in the Three Feudatories Rebellion.

The inability to absorb masses of new adherents into the Eight Banners after 1645 combined with the Three Feudatories Rebellion, with evidence of cultural assimilation or diversification among the Eight Banners garrisons in China, and with the growing desire of the Shunzhi and Kangxi emperors to co-opt the Chinese intellectual and bureaucratic classes, to bring about elemental changes in the ideology of identity. The result was an admission of genealogical discourse in efforts to stabilize the criteria of identities in the post-conquest era, to erect a very explicit Confucian persona for the state in civil affairs, and to rewrite the historical character of the Chinese-martial bannermen. These elements, all discernible in the Kangxi era, were originally embedded in a regime intent upon distinguishing itself from powerful rivals—first the Ming, then the Chakhar and Khalkha leaders, and finally the Romanov empire—and enforcing terms of particularistic appeals to loyalty and legitimacy. The period of early transformation of the Qing logic of identity roughly conforms to the period of the forty-year effort to consolidate control over Inner Mongolia and south China, for the Qing were unable to achieve conquest without a means of transforming the conquered into conquerors. To this was later added the retrospect of the eighteenth-century court: that the populations of western Liaodong and north China had never been primarily conquered or conquerors but had been fixedly "Chinese," owed their allegiance to the Ming emperors, and in opportunistically aiding the Qing had transgressed the abstractions of loyalty that the Qing emperor, as universal monarch, was bound to enforce. Yet the brand of traitor or opportunist would never fall upon the Tong of Fushun or others of the founding Nikan populations. In 1740 the Qianlong emperor commanded that selected Mongols, Koreans, *tai nikan* (the Nikan population of eastern Liaodong and Jilin), and all "Fushun *nikan*" be enrolled in the Manchu banners.[80] It was the last word in the re-identification—or de-identification—of a population that was ancestral to Qing society, had been indispensable to the creation of the state, had intermarried with the imperial lineage, but in the seventeenth century had been sinophone, urban, and—however tenuously—under Ming dominion. That Liaodong population was severed from the Chinese-martial banners and re-created Manchu, which meant that the monolithic association of the Chinese-martial population as a whole with the population of China proper as a whole was no longer obscured by lingering historical shadows. This act of 1740 was made possible by the rehistoricization of the old Liaodong Nikans as Manchus and of the conquest "functionaries" of western Liaodong as typical Chinese literati unhesitatingly sacrificing their lives for the Qing. It was the act of a universalist state, whose evolution will be explored in following chapters.

---

80. Reproduced in the précis to the *BMST*, 4a, dated Qianlong 5:12:8 (i.e., January 24, 1741). See also Fu Kedong and Chen Jiahua, "Baqi zhidu zhong de Man Meng Han guanxi," in *MY* 6 (1980): 24–49 (31–32). In spite of the emperor's syntax, the Fushun *nikan* (whom he has singled out for emphasis) were a subgroup of the *tai nikan*.

PART II
THE FATHER'S HOUSE

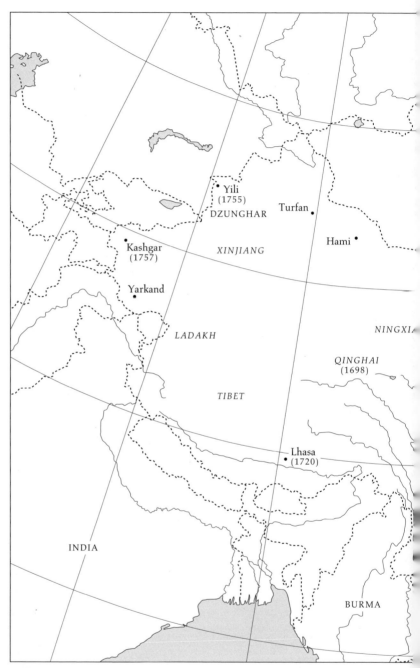

Early Qing Conquest, 1616–46

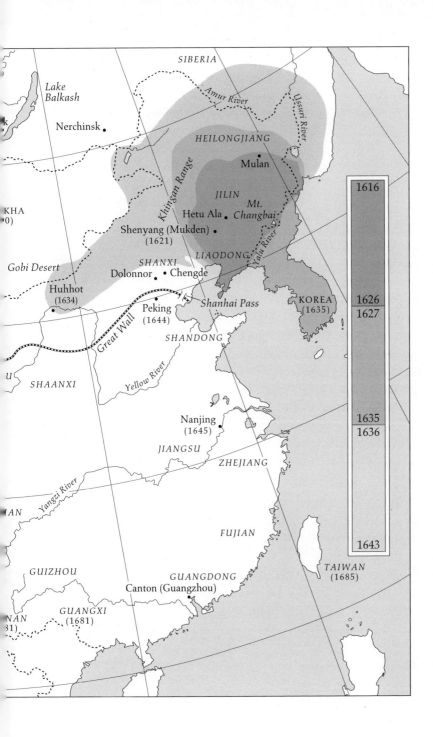

SIBERIA

Lake
Balkash

Nerchinsk .

Amur River

HEILONGJIANG

Ussuri River

Mulan .

JILIN

KHA
0)

Hetu Ala . Mt.
Changbai

Shenyang (Mukden) .
(1621)

Khingan Range

LIAODONG

Yalu River

Gobi Desert

SHANXI
Dolonnor . Chengde

Huhhot
(1634)

KOREA
(1635)

Peking
(1644)

. Shanhai Pass

Great Wall

SHANDONG

U

SHAANXI

Yellow River

Nanjing
(1645)

JIANGSU

ZHEJIANG

Yangzi River

AN

FUJIAN

GUIZHOU

GUANGDONG
Canton (Guangzhou)

TAIWAN
(1685)

NAN
31)

GUANGXI
(1681)

1616

1626
1627

1635
1636

1643

W HEN NURGACI DIED IN 1626, HE WAS SUCCEEDED BY A
council of his lineage members, including his fourth son Hung Taiji.
Within a short time Hung Taiji pared away the power of his co-rulers and
became not merely khan but monarch of the Jin order. Thereafter he accelerated change in the regime until in 1635–36 it became a centralized but segmented order—an empire—which he called "The Great Qing," *Da Qing*.
Hung Taiji magnified the military endeavors of the new state, incorporating the populations of eastern Mongolia and subjugating Korea. He not
only moved toward the conquest of north China, but also undertook extensive campaigns against the hunters, fishers, and gatherers of northern
Jilin and Heilongjiang.

The empire created under Hung Taiji bore little resemblance to the government of Nurgaci. The father had been the khan of a regional, commercially based realm and had few apparent ambitions beyond the large one of
securing the Liaodong territory, where his wealth originated. The son was
an emperor whose ambitions increased in proportion to the burgeoning
material and human resources he acquired. The khanate of Nurgaci had
given little weight to matters of genealogy in the ascription of status, being far more concerned with functions that individuals were able to perform. The empire of Hung Taiji developed means for giving individuals the
functions it required and used genealogical criteria to create divisions and
promote unity wherever it best served the strategies of the moment. The
khanate of Nurgaci had been hesitant to create institutions—particularly
dealing with literacy, literature, education, and history writing—that
could become indispensable to the transformation of the terms in which the
rulership presented itself to its subjects (who inevitably became its objects).
In contrast, the empire of Hung Taiji was aggressive in creating the institutions necessary to increase the ideological reach of the state. Perhaps most
striking, the Nurgaci khanate had absorbed simultaneities cast upon it in
the process of securing Liaodong. The Hung Taiji state actively sought, ma-
nipulated, and generated new simultaneities, using them to construct the
constituencies that legitimated past conquests and forecast new campaigns.

The war on multiple fronts demanded invention of a sophisticated rhetoric. Where Nurgaci had invoked the imperial mantle of the Jin Jurchens
and claimed Liaodong (including the Nikans) as his natural domain, Hung
Taiji in time sublimated the rhetoric of the Jin heritage. Instead, he invited
the Ming court to look upon his rule as heralding an epochal change in the
geopolitics of the world. To the Mongols, the Koreans, and the hunting
peoples of the Northeast, Hung Taiji insisted that his lineage sprang from
the same root as themselves, and he produced mythologies to prove it. His

retrospective identification of himself and his lineage proved fundamental to establishing terms of a new "Manchu" identity. In the metamorphosis of the khanate into an empire, past, present, and future were remolded. Nurgaci was made the emperor he had not been, the Great Qing was given a mandate for undelimited rule, and the habits of mythologizing, historicizing, genealogizing, and ideologizing for future generations of Qing emperors were established.

The simultaneities that Hung Taiji constructed for his emperorship derived from the specific constituencies incorporated in the empire. From the Nikans were drawn the early civil capacities of the state and the ideological fundamentals of a claim to rule over China. From the peoples of Northeast Asia came elements essential to identification of a "Jurchen" cultural world that could be considered ancestral to the Manchus and the unique status of the Nurgaci lineage within it. From the Mongols were learned new religious extensions of rulership and new claims of legitimacy. In each case, ambiguities in cultural identity that had been a necessary part of the state-building under Nurgaci were progressively (and with some deliberation) clarified by the Hung Taiji court. Nikan was distilled from Jurchen and Jurchen from Mongol. These processes were reflected in the narrative of rulership, which by the historiographical authority of the Hung Taiji emperorship was gradually disembarrassed of the personal complexities and administrative simplicities with which it had been imbued under Nurgaci.

3   Boundaries of Rule

Qing imperial narrative, folklore, and history all converge at the point of the "Seven Great Grievances,"[1] Nurgaci's earliest known expression of the direct sources of his right to sovereignty. He made the announcement in 1618 *[margin: 1618]* April 1618 from the fort town of Hetu Ala.[2] The khanate that had existed since 1616 under Nurgaci would henceforth be known by the dynastic name of Jin, "Golden." And war with the Ming empire would commence. *[margin: launch pad for war]* A religious ceremony accompanied the announcement. Inside the ritual building, the *tangse*,[3] Nurgaci burned upon an altar a yellow paper on which was written an oath to Heaven, then enumerated the causes for war. Within

---

1. After the convention of *KF* (*qi da hen*). The phrase evidently comes from *MR TC* 1:1:8, *amba koro ere nadan tere*, "thus the great grievances (sorrows, injuries) are seven."
2. The "Ro-sŏng/Nucheng" of Yi Minhwan's report; see di Cosmo, "Nuove fonti," 146.
3. Some license has been taken in the description of the ceremony here. *MR* records indicate the oath, including the burning of the written oath, on this occasion in 1618. But other particulars of the ceremony, including the opening words of Nurgaci's prayer, are taken from the *KF* description of the war-initiation ceremony performed by Nurgaci in 1588, on the occasion of the beginning of hostilities with the Yehe. There is nothing there inconsistent with information on the ceremony of 1618, for which fewer details are offered than in the earlier account. On the matter of burning paper in connection with religious rites: The Qing later banned this, at least among those who were not members of the Aisin Gioro lineage. They considered it an imitation of Chinese practice.
  The Later Jin and early Qing records use the word *tangse*, from Chinese *tangzi*, to indicate the ritual building associated with shamanic activity. This loan-word is the only word in Manchu for such a structure, suggesting that in earlier times no building was used. The construction of a building like the *tangzi* may coincide with the tendency of Jurchen leaders to absorb the shamanic role in the evolution of dynastic rituals. The use of paper and writing here may also be an innovation, associ-

weeks Fushun was taken, its armaments appropriated, and its population incorporated into the new Jin state. This victory was followed by a steady advance against the Ming forces in Liaodong. The provincial capital, Shenyang, was captured in 1621 and—as Mukden—eventually became the new capital of the khanate. Jin control over central Liaodong was consolidated in 1622 and 1623, and at roughly the same time Nurgaci concluded his campaigns to gain decisive hegemony in northern Liaodong. As his military momentum peaked, so did the political problems of attempting to rule on newly gained ground. Nurgaci combined traditional practice and innovation to keep his growing realm under control. He was determined to press his campaigns westward, into the Ming pale, and perhaps eventually toward the Great Wall. In February 1626 Nurgaci suffered his only serious military defeat, in the assault on the Ming stronghold at Ningyuan, where the canny Ming general Yuan Chonghuan (1584–1630) was in command. Nurgaci was gravely wounded, and died on September 30, 1626, while convalescing. A tomb was built outside of Mukden, and he was interred there before the end of the lunar year.

Though Nurgaci was a well-documented figure to the Ming and Yi courts, little was written of him in his own domain until he created a state in 1618. During the reigns of his son Hung Taiji (r. 1627–36, 1636–43) the annals from that period were rewritten, given a continuous narrative, and published for use by the court. An eighteenth-century imperial account drawn from these revised records and other materials, synthesized as "[Imperially Commissioned] Narrative of the Founding of the Regime" (*Han-i araha fukjin doro neihe bodogon-bithe, Huang Qing kaiguo fanglue*), depicts Nurgaci as native to a cultural space somewhere between Ilantumen in the north and Mt. Changbai in the south, where he succeeded to a regime reputedly founded by Möngke Temür among the Odori in the fifteenth century but recently ruled by Nurgaci's own grandfather and father. When Ming authorities assassinated these latter two ancestors in 1582, Nurgaci is reported to have begun a furious campaign to capture and punish the collaborator, "Nikan Wailan," who had aided the Ming in their perfidious act. In the course of these campaigns, Nurgaci united the Jurchen people under him and bestowed upon them the rule of law. In 1618, having unified the peoples of the Northeast, Nurgaci announced his "Seven Great Grievances,"

---

ated with the developing scribal functions. On the *tangse* see also Rawski, *The Last Emperors*, 236–38.

declared war on the Ming, and enjoyed victories in his pursuits until the fateful battle at Ningyuan in 1626.

In the Hung Taiji reigns, the state created slowly under Nurgaci was rapidly and graphically transformed. So profound was the change in the view of the Hung Taiji court that his first reign period was broken off and a second initiated under an emperorship in 1636.[4] Indeed the newly created emperor advised all, and particularly the Ming empire, to regard the transformation of the state as marking a new age in political relations, one in which the "mind of Heaven" (*tianxin, abka i mujilen*) guided Hung Taiji's power. He encouraged religious and philosophical language granting him the status of a Buddhist enlightened soul, a Confucian sage-king, and an heir to Chinggis Khaghan.[5] In his search for an imperial form he was drawn first to the spiritual and temporal legacies of the Mongol empires, though his departures from Mongol tradition were frequent. His chosen reign titles were complementary. The first—Tiancong/Abkai sure—denoted the capacity to transform, the second—Chongde/Wesihun erdemungge—the achievement of transformation. In both cases, they connoted "genius," that which both personifies and completes the age. The means of metamorphosis was acknowledged in the emperor's posthumous title: *šu hūwangdi/wen huangdi*, the "emperor of letters."

Though Hung Taiji is sanctified in the early Qing documentary process, Nurgaci is written as the source of this sanctity. He is carefully depicted in the Hung Taiji revisions as emperor, god, conqueror, and law-giver. The Nurgaci annals (as collated under Hung Taiji) give an overtly sentimental account of the union of Nurgaci with the second khan's mother, Monggo-gege. Nurgaci is recorded as pronouncing her his "beloved wife" (*haji sargan*).[6] He appeared to be so distraught over Monggo-gege's death in 1603, when Hung Taiji was eleven years old, that he abandoned the capital at Fe

---

4. Only one Ming ruler had two reign periods. He was the hapless Zhengtong emperor, captured by the Oyirod under Esen Khan in 1449 and not ransomed until 1451; he reascended the throne as the Chenghua emperor after his brother, who had assumed the emperorship in his absence, then died. All other emperors of the Ming and Qing periods abided by the late imperial convention of one reign period per ruler.

5. Khaghan here is the retrospective, ritual title of Temüjn, who so far as can be determined was not *khaghan* but *khan* in his own time.

6. In the edicts and legal records of the Hung Taiji period, *haji sargan* becomes a defined status, meaning something close to "wife," or "sole legitimate wife." Only *haji sargan*, for instance, was permitted to sacrifice herself at her husband's death, and her sons were given certain advantages in inheritance. As discussed in Chapter 5,

Ala and returned to the ancestral site of Hetu Ala to create a new head-quarters. It was in her honor, continued this narrative, that Hung Taiji was favored for power, since his father called him "the only offspring of the beloved wife of me, your father." Hung Taiji did indeed succeed his father as khan of the Jin in 1626 (and was invested on lunar new year's day, 1627). Some of these revisions, of which we can find concrete traces, occurred early in Hung Taiji's reign, even before compilation of the Nurgaci annals and before creation of the Qing emperorship in 1636. And the rebuilding of Nurgaci continued well into the eighteenth and nineteenth centuries, de-pending upon the needs of the times. His posthumous title of "Martial Em-peror" (*Wu huangdi*) was not entirely palatable to the politically acute Kangxi court, which in 1662 changed it to "Highest Emperor" (*Gao huangdi*—that is, the emperor from whom all others descend); but the Jia-qing (1796–1820) and Daoguang (1821–50) reigns were those that most strongly promoted Nurgaci's spiritual presence throughout the Northeast, Mongolia, and northern China as a local god of war.

ORIGINS OF THE KHANSHIP

Nurgaci aspired long to the title of khan (*han*) and achieved it by degrees in the very late stage of his career. The term "khan" had been known in North-east Asia since at latest the fourth century and was a local political tradition influenced by parallel development of the same title among the imperial Mongols.[7] In Jurchen political vocabulary, "khan" meant a leader. With qualifications, the word was applied to emperors—for instance, "emperor of the Nikans" (*nikan i han*), the Ming emperors; to "kings" (normally in Chinese *wang*, sometimes translated into English as "prince"), as the kings of Korea (*solgo i han*); or to the Buddha (Mongolian *Burkhan*, Manchu

---

it was typical for Manchu political and legal language to use ostensible sentiment to distinguish between groups and individuals in administrative practice.

7. See Lawrence Krader, "Qan-Qaɣan and the Beginnings of Mongol King-ship," for a summary of the debates on etymologies and relationships of the Mon-golian terms *khan* and *khaghan*. It appears that *khaghan* was the earlier of the two and that it is present in attestations from languages at the two extremes of the ge-ographical spectrum, Old Bulgarian and Korean. *Khan* and its Manchu cognates could have resulted from a contraction of the weak consonant. There is evidence of awareness of the term *khaghan* in the Northeast in the Tang period, and the Jur-chen word upon which Manchu *han* was based has been traced by Jin Qizong to the Jurchen disyllabic *ha-(g)an*, which appears on the stele of the Yongning si (Jin, *Nuzhen wen cidian*, 122).

[margin notes:]
HT- succeeds as khan in 1626

from martial Emp to Highest Emp (Kangxi) to spirit, God of war (after 1796)

aspiring to Khan

= imperial Mongols

Burhan). The style in which any khan ruled was determined by the realm that he ruled. Though the prestige of the term in the Northeast during the seventeenth century was probably associated with its use by the Mongol Great Khans, the regional khanship had a distinct local tradition behind it. *Khan* It depended upon frequent engagements in war and originally may have *qualities* existed solely for the purpose of uniting multiple federations for more effective attack or defense. As such larger orders gained political stability the khans sometimes became dynastic, attempting to pass the khanship through a single lineage. This does not imply primogeniture, nor did it prevent internecine strife.[8] Indeed the khans were those men who through intense struggle against their rival candidates had demonstrated Heaven-favored gifts of agility, strength, eloquence, and insightfulness. Such struggles occur in the Manchu records as contests for the judgment of Heaven; to be judged affirmatively (*urušembi*) was justification in itself, since Heaven is the highest (if impenetrable) intelligence. The qualities likely to merit this support had been called by the Turks *kut,* by the Mongols *sechen,* and by the Jurchens *sure*—the power that guides an arrow to its target. In English both are normally translated "intelligent," though in context its meaning is closer to "gifted," or "charismatic."

Nurgaci's earliest model as khan was Wan (d. 1582), the leader of the *the Wan* Hada federation, who dominated commerce at Guangshun Pass, east of *model* Kaiyuan.[9] Wan was extremely successful in negotiating the rivalries and intrigues of the area. The Ula, Yehe, and Hoifa federations had been subordinated to him and combined with his Hada to form the regionally domi- *Hulun* nant Hūlun alliance in the 1570s. To his headquarters he regularly drew *fed* talented men who feared for their safety or their positions in their home territories. He was frequently paid tribute at his palace in Hada by ambassadors from the Jurchens and Mongols, he employed Nikans as his secretaries, and he incorporated aspiring Nurgan magnates, whether Mongols or Jurchens (including Nurgaci), into his household as sons-in-law. Wan passed laws, participated in a strategic partnership with the Liaodong governor Li Chengliang, considered himself head of a court, and attempted to institutionalize his khanship by passing it to his son Hurhan.[10] The Qing

8. Fletcher, "Turco-Mongolian Tradition," 240–41.
9. Wan was one of a group of Northeastern leaders who were descended from Nacibulu, the chieftain of what would later be recognized as the Nara lineages. The Nacibulu descendants enjoyed noble precedence in Nurgan and rose to leadership in the Yehe and Ula federations, as well as the Hada.
10. This is not Hurhan (Dargan hiya), the son of Hōhōri and nephew of Nurgaci. Hurhan of Hada appears in the orthodox Qing narrative as an almost stereo-

narrative acknowledged Wan as the definer of the "Manchu" political realm, referring to him as "Wan Khan of the Hada nation, Lord of the Manchu nations" (Manju gurun i ejen Hada gurun i Wan han, Manzhou guo zhu Hada guo Wan Han).[11] The formulation is noteworthy not only because it acknowledges a Manchu ruler before Nurgaci ("Manchu" is in eighteenth-century fashion substituted here for "Jurchen") but also in its use of *zhu*, which represents Mongolian/Manchu *ejen*, "lord."[12] With its meaning of "lord," "owner," and "ruler," *ejen* would remain the fundamental self-description for the Qing dynasts.

As a khan, Nurgaci became as a political person the primary owner of slaves.[13] The "slave" (*aha*) is a child, and the owner is the parent. A benign owner might make his slaves rich, seek the best for them in all ways, and depend upon their wisdom and support. A malignant owner would be punished by Heaven, but to forestall supernatural wrath the lord's own superiors might remove slaves from him. In his relationship with his slaves the owner gives protection and sustenance. In return, the slave gives loyalty and obedience. From Nurgaci on, the Later Jin and Qing rulers would allude again and again to the subject of proper relations between owners and slaves—rarely distinguishing between the discrete institution of social and economic slavery and the political and ideological forms for which it was the basis. In this they borrowed not only from Northeastern traditions but also from Mongolian great khanship, in which the *khaghan* had also ruled his Mongols as a master rules his slaves.[14] From this idea, the fundamental political vocabulary of the Qing emerged under Nurgaci. The acquisition of populations was originally not the action of the subjugated ("joining, returning or submitting," *gui*) as it would become in the later narratives, but the action of the subjugators, simply "taking" (*de, bahambi*). In con-

---

typical "bad second emperor," who squandered his father's achievements and led the Hada nation to destruction at the hands of Nurgaci.

11. *KF* 1:2a. Despite Wan's status as "Lord of the Manchu Nations," Nurgaci later drew a pointed dichotomy between "Manchu" (i.e., Jurchen) and "Hūlun" as political identities (*KF* 3.3).

12. Jurchen had this word (*ədzen, ədzehei*), meaning "office, function, role, status, service," and the meaning survives in Manchu *ejehe*, "general, authoritative." But the late Jurchen and Manchu sense here comes from Mongolian *ejen*, "lord."

13. This is not chattel slavery, but the sort of unfree political and economic state that was long attested in the Northeast and other societies of eastern Asia. On the complexity of Qing court institutions of service see Rawski, *The Last Emperors*, 160–94.

14. For an overview in the continuity of this conceit, see Sinor, "The Inner Asian Warriors," 134–35.

text it is evident that the terms for fatherly support (*ujimbi, yang, yu*) that Nurgaci and Hung Taiji normally used to describe their relationship to the peoples under their control were extensions of the basic master-slave model.[15] In exchange for his total service the slave gained the formidable protection and symbolic (or real) intimacy of the khan. The term of affiliation was simple and level, applying to all regardless of language, custom, or habitat. It was also strongly marked by the affective basis that Manchu political vocabulary would retain: The lord and slave are linked by love, they are moved to action by passions—indignation, pity, protectiveness—and in the description of their mutual obligations there is little of the ethical vocabulary that distinguished state Confucian rhetoric.

Nurgaci had begun his career as *beile*,[16] or headman, of the Jianzhou, and as khan he formalized the subordination of other *beile* to himself. *Beile* were considerable landholders in their own right (and had their working villages, or *tokso*, administered by trusted servants) but were putative original owners of all lands, goods, and peoples in their domains. They had assumed their positions in most cases by force or the threat of force, and had the exclusive right to designate other headmen within their federations as owners and to grant them working villages of their own. It appears that distribution and redistribution of property by the *beile* was an extension of shamanic rights, suggesting (like the rituals Nurgaci affected first as *beile* and then as khan) either an amalgamation of political and spiritual functions or displacement of the latter by the former. In earliest times, for instance, it was shamans who punished murderers by the removal of their flocks and property and shamans who condemned evil households to ruin by damning their herds.[17] As the primary owner, the *beile* was the first defense against theft and violence. Villages coming under the hegemony of a *beile* usually lost control over weapon making; thereafter the *beile* monop-

[handwritten margin note: Nur- 1st a headman of Jianzhou]

---

15. The vocabulary remained a part of imperial usage and evolved into prominence (in the form *aiyang*, "love and support," or "loving support"), in *Dayi juemi lu* (hereafter *DJL*) 1:a, 14a, 3:2a (see Chapter 5). The association of bondage, affection, and basic social relations suggested here is not very different from the history of the word "family" in English and its Latin roots.

16. See also Crossley, *The Manchus*, 42–44; 206. In the sixteenth century there was a rough correspondence between the title *beg* in Mongolia and *beile* in the Northeast. These were the headmen of federations ("tribe," in Chinese usually translated *bu*, but in Mongolian *aimakh*, borrowed into Jurchen as *aiman*). *Beile*, which is linguistically related to *beg* and probably comes by its own route from Turkic, was the earlier of the two borrowings.

17. Franke, "Some Folkloristic Data in the Dynastic History of the Chin," 138. Also *coohai janggin*.

olized the manufacture of arrows and iron weapons and forbade artisans to work at these enterprises in the free villages. Those who wished to purchase weapons had to come to the *beile's* residence and apply for permission. In times of military mobilization, the *beile* authorized his lieutenants to distribute arrows to the village headmen. By the sixteenth century a war leader, whether a *beile* or a lineage headman, could be known by the title "lord of arrows" (*nirui ejen*).[18] The *beile's* position as putative original owner in his lands was also the foundation of his right to dispense justice (that is, the taking and giving of goods). Corporal and capital punishments were, under the most desired circumstances, meted out to lineage members by their elders before the *beile* was burdened with judgment himself; if judgment should for some reason be referred to him, administration of punishments by lineage elders was expected to be swift. In this way, lineage leaders hoped to keep discretionary power from falling completely into the hands of a very powerful *beile.* There is evidence that lineage leaders continued well into the period of Nurgaci's khanate to preemptively administer punishment to their members to retain some autonomy by minimizing the amount of Nurgaci's judicial initiative.

In his youth Nurgaci had to struggle to attain the title of *beile.* It had evidently been used by elders of his lineage, perhaps by more than one of them, among the Jianzhou. But his involvement with the court of Wan may also have firmly fixed his ambitions on attaining the title of khan. If so, it was a long time in coming, and when it did come, it was not from Nurgaci's Jurchen followers. The first to title Nurgaci "khan" were Mongolian-speaking Khorchins. After their defeat by Nurgaci in 1606 they made

18. There is a connection here with some Mongol practices in which marked arrows were used as tokens of affiliation and of status. See, for the fullest secondary treatment, Serruys, "A Note on Arrows and Oaths among the Mongols." In Chinese records of the Yuan and Ming periods they are referred to as *lingjian,* "arrow(s) of command," and producing one was sufficient to identify a visitor to any part of the Mongol world as a messenger or emissary of high commanders, or as couriers (very like some incidents described by Shin Chung-il), and the placement of arrows with distinctive markings was used to claim places and things as well as people. In Qing times the banner affiliations and rank of officers was indicated by the attachment to their symbolic arrows of small flags of varying shapes and colors. The distribution of these rank tokens was so well known in Qing times that the practice was satirized in Cao Zhan's "Dream of the Red Chamber" (in which a chief rat distributes marked arrows as he deputizes his underlings to scrounge up supplies for a New Year's celebration). Serruys comments that Antoine Mostaert saw the practice still in use among Santa troops of the warlord Ma Fuxiang, in Gansu, around 1917. The Santa in question were Muslims but spoke an archaic form of Mongolian.

themselves amiable by acknowledging him as *Kündülün khan* (Jurchen *Kundulen han*).[19] The superiority the title implied was directed at Nurgaci personally (not at the Jianzhou Jurchens generally), and his khanal rank was derived from—and limited to—his relationship to the Khorchins. To his Jurchen followers he remained "Wise *Beile*" (*Sure beile*,[20] which may have been inspired by the Mongolian *Sechen khan*). It was a simple but crucial form of simultaneous leadership that Nurgaci incorporated into his ruling persona as he incorporated the Khorchins into his regime. The Qing narrative states that in 1616 Nurgaci combined his Jianzhou title—"Wise *Beile*"—with his Khorchin title and became the Jianzhou/Khorchin ruler "Wise and Revered Khan."[21] Within a short time he changed his title again, to "Enlightened Khan" (*Genggiyan han*).[22] How soon this happened and precisely what it signaled is a question. The imperial history bundles together the title of "Enlightened Khan" with a reign title, and the dynastic name of Jin. But the correspondence with Korea is not consistent with this. In 1616 Nurgaci announced himself to the Yi court as Khan of the Jianzhou; not until 1618 did he share the dynastic name Jin with them.[23] A reign name (as distinct from a dynastic name) would have unequivocally marked initiation of the state, with its ability to document events and formalize the passage of time, denying Jurchen subordination to the authority of the Ming. The evolution of the record on Nurgaci leaves some doubt whether he used a reign name in his own time at all or whether it was imposed by the historians of the Hung Taiji period.

The name chosen for Nurgaci's reign was *abkai fulingga*, a phrase rich with political pretention. Grammatically the reign name was a near equivalent to Chinese *Tianming*, "Mandate of Heaven," though the Manchu is slightly more precise: "That which has been mandated by Heaven."[24] This

---

19. *Manzhou shilu* gives *wushen huangdi* ("Emperor of Martial Spirit") as the meaning for the title, which is followed by Hummel et al., *ECCP*, 596. The phrase *wushen* appears as a description of Nurgaci in *KF*, and the gloss also may be due to a confusion with Nurgaci's first temple name, *Wu huangdi*. The Mongolian title means, as Farquhar has pointed out, "respected, revered," related to modern *qündülqü*, "revered." See also Manchu *kundulembi*, "to respect." The word was correctly glossed from its first appearance in the Qing annals: *Wu huangdi shilu, juan 2*, p. 2.

20. In *KF*, *zongrui beile*.

21. *Sure kundulen han. TM 1.*

22. *TM 1.*

23. Zhu Xizu, *Hou Jin guohan xingshi kao*, 21. See also Yan Chongnian, *Nurhachi zhuan*, 158.

24. Cf. Jurchen *fuli[n]gi* (*fuli[n]gi gaibi*, etc.), to command (Jin, *Nuzhen wen cidian*, 226).

may appear to suggest that the mandate—in the universalist sense entrenched in Chinese political rhetoric by this time—was passing to a new order. There is no contemporary evidence, however, to suggest that Nurgaci ever resolved to succeed the Ming in their own realm. The change of regime suggested by the reign name (if Nurgaci in fact used it) was to occur in the Northeast, where Ming authority would give way to Nurgaci's control. Equally striking, in Nurgaci's own time such a reign name would have signaled the coming of a "mandate of Heaven," or centralized political rule, to the Northeast for the first time since the demise of the Jurchen Jin empire.

Fulingga was a noun for the fruits of the "intelligence"—the natural worthiness, or charisma—that wins the judgment of Heaven after a struggle. It connoted good luck, fortune, and favor by Heaven, and was one of a series of words related to speech, speaking, articulateness (or the lack of it).[25] *Fulingga*, the "good luck" of the natural ruler, was the ability of Heaven to express its wishes in the world. Its use in the phrase *abkai fulingga* was a statement not only of the manifestation of the will of Heaven, but of the ability of Heaven to speak through the khan. It identified the khan as a political shaman, a meaning neither far removed from Chinese *tianming* of ancient times nor from the more immediate sources of shamanic political legitimation in the Northeast.

Whether or not Nurgaci used a reign name in his own lifetime, he certainly resurrected the dynastic name Jin, "Golden." The single word "Jin"— in Manchu, Aisin[26]—invoked a powerful historical reflection. In the thirteenth century China had been divided between the Jurchen Jin empire in the north and the Song in the south (both had later been destroyed by the Mongols). Now, in 1618, Nurgaci claimed descent from the Jin Jurchens. Historically, this could be justified only in the loosest sense; the Wanyan federation, descendants of the Jin imperial family, were far to the east of the Jianzhou, and had been subdued by violence in the 1580s. The language of the Jianzhou Jurchens, which would someday become reformed as Manchu, was a recognizable cousin of the language of the Jin Jurchens, but certainly not its direct descendant. It was both grammatically different and permeated by a large number of loan-words, most from Mongolian and

25. See also Crossley, "*Manzhou yuanliu kao* and the Formalization of the Manchu Heritage."

26. By convention historians refer to the Nurgaci and early Hung Taiji period as the "Later Jin," Hou Jin, but contemporary records refer to the state only as "Jin."

Chinese but a smaller number—mostly via Mongolian—from Turkic, Arabic, Russian, and Aramaic.[27]

These facts were irrelevant to the historical imagery Nurgaci intended to use. He first of all established himself as inheritor of a tradition of rule over the Northeast, and not only over the Jianzhou territories, or even all Jurchen territories. The medieval Jin had controlled Siberia, the Northeast, north China, and parts of Mongolia, and their tributary peoples had included not only the Turks, Uigurs, and Kitans whose powers had passed, but also the Mongols who would someday succeed them. Capitals, bureaucracies, and decimally organized armies had been the foundations of Jin administration—a fact not of much interest to Nurgaci but quite important to Hung Taiji. The old Jin had commanded the loyalties of and successfully incorporated the population of north China, the Han. The new Jin, with the conquest of Liaodong, would do this, too. The old Jin had resisted Song attempts to dislodge them from the north and referred to the Song as the "southern court" (*nan chao*). The new Jin proposed to do something similar with the Ming. Though hardly persuaded by Nurgaci's Jin pretensions as promulgated in 1618, the Ming proved sensitive to the images he had invoked. They did not deny the historical link of the later Jin Jurchens to the imperial Jin Jurchens of the twelfth century; on the contrary they desecrated the Jin tombs at Fangshan, near Peking, "to celebrate it."[28] Nurgaci's rhetoric might also have intensified Ming suspicion of their border officers who acknowledged or were suspected of Jurchen ancestry, a suspicion that turned to persecution after the Ming reverses of 1622 and 1623 in Liaodong and may have contributed to the desertion of high-ranking Ming officers, as well as the trials of Tong Bunian, Li Rubo, and others.

In his early years as khan Hung Taiji continued his father's practice of referring to the Jin/Song era as a model for relations between Ming China and the new Jin state. He ordered the histories of the (Kitan) Liao, (Jurchen) Jin, and (Mongol) Yuan empires translated from Chinese into Manchu and was reported to have been a reader of the Jin history (possible, though there is room for doubt, since these translations were not completed in Hung Taiji's lifetime). During the Jin raid upon Peking in the summer of 1629—the only time Hung Taiji entered China proper—he traveled out to Fang-

---

27. Franke, "Etymologische Bemerkungen zu den Vokabularen der Jürcen-Sprache."

28. When the Qing armies invaded China in 1644 Dorgon sacked the Ming tombs north of Peking "to get even." See Mo Dongyin, *Manzu shi luncong,* 75.

shan and made sacrifice at the tombs of the Jin emperors Agūda and Shizong. Equally striking—even obtrusive—is the insertion in the Manchu
annals revised under Hung Taiji of a sequence of passages drawing strong
parallels between the personal careers of Nurgaci and the medieval Jin
founder, (Wanyan/Wanggiya) Agūda. Like Nurgaci, Agūda had first participated in the imperial conventions of the predominating empire, then rebelled against them. Like Nurgaci's, Agūda's life was saved by a conde-
scending official of the empire. Like Nurgaci (it was implied), Agūda had
been forced to wage war against the empire to resist its aggression. Like
Nurgaci, Agūda had first battled the fortified lineage villages of the Northeast and united the Jurchens before declaring war on the empire. Like Nurgaci, Agūda had awed a variety of local peoples, all of whom flocked to his
standard.[29] And like Agūda, Nurgaci would formalize and bureaucratize
the basic social forms of the Jurchens.

The reorganization of social hierarchies and affiliations celebrated in
these passages from the annals proceeded apace with growth of Nurgaci's
power. With each new village that surrendered or was conquered, or with
each group of nomads or hunters who surrendered from afar, Nurgaci marginally increased his ability to redistribute wealth and to rearrange social
structures within the newly incorporated peoples. As a *beile,* his roles as
gift-giver and law-maker were actually one. As his regime became more
complex, he was forced to differentiate and in some cases delegate these
powers. To establish that these powers (or their effects) proceeded from
him to others, he had to fix himself as a center. This was difficult for two
reasons. Like his immediate ancestors, Nurgaci had been rather casual about
where he lived and how his home was arranged (apart from having stout
fortifications). Few, apart from Wan of Hada, had achieved a degree of centralization in living memory. The locations and disposition of Nurgaci's
homes have been historically interpreted as representing his status and his
ambitions. This may not have been an obvious consideration to the young
Nurgaci. He was born and raised at his father Giocangga's homestead at
Hūlan Hada, the "Chimney Cliffs," believed to have once been the base of
Li Manzhu (see Chapters 2 and 4).[30] Nurgaci's first independent home indicated merely his condition as a free and adult man; it appears that at the
traditional age of nineteen he left his father's house, married, and established a household for himself. The location is unknown, but remarks by

[handwritten margin note: Nur's — need to affix himself to a center — needing a home]

29. For Agūda's narrative see *TM* 3:3 (232–36; 300).
30. Leader of the Jianzhou Jurchens before his power was destroyed by Möngke
Temür and Fanca. See Chapter 2.

Shin Chung-il suggest that it could have been at Ninggūda, less than a half
day's travel from Hūlan Hada. Ninggūda, supposed to have taken its name
from the fact that Giocangga and his five brothers had once lived there,
could not have been a grand setting. When Shin Chung-il saw it in 1596 all
that remained was a neglected watchtower and eight deserted houses; the
grounds of Ninggūda had been given over to grazing for horses and cattle,
and a new village, of perhaps forty households, had begun nearby.[31] After
the deaths of Giocangga and Taksi, Nurgaci assumed their homesteads back
at Hūlan Hada. He greatly improved upon the site. In 1587 the first walls—
a wooden palisade—went up, and a three-story palace was built. But when
Shin Chung-il passed Hūlan Hada a little less than a decade later it was a
disappointing sight too, with fewer than fifty households and no remaining fortifications, all under the control of an undistinguished headman.[32]

In 1592 Nurgaci moved to Fe Ala ("Old Hill"), sited in a such way that
it was at the nexus of Ming and Nurgan territories. Indeed its connections
favored the Ming. It was only two nights' journey from Fushun, but three
or four nights from Jurchen settlements of any size. The Korean town of
Huanyang was three days to the southwest, at the Yalu River. Ten days to the
east was the mountain sacred to many Northeastern peoples, Mt. Changbai.[33] Further east of that, two weeks away, was the ancestral territory of
Möngke Temür and the Odori Jurchens, at Huncun. The residence of the
powerful leaders of Ula—Bujantai and Mantai—was a month away to the
northeast. Thus Nurgaci was based at the eastern extreme of the Ming territories and the western extreme of the Jurchen political continuum. His
locations marked the westward progress of the Jurchen political center,
which since the time of Möngke Temür had moved from Huncun to northern Korea to "Tunggiya"—the region of Hūlan Hada and Ninggūda. Now
Ming Liaodong was familiar territory to the Jianzhou leaders, and Huncun
was a distant, unfamiliar place.[34] In 1603—the year that Monggo-gege
died—Nurgaci moved to Hetu Ala, the "Level Hill" (*Ping gang*),[35] named

---

31. *KJD*, 14.
32. Hūlan Hada (Hulao ling) Shin, *KJD*, 14. It had been ten years, Shin was
told, since Nurgaci had left Hūlan Hada (an error, though not a big one).
33. *KJD*, 29.
34. *KJD*, 10; 16; Crossley, *The Manchus*, 56–57.
35. For background on Hetu Ala see Rawski, *The Last Emperors*, 18–19. Giovanni Stary, excoriating Wakeman's discussion of Hetu Ala, states that Hetu Ala is
correctly translated as "little hill." "Hetu" means "level," or "table-like" (a mesa),
which is reflected in the Chinese name "Pinggang." The word *hetu* is related to the
common Qing bureaucratic term *heturi*, "horizontal."

for its peculiar conformation, with steep sides and a flat, easily defended top. The region was fertile, since Hetu Ala lay along the Giyaha River. The city (now Xingjing in Liaoning province) remained Nurgaci's headquarters until the conquest of Liaodong and removal of the capital to Mukden (Shenyang) in 1625.

The imperial narrative celebrates the fortification of Hūlan Hada in 1587 as the building of a capital and associates it with Nurgaci's new role as a law-maker. The history specifically states that Nurgaci promulgated a legal code at this time.[36] Shin Chung-il affirms that certain rules were known to be in force among the Jianzhou and that Nurgaci was their source. Many related to keeping the growing wealth in land, minerals, furs, animals, and people in the hands of those to whom Nurgaci had given it. There seems no need to assume a set of written regulations. Whatever system was in place was probably not complex and still relied upon the lineages to execute justice. And the timing is reasonable. It is close in time to (though very slightly in advance of) the great expansion of Nurgaci's base of support in 1588, during which he recruited the men who would later be known as his five "judges" (jargūci, from Mongolian yarghōči). Through the judges, a standardization of legal practice, however simple, was probably instituted sometime before 1590.

Wealth was the primary focus of all Nurgaci's political activities, from his early struggles to retain and enhance his family's properties to his late role as ruler and spokesman for the political interests of the region. Development of agricultural lands within Nurgan, as well as importation of slave labor from Liaodong and northern Korea, appears to have contributed to population growth within the Jurchen territories in the later sixteenth century. At the same time, Jurchen agricultural land was occasionally appropriated by Ming forces. Li Chengliang had claimed lands south of Hetu Ala—probably with the acquiescence of Giocangga and Taksi—in the 1570s, and the military establishment there continued to encroach upon the surrounding Jurchen areas. Ming authorities encouraged emigration from north China (particularly Shandong) to the region, and the growing Jurchen population was feeling the pinch. The Ming held the line against further westward expansion, while the Yi kept pushing the Jurchens north from Korea. By the 1580s, it seems, to acquire wealth was dangerous. The later Qing view of the situation would emphasize the deep chaos of the re-

36. KF 2.1a.

gion and the urgent need for a pacificator. "Bandits were like bees, arising one after the other and calling themselves *han, beile, amban.* Every village headman set himself up as a magnate, every lineage leader set himself up as a statesman. . . . And those with the strongest lineages attacked and subjugated the weakest."[37] As a contemporary witness, Shin recorded the testimony of Jianzhou, who credited Nurgaci with literally making the roads safe to travel and money safe to keep in the house. The effect of Nurgaci's laws, evident all through the Manchu annals and through the history of the conquest, was that individuals were permitted to acquire wealth given by Nurgaci but never to hoard anything—money, goods, or people—without his knowledge and consent.

During the Nurgaci era lineages became institutions seriously involved in the negotiation of justice and policy. In general it appears that the leaders of prominent lineages attempted to slow the incursion of khanal authority over their members by administering the punishment themselves, their traditional right. Within his own lineage, Nurgaci repeatedly refused to delegate the power of life and death to anyone; in 1620, for instance, he refused Daišan (Guyen baturu) permission to execute his own wife, who was accused on good evidence of adultery, and in 1622 refused permission to Daišan and Amin to execute their sons (Yoto and Soto, respectively), who were suspected of trying to desert.[38] Until the very late seventeenth century, lineages among the bannermen were not the legal corporations they were often considered under the civilian Chinese.[39] Wrongdoers did not pollute their family members with their criminality, and the laws of Nurgaci did not provide for the punishment, execution, or posthumous desecration of the family members of the convicted. Indeed Nurgaci's court reconciled itself to the widows and mothers of his personal opponents Bujantai, Mantai, and Gintaisi with gifts and public honors,[40] and many Aisin Gioro descendants of the disgraced or executed—such as Šurgaci or Cuyen (Argatu tumen)—prospered afterward. The alteration and command over the higher levels of lineage structures made the organization of Nurgaci's

37. Quoted in Mo, "Mingmo Jianzhou nuzhen," *Manzu shi luncong*, 91; Wakeman, *The Great Enterprise*, 49 n 61.

38. Okada, "How Hong Taiji Came to the Throne," 254.

39. On legal functioning of the civil lineages, or *zu*, see van der Sprenkel, *Legal Institutions in Manchu China*, 80–89.

40. *TM* 10:1:7.

political regime possible. With these mechanisms he shaped, promulgated, and enforced his laws; mobilized the military forces he required; formalized relationships with prospective or accomplished allies; and established a council of his own family to aid in managing what he had acquired. It is clear that in all these matters Nurgaci preferred the smallest amount of innovation necessary to accomplish his purposes. He had no ambition—and no means—to effect a thorough reorganization of society, either in Nurgan or in Liaodong.

The "lineages" of Nurgaci were plastic indeed. The word for them, *mukūn*,[41] occurs no later than the records of the medieval Jin empire as a term for lineage associations among the Jurchens. There *mukūn*—rendered *mouke* in the Chinese records of the Jin—was a term for a hunting or gathering collective, whether a migrating group or a village. After the founding of the Qing state, *mukūn* would become a definitive lineage term, and is now (after Shirokogoroff) frequently translated "clan." But it is important that the elaborate, formalized lineage constructions of the Qing period not be read back to the earlier seventeenth century. The environment out of which early Qing society was formed was one of oral and rather vague accounts of descent, fragmented and frequently removed settlement groups, and pragmatic political alliances. Communities were crucial to survival and were in no way superficial to Jurchen life, whether material or spiritual. But the association of eternal and immutable lineage identities with consanguinity was a later imposition on the cultural history of Nurgan. Records relating to the Nurgaci period commonly do not make a rigid distinction among *mukūn*, villages (*gašan*), or hunts (*tatan*). Linguistic evi-

41. Early discussions of Manchu kinship have provided the Qing neologism *halamukūn* as the usual term for a "clan," or lineage (see Shirokogoroff, *Social Organization of the Manchus,* and Ling Chunsheng, *Songhuajiang xiayou de hezhe zu*). This, it has been suggested, was cognate to Chinese *shizu*, which also suggests the latter word as a unit of the former: That is, that *hala* (or *shi*) is a "clan" and *mukūn* (or *zu*) a sub-clan, or lineage. In fact *mukūn* is the older of the two Manchu terms and (like *zu*) was originally not a word that unambiguously indicated a blood-related group. *Hala* came later to indicate federations of *mukūn*, and in the Qing period *mukūn* remained the normal word for a lineage or extended family, with *hala* being an infrequently invoked reference to totality of people sharing a lineage name (whether they were actually related or not). This term is attested for Jurchen in the Ming period (see Jin, *Nuzhen wen cidian,* 188, *hala moumuhuwe*). This is usually glossed as Chinese *shizu*, which also suggests the latter word as a unit of the former: That is, that *hala* (or *shi*) is a "clan" and *mukūn* (or *zu*) a sub-clan, or lineage. See Chapter 3; see also Crossley, "Thinking about Ethnicity" and *Orphan Warriors.*

dence suggests that lineages as entities were easily distinguished from villages as entities, but in practice the differences could be insignificant. To continue his quest to control borders and trade with both Korea and the Ming empire, Nurgaci had to apply his powers to the reorganization of life among the Jurchens. He utilized the deep tradition of household and village defense. Every man was expected to purchase his own arms and equip himself (typically with an ox, grain, jerky, and eighteen taels of silver for ransoming himself should he cross into Korean territory) on the occasion of a campaign, on the assumption that every man was part of a family and every family was experienced in the needs of a man doing battle. Nurgaci himself paid nothing to mobilize forces. Men enlisted in the defensive campaigns because this was the best way to protect their homes from depredation by Ming forces or their mercenaries, and they joined the attack forces anticipating a share of the rewards. Households worked together to supply the soldier in hopes of partaking of his booty. They shared in his misfortunes, too, and this went beyond death or injury. Nurgaci's custom required, for instance, that families too poor to provide their soldiers with ransom money would be required to go to Korea themselves to redeem their men if they were captured.[42]

The mutability of lineage functions, structures, and names before the conquest is suggested by the fact that Jurchen had no word for a higher level of organization—a confederation of lineages, or a "tribe." Mongolian *aimaleh,* which denoted a collection of lineages under a single leader, was borrowed (as *aiman*) to describe a federation normally under the command of a *beile.* In practice it corresponded in the late Ming to the "garrison" divisions in the Northeast (see Chapter 1), but in other instances its meaning was not distinguishable from Chinese *bu,* normally translated "tribe." The date of the Jurchen term's introduction is not known, but it most probably is of Ming vintage, and may have become widespread during the period of migrations, political amalgamations, and warfare of the fifteenth and sixteenth centuries. It was this term—and this organization—that was the obstacle to Nurgaci's ambitions. In his wars against his Jurchen neighbors, their *aiman* were dismantled, not their *mukūn.* On the contrary, the *mukūn* became the vessels for Nurgaci's early organization for war. Instead of joining *beile* in fighting against other *aiman* for survival or enrichment, the headmen (*mukūnda*) of the *mukūn* became captains in Nur-

42. *KJD,* 25.

gaci's "companies" (*niru*). In 1596 Shin observed that wherever Nurgaci
went outside his private compound, whether on foot or on horseback, he
was accompanied by a rather elaborately armed guard, each man supplied
with bows and arrows and each carrying his own supply of grain. These

institutional-
izing
the
banner
men

guards were part of a large, well-organized army. Undoubtedly what Shin
saw was a group of very early bannermen. He also found that at Fe Ala the
space between the inner living quarters of Nurgaci and Šurgaci and the ex-
terior walls of the city were occupied by "the families of soldiers," with the
emphasis here on "families"—it would remain Qing practice that bannermen except in unusual circumstances lived with their families (who originally supported them). These families would usually share in the fortunes
of war and in the end shared in the fortunes of identity, all being cast in the
mold—for good or ill—of the professional, salaried men who always made
up a minority of the banner populations.[44] By 1601 they were recorded as
formally amalgamated into four "banners" (*gūsa*)—in descending order,
the Yellow, White, Red, and Blue.

The ancient pressures of defense and attack caused families and villages
not only to strengthen and regularize their bonds of mutual aid but also to
represent themselves corporately to their banner lords and ultimately to
Nurgaci. In this Nurgaci had an unprecedented impact upon the region,
and rooted the heart of what would later be Qing state-building in the reconstruction of household, lineage, and village life. Nurgaci's attempts to
control the judicial autonomy, identification, growth, and wealth of *mukūn*
can be discerned from the time of the creation of the state and must have
begun no later than this. His campaigns to reunite a portion of the Jurchens

constructing
lineages

in the late sixteenth century uncovered profound disarray in lineage affiliation.[45] As he proceeded to establish the banner system and then the state,
Nurgaci determined that for purposes of registration the lineage affiliations
of his followers should be codified. Unaffiliated individuals were assigned

✓

to lineages. Those lineages in good working order and distinguished for
their service to Nurgaci were given hereditary companies within the banners. Each banner (*gūsa*, *qi*) was based upon a collection of companies (*niru*,
zuoling),[46] and each company was, in the late sixteenth century, based upon

44. *KJD*, 17.
45. "Précis" (*fanlie*) to *BMST*, p. 3a–b.
46. The Jurchen/Manchu word, *niru*, literally meant "arrow." Its use to denote
a hunting or military company has not been entirely explained. Ming accounts
describe the *niru i ejen* as being those who on the occasion of the hunt or of battle
distributed arrows to their followers. Shin Chung-il found that Nurgaci, as *beile*,

some preexisting social unit. Large lineages within villages could form companies, in which case their headman (*mukūnda*) would act as captain, or "lord of the arrows" (*niru i ejen*). Villages (*gašan*) with smaller lineages might form a company, in which case the village headman (*gašanda*) would act as captain. In accord with Northeastern tradition, eligibility for *niru* leadership was hereditary. To compete for command of the companies—and receive the stipends and privileges attending it—a lineage name and an account of origins had to be produced. In this need lay the origins of many of Nurgaci's programs for the regularization and institutionalization of lineage identity. The immediate object is clear enough, for the *mukūn* were the units upon which the banners were based. But under the pressure of impending war with the Ming, it was equally important that in building and propagandizing his new state Nurgaci should invoke repeatedly the twelfth-century dynastic heritage of the Jurchens. The adoption of the Jin heritage as part of Nurgaci's propaganda reinforced the development of lineage-based public affiliation, since certain lineage names were easily associated with the Jin heritage. The lineages Nurgaci was uniting were, the imperial history would later claim, the lineages of the imperial Jurchens.

In the banners as in the khan's court, marriages were an important aspect of all lineage relationships.[47] Prior to organization of the banners many *baišin* men had been adopted into their wives' families, and as suggested above the administration of justice was generally guided by lineage affiliations. Nurgaci's marriages played a critical role in stabilizing his political relationships and with the Eight Banners formed a bridge between personal rulership and creation of the state. In his youth this was only a matter of securing his place in his native locality and his place in his lineage. His first marriage, in 1577, apparently was to Hahana Jacin,[48] daugh-

---

adhered to the traditional practice of monopolizing the manufacture of arrows, which took place in special workshops either at Fe Ala or at the *tokso* under Nurgaci's control. Nurgaci was himself a "lord of arrows" and on the occasion of a battle distributed arrows to his lieutenants, who then acted as "lords of arrows" and distributed them to their followers. *Niru i ejen* continued as the name of company captains through the Qing period. The designation of companies as *niru* in Nurgaci's time was certainly related to the arrow tradition and may have come through domination by the term *niru i ejen*—the *niru* being in both cases that over which the lord has control.

47. *KF* 2 opens with a celebration of the gifting of women to Nurgaci, as evidence of his waxing fame and power.

48. The facts associated with Nurgaci's taking of wives and concubines are difficult to sort out, since Hung Taiji, who first ordered the revisions of Nurgaci's chronicles, insisted that his own mother, Monggo-gege, should be an empress (*gao*

ter of Tabun Bayan of the local Tunggiya lineage.[49] This marriage, which preceded Nurgaci's wars of consolidation, was a normal contract between neighboring lineages. His second marriage was occasioned by exigency: When Nurgaci's older cousin Weijun was killed around 1584, Nurgaci in accord with the marriage practices of the Jurchens took his widow Gundai — daughter of Mangse Dujuhū (that is, *duzhihui,* the Ming rank "commander") of the Fuca lineage at Šaji—as wife.[50] Next was Monggo-gege,[51] daughter of Yangginu of an Ula lineage of Yehe. This marriage, arranged in 1588 in recognition of the fleeting amity between the Yehe and Nurgaci, was his first diplomatic marriage. Still later came a marriage to Abagai,[52] daughter of the late Mantai of the Ula Nara lineage, who was sent by her uncle Bujantai as tribute to Nurgaci in 1601.[53] Nurgaci married or took as

---

huanghou) and all other concubines, various ranks. Zhang Caitian, *Liechao hou qi zhuan gao,* describes four of the women by the Manchu word for wife, *fujin,* and all others as concubines or secondary concubines.

49. That is, the Tunggiya *mukūn* formed in the sixteenth century in Tunggiya, descended from Bahu Teksin (see Chapter 2). Okada, "How Hong Taiji Came to the Throne," 251–52, supposed Hahana Jacin was a Tong of Fushun, which appears an error based on *BMST.* Nurgaci married Hahana Jacin in 1577, when he left his father's house, aged nineteen. The date of Hahana Jacin's death is not known but must have been after 1583 or 1584, when she and her daughter and two sons are mentioned in *Manju i yargiyan kooli.*

50. She was first married to Weijun, a second cousin of Nurgaci (second son of Utai, second son of Soocangga, third elder brother of Giocangga), and had three sons: Alantaiju, Cungšan, and Anggara. Weijun was killed in battle at age twenty-nine, and Gundai married Nurgaci. According to Okada, these circumstances are mentioned only in *Aixin jueluo zongpu.* The date of Weijun's death is not known, but Gundai's remarriage appears to have been in 1585 or 1586, since Alantaiju and Cungšan were born in 1583 and 1584, respectively, and Manggūltai was born in 1587.

51. "Xiaoce." "Monggo-gege" is not a name but an epithet, "Mongol lady" (*gege,* from Chinese *jiejie,* "older sister").

52. "Xiaolie." Zhang Caitian, *Liechao hou qi,* 38, notes that she was installed as *amba fujin* ("empress") after the death of Monggo-gege (see below). Nurgaci, attempting to return to Mukden from a visit to a hot spring in the winter of 1626 to recover from battle wounds, is reported to have fallen mortally ill at Aijibao, about four miles from Mukden. A messenger sent to the city for Abagai, who traveled with two lesser concubines to Nurgaci's side. Nurgaci died and Abagai, then aged thirty-seven, killed herself, as did the two other women who accompanied her. This is the account of Zhang Caitian; according to *ECCP,* 1, Abagai was forced to commit suicide by Hung Taiji, Daišan, and Manggūltai.

53. *MR TM* 10:1:7 notes Mantai's wife (*sargan*) as a mother-in-law (*emhe*) of Nurgaci, among the affiliates whose ranks were clarified in an announcement soon after New Year's, 1625.

concubines women of the Irgen Gioro,[54] Nara of Yehe (one of the daughters of Yangginu, *beile* of the Yehe), Bojirgids (twice),[55] and Nara of Hada (daughter of Wan, khan of the Hada). His lesser concubines included the daughter of Lakda of the Joogiya (mother of Abai), the daughter of Bokdan of the Niohuru (mother of Yanggūdei and Tabai), the daughter of Legun Bayan of the Gioro of Giyamuhu (mother of Babutai, Babugai, and three daughters), and the daughter of Doduri Hasinggū, of a Gioro lineage that would later be distinguished as the "Silin" Gioro (mother of Laimbu). They were part of the process of negotiating with hostile lineages and federations. Nurgaci's marriage to Monggo-gege, for instance, did not actually create much good feeling between Nurgaci and Yehe; when she fell mortally ill in 1603 and asked that her mother be allowed to visit her, the Yehe rulers sent two concubines instead, an act that enraged Nurgaci and in the long run gave him another excuse for stepping up his war against Yehe.[56] These marriages were instruments of diplomacy (as in the case of Monggo-gege) and not mere symbols of accomplished alliances; in fact, the lineages who were closest to Nurgaci, such as the Niohuru or the Gūwalgiya of Suwan, were not well represented among Nurgaci's women. As the women of Nurgaci circled him, representing the pieces of his mosaic of negotiations and alliances, so his children helped cement his growing number of incorporations in their own marriages.[57] Hahana Jacin's daughter Nunje (Gulun) married Hōhōri of Donggo, on Nurgaci's east flank; this helped end generations of enmity with Donggo and brought into Nurgaci's camp one of his ablest commanders. Hahana Jacin's two sons, Cuyen (born in 1580) and Daišan (born in 1583), became second and third in command of the federation in 1611 and 1612. Gundai gave birth to the sons Manggūltai

54. Zhang Caitian, *Liechao hou qi*, 44: "a secondary concubine, daughter of Jacin Bayan." She was the mother of the sons "Huang qi zi" and Abatai, and of the daughters "Huang er nu" and Hoso.

55. Zhang Caitian, *Liechao hou qi*, 45–46, describes the wedding celebrations in 1618: Minggan-monggo ("Thousand Monggols"), *beile* of the Kharachins and father of the bride, came to Nurgaci's compound and gave to his new son-in-law ten camels and a hundred horses and stayed a month. Nurgaci gave to his father-in-law forty households, forty suits of armor, money, and silk, and then rode the ten miles back with Minggan-monggo to the Kharachin camp and stayed overnight before going home. According to Jurchen custom, a son-in-law was obliged to spend the first night after the wedding at the home of his bride's family.

56. Zhang Caitian, *Liechao hou qi*, 29.

57. On the history of women of elite station connected to the Aisin Gioro see Rawski, *The Last Emperors*, 127–59.

(who eventually killed her) and Degelei, and the daughter Monggoci-gege, who married Menggebolo and sealed the incorporation of Hada into Nurgaci's league in 1601.[58] Monggo-gege, in her turn, was the mother of Hung Taiji. Abagai was the mother of Ajige, Dorgon, and Dodo. These four women, in contrast to those many coming afterward, were recognized as "wives" (fujin), which later records would upgrade to "principal wives" (da fujin) and later historians would construe as "empresses." Among Nur-gaci's sons, only those—Cuyen, Daišan, Manggūltai, Hung Taiji, Ajige, Dorgon, Dodo, Degelei—born to these four wives were considered eligible to govern.

One of the Ming charges against Tong Bunian had been that other Fushunese lineages who had joined Nurgaci's command ranks—including but not limited to the families of Tong Yangzhen and Tong Yangxing—had received the rank of efu.[59] This rank primarily indicated membership in the emerging aristocracy under Nurgaci, but its enabling mechanism was ap-parently the establishment of a marriage connection with Nurgaci's lin-eage. It did not entail that Nurgaci himself should marry with a woman of an efu family, but it cannot at this time be shown that he did not include Nikan women in his own collection. Tong Tulai's daughter, who was a wife of and eventually became recognized as the empress of the Shunzhi em-peror Fulin, is the first Nikan woman to be prominent in this respect, but it is reasonable to suppose that she had predecessors who are now difficult to identify. Tong Bunian's Ming prosecutors were well motivated to claim that Fushunese deserters had become proto-aristocrats in Nurgan, but that does not explain why they chose this particular charge, among many that could have been very damaging, to make.[60] The willed political indistinct-ness of Nikans of the Fe Ala and Hetu Ala periods also makes it impossible to assert, as some historians do, that there were no Nikan families repre-sented among the wives of Nurgaci or Hung Taiji.[61] This presumes that

58. Another epithet, from Mongolian monggholcin, the feminine for mongghol.

59. I have used a slight anachronism in order to keep the meaning clear. The Manchu documents of this period use the word fuma, a loan-word from Chinese, for sons-in-law of the khan. Efu was later introduced on the instruction of the court in order to make Manchu more ostensibly native.

60. Liu Lu, "Qingdai huanghou cili yu baqi da xing shi zu," 61, from a separate perspective, makes a similar observation that the chances are overwhelming that Nurgaci's collection of twenty-eight women was far more likely to have included Nikan women than not.

61. If, for instance, the Joogiya lineage were from Joogiya-hoton and were the inspiration for the village's name (rather than the other way round), Lakda of Joogiya, who supplied a daughter to Nurgaci, may have been Nikan.

names are sufficient to identify individuals as Nikan or Jurchen, which is manifestly not so.

For Nurgaci the presence under his figurative roof of representatives of the populations under his control was a natural product of this political exigency. For the Qing sovereigns coming after him, the emperor's collection of women and its obverse, the collection of imperial sons-in-law, became fundamental field for the representation of the imperial constituencies. In one of his retrospective fancies, the Qianlong emperor would later celebrate the *efu* system as akin to the marital alliances (*heqin*) of pre-imperial China.[62] As with all other politically influential aspects of identity, these affiliations were subject to imperial adjustment. Concubines drawn from the bondservant companies (which were overwhelmingly Nikan) whose sons became emperors had their registrations retroactively altered to the Manchu banners. In Nurgaci's time, however, he accepted women from all sources contributing to the stabilization and extension of his rule.[63] Moreover, as Nurgaci's practices reinforced the traditions permitting senior women to participate in political consultation—especially those recognized as wives of the khans (*sargan*, and later *fujin*)—the women themselves became anchors of their sons' status among the eight *beile*. For this reason, senior women or those with the capacity to become senior were frequently the targets of Hung Taiji, who perceived them and their status as obstacles to his personal monopolization of power.[64]

THE COLLEGIAL IMPULSE

Historians of the Qing have studied in detail the two great periods of rapid centralization of rule: the first, under Hung Taiji, from about 1630 to his death in 1643, and the second, under the Yongzheng emperor, from 1725 to about 1730. The trend toward centralization is seen to have peaked in the Qianlong reign. In this view, the nineteenth century is seen as a period of unraveling of centralization, disintegration of imperial political initiative, and general "decline." It is certainly true that there was marked movement toward political centralization in the Hung Taiji emperorship and in the reign periods of Kangxi, Yongzheng, and early Qianlong, and that there

62. For a very short but direct discussion see Liu Guang'an, "A Short Treatise on the Ethnic Legislation of the Qing Dynasty," 98.

63. Liu Lu, "Qingdai huanghou cili," 61.

64. This point is made and elaborated with citations from the imperial genealogical records in Liu Lu, "Qingdai huanghou cili," 63–65.

was graduated decentralization beginning in the later eighteenth century. But it is probably unwise to think of centralization—that is, the movement toward concentration of decisive power in the hands of a single ruler—as the normal, or more vital, motive in Qing political culture. Nurgaci was at best ambivalent about it, warned repeatedly against the centralizing ambitions of Hung Taiji. He attempted to formalize a style that is often called "collegial" or corporate rule that was of long standing in Nurgan, became embedded in Qing court tradition, and continued for some time in the nineteenth century to compensate for real loss of political momentum in the emperorship.[65]

Nurgaci did not inherit rulership among the Jianzhou but succeeded to a leading lineage of sorts, and it appears to have been of a socially conservative type. Möngke Temür had been recognized both by the Ming and by the Yi as leader of Odori, and his authority might have derived from his father's recognition as Odori headman by the failing Yuan empire of the Mongols. Giocangga, Nurgaci's grandfather, claimed to be a fourth-generation descendant of Möngke Temür and to ascend to the headmanship through his father Fuman and grandfather Cungšan (see Chapter 4). Fuman had received the garrison title of *qianshi dudu* from the Ming court; no known document indicates that it passed to Giocangga, but it was used by Nurgaci in the 1590s. Within Nurgan, Giocangga was not without rivals, of whom the best known were Wanggoo and Yangginu. In his own Jianzhou territories, Giocangga shared power with his older brother Soocangga and Soocangga's son, Utai, as well as with his own son, Taksi. When Giocangga and Taksi died in the incident that will be discussed below, Nurgaci—Taksi's oldest son and second child—was nearly twenty-four years old.[66] Next in

---

65. Central and Inner Asian specialists might well ask whether the problem raised in the following passages relates to the dual or bifurcated rulerships well attested in the Turkic empire, in Khwarasmia, and the Khazar khanate, strongly suggested in the history of the Liao empire and its Karakhitai successor in Central Asia, and possibly persisting in a residual form in the Mongol segmented empire. My own position is that the similarity is superficial; as with the name and institution of "khan" itself, Mongolian and Central Asia political practices had at most a very indirect effect on eastern Liaodong in the sixteenth and early seventeenth centuries. More persuasive is the contemporary, proximate evidence for the development of corporate—often dual, but sometimes more complex—leadership of the Jurchen and Hūlun federations, predating but strongly marked in the generations of Giocangga and Taksi.

66. *KF* 2.2a. Taksi's oldest daughter was married to Hurgan (1576–1623), the son of Hūlagū, who had used the Tong surname but resided in the Yargū village; Nurgaci would later take in this nephew as his foster son and give him the Gioro name. Hurgan is the Darhan hiya, "valiant guard," of *MR*.

age was Murgaci (1561–1620), aged twenty at the time of the deaths of Giocangga and Taksi; then a sister who was married to Cinggiha; then Šurgaci (1564–1611), aged eighteen; then another sister married to Puhaha.[67] There were minor children, too, including at least two other sons, Yargaci and the newborn (or unborn) Bayara (1582–1624).[68] Nurgaci joined with Utai and Soocangga in leading the federation, but he quickly propelled himself to the forefront of Jianzhou leadership.

The imperial narrative presents a picture of Nurgaci's leadership of the Jianzhou between the very late 1580s and the early seventeenth century that is in rather bald contrast to that presented by other sources. The Yi court, for instance, knew of two leaders of the Jianzhou Left Garrison, one "Chief Nu" (or Niu) and one "Chief Siu," both of whom sent embassies and missives to the Korean court. When Shin Chung-il was finally on the scene in Fe Ala in 1596 (thirteen years after Nurgaci began the campaigns of unification), he was bemused by the relationship between Nurgaci and Šurgaci. After Shin was at length admitted to the inner sanctum, he found Nurgaci's family, Šurgaci's family, and the leading soldiers of the Jianzhou in residence there. Nurgaci's and Šurgaci's compounds were at the center, Nurgaci's on the north facing south (the superior position), Šurgaci's on the south facing north. They shared a greeting yard and a religious shrine. Shin commented on a striking physical contrast between the brothers. Nurgaci was neither fat nor thin, in physique strong and erect, nose straight but large, face long and rather dark. Šurgaci was heavier than his brother, square-faced and fair, with silver hoops in his ears.[69] At a New Year's banquet Nurgaci wore a hat of sable fur, with ear flaps and a pointed crown, topped by a feather and a small decoration shaped like a man seated on what Shin called a "lotus platform" (*lian tai*); Šurgaci wore a similar hat. Nurgaci had a long sable robe, with silk appliqués in five colors. So did Šurgaci.[70] Whatever prerogative Nurgaci displayed, whether in dress, seating,

67. Puhaha used the Tong surname (see Chapter 1). He was a grandson of (Tong) Qianqiuli, who had been headman of the defunct Wenhuo federation. Remarks by Shin Chung-il suggest that after the Wenhuo were absorbed by Nurgaci they continued to function as a military unit under Puhaha's command, possibly with six divisions that represented the original six communities of the Wenhuo federation; in 1596 their numbers were slightly over a thousand (*KJD*, 25).

68. *KF* recognizes Yargaci instead of Murgaci as one of Nurgaci's full brothers; Murgaci is absent from the description of the family there.

69. *KJD*, 24.

70. An item in the Qing portrait collection of the Arthur M. Sackler museum shows an almost lifesize representation of such a robe; it is identified as a portrait of "Dorgon."

hospitality, ritual centrality, entourage, or verbal grandiloquence, Šurgaci evinced something similar—but ever so slightly less. The relative standing of the two brothers was on some occasions even quantifiable: When Laba of Ula surrendered to the Jianzhou, his tribute included a hundred horses, sixty given to Nurgaci and forty to Šurgaci.[71]

Whether the point represented by the record of Shin's visit lies on the rising or falling slope of Šurgaci's power is a problem in early Qing political history. At the time of the deaths of Giocangga and Taksi, rulership of the federation could not have fallen automatically to any single person, for Soocangga and Utai were older and were experienced at governing. Nurgaci may have been explicitly fulfilling the role of fictive younger brother to Utai's son Weijun when he took in Weijun's widow in 1585 or 1586. It was not merely the case that Nurgaci was not by default the Jianzhou leader. There was active opposition from at least two of the brothers of Giocangga, and only the descendants of Desikū—including his son Wambulu and Nurgaci's trusted companion Anfiyanggū—were early supporters of Nurgaci's leadership.[72] Against these ambiguities, Li Chengliang's acknowledgment of Nurgaci as the representative of the lineage was clearly of distinct value. It is likely that both Murgaci and Šurgaci acted as Nurgaci's lieutenants in the early campaigns, during which Nurgaci established personal control over villages within the Tunggiya region that Soocangga and Utai would otherwise have been entitled to rule jointly with him. What Shin observed of Šurgaci's status in 1596 was evidently the result of Šurgaci's aggrandizement of his own status at the expense of Murgaci. Though the orthodox narrative of Qing origins gives little attention to Šurgaci, his ambitions profoundly shaped the early state—so profoundly that he paid with his life, while Murgaci lived to die a natural (if obscure) death. The Šurgaci problem framed not only the development of Nurgaci's relations with Ula— and thus indirectly with all the Hūlun nations and the Khorchins from whom Nurgaci first derived his status as khan—but also the institutionalization of Nurgaci as khan in 1616.

The problem of Šurgaci and the problem of the Ula federation under Bujantai are related. Despite the official insistence that indignation over abuse of his daughter spurred Nurgaci to finally shatter Bujantai's power in Ula, it seems more likely that Nurgaci was intent upon destroying both Bujan-

71. KJD, 24.
72. ECCP, 13, notes "Janggiya" and "Nimala" as the names of two settlements that attempted to rebel against Nurgaci and were really the settlements of two of Giocangga's brothers.

tai and Šurgaci, because they had formed a covert alliance against him. At the time that Nurgaci released Bujantai to return to Ula in 1596, Šurgaci had supplied Bujantai with two of his daughters as wives, and the two men remained in regular contact. In 1607, as Nurgaci's forces pushed into the north, warfare erupted between Ula and Jianzhou. Bujantai quickly agreed to cease hostilities and this time became a son-in-law of Nurgaci. But Šurgaci remained his protector within the Jianzhou command. After Bujantai's capitulation, Nurgaci proposed to remove the population of the Ula village of Fio-hoton, about twenty miles north of Huncun, to Fe Ala. Šurgaci, disliking to see the resources of his ally diminished, asked to accompany the expedition and did all he could to thwart it. Over his objections Nurgaci's sons Cuyen and Daišan, together with the judge and general [Suwan Gūwalgiya] Fiongdon, went to Fio-hoton and accomplished the objective. The campaign gave Nurgaci his first foothold in the Mt. Changbai region and was the beginning of his complex relationship with the "hunting and fishing" (*butha*) people of the Northeast. The expeditions also marked a sharp rise in the political profiles of the successful commanders and a rapid imperilment of Šurgaci. In 1609 Nurgaci ordered the confiscation of Šurgaci's property, including his people, giving most to Cuyen,[73] which marked him as heir to Šurgaci's position as co-ruler. The next year Šurgaci's eldest son Altungga and third son Jasaktu were found guilty of treason and executed. In 1611 Šurgaci was assassinated; those of his sons whom Nurgaci favored (Amin and Jirgalang) were taken into his own household.

Šurgaci had risen as high as he had not only due to his own energies but also because Nurgaci found it useful to share the responsibilities for command.[74] Upon Šurgaci's demise, Nurgaci turned immediately to a new co-

---

73. *Jiu manzhou dang* (hereafter *JMD*) 1610 (Wanli 38): describes this slightly differently. In the last year of Šurgaci's life, when his household was experiencing many troubles, the banner troops were divided into a major portion shared by Nurgaci and Cuyen and a minor portion shared by Daišan and Šurgaci.

74. I cannot agree with George Kennedy's comment in *ECCP* (694) that Šurgaci's career was "unimportant" since I suspect that it was responsible for shaping much of Nurgaci's political style. It is possible that Kennedy followed the pose of *KF* 1.10.b, which dismisses Šurgaci without naming him: "[The records also say] that Taizu [Nurgaci] and a younger brother were both very valiant and influential. Older and younger brother began their ascendancy by consultation, and thus established their foundation. In the process of establishing their policies, it was not the practice for a single individual to collect information. And never for a single day did they forget the sacrifice of [their grandfather and father]." Exit Šurgaci. This is an interesting treatment because the identity of this mysterious younger brother was well known to all readers of *KF* and some of them may have had some feelings about it: The descendants of Šurgaci were the princes Zheng (later Jian, then

ruler, his son Cuyen, who had been recognized as a *beile* for his war exploits as early as 1598, when he was eighteen years old, and shortly afterward had been granted the honorific *hūng baturu*. At some point he assumed the Mongolian title "prince," *taiji*, and in 1611—that is, on Šurgaci's death— he was also given the title *taise*.[75] Later historiography would construe *taise* as denoting an heir apparent. In fact, it appears to have identified Cuyen as Nurgaci's co-ruler. Cuyen assumed responsibility for running the federation, while Nurgaci, now aged fifty-two, concentrated on the battles that allowed his power and wealth to increase exponentially by the year. An allusion in the old documents indicates that Nurgaci had to overcome some skepticism about Cuyen before giving him these responsibilities.[76] But complaints against Cuyen's governance immediately began reaching Nurgaci. As they would on other occasions, Nurgaci's sons and nephews came to him in a group to indict Cuyen's injustices in the distribution of booty; he was alleged to be slighting Daišan, Manggūltai, Amin, and Hung Taiji, all his primary rivals for power. Nurgaci, in an equally characteristic response, upbraided Cuyen in front of the others, then left him free.[77] But Nurgaci was bitterly disappointed. When he left Hetu Ala to pursue the destruction of Bujantai in 1612, he received reports that in his absence Cuyen had plotted against him and even employed shamans to bewitch the entire family. Nurgaci ordered Cuyen imprisoned under Daišan's authority. In 1615, apparently despairing of Cuyen's return to acceptable behavior, Nurgaci killed him.

The moment of Nurgaci's creation as khan is probably related to the reason he became khan. Evidence suggests that, after monopolizing leadership of the Jianzhou federation, Nurgaci attempted to revert to older practices of collegial rule—perhaps because he wished to lead battles without being encumbered by management of the growing economic, demographic, and

---

changed back to Zheng again, see Chapter 6), inaugurated by Jirgalang, and held during the composition and publication of *KF* by Depei, Citungga, and Jihana, consecutively. Lesser-known descendants of Šurgaci were also well represented in the military and civil ranks.

75. Another example of attempts to enrich the political nomenclature. *Taise* is the Jurchen plural of the loan-word *taiji* and—as in the case of *beile* and *beise*—is used in the singular in order to provide a new and definitive title.

76. *JMD*, 1613.

77. This may not be entirely the way to put it—Fang Chao-ying has suggested that Nurgaci may have assigned Daišan to Hetu Ala when Nurgaci himself was on the battlefield in order that Daišan might keep an eye on Cuyen's conduct (*ECCP*, 212).

political resources under his control. It was after the collapse of the second collegial rulership that Nurgaci announced himself khan in 1616.

The "cardinal *beile*" (*hošoi beile*)[78] were the established princes of Nurgaci's lineage, or, more properly, of Giocangga's; they included not only Nurgaci's sons but also his nephew Amin, who had been taken into Nurgaci's household after the death of his father Šurgaci in 1611. They owned, with consent of the khan, the Eight Banners, which were not only military but also social organizations. In Nurgaci's time the banners were not differentiated, as later they would be, as "Manchu," "Mongol," or "Chinese-martial." They were distinguished only by the lord to whom they belonged and to whom they answered in all matters of battle, preparedness, land rights, animal use, booty distribution, rank, promotion, housing, marriage, and burial. The princes of the banners were also empowered to guide succession to the khanship after Nurgaci's death.

At that time, the ambiguous and rather common rank of *beile* was formally subordinated to the khan, and a declination of ranks below the *beile* promulgated: *beise, amban,* and, for the Nikans particularly, *hafan.* Nurgaci appointed seven of his sons and a nephew as *beile* and granted each a banner—which required splitting each of the existing four banners into two. Nurgaci repeatedly instructed the cardinal princes to rule jointly after his death, consulting on all affairs, and executing all laws as equals. But it is possible—though only revisions of the Hung Taiji era attest to it—that in various ways Nurgaci had suggested his preference for his fourth son, Hung Taiji. The favoritism may have been widely noted and even taken for granted by Hung Taiji himself. An incident preserved in the Manchu annals relates that in 1623 Hung Taiji was, together with Degelei, Jirgalang, and Yoto, found guilty of having accepted bribes from (Nikan) officials. Nurgaci punished Hung Taiji along with the others (by reducing their estates) and scolded him: "You pretend that only you yourself are right and act arrogantly to others. Are you thinking of sitting on the khan's throne over the heads of your elder brothers?"[79]

When Nurgaci brought eastern and central Liaodong under his control in 1621, he wished again for help in managing his territory (which had more than doubled in size) and instituted a revolving co-rulership, which

78. That is, cardinal as in the points of a compass. Later records suggest that there were four *hošoi beile,* as in the points of a Western compass, but there were, as will be discussed below, eight—as in the eight cardinal points of the shamanic compass of the Northeast.
79. Okada, "How Hong Taiji Came to the Throne," 258.

four of his *beile*—Daišan, Manggūltai, Amin, and Hung Taiji—each assumed for one month, in cycles. The early history of this institution is clouded in the record and appears to have been disturbed by constant rivalry among the four *beile*. Indictments and counter-indictments were thick between 1621 and Nurgaci's death in 1626. Daišan, for instance, was severely reprimanded by Nurgaci for nepotism, and Hung Taiji was found guilty of accepting bribes from Nikans hoping to gain privileges for themselves. Nurgaci constantly reminded his sons that collegial rule, if done well, was not only the most practical but the most wise: A collegial government might avoid the excesses that would bring down the divine wrath. "My successor shall not be a strong man, for such a man may, once he is on the throne, be inclined to wield his power in such a way that he offends Heaven." Nurgaci went on to advise that an excessively ambitious khan should be deposed by the *beile*.[80] But on the whole it appears that in these years Hung Taiji—clearly the "strong man" Nurgaci was wary of—gained ground at the expense of his co-rulers. Prior to Nurgaci's death Hung Taiji's closest associates had been his cousin Jirgalang, his younger brother Degelei, and his nephew Yoto (Daišan's son). Yoto's devotion to Hung Taiji may have been partly due to the fact that they shared maternal ancestry; Yoto's mother (Daišan's hated second wife) was the daughter of the Yehe *beile* Bujai, who was a first cousin of Monggo-gege. After Nurgaci's death, it was Daišan—evidently at the urging of Yoto and Sahaliyan—who proposed that the *beile* elect thirty-five-year-old Hung Taiji as khan. He was invested at Mukden on New Year's Day 1627. Historical records compiled in his own time and recounting the period of his father Nurgaci's reign as khan refer to Hung Taiji only as the "Fourth *Beile*" (*duici beile*).[81] The Chinese versions of the same records give him the name Hung Taiji, or Prince Hung, and Korean

---

80. Li Hsüeh-chih, "An Analysis of the Problem in the Selection of an Heir during the Reign of Nurhaci of Emperor Taitzu of the Ch'ing Dynasty," 114, from *Wu huangdi shilu* 1622: March 3.

81. This despite the fact that a Korean visitor in 1619 heard the man referred to as Hung Taiji (see di Cosmo, "Nuove fonti," 147). Because by the late seventeenth century emperors' personal names were considered sacred, they were replaced with titles and epithets in each revision of the documents. The originals, where they survived, evidently contained the names, but they were normally covered with a yellow slip to preserve the sanctity of the name by hiding it from the view of lowly scribes. As surprising as it is to contemplate, it would be possible to lose Hung Taiji's name (if he had any other) by these means, but concealment is also possible: The Fifth Dalai Lama, with whom Hung Taiji began to have some correspondence in the last years of his life, had a concealed name.

records concur.[82] In Chinese it is often written as Huang Taiji, "imperial prince," suggesting that the name indicated the holder's status as heir apparent. This is certainly not what his name meant. An historiographical error in European scholarship has given him the attractive but erroneous name of Abahai.[83] Under the temple name of "Great Spirit, the Culturing Emperor" (*Taizong wen huangdi*), Hung Taiji was the second khan, and first emperor, of the Qing period.

The Nurgaci government had consisted of little besides the Eight Banners and the khanal lineage, and Hung Taiji quickly consolidated his control over a critical portion of the banners as a means of controlling both. For reasons that are not entirely clear, Hung Taiji at the time of his election as khan in 1626 owned two of the eight banners (Bordered Yellow and Plain Yellow). Nurgaci had expressed a wish for his young son Ajige to have a banner, but Hung Taiji instead kept it for himself. He was able to add to the banners under his personal ownership by absorbing the Bordered White at the time of Manggūltai's death in 1633. These three banners, known afterward as the Three Superior Banners (*ilan dergi gūsa, shang san qi*), would remain the patrimony of the direct imperial line. Hung Taiji also dismantled what remained of the oligarchy Nurgaci had attempted to reestablish in his last years. In 1629 he abolished the revolving co-rulership, which just prior to its cancellation had moved alternately between Daišan and Manggūltai. The campaign to deprive the *beile* of their oligarchic functions was accompanied by moves to discredit each of them personally, in this way striking against the traditional authority they might have continued to wield. Amin, who had stood second among the *beile* under Nurgaci and had been indispensable in subjugating Korea for Hung Taiji, was imprisoned in 1630 for relinquishing control of Yongping to the Ming. The circumstances were ambiguous. The charges against Amin included desertion of his post, failure to engage the enemy in battle, suffering unnecessary losses among his

82. This title is of Mongolian inspiration and borrows a word, *hung*, that occurs elsewhere (i.e., *hūng baturu*) and may be related to Mongolian *khung*, which occurs in some titles (for instance, that of the Khalkha prince who became the Fourth Dalai Lama and that of Galdan's father). It may be related to modern Mongolian words associated with bells and the sounds they make, but use of this name/title among near contemporaries of Hung Taiji is probably related to his own use of the name.

83. The mistaken appellation in Erich Hauer's translation of the *Kaiguo fanglue* was noted by Gertraude Roth [Li] in "The Manchu-Chinese Relationship," 7. Giovanni Stary, "The Manchu Emperor 'Abahai,'" notes the introduction of "Abahai" into English-language scholarship in Herbert Giles' *China and the Manchus* (1912).

forces, and allowing his troops to loot the town (a transgression against the appropriative rights of the khan). A commission of *beile* and ambans (perhaps with the covert encouragement of Hung Taiji) sentenced Amin to death, but the khan commuted the sentence to imprisonment—a life sentence, as it happened, since Amin died in captivity in 1640. His Bordered Blue banner was transferred to his younger brother and long-time Hung Taiji supporter, Jirgalang.

Manggūltai, who had also distinguished himself at the battle of Sarhū (in imperial historiography destined to become the special victory of Hung Taiji alone), came next into the disfavor of the khan. Soon after Amin had been destroyed by charges resulting from the battle at Yongping, Hung Taiji's political mouthpieces suggested that Manggūltai was similarly culpable for losses at Dalinghe in 1631. Outraged that the snares that had trapped Amin were now being laid for him, Manggūltai went so far as to draw his sword in Hung Taiji's presence, though he was quickly restrained by his younger brother Degelei. The *beile*, in private session, decided to deprive Manggūltai of his rank of cardinal *beile*, and levied a huge fine against his estate. Daišan, who had been first among the *beile* under the Nurgaci khanate, feared that Hung Taiji's sights would next be trained on him. In his oldest surviving brother Hung Taiji had a rival who had never shown an inclination to risk his personal well-being on political ventures—who had in fact sacrificed his wife (by whom he was previously reported to have been continually bullied) to avoid trouble with his father in 1620. In 1627, faced with Hung Taiji's determination to be khan, Daišan had not only stepped aside but become his younger brother's sponsor for election. Now Daišan, pressured by his energetic son Yoto, made no effort to resist Hung Taiji's aggrandizement and in 1632 proposed that both he and Manggūltai should content themselves to share the ceremonial dais with Hung Taiji by sitting at a removed and physically subordinate position. Manggūltai was killed in battle the next year, and among the original cardinal *beile* only Daišan remained a free and living relic of the days of corporate government under Nurgaci. The personal and subsequently institutional degradation of the cardinal princes was only the superficial expression of a process under Hung Taiji that systematically pared away the cultural, economic, and legal foundations of the Jurchen elite, and of the Nurgaci lineages particularly. Hung Taiji himself had undertaken the very formidable task of centralizing political power in his own hands in opposition to the collegial practices that were traditional to the Northeast, inherent in the institution of the khanship, and explicitly affirmed by Nurgaci on the eve of his death. Centralization of power and professionalization of the bureaucracy went together in this process, for which Hung Taiji's model was the emperorship as it had been developed and refined in China.

Nurgaci's preference probably would have been for some form of oligarchic, consultative government, which had the force of tradition behind it and might have convenienced Nurgaci in many respects. But in practice the two co-rulerships he allowed were unsuccessful, and in each case his kinsman and erstwhile colleague was killed. Nevertheless, Nurgaci is in the early Manchu records credited with lectures to his sons and nephew on the virtues of joint rule, and after the occupation of Shenyang in 1621 he reestablished a sort of co-rulership. Perhaps he feared challenges should a single younger man be identified as a co-ruler or heir apparent. It is equally possible that Nurgaci believed that, if practicable, collegial rule was the best system. In combination with other elements in the narrative, including the polite comments on the collegial role of the otherwise purged Šurgaci, there lingered in Qing political tradition an ulterior impression of Nurgaci as an advocate of collegial government. The persistence of this impression is linked to the survival of collegiality as a Qing political value through the nineteenth century, quickened as it was from time to time by the need for regencies and the enduring interests of the Aisin Gioro lineage as a political class.[84]

THE REINVENTION OF TREASON

Nurgaci was conscious of the ways in which his rule of the region represented a dawning of social order and centralized political authority in the Northeast. But he was no revolutionary. The changes he oversaw had been slow in coming, and all were necessitated by his uncompromising if limited program to preserve and enhance the fortune to which he was heir. To protect his wealth, Nurgaci needed to control those portions of Liaodong encompassing the trade routes and market towns upon which he depended. To control Liaodong, Nurgaci had to quell his Jurchen rivals, increase his influence with the Mongols whom the Ming employed as mercenaries, and convince the Koreans to honor his commercial independence. In the space of forty years Nurgaci had indeed organized the Jurchen world under his rule. But Korea and China remained unconvinced of his intention to dominate the commercial centers necessary for his security. To persuade them he had to declare war, and to justify war he had to make himself the moral

84. See also Rawski, *The Last Emperors*, 9.

equal of the emperor of China. The connection in the "Seven Great Grievances" of the deaths of Giocangga and Taksi with a violation of Jurchen territorial sovereignty was an intimate feature of Nurgaci's nascent political rhetoric and was firmly institutionalized in the documentary processes of the Hung Taiji years. The importance of the construction of borders, both spatial and cultural, is much connected with the appearance in the Qing narrative of the shadowy figure of Nikan Wailan. Some of this was a retroactive association, coming after a series of developments in which Nurgaci did in fact wring informal recognition of his borders from Ming officials. But it was equally a reflection of what in Nurgaci's youth was already a burning topic among Jurchen leaders: protection of Jurchen economic enterprises, fields, and routes of transport from harassment by Ming troops and officials.

Among the Jianzhou, this struggle for territorial definition had begun well before Nurgaci's time. Cungšan, a son of Möngke Temür, had attempted to fight for his independence while he was leader of the Jianzhou federation in 1478. Though his uprising was suppressed, Jurchen leaders petitioned repeatedly for a border monument acknowledging the differentiation of their territory from that of the Ming.[85] Nurgaci pushed the same program vigorously from the time he became one of the leaders of the Jianzhou in 1582. A conference between Koreans and Jianzhou at Mamp'ojin in 1588 had been taken by Nurgaci as a tacit recognition of Jurchen economic sovereignty north of the Yalu. He argued for similar recognition from Ming officials in Liaodong, but was unsuccessful. During his visit in 1596, Shin Chung-il was repeatedly harangued by Nurgaci's surrogates on the necessity that China recognize borders with the Jurchens. He was sent back to Korea with a letter recounting the travails of the Jurchens in maintaining their Ming border (reported there to be about 315 miles [950 *li*] in length). "In future," Nurgaci had advised the Yi court, "when the officials of the Heavenly [i.e., Ming] Court harm us, you will represent us and speak out, you will remonstrate with the officials of the Heavenly Court, and I will appreciate it."[86] The Yi were unmoved by the letter and suspended Jur-

---

85. The uprising was quelled by forces under the command of the eunuchs Huang Shun, Zhao Fu, and Li Bing (d. 1489)(Chenghua 14). Li Bing was a *jinshi* of 1436. See *DMB*, 495. He had been recalled from the Ordos and sent to the Northeast because of being disgraced after criticizing the throne. *KF* complains of this incident (though gives a different date, 1466) but, according to its habit, did not name the Jianzhou commander involved; Cungšan had already been introduced elsewhere as the mythical Emperor Xingzu.

86. *KJD*, 30.

chen trade at Mamp'ojin. For their part, the Ming seemed to grant some recognition to Nurgaci's political dominion in 1608, when they agreed to a Liaodong border treaty that forbade Chinese entry into Nurgan; according to Qing records, the stele commemorating the event and marking the border described the ceremonial sacrifice of a white horse to Heaven and a black ox to Earth and promulgation of a law providing that "Ming people" (*Ming i niyalma*) crossing into Jurchen territories would be killed by Jurchens, and Jurchens crossing into Ming territory would be killed by Ming people.[87] Exclusion of further Chinese settlement outside Liaodong was a condition intended to preserve the Jurchen monopoly on the regional products that commanded a high price in China and Korea and later would be absorbed into Qing policy toward the Northeast.[88] For a short time Nurgaci continued to send envoys to Peking to present tribute and beg titles and trading patents, but he later accused the Ming of failing to observe the border agreement and after 1609 seems to have stopped sending embassies to China altogether. Nurgaci's grievance against the Ming accused the military governor Li Chengliang of trespass in the deaths of Giocangga and Taksi—that is, Nurgaci claimed that the deaths took place on Jianzhou soil, where Li had no right to be. The complaint was one of several in the grievances of 1618 directed against the manipulation of Jurchen internal affairs by Liaodong officials. The second complaint, for instance, was that the Ming had failed to confine themselves to their proper sphere when they had attempted to intervene on behalf of the Yehe Jurchens during Nurgaci's wars of unification. The sixth was that the Ming had persistently slandered Nurgaci to the Yehe to undermine the alliance between the two Jurchen groups. The seventh was that the Ming were now attempting (in the spring of 1618) to undermine the Jurchen alliance by promoting suspicion and hostilities among the various groups, particularly the Hada and Yehe.

In the time of Nurgaci's grandfather Giocangga and father Taksi, who had been part of the oligarchy of the Jianzhou Jurchens, loyalties were personal, negotiable, and intensely small-scale. The notion of being allied exclusively with the Ming empire or with a Jurchen entity was not consonant with the conditions of political life. Giocangga and Taksi had gone so far as to cultivate and then betray Nurgaci's own grandfather, Wanggoo, and

---

87. *MR TC* 1:1:8. The provisions are interesting to compare to the treaty Nurgaci tried unsuccessfully to set up with the Yi in 1596, which provided for the safe return of those crossing the border either way, as well as the return of property (primarily cattle that had wandered over the border). *KJD.*

88. See Robert H. G. Lee, *The Manchurian Frontier in Ch'ing History*, 20–21.

uncle, Atai, in hopes of raising their standing with the nominal Ming commander Li Chengliang. Nurgaci himself was attempting to ingratiate himself with the Ming in 1596, even as he complained so bitterly of his treatment by Ming officials in the Northeast. In 1590 he had in fact won rewards from the Ming court for his nearly unprecedented generosity in returning—instead of killing, enslaving, or holding for ransom—two "Ming people" who had come into his hands during a confrontation between Jurchen groups, and in 1592 he had offered to join the Ming cause in Korea against Hideyoshi. As late as 1608, when he finally won a measure of Ming acknowledgment, Nurgaci was still making embassies to Peking. Any idea that "Jurchens" should unite to keep the powers of Liaodong from interfering in their affairs was some time in the future. Even in the imperial narrative, the earliest reference to Nurgaci's idea that Jurchens represented an integrated society naturally opposed to the Ming is the description of him lecturing Yehe envoys on the importance of Jurchen unity after their attempt to ally with the Ming against him in 1599.[89] But as Nurgaci, a product of the fragmented and opportunistic political culture, announced himself khan and promulgated his "Seven Great Grievances" in 1618, the depiction of Giocangga and Taksi as innocent victims of foreign political machinations remained a problem.

When Nurgaci was still a teenager, Li Chengliang and Wan of the Hada federation cooperated in the domination of Liaodong and the near Nurgan territories. Wan supplied Li useful information and aided in the suppression of ambitious *beile*. Li Chengliang, in return, commended Wan to the Chinese court, accompanied him on embassies to Peking, and generally ensured a flow of rewards to Hada. Between them they kept the peace and enriched themselves. In the collaboration of Li and Wan, the Jianzhou leaders found a tempting opportunity for advancement. One of Li's most pressing problems in the 1570s and 1580s was Wanggoo (d. 1575),[90] *beile* (and *dudu*) of the Jianzhou Right Garrison,[91] and his son Atai, who were harassing Liaodong with frequent incursions of plunder and kidnapping.[92] Giocangga and Taksi tried to exploit the Atai problem to compete in the power game controlled by Li and Wan. Giocangga was one of the hereditary leaders of the Jianzhou federation, but he appears to have been eager

89. *KF* 2.3a.
90. Wang Gao, *ECCP*, 595.
91. Founded by Šigiyanu; see Chapter 1.
92. *KF* 1.10a provides an example of Wanggoo's lawlessness in the murder of Bi Cheng, commander of Ming forces at the Qing River.

to raise his standing not only in relation to other Jurchen leaders but also in relation to an elder brother, Soocangga, superior to him in the Jianzhou command. As a self-elevating measure Giocangga had offered one of his granddaughters as wife to Atai. In return, Wanggoo had given a woman of his lineage to Giocangga's son Taksi, and among the children borne him by her was Nurgaci.[93] Giocangga and Taksi learned that Li and Wan desired to destroy Wanggoo, and they joined in plotting his downfall. In 1574 Wan captured Wanggoo and remanded him to Li, who sent him on to a Peking prison as a bandit; Wanggoo died there the next year. As a consequence of the suppression of Wanggoo, rewards flowed richly to Li and his sons and from them to Wan and Giocangga thereafter; indeed in 1576 Li accompanied Giocangga and Taksi to Peking to allow them to personally partake of the gratitude of the Ming court. But Atai succeeded Wanggoo, and it eventually became necessary to remove him, too. In 1582 Giocangga and Taksi decided to help Li destroy Atai's fortifications at Gure.[94] It was a time when opportunists—which Giocangga and Taksi appeared to be—could be tempted; Wan of Hada had just died, and the Hūlun alliance was in danger of coming apart. They made the fatal error, however, of being present at the attack at Gure. Either Li took advantage of the opportunity to rid himself of Giocangga and Taksi as well as Atai, or the confusion of the melee led to their accidental deaths.[95] Giocangga was burned alive when a building in which he had taken refuge during the fighting was torched, and Taksi was shot in the back during the battle.[96]

It is probable (as *Eminent Chinese of the Ch'ing Period* suggests) that Nurgaci was also present at Atai's fort that day and by luck or by the favor of Li Chengliang escaped the fate of his father and grandfather. Even as a teenager Nurgaci had made himself famous for his energy in the service of Li. Ming informants in Fushun described the youthful Nurgaci as something over six feet tall, extraordinarily intelligent, and the first to fling himself into a fight on behalf of Li Chengliang. In return, he enjoyed Li's

93. Qing genealogical records and *KF* identify the woman's father as Lidan, of the Kitala lineage. There is no mention of Wanggoo. Lidan was presumably a son of Wanggoo, and the lineage was in Qing times publicly acknowledged as the Kitala.

94. Present-day Gulou Production Unit, in northwest Xinbin County, Liaoning (Yan, *Nurhachi zhuan*, 25).

95. *KF* provides a detailed account of the lone Giocangga entering Atai's fort and braving enemy arrows in order to save Atai and his wife (Giocangga's granddaughter) from the henchmen of Li Chengliang; Atai, in the narrative, refuses to flee.

96. Qing records do not detail this incident but only refer to it in the context of the "Seven Great Grievances." This narrative is based on the contemporary account of Ma Wensheng.

"support" (*chi*).[97] After the Gure incident Li Chengliang recognized Nur-gaci as leader of the Giocangga lineage and returned Taksi's body to him. Though Li consistently refused to pay reparations to the family, he never-theless met with Nurgaci at least twice at Fushun to discuss the matter.[98] Contemporary evidence suggests that Nurgaci continued to be aided, politi-cally and materially, by Li Chengliang and his sons (whose own sons would someday be prominent in the Eight Banners and in the conquest of China) after the initiation of the Tunggiya campaigns.

The role of "Nikan Wailan" as betrayer of Giocangga and Taksi (the im-perial narrative describes him pointing out the location of Giocangga and Taksi to Li's troops, an image used in subsequent imperial historical narra-tive as an indicator of the difference between loyalty and treachery, right and wrong, and authentic identities in a world quite as chaotic as the Gure battlefield), and the story of his subsequent demise at the hands of the fu-rious and righteous young Nurgaci, are all that is really known of him.[99] The tradition has developed, both in Chinese and European scholarship, that "Nikan Wailan" was not a name but a title or epithet meaning "Chi-nese official" (or "agent"). Why scholars have taken "Wailan" (a loan into Manchu of the Chinese term *wailang*, a minor official) as a title and not a name is unclear. Chinese and Korean words, including both "Nikan" and "Wailan," certainly did enter Manchu, and many became elements in

97. Yan, *Nurhachi zhuan*, 19. Nurgaci's height is put at eight *chi*, or Chinese feet, which was a variable measurement. In no case, however, could it have exceeded ten inches.

98. *KF* 1.10b states that Nurgaci continued these negotiations with Li Cheng-liang for four years.

99. More can be speculated, particularly on the basis of Nikan Wailan's evoca-tive name. Zheng Tianting argued that Nikan Wailan must have been a slave of Giocangga. Undoubtedly Giocangga had slaves who were Nikans, but no definitive evidence suggests that Nikan Wailan was one of them, or how he might have risen from slavery to be headman of Turun-hoton, which the original Nikan Wailan was reported to be. Wakeman, *The Great Enterprise*, 51, designates Nikan Wailan a "transfrontiersman." It is not at all impossible that Nikan Wailan had ancestors from Liaodong or from China proper; indeed given the social history of the Liaodong/Nurgan interface it would be surprising if among his ancestors there were no Chinese or Koreans at all. But that Nikan Wailan himself was an immi-grant is not suggested by any known evidence apart from his name. *BMST* claimed that Nikan Wailan was a member of the Tunggiya lineage (*juan* 19) but the testi-mony of that collection is suspect. Nikan Wailan is one of the sketchiest characters of the early Qing records and has no identity apart from Nurgaci's hatred of him, and this reinforces my speculation that Nikan Wailan was an archetypical figure, probably based upon the headman of Turun-hoton. *BMST* (1745) 19:1a,18a. For Nikan Wailan's biography see *ECCP*, 591.

names. Wan of Hada's uncle, Wangji Wailan, had it in his name, and it does not appear to have been other than a name. Nevertheless, in Chinese scholarship the idea that "Nikan Wailan" was really a title is so strong that translations from Manchu documents of the period into twentieth-century Chinese write it as *hanren wailang*. But "Nikan Wailan" is more likely to have been a name, and perhaps the name of a real person—as some records suggest that he was the headman of Turun-hoton, a village slightly west of Nurgaci's home at Hūlan Hada that was conquered with some difficulty in 1584.[100] In subsequent years Nurgaci pressed his campaigns northward, always seeking his prey, and bringing more Jurchen settlements under his control. In the meantime he held Turun-hoton as well as Joogiya-hoton ("fortified town of the Zhao family place") and Barda-hoton in his immediate vicinity. By the fall of 1584 he also took Donggo, to his west—the seat of a group of Warkas led by Kecen Bayan, who had vexed Giocangga and his brothers when they lived at Ninggūda. In 1585 Nurgaci captured the Antu region. The elusive "Nikan Wailan" still kept ahead of him, and tried to flee to Fushun in 1586. The Fushunese refused him, and he ran to the Jurchen settlement of Elehūn. Soon Nikan Wailan was apprehended there by Liaodong authorities, who, in accord with Nurgaci's wishes, executed the captured fugitive in 1587. This is the year the imperial narrative (*Kaiguo fanglue*) celebrates—the same year that the first wooden fortifications went up at Nurgaci's capital at Hūlan Hada—as the initiation of Nurgaci's status as a recognized magnate and law-giver. Delineation of larger-scale lines of affiliation became Nurgaci's goal in the 1580s. First icon of these divisions was Nikan Wailan, on whom centers the opening chapter of the imperial narrative. In the subsequent Qing interpretation of the incident at Gure, Giocangga and Taksi had gone to Atai's fort to help their kinsman repel an invasion by Li Chengliang. There, somebody called Nikan Wailan betrayed them into the hands of Li's troops. This fabrication was imposed not only to extol Giocangga and Taksi but also to introduce ideas of native and foreign, of loyalty and betrayal, that had little actual meaning at the time of the Gure incident. But Nikan Wailan, the "Chinese agent," is the figure onto whom the complexities of Northeast politics are projected; Giocangga and Taksi become pure to the same degree that Nikan

---

100. The suggestion that Nikan Wailan was really a title (that should be translated as *hanren wailang*) may originally have been made by Meng Sen (*Ming Qing shilun zhijikan*, 185); it was evidently Meng's hypothesis that was alluded to in George Kennedy's entry on Nikan Wailan in *ECCP* (591). Meng's suggestion was long ago disproved by subsequent research (see Ch'en Chieh-Hsien, "The Value of *The Early Manchu Archives*," 75, 77).

Wailan is stained by duplicitous associations with Li Chengliang. Nikan Wailan is the necessary ingredient in the definition of a Jurchen political identity, since he is the essence of Jurchen treason: a native who betrayed the regional interests by betraying its leaders, then fled to his false masters for safety, only to be destroyed by the widening reach of Nurgaci's political authority (which in this instance is depicted as penetrating Liaodong to define Nikan Wailan as a Jurchen under Nurgaci's authority, and subject to his sentence).

With Nurgaci's death the political primordium of the new state had come to an end. In the cooling process under his successors would emerge the asymmetries and solidities that would shape him as a historical presence. Yet certain political features that appear consistent with contemporary information on Nurgaci would become permanently, if troublesomely, embedded in the Qing historical consciousness. Nurgaci persisted, in Qing imperial ideology, as the first of many political persons who would ultimately inhabit the emperorship. Some legendary attachments to Nurgaci's history are factually moot.[101] The orthodox Qing narrative states that he was the product of a thirteen-month pregnancy (one of the universal attributes of prodigies who emerge from the womb curiously advanced in ability), insists that he was not only literate but loved to read[102] and at the age of sixteen had already begun to pursue his ambitions. With the declaration of the "revival" of the Jin empire and the initiation of the war in Liaodong, Nurgaci was depicted in the records as a man of acute historical sensibility—a characterization that coincides with his remarkably transformed attitudes toward literate Nikan, as depicted in the invented encounter with Fan Wencheng. The sudden historical erudition on the Liao, Jin, and Yuan empires, the lightning-like grasp of the work and descendants of Fan Zhongyan, the seizure of somber respect for the literati, and the turning of Nurgaci's putative gaze toward Shenyang—beyond which lay Peking—were all integral to the Hung Taiji construction of the "first" Qing ruler.

Nurgaci is depicted as hot-tempered and quick to shout down underlings who were slow to agree with him or do his bidding. These are not only the valued traits of the warrior, they were, like his debut passions, corollaries

---

101. The legends of Nurgaci, not treated here, are discussed in Rawski, *The Last Emperors*, 243; and Crossley, *The Manchus*, 47–74.

102. *KF.* Literacy is a very elastic concept, and it must be true that Nurgaci was able to verify the contents of oaths he burnt to Heaven. Nevertheless, the idea that he spent a lot of time reading books (in Mongolian, presumably) strains credulity.

of his legitimacy. His righteous vengeance propelled him to leadership of the Jianzhou; his outrage against the treatment of his daughter led to the destruction of Ula under Bujantai; and his great love for Monggo-gege justified accession of her son, Hung Taiji, to the khanship. The resonance of these images for the political ideologies of the Northeast was strong. The usual phrase for explaining the victory of one contestant or another in a war was that "Heaven agreed [*urušefi*] with him," meaning that the struggle itself was prerequisite to attaining Heaven's favor, and that only in the fury of a conflict could Heaven's will be discerned.[103] More important, the medium of relations between master and slave was love: protective, beneficent love from the master downward; total, unquestioning, obedient love from the slave upward. To the end of the Qing empire, the Manchu political vocabulary would be based upon an affective rhetoric that contrasted vividly to the ethical vocabulary of Chinese political expression. Finally, Nurgaci's apotheosis as a war god, which would become important in later relations with Mongolia and Tibet, was at least partly derived from his characterization as a valiant firebrand (consonant with the literary persona of his spiritual twin in the war god cult, Guan Di).

The imperial account aside, other sources more clearly depict the conquest of Liaodong not as the achievement of a youthful and visionary regime but as the final act in the career of a shrewd, willful, but determinedly local strongman. When Nurgaci gained strategic control of Liaodong in 1621 he was sixty-three years old. He demonstrated a preference for simplicity in administration, of the sort that arose from relative decentralization of command and strong reliance on his sons, nephews, and companions who had joined his campaigns. He was content for civil responsibilities to rest primarily with his heirs, who would receive not only his power but his fortune and who would, in his view, be best motivated to husband both. As he extracted the khanate from local examples, so he extracted from the same source some simple codes of affiliation. He denounced the corruption of Ming officials in the Liaodong; he fulminated against the destruction of crops in the Jianzhou territories (or what he claimed as Jianzhou land), disruption of commerce, and sabotage of the roadways. Since affinity for his cause could not be ascertained on the basis of any individual's genealogy, it was sealed by the process of incorporation into the banners. This incorporation was, in both institutional and symbolic terms, nothing other than induction into slavery.

103. *MR Taizu* I:300.

Liaodong, however, would force changes in all that. In Liaodong, Nikans were the majority, not the minority. The population of Liaodong could not be carried entirely away to the Nurgan territories. In Liaodong were men who demanded a different price for capitulation. Nurgaci knew that slaves had been shaking down their masters for as long as people had lived in the Northeast, but he resisted. His contempt for literate Nikans of Liaodong—whom he regarded as treacherous, greedy, ungrateful, and cowardly—never died. If anything it intensified as the Jin conquerors came to identify the *shengyuan,* or licentiates, of Liaodong as their most implacable enemies. But in the end Nurgaci had to compromise his policies, if not his opinions. Under the weight of armed resistance, terrorism, sabotage, opportunism, and the sheer numbers of the Liaodong population, Nurgaci was forced to allow his state to invent statuses it had never recognized before, to create bodies of government it had never tolerated before, and to project a monarchical image that was at the far end of the spectrum from the militarized private commercial monopoly that Nurgaci had worked nearly his entire life to build and protect.

4   Empire and Identity

As Hung Taiji worked systematically to attenuate inherited obstacles to the concentration of power in his own hands, he had also to create the ability for his state to sponsor a history of such a style of rule, to make that history point to him and to use that historical anointing to extend his power of enunciation in as many directions as his conquest ultimately extended. The written Manchu language changed. The first lexicons standardizing the language for formal instruction were drafted, and the nomenclature of the state was revised. Some of the changes appear prosaic on the surface, no more than the substitution of invented "native" words for familiar loan-words from Chinese: imperial sons-in-law became *efu* instead of *fuma;* the *Monggo yamun* (Imperial Colonial Office) became *Tulergi golo i jurgan* (Department of Border Provinces). The ranks of the Eight Banners, mostly identified by obvious loan-words from Chinese, were commanded to be altered to ostensibly native words.[1] Other changes were more ideologically potent, as in the case of eradicating the title "khan" (*han*) where it referred to Nurgaci in the annals collated under Hung Taiji, and replacing it with "emperor" (*hūwangdi*).[2] The latter example suggests how inadequate the words "substitution" or "translation" are in describing the massive lexical shift of the period between 1626 and 1636. Yet the idea of transformation

[marginal annotations: "Language changes", "Khan to emp"]

---

1. Though this was the stated intention of the edicts (mostly from the fourth and fifth lunar months of Tiancong 8 [1634]), it was a bit hopeless. The rank of *zongbingguan,* for instance, was changed to *amba janggin.* Though possibly an old word among the Jurchens (it appears in "Tale of the Nisan Shamaness," for instance), *janggin* was originally Chinese—from *jiangjun,* "general."

2. See *Manju i yargian kooli,* Number One Archives, Beijing (1639 edition), p. 5, introduction of *enduriningge hūwangdi* to displace *enduringge han* used in earlier lines.

falls short, too, when it comes to matters of identity under the new khanship and the emperorship that followed. Jurchens, for instance, were not
transformed or translated into Manchus, nor were Nikans into Chinese,
nor were Hūluns into Mongols. New categories of identity were literally
invented, in some cases attached to putative precursors to lend them authority, in all cases attached to living individuals at the discretion of the
emperorship.

SUBJUGATION AND EQUALITY

In the last year of his life, Nurgaci oversaw a New Year's ceremony that followed the order established in the previous few years. It was a public performance of the ranking of individuals and, as a new phenomenon, of groups
within his increasingly elaborate khanate. All prostrated themselves before
Nurgaci, who alone was acknowledged as ruler. He proceeded to his most
ancient role as provider for his dependents, usually distributing silver, pelts,
or silk. Individuals came forward in the order now stipulated by written
regulation and reflected in the New Year's reports of the Manchu annals:
first, the khan's wives (*han i fujisa*), then the "various" *beise* of the Eight
Banners (*jakūn gūsai geren beise*), then the wives (*fujisa*) of these *beise*,
then the *beise* of the "Mongols" (*monggo i beise*, that is, Mongol nobles
not in the Eight Banners), then their wives (*fujisa*), then the Nikan officials
(*nikan hafasa*), then the wives of the officials (*hafasai sargata*). The court
ceremony was followed by games on the ice, and as games often do, they
reflected more archaic values than those represented in the newly contrived
court protocols: Men and women, of all ranks and categories, scrambled in
individual races and team competitions for additional prizes. Over the
course of a New Year's Day, then, one saw both the past and the future of
regional stratification pass before one's eyes.[3]

In the early ideological grammar of Nurgaci's khanate, the object of the
khan's supporting, nourishing, and cherishing (*ujimbi*) was the "diverse

---

3. See, for instance, *MR TM* 10:1:2. I think the differential use here of *fujin*
(for the wives of the khan and the princes) and *sargan* (for the wives of the Nikan
officials) is related to the fact that the Mongol and Banner women presented in the
ceremony were the spouses of noblemen, while the Nikan "wives" were married
to men without hereditary rank. Among the crystallizing aristocracy, both *fujin*
(as principal wives—"princesses," "empresses," and so on) and *sargan* (for more
humble women—"concubines") were identified in the Manchu genealogies and
regulations.

peoples" (*geren gurun*).[4] As suggested in Chapter 2, the original object of
the khan's political affections was probably the Nikans of Tunggiya, whose
"cherished soldiers" appear as part of his military force at an early date. In
the years just preceding the creation of the khanate, the "various peoples"
grew to include the Khorchins and Kharachins, the former Hūlun alliance,
and the various Mongolian speakers of Nurgan. But the appeal of "cherishing the various peoples" was its futurity, its infinite expandability. In
Nurgaci's time the intentioned objects of the phrase certainly included inhabitants of northern Korea, the unacculturated peoples to Nurgaci's northeast and east, the Tibetan *lama* who were introduced to his court by the
Khorchins, and the inhabitants of Liaodong. The construct served later
Qing emperors in good stead as they directed their rhetoric, and then their
armies, toward farther Mongolia and Central Asia.

Though the historian hardly expects to see equality in the livelihood
and treatment of Nikans in Nurgan before 1618, the evidence that Nurgaci
seriously attempted to make immigrants—whether they had willingly
come or been coerced in some manner—level with natives is striking. Shin
Chung-il remarked that it was sternly enforced in Nurgaci's regime that
there should be no sartorial distinctions between natives and incomers. The
Nikans of Liaodong were required to show their submission to Nurgaci by
having their heads shaven in the Jurchen style, adopting Jurchen dress, and
performing the curtsy, all of which were extensions of Nurgaci's insistence—perhaps based upon the example of Wan and others—that invidious distinctions among the khan's population should be avoided. This became known to the Liaodongese as a Jurchen law in 1618, at the time of Li
Yongfang's surrender. After the conquests of Liaodong and of China the
conquered were treated as immigrants had formerly been, resulting in the
imposition of the queue upon the general Chinese population.[5] The ostensible egalitarianism of Nurgaci's social code was also a strong political advantage in his competition against Ming authorities for the loyalty, or at
least the neutrality, of the Liaodong population. It was designed both to win
the affection of those who were not rich and also to undermine the power
of native elites—as similar rhetoric in Nurgan had enlarged the khan's
power at the expense of the older social and economic powers of the Jurchen world. "Instead of letting the rich accumulate their grain and letting

4. *Abka geren gurun be ujikine seme sindaha genggiyan han*, "the Heaven-
designated enlightened khan who cherishes the various nations" (*MR TM*:1:1:1).

5. Deng, *Nurhachi ping zhuan*, 10–12, provides citations from *Guanghai jun,
Shen guan lu*, and the *shilu* of the Qing.

it rot away, or letting them pile up the goods for no use, one should nourish the begging poor."[6] By 1619 the invasion of Liaodong was in full gear and treatment of the Liaodongese had become a political matter. Nurgaci desired to attract Nikans with promises of equal or favored treatment, even going so far as to demand in some instances that "the houses, stores and grain of the Jurchens will be given to the immigrated Nikans."[7]

All Nikans were entitled equally to enjoy the beneficence of the khan ("Whether they are newly surrendered or have been with us a long time, all will be befriended, and graciously nourished"[8]), and they were not to be subjected to legal restrictions or punishments that did not apply also to the Jurchens; "Manchus and Han are level and of one body (yiti)."[9] But strategically important Nikans were treated in a manner suitable to their function in the developing relationship between the monarchy and the traditional, regional elite: They were granted estates composed of the forcefully extracted wealth of the Jurchen nobles.[10] The latter development, which became more strongly apparent in the Hung Taiji period, is a reminder of the role played by Nikans, of the extension of their political role in the early state, and of their ultimate definition as a distinct population in the centralization of power—minimally under Nurgaci, and very intensely under Hung Taiji. The incorporation of some Nikan lineages into the new aristocracy was an instrument for the redistribution of lands, people, and goods from natives to newcomers, and subsequent diminution of the wealth—that is, the power to gift—of the older lineages. At the same time, Nikans in general contributed to the ability of the khanship to create new capacities for documentation and control of matters that had previously been discretionary to the lineages, the more powerful lineages having previously the greatest discretion and losing the most to the new rulership. Finally, the ability to attach identities to individuals and to encase those identities in formalized codes of obligation and privilege cannot be demonstrated to have been limited to any identity group at any time: As it proceeded among the Nikans, so it proceeded apace among the Jurchens, Hūluns, and other inchoate constituencies of the rulership.

6. Translated in Roth [Li], "The Manchu-Chinese Relationship," 9, from *MR* 2:579.

7. Zhu Chengru, "Qing ru guan qian," 76, from *MR Taizu juan* 47.

8. Zhu Chengru, "Qing ru guan qian," 78, from *Donghua lu, Tiancong* 10.

9. Zhu Chengru, "Qing ru guan qian," from *MR Taizong shilu juan* 41.

10. This general interpretation of the Hung Taiji policies was sketched by Liu Chia-chü, who also provided many citations of instances of forced transfers of wealth. See "The Creation of the Chinese Banners," 64–65.

Nevertheless, Liaodong was achieved by military conquest, and the early practices of conquest did not differ fundamentally from the techniques used against the Jurchens, the Hūluns, and the Khorchins during decades of war. Captured populations, at Fushun in 1618 as at Fio-hoton in 1609, were removed to the Jurchen heartland. There they were divided up and distributed to the *beile*. In this regard it must not be forgotten that the superficial paternalism and affection of Nurgaci's rhetoric—and to a certain extent his social code—was merely an aspect of a rather ruthless approach to the acquisition and control of people. His demands upon the Fushun population he acquired in 1618 were not in essence less stern than had been his earlier demands upon Jurchen villages in the 1580s and 1590s. Having chosen surrender over defeat in war, the new acquisitions were to be parsed among Nurgaci's followers and territories as he, in consultation with his councilors, dictated. They were required to remember that they were his property and additionally that they had no property rights of their own apart from what was given them by him. This legal principle was inviolable by any follower, no matter how high-ranking. But for a large proportion of Nurgaci's subjects, slavery was not merely a political construct or a principle for adjudication. Many lived as permanently indentured at hard and filthy labor, and in the Nurgaci and Hung Taiji regimes commoners were treated as servile whether they were Jurchen or Nikan. One of the stranger demonstrations of this occurred when Hung Taiji wished to ban the smoking of tobacco. He learned in 1634 that his strictures were not being followed and furiously called together the *beile* to demand to know why smoking was continuing. The *beile* pointed out that they alone had not been forbidden to smoke, and this was possibly leading the commoners into error. To this the khan replied that the *beile* were responsible for preventing commoners from smoking (there seemed to be no question of his attempting to impose an interdiction on the *beile*). When Sahaliyan, Hung Taiji's cousin, commented that the commoners might be discontented by this treatment, the khan turned in astonishment at such a sentiment, and shouted, "Am I taking away their food?" As the khan, he was obliged to feed his slaves if they pleased him, but no more; they certainly could not smoke.[11]

As the conquests moved westward, a majority of the illiterate Nikans fell into the servile categories. Following the conquest of Shenyang and the domination of central Liaodong, Nurgaci's familialism became literal. Because it was no longer possible to transport conquered populations to the

11. *MR TC* 8:12:22.

Jurchen territories, a method had to be devised, for the first time, of controlling them in their own places. Households became (as they had become in the construction of Jurchen political order in Nurgan) the fundamental units of the Liaodong conquest regime: By Nurgaci's decree, Jurchens and Nikans were to occupy the same (formerly Nikan) households. They were to work the fields together, maintain the house together, and report to the state together. The proximate inspiration for the policy is obvious enough: to provide quick housing for Jurchen occupiers.[12] Indeed some Manchu records present the policy as being of local, Chinese inspiration. The original plan of Nurgaci was to move Chinese from their homes on the western and southern fronts and to concentrate them in the cities of central and eastern Liaodong (a continuation of the old Nurgan practice of removing populations from enemy domains). In 1621, in response to Chinese requests that they be permitted to stay in their homes and take in the Jurchens as housemates, the policy of cohabitation was initiated.

As a by-product, a potentially profound policing system was also introduced. Members of a household were enjoined to report calumnies against the occupation state, plans to aid in the resistance, or intentions to escape. Seditious speech was required to be reported to the khan's inspectors, for the specific reason that further capitulation of the Liaodong cities could be endangered if harsh opinions of the invaders were circulated. At the same time, Nurgaci personally instructed his high officials and judges never to show prejudice against the Liaodong Nikans, never to allow them to be abused by banner soldiers, never to separate their families. Jurchen abuses of the cohabitation policy were frequently reported. Like pillage, extortion and theft were viewed both as violations of the khan's sole right to distribute property and as subversions of the khan's wish to facilitate the Liaodong conquest by treating capitulating Nikans well. Nikans also were reported to be abusing the cohabitation policies—usually by taking advantage of their closeness to the Jurchens to murder them, primarily with poison. Paranoia spread among the Jurchens, who soon came to feel that eating and drinking could kill them, and there were no measures to make them absolutely secure. The cohabitation policy finally ended after it was blamed for a series of violent episodes among the Nikans in 1623.[13] In the aftermath, the state had not only to provide for separate housing and maintenance of the Jurchens but also for the clear legal distinctions between Nikans

12. Zhu Chengru, "Qing ru guan qian," 76, from *MR Taizu juan* 47.
13. The best treatment of this episode is Roth [Li], "The Manchu-Chinese Relationship."

and Jurchens. Nikan military leaders continued to surrender to Nurgaci, to the end of his life, and all were created Chinese-martial by the state, awarded significant lots of people, livestock, and land, and in many cases ennobled. Nikan civil officials, however, continued in the functions that they had fulfilled for at least forty years in Nurgan before the conquest of Liaodong: as servants of the khan and the *beile*, as scribes, as advisors, and as intermediaries with the Chinese and Koreans. The difference was that, in Liaodong, the overwhelming portion of functional Nikans in fact understood themselves to be ancestral Chinese, to have grown up in Ming territory, and to be not only subordinate to, but immutably distinct from, their military overlords.

This was reflected in political rhetoric of the Hung Taiji era on the question of the solicitation of Nikan submission to the conquest state in Liaodong and magnanimity of the state in providing the Nikans livelihood and protection. The elevation of the Nikan classes was strongly connected to refinement of monarchical power. Following the conquest of Liaodong, all Nikan capitulators were put under the khan's personal jurisdiction. "Those civilians [*minren*] who surrender are my people,"[14] Hung Taiji declared in straightforward khanal fashion in 1631. Any action, whether deliberate or not, by the *beile* to impede the surrender of Nikans or harm them as they arrived was to be swiftly punished, and new laws to that effect were generated. "From today those who are coming to surrender, if the *beile* know of it and kill them, they will be fined ten households. If the *beile* do not know of it and the commoners riotously murder them, they [the commoners] will suffer death, and their wives and children will be enslaved."[15]

Manchu annals hint at the khanal posture obscured behind these policies so gentle and alluring to educated Nikan men. On the eve of his elevation to the khanship, Hung Taiji's remarks on the Nikans showed him to have an opinion on the Nikan political personality similar to his father's. "The Nikan officials [*nikan ambasa*] among our people, and the common Nikans [*irgen nikasa*], have always been self-seeking and apt to flee. Even today there are traitors who come and go, or live among us [expecting to do that someday]."[16] This was the period in which Fan Wencheng[17] became prominent in the khanate, and it was this era that the narration of his story in later Qing annals attempted to revise. The period of stern rhetoric to-

14. Zhu Chengru, "Qing ru guan qian," 78, from *Qing Taizong shilu juan* 5.
15. Zhu Chengru, "Qing ru guan qian," from *Qing Taizong shilu juan* 4.
16. *Qing Taizong shilu*, 1.
17. See Chapter 2.

ward the Nikans of Liaodong was, moreover, coterminous with huge people-taking raids inside the Great Wall, which brought to Liaodong, and frequently to the ranks of slaves in the khanate, a population that in the records cannot always be clearly distinguished from livestock. The first of these, in 1629, Hung Taiji headed himself. In 1636 his younger half-brothers Dolo and Ajige raided points around Peking and netted a reported 180,000 "head," of which an unknown quantity were people and the rest animals. In 1638 the imperial half-brother Dorgon and nephew Yoto entered the Great Wall at Tanzi Range and Qingshan Pass, followed the Grand Canal south of Mt. Taixing, and invaded Shandong as far as Jinan. In a six-month campaign, they collected 462,000 head of people and animals. In 1642 Hung Taiji's younger half-brothers Dolo and Abatai (1589–1646) led an expedition through the Great Wall as far as the Jizhou environs, and then turned to invade Shandong again. In eight months the Qing forces collected 370,000 "head." In ten years, five campaigns, it appears that Hung Taiji collected over a million "head."[18] A much later imperial source estimated that the human population of Liaodong was increased by 50,000 or 60,000 by this method alone in the years between 1629 and 1641, which suggests that prior to the conquest perhaps a hundred thousand people from inside the Great Wall were driven, along with livestock, to Liaodong. Younger men, who were probably the vast majority, were enrolled in the banners, most likely as bondservants in the imperial companies. The old, whom we may assume were a very small minority, were made dependents of the khan.[19]

Nikans were afforded increased legal protection in the civil sphere by the creation of new laws protecting them from claims by Jurchen nobles upon their services or their property. In essence the new system was one of segregation and has often been portrayed as an attempt by the state to improve the lot of Nikans, contributing to the political appeal of the khanate in Liaodong and in northern China. The rhetorical value of the new legal system may, indeed, have been great, but of more significance in the long term was the newly created state power to identify individuals as "Nikan" or "Jurchen" and to assign them residences, livelihoods, and legal protections based on those state-assigned identities. This was the civil corollary to the incorporation of the Nikan military units, long represented under their black banners in the Nurgaci period, as the "Chinese-martial" banners, full units of the Eight Banners, in 1642. It was accompanied by more

18. Zhu Chengru, "Qing ru guan qian," 78–79.
19. Zhu Chengru, "Qing ru guan qian," 78, cites *Donghua lu.*

state activity on the construction and confirmation (much of it through newly composed genealogies) of the new "Chinese-martial" identity.

GENERATING IMPERIAL AUTHORITY

The legal distinction between Nikans and Jurchens was slow in coming and was originally made, as discussed, along lines of culture and function. Evidence remains to be explored that those who in life functioned as Nikan could be retrospectively—and again for fairly transparent reasons—historicized as Manchu. The story of Erdeni[20] is significant in this regard. As recounted in the Manchu annals, his case captures the dynamic interactions among state-building, institutional function, and identity in this early period. Though Erdeni is best remembered as one of the putative inventors of *ē ɹ ūnī* Jurchen / Manchu script, he was also one of the most prominent figures in the Nurgaci state. He was a judge, a diplomat, a military commander, and a strategist who made substantial contributions to the early conquest of Liaodong. His epithet, *baksi*,[21] was the special title given to literate men. Like those of many leaders of the Nurgaci period, Erdeni's origins are difficult to characterize. He had a Mongol name and certainly could write Mongolian; he may have been a native of a Mongolian-speaking region. But the early Manchu records suggest that he was also expert in Chinese, and that in his contemporary frame he functioned as a Nikan.

The imperial narrative asserts that in 1599 Nurgaci commanded Erdeni and Gagai[22] to adapt the Mongolian script for the writing of Jurchen.[23] A new script was commanded, explained the khan, because the Chinese and

---

20. *ECCP,* 223–24; *Qingshi gao* (hereafter *QSG*) 234.

21. From what in modern Chinese is *boshi*. It was transmitted to the Jurchens through Mongolian *baghši*, which like the Jurchen word meant not an erudite (the Chinese meaning) but a literate. See also Mair, "Perso-Turkic Bakshi."

22. Gagai was a military man as well as a civil functionary. In 1596 he was one of the leaders—with Cuyen, Bayara, and Fiongdon—against the Warkas of Anculakū (*KF* 2.7a).

23. The script of the Jin period Jurchens, which had been adapted from Kitan script, continued in use among the Haixi (predecessors of the Hūluns) until the sixteenth century but at a relatively early date was lost by the Jianzhou and their neighbors, who when necessary wrote in Mongolian. Its last implementation in Nurgan may have been at the Yongning temple in Nurgan, where the Ming caused Buddhist prayers to be inscribed in Chinese, Mongolian, and Jurchen at the beginning of the fourteenth century. Xu Zhongshu, "Mingchu Jianzhou nuzhen," 164; Serruys, *Sino-Jürched Relations,* 37, and "Remains of Mongol Customs in China during the Early Ming," 141; Yan, *Nurhachi zhuan,* 134; Crossley, "Structure and Symbol," 51–54.

the Mongols were able—unlike the Jurchens—to write their own languages in their own way; the Jurchens must have the same ability.[24] It is probably not coincidental that in these same months Nurgaci gained hopes of winning his war against the Yehe. He lectured Yehe emissaries that they should acknowledge Jurchen unity and come under his aegis, and he hoped to conclude a written agreement with them—all the better if it could be in a Jurchen script.[25] Gagai died in 1599, and if he was really involved in the enterprise it must have happened that early. But there are no extant Jurchen documents in the Mongolian-derived script from this period, and evidence suggests a slow adaptation of the Jurchen syllabary or massive destruction of the documents of this period. For a considerable time communications between Yi and the Jurchens were handled just as they had been before; Mongolian remained the *lingua franca*.[26] The new device was unvocalized and confused many readers who could not easily associate the written word with the spoken, because of the impracticability of using Mongolian vowel harmony in deciphering Jurchen words. Hung Taiji's decision after 1626 to make written Jurchen a pillar of governance required that he be an energetic sponsor of literature in the language. In order to accomplish this he had to commission improvements in the orthographic system that had been developed under his father's rule. Not until 1632 did Dagai, with license of Hung Taiji, begin to invent a means of vocalizing the script by the addition of circles and dots, which was thereafter called the "circled and dotted script" (*tongki fuka i hergen*).[27] This allowed the state, for the first time, to represent the actual sounds and mechanisms of the language that would soon come to be known as "Manchu."

In early spring of 1623 a member of a banner company under Erdeni's command went to Nurgaci's grandson Hooge[28] and reported that two other

[handwritten margin note: 1632 / Dagai devises script]

---

24. *MR TC* 1:3

25. The only source for the event is *KF*, which is based upon a variety of sources, some written and some clearly oral.

26. Koreans retained materials and a curriculum for instruction in Jurchen as part of their court bureaucracy, long after Jurchen communications had been overshadowed by a revival of communications in Mongolian. See also Hiu, *Die Manschu-Sprachkunde in Korea*, 14–17, and Song Ki-Joong, "The Study of Foreign Languages in the Yi Dynasty (1392–1910)," *Bulletin of the Korean Research Center: Journal of the Social Sciences and Humanities* 54 (1981): 1–45.

27. The inspiration for this innovation may well have come from the *han'gul* script of Korea. This has been hypothesized by J. R. P. King and others. See King, "The Korean Elements in the Manchu Script Reform of 1632."

28. Hooge was the first son of Hung Taiji and in 1623 could not have been more than fourteen years old.

members of the company were planning to desert. The family of Erdeni undertook a search for the men. In the meantime "Nikan officials" (*nikan hafasa*), as Erdeni's representatives, streamed toward Nurgaci's palace to offer meat, grains, silk, and cotton as evidence of Erdeni's shame over the event. In view of the severity of Erdeni's offense, the goods of the Nikan officials were deemed inadequate, and more reparations were demanded.[29] Moreover, the Nikan officers of Erdeni's company were to be sacked and the company given to Nurgaci's kinsman Munggatu. The punishment imposed upon Erdeni, as was customary, was a fine on his goods. In Erdeni's case compliance with the demand to surrender his property could probably have saved him, but in a moment of confusion he supposed his wealth was his own: He attempted to preserve his gold and pearls by concealing them at a relative's house. The ruse was discovered, and Erdeni and his wife were arrested and executed. Nurgaci did not consider the loss of one of his accomplished literate officials as intolerable; only the wish of his officials to shirk responsibility for the actions of their underlings and to surreptitiously control their own wealth were intolerable to him.[30] A colleague of Erdeni, Dagai, was also judged guilty of neglecting to control the actions of the Nikans and had his nose and ears mutilated with an arrow.[31] The passage insists upon Erdeni's and Dagai's intimate connection with the Nikan officials: The Nikans worked under them and represented them to the khan. After Erdeni's execution his companies were transferred to an imperial kinsman; the Nikan officers who had worked for Erdeni were replaced by Jurchen-speakers.

These are vivid examples of the congruence of function and identity in the early state. Erdeni and Dagai constituted the literate resources of Nurgaci's regime after 1616, and at the time were capstones of his bureaucratic infrastructure. This was the reason Erdeni was seated at Nurgaci's side at the time the khanate was declared in 1616; he had, on this occasion, displaced the warriors and bodyguards whom Shin Chung-il had seen sitting

29. Six pairs of slaves, seven horses, and three oxen, all of which were to be given to Nurgaci's son Abatai.

30. *MR TM* 7:1.

31. This was probably not a specific borrowing from Mongol practice but was a version of an ancient punishment attested throughout East Asia (earliest in China) and documented in some detail in the account of the execution of Lawrence Imbert in Korea in 1837. Presumably all these punishments could have been inflicted with swords or knives, but arrows were very particular symbols of authority, and explicitly of ownership (as they were themselves marked as the property of their owners). See comments in Chapter 3, but also Serruys, "A Note on Arrows and Oaths," 287 n 48.

in that position in 1596. Onoi, Tuša, Erdeni, Gagai, Dagai, Kanggūri, and others may all have been of Nikan background, but in fact it was irrelevant. Because of their responsibility for literate acts under the state they lived as Nikans, being answerable for the welfare and for the actions of other Nikans (and these Nikans reciprocated, as was observed in their rendering of their goods to Nurgaci as reparations for Erdeni's negligence in 1623). Nevertheless, Erdeni's retrospective biography in the "General History of the Eight Banners" makes no allusion to the ambiguities of Erdeni's identity in his lifetime and confidently states that he was a Manchu, of the Nara lineage once living at Duyengge.[32] As will be discussed below, that group was later seen as ambiguously Mongol or Manchu, and so, under Hung Taiji, Erdeni was posthumously made a Hešeri (that is, decidedly a Manchu).[33] Dagai became a Giolca, an identification for which no evidence is cited, and indeed there is no evidence of this in extant documents of the very early seventeenth century. The sudden resolution and subsequent revision of Erdeni's and Dagai's ancestry is characteristic of the reconstructivist impulse of the Hung Taiji state. By genealogizing Erdeni and Gagai, the khanate became in origin Manchu, and the Manchu script—in the records the creation of Erdeni, Gagai, and later Dagai—became purely Manchu in invention. The recounting of Erdeni's story in the Manchu annals and the assignment to him of Manchu lineage status occurred at the cusp of the state's ability to ascribe. Writing—originally lists of property, tribute objects, or missives between Jurchen leaders and the Ming or Yi courts—had previously been the function of Nikans. It had been both a lowly skill and an intimate one, since those with the ability to read and write could neither be wholly trusted by nor ever divorced from the khan. As the small bureaucracy under Nurgaci became the means for the khan's inroads against the discretionary powers of the nobles, however, the power of the scribes as a group increased, and Erdeni was one of those who achieved a visible and influential place on the khan's dais. Hung Taiji evidently did not intend for these

32. *ECCP*, 225–26, from *Qingshi gao*. Duyengge stood at the confluence of the Nani and Songari Rivers and was a central point of trade and settlement for the Ula federation and the Mongols coming from the west. See Grupper, "The Manchu Imperial Cult," 38.

33. The lineage affiliation was awarded in 1654, evidently to associate Erdeni with (Hešeri) Khife, who helped design the early Manchu examination system, and (Hešeri) Asitan, who was responsible for the early translation of novels. At the same time the court gave Erdeni the posthumous title of *wencheng* ("perfection through letters," the personal name of Fan Wencheng).

powers to remain preponderantly Nikan. The further development of scribal functions under Hung Taiji would emphasize differentiation of literacy into Manchu, Mongolian, and Chinese channels, as the simultaneous expression of the rulership became more sophisticated.

When annalistic activity began is uncertain, though the pattern of surviving information suggests that it dates only from shortly before the declaration of the khanate, perhaps sometime between Cuyen's imprisonment and his death. Records before that time allowed Qing historians to reconstruct a sketch of Nurgaci's campaigns of conquest, but the years between 1582 and 1615 are notable primarily for the discrepancy between the wealth of action and the paucity of records. Lists of slaves, lists of lands, lists of gifts, lists of dependents and ancestors, lists of soldiers enrolled in the banners, these were the matters that constituted the early documentary concerns of what would become Nurgaci's state. Writing in Chinese and Mongolian was important to Nurgaci because it allowed him to communicate with the Ming and the Yi when he desired. But his pool of literate men before the taking of Fushun was small, and their cataloging duties were heavy. The establishment of a scribal capacity in the state, which also established a civil, literate, bureaucratic identity, allowed Nurgaci simultaneously to refine his control over the resources at his command and to regulate a certain amount of social and economic activity among his subjects. The power to document was clearly defining for the Hung Taiji emperorship, and demanded control over the spread of literacy, which both depended upon and was generated by evolving terms of identity. The Documentary Department (*wenguan*),[34] initiated in 1629 as the khan's bureau, had by 1636 (the year the empire was created) become the Three Imperial Offices (*sanyuan*). By 1635, the production of documentation in Chinese, Jurchen (soon to be "Manchu"), and Mongolian had become a routine function of this bureaucracy. These mechanics were not only functional but also ideological—the simultaneous documentation was an early, palpable representation of the components of the emperorship. It is not too much to say that the production of multilingual documentation was in fact the raison d'être of large sectors of the early state (specifically the *wenguan*) and that the temple name of Hung Taiji is at least partially a reflection of the signifi-

[handwritten margin note: 1636- year Empire created]

34. The keeping of the records on the activities of the emperor (*qiju zhu*) was originally an extension of these bureaucratic structures and got a rather fitful start under the Qing. On the historical background of such record-keeping in Manchu and the status of current holdings in Taiwan, see Ch'en Chieh-hsien, "Introduction to the Manchu Text Version."

cance of this enterprise.[35] Not surprisingly, the first of the Three Imperial Offices as they were composed in 1636 was the Imperial Office of Historiography (*guoshi yuan*), an organ fundamental to the articulation of imperial legitimacy and prerogatives in the Jurchen polity. It was this office that assumed responsibility for the writing of the annals for the Nurgaci years. An illustrated version of the Nurgaci annals in both Chinese characters and in Manchu script was completed in 1635 and included illustrations of the mounted, mustachioed, hook-nosed Nurgaci leading his troops into battle at various celebrated encounters. The next year the first formal narrative, in the Chinese style, of the Nurgaci reign was completed: "Annals of the Martial Emperor" (*Wu huangdi shilu*). Now the inventor of the Qing empire (Hung Taiji) had a pedigree (Nurgaci).

There was still no Jurchen literary corpus by the time of Hung Taiji's ascension to the khanship in 1627. The original texts are not extant, but there are indications that during Hung Taiji's regime a broad collection of Chinese philosophical and historical texts[36] were translated, and the translation of the histories of the Liao, Jin, and Yuan empires (from all of which Hung Taiji was claiming legitimacy) was ordered.[37] The flagship of Hung Taiji's translation project was the history of the Jurchen Jin empire, of which Hung Taiji proclaimed himself an avid reader and from which he learned both the necessity and the dangers of bilingual education for the Manchus.[38] Among Hung Taiji's intentions in sponsoring these translations was an obvious program for the importation and legitimation of terms and concepts, primarily emperorship and its corollaries, that were not well established

35. For recent Chinese translations of pre-1644 Manchu documents, see *Chongde sannian Manwen dang'an yibian*, trans. Ji Yonghai and Liu Jingxian (Shenyang, 1988), and *Shengjing xingbu yuandang — Qing Taizong Chongde sannian zhi Chongde sinian*, comp. Zongguo renmin daxue, Qing shi yanjiu suo, and Zhongguo diyi lishi dang'an (Peking, 1985). On the rewriting of pre-1644 documents during the Qianlong reign, see Guan Xiaolian, "'Manwen laodang de xiufu yu chongchao,'" 115–22, 135.

36. The *Xingbu huidian, Sishu, San lue, Mengzi, San guo zhi, Tongjian gangmu, Xingli*, and *Da chengqing*.

37. Sun Wenliang and Li Zhiting, *Qing Taizong quan zhuan*, 310. Though Hung Taiji is well known to have commented particularly upon the Jin history *Aisin gurun-i suduri*, the translation was originally commissioned together with those of the Liao (*Dailiyoo gurun-i suduri*) and Yüan (*Dai Yuwan gurun-i suduri*) histories. The value of translating the histories was noted by Nurgaci, but it was Hung Taiji who appointed the translation staff—probably (Hešeri) Khife, Jamba, Cabuhai and Wang Wengui—who undertook the projects. The finished works seem to have been presented to the court in 1646.

38. *XZ, chüan* 1:1b–2b.

within the Jin khanate. Hung Taiji's insistence that his bannermen and bureaucrats be conversant with Chinese history was inspired by his interest in naturalizing the imperial institution in the Manchu language. Though, as shown in Chapter 3, in his own career the introduction of the emperorship was seen as a usurpation and the cause of political turmoil, the histories developed under Hung Taiji showed the institution to have a long history and an extensive ideological vocabulary. This history, it was important to show, was not limited to the periods of the "Chinese" empires: The alien empires, and all the Northeastern empires, had also had the emperorship, and that included the twelfth-century empire of the Jin Jurchens.

Translations from Chinese into Manchu proceeded apace with the development of a bilingual bureaucracy under Hung Taiji. The first Board of Appointments (*libu*) was headed by (Suwan Gūwalgiya) Garin (Ganglin), who was granted a "provincial" (*juren*) degree in 1634. Together with two other Manchus and three Oyirods he continued to draw up the plans for elaboration of the civil government. For the state to grow, examinations would have to be established, and it appears that the first examination of Manchus, Mongols, and Nikans was held at Mukden in 1638.[39] The content of subsequent examinations, in both Manchu and Chinese, was established by Cabuhai and Giyanghedei in 1639.[40] Hung Taiji also commissioned a group of "Confucian officials" (*ruchen*)—who should not be imagined as "Chinese" since they included Garin, Cabuhai, and others registered as Manchus—to translate selected works into Manchu "in order to instruct the national population [*guoren*, i.e., bannermen]."[41] The basis for any individual bannerman's participation in these examinations was ascribed identity, since the syllabus and the standards were determined by one's classification as Manchu, Mongol, or Chinese. Development of the examination system, which was fundamental to development of the bureaucracy, thus proceeded apace with other developments producing new distinctions among the imperial constituencies.

The elaboration of the Jurchen state during the first nine years after Nurgaci's death and the ascension of Hung Taiji as khan compromised much of the simplicity that Nurgaci himself had valued in his relations with the Jurchen elite and the growing mass of conquered and incorporated peoples. Most relevant to the present discussion, Hung Taiji's expansion of the civil institutions of the state created a greater role and a greater need

---

39. Zhang Zhongru et al., *Qingdai kaoshi zhidu ciliao* (hereafter QKZC), 1.3a.
40. QKZC, 1.9a.
41. (Aisin Gioro) Zhaolian, *Xiaoting zalu 1*, p.1b.

[margin note: need for Nikan]

for educated men of the Nikan classes to be introduced to official life. Nurgaci had admitted such men to his confidence reluctantly and insisted that they fulfill the traditional criteria of slavehood in the same proportion as Jurchen adherents. Under Hung Taiji, the numbers of Nikan subjects increased radically as the Jurchen conquests subsumed western Liaodong and northern Zhili. The larger state demanded a larger and more professional bureaucracy, which could hardly be staffed by illiterate hunters, fishermen, or farmers. The design of the early Hung Taiji state made it possible for the recently formalized Manchu orthography, and by extension the Manchu language, as a political device to survive. It was unavoidable that in its early stages the state would be partially dependent upon a class of Nikan scribes who were competent in Chinese, Mongolian, the new Manchu script, or all three. There seems, however, to have been a strong desire to bring an increasing number of state functions into the hands of Jurchen / Manchus after initiation of the empire. This political concern may have been the impetus behind the creation of a formal Manchu literature, education, and examination program in Manchu and for Manchus, as well as the elaboration of state organs accommodating selected political traditions of the Northeast, the primary military role of the bannermen, and the strategic advantages and increasing symbolic significance of Manchu as a medium of official communication.

AUTHENTICITY

In a letter to Nurgaci's nemesis Yuan Chonghuan[42] in 1627, Hung Taiji did not bother to pay his respects to the Ming court or even to reason out an argument on the parity of the Jin and Ming regimes. He satirized Ming attempts to claim Heaven's aegis for themselves: "The reason why our two nations have sent armies against one another was originally because the officials quartered in Liaodong and Guangning considered their emperor to be as high as Heaven itself, while considering themselves as those who live in Heaven; and the khan of another nation merely created by Heaven was unworthy of any degree of independent standing. Not able to bear the in-

---

42. Yuan (1584–1630) was appointed to protect the Shanhai Pass from invasion by Nurgaci's forces in 1623. He was successful in preventing Jurchen capture of Ningyuan in February of 1626, five months before Nurgaci's death. Hung Taiji, in an effort to avoid a two-front war against both China and Korea, agreed to a truce with Yuan in October of the same year. See *ECCP,* 954–55.

sults and contempt, we have taken our case to Heaven, raising troops and beginning war with you. Since Heaven is, in fact, just, and heeds not the magnitude of the nations but only the righteousness of the issue, it considers us in the right."[43] Hung Taiji's boasts all came true. Shortly after, he entered and pillaged China by way of eastern Mongolia, leaving Yuan at the political mercy of his enemies at the Ming court, who eventually had him prosecuted and executed. But by 1631 Hung Taiji had decided to soften the rhetorical emphasis upon the Jin heritage. It was imperative that a diplomatic channel should be opened with the Ming; Jin had come to open warfare with the Chakhar Mongols, and the khanate's resources were not sufficient to sustain a two-front war in Liaodong. Now Hung Taiji wrote to the Ming court through Zu Dashou, "The princes and officials of your country see only the reflection of the events of the Song period, and do not have a single good word to say about us. But you Ming rulers are not the descendants of the Song. Nor am I a son of the Jin." In the reforms of 1635 and 1636 Hung Taiji, who had by then effectively destroyed the political structure created by his father, would discard the Jin image as well as the name.

As he neared the completion of the political process leading to the emperorship, Hung Taiji declared in 1635 that those previously known as "Jurchens" should now be called "Manchus."[44] The reason for this change is not stated in the imperial narrative, and though explanations have been forwarded over the centuries, no very satisfying analysis of either the motive for this change or its timing has been established. One might note, first of all, that the group being created "Manchu" in 1635 was not the entire body of Jurchens. Negotiation of Chinese-martial and civil Nikan status had absorbed some number of those who had previously been considered "Jurchen," and some others were being incorporated into the Mongol banners as the decree was promulgated. Jurchens settled in the extremes of Heilongjiang continued to be called Jurchens as late as the Treaty of Nerchinsk in 1689, when the Kangxi emperor used this name to refer to them. "Manchu" was the name restricted to those joining the Eight Banners, none of whom could have honestly been called a "Jurchen" (a word meaning "free man") under the metamorphosing state. The traditional links of Jurchen commoners to Jurchen nobles were being severed; their functions

[margin annotations: discarding the Jin tie; Jurchens to Manchus]

---

43. *JMD* (*Qing Taizong chao*, vol. 1), Manchu on p. 2 [2564] and Chinese on p. 161.

44. He claimed "originality" for the Manchus and condemned those who continued to use the word "Jurchen." See also Rawski, *The Last Emperors*, 36, citing the annals for Taizong 9:10:13.

and in increasing numbers their livelihoods were being transformed from those of hunters, fishers, ginseng gatherers, merchants, shepherds, cowherds, livestock breeders, and farmers to that of full-time soldiers; their household cultures were being radically affected by the westward movement toward Chinese-speaking regions. "Manchu," as the new status name for those speaking the khan's language, worshiping in his religion, and honoring ancestors from erstwhile Nurgan, was only a part of the program. Unlike "Jurchen," "Manchu" was not an identity that was subject to the cultural ambiguities and tides of the Northeast. On the contrary it was to be fixed by criteria (genealogical affiliation, the requirement to serve in the Eight Banners and to perform in the Manchu examinations) that were enunciated by the state, and were as permanent as the state itself. Once established, Hung Taiji used these criteria aggressively, as in his continual pressure on Yi Korea—which signed an accord of amity with him in 1627 and ten years later acknowledged him as its overlord—to "return" to him Koreans of Jurchen descent.

When Nurgaci had attempted to control Liaodong, he had also been challenged by a second front, to his east and north. In his time this region was politically limitless and amorphous, a condition that would change dramatically for his successors. It was soon after the consolidation of his control over Tunggiya, and before he turned his military goals toward Fushun, that Nurgaci began to train his attentions on the regions of the Warkas, Woji, Hurkas, Evenks, Sibos, Giliaks, and others of the "wild men" who had not been brought into his federation. It happened that through their Tungusic linguistic links the traditional peoples of the Northeast, with a few exceptions, were distant cultural cousins of the Jurchens and the northern Koreans. But there is no evidence that this was a driving consideration in Nurgaci's approach to them. His interest appears to have been stimulated by his hostilities against Bujantai and the Ula federation. The first known Nurgaci campaign in this area was under the command of Fiongdon, who subdued some Warka villages and gained control of part of the Ussuri River in 1596. Two years later Nurgaci's sons Cuyen and Bayara led a force (including Fiongdon and Gagai) against the inhabitants of the Anjulakū region; a sweep of some twenty villages netted a captive population of over ten thousand people, who were herded back to Fe Ala.

Word of the invasions must have spread quickly. The next year, in 1599, six headmen of the Woji and the Hurka, under the leadership of the brothers Wangga and Jangga, appeared at Fe Ala. They contracted to supply Nurgaci with an annual tribute of black, white, and red pelts, and requested wives to seal the bargain. In return Nurgaci awarded six of the daughters of his highest-ranking officers, and personally oversaw a week-long celebration with his newfound brethren that is reported to have made a deep impression upon their hearts. By the time of the 1609 expedition to Fio-hoton, the strength and determination of Nurgaci were familiar in the region, and by 1610 most of the federations had subscribed to Nurgaci's multiplex diplomacy of tribute and marriage. As he would with the Khorchins or Kharachins and the Nikans of Liaodong, Nurgaci used his familial propaganda to justify his military domination of the Northeast. "We are one nation," he informed the Warkas of Fio-hoton, "but because you live so far away from us you are oppressed by Bujantai. Today, our nation has a khan, and he has defeated the soldiers of Ula. Now you will follow your kin, and your khan." [45]

[margin note: Nur.'s interest/success in the ne.]

Hung Taiji may have shared his father's nostalgic interest in the Amur, but he had an increasing strategic interest as well. From the time of his ascension as khan, Hung Taiji had directed kidnapping raids against the Amur peoples, as he had against those of western Liaodong and northern China. The numbers seized in these undertakings were, in comparison to the numbers of people brought from the western regions, modest. A report of May 1640 specifies a total seasonal catch of "3,154 men, 2,713 women and 1,819 small children . . . together with 424 horses, 704 cows and bulls and, on different occasions, more that 5,400 sable and miscellaneous furs." [46] The numbers were perhaps less a consideration than the quality. Men taken in these raids were sent not to the Eight Banners but to the special Hunting and Fishing (*butha*) Banners, with special duties in their attendance on the emperor. And the livestock and pelts were all of extremely high quality, consistent with the local standards that had earned a fortune for Nurgaci's ancestors but would diminish the fortunes of his descendants should they be required to purchase instead of seize them. Nurgaci had sent his raiding parties toward the Amur in order to weaken Bujantai. Hung Taiji

[margin note: Amur's captives]

45. *MR Wanli* 35 (*dingmo:* third month).
46. *Taizong juan* 51:9a/b. Also Melikhov, *Man'chzhury na Severo-Vostoke,* 16. Compare to the numbers recorded in *MR TM* 10:3:5 on the numbers of men coming willingly to perform the kowtow (*hengkilembi*) by their headmen Tayu, Garda, and Fukana in 1626: 120 Hurka, 222 Warka. Additional but similar figures to the abduction numbers cited here are provided in Melikhov, "The Northern Border," where the story of Hung Taiji and subsequent Qing violence against the peoples of Amur is argued to delegitimate modern Chinese claims to the region. See also Introduction, nn 40 and 41.

wished to weaken the Evenks (Solons), a Tungusic-speaking group with some culture in common with the Jurchens.[47] The Evenk federation, under the leadership of Bombogor, represented a considerable obstacle to the consolidation of Qing power in the east. On at least one occasion the Evenks fielded 6,000 men against a Qing squadron, impressing the Hung Taiji court with the necessity of coordinating a large campaign against the Amur populations. Hostilities peaked in 1640, the year Bombogor himself was run to ground in an Evenk village and brought to Mukden for execution. By the time of Hung Taiji's death in 1643, the Evenks had by and large been absorbed into the banners, resettled in more southerly and secure Qing territories, or slaughtered. Very small groups of bannermen were stationed in some villages, with one of the smallest and most remote at the trading village of Ningguta. As the newborn Qing empire expanded to include more of the peoples of the Northeast, Hung Taiji speculated upon the roots of the Aisin Gioro among the Warka and other Jurchen peoples.[48]

From Hung Taiji's speculations arose a foundation myth of the Qing imperial lineage, a myth that would be elaborated and refined over the next century or more. Wars in this period against the Evenks and other Amur peoples brought the Qing court into close contact, for the first time, with the region of Mt. Changbai, the sacred mountain of the Tungusic peoples for as long as the history of the region was known. Möngke Temür, the Jianzhou commander from whom Nurgaci had claimed descent and legitimacy, had been a native of that area, and like his putative descendants he had spent his adult life warring against the peoples of the Amur and of northern Korea. Hung Taiji was as curious about the Mt. Changbai region as Nurgaci had been, but he was bolder in declaring an ancestral claim. Möngke Temür, Hung Taiji reminded the Amurians, had been lord of Mt. Changbai and of Omohoi (northern Korea). Hung Taiji was his descendant, and so Hung Taiji was the rightful lord of Mt. Changbai in the present. More important, the peoples of the east were the kin of the Manchus. All were descended from a single ancestor, Bukuri Yungšon. The method of proof of this dramatic and profound claim was folklore. During the eastward campaigns of Hung Taiji, ever greater numbers of traditional peoples were incorporated, and in a short time Hung Taiji's military agents became familiar with the folk histories of the area. From these accounts was woven not

47. On early- and middle-seventeenth-century Jin/Qing campaigns in the Amur region see also Mancall, *Russia and China*, 20–32.
48. Jiang Xiusong, "Qingchu de Hurha bu," 139.

only a dramatic change in the self-representation of the Qing, but also the invention of the imperial lineage, which assumed the name of Aisin Gioro.

Bukuri Yungšon was magically conceived[49] when his mother Fekulen[50] held a fruit that had fallen from the mouth of a sacred magpie (*saksaha*).[51] The child Bukuri was barely grown when he pacified the warring factions of the "Three Surnames" (*sanxing*) people, and was elected *beile* by them. He then lived at Odori, a town on the heaths of Omohoi, east of Mt. Changbai, and he called his group *manju*. The Yuan empire established a military myriarchy here, and in the early Ming it became the Jianzhou garrison. After several generations the lineage of Bukuri Yungšon became unfit to govern the people. When the local people rebelled, Fanca, a scion of the lineage, escaped. Generations later the garrison commander Möngke Temür was born into the lineage.[52] The myth insisted upon some particulars of the status of the Aisin Gioro ancestors at Ilantumen as formulated from Hung

[margin: san xing]

49. Without reference to Hongli's comments, Sun Wenliang and Li Zhiting, *Qing Taizong quanzhuan* 1-3, discuss some similarities between the Qing foundation myth of Bukuri Yungšon and the legends of Qi, founder of the Yin (later Shang) dynasty, on the basis of the "Yin benji" and "Qin benji" sections of Sima Qian's *Shiji*, and the "Shi jun lan" section of the *Chunqiu*. In brief, they note the roles of sacred birds, supernatural conception, and heroes with unknown fathers. For an extended discussion of comparative themes in East Asian and in European folklore, see Peter H. Lee, *Songs of Flying Dragons*, esp. 102–23.

50. That is, Fekulen, mother of Bukuri Yungšon and hero of her own story cycle. There are two similar but not identical Bukuri/Fekulen narratives in early Qing documents, one in the *Manzhou shilu* (*juan* 1, 1–2b) and one from Mukesike, in *Mambun rōtō*, 9. There is also a similar Oronchon myth: see *Elunchun zu minjian gushi xun* (Shanghai: Wenyi, 1989). See also Crossley "An Introduction to the Qing Foundation Myth," 13; Meng Huiying, "Man—Tungusi yuzu minzu shenhua," 57–59.

51. Mark Elliott suggested to me in 1986 that *saksaha* is best translated "magpie." Natural history reference texts in English are slightly ambiguous on the exact meaning of "crow" and particularly to what extent it would include or exclude the magpie. Norman identified "magpie" as *pica pica*, which is not the North American magpie but what Matthews glosses as "the Chinese magpie" (*xiqu*, cf. Liu Housheng, *Jianming Man Han cidian*, "*saksaha*"). But given elements cropping up in various places in Qing folktales, a marked bird is certainly what is indicated, and so I think "magpie" is indeed the preferable translation. *Saksaha* is important enough in Manchu studies that it has been chosen as the name of the small research journal dedicated to Manchu language and culture. The word is related to other words for sticking together, inserting, or building (including the buildings used in shamanic rituals and celebrations).

52. The preceding paraphrase is from *Qingshi gao* (1928), 1:1a (1977 edition p. 1). It is a condensation of an earlier version. Compare *Manzhou shilu*, unnumbered pp. 1–16, *Donghua lu* 1:1a–b (1980 edition, p. 1). A more elaborate treatment is *Mukden i fujurun bithe* (1743), discussed below.

Bukuri's new old lineage (margin note)

Taiji on. Bukuri was elected *beile;* he founded a walled town at Odori in Omohoi, where a Yuan military myriarchy had once been and later became the Jianzhou garrison; and he called his followers *manju.* The last point, as with the story of Fanca, is historically moot; the name Manchu was officially adopted in 1635 by Hung Taiji, though the word's source, meaning, and history of usage before that time is obscure.[53] But in light of the ideas informing the tale of Bukuri, the introduction of the name *manju* at this point is significant. It invokes a complex blend of fact and symbolic fiction.

The career of Möngke Temür does not figure prominently in the Qing foundation myth. His status as an early ancestor of the Qing imperial line was not questioned, and was copiously though variously documented in the early Qing years.[54] Elements of Möngke Temür are admitted into the tale in sometimes garbled form. For instance, the Fanca who led his people to safety after the rebellion of the *sanxing* people before the birth of Möngke Temür was evidently inspired by the Fanca who in life was Möngke Temür's younger brother.[55] Like his legendary namesake, the historical Fanca led a Jurchen exodus. We know that he brought his group into the present Tunggiya River (then the Pozhu River) valley in 1435 or 1436, but the precise reason for quitting their home near present Huncun, in the extreme eastern corner of Jilin province, is not known. In light of the fact that Möngke Temür died fighting the so-called "wild" Jurchens who regularly harassed Korean outposts, it is not unlikely that the move was inspired by rising danger from hostile Jurchen neighbors or even a break within Möngke Temür's Jianzhou group.[56]

Fanca the escape who carries on that line (margin note)

As a subplot, the Fanca story hinges upon a critical issue in its reference to the *sanxing* people. In the Qing myth, the *sanxing* people are first men-

<hr>

53. *Manzhou yuanliu kao* 1:1 states that *manju* was originally the name of an early Jurchen tribe; no such name has been discovered in the records. Many possible explanations of the name's meaning have been suggested, but the etymology remains a mystery.

54. Zhu Xizu offered an exhaustive review of the early Qing generations and their variations in his *Hou Jin guohan xingshi kao* (1932). See also *Qingshi gao* (1928) (1977 edition, pp. 1–2).

55. Fanca has some independent importance as a frequent spokesman for his brother at the Yi court and as the Wodoli leader after his brother's death. See *Qingshi gao,* 222 (1977 edition, pp. 9119–20), and Wang, *Chaoxian "Lichao shilu,"* 38ff.

56. The Korean records indicate an intensifying conflict between the Yi Court and Fanca over Jurchen occupation of the Omohoi region. It is also possible that a concerted Yi military effort combined with Jurchen disaffection to force Fanca's remigration. See Wang, *Chaoxian "Lichao shilu,"* 39–49; Edward Willett Wagner, *The Literati Purges,* 8–10.

tioned in connection with Bukuri Yungšon, originally a stranger to them whom they brought into their midst and elected *beile* (a conventional element that is also present in the Nurgaci folk tales). Literally *sanxing* means "three lineages," or possibly "three federations." In both the Chinese and Manchu text, the phrase is used in such a way as to leave itself open to construction as either "the people having three lineages" or—as with Jurchen lineage names, discussed in Chapter 1—"the people of the place called Sanxing." During the Qing period Sanxing was the name of what is now Yilan in Heilongjiang province. Linked to this locality, the inconsistencies of the Bukuri story and the ambiguities of Northeastern history fold into a coherent if vague account of the provenance of the Qing imperial lineage. There is first of all a historical referent, linking the history of "Ilantumen" to the Jurchen settlement of Liaodong, which Nurgaci sometimes invoked in his propaganda and was acknowledged in some of his titles. The historical sequence within which the myth embeds itself begins far away from the northern Korean site that is the ostensible home of Bukuri Yungšon.

The interplay of ambiguities of affiliation and identity in this mythicizing process are displayed in the case of the Urianghka. The Qing court after Hung Taiji regarded the Uriangkha as an alien and troublesome presence. But Uriangkhad affinities with the Jurchens were well established. Several references in the history of the Liao empire (907–1121) indicate the presence of the Uriangkha in Liaodong in the early tenth century.[57] By the earliest years of the Ming the Uriangkha were situated well north and west of this region, and by the late Ming they were identified as part of the "western" Mongol alliance.[58] In the chronicles of Rashid ad-Dīn the thirteenth-century Uriangkha are described as "forest peoples,"[59] a term much more appropriate to the Evenks and other peoples who later became Manchu than to the Mongols as they are generally known. Korean records of the fifteenth century specifically identify the Jurchens as the "Uri-

57. Yanai, *Wuliangha ji dadan kao,* 4–5. The name occurs in the annals of the reign of Liao Taizu (Abaoji) as Wenlianggai and Wolanggai. *Liao shi* 116 calls Wolanggai a place name, but Yanai identifies it as the lineage name of Sübüdei.

58. Henry Serruys, "Yellow Hairs and Red Hats in Mongolia," discusses the Uriangkha in the east and their later reappearance in western Liaodong.

59. O. J. Maenchen-Helfen, "Akatīr," *Central Asiatic Journal* 11, no. 4: 275–86. *Woji,* a Jurchen / Manchu word for a forest dweller, was a common appellation for certain Jurchen groups in the Ming period. Possibly the Kangxi emperor ascribed a similar meaning to the name *wulianghai,* suggesting that in the seventeenth century a cultural and etymological link between the Uriangkha and the *woji* may have been assumed (Wilhelm, "A Note on the Migration of the Uriangkhai," 175).

angkha."[60] Modern scholars, too, have stressed the relationship between the Uriangkha and the medieval Jurchens.[61] The three myriads settled at Ilantumen during the Yuan period were called Wodolian, Huligai, and Taowen; when in the late fourteenth century the Jurchens who had migrated southward began to encroach upon Yi Korean territory, the three myriads mentioned in Yuan records appeared to be still intact. Korean records speak very particularly of the Jurchen headmen who led the newly arrived barbarians, collectively calling themselves "Uriangkha": Ahacu, leader of the Huora;[62] Burku, leader of the Taowen; and Möngke Temür, leader of the Odori.[63] The illustrated version of the Manchu annals completed under Hung Taiji in 1635 depicts Bukuri Yungšon standing before a very imposing fortification that is identified as Odori town. In reality, Odori was the original name of the group led by Möngke Temür in the days before the Ming court assigned the eastern Jurchens as the Jianzhou "garrison" in the Yongle period. The Odori people were part of the myriarchy created by Yuan administrators at Ilantumen in the thirteenth century. When the Odori, like the other Jurchens of Ilantumen, migrated south-

60. *Yijo sillok* distinguishes primarily between the *orankha tumen* led by Ahacu, Möngke Temür, and Burku (in Ming records, the Jianzhou Jurchens), the *udika* (Ming *woji*), and the *yain* (Ming *yeren*). The *udika* and *yain* were tribal peoples not included in the Ilantumen/Janzhou federations and constantly under military pressure from both Korea and the Jurchens proper. Henry Serruys noted on the basis of the work of G. J. Ramstedt that the Korean term *orankha*, "savage," was a clear reference to the Jurchen invaders of the fourteenth and fifteenth centuries; see *Sino-Jürched Relations*, 32. See also Jiang Xiusong, "Qingchu de Hurha bu," 139 n 2 (on Meng Sen). In addition to the Yi annals there is an extended reference to the Uriangkhad Jurchens in *Yongbi o'chon'ga* (1445), which has been translated into English with critical discussion by Peter H. Lee, *Songs of Flying Dragons*. See also Mitamura, "Ryūhi gotenka ni mieru joshen to udika," in *Shinchōzenshi no kenkyū*, esp. 74–75.

61. For examples see Wilhelm, "A Note," 74; Yanai, *Wulianghai ji dadan kao*, 8–9; Abe Takeo, "Shinchō no seijireki to manshūhakki to no kankei," in *Shindai shi no kenkyū*, 99–101; Mitamura, "Irantōman to sono genryū," in *Shinchō zenshi no kenkyū*, 97–106; Nicholas Poppe, "On Some Mongolian Loan Words in Evenki," *Central Asiatic Journal* 16: 102–9; idem, "On Some Ancient Mongolian Loan-words in Tungusic," *Central Asiatic Journal* 11, no. 3: 187–198.

62. The Huora (Huligai of the *Yuan shi*, see *juan* 59:1400) shared a name, and probably some history, with the Hurka, who were historically distinct from the Jurchens but later incorporated into the Qing banners as "new" Manchus. See Jiang, "Qingchu de Hurha bu." Ahacu was the first recognized commander of the Jianzhou garrison at the time of its creation in 1411. Möngke Temür and his kinsmen eventually usurped the commercial power and political recognition of Ahacu's lineage. See also Wu Han, "Guanyu Dongbei shi shang yiwei guaijie xin shiliao," and *Qingshi gao* 222:1a (1977 edition, pp. 9115–16).

63. *Yongbi o'chŏn'ga* 13; Wang, *Chaoxian lichao shilu*, 1–50.

ward toward Korea, they took their name along, and as is often the case the
federation name later became a toponym—one that was in this instance
associated with the peoples who later were loosely collected under the
Jianzhou rubric. Omohoi, where the Odori settlement was supposed to
have been located, was an ancient name for the plain that is now the northeastern sector of North Korea, and is indeed to the east of Mt. Changbai.

If the myth is partly a recasting of the history of Jurchen migrations
and partly an abridgment of the history of Möngke Temür and the Jianzhou garrison (all now caused to revolve around the sacred mountain of
Mt. Changbai), how is Bukuri Yungšon to be accounted for? His epithet,
Yungšon, is not a Manchu but a refracted Chinese word. Though Qing
records write it as Yongshun, it is evidently a corruption (perhaps via Korean) of *yingxiong,* "hero," which was noted by the compilers of *Manzhou
shilu.*[64] As a title, Bukuri Yungšon is an obvious translation of Bukuri
baghatur, the Mongolian word "hero," that was later borrowed into Manchu
as *baturu* and frequently used as an honorific. The title may well have been
bestowed upon Jurchen headmen at Ilantumen who proved helpful to Yuan
administrators, and a father or grandfather of Möngke Temür may have
enjoyed such a title, as some Qing genealogies suggested. But the name
Bukuri was originally not the name of a man, real or mythical. It was a
mountain spirit of the Amur region. There is evidence that Bukuri-alin
(Mt. Bukuri) was the original setting for the legend of the hero Bukuri before he was impressed as the mythical ancestor of the Aisin Gioro. In the
folk story, however, Bukuri mountain and its Bulhūri pool (*omo*) were
the scene of Bukuri's conception and birth; and he was not the ancestor of the
Aisin Gioro, but was a "kinsman" (*tongzu*) of theirs—just as the regional
peoples were the historical cousins of the Jurchens.[65] The story was probably originally related to the court by Evenk informants, though some of
its elements strongly resemble myths of the Oronchon; in all likelihood all
peoples of the Amur were familiar with the story, and many may have used
it as a foundation myth.[66] The Manchu narrative completed under Hung

64. Zhu Xizu, *Hou Jin guohan xingshi kao,* 21, discusses the notations to the
source materials for *Manzhou shilu.*

65. Sun Wenliang and Li Zhiting, *Qing Taizong quanzhuan,* 4, cite an edition
of the *Mambun rōtō.*

66. Stary, in "Mandschurische Miszellen," provides not only transliteration of
the earliest documents associated with Qing appropriation of the myth but also the
history of scholarship on the problem. Walter Fuchs was evidently the first scholar
to write on the myth, in "Bulhûri Omo: Die altäste Fassung der mandjurischen
Stammessage," in *Sinologische Arbeiten I* (1943), 47–52, which was inspired by a

Taiji in 1635 wove together Bukuri-alin, the mythical place of origin of the Amur peoples, with Mt. Changbai as a place of origin for the Manchus.[67] Baldly, the myth appropriates to the Aisin Gioro not one but two sacred sites of the Amur, Mt. Bukuri and Mt. Changbai. Called by various names in the Chinese records, Mt. Changbai could be traced at least to the records of the Han empire as the single most sacred site for the peoples of the region. Early inhabitants of the Northeast called the mountain Tutai,[68] but from Han times on the Chinese called it, probably because of its volcanic crater, the "incomplete mountain" (*buxian shan*). By the Northern Wei period it was called, because of its appearance, the "great white" (*taibai*) or "perpetually white" (*changbai*) mountain.[69] The Tang had known it as "white headed mountain" (Baitou shan), which is preserved in the Korean name, Paekt'u san. In the Qianlong emperor's "Ode to Mukden" (see Chapters 5 and 6) it became Šanggiyan (Šanyan)-alin, the "white mountain," and its crater lake, Tamun.

It was not immaterial to Hung Taiji's campaigns in the Amur to have a totemic rhetoric linking his own ancestors to those of the people of the region, at the same stroke establishing his lineage as supreme there since the "time" of the mountain spirit, Bukuri. But as a political myth the foundation story was also useful in the definition of the Manchu population within the banners. It aided in the Qing project, which continued into the eighteenth century, of standardizing the cultural and spiritual life of the

---

passage in Hauer's "Das mandschurische Kaiserhaus, sen Name, seine Herkunft and sein Stammbaum" in *MSOS/OS* 29 (1926): 1–39. Hauer and Fuchs both noted, as have more recent scholars such as Sun Wenliang and Liang Zhiting, that some themes—most strikingly miraculous birth—had appeared in Chinese mythology very early and left their traces in Han-period works such as the *Shujing* and Sima Qian's *Shiji*. The suggestion appears to be that some diffused Chinese influence could account for these elements, but as they are very common in mythology from many cultures this seems an unnecessary inference. As a result of research by Matsumura Jun, a letter from a Hurka, Muksike, was discovered (its content is also contained in *MR* 9), and its text is now considered the source of the Qing myth as it is redacted in the *Manju i yargiyan kooli*, 2–6. Stary provides both texts. More comparative comment is provided in Meng Huiying, "Man—Tunggusi yuzu minzu shenhua," and for comparison the Oronchon myth of the Heavenly Maiden, *Elunchun zu minjiang gushi xun*, may be consulted. See also Introduction, n 35.

67. The original importance of incorporating Bukuri-alin into the Qing foundation myth was lost on the later Qing court, which gradually edited "Bukulishan" out of the myth. In the last dynastic narrative, *Qingshi gao*, Bukuri-alin is not mentioned at all.

68. *Wei shu,* 100.

69. *Xin Tang shu* 219:71.

Manchus, primarily by generalizing the self-narrative and religious practices of the imperial family. The introduction of the sacred magpie, for instance, is a direct appeal to the shamanistic traditions of the Qing imperial
line. Prior to Nurgaci's unification, lineages worshiped various animals in
connection with their shamanistic rituals, which were also likely to differ
from lineage to lineage and were protected by a code of secrecy.[70] The myth
very clearly identifies the magpie as the spirit of the Aisin Gioro lineage,
and it was probably on the basis of this association that magpie worship began, in Qing times, to supplement and in many cases supplant altogether
the worship of other spirits among the lineages. The first steps toward state
codification of religion were taken, and the process would accelerate under
succeeding emperors.

[handwritten margin: sacred magpie]

The primary intention of the Bukuri myth is to establish its hero as the
personification of the Aisin Gioro lineage, and the Aisin Gioro lineage as a
manifestation of the newly unified Manchu people. It is a lineage fable bent
to genealogical uses, and as such was an indispensable part of the lineage
reorganization of the early seventeenth century. The lineages were and
continued to be the Manchu link with the past. They were important to
Nurgaci's claim of descent from the Jin Jurchens of the twelfth century, and
they were crucial to the social organization that made the Eight Banners
possible.[71] But the migrations of the fourteenth and fifteenth centuries had
left the ancient lineages in chaos. Nurgaci ordered that all who were brought
under his authority should be registered in a lineage, a measure that necessitated the assignment of false lineage associations in many instances.[72]
In many ways, Bukuri Yungšon was the counterpart of the hundreds of
legendary lineage founders to whom the Jurchens looked for their ancestors.[73] For while the preceding generations in Nurgaci's own lineage were

[handwritten margin: ll { Bukuri myth .]

70. The introduction to the *Manzhou jishen jitien dianli* indicates that prior to
the Qianlong period the lineage had all evolved their own traditions in sacrifice and
liturgy, to the point that the members were now confused as to proper practice. The
compilation was intended to remedy the situation by opening the Aisin Gioro rituals to approved readers and urging their adoption as standard. See 1a–b.

71. Zhou Yuanlian, "Guanyu baqi zhidu de jige wenti."

72. The introduction to the *BMST* (1745) speaks of the disarray into which the
ancient clans appeared to have fallen by the time of Nurgaci's rise and the measures
adopted in an attempt to supply lineage affiliation for each individual. See 'Précis'
(*fanlie*) 3a–b.

73. Compare to redacted genealogies of the *BMST*. Most trace lineages to a pro-
totypical ancestor, living in an unspecified time. It must not be supposed that because the genealogies were previously unwritten they were as a consequence completely fabulous. The point here is that like all oral traditions the genealogies

comparatively clear, the Gioro lineage of which he was a nominal part was in as great a state of disarray as any other. He assumed the lineage name "Aisin" (Golden) Gioro to distinguish his lineage from those who might claim parity, and the Bukuri myth decisively separated the Aisin Gioro origins from those of the mass of Jurchens.[74]

For the most part, Qing documents do not confuse the immediate genealogical antecedents of the Qing emperors with this larger myth of regional origins. The Manchu annals open with the story of Bukuri Yungšon, but by the time the Shunzhi annals had begun to be influenced by the Chinese form, the convention of "four original" ancestors was being observed, in accord with the standardization of lineage ritual that occurred in the early Kangxi period.[75] Nurgaci's "four original" ancestors were Möngke Temür, Fuman, Giocangga, and Taksi; all had posthumous titles, all had rituals established acknowledging them as imperial antecedents, and all had tombs very near the site of Hetu Ala (the installation is now called Yongling). This specific and archetypical arrangement of personal identities had some mysteries of its own. Möngke Temür died in or around 1434, and Giocangga and Taksi both died in 1582. This implies an impossible lifespan for Fuman and also neglects the well-attested Cungšan, who was leading the Odori / Jianzhou Jurchens in the later fifteenth century and was evidently a son or nephew of Möngke Temür. Moreover, Möngke Temür was killed in Korea, and though it is possible his younger brother Fanca brought his body to the Tunggiya region, or at least to the vicinity of Hetu Ala, there is no indication of it in the records. The tombs might well have originally been built for a reburial of Giocangga and Taksi, if the attested date of 1598 for their original construction is accurate. But who the others buried there really are[76] is not more certain than how many individuals in the lineage—if it truly goes from Möngke Temür to Nurgaci—are omitted between Möngke Temür and Giocangga in the conventionalized "original four ancestors" sequence that the records have established. More important, the imperial narrative does not pretend that the imperial myth of descent from Bu-

---

adhered to a conventional structure and that Bukuri's story follows the structure in its general outlines. This is particularly true for the story as it appears in *Qingshi gao*, where it is overtly presented as a genealogy.

74. Only the *Qingshi gao* refers specifically to the theme of Jin descent.

75. Kai-wing Chow, *The Rise of Confucian Ritualism in Late Imperial China*, 161–66.

76. Records of the Kangxi period, when the tombs were rebuilt for the first of several times, indicate the bodies of Möngke Temür, Fuman, Giocangga, Taksi, two others of Giocangga's sons, and assorted concubines are present.

kuri Yungšon needs to be reconciled with the incompatible myth of familial descent.

SURPASSING LIMITS

Nurgaci's early regime, based upon models provided by Wan of Hada, by Jianzhou leaders such as Giocangga, Taksi, Soocangga and Utai, and Li Chengliang, had for most of its existence remained firmly fixed on local political rhetoric and local ambitions—if by that we may acknowledge that the scope of Nurgaci's power enlarged by several orders of magnitude of the "locality" to which his predecessors had aspired to dominate. It was only in the last years of his life that Nurgaci began to discern, and on occasion to exploit, an avenue to a style of rule that in comparison to his earlier models was virtually unlimited in space or in time. The road to that new form of dominion lay through the Mongol-affiliated peoples of northern Jilin and Liaodong, and farther west. Though there is no contemporary evidence indicating that Nurgaci grew truly expert in the details or the cosmology of that other political universe, he certainly knew it had something to do with specific forms of Buddhism, it had something to do with the Great Khans descended from Khubilai, and it had something to do with gaining the allegiance of those identifying themselves—or who could be identified—as Mongols.

This "Mongol" identity was not easy to pin down. Partially or fully pastoral groups roamed the open areas of the Jurchen territories. They included representatives of the northern cultures of Ula and Yehe, a region with a distinct milieu more strongly attached to the northerly populations of Liaodong and Jilin than to the southerly groups affiliated with Nurgaci. From the late fifteenth century the Ula and Yehe were part of the large Hūlun federation, all of whom were called "Mongols" (Manchu *monggo*, old Jurchen *munggur*) by the Jianzhou and regarded them as foreign. A majority of the Hūluns must have been of Jurchen descent, and their languages were mutually intelligible with that of Nurgaci's Jianzhou.[77] But by the late 1500s the Hūluns spoke distinct dialects, with a much larger portion of Mongolian loan-words, and among them occurred a very high incidence of Mongolian names, marriage into Khorchin or Kharachin lineages, and extensive acculturation with the Khorchin or Kharachin populations.

[margin handwritten note: Mongol ID - included Ula + Yehe areas - part of Hulun fed of Jurchen descent]

These things happened among the southern population where Nurgaci had his base, also, but to a sufficiently smaller degree that there was a regional consensus that those living north of Liaodong, in the general Khingan region, were "Mongols," no matter what their ancestry.[78] While the Jurchens before and during Nurgaci's time used the word "Mongol" (*monggo*) for the Hūluns, they did not always use this name to refer to the Khorchin and Kharachin immigrants to Liaodong and what is now Jilin province.[79] Many had come into the region to serve as mercenaries in the Ming forces in Liaodong, and others remained pastoral, fleeing famine or the increasingly chaotic political situation of the Chakhar-Khalkha region. The Korean visitor Shin Chung-il saw nomadic bands in 1596, dressed in furs, with their felt yurts on wagons, moving their herds toward appropriate pastures. Many, he noted, were also agricultural, and would sow fields in the spring to which they expected to return in the fall to reap a meager crop of wheat or millet. Like the Koreans, the Jurchens called these populations "Tatars" (*dazi, daji*).[80] Shin Chung-il noted the economic segregation of these nomads, who were still primarily pastoral. They kept their yurts on wagons, as their steppe cousins did, and almost always dressed in furs. Nurgaci gave these Mongols a distinctive role in his early operations, employing them primarily as guards and cowherds. In the meantime, the Khorchins and some portion of the Khalkha worked toward an agreement of submission to Nurgaci that would spare them the slow but inevitable obliteration to which the Hūlun populations were being subjected. As early as 1594 Nurgaci may have received an embassy from a group of Kharachins, and

78. *KF* 3.3a.

79. This early distinction between the Kharachins and the Liaodong populations, followed by their integration in the Ming period, was also noted from the other side: Zhang Mu remarked that the Kharachins had first fought against the "Tatars" (*dadan*)—that is, the peoples of northern Liaodong whom the southerly Jurchens regarded as "Mongols"—but later moved east on account of Lighdan and settled among their former enemies. This story is bound up with the eastward dispersal of the Uriangkha, who intermarried with the Kharachin leaders and then participated in this eastward migration. The federations at Ilantumen (see Chapter 2), among whom the Jurchens as well as the Hūluns took some provenance, used some of the same names as had been prominent among the early Ming federations of eastern Mongolia—particularly Doying (Jurchen Doyen) and Fuyu. Zhang's work on the Mongols, *Menggu youmu ji*, was uncompleted at his death in 1849 but was revised by He Qiutao and printed by Qi Junzao in 1867 (Qi had earlier published a chronology of Gu Yanwu, about whom Zhang Mu had also done a study). See *ECCP*, 47; Hyer and Jagchid, *Menggu youmu ji*; and Chapter 5, n 43. The three groups of early Qing Uriangkha are reported in great detail (but with no reference to their amalgamation with the Jurchens) in *Qingshi gao* 524:14511–27.

80. *KJD*, 21a–22a.

[handwritten margin notes: "juén wt", "Nur— to avoid losing ID"]

certainly, in 1605, the Khorchin headman (and Borjigid descendant)[81] Enggeder presented Nurgaci with twenty horses. By this time the Khorchins were ready to formally transfer their loyalty to Nurgaci and in 1606 presented him with his first title of "khan"—*Kündülün khan* (Jurchen *Kundulen han*) or the "Revered Khan." The title was clearly directed at Nurgaci personally, and his khanal rank was derived from—and limited to—his relationship to the Khorchins. To his Jurchen followers he was still "Wise Beile" (*Sure beile*,[82] which may have been inspired by the Mongolian *Sechen khan*, applied to Nurgaci by some portion of his Khorchin contingents).

When, in 1596, Nurgaci referred to the "Jurchen Nations" in his self-description (partly derived from Wan of Hada), it signified the nearly completed subordination of the Yehe, Hada, Hoifa, and Ula federations, and was novel.[83] By 1599 Nurgaci felt that his followers were well-enough distinguished from the Khorchin-Hūlun populations for him to style himself headman of the "Jurchens and Wildmen" (Manchu *weji*, Chinese *yeren*, Korean *ya'in*—the Tungusic hunting and gathering peoples of the Northeast) and to sponsor the development of a script derived from Mongolian (which had been the *lingua franca* of the region) for the writing of the Jurchen language. This new stage of Jurchen definition (reinforcing the new solidarity of the Jianzhou and the Hūluns, by means of defining the Khorchins as "Mongols") opened as wars against the Khorchins and the Hūluns reached crisis. Nurgaci had captured the leaders of some Hūlun federations and begun negotiations that, after twenty years of fits and starts, would obliterate not only Hūlun power in the Northeast, but the federations themselves. During the defeat of the Hūlun allied forces in 1592, the Ula leaders Bujantai[84] and Laba were captured. Together with his older brother and co-ruler Mantai, Bujantai had decided in 1592 to join the effort by the Hūlun confederacy and the Khorchins to prevent a northward spread of Nurgaci's power. But the forces were defeated at Mt. Gure (Gure alin,

---

81. The Khorchins were believed to be descendants of followers of Chinggis' brother Khasar, and so although not Chinggisids the Khorchin leaders were of Chinggis' Borjigid lineage.

82. In *KF*, *zongrui beile*.

83. Hung Taiji's declaration in 1635 that the nation (*gurun*) had "originally" consisted of the "Manchu, Hada, Ula, Yehe and Hoifa" was a purely ideological imposition. See also Rawski, *The Last Emperors*, 36.

84. Shin wrote Bujantai's name with the Chinese characters Fuzhetai and described him as a "Mongol general." Bujantai was a grandson of Buyan, the first *beile* of the group who called themselves Ula ("river"), a reference to the Songari. Buyan was descended from Nacibulu, who would someday be acknowledged as the progenitor of the Nara lineages of the Yehe, Hada, and Ula territories.

near the scene of the demise of Giocangga and Taksi) by Nurgaci.[85] Bujantai became the stepping stone (if a slippery one) to bridging differences
with Ula, opening the way to the unstable alliances that Nurgaci complained the Ming were trying to undo in 1618.

In 1591 Nurgaci began the confrontation with the Hūlun alliance to his
north that would determine whether he or they would dominate the Jurchen territories of Liaodong and Jilin. He resisted a demand from the Hūlun leaders Baindari, Yangginu, and Narimbulu that he return land to the
Yehe and in 1592–93 successfully defended his villages against a concerted
attempt by the Hūlun, Khorchins, and other groups to dislodge him—as a
result of which Bujantai and Laba were brought into Nurgaci's camp. In the
spring of 1596 Bujantai was sent back to his people to act as *beile* after
Mantai's death.[86] Nurgaci assumed that Bujantai had learned his place and
released him to act both as *beile* of the Ula and as tributary to the lord of
the Jianzhou. If Ula could be brought under Jianzhou control, they would
represent the northernmost and easternmost extent of Nurgaci's hegemony. The geographical sway Ula promised to add to Nurgaci's domain was
considerable. In comparison to Fushun, only two days away to Nurgaci's
west, and Korea, only four days away to his south, Ula was far removed, demanding eighteen days to a month to reach their villages from the Tunggiya valley. The apparent submission of Bujantai put his neighbor, the Yehe
confederacy, in an untenable position, and in 1597 Yehe concluded a truce
with Nurgaci. The uneasy Jianzhou peace with the Hūlun alliance was
short-lived—in fact, it survived only long enough for Nurgaci to receive
as wife a Yehe woman who would become the mother of Hung Taiji. By
1599 the Yehe entered into an alliance with the Liaodong military authorities in an attempt to throw off Nurgaci's hand and resumed the hostilities
with Jianzhou that would not be concluded until 1620. The Hada (now under Wan's son Hurhan), also, resented Nurgaci's intrusion upon their independence and embarked upon the disastrous war that ended with their destruction as a separate entity less than a year later.[87] Under Bujantai, Ula

85. Bujantai, with 20 fully armed and equipped men, was taken prisoner. Laba,
another influential member of the Ula, had surrendered at the same time, bringing
with him another 20 armed men, 120 foot soldiers, and 100 war horses. Mantai offered Nurgaci another 100 horses for Bujantai's freedom, but he was rejected.

86. During Bujantai's stay at Fe Ala, his elder brother Mantai had assumed the
status of sole *beile* of the Ula. Not long afterward both Mantai and his son were put
to death by the confederacy.

87. They were defeated in July at Fulegiyaci and incorporated into the Jianzhou
federation under the nominal command of their headman, Monggobolo, in 1601.

attempted to lie in the middle, sometimes fighting Nurgaci, sometimes ne-gotiating with him, always seeking leverage from Liaodong, the Khorchins, or enemies of Nurgaci within the Jianzhou camp. Warfare briefly broke out between Ula and Jianzhou in 1607, as Nurgaci's forces secured his su-premacy over the Khorchins and Bujantai tried briefly to come to their aid. Qing records give a very obscure account of the final push against Bujan-tai, claiming that Nurgaci was enraged by the mistreatment of the daugh-ter he had given to Bujantai in marriage. The young woman had "whistling arrows" shot at her, which the records suggest was a violation of her dig-nity. But "whistling arrows" were judicial instruments among the Jur-chens.[88] As the woman's only kinsman among the Ula, Bujantai would have been the proper executor of her punishment. Though it is probable that Nurgaci's daughter was in this case the object of a legal process, the Qing records describe Bujantai's behavior as wanton. As a result of it Nurgaci's wrath was pricked and the final war with Ula begun. The Jianzhou forces quickly overwhelmed Ula, and Bujantai fled to his allies the Yehe, against whom Nurgaci was still warring at the time he promulgated his "Seven Great Grievances" in 1618. Indeed his fourth grievance was that a negoti-ated ending of that war had been frustrated by Ming agents who kidnapped a Yehe princess promised to Nurgaci as part of the settlement and diverted her to their own Mongol allies.

As khan, as when he was *beile*, Nurgaci had been a sponsor of the shamans and expected them to support him in turn. But it appears that he had other religious involvements as well. When in his own reign Hung Taiji defeated the Chakhars[89] and assumed the religious functions of their erstwhile Chinggisid khan, he was inclined to have his historians cast those functions earlier in Qing history, back to the time of Nurgaci. It is certainly

88. Nurgaci did not use the bamboo rod for corporal punishment. Instead, the convicted were lashed to trees or frames and had their backsides shot full of small "whistling arrows"; the greater the crime, the more arrows were injected. Shin Chung-il saw them used by Nurgaci's judges, and Qing records as late as the Hung Taiji period speak of punishments inflicted by being shot with or mutilated with ar-rows. Passages in the early Manchu records also speak of concubines being pun-ished by being mutilated with arrows.

89. Manchu Čagar. The antecedents of the Chakhars are somewhat obscure. The name occurs in connection with Chinggis Khaghan only during the conquest of the "Chakhar" region around Kalgan in the campaigns of Mūkhali against the Jurchen Jin in 1211–12. This remains the territory most consistently associated with the Chakhars. As discussed below, the Chakhar rulers were Chinggisid and Khubilaid descendants, who achieved a political recentralization of eastern Mongolia under Dayan Khaghan in the fifteenth century, which Lighdan attempted to revive in the early seventeenth century.

enter
Tibetan
sects

not true that Nurgaci functioned in his own time as a Buddhist monarch. He did, however, initiate the complex relations between his lineage and Tibetan esoteric sects that would come to define and redefine Qing imperial universalism. When Shin Chung-il had visited Nurgaci's capital at Fe Ala in 1596, he had noticed that both Nurgaci and Šurgaci wore caps with a small figure on top in the shape of a man seated on a "lotus platform" (*lian tai*). If Shin construed this tiny figure accurately, it suggests some Buddhist imagery already was being used by the Jianzhou leadership at this time.[90] From the middle sixteenth century, the powerful Chakhars to Nurgaci's northwest had patronized the Sa skya pa sect,[91] and in return their khans were recognized as universal Buddhist rulers (see Chapter 5). Mongol documentation for the late sixteenth century explicitly recorded the actions of Sa skya pa missionaries based among the Chakhars and working eastward, into the Jurchen territories.[92] In this early period as *beile* of the Jianzhou, Nurgaci and Šurgaci may have adopted the Buddha image as a political talisman, perhaps at the prompting of early missionaries from the tantric sects of the Khorchin, Kharachin, Chakhar, and Khalkha regions. The point at which Nurgaci entered into a formal relationship with the Sakya sect is unclear. Presumably the capitulation of the Khorchins in 1606 brought not only the title of "khan" to Nurgaci but also a direct influence from their

90. The idea that Shin's "shape of a man seated on a lotus platform" was a representation of a Buddha was very kindly suggested to me by Kam Tak-sing in February 1993. It is mystifying that Shin would describe this figure as that of a "man" if he in fact recognized it as a Buddha, which any Korean would indeed recognize. I can only surmise that iconographic inspiration for the small figure possibly was derived from the Chakhars and other groups to the north and west, and that Shin suspected it represented a particular *bodhisattva* image, without being sure which one. In Qing imperial times, day caps for emperors often had a Buddha embroidered on the fabric over the front and normally had a jewel on their crown, either a pearl or a ruby. But in the funeral portraits in which emperors wear their "dragon" robes and caps, there is an ornament whose shape is indeed ambiguous and may recall the figure Shin saw. It is a gold knob encrusted with jewels or pearls, shaped in such a way that the head, shoulders, and knees of a seated figure may well be suggested (in some instances, it appears to assume almost a pagoda shape). If the shape of Qing times represents very closely what Shin saw in 1596, it may indeed have been so ambiguous that he felt only justified in saying it resembled a figure seated on a lotus.

91. The Sakya sect, which takes its Tibetan name from the Sa skya region of west central Tibet, was founded in the late eleventh century and like other tantric sects of the time was based upon a community of celibate monks led by a noncelibate practitioner of tantrism—who may have been regarded by the popular society as having "shamanic" powers (on the latter point see Samuel, *Civilized Shamans*, 473–74).

92. See Grupper, "Review of Klaus Sagaster, *Die Weisse Geschichte*," on basis of *Erdeni-yin tobchi*, 200/9–18.

own Tibetan *lama*. Not later than 1617, as the Chakhars emerged as the major rivals of Nurgaci for control of Liaodong, Nurgaci had become a Sakya pa patron, too. The date may have been slightly earlier, at his formal installation as khan of the Jurchens as well as the Khorchins in 1616. Indeed his attested khanal title, "Enlightened Khan" (*Genggiyen han*) is considered by S. M. Grupper to have been of Buddhist inspiration and may have been intended as a direct claim to the legacy of the Yuan emperors.[93] And it may be meaningful that, like the Oyirod leaders who could not claim Chinggisid legitimacy for themselves, Nurgaci found a marriage connection to the Borjigid lineage: his "best loved wife" (*haji sargan*) and mother of his successor Hung Taiji.

Very soon communications and amicable overtures came to Nurgaci from other groups of eastern Mongolia—particularly the Khalkhas, who though nominally subjects of the Chakhar khans were actually suffering under the fierce recentralizing of the Chakhar ruler, Lighdan Khaghan. The headmen of parties of significant strategic status were, like others with whom Nurgaci was forging alliances, incorporated into Nurgaci's family by marriage. The most highly favored married Nurgaci's daughters and sat at his court (after he declared himself khan of the Jurchens) as *efu*. The institution of the "five princes" (*tabun ong*) was the early definition of a "Mongol" elite within the Nurgaci state, and the delineation of a new pattern of leadership for those Khorchins, Kharachins, Khalkhas, and Oyirods who had offered their followership to Nurgaci instead of to Lighdan.[94] After the conquest of central Liaodong and establishment of the new Jin capital at Mukden (formerly Shenyang) in 1625, Nurgaci sponsored the rebuilding of Lianhua temple outside of Liaoyang. The *lama*, Nangso, was a Tibetan or possibly a "Tibetanized Uigur,"[95] who by 1621 had assumed some political status with Nurgaci. In the last years of his life (and presumably at the height of his power) Nangso made two trips to Nurgaci's court at Mukden, and Nurgaci not only underwrote the expenses of the lamasery (and exempted all lamasery property and personnel from the tax) but also built a stupa to receive Nangso's remains after the *lama*'s death. So, though there is no contemporary evidence that Nurgaci's investiture in 1616 was accom-

---

93. For evidence see Grupper, "Review of Sagaster." He observes, "One need only note that such titles were conveyed at the time of imperial investiture to see that they have religio-dynastic connotations."

94. For a very short but direct discussion see Liu Guang'an, "A Short Treatise on the Ethnic Legislation of the Qing Dynasty," 98.

95. Grupper's phrase, based upon his speculation that Nangso might have been from Amdo or Western Gansu, where tantric Buddhism was influential.

panied by Buddhist ceremony, nor a suggestion that Nurgaci capitalized upon the ideological contributions that Buddhism was offering him, his interest in Buddhism appears earliest to have been inspired by a general notion that Buddhist iconography was politically effective, and later, that patronage of the Sakya pa would give him an advantage in his struggle against Lighdan Khaghan for influence in Liaodong and among the Khorchin and Kharachin populations of the Northeast. From this rather casual association, subsequent rulers would spin a powerful ideology of dominion.

Lighdan had trading rights in the town of Guangning, to Nurgaci's north and west, which he wished preserved from assault by Nurgaci's khanate. In 1619 the two leaders engaged in a short but intense correspondence on the question, and it is clear that Nurgaci's quick temper and sarcastic epistolary style were both stimulated by Lighdan's presentation—in which he signed himself "Chinggis Khaghan of the Mongols"—and reminded Nurgaci that the Chakhar forces numbered 400,000 as opposed to the Jin khanate's 30,000 bannermen. Lighdan, who proclaimed himself a universal Buddhist ruler in succession to Chinggis and Khubilai, had not only what he claimed was the imperial seal of Chinggis, but also patronized the Mahākāla cult of the Tibetan Sakya sect. This cult was regarded by many elites of Mongolia as the key to universal dominion, since it alone gave rulers access to the consciousnesses of past Great Khans. But so long as Lighdan Khaghan ruled in Chakhar, the Jin claim to universal Buddhist kingship would be unconvincing to the majority in eastern Mongolia. After Nurgaci's death, Hung Taiji continued the war against Lighdan. In the early 1630s, as Hung Taiji was eliminating his rival *beile* as obstacles to his power, he pushed very hard for destruction of Lighdan's khanate. The effect was as Hung Taiji expected; Lighdan's forces withdrew to the west to recoup and began extraction by force of grazing land from the residents of the Khalkha region. Soon Lighdan had internal rebellions on his hands as well as full-scale war with the Jin. In 1633 Lighdan fled Hung Taiji's troops (and died soon after) and the Chakhar surrendered. They delivered to Hung Taiji (who was through his mother a descendant of Chinggis' lineage, the Borjigids) what they said was the seal of Chinggis and acknowledged him both as the Chinggis incarnation and as the universal Buddhist ruler. Hung Taiji convinced Lighdan's son Erke Khongkhor Ejen (Eje-khoghor) to surrender and become a prince of the first degree (*qinwang*) by marrying one of the Hung Taiji's daughters. This began the remarkable process that between 1634 and 1636 ended both the Northern Yuan and the Later Jin khanates, initiated the Qing empire that amalgamated both, installed Hung Taiji himself as an emperor, and saw the creation of new institutions for the identification of "Mongols" and administration of their life in the new order.

As Hung Taiji assumed Lighdan's role, he also assumed his problems, including resistance or rebellion from groups who did not wish to join their neighbors in submission to the centralization and reorganization of the nascent Qing empire anymore than they had wanted to submit to similar impositions by Lighdan. The problems persisted for the regime after the premature death of Hung Taiji in 1643 and after the conquest of Peking by Qing forces in 1644. A major outbreak occurred in 1646, when Tsetsen Khan rebelled. The uprising was suppressed near Urga in 1648 and featured a stratagem that would be used by the Qing repeatedly in their progressive conquests of Mongolia and Turkestan: Commanders of "Mongol" ancestry (that is, Khorchin, Kharachin or Chakhar) were dispatched by the empire to suppress uprisings of "Khalkha" or "Oyirod" groups—in the case of Tsetsen Khan, the Qing forces were headed by Minggadari (d. 1669, Surut lineage of Khorchins). He was exemplary of the population that was regarded by the Qing as truly "Mongol"—those who submitted early, who supplied Nurgaci with his first khanal title, whose leaders intermarried with the Aisin Gioro, who brought to the Qing emperors descent from and the symbols of legitimacy of Chinggis, and who formed the core of the Mongol Eight Banners. The eighteenth-century and nineteenth-century Qing nobility was adorned by the descendants of these early "Mongol" adherents, including Songyun (1752–1835, of the Marat lineage of the Khorchins), Changling (1758–1838, of the Sartuk lineage of the Khorchins),[96] Qingxiang (d. 1826, of the Tubet lineage of the Kharachins), Qishan (d. 1854, a descendant of Enggeder), and Senggerincin (d. 1865, of the Borjigid lineage of the Khorchins). The early adherents of western Liaodong and eastern Mongolia were the foundation of the Mongol Eight Banners.

They were joined there by some Hūlun descendants who were indistinguishable from others who had joined the Manchu Eight Banners, and who were significantly changed by the incorporation process. Some, such as the Uya lineage of very obscure origins in the Hūlun territories, had become close to the Aisin Gioro lineage by marriage (indeed the Kangxi emperor's Uya wife, later canonized as Xiaogong, was the mother of Yinzhen, later to be the Yongzheng emperor). Shortly before his death, the Kangxi emperor ordered the lineage removed from the bondservant companies and enrolled

96. Son of Nayentai (1694–1762).

in the regular Manchu Bordered Blue banner. In the last year of his own life, 1735, the Yongzheng emperor ordered a very similar clarification for his senior wife's lineage, having them removed from the bondservant companies and their obscure Hūlun origins clarified by enrollment in (and genealogical regularization in) the Manchu banners.[97] But a majority of Hūlun descendants were within a generation of the conquest of China enrolled as "Mongols." This sudden re-creation as Mongols, accompanied as it was by the requirement to be proficient in written Mongolian and to play the Mongol role in the state religious cult, represented a distinct alteration in their lives and careers. And, as with his criteria of Manchu identity, Hung Taiji applied the criteria of Mongol identity aggressively, insisting that Mongols in the employ of Ming fortifications in western Liaodong defect to him, as the new spiritual and temporal ruler of Mongolia.

Hung Taiji's design for a rapid expansion of the Qing bureaucracy was from the first predicated upon offices for the management of communications with his "Mongol" components and management of their economic and cultural affairs. Most important among these was the institution later known as the Imperial Colonial Office (Chinese *lifan yuan,* Manchu *tulergi golo be dasara jurgan*).[98] It began life in 1636 as the "Mongol Department" (Manchu *monggo yamun,*[99] Chinese *menggu yamen*). One of its chief duties in these days was to track the titles awarded to Khorchin, Kharachin, and Khalkha nobles who declared allegiance to the Qing. In the case of the leaders of the three large divisions of the Khalkhas—the Tusiyetu khan, Joriktu khan, and Jasaktu khan—the "Mongol Department" had not only to record their domains and the details of their estates but also to record their entitlement by Hung Taiji as first-degree princes (*qinwang*) in 1636 and arrange their ceremonial presentation. The "Mongol Department" also began assuming responsibilities—previously vested in the khans of eastern Mongolia—for the adjudication of disputes among the Khorchin, Kharachin, Chakhar, and Khalkha populations. This meant on occasion delineating boundaries and institutionalizing new terms for economic interaction, two functions that were soon generalized to relations with the Romanov empire, so that by the 1650s the "Mongol Department" had in fact become the diplomatic office and colonial authority of the Qing empire

97. Guan Tianting, "Qingdai huangshi shizu," 62.
98. See Chia, "Li-fan Yüan," and Zhao Yuntian, *Qingdai Menggu,* 45–69.
99. *Yamun* being a loan from Chinese *yamen.* In the eighteenth century the Manchu name of the institution was changed to *monggo i jurgan,* after the Manchu word *jurgan* (which originally had no meaning associated with government) was invented to mean a bureaucractic department and displaced the Chinese loan-word.

in Inner Asia. Hung Taiji was not satisfied to allow the state to perceive and legitimate existing affiliations. He used categorical identities to extend affiliation to those not yet conquered or otherwise incorporated, as Nurgaci had done only in the instance of Liaodong. The best-known examples, perhaps, were his demands that Jurchens living in Korea be returned to the Manchu territories and that Mongols living in Liaodong and working under the Ming system defect to him. His claims on these people were integral to his claim not only to the khanship of his father but also to the Great Khanship of Lighdan. Both occurred after his defeat of the Chakhar Mongols and his formal claim to the succession of Chinggis and Khubilai. The basis for the claim was like the bases for the reorganization of the banners in Hung Taiji's time: that geocultural affiliations entail political identity. This was characteristic of Hung Taiji's uses of ideology of identities. In his explicit association of the integrity of the emperorship with the ascription of identity, Hung Taiji adumbrated the taxonomic ideology of the Qianlong era.

PART III
THE CELESTIAL PILLAR

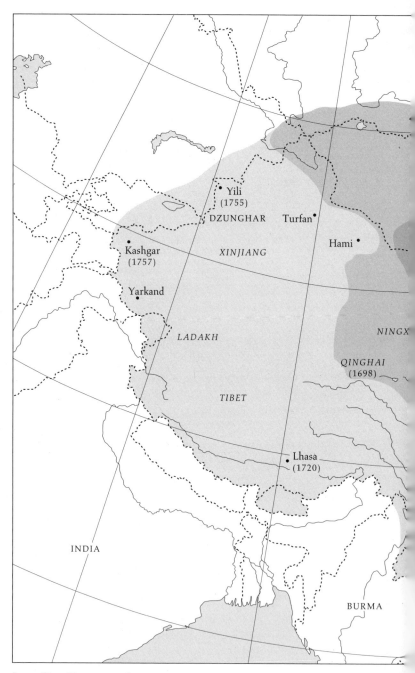

Later Qing Conquest, 1644–1750

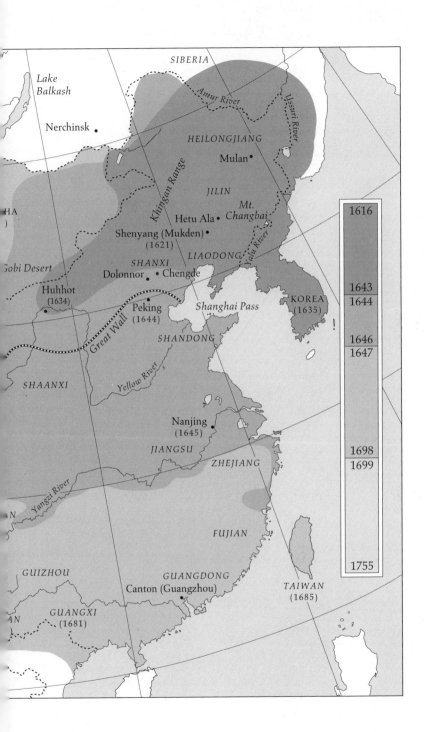

SIBERIA

Lake
Balkash

Nerchinsk .

Amur River

Ussuri River

HEILONGJIANG

Mulan•

Khingan Range

JILIN

Mt.
Hetu Ala • Changbai

Shenyang (Mukden)•
(1621)

LIAODONG

Yalu River

SHANXI

Gobi Desert

Dolonnor • • Chengde

Huhhot
(1634)

Great Wall

Peking
(1644)

Shanghai Pass

KOREA
(1635)

SHANDONG

SHAANXI

Yellow River

Nanjing
(1645)

JIANGSU

ZHEJIANG

Yangzi River

FUJIAN

GUIZHOU

GUANGDONG

Canton (Guangzhou)

TAIWAN
(1685)

GUANGXI
(1681)

1616
1643
1644
1646
1647
1698
1699
1755

UNDER HUNG TAIJI THE ESTABLISHMENT OF THE EMPERORSHIP
required transformation of Northeastern society and elite political culture. The conquest of China, Mongolia, and a large portion of Central Asia
can be seen as by-products of the imperializing process under Hung Taiji.
The essential geopolitical orientation of Hung Taiji's time—that China
would be a component, if a fundamental one, in the Qing empire—persisted and was, indeed, accentuated in the Qianlong era. A large part of
Turkestan and virtually all of Mongolia were conquered. The capital of
Tibet was brought under military occupation. Populations of south and
southwest China were subjected to unprecedented military and political
pressures. Tributary and "local headman" (*tusi*) systems, both adapted from
the Ming, were magnified in scope. The universalist pretensions of the emperorship were expressed in various ways, some of them long predating the
Qing period. As suggested by the reign title Qianlong ("supported by
Heaven," but also "Heaven's support"), the idea was a central, unique point
upon which depended, or from which radiated, meaning. Eventually Qing
imperial ideology wove many distinct but consonant images into its universalist cloth: the "pivot" in the classical image of "The Mean"; the metaphor of Geser as a central tent pole; the ancient royal image of the Chinese
king as the Pole Star; the Buddhist trope of King Ašoka as the point at
which the spokes of the wheel of time joined.

The Qianlong emperor's universalist ideology was distinctly centered
upon himself, as the sole point where all specifics articulated. He was a
grand impersonator, controlling cultures by incarnating them, commanding their moral centers through the conduct of their rituals. The Qing empire was universal because the Qianlong emperorship was culturally null,
and through his actions (including the commissioning of literature, architecture, painting, and portraiture) he brought reality and meaning to all
cultures. He was by these virtues a sage-king (*shengwang*), and he was the
unique "son of Heaven" (*tianzi, abka i jui*), the sole intercessor between
human cultures and their deities. But as words must be defined and their
usage clarified (and the Qianlong emperor was a great enthusiast of dictionary and encyclopedia projects), so must the cultures the emperor represents to Heaven be distinct, hierarchical, and historicized. He could not
incarnate peoples who were in their fundamental identities chaotic or ambiguous. Manchus, Mongols, and Chinese were to become whole and un-
corrupted exemplars of their "own" cultures. Not only historical literature—much of it new but given an implied classical pedigree by the "Four
Treasuries" (*siku quanshu*) process—but also educational programs and
administrative measures were applied to encourage bannermen in particu-

221

lar to adopt cultural lives based upon the genealogical identities attributed to them by state documentation. In its prescription that genealogical identity accord with cultural destiny, the Qianlong court institutionalized genealogical concepts and bequeathed to the nineteenth century both a literature of descent and a political imprimatur for racial thinking. Cultural knowledge became valued for its ability to complete the imperial universe through the contribution of symmetries and dichotomies. In the process, "Han," "Manchu," and "Mongol" identities were historicized anew, given documentary institutionalization and political status that would survive when the empire that affirmed them had crumbled.

5 The Wheel-Turning King

In the Qianlong period, conquest designs begun under the Kangxi (1662–
1722) and Yongzheng (1723–35) emperors were largely concluded. In *1736-95*
some cases this resulted in the establishment of lasting if not peaceful Qing
control, as in Inner Mongolia and eastern Turkestan (now the province of
Xinjiang). In other cases—for example, Tibet and regions of southwest
China—institutions of Qing dominion were planted but developed complex layers of accommodation with local patterns of government. In still
other instances, the expansion of the empire ground to a halt in failed campaigns that have been explained as results of mismanagement and corruption, poorly chosen targets, or a declining ability to direct resources from
one region of the empire to another. The explanations lie outside this work.
The relevant points are that over the long Qianlong reign, conquest came
gradually to a close, that the court in its later years made conscious expression of its sense of completion, of apex, of perfection that transcended
the very considerable territorial and economic sway of the empire. Nevertheless, Qianlong rhetoric tended not to describe the completeness of the
empire in terms of its territorial reach but in terms of the infinity at its center. Nurgaci and Hung Taiji had often invoked the length of their boundaries in their expositions on the size or importance of their domains; the
Shunzhi, Kangxi, and Yongzheng emperors had devoted considerable political energies and military resources to expansion of boundaries in Mongolia, Turkestan, and Tibet, while seeking to negotiate management of a
common border with the Romanov empire. The Kangxi emperor had point-
edly sponsored map-making enterprises and missions of exploration in Inner Asia and in the Northeast. Yet for the Qianlong emperor, the key was
not the physical boundaries themselves (though it would be a mistake to

claim that as a ruler he was casual about close management of border security, trade regulation, or customs income), but increasingly spectacular ways
of reflecting those boundaries through a central, transcendent looking glass.

Those explorers, mapmakers, and weapons manufacturers who had been
the foremost agents of the great imperial undertakings of the Kangxi era
were overshadowed in the Qianlong period by scribes, scholars, poets (all
ready to act, when necessary, as imperial amanuenses), painters, and archi-
tects. The militarism of the Kangxi and Yongzheng emperors had been one
aspect of their particularistic competition with other monarchs. When ad-
dressing the Chinese literate elites, the Kangxi emperor used his public
rhetorics, leaning heavily on a severely truncated "Confucian"[1] lexicon, to
characterize himself as a benevolent, peace-minded, humble monarch working toward a sagely kingship. To the peoples of the Khalkha region, he presented himself as successor to Chinggis Khaghan, and in Tibet he was the
Buddhist ruler and student of the master priests. Even to the Jesuits and
Dominicans he was eager to appear more worthy of their loyalties than the
popes or the European emperors. In combination with his military prowess
he used such pronouncements to campaign tirelessly to be preferred by the
Cossacks over Peter the Great, to be preferred by the Mongols to Galdan,
to be preferred by the Chinese literati to the Ming court (whether its ghost
or its scrawny pretender courts in the south). In contrast, the Qianlong emperor rarely betrayed an ambition to compete with another ruler, living
or dead. He cultivated the detached, impersonally benevolent, internally
satisfied and externally omnicompetent mien of the transcendent, universal ruler.

THE CENTER

As individuals, emperors were likely to entertain serious interests in arts,
philosophies, and religions. The Shunzhi emperor was renowned (and in
some quarters derided) for his deep interest in Buddhism; the Kangxi emperor was considered a serious student of Confucianism; the Yongzheng
and Qianlong emperors were both widely known to have devoted considerable study to Confucianism, Daoism, and Buddhism. Whether their personal attractions to philosophy and religion were deep or shallow, and their
accomplishments in theory and practice magisterial or negligible, is an is-

---

1. See qualifications of this term in Introduction.

sue distinct from the uses to which the emperorship put imagery and rhetoric supplied by these systems. Individuals have beliefs, individuals who are emperors may subscribe to them, and governments may for some reason or other encourage the expression of certain beliefs and discourage expression of others. It may even happen, as we explore below, that the personal concerns and ideations of an emperor may influence the expressive habits of the state. But the state does not believe.

Beyond the distinction between the beliefs and practices of an individual who is an emperor and applications a state may make of philosophical or religious rhetoric, there are further questions to underscore. One is the difference between philosophy and ideology; another is the relationship of either, both, or neither to "orthodoxy," or the policy of enforcing certain teachings as "correct." It is a commonly encountered statement that the Qing "dynasty" had a "neo-Confucian" or "Cheng-Zhu" orthodoxy. What is probably meant by this is that the Qing court had Zhu Xi's (1130–1200) "Four Books" translated into Manchu,[2] prescribed them and certain commentaries on them as the basic syllabus for the examinations in all languages, and did not interfere with examiners who rewarded responses conforming to favored commentaries; also, imperial decrees tended to feature reasoning on benevolent government that displayed a large number of allusions to the approved texts. The orthodoxy in question, then, was not a property of the state but of certain groups of literati—mostly working or aspiring bureaucrats—who were inclined to the received "Cheng-Zhu" interpretations, wished to impress them on others, and found their paths of expression smoothed by state policy. In fact, as will be discussed below, the Qing court, while continuing to employ generous doses of rhetorical bits derived from Zhu Xi in the eighteenth century, became rather chilled toward those expounding this "orthodoxy." No real change in the way normal imperial edicts in Chinese were styled occurred, however; there was no reason why it should, since the state does not believe.

The effects of misplacing "orthodoxy" onto the state instead of onto groups enjoying the encouragement of the state has obscured the issue of imperial ideology. As suggested in the Introduction, what is meant by "ideology" is the tendency of an individual or group to organize its sensations, or knowledge, in particular ways and to attempt to express the resulting ideas. In the case of the imperial courts, the expression was intended to be dominant, which could be achieved by the sheer mass of the publishing and

2. On the details of this, see Durrant, "Manchu Translations of Chou Dynasty Texts"; Crossley and Rawski, "A Profile"; and Hess, "The Manchu Exegesis."

enforcing capacities of the state but could also be aided by a certain coherence in the ideology itself. This coherence does not entail logical perfection but was in the Qing instance—perhaps as in other contemporary emperorships—based more upon reinforcing images, allusions, and resonances with a fundamental consistency of figuration. The successive Qing courts can certainly be shown to have used selected Confucian rhetoric in this way, but it was only one of several ideological vehicles employed in the characterization of the Qing mission and its legitimacy. Long before the Qing, emperors based in China had generous access to militant Confucian rhetoric. Justifications of imperial violence—whether in military campaigns against Chinese resisters of the conquest or against border peoples, or whether in political actions against civil enemies of the court—tended toward invocations from the Confucian lexicon: the Mandate of Heaven, the need for filiality in the populace, the manifest benevolence of the ruler, the goal of peace in the world. The Qing began from the first imperial years under Hung Taiji to adapt this idiom to their purposes. Indeed the public continuity in Confucian imperial speech was critical, since it fronted such a massive transition from the Ming to the Qing regimes.

There was an irony in the adaptation of a political philosophy which fundamentally opposed great concentrations of power to the rhetorical uses of militarily expansive, coercive government. Emperorship is considered to have appeared in China in 221 BCE, when the "First Emperor" (Shihuang) of the Qin put an end to the wars that had raged among the loosely federated and competing local "kingdoms" (*guo*) of the Later Zhou period (770–221 BCE). The First Emperor tossed the Confucians into pits, burned their books, and proceeded to create a large centralized state that professed few intentions other than strengthening its armies, filling its coffers, and enforcing its tax code, with no reference to ethical concerns that had been familiarized among the literati by Confucian/Mencian teaching. The new style of rulership, retrospectively characterized as "Legalist," was explicitly an instrument for the integration of a massive polity, subordination of regions to its capital, limitation or destruction of the discretionary privileges of a hereditary elite, and command of language, religion, and all economies—whether of time, energy, or exchange—by a central intelligence. Standardization (of demographic, geographical, financial, military, transportational, and even linguistic forms) was a format for centralization, and centralization (of authority in the hands of the emperor) obviated the roles that Confucian/Mencian political thought had constructed for the bureaucracy and the nobility. The First Emperor did not invent the tech-

niques of mutual surveillance, mutual liability, and decadenal restructur- *state*
ing of society, but he was the first to cement these instruments to the em- *machine*
perorship and its goals, for which he was periodically vilified by emperors
from Early Han (206 BCE–9 CE) on. The ideological advantages to the emperorships of having in the First Emperor an icon of authoritarianism to
condemn—frequently and sweepingly—are obvious. By never again es-
pousing Legalism as an official political philosophy, emperors from Wudi
of the Han (r. 141–87 BCE) to the Kangxi and Qianlong emperors of the
Qing who were in fact enthusiastic about centralization and coercion de-
flected, at least on the rhetorical level, charges of centralization and coercion to which they might have been liable.

State rhetoric established by the Han (202 BCE–9 CE; 23–220)[3] and used *selective*
by nearly all succeeding empires in China—based upon the select empha- *use of*
sis upon a few Confucian phrases and texts, while vigorously employing *Conf.*
the state techniques developed and defended by the rivals of the Confucians—has been described by some scholars as "imperial Confucianism,"
a deliberate oxymoron. Though authoritarian, the empires could claim the
intention on the part of rulers and civil servants to guard the welfare of the
common people and to seek their moral improvement. And if fundamentally opposed to centralized, authoritarian, militaristic government, the
styles of Later Zhou thought now considered "Confucian" had at least one *e.g.*
thing in common (as it were) with it: a hostility to communities. That is to *=*
say that the imperial institution was hostile to the formation of solidarities *communities*
based on common descent, common age, common gender, common status, *threaten*
common habitat, common religion, common proximity, common skills, *by*
common pastimes, common occupation, common avarice, common secu- *Emp*
rity, common recreation, common indebtedness, or common dissoluteness.
Such organizations existed through Chinese history, but the imperial government (to simplify for a moment) is seen constantly attempting to bring
them under its sponsorship and regulation, and to blur the line between
state organizations and social organizations by shifting responsibility for
the provision of resources onto social ground (for instance, local charitable
or defense associations, lineages, and households) while attempting to attract to itself power to recognize, legitimate, reorganize, and otherwise

3. It is slightly unfair to conflate the earlier Han and Later Han (ignoring the
Wang Mang period) under the rubric of "one" empire, but I hope specialists will
agree that the differences among the regimes are not germane to the present
discussion.

manipulate the status of such groups, retaining the capacity to neutralize them as challengers to the ideological, political, or financial preeminence of the court.

This confluence of interest between the ruler and Confucian theorists against solidarities had been appreciated in the Later Zhou period by kings and princes (either could translate *wang*) eager to hasten the disappearance of the last vestiges of aristocratic obstruction to centralized rule and the emergence of larger states. The rigid hierarchies and the prescription of "five relationships" (*wu lun*)—importantly, five substances, and not merely five directions, of relationships—within the household explicitly excluded from legitimacy any level orientation of one individual to another. Instead, each person stood in a special relationship to any other individual. The central idea distinguishing Confucian political thought of the pre-imperial era was that this model of household cohesion should be the template for all political relationships. Under the influence of imperial Confucianism, the construction of familial relations changed from symmetrical to asymmetrical, reinforcing hierarchies and snaring every individual in the "bonds" (*gang*) of state-defined obligations. The relationships originally described in early texts (one usually cites "The Mean," *Zhongyong*) had been reciprocal: Between father and son there should be affection (*qin*), between prince and minister righteousness (*yi*), between husband and wife discretion (*bie*), between the old and the young order (*xu*), between friends trust (*xin*). A post-imperial imposition led to a sanctioned interpretation of relations in which superiors (sovereigns, fathers, elder brothers) were benevolent (*ren*) to their inferiors, while male inferiors had—depending on their social status and degree of education—to master a variety of relationship-specific qualities ("loyalty" [*zhong*], "filiality" [*xiao*], and "fraternal deference" [*ti*]) and women were generally "subservient" (*cong*) to everybody.[4]

---

4. See also Hsü Dau-lin, "The Myth of the 'Five Human Relations' of Confucius." A suggestion that I read as in agreement with my suggestion here is to be found in Tu, *Centrality and Commonality*, esp. 54–51, where the original codes of the *Zhongyong*, which Tu calls a prescription for "dyadic" relationships, are acknowledged to have received an interpretation in imperial times and after that been systematically distorted toward hierarchical authoritarianism. A code of relationships cannot be attributed to Confucius, who argued only for authenticity of affection and function. The transformation of ideals of relationship from symmetrical to asymmetrical may, in the earlier imperial period, have owed much to the influence of an imperially favored *yinyang* exegesis, particularly in the hands of Dong Zhongshu (179–104 BCE) and Ban Gu (32–92). Institutionalization of these relationships as central to "Confucian" social ideology had been initiated under the Mongols but was completed under the Ming.

As a theory of households, and of the household as the model for all political relations, Confucian rhetoric later came increasingly into accord with the disposition of a centralizing emperorship.

Historically, the centripetal tendencies of emperorship were obstructed by many factors in many periods. Nobilities were relatively strong in Han, Tang, and Yuan times. There have been whole ages of emperors dominated by eunuchs, by regents, by usurpers. And truly centralized, authoritarian emperorships have tended, with a few well-known exceptions, to be brief. But the essential hostility of the imperial institution to the communities surrounding it was not compromised. From later Tang times forward, as we supposedly see the intensifying despotism in the emperorship, we see also a more arch commitment to imperial Confucianism, of which the centerpiece was the Mongol Yuan court's enshrinement—in response to repeated petitions from literati of central China—of Zhu Xi's philosophy as "orthodox" in 1313. The Yuan court did not specify its reasons for making Zhu Xi's interpretations of Confucian literature the standard for the examinations and for the imperial lectures. Nor did subsequent regimes explicitly state their reasons for accepting this imposition (which was very temporarily abandoned in the early Ming, possibly as a reaction against the Mongol interference it was construed to represent). But if the content of examinations in the seventeenth and eighteenth centuries is any clue, those imperial prefaces in which the prescribed "Confucian" works—now identified as the "Four Books" that Zhu Xi had established in his syllabus—are cited suggest that the Qing court, at least, was charmed by Zhu Xi's rhetorical "dualism." I am not referring here to the dualism of Zhu Xi's metaphysics which is fundamental to his "rationalism," but to his marked and forceful use of dualistic metaphor. Especially important in this regard was his way of allegorizing the relations of moral mind (*daoxin*) to human mind (*renxin*), in which the former conquers, rules, and even enslaves the latter. The ideological result is the construction of subject-object relations between the emperorship and its domain. Morality consists in the ruler's fidelity to the desires of Heaven, and in the loyalty of followers (whom, as already discussed, Qing rhetoric already represented as slaves) to the ruler.

The commitment to Zhu Xi as "orthodox," then, is best thought of as a commitment to Zhu Xi as a rhetorical resource, represented in the "Four Books" (a very limited exposure, at best, to pre-imperial thought and open to interpretation as corrupted) and his commentaries on them. That the empires of the early modern period in China had no significant interest in the intentions of Zhu Xi's thought could be illustrated in a number of ways, but in the interest of focusing on the Qianlong period we might examine the blunt conflict between Zhu Xi's ideas on sagehood and the ideology promoted, more or less subtly, by the Qing court. The primary issue was "moral" mind—specifically, who has it, how it works, and how it manifests itself through action upon "human" mind.[5] This hinged, during the eighteenth century (and was vividly reflected in the content of the examinations) upon discourse relating to moral (*daotong*) as contrasted to coercive (*zhitong*) government. The Qing contention, to the degree that it can be reduced to a sentence, was that it was not merely that knowledge of governance (the province of the ministers) had been preserved through China's imperial history but that the virtual consciousness of sagely kingship had been transmitted to the Qing rulers. "The Mean," like others of the "Four Books," had been translated into Manchu at Hung Taiji's orders (though not completed until 1652), and in a memorial of 1632 explaining the value of this for Manchus, he had asserted that it contained "the subtle principles of the doctrine by which an emperor governs and pacifies."[6] In the Qianlong era, this idea was as urgently endorsed as in earlier emperorships and had become casually embedded in the culture of bureaucratic education. As a top essayist of 1751 put it, "the way of the sage kings . . . reappeared in the unified mind of the emperor."[7] Sagehood (and the moral mind of the polity) was thus exclusive to the emperor; moreover, the "outwardly royal and inwardly sagely" (*waiwang neisheng*) formulation so often encountered in examinations reserved sagehood only for the sage-kings of ancient times, which by implication denied a generative moral voice to Confucius himself.

It is not surprising that a favored authority for the court position on this was Zheng Xuan (127–200), a commentator of the Later Han period—that

5. On the interplay of these questions with the civil examinations in the eighteenth century, see Elman, *A Cultural History of Civil Examinations*, Chapter 8.
6. Hess, "The Manchu Exegesis," 402, quotes Durrant, "The Early Chou Texts." The first translation into Manchu was accomplished by Asitan (d. 1683 or 1684), working under the direction of Miao Cheng (fl. 1644–61); see Durrant, "The Early Chou Texts" and Crossley and Rawski, "A Profile." The "Four Books" were also published in a "daily instruction" edition for the emperor and princes, with an introduction by Xuanye, in 1677; that work was revised and republished in 1756.
7. Elman and Woodside, eds., *Education and Society*, 140–41, reflecting B. A. Elman's original conference paper of 1989. Though prior to the Qing a large body of commentary, much of it generated by those close to the examination system, had developed the idea of a transmitted mentality of rulership (in Elman's phrase the "thought-world" of the ancient sage kings), this was usually assumed to be associated with techniques of education, cultivation, or transmission that occurred between a ruler and his successor. The Qing idea of reincarnation or "appearance" is implied in the commentaries, but distinctive.

is, from the period of early refinement of imperial Confucianism. Zheng's commentaries on the issue of exclusive sageliness in kings had been repeatedly overruled by Zhu Xi but had been in favor in the early Ming (when the Hongwu court rejected Zhu Xi's Mongol-imposed "orthodoxy"). From the early fourteenth century—that is, from the accession of the self-styled *pādīshāh* of the Ming, the Yongle emperor—however, Zhu Xi was raised and Zheng Xuan was lowered, until the latter's tablet was removed from the "scholar's temple" (*wenmiao*) of the imperial city in 1530. But Zheng's place was reestablished under the Qing. In the late 1680s the Kangxi court entertained a petition from Zhu Yizun (who was at the same time also proposing a set of collected statutes that would standardize lineage practices in the empire) advocating that Zheng Xuan's tablet be restored to the scholar's temple. A call for literati opinion was not issued until 1724, in the Yongzheng reign, but the result was that in 1753, at the order of the Qianlong court, Zheng was indeed reestablished among the intellectual immortals.[8] Zheng Xuan on the one hand and Zhu Xi on the other emblemized the two sides of a debate on the spiritual transcendence of emperorship that predated the Qing but would intensify in the seventeenth and eighteenth centuries. A frequent point of contention was the passage from "The Mean" on the "trinity," a passage very close to the heart of the Qing ideology:

> Only the most sincere in the world can completely manifest his nature. Only those who can completely manifest their natures can completely manifest the nature of human beings. And only those who can completely manifest the nature of human beings can manifest the nature of all things. Those who can completely manifest the nature of all things can in this way implement the transforming and nurturing powers of Heaven and Earth. Those who implement the transforming and nurturing powers of Heaven and Earth can stand in a trinity with Heaven and Earth.[9]

8. Kai-wing Chow, *The Rise of Confucian Ritualism*, 182–84.

9. From *Zhongyong*, chapter 22. I have based my translation on, first, the vernacular rendering in *Sishu baihua jujie*, 45, which is otherwise unannotated; and on Shimada, *Daigaku • Chūyō* 2:150–151, which closely corresponds to the traditional vernacular renderings in Chinese, but with citation to earlier glossaries. For a slightly different translation see Wing-tsit Chan, *A Source Book*, 107–8 (I hardly agree that the differences between the Zheng Xuan and Zhu Xi interpretations are "immaterial"). I should make these comments for those unfamiliar with the original: the word I have translated as "completely manifest" is, literally, to exhaust, to deplete (*jin*). It means to use without reserve, to leave nothing unexploited, ungenerated, untransformed. It is not the same as, and may in fact contrast to, the meanings of "complete, fulfill" as familiarly expressed by the word *cheng* in ancient Chinese texts; but I see the ideas as complementary and so have translated

Zheng Xuan had argued that this power of transformation and ability to constitute a trinity with Heaven and Earth belonged to the ruler exclusively. Zhu Xi had argued that it applied to sages—which any self-cultivating man had the hope of becoming. On this point Zhu Xi, and those cleaving to his interpretations, were passionate, since sagehood was their avenue to salvation. Zheng Xuan had also claimed that a son showed filiality to his dead father not by following his will (or stated instructions), but by following his moral intuition (*dao*), which in Qing times was taken as the meaning of moral rule (*daotong*)—the transmission of generative moral consciousness down the lineage of emperors. Gu Yanwu had attacked this idea, along with Zheng's scholarship on lineage rituals generally, in writings known in the seventeenth century. Later the objection was taken up by Wan Sitong, who complained that Zheng had displaced ancestors as the ceremonial objects and substituted for them the abstract authority of Heaven (whom the emperors exclusively addressed and represented).[10] Zheng, in other words, had consistently claimed sagely authority for the ruler alone, which Zhu Xi and his later sympathizers abhorred as a usurpation as well as an uprooting of the relationship of the past (or at least the dead) and the present.

As seen in Chapters 2 and 4, the Qing were quick to avail themselves of the imperial Confucian lexicon as they established their rule in China. But it was critically important that they had at hand a second, equally well-developed rhetoric of aggressive emperorship, which with complex alterations could be used in regions where imperial Confucianism had little influence. Like pre-imperial Confucian thought, Buddhism was in its fundamentals a belief system that was indifferent to, if not actually hostile toward, the state. And like Confucianism, it over the long term was milked for an ideology that supported centralized and expansive rule. Until the end of the Yuan empire in China, this experimentation with Buddhist ideology was open and relied to a great extent, in the early period (Northern Wei) particularly, upon the cross-identification of Confucian, Daoist, and Buddhist rhetorical elements. For various reasons, this aspect of imperial self-representation became more obscure in the post-Yuan period.

The history of Buddhism as a source of imperial ideology is different from a general history of Buddhism in China. Buddhism provided to Chi-

---

what in English could sound very negative ("deplete") in terms of the result of the depletion: manifestation.

10. Kai-wing Chow, *The Rise of Confucian Ritualism*, 140–43. See Liu Danian, "Lun Kangxi," for the context of the Kangxi emperor's antipathy to Wan and the scholars retrospectively associated with the "Tongcheng school."

nese—indeed, East and Southeast Asian—rulers several attractive ideas linking earthly power to holy ends. Earliest were the Deva kings, which could be invoked for protection of the state. The motivation of the Deva kings, however, tended—though it was not an absolute requirement, since the Law (*dharma*) is wiser than any human—to be linked to the spiritual condition of the monarch. Like imperial Confucianism, Buddhism provided kings and emperors with missions. As the Confucian monarch was to bring human-mindedness under the control of moral-mindedness, to transform all through himself, and to pacify the world, the Buddhist monarch was to effect change in human destiny by spreading the doctrines of Enlightenment, bringing the secular age to a close, and ending misery by directing all toward bliss. For the ruler to have such pure intentions, he was unlikely to be understood as remaining in a rude human state. It was soon an axiom of Buddhist imperial ideology that the ruler was, in addition to his peculiar spiritual mission, also in a peculiar spiritual condition: he was a "wheel-turning king" (or "center-turning king") and possibly also an "enlightened one," himself ready for bliss, but postponing it to aid in the salvation of mankind. In China from the Northern Wei period to the end of the Tang, Buddhism combined with Daoism to provide imperial concepts that reinforced those already established in state Confucian rhetoric. A wellspring of this political function was the process of the translation of Buddhist texts into Chinese. Though practices changed as generations of monks became more sophisticated in this task, the early translations were done in an atmosphere of seeking equivalent words for Buddhist concepts from the philosophical vocabularies of Confucianism and Daoism (which were not always in disagreement with each other on cosmological hermeneutics). Imperial courts were quick to find the points at which Confucian sageliness could be identified with Buddhist saintliness (neither at that time being firmly established as imperial attributes in China). By the fourth century Buddhist proponents were proclaiming an additional equivalence in political meaning, and political fortunes, between Buddhism and Confucianism. Like Confucian sagehood (which would be realized, according to some Confucian scholars of this period, in only very rare instances), *bodhisattva*-hood made the emperor unlike other men and gave his mission the special Buddhist pathos of bliss denied (or postponed from) the self, for the purpose of the salvation of mankind.

This *bodhisattva* imagery for the ruler became important in the Tang period but was politically complex. Theravāda Buddhism, which prevailed in Southeast Asia and some other regions that emperors based in China would have liked to impress, did not recognize the *bodhisattva* condition.

In those areas of Central Asia and Northern Asia influenced by Mahāyāna Buddhism imported from India, *bodhisattvas* were too common. Local gods were readily absorbed into Buddhism as *bodhisattvas*, local notables became centers of *bodhisattva* cults, and among the plethora of *bodhisattvas* in the Mahāyāna lore were to be found few individuals of elevated earthly status, let alone emperors; most were poverty-bound itinerants, reputedly with no interest in earthly affairs. Still, in the early Tang period imperial *bodhisattva*-hood became a necessary though not sufficient element in the imperial ideology.[11] The establishment of Buddhism as a court-favored religion led to many political tensions. By the middle ninth century the Tang emperors and the Chinese literati were combined in an effort to oppose Buddhist political influence and limit, to the extent it was practicable, its effects on society and popular culture. This was not successful, either in a general sense or at the level of the literati; the eagerness to respond to Buddhism, anticipated by Han Yu and others of his generation, legitimated an incorporation of Buddhist philosophy into "Confucian" discourse, helping to give rise to the speculative cosmology and salvation theory that is known in English as "neo-Confucianism." In the aftermath of the political suppression of Buddhism and dissolution of the monasteries in the later Tang, *bodhisattva* representations of the emperors were infrequently regarded as appropriate when addressed to the Chinese public.

A more powerful, and explicitly imperial, Buddhist concept was that of the "wheel-turner" (*cakravartin*)—also "wheel-turning king" (*cakravartirāja*). The title does not distinguish between a center (*cakra*) and those concepts to which a center is indispensable: wheels, flowers (the lotus in particular), time, and space (both of which have Mt. Meru [Sumeru] at their shared center). All Buddhist rulers of the middle ages and later saw themselves as successors of Aśoka, historicized as the first wheel-turning king.[12] This was more than a general understanding that the goal of his regime was to spread Enlightenment. The wheel-turning conceit became locally differentiated, accompanied by various rituals, icons, and political patterns. In Southeast Asia, for instance, chakravartinism (in the context of Theravāda Buddhism) in the ruler was associated with what Stanley Tambiah has described as a "galactic" state. It is possible that Singhalese

11. Kang Le, "Zhuanlun wang guannian yu Zhongguo gudai de fojiao zhengzhi," 132–37.
12. This was the sectarian historicization imposed upon Aśoka. In his own time he expressed himself in terms of solidarity with the Buddhist community but never characterized himself as their instrument or as a monarch devoted—in his political person—to any individual religion. See Thapar, *A History of India*, 70–75.

ideas of Buddhist kingship were instrumental in reinforcing notions of chakravartinism in China in the fourth century. If so, it was incidental to the development of a strong, local complex of ideas in early medieval China relating to *cakravartin* rulership. This was founded on an imperial narrative for Ašoka, claiming him as the earthly agent who had unified the "world"— here the mythical continent Jambudvīpa—and instituted justice and bliss as agent of the Buddha.[13] This implied that China had been, anciently, Buddhist (in some accounts, converted by a daughter of Ašoka). Statuary and other remnants of Ašoka's rule were claimed to have been recovered, proving that Buddhism was not a foreign religion introduced by barbarians, but a universal truth that had been eclipsed by the political catastrophes of the later Han period. Like *bodhisattva* representations of the ruler, *cakravartin* language also went out of fashion for public presentation of emperors after the late Tang, though various forms of Buddhist practice were to be found in the personal spheres of emperors in the Song and Ming periods.

Parallel to these Buddhist imperial ideologies in China were several distinct trends of Inner and Central Asia. It is possible, though unproved, that Central Asia as far north as the empire of the Xiongnu was affected by the spread of Buddhist proselytizing in the time of Ašoka and his immediate successors.[14] Certainly Buddhist influence was very strong in the region of modern Afghanistan and eastern Iran, which were in regular contact with China via the silk roads. By one or both of these means it reached the regions of Turkic dominance in Central Asia and there combined with other influences—possibly Iranian in origin—to produce an ideology of universal Buddhist rule. Over the centuries this tradition, regarded by some scholars as a distinct variety of Buddhist imperial ideology,[15] took many forms, and generalization is risky. But, as it must be attempted, one might characterize it this way: Where developing Buddhist ideologies of rulership in South Asia and in Eastern Asia regarded the emperor as the means by which the teachings of Enlightenment would be disseminated among humanity, this Central Asian idea proposed universal rulership as an end that in itself would merit Buddha's blessing and somehow redound to the general benefit of mankind. Patronage of the teachings was important, as was recognition of the Buddhist clergy by the ruler. But the legitimation of

moving from the emp as a means to the emp as the end

13. Probably originating in the *Ayuwang zhuan, Ayuwang jing,* and other works produced by Chinese Buddhists from the third century on (Zürcher, *The Buddhist Conquest of China,* 277–80).

14. Moses, *The Political Role of Mongol Buddhism,* 13–17.

15. Moses, *The Political Role,* 14; Eberhard, *Conquerors and Rulers,* 146.

universal rule—in which Buddhism actually plays a role in concert with shamanism and an evident Zoroastrian influence—was the primary goal.[16] The late medieval reflections of this Central Asian tradition, particularly in the ideology of the Mongol empires, can be difficult to sort out. Though it is clear, for instance, that the rulers of the Liao empire of the Kitans were all Buddhist, the content of their imperial ideology is not well attested. It may have been a survival of the *bodhisattva* and *cakravartin* notions that had permeated the Tang (the Kitans liked to think of themselves as successors to the Tang in many areas relating to imperial culture). Though some elements of rulership under the Mongols can be traced to the Kitans, Buddhist imperial ideology does not seem to form one of these links. A more interesting possible link is through the Buddhist imperial ideology of the Xi Xia state of the Tanguts, who were at the interstices of Tibetan, Chinese, and Central Asian traditions.[17] Very likely there were at least two localized sources of the Buddhist elements of Mongol imperial ideology. The first was evidently the residual Buddhist elements, including the emphasis on universal dominion, in Turkic Central Asia. The second was a direct, and slightly better documented, influence from the Sakya clerics of Tibet.

In explaining the character of this second ideological influence, there is some difficulty in defining what "Tibetan" in this era was. The spectrum of Tibetan cultures stretched from Mongolia and Turkestan to southwest China, northeast India, Nepal, Burma, and Southeast Asia. In these regions, as in the Tibetan plateau, there were many religions, most sharing the imprint of early shamanic beliefs, overlaid with identifiable influences from Zoroastrian/Manicheanism, Buddhism, and—in some regions, and much later—Islam. Tantric practices—favoring the use of incantations (*dhāranī*) and spirit communications for the effecting of mundane as well as spiritual well-being—had developed as an aspect of early Buddhist teaching in India, and when Buddhist influence came to Tibet by various routes, the tantric elements found easy resonance with earlier religious ideas. The result was a cosmology that incorporated Zoroastrian ideas of eternal battle between gods and their enemies, the *asura*, in which the gods appealed constantly to Buddha for aid; in which the emanations of Buddha, which had been part of early Buddhist belief and were at least partly an inheritance from Hinduism, supplied elements of anger and violence necessary to protect the

16. See Turan, "The Ideal of World Domination among the Ancient Turks."
17. For background see Dunnell, *The Great State of White and High.*

Mazdean. overprint wɪн Budd - Tibetan style

righteous, or tenderness and brilliance to inspire them; and manifestations of Buddha demarcated the past of ignorance from the future of universal salvation.[18] At about the time the Tang empire had attempted suppression of Buddhism in the middle ninth century, a similar campaign by the king of Tibet had had an opposite result: The clergy had assumed rule of the country. Afterward, rivalries for power among the sects could be calamitous. By the time Chinggis Khaghan had established his empire in the thirteenth century, the tantric Sakya—one of the so-called Red Hat sects—had established themselves as politically supreme in eastern Tibet. When the Mongol troops under Godan attempted, for strategic reasons, to take Tibetan territory, they came face to face with the politically aggressive Sakya sect. Tibetan monks under Sakya Pandita went straight to the Mongol Great Khan, Möngke (whom European missionaries thought they were on the verge of converting to Christianity), and argued for protection under the universal authority of the empire. Möngke, evidently not without some gentleness, explained to the disappointed Europeans that he would remain above religion; they were right in asserting that there was one god, but wrong in arguing for one religion. The emperor, he explained, would be addressed by all believers (he demonstrated that the hand consists of five fingers); and he would address God alone. In this case, the Tibetan argument may have counterbalanced the European argument, but the outcome was more like the generalized imperial ideology of Central Asia than the Tibetan pattern. By contrast, the arrangement between Khubilai Khaghan— *Khubilai Khaghan - (Yuan)* the last of the Mongol Great Khans and founder of the Yuan empire based in China—and the *lama* P'agpa ('Phags pa, nephew of Sakya Pandita) was *Mongol politics & religion* distinctly Tibetan. It was characterized by an assumption of two realms, one of sacred action and one of secular action.[19] They were bridged by the practice of initiation, for the purpose of instilling in the emperor the actual consciousness of a Buddha emanation (some discussion was expended upon which emanation would best suit the circumstances) who would make his rule more effective and more righteous. More important is the relevance of the initiation ritual for imperial ideology. It demarcated the *lama* as the teacher and the avenue to contact with the Buddha-consciousness. At the same moment, the emperor was the object of the teacher's ministrations

18. For a general discussion of these doctrines, see Tucci, *The Religions of Tibet*, 47–109.

19. The source of much of this thinking was the "White History" (*Chaghan teüke*), parts of which date from the twelfth century. See Sagaster, *Die Weisse Geschichte*, and Grupper, "Review of Sagaster." See also Introduction, n 75.

Khubilai

and thereafter the earthly instrument of Buddha's intentions. Unlike the accommodation with Buddhism under Möngke, Khubilai's posited a mutual dependency, and unified identity, of the *lama* and the *cakravartin*.

After the fall of the Yuan empire in 1370, sporadic campaigns of reunification by leaders in Mongolia catalyzed development of a more tightly structured imperial cult.[20] When the Tümed leader and aspiring Great Khan Altan dominated the eastern alliance, he invited Songnam Gyamtso (bSodnams rGya-mtsho), an elder of the reformed Gelug (dGe-lugs pa) or "Yellow Hat" sect,[21] to eastern Mongolia and also requested printed lamaist literature from the Ming—who supplied it, believing that religious conversion would soothe the savage breasts of the peoples of Mongolia. Subsequently Altan Khaghan endowed the Yellow Hat leader with the title *dalai* (in Mongolian, "oceanic," "universal") *lama* ("teacher," in Tibetan). In ensuing years, rivalries between the Red Hat and the Yellow Hat sects further differentiated *cakravartin* ideologies, liturgies, and ritual practices.[22] Yellow Hat sects became the more widespread, but the older Red Hat sects retained influence, particularly through the development of the imperial cult of Mahākāla,[23] which continued for a time to depend upon Tibetan texts, language, and acknowledgment of Lhasa as spiritual center for legitimation of Mongol leadership. But regardless of sectarian specializations, spiritual companionship between the "teacher" (*lama*) and the *cakravartin* was intertwined with the right to rule Mongolia.

Nurg — + Buddh.

As suggested in Chapters 3 and 4, it appears that Nurgaci was exposed to some influence from Red Hat missionaries, probably based in eastern Mongolia, before 1596, and that by the time he had conquered and established his base in Liaodong, he had assumed the role of patron of at least one Red Hat establishment near Mukden. In 1636, two years after the destruction of Lighdan's regime among the Chakhar and assumption of his

---

20. Grupper, "The Manchu Imperial Cult," 4, 28. I am not as confident here as is Grupper that the issue is "Mongol absolutism," or "autocracy," as he comments elsewhere, though it is clear to me—and Grupper's work is essential in this inquiry—that emperorship as an absolute was an issue.

21. dGe-lugs ("Enlightened") Lamaism, also called "Yellow Hat" (as opposed to the "Red Hat" Sakya sect) or Reformed Lamaism, originated in the teachings of the Tibetan priest Tsong-kha-pa (1357–1419). The reform called for revitalization of monastic life, rejection of some older tantric teachings, and the pursuit of individual *bodhisattva*-hood. Reformed Lamaism struggled successfully for dominance in Tibet from the time of Tsong-kha-pa to the seventeenth century.

22. Tucci, *The Religions of Tibet*, 39–46.

23. For a study of the cult see Grupper, "The Manchu Imperial Cult."

symbols of rule, Hung Taiji invested himself as emperor with the attendance of Tibetan clerics, probably Red Hat, and during his reign the very
large set of temples, with Mahākāla at the center, was constructed at the new
capital. Tibetan cult objects were introduced into the Aisin Gioro temple in
Mukden well before the conquest of north China, and patronage of Yellow
Sect temples and monasteries is documented from 1639; this was followed
in 1642 by the first mission to the Manchus directly from the court of the
Dalai Lama. After the Qing occupation of north China, the relationship
with the Dalai Lamas was reinforced by at least two more embassies from
Lhasa, and in 1651 the regents for the Shunzhi emperor Fulin were successful in formalizing a ruler-teacher relationship during the Dalai Lama's
visit to Peking. Such recognition by the Dalai Lama was central to Qing
claims to rule Mongolia, and the Qing in return affirmed—until the eighteenth century—the Dalai Lama as spiritual leader of Mongolia and Tibet.[24]
Subsequent Qing rulers proved generous patrons of many Buddhist sects,
and both the Shunzhi and Yongzheng emperors were believed to be partial to Chan doctrines. But they continued to show a strong interest in
lamaisms—indeed the Yongzheng emperor gave the palace (Yonghe gong)
in which the future Qianlong emperor was born to the Yellow Hat sect to
use as a lamasery in 1722. Through the Qing period the daily schedule of
rituals at the Kunning Palace of the Forbidden City encompassed shamanic
as well as diverse Buddhist cults, including at least two varieties of lamaism.
The intimacy of lamaist doctrines to the imperial lineage was vividly expressed in the practice of draping the coffins of emperors and empresses,
exclusively, with red silk covers in which Sanskrit *dhāranī* (in the nineteenth
century accompanied by some Chinese prayers) were stitched in gold.

Among the lamaist sects with which the Qing court kept constant contact, the Mahākāla cultists had a special place. At the court of Lighdan,
from which the Mahākāla rituals were taken, the cult had proclaimed itself
as a continuation of the original relationship, beginning with the initiation,
between Khubilai and Pagpa. There is no particular evidence to prove this
is the case; but the authority in eastern Mongolia which the cult commanded
as an aspect of continuing rule of the Great Khans was very considerable,
and Hung Taiji quickly made himself the center of its liturgy. The site of
the Mahākāla complex at Mukden was carefully chosen and richly endowed,
containing a golden image of Mahākāla that had been transported to the

24. See also Zhao Yuntian, *Qingdai Menggu*, 234–47.

site by the family of Lighdan. Hung Taiji personally led visiting Jurchen and Khorchin dignitaries there on many occasions (though Nikans were not permitted to attend). After the conquest of China the Qing emperors continued to elaborate the site. In 1694 the Kangxi emperor had the image of Mahākāla transported to Peking, where it became part of a new temple complex in the southeast corner of the Imperial City (south of present-day Donghuamen Street). In the next century the Qianlong emperor had a plaque erected with his own calligraphy (an obsession with him) within the grounds of the Mukden temple complex, describing it as "garden of the gold that mirrors all," and in 1777 the monks there received from the Qianlong court an "Ode to the Temple of the Dharma" (*Falun si fu*). The new complex in Peking included a monastery for the exclusive residence and training of Mongol monks, who in fact recited the liturgies of the sect in Mongolian until the demolition of the temple in the early twentieth century.

The choice of the Mahākāla cult was dictated by circumstance. This cult was the central means of legitimation in Mongolia for those claiming the authority of the Mongol Great Khans, it had been a prized possession of Lighdan, and Hung Taiji had been determined to take it for both these reasons. The peculiar association of the Mahākāla cult with the claim to rule Mongolia was plain in the dedication of the Kangxi complex at Peking to the recitation and printing of Mongolian liturgies. Yet the associations of the Mahākāla persona must be noted. Mahākāla was a clear inspiration of the Hindu deity Šiva that had been adopted as a Buddhist fearsome spirit, handy at protecting Buddhist rulers, monastic institutions, spiritual leaders, and the gentler Buddha manifestations with which Mahākāla often kept company (particularly Avalokiteśvara). He had become, under the name Gompo, a favorite demon fighter and protecting spirit of the Red Hat monasteries in Tibet. He also had a special association with death; he appears in the Tibetan "Book of the Dead" (*Bardö thodöl*) as one of the psychopomps conducting souls toward judgment, and like Yamantaka and Cakrasamvara, is often depicted in proximity to skulls, weapons, and monsters. Mahākāla is in short a war god in heavy Buddhist trappings. Others of these fearsome spirits had, like Mahākāla, intensely tantric cults with elaborate initiations and powerful advantages conferred through the teacher-initiate relationship. In the case of the Qianlong emperor, there were several tantric initiations—clearly that of Mahākāla, through which he received the consciousness(es) of Tang Taizong, Chinggis Khaghan, Khubilai Khaghan, and Hung Taiji, but also the cult into which he was initiated by his personal teacher, the Gelug adept Janggiya (lCangs skya Khutukhtu Rol pa'i rdo rje, 1717–

86) *khutukhtu*.[25] It helps in understanding the general themes of the imperial literature, art, and architecture of the Qianlong period to know that the central idea of Gelug teaching is luminosity (*sems*), the pervasive universal intelligence, accessible through instruction, that makes "Enlightenment" possible.[26] It takes its basic qualities from the ancient concept—possibly predating Buddhism, but certainly pervading the early texts—of *šunyāta*, usually translated "emptiness." But what it more precisely means is the quality of being undifferentiated and without actions (the literal meaning, too, of the Chinese *wuwei*). For the Qianlong emperor as a Gelug initiate, this essential nullity was the only absolute, which is to say the only reality. The purpose of his religious instruction was, in the words of G. Tucci, "to overcome the world of relativity," and as a *bodhisattva* the emperor's identifying mark was commitment to work for the salvation of others. As a *cakravartin*, the vessel of the intuitions of the greatest emperors, the object of the protecting spirit of Mahākāla, and a *bodhisattva* working for the most humane goals, the Qianlong emperor could affirm through his Buddhist expression the same notion of having access to the *dao* of the sage-kings that had been indicated in the court's favored interpretation of the Chinese classics.

But the expression of this spiritual centrality was necessarily subtle. David Farquhar, in discussing the *bodhisattva* role of the Qianlong emperor, commented upon imperial "discretion." Though he could show by circumstantial documentation that the Qing emperors were acknowledged by the Mongols as *bodhisattvas* and in fact played the role of *bodhisattva* in their relations with the Mongols, Farquhar could find no document in which the emperor named himself as *bodhisattva*—it seemed mystical indirection was essential to the efficacious representation of the *bodhisattva* incarnation.[27] Farquhar did, however, discover a text of sorts, a visual representation from the imperial collection, of the *bodhisattva* Manjušri (the emanation of erudition, usually shown holding a book, and associated with China), whose face was a posthumous portrait of the Qianlong emperor. The significance of the scene depicted and the representation of the person of the Qianlong emperor were far more powerful invocations of the *bodhisattva*-hood of

25. Manchu *hutuktu*, Tibetan *trulku*, an incarnate lama (for explanation see Samuel, *Civilized Shamans*, 281–86). On the Qianlong emperor's initiation under Janggiya Khutukhtu see Rawski, *The Last Emperors*, 252–53; 256–57.
26. Tucci, *The Religions of Tibet*, 69–73.
27. Farquhar, "Emperor as Boddhisattva in the Governance of the Ch'ing Empire."

the emperors than self-glorifying documents could have achieved. More-over, the portrait to which Farquhar made reference does not represent the Manjušri incarnation exclusively. The imperial figure is seen to hold in its left hand the Wheel of the Law (*dharmacakra*), that is, the wheel that the "wheel-turning" (*cakravartin, zhuanlun*) king propels in his role of bringing the world closer to the age of salvation. As such it is a simulta-neous representation of the Manjušri and Avalokitešvara (the emanation of compassion and, as Chenresig, the patron *bodhisattva* of Tibet) aspects. Incarnation as *bodhisattva* and as Manjušri had, as Farquhar demonstrated, placed the emperor in China and established the Chinese seat as the ful-crum in the relationship with Mongolia and with Tibet. Manjušri, how-ever, was not only the patron of learning in Tibet, Mongolia, and elsewhere in eastern Asia, but the emanation of "insight" (*prajna*), particularly—in G. Samuel's apt phrase—"insight into the nondichotomizing nature of re-ality,"[28] an appropriate spiritual font for a self-consciously universal ruler.

The Qianlong emperor's claim to be recognized as a *cakravartin* was im-plicit as an heir of Hung Taiji, and he certainly expected his coffin to be cov-ered in the *dhāranī*-laden shawl (which it was, until his grave was robbed and corpse demolished in 1928).[29] But, characteristically, he decided to be slightly more public in his *cakravartin* role. The text in this case is his mau-soleum, Yuling, at the Eastern Tombs site (Dongling) Malanyu, designed by the emperor himself. The walls of the antechambers to the tomb are completely incised with *dhāranī* in Sanskrit, which the Qianlong emperor, unlike his ancestors, had actually learned to read during his instruction by Janggiya *khutukhtu*. In the burial chamber, directly over the emperor and his empresses' funereal platform—that is, directly in an imaginary line of sight of the emperor's coffin—is inscribed in the ceiling the wheel of the *cakravartin*.

Late in the Qianlong reign another image of imperial centrality was de-veloped through links with the Tibetan and Mongolian war god, Geser (Ti-betan Gesar). Despite a veneer of Buddhist rectitude (which had already been part of the tale in its Tibetan folk milieu), the cultic communication in this case was with the popular religions (including shamanism) of Mon-golia. The logic of the adoption of the Geser cult parallels that of the more

---

28. Samuel, *Civilized Shamans*, 281.

29. The emperor's shroud was closely copied in the shroud of the "empress dowager," who was buried in 1909 and whose grave was looted at the same time as the Qianlong in 1928. They are presently on display at the Dongling tombs at Malanyu.

literate and more liturgically based appeals to Confucian and Buddhist elites. Geser was a Tibetan god, originally localized in the region of Ling in eastern Tibet. He was part of a pantheon of horse-riding war gods who by the eighteenth century were as well established in Mongolia as in Tibet; as Red Hat (Sakya) and Yellow Hat (Gelug) Buddhism became more pervasive in most regions of Mongolia, so did the influence of Tibetan folk religions, including varieties of shamanism, that had easy resonance with the shamanism that continued to cohabit with Buddhism in most social organizations in Mongolia. But it is improbable that before the seventeenth century the Geser story itself was widely known in Mongolia. The Kangxi court became aware of a Mongolian redaction of the tale and as a sign of amicability had the first six chapters published in Peking in 1716 for presentation to the Khalkha leaders (see Chapter 6). The specifics of the Mongolian Geser epic may explain the readiness with which it was adopted by the Qing court as a figuration of centrality. In it, Geser (which is a title, like its inspiration *ceasar*, for a god named Joru),[30] is the son of the king of the gods (*tngri*), Khormusda (that is, Ahura Mazda, the Zoroastrian supreme deity). The gods are engaged in battle with their enemies, the *asura*. Khormusda has submitted himself to Buddha at Mt. Meru (the center of all centers) and continues the battle against evil in the name of Buddha. In the epic, Khormusda remains in the "west," and Geser is sent to quell the forces of evil in the "east" (probably originally the Tibetan region of Ling but now understood to be the eastern part of Eurasia). Geser was an important choice for adoption as a state deity. His earliest function was that of a Deva king, a state-protecting deity of the sort known in eastern Eurasia since the time of the Later Han empire.[31] At the same time, his imagery was strikingly

30. Hence Geser is given the geographical epithet of "Ling," an alternate name for the Tibetan region of "Khrom," that is, the Rūm (Anatolia) of the Seljuks. The likeliest inspiration for the story cycle was the Sassanian hero, Gesar of Rūm. Geser of the Mongolian epic is described as "from the land of Khormusda," the latter being king of the gods, and Gesar's "father". On the 1716 edition of the Geser, and particularly the prominent injection of the term *Mongghol ulus* ("Mongol people") into its text, see Choirolzab, "Guanyu 'Gesir' zhong chuxian de 'Menggu' yici," 50–52 (issue's table of contents is in error); see also German translation by I. J. Schmidt (St. Petersburg: Imperial Academy of Sciences, 1836, 1839) and English translation *Gessar Khan* (New York: George H. Doran, 1927). See also Chapter 6, n 63. On the Gesar cycle in Tibet and its association with Sakya teachings see Samuel, *Civilized Shamans*, 68–70, 292–93, 571–72.

31. One of his liturgies describes him as one who "grinds into dust the enemies and devils who alarm the state and religion" (Heissig, *The Religions of Mongolia*, 93, from B. Rinchen, "En Marge du culte de Guesser Khan en Mongolie," *Journal de la Société Finno-Ougrienne* 60:1–51 [28]).

like that of the *cakravartin*, since he is described in his worship as "the supporting beam of the dwelling-house and the spokes of the cartwheel."[32] Finally he is a "son of Heaven" and, more, an "incarnation of the *tngri* [gods] who rule all those who live on earth."[33] The iconic figure of Geser allowed the court not only to cement its ritual and cultural identifications with Tibet and Mongolia, but also to reinforce connections between its cultic life—secluded from commoners but not from the Eight Banner elites—and its ideology. Geser as a single figure, because of the antiquity of his cult in the Buddhist territories of Inner Asia, retained a host of ideological allusions, from the Deva kings, through *bodhisattva*-rulers, to *cakravartin*.

For the Qianlong emperor the undifferentiation of substance in his own being was a separate issue from the expression of specific qualities to specific constituencies. Inevitably, the consistency of figuration to which the emperors were attracted in their roles as ideological propagators encouraged some conflation of ritual idioms. By the eighteenth century, Qing court festivals and rites had effected a limited convergence around Nurgaci. His hunting prowess (now borrowing from elements of Northeastern sagas) was reenacted with the participation of shamans, inside the Forbidden City, each lunar New Year and on other auspicious occasions (including imperial marriages). At the same time, Qing court iconography and Confucian New Year's rites explicitly identified Nurgaci and the Chinese folk hero (and war god) Guan Di, whose worship had originally been encouraged in Liaodong by the Ming.[34] The insistence that Nurgaci and Guan Di be worshiped as the same war god was consciously encouraged by the early Qing empire under Hung Taiji, who ordered translation into Manchu of the Chinese novel "Romance of the Three Kingdoms" (*Sanguo zhi yanyi*),[35] at least

[margin handwritten: Guan Di]

---

32. Heissig, *The Religions of Mongolia*, 94, from Heissig, *Mongolische volksreligiöse und folkloristische Texte aus europäischen Bibliotheken, mit einer Einleitung und Glossar*, Verzeichnis der orientalischen Handschriften in Deutschland, Supplementband 6 (Wiesbaden: Steiner, 1966), 149.

33. Heissig, *Religions of Mongolia*, 140–49, from Rinchen, "En Marge du culte de Guesser Khan en Mongolie," 28.

34. This subject is continued in Chapter 6. For an introduction to the Guan Di cult in some parts of China, see Duara, "Superscribing Symbols."

35. Guan Yu, a historical figure and inspiration for the Guan Di cult, was a follower of Liu Bei in the attempt to reestablish the Han dynasty in the third century. The history of the era was later the subject of story cycles and fiction, the best known being Luo Guanzhong's sixteenth-century *Sanguo yanyi*. The novel was translated into Manchu as *Ilan gurun-i bithe* by Kicungge and others in 1650 and was reproduced at least twice, in 1721 and in 1767. A special illustrated edition (*Ilan gurun-i bithe nirugan*) was produced in 1769. See also description of anomalous

partly to more familiarize bannermen with the character of the "Guan Di" image they knew had been worshiped at Ming military garrisons. In the Qianlong reign, the court continued to encourage worship of this amalgamated Nurgaci/Guan Di war god, and Janggiya *khutukhtu*, the emperor's own teacher, created the prayer (simultaneously) in Tibetan, Manchu, and Mongolian, with a distinctively tantric twist: Now Guan Di was specifically identified as a "protecting deity" (Mongolian *yeke sülde tngri*, Tibetan *dgra lha*), in the Tibetan-Mongolian sense, of the Qing empire. This meant, in essence, that he was no longer merely a patron god of soldiers, but a demon-killing, death-dealing collaborator of the Gelug emanations of violence such as Guhyasamaja, Cakrasamvara, and Yamantaka. Nurgaci/Guan Di had, in short, joined the gods in the campaign to "spread the Buddhist religion and pacify those who live in the Empire."[36] The integration of Nurgaci with Guan Di underscored the centrality of the Aisin Gioro lineage as a supporting structure and the required loyalty (as exemplified in Guan Di lore) to it. By the turn of the nineteenth century the larger cult of Nurgaci/Guan Di/Geser/Vaiśravana provided encyclopedic cross-references—ritual, narrative, iconographic—to reinforcement of the position of the Qing ruler as singular agent in the integration of the spiritualities of the Northeast, China, and Central and Inner Asia.

This was handy magic for dealing with the increasing violence in Turkestan, Tibet, and southwest China that will be discussed in the next chapter, but it was the sort of conflation of personae that was not highly valued by the Qianlong emperor and in fact did not develop much, either as a court practice or in popular religion, until the period after his death. A consistency of ideation was clearly more to his taste than was a confusion of expressive modes (as when the nineteenth-century emperors and empresses smattered their funerary *dhāranī* shawls with Chinese prayers), whether orthographic, iconographic, architectural, or narrative. Though the "trinity" formulation of state-encouraged Zhu Xi idiom was cognate to the "wheel-turning" of the *cakravartin*, it was addressed to a discrete constituency and in the eighteenth century maintained both the coherence of that constituency and the universality of the emperorship through that discretion. In different media, it carried a similar message: that only through the exclusive generative power of the emperorship could all things achieve

[margin note: Q/L. did Not so for it.]

editions (one from the collection of Klaproth) in Puyraimond, *Catalogue du fonds mandchou*, 66–68.

36. Heissig, *Religions of Mongolia*, 99–100.

salvation. A requirement of this formulation was that the emperor as a cosmic address and as a person should be morally absolute and culturally null. He inhabited a mandala-like field in which infinite cultures and histories were represented around him in a most idealized way. The emperor himself was a point of originality, or revelation, of historically unbounded character. This is characteristic of Qianlong art, architecture, and imperial literary expression. It mandated a rigid imposition of cultural formalism and ideal identities. And behind this was posited a history that would by its process define the cultural nullity and moral universality of the emperorship.

DEBATING THE PAST

Qing emperorship as a point of integration for the moral and spiritual systems of eastern Eurasia—and, under the Qianlong court, of the "world"—was an idea consistently pursued since the time of Hung Taiji. But how the center achieved this integration was not represented with the same consistency. The Kangxi and Yongzheng emperors, when pressed, leaned toward conventional interpretation of the pre-imperial Chinese texts as presenting a narrative of transformation and progressive moral improvement, as men of all stations learned of moral principles and brought their actions into harmony with them. For rulers personal moral improvement would entail the uplifting of all whom they governed, an unexceptional interpretation of "The Mean"'s trinity passage. The Kangxi and Yongzheng emperors, aware that there were literati who argued that the Qing rulers were irremediably barbaric and their rule incorrigibly illegitimate, were inclined to rely upon this tenet to maintain that they, too—both the Aisin Gioro imperial lineage and the Manchus—had been morally transformed, and their rule was just and benevolent. In 1730 the Yongzheng court found itself in intense debate with a dead writer who had decried the barbarism of the Qing, and it relied upon the transformationalist argument to refute him. But in the ensuing sixty years, the Qianlong court would take up its own debate with the past. Under the Qianlong emperor's leadership, the court made a shocking early rejection of the Yongzheng ideology and then proceeded to present its own view of how emperorship, as the transformer rather than that which is transformed, worked.

In some periods of Chinese history—notably those devising a historical retrospect on conquest regimes—the latent conflicts between the fundamentals of pre-imperial thought and those of the institution of emperorship became explicit. Some writers were able to extract from the Confucianist ambivalence toward the emperorship a coherent philosophy of the primacy of moral rule (*daotong*) over rule by force and to see themselves as working in that tradition.[37] During the Qing period, such scholars associated the emperorship with repeated rule by alien peoples and with forced integration of Chinese and barbarians. They found the confusion in philosophy regarding the emperorship to be linked with a basic neglect of the "Chinese/barbarian distinctions" (*huayi zhi fen*) that had been, reportedly, established by Confucius and elaborated by Mencius in his critiques of Mo Di and Yang Zhu. For these scholars, barbarian emperorship in China meant a usurpation of the moral absolutes inherent in the ideal of the world ("all under Heaven," *tianxia*). It was an ethical contradiction that was also an inevitable outcome of the development of the imperial instruments since Han times. Those cleaving to the recessive opposition to emperorship have come to be characterized as "loyalists," "dissidents," "eremetists," or, in the late Qing years, "nationalists." The association of opposition to emperorship and opposition to foreign rule was not an innovation of the late Qing years; indeed it appears to have developed in the Ming as a retrospect on Yuan rule, had been occasionally aimed at the Ming emperorship while it dominated, and then found its last object in the Qing.[38]

Wang Fuzhi has previously been discussed (Chapter 1) in connection with his advocacy of an ideology of genealogical identity in the late Ming. This was directly connected to his concern with the difference between barbarians and civilized people. His terms of identity were both historical and biological, which is to say that they were both handily subsumed under the metaphor of genealogy. In his cosmology, all dynamics—physical, social, historical—are the products of the propensity of "matter" (*qi*) to concentrate itself irregularly, into globules or lumps, and for these concentrations to either be repelled by or attracted by others.[39] Like attracts like, unlikes

---

37. See also de Bary, "Chinese Despotism and the Confucian Ideal."

38. Onogawa, "Shinshu no shisō tosei o megutte"; Hsiung, "Shiqi shiji Zhongguo zhengzhi sixiang zhong fei chuantong chengfen de fenxi."

39. Santangelo ("'Chinese and Barbarians' in Gu Yanwu's Thought") suggests on the basis of this that Wang's thought may have been, in contrast to Gu Yanwu's, "objective." This is in connection with his characterization of Wang's notion of difference as being entirely "material." Though Wang would have appreciated being described as a materialist, he did not proceed to call the actual differences between peoples material; it was a matter of consciousness, and of morality, and thus I quibble a bit with Santangelo's passing characterizations of Wang's thought. But for

repel. Wang notes the same pattern in the interrelationships between human societies. People are attracted by their own kind, repelled by others. This is a desirable situation, primarily because human societies are at different points on the ladder of development. Under this conviction of the moral differences between Chinese and barbarians, the Ming emperorship took on a powerful moral posture. It was, for Wang Fuzhi, the avatar of moral and historical rectitude—which was now the exclusive birthright of the people recognized by the Ming court as "Chinese" (*han*)—and inhabitants of the amoral barbarian pale were subject to the imperial sword. "Destroying barbarians to save our people may be called humane [*ren*], deceiving [barbarians] and treating them as they hate to be treated may be called loyal [*zhong*], occupying [barbarian] territory to displace their customs by the power of our letters and beliefs, as well as confiscating their property to increase the supplies for our own people may be called righteous [*yi*]," he had advised.[40] *Ren, zhong,* and *yi* are invoked in the passage not only with reference to Chinese advantages, but also in the interest of barbarians, who inhabit a kind of limbo of consciousness from which they can be freed only by the destruction of their culture and their lineages—that is, the "material" framework of their identities—and subsequent absorption into Chinese society. Because—as in the case of Tong Bunian—the Ming court had delineated ostensibly natural lines of difference and had enforced them in policy, it had in Wang Fuzhi's view used coercion legitimately (despite its numerous other failings). By the same criterion, the Qing empire, under which Wang lived his later life, was necessarily illegitimate in its use of power. Instead of clarifying differences and enforcing them through policy, it had obscured them and used its power to force a coexistence of different peoples—with the, for Wang, predictable outcome of amoral distinctions of status between the barbaric and the civilized, and the suffering both of the Han as people and of China as a civilization.

It is tempting to see in Wang Fuzhi the antecedents of racial thought among the early modern Chinese elite. But to understand the transition represented from seventeenth-century literati thought in China to the imperial ideology of the eighteenth-century Qing court, a few qualifications

---

more on Wang's contribution to the foundation of the "evidentiary scholarship" movement see Onogawa ("Shinshu shiso"), who ranks him with Fang Yizhi and Lü Liuliang.

40. This is from *Chunqiu jiashuo*, but a similar passage appears also in *Quanshan quanji*. This material is also translated in Wiens, "Anti-Manchu Thought during the Ch'ing"; Santangelo, "'Chinese and Barbarians' in Gu Yanwu's Thought."

in this characterization of Wang might be considered. First of all, as sternly as Wang insisted upon unnegotiable moral differences between Chinese and "barbarians"—he meant primarily the Mongols and the Manchus— he did not believe that time worked no transformations upon barbaric peoples. Indeed he proposed that the predecessors of the Chinese—before the emergence of the Hua, or Xia, people—had been barbaric, and that civilization was by definition a condition of progress away from chaos and toward moral order.[41] Both conditions—barbarity and morality—were absolutes for Wang; identity itself was not. His strong position on the role of the state in recognizing differing conditions of development and enforcing barriers between them in the present was based upon his understanding of the rate of change. It was slow enough—and China's own barbaric antiquity so distant in time—that in the course of "history" it was not discernible. Acceleration of this transformation was in Wang's view invariably disastrous. It required nothing less than, as he noted, the total destruction of a barbaric peoples' social structure and economic life, as well as any means of reviving them. As painful as such enforced change was, it was still an acceptable alternative to the greater cataclysm of the shattered infrastructure of civilization—the social structure and economic life of China, which Wang believed was profoundly damaged in his own lifetime by the Qing conquest.

Wang was among a group of scholars who, at the end of the Qing period, would be apotheosized as early prophets of nationalistic thought in China, and still later targeted by historians as conduits of racism, "ethnocentrism," and general condescension toward other peoples, both within China and without. Generally Wang is lumped with Huang Zongxi,[42] Gu

41. Specifically, in the time of Tai Hao the Chinese had been at the level of beasts, and by the time of the Yellow Emperor they had reached the level that barbarians had achieved in the time of Wang's readers (from *Siwen lu waibian, ye* 25a). Similar comments appear in *Du tongjian lun* 1:3a; see also McMorran, *Passionate Realist*, 150ff.

42. *ECCP*, 351–54, from Yuyao, Zhejiang. Huang's father Huang Zunyu had been a "loyal member of the Donglin faction" and was ordered executed in prison in 1626 for his opposition to Wei Zhongxian (the Ming court later canonized Huang Zunyu in 1644). Zongxi plotted a revenge assassination of Wei Zhongxian but was prevented from carrying it out by, among other things, Wei's natural death. Early in the 1630s Huang joined the Fushe, to oppose a resurgence of eunuch power. In 1644 he joined the court of the Prince of Fu at Nanjing, but internal disagreements there soon led to the persecution of Donglin and Fushe members and their families. Huang transferred to the Prince of Lu and participated in the defense of Shaoxing in 1645. By 1649 he abandoned the Ming effort and retired to read and write. Qian Qianyi remained one of his few contacts outside of Yuyao, and Huang revived the

Yanwu,[43] and Lü Liuliang (1629–83),[44] as the "loyalists," "dissidents," or "eremetists" of the early Qing conquest period.[45] But each of these thinkers was distinctive. Huang Zongxi (a student of the Donglin activist and accuser of Tong Bunian, Liu Zongzhou), for instance, was more liberal than Wang in assessing the transformative forces of civilization and considered

---

academy formerly directed by Liu Zongzhou. In 1678 the Qing court ordered that Huang's writings on Ming history should be reproduced for the convenience of the Ming history project, and in 1909 the Qing installed Huang's tablet in the Kongzi *miao*. Fifteen works by Huang Zongxi were entered into the "Four Treasuries," though *Xingchao lu* was banned. Huang's two best-known works, *Mingyi daifang lu* and *Mingru xue'an*, were completed in 1662 and 1676, respectively. See also Struve, "Huang Zongxi in Context," 474–502.

43. *ECCP*, 421–26. Gu is best known as a progenitor of the critical textual methods that underlay the so-called Han Studies movement of the Qing period. He was a native of Jiangsu and changed his personal name to Yanwu ("blazing battle") after the Qing conquest. In 1645 he defended his native city of Kunshan against the invaders. His foster mother starved herself to death in despair over the conquest. Gu himself joined the resistance of the Prince of Tang but from 1647 on was a fugitive as a result of a complex personal vendetta. Gu was a landowner who made a name as a consultant on financial and industrial matters. In 1668 he was imprisoned for about six months on sedition charges, from which he was exonerated by the state. When his collection of essays, *Rizhi lu*, was brought into print in 1670, it is reported to have been purged of "anti-Manchu" comments by Gu's student Pan Lei (a comparison of the manuscript and the Pan edition was published by Huang Kan in 1933). Gu's work was the best known of the "loyalists" in his lifetime, and he continued to grow in influence through the eighteenth century. In the nineteenth century he was the object of a new wave of scholarship and commentary, including work by Zhang Mu—best known for his study of the eastern Mongols—and Zhang's publisher, Qi Junzao (see Chapter 4, n 79). The Qing placed his tablet in the Kongzi *miao* in 1909. See also Thomas Bartlett, "Ku Yen-wu's Response to 'The Decline of Human Society'" (Ph.D. diss., Princeton University, 1985); Peterson, "The Life of Ku Yen-wu."

44. *ECCP*, 551–52. Lü, the most obscure of the "loyalists" and the least committed to criticizing the Song philosophers, was a grandson of a woman of the Ming imperial line. A nephew of Lü's was executed at Hangzhou in 1647 for resisting the conquest. Lü continued his studies until 1666, then decided to work as a physician rather than as an official. In 1674 he ceased medical work. Thereafter he operated his bookshop in Nanking, edited examination preparation texts that were sold through the shop, and consulted on examination questions. In 1680 he decided to renounce the world and become a Buddhist priest. One of his daughters married a son of Huang Zongxi. Lü's writings that bear upon the conquest were not published. They were summarized in several forms in *Dayi juemi lu*, which was issued pursuant to the first inquisition of Zeng Jing in 1730. The Qianlong court later banned all of Lü's works (and suppressed *Dayi juemi lu* itself), and only fragments of nonpolitical writings survive. See also Fisher, "Accommodation and Loyalism: The Life of Lü Liu-liang (1629–1683)," *Papers on Far Eastern History* 15.

45. As examples Weins, "Anti-Manchu Thought during the Ch'ing"; Dikötter, *The Discourse of Race in Modern China*, 25–30; Hsiung, "Shiqi shiji Zhongguo zhengzhi sixiang"; and forthcoming work by Edward J. M. Rhoads.

that the Mongols living in China since Yuan times had already been civilized—that is, become Chinese. On the other hand, Gu Yanwu and Lü Liuliang were far more conservative than Wang on this very point. Indeed each came close to unqualified assertion that there were virtually no historical forces capable of turning barbarians into civilized people. Instead, they saw civilization locked in a life-or-death struggle against its surrounding barbarities. They saw the political leadership of China—and those who had served it—as justified in a wide range of ruthless actions whose morality lay solely in the object of protecting Chinese territory from depredations by aliens. For them, political morality was never an absolute but must be always judged in relation to its effectiveness in maintaining the distinction between Chinese and barbarians. A large, undelimited, ruthless rulership may be perfectly moral, if it defends civilization where other measures have failed.

In this discourse, the eighth-century BCE political philosopher Guan Zhong became the paradigm of service to a centralized power defending civilization from barbaric assault.[46] He had been a problem in political morality from the time that Confucius had praised him and been questioned about it by his pupils, a dialogue that is preserved in the "Analects" (*Lunyu*). Because Guan Zhong had been an apparent champion of centralized power (under Duke Huan of Qi) and servant of the killer of his former master, Confucius' listeners expected to hear Guan Zhong condemned. Instead, he was cited for his service in time of crisis, when the Zhou federation was threatened from without. It was imperative to note, as Lü Liuliang explained, that Confucius' praise of Guan Zhong had reference only to a very particular situation: the preservation of civilization against barbarian invasion. Those who would use Confucius' praise of Guan Zhong to ex-

---

46. Guan Zhong (d. 645 BCE), minister to the first *ba* of the Zhou federation, Duke Huan of Qi, whose personal name was Xiaobo. Leadership of Qi was contested between Xiaobo and his younger brother Jiu, and Guan Zhong (Guan Yiwu) was a vassal of Jiu. Guan came close, once, to killing his future master, but the arrow struck Xiaobo's belt buckle. When Xiaobo attained power (and killed Jiu), he forgave Guan's assault upon him and hired Guan as his counselor, an objective appreciation of Guan's talents for which the *Zuo zhuan* seems to praise Xiaobo. Guan Zhong, in loyal appreciation of the need to strengthen the hegemon in order to preserve Zhou civilization from an attack by the barbarous state of Chu, accepted the appointment and did not avenge Jiu, for which the *Lunyu* praises him. Sydney Rosen has commented that the *Zuo zhuan* account appears to be the more factual and the more pertinent, since its focus is upon Xiaobo as an ethical and strategic hero; later discussion depicting Guan Zhong as the center of the ethical drama here is consonant with the tendency of the shi to center themselves in the political and cultural arena. See Rosen, "In Search of the Historical Kuan Chung."

cuse themselves for serving barbarian monarchs were neglecting the paramount Chinese/barbarian distinction, at which—for Lü—all moral reasoning began. They were also ignoring the "secret counsel" of the "Spring
and Autumn Annals," which was to "revere the emperorship [only for the
purpose of] resisting barbarians [*zunwang rangyi*]."[47] Lü emphasized that
emperorship was the key to the barbarian problem. It was, first, a model of
the proper relations between Chinese and barbarians; the Chinese (that is,
"people," *ren*) occupied the status of sovereign, the barbarians (*yi di*) that
of ministers (*chen*). It was, second, an instrument in the proper hands for
the protection of civilization from designs of the barbarians. Lü remarked,
"Guan Zhong forgot vengeance for his lord and Confucius could hardly
find a justification to characterize this as benevolent [*ren*]. But using the
principle of sovereign and minister to distinguish between Chinese and barbarians, inner and outer, demarcating Chinese from barbarians and people
from animals, is the first meaning of 'center' and 'periphery.' It was for this
reason that Confucius acknowledged the merit of Guan Zhong."[48] For Lü,
no other program for the aggregation of imperial powers could be justified.
The Ming had fallen because of the excesses of the imperial institution, and
among the Qing evils was their intention to sustain and if possible refine
imperial despotism. Huang Zongxi, in commenting upon the perverted political history of the emperorship, introduced his famous "host" and "guest"
analogy: In ancient times, the sovereigns had been the guests of the people,
but in recent times the sovereigns had become the hosts (in Chinese, *zhu*,
the same word used to translate Manchu *ejen*, "lord"). "Thanks to the sovereign, the people can find no peace and no happiness."[49] The remedy (here

47. Zhang Binglin (see Postscript) indicted his own teacher, Yu Yue, for supposedly forgetting this principle. He berated Yu for being deluded into thinking
that there could be just grounds for serving foreign rulers and backs up his argument with citations from Gu Yanwu's own denunciations of the Northern Wei minister, Cui Hao. See also Leung Man-kam, "The Political Thought of Chang Ping-
lin," 36. This attack on Yu may have been in response to Yu's rebuke of Zhang for
putting his radical political rhetoric (his "nationalism") above Yu's preferred ethic
of humanity (*ren*). See Crossley, *Orphan Warriors*, 182.

48. Lü's views were supposedly recorded in his private writings, which were destroyed during the first inquisition of Zeng Jing. His argument is known only from
its reflection in Zeng's deposition, *Zhixin lu*, and in the rebuttals offered by Zhu Shi
and Wu Xiang on behalf of the Yongzheng emperor and now included in *Dayi
juemi lu*. On the question of a "secret counsel" in the *Chunqiu* tradition see also
Wiens, "Anti-Manchu Thought during the Ch'ing"; Bernal, "Liu Shih-p'ei and
National Essence."

49. From *Mingyi daifang lu*. See also Laitinen, *Chinese Nationalism in the Late
Qing Dynasty*, 22, 167; de Bary translation in *Sources of Chinese Tradition*, 533.

Gu Yanwu, in particular, looked back to the Song scholar Shen Gua) was decentralization—a revitalization of the noble classes (particularly in the local context), of the lineages and of the villages.[50] Huang Zongxi's prediction, which was shared by many of his sympathizers, would sting late-nineteenth-century readers with its fatal insight: The emperorship was incorrigible (more so, in his own view, than any "barbarians" were without it) and incompatible by its nature with the welfare of the people.

Zeng Jing (1679–1736), forty-eight years old in 1726–27, was a scholar of humble origins from Hunan with an interest in the writings of Lü Liuliang.[51] Zeng had heard, apparently, that although Lü's career did not conform to that of a typical Ming loyalist "hermit scholar" (*yilao*)—he worked as an educational bureaucrat for the Qing shortly after the conquest—his private writings were full of "anti-Manchu" polemics. Zeng dispatched his friend Zhang Xi to Zhejiang to examine these writings, and later Zhang brought them to Zeng's house. Moved by them, Zeng determined to foment a rebellion against the Qing and sent Zhang Xi to contact the governor-general of Sichuan and Shaanxi, Yue Zhongqi (1686–1754), with Lü's writings in hand. He apparently supposed that Yue, who was a descendant of the Song patriotic martyr Yue Fei, would throw his weight behind the rebellion. Instead, Yue reported the incident to the imperial censors and took Zhang and then Zeng into custody.[52] The mild treatment given both to Zeng Jing and to his polemics by the Yongzheng emperor in the original process was remarkable. Though it was not frequent for emperors to publicize the views of their political enemies, it was not unprecedented. "Great Righteousness Resolving Confusion" was the name of the collection of documents published and distributed together in 1730.[53] It was a distinc-

[handwritten margin note: Yongzheng's mild treatment of Zeng Jing]

---

50. From *Rizhi lu*, but see also Thomas Bartlett, "Ku Yen-wu's Response to 'The Decline of Human Society.'" For an overview of Gu and localism, see Kai-wing Chow, *The Rise of Confucian Ritualism*, 80–84. There is a strong echo of Shen Gua and Gu Yanwu in Zeng Jing's claim, as quoted in *DJL*, that "feudalism (*fengjian*) is the main means by which sages govern the world" (*DJL* 2:21b–25b).

51. There is an excellent narrative of Zeng Jing's first inquisition in Feng, *Yongzheng zhuan*, 222–37. It includes lengthy commentary on Lü Liuliang which, alas, is drawn almost entirely from *Dayi juemi lu*.

52. *QSG* 9:326 (YZ 7:5: *yiniu*) 1729. "Yue Zhongqi says that a Hunanese, Zhang Xi, has given him a 'treasonous letter' (*nishu*), on orders of his teacher Zeng Jing. [It has been ordered] that Zeng and Zhang be brought to Peking. Zeng deposes under questioning by officials that he fell into error by reading the works of Lü Liuliang of Zhejiang. Lü is blamed for this incident, and officials both at the capital and in the provinces are ordered to discuss his crimes."

53. The "great righteousness" to which the title refers is the proper relationship between ruler and official, which in the view of the Yongzheng court was morally and not genealogically prescribed (*DJL* 1:3a; 11a; 2:10b).

tively Yongzheng document in the sense that it was a long imperial polemic with a fairly topical focus in the style of the "Treatise on Factions" (*Pengdang lun*) of 1725.[54] It also was a product of a literary inquisition that in itself was intended to become seminal material in all future examination preparations—a point that cannot be emphasized enough—and thus was partly modeled on *Mingjiao zuiren*, the volume of 385 poems and an imperial preface excoriating Qian Mingshi, which Qian was forced to publish and distribute at his own expense in 1725.

There was, additionally, a secular change in the legal posture toward literary crimes in the eighteenth century. This change took the form of a much more severe approach in the Qianlong period, particularly in those cases that in the previous period would have been mitigated by pleas of insanity or instability—that is, the grounds of offense were broadened in the Qianlong period, as L. C. Goodrich noted long ago, and the grounds of defense were markedly narrowed, as Guo Chengkang has recently documented. In fact the Qianlong court was almost unprecedented in its unwillingness to admit madness as a defense in literary crimes. There may originally have been some indirect relevance here to the Zeng Jing case, particularly in light of the portrait, suggested by the Yongzheng court, in "Great Righteousness" of Zeng Jing as a poor Hunanese peasant whose judgment may have been unhinged through his experience of natural and economic calamities in his home province.[55] Indeed, in his reply to Zeng Jing the Yongzheng emperor seemed to go out of his way to indicate the distressing conditions of Zeng Jing's youth, in a bald appeal to the instability defense and an obvious show of imperial compassion. Politically the court's release of Zeng Jing was a canny move, which took much of the sting out of the polemics of the anti-Qing underground. It also opened the imperial window on seditious literature and may have optimized the possibilities of voluntary surrenderings of such works. These factors do not, however, explain the "Great Righteousness Resolving Confusion," which was a more than ten-thousand-word historical and philosophical treatise that was clearly intended to become study material for the examination system. To understand this single event with two components—the release of Zeng Jing

54. The essay was another kind of debate with the past: the emperor wished to refute Ouyang Xiu's observations in an essay of this same name (see *Guwen guanzhi*, 268–69) that factions were an inevitability and healthy: communities of good could combine to combat communities of evil. The emperor pointed out, not surprisingly, that factions always lead to corruption and instability. See also Pei Huang, *Autocracy at Work*, 93.

55. *DJL* 2:62a–63b; 3:30a–32b.

in 1730 and promulgation of the "Great Righteousness Resolving Confusion"—it was necessary to consider the content of the work and its import.

It was organized into four large chapters (*juan*). The first opens with a
series of imperial pronouncements on history, sentiment, rectitude, and
culture. It also contains the first of Zeng Jing's articles of deposition, in
which the imperial inquiries, in large characters, loom over the represented
replies of Zeng Jing, in small characters; these continued through the second and third chapters. The fourth was divided among an *ad hominem* attack upon Lü Liuliang, a relative dismissal of the role of Zeng Jing, and
Zeng Jing's own "Why I Have Submitted to Benevolence" (*Gui ren shuo*).
The collection was originally published and distributed together with "A
Refutation of Lü Liuliang's Interpretation of the Four Books" (*Bo Lü Liuliang sishu jiangyi*) by Zhu Shi and Wu Xiang. "Great Righteousness Resolving Confusion" fundamentally expressed an ideological struggle between the Yongzheng emperor and the thought of the late Lü Liuliang (that
is, a dialect of the Ming ideology of identity). Throughout, the argument
was made that Zeng Jing was a mere dupe, born without the advantages of
Lü, struggling to gain an education, receiving in an innocent fashion the argument of Lü and his associates that the misfortunes of Zeng Jing associated with his own youth were caused by the depredations of the Qing.[56]
With his recantation, Zeng's record was clear and he was free to go his own
way. The emperor's indictment of Lü Liuliang, however, was thorough.
There has been trouble in Zhejiang for years, the emperor grumbled, including the inquisitions of Wang Zhongqi (1672–1726), Zha Siting, and Lü
Shengnan. These events, it was now clear, were all fruit of the seeds of treason sown by Lü Liuliang. Despite the fact that he and his son, Lü Baozhong,
had enjoyed the bounty and the confidence of the Qing, they had spent
their lives devising falsehoods and clever arguments to attempt to deceive
honest literati into treasonous beliefs. Their works must be banned eter-
nally and their crimes remembered as the most heinous. The bodies of Lü
Liuliang and his eldest son Lü Baozhong, as well as the corpse of Lü's colleague Yan Hongda, were dug up and their bones exposed.

The line of opposition taken by those writing for the Yongzheng emperor was conventional. The points at which Lü Liuliang had transgressed
against the fundamental Confucian ideal of cultural transformation of populations and moral transformation of individuals were obvious. "In your
seditious book you have said that 'the world is one family, and all things

56. *DJL* 1:2b–3a; 48b.

have a single origin' [*tianxia yijia, wanwu yiyuan*], so where does this 'distinction between the Chinese and the barbarians' [*zhonghua yidi fen*] come from?"[57] The fundamental argument was prosecuted simply, with few digressions into difficult or difficult areas of thought: The Qing had successfully assumed the vessels, rituals, and functions of the emperorship in China; the people were cared for; the natural processes were facilitated; and the peoples of the earth were united in their awe of and love for the ruler.[58] There was no surer test of the Mandate of Heaven.[59] For this to be the case, it must be that the Manchus had been morally transformed (*hua, xianghua*) in the course of their history. They could not be condemned as the barbarians that their ancestors had been. They were civilized, and their rule was righteous. For a century the court and the people had enjoyed a relationship of intimacy and reverence, and the dynasty had acted as the lords of the officials and the common people of China and other territories. How could a court so solicitous and loving of the people make invidious distinctions between "Chinese" and "barbarians"?[60] Moreover, Lü and his ilk (all "treacherous thieves," *nizei*), in comparing barbarous peoples to livestock and insisting that no transformation had occurred, had suggested that the people of China, being ruled by livestock, must themselves be inferior to livestock.[61] On the contrary, the emperor insisted that, as in the successful campaigns against the Mongols or the rebellious peoples of the southwest, the victories of the Qing court were in fact the victories of Chinese civilization and of the march of morality generally.[62] The "five relationships" were also invoked: The relationship between ruler and official was the chief of these, and people without a ruler could hardly be called "people"; it was

defending the CD's

---

57. *DJL* 2:13b. There is a slightly different allusion in the preface (*DJL* 1:1a), *tianxia yijia wanwu yiti*, "the world is one family, all things have one substance."

58. *DJL* 1:1b–2a; 4a.

59. "Traitors" (*jianmin*), a major theme of *juan* 1, could not recognize the Mandate of Heaven (*DJL* 1:11a).

60. *DJL* 1:2a. In a subsequent passage, the writers take this further, indignantly claiming that the "barbarian" label put upon the Manchus by Lü Liuliang did not distinguish between the Manchus and, for instance, the Dzunghars, who despite their own deficiency of civilization often made bold to denigrate the Manchus themselves. In the Yongzheng classification scheme, the Manchus and the "people(s) of China" belonged in one category, the Dzunghars in another—but none, the work repeatedly insists, are beasts (*DJL* 1:43a).

61. *DJL* 1:4b–5a; one notes with some irony (which would be lost on Hung Taiji) that the livestock theme is sarcastically belabored in 1:42a–43a, 44a; 44b; 51a; 54b–55a; 2:15a–17b.

62. *DJL* 1:5a; 7a–b; 41b; 42b.

the Qing who alone had proved capable of establishing order in China and the Qing alone who provided the demarcation between Chinese and animals; indeed in natural law (*tianli*), the fundamental distinction was not between Chinese and barbarians but between people and beasts.[63] The strength of the imperial reply appeared so unimpeachable to the court, and the basis of the Lü/Zeng attack on the empire so philosophically faulty, that publication of the deposition of Zeng Jing and repudiation of Lü Liuliang was an opportunity for advertisement of the Confucian rectitude of the regime that the court could not ignore.[64] Zeng Jing, the stress-crazed innocent from Hunan, was rewarded with freedom and employment. The inquisition of Zeng Jing forms the body of work that was ultimately intended to be used in a very widespread program of indoctrination on the origins of culture, identity, and morality—that is, to establish a mode of argument, based upon the transformative power of civilization, that would become the official creed. Zeng Jing had provided the court with an opportunity to clarify and institutionalize this creed, while gaining greater control over the essentialist discourse which Lü had represented.

But in addition to the dispassionate voice condemning Zeng's cosmological errors, another voice was present in the text. Zhu Shi, the primary writer on behalf of the Yongzheng emperor, was both an adherent of the "materialist" school of thought represented by Lü Liuliang (commissioned to refute Lü on his own terms) and a student of the Manchu language who understood well its habits in the expression of political ideas. This second voice—the voice of the Nurgaci and Hung Taiji khanates—was obsessed with supernatural signs, insisting that auspicious plants have sprung up in auspicious places, water levels have risen and dropped in an auspicious pattern, and badgering Zeng Jing to name even one mountain that has fallen or one river that has dried up since the inception of the Qing regime.[65] The philosophical voice explained calmly that the Qing were invited to China by Wu Sangui, as a representative of the Ming court, to quell internal troubles, and stayed only to stabilize the country afterward. This voice repeatedly invokes the phrase (a revisitation of the "trinity") from the Book of Odes (*Shujing*), "The ruling Heaven [*huangtian*] has no intimates [*qin*]; virtue [*de*] alone is his support."[66] The khanal voice insisted that Heaven gave us Mukden, Heaven gave us Peking, Heaven gave us China; it speaks

63. *DJL* 1:11a–11b.
64. *DJL* 1:12a–13b.
65. *DJL* 1:45a–47b; 55a–58b.
66. *DJL* 1:1a; 41b.

long and bitterly about the comparative family histories of the Ming and Qing orders.

The two personalities of the "Great Righteousness Resolving Confusion" are recognizably two of the distinct personae of the Qing emperorship. One persona was the khanate out of which the Qing empire was born. The central concept in this schema of khan-emperor of the Hung Taiji period was that of the "mind of Heaven" (*abkai mujilen, tianxin*). The khan-emperor owes his moral intuition (which in Qing discourse, as already suggested, came to be represented as *daoxin*) to the fact that his consciousness reflected this Heavenly mind (as Hung Taiji had indignantly informed Yuan Chonghuan). It is, moreover, the motive force in history and the achievement of Heaven's intentions manifest. This would remain a pervasive concept in Manchu political expression, from the fulminations of Nurgaci and Hung Taiji against the Ming court through the large literary production of the Qianlong era. The khan was the khan because his consciousness was an extension of the mind of Heaven. Because of this endowment, the khan was superior in all things. His access to intuition was exclusive, his obligation to use his moral powers for the completion of the universe absolute. The Kangxi emperor had been remarkable for his ability to compartmentalize these two personae, these two idioms, and to express himself in a rigidly Chinese imperial tongue that many times betrayed nothing at all of the conventions of khanship. But the Yongzheng document blended these two legacies. The emperor provides historical justification for the Manchu conquest of China and views with satisfaction the moral health of the empire, while the khan states that China has been given to him by the decree of Heaven (what in the Manchus annals was likely to be expressed as *abka urušefi*, " . . . Heaven, having supported our struggle . . . ") and cites endless supernatural indications of the fact. The emperor depicts Lü Liu-liang as a man of cultivated mind but deceitful heart, trespassing upon time-honored rules of ministerial propriety, while the khan excoriates him as a crude ingrate who ate from the Qing stores and failed to return the love that was due.

In 1736 the Yongzheng emperor died. At the time of the Zeng Jing incident Hongli, later to be the Qianlong emperor but in 1730 an eighteen-year-old prince, had had deep feelings about the error of his father's approach to the Zeng Jing problem.[67] When the Yongzheng emperor died,

---

67. There is a traditional explanation, to be found in *ECCP* and elsewhere, that Hongli destroyed "Great Righteousness" because of embarrassment over the discussion contained in the work (see *DJL* 1:14a–37a; 3:30a–49b) of matters relating

Hongli did not observe the traditional hiatus between the death of a sitting emperor and the lunar New Year, when the ascending emperor is invested. Instead he moved only weeks after his father's death to undo the Zeng Jing denouement. He ordered the rearrest of Zeng Jing and Zhang Xi.[68] A new investigation was conducted, resulting in Zeng Jing being sentenced to death by slicing. It was ordered that all copies of "Great Righteousness Resolving Confusion" were to be collected and destroyed. By this last act the new emperor appeared to grossly contradict and insult his father's faculty of reason—particularly since the rearrest of Zeng Jing and the destruction of "Great Righteousness" were followed very closely in time by the pardoning of the relatives of Wang Zhongqi and Zha Siting, who had been condemned by the late emperor in connection with their factitious conspiring and treasonous commentary.[69] The new emperor was in haste to suppress both the redaction in "Great Righteousness" of Lü Liuliang's thought and the defenses—no matter whether reasoned or impassioned—that his father had offered. Qianlong literary acts thereafter (which may have been on a scale rivaled by no one else, anywhere) suggest that his objection was not to the specifics of his father's defense against Lü's accusations but to the implication that any defense, any response, was even necessary. The rearrest of Zeng Jing was a forced return to the point where (in the view of the Qianlong emperor) all had gone wrong; as the counting of years would begin again with the new reign, so would the response to Lü Liuliang's indictment.

[margin note: Hongli revisits his father's view.]

---

to the imperial family and especially to the circumstances of the Yongzheng emperor's succession. The treatment certainly appears extravagant and betrays the legendary (and justified) defensiveness of the Yongzheng emperor over his apparent usurpation of the throne. Nevertheless the discussion fits into the themes of the work generally, insofar as it is an apologia on the moral preparedness of the Yongzheng emperor for rule, is an indictment of the disloyalty and selfishness of his princely rivals and their equally malicious bureaucratic supporters, and is ostensibly offered as a case study for the importance of order over chaos. It also leads into a narrative of the earlier history of the lineage, as Nurgaci and Hung Taiji are depicted as bringing order to the chaos of motley peoples of Mt. Changbai, Korea, and Mongolia, and this history is explicitly connected to the mission of the Qing conquest in China (to restore the order that the Ming had abdicated). If Hongli's intention was to suppress the passages relating to the Yongzheng succession particularly, he could have found many less obtrusive ways to do it than to sponsor a spectacular retrial of Zeng Jing and destruction, rather than revision, of "Great Righteousness."

68. *QSG* 10:345 (10 *yue, renshen*).

69. *QSG* 10:348 (3 *yue, gengzi*). In Zha's case, treason had consisted of the use in a composition of two characters which, without their top strokes, resembled the characters of the Yongzheng reign name; this was taken as a covert call for the emperor's beheading.

There were points of agreement as well as disagreement between "Great Righteousness Resolving Confusion" and the views of the new Qianlong emperor. The agreements consist primarily in the historical narrative of Qing origins and of the Qing entry into China, the latter portrayed not as a premeditated conquest but as a response to the Ming call for aid (relayed through the Liaodongese Wu Sangui), and as an attempt to ensure stability in the country after the suppression of the rebel Li Zicheng.[70] The fact that the account in the "Great Righteousness Resolving Confusion" was the approved line, and would remain the model for discussions of the past, did not make "Great Righteousness" appealing to the Qianlong emperor. On the contrary it threatened the original authority of the universal Qianlong emperorship, and it was desired that it should disappear (this was an adumbration of the fate of much literature with which the court was in basic agreement in the Four Treasuries process). There was a rivalry for authority here, and the Qianlong emperor would become accustomed to winning such contests. But more damning was one very profound point of disagreement. This was the consistent, underlying argument of "Great Righteousness Resolving Confusion" that the Aisin Gioro lineage (and by a vague connection the Manchus) had been culturally and morally transformed and for this reason were fit to rule China. This concept of cultural and moral transformation, so well tailored to the Cheng-Zhu rhetoric that the court normally employed and so admirably calculated to heresize the position of Lü Liuliang, was unacceptable to the Qianlong emperor. He did not believe in mass cultural transformation, except as a state of corruption. He believed in cultural refinement, cultural purification, through the agency of the universal emperorship. It was not because the Manchus had somehow been transformed through the improving influence of Chinese civilization that the Qing empire was fit to rule China. The Qing were fit to rule China because Heaven had backed the struggles of Nurgaci and Hung Taiji against the Ming, and because the emperor's consciousness was an extension of the mind of Heaven, he maintained this connection through an encyclopedic collection of rituals, and he reified Heaven's will in the magnificence of his regime.

The dramatic contrasts between these two imperial worldviews can be illustrated closely in their use of a common reference from the ancient Chinese texts. This was Mencius' characterization of Shun (the second sage king) as a man of the "eastern barbarians" and King Wen, founder of the

---

70. *DJL* 1:3b–4a; 6b–7a; 37a–40a; 42a–b.

Zhou dynasty, as a man of the "western barbarians." These are the best-known, though obviously not the only, examples of worthy barbarians from the early texts. By Qing times, partly because of the philosophical and political developments of the late Ming period, these were regarded as strange and perplexing allegations. The reference occurs in "Great Righteousness Resolving Confusion," where it was argued that though they came from barbarian territories, Shun and King Wen became sages by virtue of their subsequent moral improvement ("repair," though the word is normally translated as "cultivation" [*xiu*]).[71] The process of transformation was acknowledged and made explicit, and was obviously intended to apply not only to the Qing but to the Yongzheng emperor himself, who despite barbaric origins for his reign may be seen as a transformed sage-king. But the same reference occurs in the Qianlong emperor's introduction to the "Researches on Manchu Origins" (*Manzhou yuanliu kao*).[72] There, the emperor argues that Mencius cites the origins of Shun and King Wen without shame because there was indeed no shame in their origins. They ruled China because, regardless of their origins, they were fit to do so, and no question of transformation was admitted.[73]

In rejecting the idea of cultural transformation (that is, moral reconstruction) of the Aisin Gioro as a ruling caste, the Qianlong emperor was necessarily also rejecting the proposition of the Qing emperor as a Confucian sage-king. That is, the claim that the Qing emperors were righteous rulers because they were attentive to the counsel of cultivated advisors, and had indeed surpassed their moral teachers, was a function of the idea that

71. *DJL* 1:2b–3a; 42b–43a.
72. See Chapter 6.
73. Both of these interpretations of Mencius appear to me wide of the mark. The original passage seems to have nothing meaningful to say about the particular origins of either Shun or King Wen. It is rather a comment on the power of *institutions of leadership* to overcome the parochial differences in outlook that were clearly to be found within the boundaries of the late Zhou federation. See Mengzi, *Li lou zhangju (xia), Shun sheng yu Chufang, qian yu Fuxia, zu yu Mingtiao, dongyi ren ye. Wen wang sheng yu Chizhou, zu yu Biying, xi yi ren ye.* It is clear from the context that Mencius intended not to emphasize any barbaric origins for Shun or Wen wang but the fact that they were widely separated by time and geography but were able to unite the country by their adherence to basic principles of governance. For an exegesis of Mencius' geographical references here see Legge, trans., *The Works of Mencius*, 316 n 1. I am obviously in disagreement with Legge's translation of *dongyi ren ye* and *xiyi ren ye*, which I think distorts the plain meaning of Mencius' lines in response to later anxieties over their meaning. Mencius appears to have attached no importance to the origins of Shun or Wen wang, but the utterance received a great deal of attention in later ages.

the Aisin Gioro (including the emperor) had been elevated in their moral consciousness through their exposure to civilization. The sage-king role had been assumed by the emperor's predecessors, most brilliantly by the prodigy, the Kangxi emperor. He had spoken to the "Outside the Wall" (*guanwai*) sector of his empire in the region's traditional idiom of master to slave and to the "Inside the Wall" (*guannei*) sector in that region's traditional idiom of patriarchal dominion. This had entailed a programmatic co-optation of the sage-king concept. But the Qianlong emperor denied that the Aisin Gioro or the Manchus had been transformed through the influence of Confucian civilization or anything else. He asserted, through various media, that cultural identity was absolute, that the Aisin Gioro lineage represented the apex of the autochthonous civilization of the Northeast, and that they ruled China because of their unique and inherent favor by Heaven. In his rhetoric the sage-king term persisted but took on a new significance with respect to the relationship of the Qing emperor to this universalistic Heaven.

THE POWER OF SPEECH

In ancient Western Asia, the earliest relics of simultaneous expression are found. They are quite practical and mundane, their purposes having often been to mark borders. Frequently, the borders occurred at the interface of territories using different languages. One language for one territory, another for its neighbor. On second thought the simplicity disappears. The languages are not the sole languages of the regions they are now representing but the dominant ones, or perhaps the dominant written media. Moreover, it cannot be the case that use of each language reaches comprehensively to the point of the marker and then stops. Choosing the languages and placing the markers were actions of rulership, which simplified and codified regional cultures in order to represent a point on the earth where one had to pay a tax, or start observing a certain law, or dismount one's horse or camel. The planting of stelae in two languages to mark borders were milestones in the career of Nurgaci, who struggled long and furiously to get recognition of Jianzhou territory from the Ming and Yi governments. Hung Taiji marked his borders as they expanded, but the large number of epigraphical monuments[74] from his period indicate the variety

---

74. It originally seemed to me that I was taking liberties with this use of "monument," since art historians are adamant, and on firm philological ground, in attributing some element of historical allusiveness, memory, or reimagining of the

of uses to which he put his own simultaneity: Legal decrees, obituarial comments, as well as borders were signaled by his stones. Wherever they stood, the emperor was speaking simultaneously. Hung Taiji, as the first conquering emperor of the Qing, put strong emphasis indeed upon marking his expanding borders with his monuments. But they were not only to mark his own territories from somebody else's. They were increasingly used to distinguish his internal realms from one another. That meaning of the simultaneous monument would become increasingly important in the eighteenth century. The Qianlong emperor had an extensive archeology of simultaneous imperial traces about him. Since the *cakravartin* has only internal boundaries to mark, the simultaneous stelae had been one of his specialties. Ašoka's monuments, in Greek and Aramaic, are still found in Iran and Afghanistan (of course, to Chinese Buddhists, his traces were to be expected all over his unified continent of Jambudvīpa, and were frequently discovered). Tang Taizong's monument on the Orkhon River, simultaneous in Chinese and the runic script of the Turks, divided his imperial personae; on one side he ruled as khan, on the other as emperor (and in the Mahākāla liturgy is specifically named as the *cakravartin* between Ašoka and Khubilai).[75] The Mongol Great Khans had left the example of the simultaneous monument at Juyong Pass, where travelers actually progressed through a tunnel with six languages running its length.

The Qianlong emperor was especially attentive to these internal boundaries. His imperial landscapes (both natural and miniaturized) were notoriously studded with monuments in stone and wood, reminders of the emperor's ability to utter, indicate and objectify, everywhere at once, in all media. But the emperor also extended his powers of simultaneous display

---

past with the function of a "monument," and particularly the quality of "monumentality" (see the two contrasted and resolved by Wu Hung, *Monumentality in Early Chinese Art and Architecture*, 1–4). However, it must be remembered that though the intention of the "monuments" under discussion here is communication of an immediacy of presence between the emperorship and the subject (even if the literary content relates to history), the emperorship itself is a past, a narrative, and a particular construction of time (see Introduction to this book). For remarks in a similar spirit, see Kahn, "A Matter of Taste," and Waley-Cohen, "Commemorating War."

75. Like Ašoka, Tang Taizong would probably have been surprised to find himself at the center of a cakravartin cult (even though he patronized Buddhist institutions) or even as a font of imperial simultaneity. Taizong and other early Tang rulers had tried and failed to settle Turkic subjects within the bounds of China; the policy dissolved after a series of Turkic revolts, and the Tang reverted to a policy of segregation, with these stelae to mark the boundaries. See Wechsler, *Mirror to the Son of Heaven*, 121–22.

to the printed page. Much of this production took the form of the "correction" and preservation of classic works, and of informative writings on topics that included technology and medicine. But much was of a monumental nature. The antecedents were plentiful. The traditional jeweled Buddhist liturgical and divinatory texts, for instance, were only partly related to the idea of reading what was on the page; in very many cases, the words were well memorized, and their presence on the page was only a way of creating new resonance for them in another dimension (akin to the writing on prayer wheels, or displays of the Lotus Sutra in Sanskrit, where nobody actually reads Sanskrit). The production of elaborate editions of the *Kanjur* (*Kangyur*—tantric prayers) and *Tanjur* (*Tengyur*—tantric commentaries) were prominent examples of monumental literature, specifically connected to the mission of the *cakravartin*. Lighdan, as patron of the Mahākāla and other tantric cults, had sponsored printing houses at his capital, Köko khota,[76] that had produced impressive versions of these works in Tibetan and in Mongolian. From Hung Taiji on, the Qing emperors had firmly claimed this role as publishers of Tibetan texts, both at Mukden and at Peking, which by the end of the seventeenth century was the primary source for many works in Mongolian, not only of a religious nature.[77] A second source was the encyclopedia project of the Yongle emperor of the Ming (the Chinese *pādishāh*, builder of the Forbidden City, sponsor of Zheng He's expeditions and other acts of spectacle that suggested his own succession to the status of the Great Khans). Though financial and political tangles had frustrated the Yongle ambition of a completed and disseminated encyclopedic project, the meaning of this enterprise was not lost on any of the Qing emperors. The Kangxi and Yongzheng courts had sponsored large projects compiling cartographic, medical, strategic, and technical information, and each had commissioned works of exploration, genealogy, and history that would become cornerstones in the literary panorama of the Qianlong age. Standing on these earlier collections, and having no intention of allowing cost to be an object, the Qianlong emperor over the course of his career achieved the most profound influence over the scope and content of the literary milieux in Chinese, Manchu, Mongolian, and Tibetan of any individual who has ever lived.

There was finally a homely source for the Qianlong emperor's monumentalism. Since Tang times, various small offices for the handling of written communications between empires based in China and their "tributary"

---

76. Now Huhhot, capital of the Inner Mongolia province of China.
77. Crossley and Rawski, "A Profile."

states in various parts of Asia had been collecting bits of foreign writing. Until Ming times—when continuing communications with the Mongols became of some political moment—the functions of these offices had been negligible: Foreign envoys were seen after by interpreters who might or might not be able to read; court rituals involved no communication of information in writing; and political or economic discussions could be handled either entirely in Chinese or with the aid of those who could interpret speech. The libraries of these offices had over the centuries piled up bits of thing—books, plaques, scrolls, inscribed gifts—on which were displayed foreign writing that nobody understood. A few scholars, mostly of Mongol or Muslim descent, did some serious work in these departments during the Ming, out of which was produced the "Secret History of the Mongols," which the Qing had revised and reprinted (after translation into Mongolian script) several times.[78] The same scholars were responsible for working out the technically difficult but influential Chinese–Mongolian lexicon, the "Chinese-Barbarian Glossary" (*Huayi yiyu*). The mystique and display value of the objects interested the Qianlong emperor, and as the tide of philological interest rose, he demanded not only that a philological review be undertaken of earlier imperial histories but that new lexicons be produced as well. Some of these were clearly designed for practical use in language programs he would also prescribe. But others were monuments intended to impress upon the viewer, with their lines of two, three, four, or five languages running across the enormous pages, the profound and vast simultaneity of imperial expression. These lexicons—the largest striped in Manchu, Mongolian, Chinese, Tibetan, and "Uigur"—were called "mirrors" (*jian, buleku, bilig*), reflecting the luminosity of imperial intelligence in the eyes of a staggered public.

This simultaneous, monumental quality is not always emphasized in discussion of the single greatest literary campaign of the Qianlong era, the [the libraries] "Four Treasuries" (*Siku quanshu*). It is perfectly true, and of no small importance to the Qianlong court, that assuming curatorship over all the literature of China meant suppression as well as expression. As libraries were combed for significant works or families surrendered their valuable libraries to the court officials directly, the search for undesirable literature was ongoing; those caught with evil works (as distinct from the merely unimportant, unconvincing, or badly written) risked very serious consequences. But the authority wielded was over not only Chinese literature

78. Crossley, "Structure and Symbol."

but all the literatures of the empire, and the ultimate aim was to make all true expression, in any language, the property of the emperor. He would (through his extensions) review it, study it, meditate on it, correct it where hermeneutical techniques demanded it, catalog it, rank it, produce it anew, and make it available in his own libraries built for that purpose (seven in various parts of China and the Northeast). Not only hoary classics, but newly generated works on history, linguistics, and "customs" would all become emanations of the imperial mind. The new libraries (all built on what was an idealized basic pattern) were monuments, and within them were monuments (books), which contained within them more monuments (written words).

The proprietariness of the Qianlong court over words may have helped intensify a scholarly battle of the late seventeenth and eighteenth centuries. The depths of these struggles have been explored by Benjamin Elman and other scholars, and here we will touch only on the areas of conflict that interested the Qianlong court. To oversimplify, there had arisen over the course of the seventeenth century a scholarly point of view (related to the "materialist" philosophies of Wang Fuzhi, Gu Yanwu, and Lü Liuliang) that promoted the use of systematic methods of inquiry into various forms of knowledge. These methods were in time applied to the texts that were presumed to date, in their known form, from the pre-imperial era, but some scholars had used etymological and ideographic studies—a species of "evidential" (*kaozheng*)[79] scholarship—to demonstrate that certain of these very prestigious works had been significantly altered, or even invented, in imperial times, particularly in the Han era. They were, in addition, able to suggest that the forms of the texts used by Zhu Xi—who had himself al-

---

79. Scholars working in what has come to be known as the *kaozheng* ("research and correct") mode drew upon the so-called materialist philosophical orientation of the middle seventeenth century—in this book discussed generally in connection with Wang Fuzhi—and developed a method of critical scholarship. It was strongly oriented toward the study of the evolution and meaning of the Chinese writing system, the study of textual integrity, and the construction of criteria of authenticity, and it discredited some texts that had been conventionally accepted in the classical canon. In many quarters the discipline inspired a new skepticism toward the intellectual tradition and those parts of the state that were dedicated to its preservation and enforcement. From time to time modern scholars have viewed the *kaozheng* movement as evidence of objectivism, empiricism, and even scientific inquiry in early modern Chinese thought. The most prominent recent scholar of this subject and its received characterizations is Benjamin A. Elman (who has generalized the term "evidentiary scholarship" for the *kaozheng* trends). See his *From Philosophy to Philology; Classicism, Politics and Kinship;* and the early chapters of *A Cultural History of Civil Examinations in Late Imperial China.*

tered some works to make them, in his eyes, more "correct"—were not authoritative, and by implication Zhu Xi and those on whom he based much of his work were not authorities (moral, cosmological, or hermeneutical), either. Scholars subscribing to this view were in time identified as the "Han Studies" school. There was great variety in the thought of the Han Studies group, but in general they tended toward the line of analysis already referred to with respect to Zheng Xuan: that the texts have no charismatic qualities but are suitable subjects for objective analysis, that the state is rooted in history and not in the "original" nature of man, that imperial authority is distinct from social affirmation and instead derives from its control of and relationship to historical sources. The opposition to this view in the writings of Zhu Xi and others of the Song period was already clear and had already been, to some extent, a topic of contention in the early Ming period. Now, those who continued to advocate Zhu Xi's conclusion that the texts were sources of metaphysical insight, that meditation upon them could lead to sagehood in any man, and that language had an inalienable quality of moral generation were opposed to the Han Studies school as the "Song Studies" school. The contradictions and ironies of the eighteenth-century debate need not be detailed, though it should be pointed out that the Qing court's preference for the "Han Studies" position—manifested in its promotion of scholars of that bent to high bureaucratic, research, and editorial positions, the friendly reception of "Han"-like answers to examination questions—was clear and was related to the "Han Studies" commitment to exclusive sagehood in the ruler.[80] This in no way interfered with the court's formal support for Zhu Xi and the "Four Books" as the basis of the examinations themselves or as the favored source for obligatory opening comments to imperial edicts or introductions to revisions featured in the "Four Treasuries."

One of the effects, which would influence much later thinking on the relationship of ruler and ruled, was a gradual dislodgement of Mencius from

---

80. See also the argument by Zhu Shi that the "Chinese-barbarian theory" (*hua di shuo*) was an imposition of Eastern Jin times and later, and was alien to Confucius (*DJL* 3a–3b). Qing use of the examinations to ensnare the interests of and inculcate beliefs in the literati was attacked by Lü Liuliang and Zeng Jing; *DJL* quotes them as claiming that the "examination system is a greater [evil] than and more widespread than the evils of Wang Yangming" (2:19a–21a). In the subsequent section, Zeng's explicit placement of Lü Liuliang on a level with Zhu Xi and Cheng Yi is attacked, clearly indicating that Zhu and Cheng were important icons in dissident, not exclusively in orthodox, rhetoric (2:20a–21b). On the examinations as a very imperfect vehicle for ideological indoctrination, see Elman, *A Cultural History of Civil Examinations*, Chapters 8 and 9.

his place at the center of China's philosophical tradition (a centrality for him that Zhu Xi had inherited from Tang scholars but very forcefully confirmed). The early mile mark in the repudiation of Mencius as the authoritative interpreter of Confucius may have been during the career of Dai Zhen (1724–77). For his neglect of the role of the emotions in human consciousness, for his conflation of public and private in his discourse, for his marrying of political legitimacy to the personal morality of the sovereign, Mencius came to be perceived as the apologist of tyranny. A similar phenomenon occurred for much the same reasons (criticism of the archaism of legal and social institutions) in Tokugawa Japan, particularly in the work of Ogyū Sorai.[81] Even partial displacement of Mencius meant, most immediately, a revival in the prestige of Xunzi, who was perceived not as a philosopher of human nature but as an engineer of political systems, a "statecraft" pioneer who placed the rule of principle and law above the personal qualities of the sovereign. It was a first step in the resegregation of government from society that would be critically important, if vexing, to nationalists of the late nineteenth century.

As the emperor's hired scholars were defending the "Han" view of the historicity of the texts and the moral uniqueness of the ruler, the Qianlong emperor was finding ways of expressing it in more direct fashion. Having rejected the attempt of his father to characterize the Aisin Gioro as culturally transformed monarchs who justified themselves by their impersonal benevolence toward the "world," he set out another case. To the "Ode to Mukden" (see Chapter 6), he contributed a preface in 1743 that began to make the new argument. The main theme of the "Ode" is precisely in opposition to that of "Great Righteousness Resolving Confusion": Instead of emphasis on the importance of transformation, emphasis on the persistence of consciousness (*mujilen, xin*) from the remotest ancestors to the present and the unique source of imperial consciousness in the Heavenly mind. A similar essentialism is seen to imbue the distinct consciousness of the emperor, the nobility (that is, the Aisin Gioro), and the common people. "Of those who receive their minds [hearts] from fathers and mothers,

---

81. Liang (to be discussed in the Postscript) was aware of the new roles that materialism, *zhuzi* scholarship, and a new attention to Xunzi had played in Tokugawa nationalist thought, and approved of it. After all, the inspiration for it all came from China. It was for this reason, I speculate, that he placed his biography of Zhu Shunshui, who transmitted Ming-Qing materialistic thought to Japan, on an equal level with that of Wang Fuzhi. See "Two Extraordinary Confucians (*liang qi ru*)," *Zhongguo jin sanbainian xueshu shi*, 83–84. Wang Fuzhi's belief in the basic transformability of peoples' consciousness (*xin*) is emphasized.

there is none under Heaven who does not feel fraternal toward brothers. Of those who receive their hearts [minds] from ancestors, there is none who does not feel affection toward those of his lineage. Of those whose hearts come from Heaven and Earth, there is none who does not clasp to himself the myriad things."[82]

The passage might first be noted as a reminder of the great difference in affective content between political expression in Chinese and in Manchu. In the first stanza, what I have translated as "feel fraternal" is in Chinese the word *you*, to "treat as a friend, be amicable," while the Manchu, *senggime*, is related to the Manchu word for "blood" and connotes intimacy. In the second stanza, "feel affection" translates the Chinese *mu*, "to be kindly to, feel friendly toward," but the Manchu noun *hajin*, "love"—the sort of love that the Nurgaci of the *Mambun rōtō* documents invoked when he described Monggo-gege as his "beloved wife" (*haji sargan*) and retrospectively legitimated Hung Taiji as the new khan. In the last stanza, "clasp to himself" translates the Chinese *ai*, "like, love, covet," but the Manchu *hairarūngge*, "the loathing to part with, inability to live without, passionate, tender devotion to." The contrast in the two voices (now, in Qianlong style, each contained within its own language) is typical of the differences in the two political voices of the Qing that had been blended in "Great Righteousness Resolving Confusion": The benevolent, upright, dispassionate voice of the emperor (the icon of harmony), the passionate, temperamental, sincere voice of the khan (the hero of strife). The Manchu voice is palpably continuous with the historical characterization of Nurgaci as conqueror motivated by a passion to avenge his ancestors betrayed and murdered by the Ming and his daughter violated by Bujantai; with Nurgaci's contemporary encompassment of a growing pantheon of war gods; with the Aisin Gioro claim to have been legitimated by Heaven's support of their

82. ama eme i mujilen be mujilen oburengge
abkai fejergi ahūn deo te senggime akūngge akū.
mafari i mujilen be mujilen oburengge,
abkai fejergi mukūn niyalma te hajin akūngge akū,
abka ni i mujilen be mujilen oburengge,
abkai fejergi irgen tumen jaka be hairarakūngge akū.

yi fu mu zhi xin wei xin zhe,
tian xia wu bu you xiong di.
yi zuzong zhi xin wei xin zhe,
tian xia wu bu mu zhi zu ren.
yi tian di zhi xin wei xin zhe,
tian xia wu by ai zhi min wu.

struggle (whatever Heaven's reasons might be); and with the continuing dialogue with the banner slaves of the khan abiding within the emperor—the father who is not merely benevolent toward his children, but loves them. Second, the logic of the passage forcefully implies the source of the emperor's exclusive moral dominion. The more remote and powerful the source of one's "mind," the more intense (authentic) and unlimited is the power to love. Commoners take their minds from their parents, nobles from their ancestors, but the emperor from Heaven and Earth. Heaven and Earth were the dual gods to whom the leaders of the Jianzhou Jurchens had been sacrificing (a white horse and black ox, respectively) since at least the fifteenth century, in a Central Asian tradition that was generalized throughout the Northeast; Qing sacrifices to Heaven and Earth, both in the Chinese and the Northeastern ritual idioms, took place at their prescribed intervals and their prescribed places within the Forbidden City. Beyond these standard accesses to Heaven and Earth, the Qianlong emperor had also his tantric initiation, in which he had literally received his "mind." The passage leaves no doubt, and little to construe to make the connection, that the emperor has, as "The Mean" prescribed, formed a "trinity" with Heaven and Earth (as their only son, tianzi, abkai jui). His alone was the morally generative voice (that could take unlimited forms) in all worlds.

In his way of relating the authority of the emperorship to concepts of identity, the Qianlong emperor achieved, over the course of his long reign, a radical departure from the ways these ideas had been linked by previous emperors. For the Yongzheng emperor and his amanuenses in "Great Righteousness Resolving Confusion," civilization was absolute. The emperor is the personal embodiment of civilization, and due to his moral perfectedness he is benevolent, even empathetic, toward his subjects. For the Qianlong emperor, identity is the absolute, not civilization. The emperor is the single consciousness that transcends all civilizations, and due to his perfect intuition he apprehends all souls. For the Yongzheng emperor, the erosion of cultural differences (and the achievement of a morally correct world) is the mission of the ruler. For the Qianlong emperor, the clarification of cultural differences, and subsequent proof of the universal competence of the emperorship, is the mission of the ruler. He is the servant not of Right but of Time. He is the cakravartin prescribed a thousand years earlier by the monk Huiyuan: "It is said in a sutra: 'The Buddha is naturally endowed with a divine and wonderful method to convert [all] beings by means of expediency [upāya], widely adapting himself to whatever situation he may meet. Sometimes he will become a super-natural genie or a saintly emperor

Turner of the Wheel (*cakravartin*), sometimes a chief minister, a National Teacher or a Daoist master.'"[83]

In ideological representation to its separate constituencies, the Qianlong emperorship mediated its legitimacy through the precise manipulation of historical symbols of the early Qing court. This was only symptomatic of the movement of the state toward a comprehensive legitimation of genealogical and eventually racial thinking, symbolic legal segregation, and cultural idealization, all of which reached highest development during the Qianlong years. Under the universalistic prescriptions of the Qianlong court, culture was an ideal, rigidly fixed by descent and by geography. The Qing ruled a complex geocultural realm by the power of the emperor to command the moral center of all civilizations. The Manchu homeland in Northeast Asia and the history of Nurgaci's formation of the state there remained indispensable to the historical legitimacy of the empire.[84] Yet the status of the emperorship in China and newly conquered Central Asia was in some opposition to its pre-conquest career, for the regional and particularist elements that had made the earlier state possible had receded before the universalistic, the taxonomic, the ideal, and the abstract. The solution for the eighteenth-century court was not to fulfill the logical extension of the genealogical criteria that would have extinguished Chinese-martial identity, for instance, and with it the pre-conquest history of the Qing. The court chose not to obliterate but to colonize its own history. This became a thread in the tapestry of Qianlong literary management, over which the emperor sat in the pose of holy regimentor.

Neither the behavior of the emperor nor his way of conceptualizing his relationship to the word was completely unlike those of other emperors of early modern Eurasia, and it may be fitting that one of the frankest depictions of the Qianlong emperor as regimentor was contributed by Giuseppe Castiglione (Lang Shining, 1688–1766).[85] The Jesuit was not merely an observer of the emperor at his work but a facilitator: He had helped design and engineer some of the most universalist of the Qianlong architectural

83. Zürcher (*The Buddhist Conquest:*, 435n1) notes that Huiyuan paraphrases the passage from the *Taizi ruiying benqi jing,* and that there is an analogous passage in an anonymous fourth-century version of the *Mahāparinirvānasūtra.*

84. Crossley, "*Manzhou yuanliu kao.*"

85. For general background on Castiglione (from Genoa, and apparently unrelated to the Mantua family with the same name) see Turner, ed., *Dictionary of Art,* vol. 6, 39–41; Beurdeley and Beurdeley, *Castiglione;* and the issue of *Orientations* devoted entirely to essays on Castiglione's work in November 1988.

projects,[86] had contributed to the "unifying" (*yitong*) cartography of the whole empire, and before his death would participate not only in writing and illustrating the narrative of the conquest of the Turkestan and southwest China but actually managed to have the plates for the edition cast in Paris. He made visible the camp life, troops' movements, and individuals' struggles in battle of the Qing armies, not only for contemporaries not present at the scene but for future ages. The Qianlong emperor, certainly, considered Castiglione and those working under him as integral to the process of conquest, as integral as those who later produced literary narratives that became part of the "Four Treasuries." [87]

Castiglione's best-known and most striking personal contributions were his portraits of the Qianlong emperor and his court.[88] The emperor was himself fascinated with the ability of the long-lived Castiglione to capture him at so many stages of his life from youth to later middle age. When he was himself aged, the emperor more than once in his poetry commemorated his wonder at being able, as a bent and blanched old man, to enter a room and be confronted by his own youthful self—always noting that he hardly knew at whom he was looking. He made such a comment in reference to the 1758 work known as "Qianlong Reviewing the Troops," which one may take as the most intimate and most complete portrayal of the universal emperor.[89] The emperor is not surprisingly super-centered in the composition. The very high tassle of his helmet combines with the line of

86. See most recently Pirazzoli-t'Serstevens, "The Emperor Qianlong's European Palaces."

87. On Castiglione as a witness of conquest see Beurdeley and Beurdeley, *Castiglione*, 79–88.

88. He also oversaw the imperial painting workshops where his Jesuit collaborators (especially Jean-Denis Attiret and on occasion Ignatius Sickelpart) and Chinese students (most important Jin Kun, Chen Yongjie, Ding Guanpeng, Ding Guanhe, and Cheng Liang) developed a genre of imperial portraiture and activity painting that was distinctive. See also Zhu Jiajin, "Castiglione's *Tieluo* Paintings"; Hou and Pirazzoli, "Les Chasses d'automne de l'empereur Qianlong à Mulan."

89. See previous comments in Crossley, "The Rulerships of China," 1483. The known history of the painting is treated in Zhu Jiajin, "Castiglione's *Tieluo* Paintings." The painting is not reproduced in Beurdeley and Beurdeley, *Castiglione*, evidently because they worked almost exclusively with paintings held by the National Palace Museum in Nankang, Taiwan, while this work is at present in the Palace Museum in Peking. Until the publication of Zhu's article in 1988, it was supposed that this painting dated from 1739; Zhu has used evidence from the emperor's poetry to date it to 1758. For reasons that are unclear, the authorities of the Palace Museum at Peking, who have the painting (displayed again as a *tieluo* on a palace wall in the Forbidden City) date the painting to 1748. In 1748 the emperor was about thirty-

his riding posture to define the spine of the picture. But more than being central, the emperor is radiant. The *dhāranī* encircling his conical helmet form part of an ideal arc continued by the feathers of his bows, and the perfectly positioned feet of his horse suggest a further concentric circle in the outer portions of the painting. The portrait's representations of the emperor's simultaneity—his Northeastern warrior skills in riding and shooting, his Chinese-patterned raiment, and Sanskrit prayers of the *cakravartin* engraved on his helmet—are obvious enough and were evidently pleasing to the court. The painting was never taken to the Forbidden City during the imperial period but was kept at the Southern Park (Nanyuan), where the emperors conducted their hunting parties and ceremonial troop reviews (the terrain of the Southern Park is visible in the background of the picture). The painting was in the special form of a "hang and remove" (*tieluo*) canvas, which could be posted to a wall and later taken down and stored. In fact, the painting stayed for the remainder of the imperial period in its place of honor on the central wall of a banqueting hall at the Southern Park, where the emperor often hosted the leaders of conquered or amicable peoples from Mongolia, Central Asia, and the Northeast.[90] Despite the emperor's obvious pride in the painting and his conviction that it had a distinct role at the Southern Park, what is, perhaps, most important for the historian is the meaning of the portrait's iconography to its painter Castiglione and what it suggests the Qianlong emperor shared with other rulers of early modern Eurasia.

From Tang times on there are many paintings of emperors riding, usually with their retinues, and at least one painting of the Yongle emperor of the Ming on his way to the battlefield. The same emperor was also careful to have himself depicted riding with a falcon to the hunt, another of his Great Khan references—this time to a well-known painting of Chinggis Khaghan at the hunt. Though mounted emperors were depicted in Chinese painting before Qing times, the fact that they are mounted was clearly not the emblem of rulership in these compositions. Indeed the emperors tend

---

seven years old, and in 1758 about forty-seven. For reasons I discuss below, I believe on evidence independent of Zhu's that 1758 is more likely the correct date.

90. The painting remained in place after 1912, and after 1917, when Puyi and the remnant imperial household moved to the Southern Park from the Forbidden City. It was evidently after that time that Duan Qirui had the painting removed from the wall there—ostensibly to preserve it, but since there was an ongoing debate about the ownership of imperial art one suspects a plan to centralize the imperial holdings within the Forbidden City and out of the hands of Puyi and his entourage.

to be tiny figures, among many others, and the expression of power lies in the arrangement of other figures, flags, and equipage around the emperors (as in the scroll by Wang Hui and others of the Kangxi emperor's inspection tours, now in the Musée Guimet). Castiglione painted several narrative scrolls of the Qianlong emperor in this sort of frame, as in the well-known "Deer Hunting Party" (*Xiaolu tu*) of 1741, and the slightly less well-known series of acrobatics shows at Mulan, or the undated depiction of the emperor's party entering a town (probably during a Southern tour). As a portrait, "Reviewing the Troops" is unique not only in its melding of the emperor and his horse into a solitary figure, but also in its eerily realistic details (even the emperor's slight strabismus is carefully captured). While European rulers of Castiglione's time certainly had ceremonial armor that was readily distinguishable from battlefield dress, the difference was not so dramatic as for the Qing, who substituted lacquered ox-hide helmets for steel and padded satin jackets (of elaborate dragon and cloud embroidery on an imperial yellow background) for leather and steel body armor. Castiglione, perhaps reluctant to lose the hint of martial magnificence that glinting steel offered, has supplied some where it should not be—on the *dhāranī*-encrusted helmet, on the shoulders, and at the wrists. He has also supplied the emperor with the faint near-smile favored in European portraiture of eminent persons. The most striking element, however, is the emperor's horse, which certainly has no comparison in any Chinese painting and is also unique in Castiglione's numerous paintings of horses. Before the Qing, when Castiglione and his apprentices produced hundreds of horse paintings, only the Tang empire in China was fond of horse portraiture. In ceramics, watercolors, murals (often tomb murals), and in stone friezes, horses (with or without their grooms) were popular imperial subjects. In some cases (as with the friezes from the tomb of Tang Taizong), the names of the horses can be discovered. In the instance of "Reviewing the Troops," the horse was a real horse and was faithfully depicted. It is the emperor's Kazakh steed, whose presentation as part of a tribute gift to the court was the subject of another Castiglione painting.[91] The horse figures

91. Paintings by Castiglione or those working under him include many hundreds of horses, in various formats. A series of paintings, of which several dozen may survive, are careful depictions of horses presented in tribute, with their names and almost always with a few remarks by the emperor himself on their virtues. These paintings have some kinship with the materials (which I believe are a Jesuit inspiration) in "Illustrated Tributaries of the Qing Empire," in that their specifics relate to commerce, commercial value, material culture, and so on, all as mediated through the "tribute" system. So far as I have been able to discover, this particular

in several other Castiglione works of the emperor at the hunt. Its tobiano markings are consistently portrayed, and its small ears, wide face, part-colored mane, and white stockings had evidently made a very strong impression on the painter. The horse is not at all an archetype and in fact may be the most extensively and accurately depicted horse of its time. But its presence in this portrait is virtually entirely archetypical. It is striding in the "Spanish" mode favored in all equestrian portrayals of early modern European emperors, one knee raised, head alert and forward, tail slightly raised. Presumably the horse could have been depicted standing still (and in most Qing scrolls of the period that depict military exercises or reviews, the emperor and his retinue are in fact still; the troops move, not the emperor, as befits his "pole star" station in the cosmos)[92] or in the gallop favored, as will be discussed below, in depictions of Tibetan war gods. Were it not for the horse's conspicuous role in the overall proportions of the painting the position of its legs would not necessarily recall the European idiom. It is in combination with the emperor's posture that the horse's attitude becomes definitive. The emperor, his left hand holding the reins, his right a riding crop, is in the traditional pose of the European mounted emperor. In fact, the portrait is in virtually every way an exact cognate of the European imperial archetype, usually traced from the statue of Marcus Aurelius (which had much earlier antecedents in provincial art and folk religion), and widespread across Eurasia—whether in statuary or in portraiture—by the end of the seventeenth century.

Castiglione might be expected to have made reference, sooner or later, to the artistic traditions in which he had been trained, but it is equally reasonable that he took the iconography he imposed upon the Qianlong em-

---

horse is not included in the paintings of this type, and so I do not know its name. I believe the horse is depicted in the 1757 painting "Kazakhs Contributing Horses" (*Hazake gong ma*), also by Castiglione (seized by a Colonel Frey during the suppression of the Boxers in 1900 and presented by him to the Musée Guimet in 1925). For this reason, I believe that "Reviewing the Troops" and other paintings in which this horse appears (for instance, the portrait of the emperor aiming his rifle at a deer while this horse stands by) do not date before 1757 (Zhu, on independent evidence, dates "Reviewing the Troops" to 1758).

92. Another way of looking at it: All movement, on the field of battle or hunt, might be defined consistently with respect to the emperor's position. Thus the directional flags grouped around the emperor should always have represented the position of the detachments relative to him (see also Chapter 2, n 17), and the movements at the hunt would reflect not only the position of individual bodies in relation to him but the elements of the state which they constituted (for graphic representation see Hou and Pirazzoli, "Les Chasses," 34–35).

peror seriously.[93] Castiglione was among the last generations of Jesuits to live and die in China.[94] The period of marked Jesuit influence on the culture and politics of the court had closed after the Kangxi emperor's rancorous exchanges with the Vatican over the adaptation of church practices in China to accommodate certain local beliefs and the emperor's consequent suspicion that Jesuits might not prefer his authority to that of the pope.[95] For the Qianlong court, Jesuits were enablers of the imperial agenda, not teachers or debaters on philosophical issues.[96] They continued their role in the empire as technicians, completing the great map projects, working as draftsmen or in architectural roles on the building projects in the palaces and parks, and contributing many of the illustrations to the military narratives published under the sponsorship of the court. It is also probable that they were the strongest influence on the form of the "Illustrated Tributaries of the Qing Empire" (*Huang Qing zhigong tu*), which is like the

93. Or the emperor and Castiglione may have shared this idea. See the suggestion in Waley-Cohen, "Commemorating War," 892, that the Qianlong emperor may have known something about the Philip II triumphalist murals at Versailles and at El Escorial. The conscious use here of a European-derived universal representation is underscored by the existence of a superficially similar painting, attributed—not entirely credibly—to Castiglione. In the painting the emperor wears similar armor and is seated on a white horse that is similarly tacked out. But the emperor faces the viewer's left, is not in full face, appears ill at ease, and has no background behind him; also, the legs of the horse are haphazardly placed, and overall the painting is rather clumsily executed. There is very little information about this painting, which is evidently in the collection of the Palace Museum in Peking (there is a very small reproduction in Beurdeley and Beurdeley, *Castiglione*, 179 [plate 86]). The painting shows awareness of "Reviewing the Troops" but seems oblivious to the European imperial nuances in that painting, and is most probably not the work of Castiglione.

94. The tombs of many of the best-known Jesuits, including Castiglione, are preserved in Peking, presently within the grounds of the cadre school of the Chinese Communist Party (once the precincts of the Nandian Tang, or Southern Cathedral, which the Jesuits constructed in the capital with imperial permission). Many of the tombs still retain the stelae with inscriptions in Chinese and Latin.

95. It was in the midst of the contention between the Kangxi court and the Vatican that one of Xuanye's Jesuits, Bouvet, was sent to Versailles to present his *L'Histoire de l'empereur de la Chine* in 1699. Partly on the basis of the work of Bouvet and that of another Jesuit historian, Martino Martini, the eighteenth-century literati of France—most famously Voltaire—had developed the idea that the emperors of "China" were near philosopher-kings, opposed to superstition (that is, the church) and the aristocracy. The impression was reinforced by Amyôt's publication of the "Ode to Mukden," see below.

96. The Qing court remained important to the Jesuits as a base for proselytizing, however, particularly among Korean envoys to Peking, several of whom were baptized and vigorously promoted Catholicism in Korea well into the nineteenth century (Gari Ledyard, "Korean Diaries," unpublished ms., 17).

standardized portraits of American peoples presented by the Jesuits to the courts of Louis XIV and XV but unlike any tributary works done in previous empires based in China.[97] But Jesuit influence outside art and architecture declined in the empire at about the same rate as the conquest itself, and in 1805 the Jiaqing emperor would ban foreigners from learning Manchu, in order to end proselytizing among the court and aristocracy by Jesuits, Dominicans, and Lazarites.

In view of the history of Jesuit involvement in the imperial representation of Louis XIV (as discussed in the Introduction), the role they assumed at the Qianlong court might have been a comfortable one for them. Jesuits had been active in propagandizing Louis as the "new" Theodosius, or Charlemagne, a universalist conqueror who would reunite the various peoples of the world (a new possibility in the age of discoveries and sea empires) under a single moral authority. They pressed him to pursue policies reestablishing the political authority of the church and had a few successes. But the lack of complete victory did not prevent Jesuits from repeatedly working for the promotion of Louis as a universal ruler. They counseled him on how best to cultivate an imperial mystique, they promoted him as peacemaker of "four continents" (that is, the "world"), they aided embassies to his court by representatives—of one kind or another—from Russia, Guinea, Morocco, Thailand, Annam (Vietnam), Algeria, China, and the Iroquois. And, by direct or indirect influence, they facilitated the diffusion throughout Europe of a Louis-derived universalist complex that included the founding of universities, gazettes, observatories, imperial research institutes, hospitals, the publication of encyclopedias, the building of grand architecture for cradling the imperial presence, and dissemination of a transcendent imperial persona, classically rooted but chronologically undelimited. Louis was the epitome of this idiom but not its source, since earlier models could be found in François I, Philip IV of Spain, Charles I of England, and Cosimo di Medici.[98] Contemporaneous or subsequent subscribers in response to Louis' success included Karl XII of Sweden (another "pole star" ruler), Charles II and William III of England, Philip V of Spain (Louis' grandson), Leopold I and Joseph I of the Holy Roman Empire, and Peter the Great. Some were imaginative in their elaboration or adaptation of the model; others were more literal. Among the more fundamental quotations

97. See as examples depictions of peoples of northeast America from the Jesuit mission settlements, now preserved in Bibliothèque nationale de la ville de Montréal and National Archives of Canada.

98. Burke, *The Fabrication of Louis XIV,* 180–81; 184.

from Louis were a Versailles palace (the Trianon was favored) and the equestrian pose. The Qianlong emperor had both an imitation Trianon and an equestrian portrait, each facilitated by Castiglione, his contemporary Jesuits, and their collaborators at the Qing court.

Castiglione had two choices of equestrian pose: the emperor on a rampant horse, obviously in the midst of battle, or the review mode used in this case. The rampant pose, which was occasionally used for Louis and other monarchs (famously the van Dyck portrait of Charles I, now in the National Portrait Gallery) in specific representations of war or battle, would have been slightly preposterous, since the action was derived from specific European riding idealizations (evidently an inspiration of mosaic scenes of Alexander in battle) and is not known to have been used in battle in eastern Asia. More important, the rampant pose was for the conqueror in process, not the universalist emperor ruling over an accomplished domain. The review pose was not a reference to military action specifically but to the emperor as controlling the power and direction of the government, keeping stately pace, and usually holding in his right hand an instrument of authority—in many European instances an upraised sword (of victory, not of battle), or a scepter. In the Qianlong emperor's case this instrument is a crop—not in itself deadly, but the means of controlling power, and directing it where he wills (the impressive handle of his sword is subtly visible on his left side, away from the viewer). This particular pose, which is not overtly warlike but amply conveys the sense of huge power under steady rein, was well embedded in European imagery of rulership but more than a bit out of place in the Qing context. In Castiglione's reference, it had connotations that even the Qianlong court may not have appreciated, though Castiglione himself understood them well. Not only rulers, in the European gloss of this image, but saints also, were likely to be portrayed in this manner. In most cases, frequently depicted rulers or saints would appear in both rampant and review styles, depending on the taste of the artist or the intentions of the scene. Thus Saint George—intimately associated with many rulers—sometimes fights his dragon in the rampant posture, and sometimes serenely tramples the dragon under the steady footfalls of his steed. From Roman emperors on, Gauls, Basques, Muslims, Protestants, and Africans were all depicted as getting themselves under the feet of the imperial warhorse.[99] Perhaps the icon most acutely centered at the conver-

---

99. It is not critical to this argument but still interesting that ancient depictions of enemies trodden under the foot of a progressing horse may have had strong religious connotations. Dent and Goodall trace the earliest representations of a mounted

gence of the saintly and imperial missions was Saint James (originally of Campostella, a center of horse breeding in early and medieval times), who in both rampant and review postures was seen first trampling Moors under his hooves (Santiago matamoros), and later crushing American peoples (Santiago mataindios) in his progress (a nice extrapolation from the continental imperialism of Spain to its sea-spanning descendant). He even appeared (as Yagappan) in this guise in the ideology of some kingdoms of Southern India in this period.[100] The Spanish as well as Indian manifestations of Saint James were certainly among the allusive schemes within which Castiglione worked. It is the icon of the empowered universal ruler, holding the reins of orthodoxy, disinterestedly riding over chaos, dissidence, and heathenism.

The attraction of the image for Castiglione may have been intensified by details that more insistently invoked the identification of the mounted saint or ruler with religious militancy and doctrinal vigilance. In the European imagery to which the painter had access, there were a variety of choices regarding the object to be held in the rider's hand. In the Tibetan and Mongolian depictions of what Walther Heissig has called the "equestrian gods," however, there was a more limited selection. In a few cases the deity, always on a galloping horse, holds a flag (inhabited, by Mongolian tradition, by a divine consciousness), sometimes with a prayer-wheel attached. More often, he holds a riding crop. There is even an archetypical depiction of such war gods in block prints from Mongolia and Tibet in which his helmet and bows suggest the same ideal circle present in the Castiglione portrait. That Castiglione was ignorant of this idiom is very unlikely. The Jesuits had their own history of exploration and contact in Tibet, predating the Qing empire, and in the eighteenth century were still actively engaged in attempts to win the Tibetan nobility away from lamaism. The Jesuits were accompanied (rivaled) in Tibet by the Capuchins, who had in fact been ordered to evacuate Lhasa only in 1747, the year before Castiglione completed this painting.[101] But church sources may have been incidental for

hero—possibly a pre-Roman Gallic god—trampling an enemy under hoof to the western European provinces of the Roman empire, probably not earlier than 100 BCE. Identification of the motif is difficult because of the overwriting of native religious symbols with novel Roman translations. See Dent and Goodall, *A History of British Native Ponies*, 13–14, and plates 10, 11, 12.

100. See also Susan Bayly, "Saints' Cults and Warrior Kingdoms in South India," 119–20.

101. Tucci, *The Religions of Tibet*, 253–54; Snellgrove and Richardson, *A Cultural History of Tibet*, 202, 221–24.

Castiglione. As a denizen of the Forbidden City he certainly knew the importance of, and may have been knowledgeable of many of the details of, Qing devotion to the war god cults of Tibet and Mongolia, which combined shamanism, Buddhism, and imperialism in ways most pleasing to the Qing ideology. Most important, the equestrian portrait—drawing upon both European and Inner Asian images—was implicitly but unmistakably the depiction of militant centrality, enforcing true thought and speech in the unbounded world.

6 The Universal Prospect

In the eighteenth century, the Qing imperial family developed an enthusiasm for a distinctive plaything. The Qianlong emperor, the princes, and their households commissioned and collected lacquered boxes, "cabinets of many treasures" (*duobao ge*), often small enough to fit in the lap, others large enough to rest solidly only on a table. The boxes were equipped with drawers, often dozens of drawers, some undiscoverable by any but the owner. In the drawers were miniature objects: jades, ivories, cloisonnés, stones, jewels; dwarf pens and ink cakes; tiny books and paintings; mirrors. Each was in its own customized container. The set could be opened and spread over the expanse of a good-sized rug, or folded together and slipped under a chaise pillow. Some contained a special toy, a painted portrait of the owner, not much bigger than a modern playing card. Accompanying the small portrait were glass squares of the same size, but with costumes and hairstyles painted on the glass in such a way that, placed over the portrait, the owner could see himself bedecked in the costume of a Tang official, a Ming general, a Song minister, a Daoist recluse.[1] The boxes were a Qing twist on a Ming tradition. Under the earlier dynasty, boxes were used by scholars to store and transport real objects they needed—full-sized pens, paper, ink cakes and ink stones, elbow rests. They were akin to the compartmentalized lunch boxes used by scholars and working men alike. But the Qing items had been affected by the spirit of the European "curiosity cabinet," where natural and cultural oddities were concentrated for classification, stratification, and the

---

1. Derived from this tradition were the panels depicting the Yongzheng emperor in a variety of guises—Mongol, Tibetan, European, as well Daoist monk and Confucian scholar. See Rawski, *The Last Emperors*, 53, and Wu, "Emperor's Masquerade."

general purpose of defining what is odd. As every European curiosity cabinet was the center of its taxonomic universe, so each Qing prince with a cabinet of many treasures was a point from which radiated the potential to name and transform all things, including himself. The boxes were the toys of universalism, in which reality is bestowed upon objects by subjecting them to the imperial power to stereotype, miniaturize, and segregate.

Qing art of the Qianlong period is famous for its reproduction of miniaturized, complete worlds in various media. Some were architectural, as at the summer palace at Chengde, where the Tibetan residences of the Dalai and Panchen *lamas* were reproduced within the walls of the imperial dome, or at the summer palace at Yuanming yuan, where the rough imitation of the Trianon palace was installed. It is possible that this on-the-ground replication was originally Buddhist in inspiration, a three-dimensional mandala marking a center (or one of the material markers for the Center). The earliest surviving form of it was the Mahākāla complex built at Mukden. It was a cultic variation on the temple patterns of the five "meditating" or "entranced" (*dhyāna*) Buddhas that had already been replicated throughout the Mahāyāna world, using codified representations of the directions, the past and present, and the hierarchies of the Buddhas (with the highest at the center). Remains of the Mukden project suggest a very large containment, with landscaping and architecture that presaged many Qing landmarks in China and Inner Mongolia. In the Qianlong period the Mukden complex was itself replicated on a smaller scale in Peking, east of the Forbidden City, so that the imperial capital came to enfold sacred Mukden itself within its miniature worlds.[2] Philippe Forêt has noted that although Buddhist monuments were used to anchor the four corners of Jin Mukden at sites specified by *lamas*, the city plan was an allusion to the Ming imperial capital at Peking. As a provincial capital—one constructed almost to order as an outpost of the Ming imperial presence—it would be expected to have some of these qualities irrespective of whether or not it fell under control of the Jin khanate. But the division of the city into inner and outer portions, as strongly as it resembled Peking (and, from our perspective, the future of the Qing empire), it also resembled the Jin past: Shin Chung-il had been very detailed in his description of the concentric structure of Fe Ala, where the two co-rulers lived in an inner sanctum from which their troops

2. On imperial architecture at Mukden of the Jin and early Qing periods see Grupper, "The Manchu Imperial Cult"; Forêt, "Making an Imperial Landscape in Chengde, Jehol"; and Qian and Qian, *Shengjing huang gong*. For background to Chengde see also Rawski, *The Last Emperors*, 19–23.

were excluded, and where the soldiers and their families lived segregated by an outer wall from farmers, traders and laborers.

Forêt also commented in his account of the Qing literary representations (as contrasted to physical features) of the summer palace built after 1673 at Rehe (Chengde)[3] that geomantic considerations were important in the imperial architectural programs; when they could not be fully met by the landscaping and building itself, they were perfected in the artistic and literary representations of the landscaping and buildings.[4] It was the ideal form, generated by the imperial mind and visible on the imperial plane, that counted. This may have allowed matters of scale and some detail to be infinitely negotiable, so that whole worlds could be placed inside an ivory ball—or, as at Rehe, not only the landmarks of the empire but their very terrains, their natural environments, could be captured in the gardens, grounds, and vistas of the complexes.[5] In other cases, the universalism was abridged to a self-reference, which collapsed the completeness of the universe to a single, perfect loop of mutual indication (which, it has been suggested earlier, is a necessary reflex of imperial ideology). The Qianlong emperor kept in the "Hall of Three Treasures" (Sanxi tang—his own life-size curiosity cabinet) a well-known Song period painting of a scholar admiring a portrait of himself, and had the painting reproduced with his own face for the scholar's—a grown-up version of the portrait-and-costume toys in the lacquer boxes. Similarly, the tastes of the Qianlong court tended toward the elevation of form (the manifestation closest to the hypostatic imperial intelligence of the "Ode to Mukden") to the exclusion of function, as the imperial factories turned out vases that were not vases, bronzes that were not bronzes, swords that were not swords, and a wide assortment of imitation flowers and vegetables.

The idealism of the Qianlong period—that is, its tendency to use perfection in the representation of forms (containers) as an expression of the universal "oceanism," as one might translate the Qianlong emperor's religious ideology—should be placed in the context of what preceded and what

---

3. On the history of literary celebrations of Rehe (Bishushanzhuang) from the Kangxi period, see also Crossley and Rawski, "A Profile."

4. Forêt, "Making an Imperial Landscape," 29. The design and use of the Rehe grounds can be compared in some ways to the use of the hunting grounds at Mulan, as well as the ceremonial and celebrational (in poetry as well as painting) aspects of the emperor's progress from Rehe to Mulan. See details in Hou and Pirazzoli, "Les chasses," especially the discussions of the schedule of the emperor's attendance and the symbolic arrangements of groups of people as well as objects.

5. Forêt, "Making an Imperial Landscape," 51–63.

followed it. The conquest regimes of the Shunzhi, Kangxi, and Yongzheng years put primary emphasis upon the consolidation of a conquest force, admission to its ranks, cultivation of discipline and particularistic loyalties, and the establishment of governing mechanisms in newly conquered regions. To accomplish this, these earlier Qing courts had to incorporate simultaneities of imperial expression into the rulership, had to patronize printing projects that would show a curatorial interest in conquered peoples, and contribute in fundamental ways to the literary, pictorial, and architectural diversity of the empire. There is evidence that the primary theme, especially in the cases of the Kangxi and Yongzheng courts, was consolidation. They worked, as will be discussed below, to develop a melded governing elite, and in all regions to enlist local leaders in the new enterprise of Qing conquest. The foundations for the archetypical representations of imperial constituencies were all laid in the Shunzhi, Kangxi, and Yongzheng eras. But the extreme manipulation of those representations of the Qianlong era, preserved permanently in the vast literary production and reproduction of the middle eighteenth century, was distinctive.

Moreover, though the Qianlong reign was very long, it was followed by a period in which the distillations, careful pairing of voice and audience, and concomitant transcendent cultural supremacy of the emperorship was not preserved intact. In the previous chapter it was claimed that the extraction of imperial Geser patronage from the folk tales of Tibet which were newly spread in Mongolia had contributed an additional image of centrality and supremacy to the emperorship. There is very little evidence that in the middle eighteenth century the court had done much to foster, at the popular level, any knowledge of Geser outside of Mongolia, or any association of him with the imperial lineage. But by the early Jiaqing (1796–1820) period sixty-five state-subsidized "Guan Di" temples (where Nurgaci was accepted as a presence) were spread throughout Gansu, Mongolia, Turkestan, and Tibet; indeed virtually all garrisons in China had Guan Di temples, too, but most were paid for through local contributions. In Mongolia, Tibet, and the Northeast, it appears that Guan Di had also entered the liturgies of lamaist prayers (where he was considered a manifestation of Kubera/Vaiśravana, the Buddha of the North). These were evidently local impositions on the Guan Di cult, not encouraged in any particular way by the state, and Walther Heissig has suggested that the conflation of Guan Di/Nurgaci/Vaiśravana occurred in a similar way: Mongol visitors to the Guan Di/Nurgaci shrines in the Northeast during the Jiaqing period evidently as a matter of course assumed that Geser was part of the war god fusion, and in this way oracular shamanic practices associated with Geser came to be practiced at Guan Di/Nurgaci shrines throughout Mongolia and Tibet. To the historian looking for the transition from Qianlong's simultaneously expressive emperorship to a less disciplined, more "fusion" (in Heissig's term) prone emperorship, these changes in the greater Geser cult are important. Subsequently both the Jiaqing and Daoguang (1821–50) courts pushed to have Geser embraced in the Nurgaci/Guan Di temples; they installed Manchu/Mongolian/Chinese inscriptions in the shrines throughout the Northeast and Mongolia referring to "Holy Geser, Khan of the Guan family," which could hardly leave doubt that Geser was now a channel to revering the imperial family and protecting its soldiers.[6] Evidently the imperial lineage of this era became aware of and welcomed their enlarged protecting spirit, since a Mongolian divination text used at the Yonghe gong lamasery invokes a Guan Di/Geser conflation as "Great Holy Khan." By the time of Ilghughsan Khutukhtu Mergen Bandida (Don grub rdo rje, 1820–82), who sanctioned the Guan Di/Geser cult as a protecting force for the Buddhist religion[7] (at a time, one might add, when the Qing court in Peking had lost virtually all simultaneity and had become particularistically "Confucian" in the aftermath of the Taiping War), popular participation in the provinces was being directly encouraged. The cult seems to have been a vital development in the border cultures of the Qing era, in all likelihood stimulated by the multiple imperial representations of the late seventeenth and eighteenth centuries, but its nineteenth-century form vividly contrasted to the Qianlong tendency to segregate, specialize, limit, and distill. As with many other developments of the earlier Qing, the imperial trajectory went from consolidations for purposes of conquest to archetypes for purposes of expressing imperial universality to collapse, conflation, and fusion of court representation in the period of disintegrating imperial rule and increasing influence from civilian elites, progressive military leaders, and anxious aristocrats.

THE BANNER ELITES

It had been a policy of Nurgaci that those serving him would be level in identity, but not in status. Within this identity there was hierarchy; military commanders were distinct from scribes, interlocutors or accountants, who were all distinct from the farm laborers, household servants, and traders

6. Heissig, *Religions of Mongolia*, 100.
7. Heissig, *Religions of Mongolia*, 93–101.

who were bound to one nobleman or another. It was suggested earlier that that equality of identity was severely strained by the conquest of Liaodong.

H. T.

The response of the Hung Taiji years was to institutionalize some new distinctions among the conquered, conquering, and transitional populations, while putting greater emphasis upon the ability of the emperorship to integrate them all. This integration, as suggested, was not itself done in a monolithic, universalist, or even generalized way. Rather, a distinct form of appeal and authority was devised for each of the emerging sectors of the empire, and the historicized constituencies to which each was, by more or less direct means, connected. The process was long in being refined—as long, perhaps by necessity, as the century and half of conquest in which the Qing empire engaged.

making elites from banner officers

In the early stages of that process, the Qing court harbored a plan for an imperial elite that would be a middle ground between the diversities within the emperorship and the diversities among the empire's peoples. Nurgaci had had the easiest time of it, in creating a class of elites within the banners who were of equal status before him and shared a solidarity of purpose and style. The intense pressure, after the conquest of Liaodong, to incorporate large numbers of Nikans, particularly from the area near the Great Wall, had contributed to the increasing rigidity of structure, hierarchy, and bureaucratization of the Eight Banners; this was particularly at issue in the creation of the Chinese-martial Eight Banners in 1642. Yet the express wish of the court remained that all divisions of the Eight Banners would be imbued with similar education, skills, sense of mission, and attachment to the court. An administrative expression of this intention was the plan for education of banner officers, which began under Hung Taiji and continued, with detours, on a single basic design until the eighteenth century.[8] The plan was evidently to educate a banner elite who would be prepared to act in any and all capacities in the service of the empire. They were to be educated in the Chinese classics and to know the histories of the Liao, Jin, and Yuan empires. They were to know mathematics and astronomy and the established literature on medicine. They were also to be expert horsemen, archers, and fighters with the sword and spear. By reading classics on the art of war as

8. For a more detailed account see Crossley, "Manchu Education"; Chang Chung-ju et al., *Qingdai kaoshi zhidu ciliao;* Lui, "Syllabus of the Provincial Examination (*hsiang-shih*) under the Early Ch'ing," "The Imperial College (*Kuo-tzu-chien*) in the Early Ch'ing," and "The Education of the Manchus"; and Elman, *A Cultural History of Civil Examinations,* Chapter 3.

well as the novel *Romance of the Three Kingdoms*, they were to be educated in the strategic arts (including meteorology). And they were to accomplish these studies in at least two of the three imperial languages of Manchu, Mongolian, and Chinese. The function of this class was not a reflection of the emperorship. That is, this banner elite was evidently not seen as a matrix for all peoples of the empire or a means of any man in the empire being transformed into some personal expression of its omnipotence. On the contrary the sources of the banner elite were limited to hereditary ranks of the Manchu, Mongol, and Chinese-martial (whether the old Nikan families of eastern Liaodong and Jilin or not). In later decades some negligible number of Albazinian or Muslim officers were also included. But the basic plan was to give a very select group a very broad function. That function was to perform any task necessary to further the ends of conquest and occupation, which meant mastery of not only martial skills but the technology of occupation and eventually of governance. The concept was comparable to that of the *osmanli* in the Ottoman empire, probably for the reason that the Ottomans, too, felt the need to create a universal agent class that in origin would be close or construably close to the ruling house while in function able to reach to the extremities of the realm.

In the eighteenth century, this vision was abandoned. It had been receiving diminished support from the court for some time. The original plans had never been responded to adequately by the banner elites to whom they were addressed. Between 1640 and the early eighteenth century the imperial government was constantly making adjustments, but it never provided sufficient incentives or disincentives for the program to work. Perhaps more critically, the Qing government did not provide the financial resources that would have been necessary for the program to have produced sufficient comprehensively educated officials to have served the empire's needs. The stages by which this program for education and employment of a banner elite was dismantled are relevant for understanding the changes at the same periods in the rhetoric and ideology of identity.

Educational policies of the late seventeenth century had required the bannermen to become accomplished in both military ("Manchu") and civil ("Chinese") skills. The early state was inconsistent in its requirements for formal education of bannermen. Prior to the promulgation of a comprehensive educational plan in 1687, bannermen were encouraged to develop literacy in Chinese, and skills in documentary Manchu were sporadically rewarded. This plan envisioned an ideal balance of banner accomplishment between civil virtues and martial virtues. "The Eight Banners take riding and shooting (*qishe*)[9] as their root, to their left is martiality (*wu*) to their right is civility (*wen*)."[10] The court required garrison officers to ascertain that candidates (whether Manchu, Mongol, or Chinese) were in some degree proficient in horsemanship and archery before being admitted to the entry-level examinations. The open provincial examinations, to which bannermen could be admitted after passing the entry-level tests, required those bannermen who wished to be graded on the bannerman's quota (*manzi hao*)—a less competitive pool—to contribute an examination essay in either Manchu or Mongolian. The system remained much the same through the late eighteenth century, though it was suspended for short periods of experimentation. But there was one important alteration: In 1687—six years after suppression of the Three Feudatories and less than a year before the Tong/Hūwašan petition for re-identification would be submitted—the Board of Appointments (*libu*) drew up a new plan for banner participation in which Chinese-martial examination candidates would be excluded from the usual banner quota system for grading; an additional category was created for them.[11] In addition to being excluded from the quota for Manchus and Mongols, Chinese-martial also found that over time the quotas allotted them were dramatically lowered—primarily by being exchanged for the Mongol quotas. That is to say that where, prior to about 1670, the Manchu and Chinese-martial quotas were generally set equal to each other and the Mongol quotas at half of either of them, after 1670 it became gradually institutionalized for the Manchu and Mongol quotas to be equal and the Chinese-martial to be set at half of either.[12] The circumstances relating to stipends for students preparing for the examinations were similar. Annual rates of increase were established for the Chinese-martial in 1643 (very soon after the Chinese-martial banners were created), and for the Manchus and Mongols in 1671. From that point on, Chinese-martial stipends were normally awarded at a ratio of half the number awarded to Manchus or Mongols in any given year—grossly out of relationship to the proportion of the banner population they represented. At the time of the founding of

[handwritten marginal note: Chinese martials edged out of Banners]

9. *Qishe*, literally "riding and shooting," is the Chinese term for what in all Inner and Central Asian languages is a single word (in the Manchu case, *niyamniyambi*, possibly a borrowing from Mongolian) describing the distinctive Inner Asian skill of shooting from a moving horse. See also Sinor, "The Inner Asian Warriors," and Crossley, *Orphan Warriors*, 15, 22–24. For an introduction to the history of Qing mounted archery see Rawski, *The Last Emperors*, 43–46.
10. *QSG* 108:3160.
11. *QSG* 108:3161.
12. *QKZC* 1.7a.

the Eight Banners Officers' Schools in Peking in 1728, rules stipulated that 60 percent of all matriculants be Manchu (who may have represented at most 40 percent of all bannermen), 20 percent Mongol (who may have represented 10 percent of all bannermen), and 20 percent Chinese-martial (who may have represented 50 percent or more of all bannermen).[13] In 1739 the mathematics division, to which students went last, is reported to have enrolled fifty-two students, along these quota lines: twenty Manchus, twenty Chinese civilians, six Mongols, and six Chinese-martial bannermen.[14] A proportional quota for the imperial examinations (the highest level) was introduced in 1744 that limited Manchus and Mongols to one successful candidate per ten aspirants, with absolute totals of no more than twenty-seven from either group, while Chinese-martial successes could number no more than twelve.

The ideological implications of the graduated alienation of the Chinese-martial from the Eight Banners and their identification with the "Chinese" were discussed in Chapter 2, and the relationship of these developments to the end stages of the conquest is evident; as other studies have shown, the dismantling of provisional conquest governments in the provinces and the establishment of civil governments demanded greater specialization in the roles of provincial military commanders (who were, increasingly, registered as Manchus) and of civil provincial governors (who were, increasingly, civilian Chinese). What is to be noted here is that abandonment of the liberal plan for development of a consolidated imperial elite meant the development, in the later eighteenth and nineteenth centuries, of more specialized programs for the cultural and professional preparation of the new segments of elites and also for identification of common populations. The pressure to eliminate Chinese-martial bannermen from the active rolls was effective over the long term—so effective that Europeans and Americans who observed the banners for the first time in the nineteenth century saw the "Chinese" bannermen remaining there as a small, odd, difficult-to-place group, an image that has persisted in modern scholarship on the Eight Banners. As putative "Chinese" in this system were transformed into civil servants primarily, with suitable education in the political arts, so "Manchus" were subjected to the process of military professionalization, and what had once been institutions for the liberal preparation of a conquest elite became specialized schools for the training of bannermen in riding, shooting, and Manchu speaking and writing. In the early nineteenth century the compo-

13. *QSG* 106:3110.
14. *QSG* 106:3110.

nents of bomb-making and weapons manufacture were added, so that the schools became the ancestors of technical colleges in chemistry, engineering, and military arts in the last period of the empire.

SHADY PASTS

The Qianlong emperor's flat pronouncement that the Chinese-martial bannermen were all "Chinese" (see Chapter 2) was intended as revisionist. It occurred in the context of the end of conquest in China and attempts to stabilize Qing rule in the border territories, of the pressures driving Chinese-martial out of the Eight Banners, and of the Four Treasuries projects. The latter provided unparalleled employment opportunities for Chinese literati outside the bureaucracy proper, and by definition extolled the towering literary achievements of Chinese civilization. But a secondary product of the Four Treasuries project was the institutionalization of new literature. Works of history, in particular (most produced under the directory of the Imperial Office of Historiography), commissioned in the early Qianlong reign and completed later, were cataloged on an equal basis with ancient works and in this way given an aura of authoritativeness generated by the "classics." As we will see below, some presented what were intended to be the definitive historical statements on the origins of the Manchus and Mongols. For the Chinese, no project of this kind was necessary. The ancient classics contained all that was supposed to be knowable about Chinese origins, and the best the court could do—and what it certainly did—was to encourage the scholars using "evidential" methods to review these texts to see what new things could be discovered between the lines, as it were. There remained, however, a problem in this idea of monolithic Chinese origins, now that the Chinese-martial had been cast into the pool. If Chinese were all historically identical, and Qing rule was universally legitimate, why had some Chinese joined the Qing in the very first years of the conquest and some not? The Kangxi emperor, in eulogizing the Three Feudatory martyrs Fan Chengmo and Ma Xiongzhen, had used the conflation of the Liaodongese and the "Chinese" to create a model of particularistic loyalty to the Qing empire. The difference, for those writing on his behalf, had been that some Chinese could recognize righteous rule and direct their loyalties toward it; others maintained a mistaken and morally befuddled loyalty to the corrupt Ming, or simply resisted the Qing out of narrow-mindedness (a verdict emphasized in "Great Righteousness Resolving Confusion"). For the Qianlong emperor, this explanation would not do.

Unlike his grandfather, the Qianlong emperor was the emperor of the absolute: Loyalty was loyalty, no matter to whom it was directed. The opposite of loyalty to one party was not loyalty to another; the opposite of loyalty was treachery. As the emperor of the absolute, the Qianlong emperor set out to judge those who had violated the absolute. His historians began to investigate the matter of transfers of loyalty from the Ming to the Qing. On the whole, the emperor found that the "Chinese" who had joined in early service to the Qing had been merely opportunistic in doing so, and though the conquest state had found it useful to accept their services, the post-conquest state was not going to pretend it was blind to the moral implications of their acts. Nor would it be awash in undeserved gratefulness for the service of these early "traitors."

The vehicle for forming and transmitting this judgment was "Lives of Twice-Serving Ministers" (*Erchen zhuan*).[15] In 1776 the court ordered that the draft biographies being prepared by the Imperial Office of Historiography include a category called *erchen*, or those who had served two dynasties. These were soldiers and officials who had in one way or another transferred their loyalty from the Ming to the Qing. The contrast of the *erchen* biographies with the "Record of Those Martyred for Their Dynasty and Sacrificed for Purity" ([*Qinding*] *Xingguo xunjie lu*), commissioned earlier to celebrate Ming loyalists like Shi Kefa who had died resisting the Qing invasion, spoke for itself as a mark of the emperor's thinking. What is striking is that the Qianlong emperor was not entirely free to make judgments afresh. The compact with the early Liaodongese families is still visible behind the *erchen* label. Considered together with the distinct but coterminously compiled collection of "traitors" (*nichen*) in which Wu Sangui himself is remembered,[16] the *erchen* biographies can be understood as representing a class of early Qing collaborators whom the Qianlong court now viewed in shades of condemnability.

15. Frederic Wakeman, who has made thorough use of the *Erchen zhuan* in his *The Great Enterprise,* has provided the apt translation of "twice-serving ministers" for the *erchen.* The *Erchen zhuan* was published without preface, and most of the document's intentions must be inferred from its evolution and the context of other publication programs proceeding concurrently, all of which come under the larger umbrella of the "Four Treasuries" (*siku quanshu*) projects. For discussions of the genesis and political context of the *erchen* biographies see Fisher, "Lü Liu-liang and the Tseng Ching Case," and Kanda Shinobu, "Qingchao de *Guoshi liezhuan* he *Erchen zhuan.*"

16. This collection was published together (but under separate title) with the *Erchen zhuan,* in four *juan.* Like the *Erchen zhuan,* the *Nichen zhuan* was also originally compiled as part of the *Qingshi liezhuan.*

The thinking behind the *erchen* list, though characteristic of the ideology of the Qianlong emperor, was not individual with him. A hundred years after the martyrdoms of Fan Chengmo and Ma Xiongzhen in the Three Feudatories War the dramatist Jiang Shiquan (1725–85)—a prominent academician who in 1781 would himself serve briefly as a compiler at the Imperial Office for Historiography—crystallized the Qianlong view of the Fan and Ma martyrdoms by giving Ma Xiongzhen a speech to Wu Shizong in which he condemns Wu's grandfather, Sangui, as being already "twice-serving" and now perpetrating a second treachery; the exemplars of the earliest Chinese-martial adherents had arisen from the past to excoriate all who would change sides for profit.[17] Wu, the Liaodongese who betrayed both the Ming and the Qing, was (with his Three Feudatory collaborators) virtually in a class by himself. For the *erchen* there had to be fine gradations of culpability. To represent this, the list had to be very selective, and also segmented, each subject put into a neighborhood of those who most closely shared his moral failings. Factionalists, opportunists, rebels, and those who had simply gotten too much while suffering too little were segregated and displayed. Of many hundreds, one might argue thousands, of men of stature who served at one time or another both the Ming and the Qing, 120 were initially chosen for inclusion in the list (and 125 appeared on the draft list when it was completed). It was intended not only as a personal comment upon the individuals named but also as a heuristic device, like all biographical categories in the dynastic histories, for the display of types of behavior and their estimation by the state. In many instances cited individuals are outstanding for the fact that they had been accused, alive or more often posthumously, of corruption, treason or, in the case of Zhou Lianggong, of anti-Manchu propaganda. The breadth of the *erchen* was underscored by the decision in 1778 to break the list of *erchen* into two groups (*jia* and *yi*, hereafter "1" and "2"), the second of whom were more blameworthy than the first; still later the two lists were further graded into three

---

17. See *ECCP*, 141–42, and Wakeman, *The Great Enterprise*, 1118. Since Jiang was such a precise spokesman for the Qianlong view on the loyal Chinese-martial of the Three Feudatories period, it is unclear why this dramatic speech is inserted into the story of Ma Xiongzhen as though it were a primary or even a contemporary account of events. The effect is vivid, but it grafts the interests of the next century onto the story. Jiang, the best-known dramatist of the later eighteenth century, specialized in plays dealing with historical rebellions and demonstrations of loyalty (including that of the Song martyr Wen Tianxiang, invoked in Li Yu's eulogy to Fan Chengmo). The play of Ma Xiongzhen, *Guilin shuang*, was published in the collection *Cangyuan jiuzhong qu* (for alternative titles see *ECCP*) and reprinted in 1774.

levels each—*shang, zhong, xia* (hereafter "a," "b," "c")—so that altogether six ranks of relative disreputability were distinguished.[18] Topical considerations, many of which cannot be reconstructed, were significant in the inclusion of many names on the *erchen* list. The concern, for instance, with factionalism is evident in the thorough inclusion in the lowest registers of the followers of Wei Zhongxian (for example, Feng Quan, 2b; Gao Di, 1c; Li Lusheng, 2b; Qian Qianyi, 2b) in persecution of the Donglin party that, ironically, had included many of the Ming military intendants in the Northeast who were overpowered by Nurgaci (and later became accusers of Tong Bunian). It is possible that the Qianlong emperor's suspicions of Li Shiyao (d. 1788)[19] contributed to the placing of his ancestor Li Yongfang in the 1b category of the list; by the same token it is equally possible that Ma Xiongzhen's father, Mingpei (1600–1666), a Liaodong "functionary of the western conquests" (*fu xi baitangga*) who aided in the destruction of the Southern Ming and whose career paralleled many *erchen*, was omitted from the list because of the possibility of besmirching the memory of and disturbing the delicate symbolism appended to the son. The completed work was presented to the emperor, who had been complaining for years of delays in its production, in 1785.

A large portion, though not all, of the *erchen* were non-Liaodongese Chinese-martial bannermen. Their arrangement within the collection together with the omissions of some extremely prominent Chinese-martial families provide some insight into the capacity of late-eighteenth-century imperial ideology for accommodation both of the historical importance of the early Chinese-martial adherents and of the new need to recharacterize the Chinese-martial bannermen as Chinese opportunists of the conquest period. The Qianlong emperor's insistence upon absolute standards of loyalty to the dynasty under which one has been nurtured and rewarded was paramount. Thus nearly all recipients of the highest examination degree in the Ming period rank very low; a subgroup of them are the "Peking

---

18. See Kanda Shinobu, "Qingchao de *Guoshi liezhuan*."

19. Li had been governor-general of Guangdong and Guangxi provinces for ten years, during which he regularly presented the emperor with gadgets acquired from the foreign traders at Canton. By the late 1770s, however, Li had fallen afoul of the recently risen Heshen and his network, and charges of corruption were lodged against him. The emperor's demands in 1780 for publication of the *Erchen zhuan* coincided with the trial of Li Shiyao (presided over by Heshen) that resulted in a death sentence, later commuted by the emperor. The evidence indicates (see Kanda Shinobu, "Qingchao de *Guoshi liezhuan*") that Li Yongfang was to be included in the draft list, but his original ranking is unclear.

Chinese" and unincorporated bureaucrats who surrendered at the capital in 1644 and 1645. Many of these were not "twice-serving" but "thrice-serving" (like Chen Mengxia, 2c, executed in 1654 for incorrigible corruption, and Sun Chengzi, 2c), having participated in the rebel Li Zicheng's regime before the advent of Dorgon's troops.[20] The contrast to the later seventeenth century, when the first priority had been to establish the value of Chinese loyalty to the Qing dynasty particularly, is striking. Within the context of the tensions between the pre-conquest and post-conquest ideologies, the relationship of the Chinese-martial to the *erchen* list becomes decipherable. Exclusion of all Liaodong Chinese-martial from the list would have ignored the tendency of the court since at least the time of the post–Three Feudatories encomia for Fan Chengmo and Ma Xiongzhen to characterize the Chinese-martial as being in essence Chinese—more important, as representing the desired sentiments of the Chinese population toward the Qing court. It followed, under such assumptions, that certain of even the very old Chinese-martial families must be identified as "turncoats" from the Ming. On the other hand, inclusion of pillars of the early Nikan—such as Tong Yangzhen, Tong Yangxing, Ning Wanwo, or Fan Wencheng—would by implication have condemned the history of Nurgaci's state-building. A reasonable solution, given the ideological imperative of the Qianlong emperor to establish a standard of absolute loyalty, was to promulgate a list with the graduated form of the "Lives of Twice-Serving Ministers."

Time and place have a relationship in the ideology of the *erchen* that was characteristic of the eighteenth-century Qing drive to speciate the empire's moral audiences between "Inside the Wall" (*guanwai*) and "Outside the Wall" (*guannei*). There is a superficial appearance of chronological organization to the six levels of the "Lives," which is dispelled only when a close examination reveals that none of the subdivisions is in fact consistent with regard to date of surrender, place of birth, place of surrender, or bureaucratic rank. In fact, time and place had become moral criteria by the time of the compilation of the *erchen* biographies, and thus both clusterings and diversity within the subdivisions are expected. The earliest *tai nikan* families—those organized in the aftermath of the taking of Fushun in 1618, in the period in which "there were no principles for discrimination"—would be absent from the collection except for the inclusion of Li Yongfang (the

20. Only four *jinshi* recipients rank higher than 1c: Wang Aoyong (*jinshi* 1625; 1a), Wang Zhengzhi (*jinshi* 1628, 1a), Xu Yifen (*jinshi* 1628, 1a), and Hong Chengchou (*jinshi* 1616, 1b). Of this group, only Hong Chengchou was Chinese-martial.

Qianlong emperor having at this time a strong antagonism toward his descendant Li Shiyao). *Tai nikan* incorporated after Fushun, during the struggle for Shenyang and the regions to its west, are represented by three individuals, all from Guangning, taken in 1622.[21] The "functionaries of the western conquest" (*fu xi baitangga*), or those who became prominent during the drive toward north China, are in contrast represented by twenty men.[22] In sum, Chinese-martial incorporated before the breach of the Great Wall and the full-scale invasion of China in 1644 are heavily concentrated in the 1a, 1b, and 1c ranks, indicating that they appeared on the original 1778 list of "better" men, and as a group they far outrank the surrendering Ming bureaucrats of Peking and Nanjing.

Perhaps there is no better example of the morality of time and place in this *erchen* scheme than the contrast of Ma Degong with Tian Xiong, two Ming generals responsible for delivering the Ming Prince of Fu into the hands of Qing troops in 1645. Both requested and were granted admission to the Chinese-martial banners, both distinguished themselves in coastal campaigns against rebels and resisters, and both died in honorable condition in 1663. But Ma is on the 1a list and Tian on the 1c. Ma was of Liaodong provenance, though his military career happened to have taken him to Zhejiang by the time of the Qing invasion. Tian, by contrast, was a native of Zhili, inside the Great Wall. The two personify the subliminal theme in the *erchen* list: The symbolic detachment of the Liaodong from the northern Zhili populations of the Chinese-martial, still lingering nearly a century and a half after their administrative amalgamation in the Chinese-martial banners conquering northern China. Natives of Liaodong owed the Ming no loyalties that could now be admitted; they were condemned, in small numbers and in faintly negative terms, for individual acts of duplicity or opportunism. But natives from "Inside the Wall" were by definition indebted to the Ming; they performed however meritorious a service to the Qing at cost to their own integrity, and to that of any regime that would accept their service without comment. The mass historical verdict passed on

21. In descending order, Zhu Shichang (1b), Bao Chengxian (1b), and Sun Degong (2a).

22. In descending order, noting place of surrender and *erchen* group: Liu Liangchen (Dalinghe, 1a), Sun Dingliao (Dalinghe, 1a), Kong Youde (Dengzhou, 1a), Meng Qiaofang (Yongping, 1b), Zhang Cunren (Dalinghe, 1b), Zu Kefa (Dalinghe, 1b), Liu Wuyuan (Dalinghe, 1b), Shang Kexi (Pidao, 1b), Hong Chengchou (Songshan, 1b), Wang Shixian (Zunhua, 1b), Deng Changchun (Dalinghe, 1b), Zu Zerun (Dalinghe, 1c), Zu Zepu (Dalinghe, 1c), Zu Zehong (Dalinghe, 1c), Geng Zhongming (Laizhou, 1c), Quan Jie (Dengzhou, 1c), Zu Dashou (Jinzhou, 1c), Wu Rujie (Jinzhou, 1c), Ma Guangyuan (Yongping, 2a), and Shen Zhixiang (Pidao, 2a).

them in the late eighteenth century was corollary to the contemporaneous insistence by the court that all Chinese-martial were in origin Chinese (*han*). Their present and future circumstances within the Banners were to be legitimated with this claim, and their entire history to be cast into the shadow of treason.

MANCHUNESS

In Hung Taiji's time the campaign had been to militarily secure, commercially dominate, and mythologically co-opt the Amur region as the eastern terminus of the empire and the newly identified "ancestral" source of Qing history of rule. During the reign of Hung Taiji's son Fulin (the Shunzhi emperor, 1644–61), military presence in the Amur region was increased, but very modestly: The demands of the conquest of China on the Qing military apparatus were high, and Qing troops throughout the Northeast remained thinly applied. The primary assertion of Qing dominion in Sanxing (Ilantumen) and Ningguta was the tendency to banish offending military officers and bureaucrats (whether civilian or banner) to these regions. In 1653 a civil administration, based at Mukden and extending eastward to the Amur, was constructed and the small garrison at Ningguta regularized. By this time the Qing court in Peking was also becoming worried about the possibility of growing Russian military influence in the region. Explorers and traders from the west were increasing in number, and some peoples of the Amur were reported to acknowledge Russian suzerainty through the payment of a tribute. As the Qing established a garrison and magistracy on the southwest side of the Amur, the Russians established Fort Kumarsky on the other side.

When the Kangxi emperor succeeded to the throne in 1662, strategic concerns for maintaining Qing rule in the Amur region were growing. The child emperor's regents, led by Oboi, enlarged the garrison at Ningguta. A new line of fortifications was constructed around Liaodong (now marginally broadened to the east to include the site of Hetu Ala and laying the foundation for modern Liaoning province), and a new military command site (complete with workshops for the construction of warjunks to be used on the Amur) was built at Jilin. But it was recognized that the principle of border demarcation, so emphasized by Nurgaci and Hung Taiji, had been only casually pursued in the Northeast. The Amur River had been assumed as the natural boundary with the expanding Russian empire.[23] But in the 1650s the Russians had demonstrated that the Amur was nothing sacred to them, and they would extend as far south and east as the Qing would permit. Boundary demarcation was necessary. But there was a difficulty: The Qing court had only a very vague sense of the geography of the regions of Mt. Changbai and the Amur. To draw a boundary, there must be a map. Exploration would be the foundation of the claim to rule. It was, after all, the same logic being used by the Russians, and the Jesuits who were supplying the Kangxi emperor with his cartographic knowledge could hardly have argued against this principle.

In 1677 the Kangxi emperor, now aged twenty-five and experienced at governing personally since 1669, commissioned Umuna (d. 1690) to lead an expedition to Mt. Changbai. The young emperor explained to Umuna that no one knew the "exact spot" of the origin of the Aisin Gioro lineage; Umuna's mission was to find it and to sacrifice to its gods on behalf of the imperial family. Umuna secured the services of a guide, [Fuča] Sabsu, at Jilin, and set off. The mission was difficult, not least because Umuna was being sent into a literal wasteland (by its name, a place of perpetual winter) of thousands of square miles of unexplored (by the Qing) territory, and was supposed to find the "exact spot" where the Aisin Gioro had sprung up. But he understood the unvoiced purpose of the mission as well: To establish a Qing familiarity with the region and its geographical features that would be useful in delimiting boundaries with Korea (to the south of Mt. Changbai) and Russia (to its east). After some misadventures Umuna and his mission reached the top of Mt. Changbai, accurately describing its crater lake and the five prominences around it. They found also the source of the Songari River and provided the Qing court with a detailed description of the region's topography.

The report produced by Umuna, "Finding Mt. Changbai" (*Feng Changbaishan*), was taken as the model for the geographical descriptions in the Qianlong emperor's "Ode to Mukden" (commissioned in 1743). The wording on the sacred lake, Tamun, the waters flowing from it, and the geography of the region are all quotations from Umuna's report. The long introduction (a part of which was cited in Chapter 5) expressed the emperor's intense romanticism for the natural environment of the region and of the extraordinary origins of his lineage there (see Chapter 4). The completed

23. For a very detailed and dispassionate background on the expansion of the Russians into the Amur region see Bergholz, *The Partition of the Steppe*, 7–144.

work, which was considerably shorter than, say, "Great Righteousness," was done in a Manchu version, in a simultaneous Manchu and Chinese version, and editions in each language were also done in the thirty-two "magical scripts" (*fukjingge hergen*), whimsically supposed to derive from inscriptions of extremely early times. Thus the composition co-opted the orthographic studies that were still fashionable with the "evidential scholarship" practitioners and of course attracted to themselves whatever real magic there might be in the reputedly prehistoric characters. In more or less grand editions, the "Ode" became well distributed throughout the empire. The court Jesuits were charmed by it, and Amyôt paraphrased it into French in 1770.[24] Later scholars, particularly Jules Klaproth (in 1828), excoriated Amyôt's rendition for its philosophical asides and flights of patently Christian fancy that owed nothing to the brushes of Qianlong's scribes.[25] But Klaproth's strident denunciation of the work and the extravagant ideas of the Qing that it had produced in Europe came a generation—if not a century—too late. European readers had already been enchanted by the diligent, well-balanced, and kindly genius of the Kangxi emperor in Bouvet's history of 1690; they were well prepared to read the Qianlong emperor's celebration of the imperial family's brilliant origin in a perfect land. Voltaire, it is reported, committed his admiration for the ode to writing and later modeled his deistic, rational, aristocracy-defying philosopher kings of "China" on its author.[26]

As suggested in the previous chapter, the introduction to the "Ode" gave spectacular refinement to some establishments of Qing imperial speech. Its political vocabulary is markedly affective, it places the emperor in a "trinity" with Heaven and Earth, and it strongly asserts the intuitive link between blood relations—the living with their ancestors, as well as their contemporary kinsmen. This indelible identity of lineage was a hallmark of the many new historical productions of the Qianlong era, but never was the emperor content to merely allow individuals to make empty indications of their ancestors. They had to act out their identities, for which there were infinitive verbs in Manchu ("to manchu," *manjurambi*; "to mongol,"

---

24. It appears that Amyôt was working from an earlier English translation from a Manchu-Chinese bilingual edition, possibly the work of George Thomas Staunton. See Etō Toshio, *Manshū bunka shijō no ichi shinwa*, esp. 14–16, and *Dattan*, 37–48.

25. Jules Klaproth, *Chrestomathie Mandchou, ou recueil de textes Mandchou*, i–xxi.

26. Etō, *Manshū bunka*, 15. The author suggests that there was once written evidence at Bologna that Voltaire had made comments about the work in writing.

monggorombi; "to nikan," *nikarambi)*[27] and from the middle eighteenth century the sum total of these behaviors could be nominalized—*manju-rarengge* (causative case), "Manchuness." Behaviors as a source of identity were phenomena of the Nurgaci and early Qing period. The Qianlong court was interested in behaviors as an expression of identity; where genealogical identity and behaviors differed, the Qianlong government attempted to intervene to assure conformity of behavior to genealogical identity. The establishment, for instance, of Manchu as the particular language of Manchus—a process that took more than a century—was an important step in the building of the state thesis of Manchu origins, the basic tenets of which had been established under Hung Taiji: that Manchus were the descendants of culturally distinguished, genealogically coherent successions of peoples in the Northeast. Their language, their social structure, and their customs were also descendants of distinctive Northeastern forebears. The Qianlong court generated a massive documentation on Manchu origins, all in agreement with theses of cultural descent. They were incorporated into the "Four Treasuries" collections, and by that act given a classical pedigree. The methodology of evidential scholarship, the bureaucratic structure of the "Four Treasuries" project, and the interest of the Qianlong emperor were all indispensable elements in the process that led to the completion of the collections on the history and culture of the Manchu people.

It had been under the Yongzheng emperor Yinzhen (1722–35) that the foundation works of Manchu documentary institutionalization, the "Comprehensive History of the Eight Banners" completed in 1739 and the "Collected Genealogies of the Eight-Banner and Manchu Lineages" completed in 1745, had been begun as part of the bureaucratization of the banners. The interests of the succeeding Qianlong court were more subtle, more political, and more curatorial. Works of the period included the romantic "Ode to Mukden" (*Mukden i fujurun bithe, Shengjing fu,* 1743)[28] in addition to "Rites for the Manchu Worship of Heaven and of the Spirits" (*Manju wecere metere kooli bithe, Manzhou jishen jitian dianli,* 1781), which opened Qing shamanism to bureaucratic review. After seven years of compilation, the "Researches on Manchu Origins" (*Manzhou yuanliu kao*) was completed in 1783 under the supervision of [Janggiya] Agui and

27. All have causative forms.
28. The ode was first translated into French by Jean-Joseph-Marie Amyôt in 1770 and later was retranslated and printed with the Manchu text in Jules Klaproth's *Chrestomathie Mandchou.* See also Etō, *Manshūbunka,* 114–16, and *Dattan,* 7–48; and Crossley, "An Introduction," 22–23.

Yu Minzhong. It drew together folk traditions, the historical record, and Qing political ambitions into a coherent work. The "Researches" project was initiated by an imperial edict dated September 20, 1777, and published in 1783. The editorial staff had included the Grand Councillors (*da xueshi*) [Niohuru] Heshen, Wang Jie, and Dong Gao. As with all projects of the Four Treasuries, symbolic appointments and political divisions were not absent from the junior staff of the project, which presumably included those who actually accomplished the bulk of the compilation. The conventional policy of balancing civilians with bannermen (sometimes taken by historians as "Chinese" against "Manchus") was clearly followed. The two officials in charge of revision and correction were attached to the Hanlin Academy; Pingshu was the bannerman, Dai Quting the civilian. Below them were twelve compilers, of whom six were civilian, six bannermen (four Manchu and two Mongol).

On one level the work was a scholar's gloss to the "Collected Genealogies." Like Ortai's staff, Agui's took the lineages as their starting point, seeking out and arranging references to them in the official texts, then treating of the historical geography of the Northeast in great detail, finally discussing customs and folklore. But unlike the "Comprehensive Genealogies," the "Researches" owed nothing to folk or oral sources apart from those that long before had entered the imperial record; it was a systematic guide to the Manchu ancestors (or those believed to be so) in the official literature, reaching back to the pre-imperial period. Archival research was spare, limited to the Ming annals of the Yongle reign (1403–24) and to one citation each from the annals of the periods of Nurgaci and Hung Taiji's khanates. The compilation of the Four Treasuries collection proceeded simultaneously with the work on the "Researches," on "Rites for the Manchu Worship of Heaven and of the Spirits," and the second, enlarged, and yet uncompleted edition of the "General History of the Eight Banners." Materials and citations were freely shared among the ongoing compilatory projects, and all the finished products were eventually categorized according to the conventional classification system used for the Imperial Manuscript Library—the "Researches" (*Manzhou yuanliu kao*) and "Comprehensive Genealogies" (*Baqi manzhou shizu tongpu*) as "geography" (*dili lei*); the "Rites for Manchu Worship" (*Manzhou jishen jitian dianli*) and the "Comprehensive History of the Eight Banners" (*Baqi tongzhi*) as "works on governance" (*zhengshu lei*), all within the "History" section (*shibu*). The structure of the "Researches" reinforced the court's insistence that Manchu origins and the persisting key to Manchu identity lay in the Northeast. It was divided into four general sections, whose lengths were controlled to a great extent by the documentation created or neglected by earlier empires: "Federations and Lineages" (*Buzu*) in seven *juan*, "Political Boundaries" (*jiangyu*) in eight *juan*, "Physical Geography" (*shanchuan*) in two *juan*, and "National Customs" (*guosu*) in five *juan*. The authors did not, in the end, offer a summary on the shape or meaning of Manchu history; such commentary, besides being far outside the mandate of the "Researches," would have been meaningless in the eighteenth century. In the end the work in no way exceeds its original intentions of "using our dynasty as the schema [*gang*] for examination and explanation [*xiangshu*] of the preceding dynasties."[29]

Since that edict commissioning the "Researches" certainly represents the views, both personal and historical, of the Qianlong emperor, it is worth examining in some detail for its articulation of the court's ambitions for the finished work and motives in commanding the project. The edict opens with an allusion to the "History of the [Jurchen] Jin" (*Jin shi*) empire; it had been translated into Manchu under Hung Taiji, was being revised under Qianlong, and would become a source for the "Researches." According to his reading of the Jin history, the emperor observes, the ancestors of the Wanggiya (Wanyan), the Jin imperial lineage, had lived among the Mohe confederation, within the territory of the ancient Sushens, where were found the White Mountain and the Black River. The White Mountain, he notes, was obviously Mt. Changbai, and the Black River the Amur. This was the very scene of the rise of the Manchus. In former times, it was well known, certain of the peoples who had later come to be known as Manchu had been called *zhushen*. One could with reason, the emperor suggests, suppose that *zhushen* was a fairly recent reflex of the remote name of the Sushen and that the peoples shared not only a territory and a name, but probably a language and certain traditions as well. He offers an example. According to the "History of the Later Han" (*Hou Han shu*), the Sushens had the peculiar practice of "using a stone to flatten the skull" of their infants. This was contrary to all common sense. But it was an old custom of the Manchus, the emperor reminds his readers, that infants more than a few days old were confined to their cradles in such a way that over the course of time the posterior portion of the skull did indeed become flat. Regrettably the Sushens had left no records of their customs so that those

---

29. *Manzhou yuanliu kao* (hereafter *MYK*), *juan shou (tiyao)* 1b.

coming afterward might have an informed view of their traditions rather than engaging in the sort of groundless speculation that resulted in preposterous notions.

Similarly, the emperor notes the confusion in the Chinese records over the names of the Three Hans of Korea. He is referring to Chinhan, Mahan, and Pyŏnhan, the three early states that had existed on the Korean peninsula coeval with the Lolang Commandery of the Han empire.[30] It is now impossible, he admits, to explain all the elements in the names of these early societies. But *han* in each case was clearly a reference to a ruler—a khan. The historians simply had not known that *han* was a term for a leader. With only guesses to guide them, they had somehow come to the conclusion that *han* was a word for a lineage, a notion that "is not worth a moment's attention." Such crude usage, having once taken root, was very hard to pull loose, the emperor notes. For example the name of Jilin province, once the territory of the Korean states Silla and Paekche, had been corrupted in the Tang histories[31] to "Chicken Woods," which had remained the standard transcription for centuries thereafter. Clearly, the emperor concluded, people of the past had been without methods of evidential scholarship. The Manchus and their immediate predecessors in the Northeast, the emperor went on to emphasize, had been subjected to just such mistreatment in the Chinese records. During the Ming period in particular, "propagandists of the most scandalous inclinations picked over every word, every line, every paragraph, with no object other than to defame." The scholars of the time, after all, had been only dogs barking in the service of their masters.

Take the matter, the emperor advised, of the phrase "Eastern Barbarians" (*dongyi*). Because of their geographical locations, Mencius had referred even to Shun as an "Eastern Barbarian" and to King Wen as a "Western Barbarian." This could hardly be concealed (*hui*). Indeed, the emperor insisted, there would be no motive for concealing it, and thus the emperor waved away centuries of debate among Chinese scholars who, unlike him-

---

30. In Chinese, Zhenhan, Mahan, and Bianhan. These early states or confederations were known to have existed in the southern portion of the Korean peninsula when the Han installation at Lolang (Nangnang) was founded in 108 BCE (it was destroyed in 313 CE). *MYK, juan* 8:10–11 discusses the Three Hans on the basis of materials culled from the *Hou Han shu, Jin shu,* and *Jin shi.* The topic was important enough to the court that a specially commissioned essay for *Manzhou yuanliu kao* was intended to clarify the origins and identities of the peoples inhabiting the Three Hans: "Yuzhi Sanhan dingmiao," *MYK* 2:2a–b.

31. *Jiu Tang shu,* attributed to Liu Xu; *Xin Tang shu,* attributed to Ouyang Xiu and Song Qi, 618–906. Both were sources for *Manzhou yuanliu kao.*

self, bristled at the imputation of barbaric origins to their heroes.[32] But even in the present, the emperor complains, there were those who demeaned the Aisin Gioro because they did not appear to be of the same people as the imperial lineage of the Jin Jurchens of the Northeast. He reminds his readers that in Manchu, Aisin means "gold," just like the dynastic name of the Jurchen Jin; this was sufficient proof for him that the imperial Aisin Gioro lineage were a branch of the original Jin Jurchens.[33] The fact was that in the present day those in service to the court, spread as they were over the realm, were justly united in their reverence for the Qing, and it would ever be so (an echo of the Yongzheng emperor's sense of sufficient Heavenly ordination in "Great Righteousness").

The Aisin Gioro, the emperor continues, had never been servants of the empires that had preceded them. On the contrary, it was in hopes of effecting good relations with the Manchus that the Ming had offered the Qing founder Nurgaci the title of Dragon-Tiger General (*longhu jiangjun*); to please Heaven and to protect the dynastic interests the Aisin Gioro had not scorned the honor. In due time Qing power had waxed to the point where the Ming felt insecure. This in turn created ill-feelings toward the Manchus and a desire to defile their reputation. In fact it was the Aisin Gioro who were the injured party. The wrath of Nurgaci had been provoked by the "Seven Great Grievances," and it only was to avenge them that the defeats were visited upon the Ming armies in the early battles in Liaodong. The Ming sued for peace, but the Qing were not so easily placated. The historical relationship of the Qing to the Ming dynasty, the emperor explains,

---

32. The emperor is aware of but dismisses the disturbing effect that Mencius' statement had had upon scholars over a millennium. Ho Ping-ti has called the classical passage "startlingly iconoclastic," indeed, "so iconoclastic that for ages it has baffled Chinese classical commentators" (see "The Chinese Civilization: A Search for the Roots of Its Longevity"). Above quotation from the *Mengzi* follows Ho, 553, who follows Legge, trans., *The Works of Mencius*, 316. In 1998 Ho returned to this passage, still following Legge, but now finds it not the least startling and interprets it to reflect the broad-mindedness of the "ancient Sinitic world" (see "In Defense of Sinicization," 129). As I have suggested earlier, the passage seems to be about leadership (Chapter 5, n 71).

33. The emperor elaborated on this reasoning in the imperial preface to *Manzhou Menggu Han zi san he qieyin Qingwen jian* (*xu: juan* 170), quoted in A Guanhu, "Qianlong chao chongxin Liao, Jin, Yuan san guo peixi." There, the emperor draws upon the recently completed glossary of the Jin imperial history, which tabulates apparent identifications of lineage names from the Jin history with Manchu lineage names of Qing times. The details of this may be reviewed in Crossley, "'Historical and Magic Unity,'" with the cautions outlined earlier in this book respecting ostensibly "old" (as contrasted to "new") Jurchen / Manchu lineage names.

was thus: The founder of the Han had been a stalwart of the Qin; the Tang founders had been exemplary nobles of the Sui; the Song founder had been a trusted official of the [Later] Zhou; the Ming founder had been a commoner under the Yuan. The circumstances under which each had transformed the relationship with and succeeded the earlier empire were diverse, but there was no cause for censure. In the present case, it was the Ming who had been the bandits, the fomenters of unrest. When the Ming order had faltered, it was Wu Sangui who welcomed Manchu princes and generals through the Pass to restore peace and suppress the rebel Li Zicheng.

Now the dynasty had accomplished all the tasks and assumed all the symbols of a legitimate empire, conforming to the imperial standard even in the oral tales of the dynasty, which were reminiscent of those of the Shang and Zhou, long before. With the reception of the Mandate through military victories, the Aisin Gioro had proved that they were of the same people as the imperial Jin Jurchens. The Burgeli Pool of the Heavenly Maiden was at Mt. Changbai, in the region of the Amur. And on the connection between the Manchus and the Jurchen Jin, the emperor made this final point: In the Jin annals for the Mohe peoples of the Tang period were included more than ten biographies of Parhae kings, who for generations had had a literary script and rituals. These literate Parhae were the ancestors of the Jin Jurchens. Now, the Qing script dated from the time that Nurgaci had commanded Erdeni to devise a means of written communication. But in the early Jin there had already been a script, which in the subsequent dispersions of the Jurchens had been lost. Whether or not the Qing had successfully reconstructed it cannot, the emperor allows, be ascertained with present knowledge. As with other issues related to the migrations of the Jurchens, the formation of the Manchus, and the disparities in local place-names, the question must be subjected to rigorous documentary research and analysis, the results to be compiled within a volume that would be available to the world for innumerable generations.[34]

The central conceit of the "Researches" is that Manchu state and society were the culmination of millennia of political and cultural development in the Northeast, encompassing a spectrum of heritages from the earliest Sushen and Puyŏ peoples to the medieval bureaucracies of the Parhae and the Jin Jurchens as well as the pristine, unsettled traditions of the "wild" Jurchens of Jilin and Heilongjiang. The precise evidence by which Manchu origins were to be ascertained was in the lines of descent from one people

---

34. *MYK, juan 1,* "shangyu," 2a.

to another, moving through various regionally based "federations" (*bu*) and "lineages" (*zu*). With proper respect for the ambiguity of the inherited records, the "Researches" never clearly indicates the criteria distinguishing "federations" (*bu*) from "lineages" (*zu*).[35] In fact a large portion of the extracts deal with ancient and medieval "nations" (*guo*), which does little to clarify the conclusions, if the Qing writers had reached any, on the characteristics of these early social-consanguineal-spiritual units.[36] But in practice the "Researches" uses *bu* to indicate the regionally coherent, self-governing federations that flourished before the creation of formal bureaucratic states; *zu* are those lineage parties that functioned within the more or less centralized states which successively formed and decayed in the Northeast. Thus the Wanggiya (Wanyan) are a *bu* prior to and during Agūda's twelfth-century wars of unification among the Jurchens; after the creation of the Jin state in 1115, the Wanyan (as all other Jurchen *bu*) become a *zu* (or, interchangeably, *shi*).[37] Though imprecise, the terminology of the "Researches" fits very well with the Qianlong view of the Manchu present and past ("using the present as schema for the past"). The various peoples of the Northeast are given a social history that mimics the social history of the Manchu lineages, even to the point of the inexorable demotion of their status from independent institutions of governance to working parts of a bureaucratized state.

By the eighteenth century the arguments Nurgaci and Hung Taiji had used in their own time to rule in the Northeast were in need of some qualification. Their angry denunciations of Ming failure to recognize the fact of their dominion in the Northeast, based as they were upon a conviction that righteousness is manifest in the favor of Heaven (*urušengge*), were no longer adequate justification. The post-conquest empire sought legitimation in cultural history and political legacy. While acknowledging the ethi-

35. The precise meanings, if there are any, of *bu* and *zu* in the Northeastern context is outside the scope of this study. Apart from *BMST* there was no significant effort on the part of Qing compilers to make the Chinese terms correspond to traditional Manchu vocabulary related to social organization (*gurun, hala, mukûn, tatan, gargan*). For the *BMST, shi* and *zu* correspond as nearly as possible to *hala* ("surname") and *mukûn* ("lineage"), respectively. *Bu* is used for the pre-dynastic federations of the Northeast and for unassimilated tribal peoples of that region.

36. For example, in *Manzhou shilu*, the Chinese version of *Manju i yargiyan kooli, guo* ("nation") is used alternately and quite sensibly to translate either *gurun* ("nation," "political federation") or *hala* (in these records, indicating "clan," "tribe," or "surname").

37. *MYK* 7:1a–3b; compare to use of *dang* and *shi* in *Jin shi* (hereafter *JS*) (1975) 1:2; 73:1684; 86:1916; 88:1956; 91:2011.

cal burden of traditional Chinese political thought, the Qianlong emperor
clearly was not moved to impose Confucian formulae upon the Qing experience. He did not specify the precise nature of the Manchu relationship to
the Ming but insisted that the succession fully conformed to the patterns
of China's previous dynasties. The emperor was careful to reiterate his ancestors' contention that the Manchus had never been subject to the Ming
court. Qing justification lay in their relationship to the political and cultural traditions of their native world, the Northeast. The emperor's scholars were instructed to elucidate both the sophistication of the regional imperial legacy and the undeniable ties of the Aisin Gioro with the historical
rulers of the region.

Q.
legitimacy

"We fear," the editors of "Researches on Manchu Origins" said on the
Qianlong emperor's behalf, "that in later days the banner descendants will
forget the old order and do away with riding and archery, taking up Han
customs."[38] Now that the shape and meaning of Manchu origins had been
clarified, it was time for Manchu bannermen to fit their deeds to their identities. As suggested above, Manchus had been distilled from others of the
conquest elite by special requirements that they perform militarily as
well as academically. The Kangxi emperor had proclaimed, "The Manchus
take riding and archery as the root (ben), and this was originally no impediment to book learning."[39] The noble plan of cosmopolitanism for the
Manchus, as for others of the conquest elites, was tried for a century, and
failed. Incentives had been applied, though the examinations never became
as attractive for the bannermen as the court had hoped. Preferential routes
for Manchus into the bureaucracy had been established. The plan of 1687
to balance martiality and civility had continued to control policy. But for
the Qianlong emperor, this had proved a futile attempt to remove from
Manchus their natural functions and force them to attempt things for which
they were unfit. The result was bannermen who were deficient in both
Manchu and Chinese, never handled bows or guns, and rarely saw horses.
He prescribed specialized devotion in the education of Manchu bannermen
to the Manchu language and to military skills.[40] These educational policies
became major emblems of Manchu identity in the eighteenth century. In
1746, the court noted that those studying Chinese and translation in the

38. Liu Shizhe, from *MYK* 6:13b, in "Manzu 'qishe' qianshu," 54.
39. Liu Shizhe, from *MYK* 5:48–57, "Manzu 'qishe' qianshu," 53.
40. Crossley, "Manchu Education"; Chang Chung-ju et al., *Qingdai kaoshi
zhidu ciliao;* and Lui, "Syllabus of the Provincial Examination," "The Imperial College," and "The Education of the Manchus."

Aisin Gioro Academy had inelegant composition in Manchu. Adumbrating future changes, the emperor said, "Our dynasty esteems martiality as its primary occupation. Dependents[41] of the Aisin Gioro must be thoroughly versed in literary Manchu, and they must be experts at *qishe*. I am frankly concerned that those who study Chinese will gradually become lost in Chinese ways. The Shunzhi emperor once ordered us to stop studying Chinese, the better to serve our primary interests, rather than decline to a state of dissolution (*fouhua*). From now on dependents of the Aisin Gioro may not study Chinese. They are strictly required to study the military arts, in order to preserve themselves as tools for the use of the state."

The centralization and reform of banner education came, technically, after the end of the Qianlong reign but was in fact overseen by assistants of the abdicated emperor Hongli and was very clearly imprinted with his attitudes toward Manchu identity and Manchu culture. Specifically, the idea of the bannermen as a liberally educated governing class was replaced by an increasingly specialized understanding of who Manchus were and what they were expected to do. The new reforms prescribed rigorous study of the Manchu language, both written and spoken, and of military skills. The educational programs were very deliberately designed to include young male dependents as well as active or prospective bannermen, and by virtue of this claimed jurisdiction over a much broader portion of the Manchu population than could ever possibly have exercised their new skills in the service of the state. Unlike his father and grandfather, the Qianlong emperor was not primarily interested in improving governance by elevating the competence of the bannermen. He was instead bent upon refining the cultural character of the Manchus, who were now in his eyes representative not only of the cultural origins of the Qing, but of a specialized, dedicated component in his universal realm.

At first, like his father and grandfather, the Qianlong emperor had been inclined to encourage more effective study of Chinese and continued his ancestors' practice of rewarding development of Chinese erudition among

41. The text has *zidi*, "sons and younger brothers." This was an adaptation from Ming military terminology that became a social usage among and referring to the bannermen. It originally distinguished between those who actually served in the military and received stipends and those (sons and younger brothers) who were dependents of stipendiary soldiers, aspired to be in active service themselves, and so behaved in most ways as if they were in fact bannermen. At an early point in the Qing period the term became a general term for the male populations of the banners and eventually all members of banner families. See also Crossley, *Orphan Warriors*, 17.

the bannermen.[42] Later, on the basis of better information about the garrison conditions and Manchu performance,[43] he reconsidered the policies he had inherited and in his own right encouraged. After 1765 he advised bannermen that they need no longer disturb him with notifications of their households' success in the examinations unless the candidates had also distinguished themselves at *qishe*. And again he stressed the primary importance of the Manchu language. "Speaking Manchu is the Old Way (*jiudao, fe doro*) of the Manchus," the emperor admonished four Manchu officials of the court of Colonial Affairs who had been unable to keep up their end of an audience in the winter of 1762.[44] Though the Kangxi emperor had established himself as a grand exemplar to the bannermen and frequently demonstrated his literary and military skills before them for their improvement, the Qianlong emperor had a very different concept of his relationship to the bannermen. He was a paragon of omniliteracy, the esthete of all cultures, and the universal emperor. They were not. They were to apply themselves to their language, to their religion, and to their martial skills. "Whether you have studied classical literature is a matter of no concern to me."[45] Apart from an increasingly abstract emphasis upon physical training, the Qianlong emperor had also expressed some real concerns about the impact upon the bureaucracies of declining command of Manchu speech. Despite an insistence that bannermen preparing for service in the civil or military bureaucracies learn Manchu orthography, unfamiliarity with the spoken language still wreaked havoc with communications in Manchu and Mongolian. In 1779 the emperor in exasperation ordered that translations of edicts issued in Mongolian should be submitted to him for grammatical review, as was already the practice for Manchu; thus the emperor proposed to augment his normal duties of edict review by becoming a Manchu and Mongolian language tutor as well.[46]

42. *QKZC* 1.40a–b.
43. On language customs in the garrisons, see also Crossley, *Orphan Warriors,* 84, 250–51 nn 15, 16.
44. Crossley, *Orphan Warriors;* at about this time there was a renewed demand by the court that garrison officials report only in Manchu (see Rawski, *The Last Emperors,* 37).
45. Chu and Saywell, *Career Patterns in the Ch'ing Dynasty,* 52.
46. *QKZC* 1.60b–61a. A portion of this passage has been translated in Crossley, *Orphan Warriors,* 27, and a different portion has been translated by Man-Kam Leung, "Mongolian Language Education and Examinations in Peking and Other Metropolitan Areas during the Manchu Dynasty in China," 40, from a reprinted text in Hsi Yü-fu, *Huangchao zhengdian leicuan* (Taipei, 1969). On policies for

By the latter part of his reign the Qianlong emperor was well on his way to formalization of what he called the Old Way (*fe doro*) of the Manchus. This was a prescription for Manchu immersion in the military arts, the speaking and writing of Manchu, shamanism and reverence for the lineages as the basic elements in the correct life for those whom the state identified as Manchus.[47] The educational policies were quickly reformed to promote both the speaking and writing of Manchu as a primary objective. In 1791 the emperor outlined his plan for establishment of standard banner officer schools in all garrisons. However, it was not until after his abdication of the emperorship (but during a time in which he still controlled fundamental state affairs) in 1796 that the court implemented plans for a centralized, standardized educational system for the garrisons; for the ensuing twenty years, additions to the basic program augmented reform of the banner education throughout China. Special pressure was put on the elite to respond to the court's new educational imperatives. The Aisin Gioro Academy (*zongxue*), whose enrollments had declined rather dramatically in the later eighteenth century (despite a steady population increase for the Aisin Gioro lineage), had its stipends and number of instructors increased in 1795.[48] The conditions under which Aisin Gioro students participated in the examinations were also changed. The traditional options to be examined on arts and poetry were eliminated, and performance in translation became an additional requirement.[49] The greatest change was in the provincial garrisons, where for the first time officer schools under the jurisdiction of the Board of Appointments (*libu*) were established and all bannermen became eligible to compete for admission. The curriculum, which was not intended to be distinguished for innovation, was based upon the program of the National Academy and the Eight Banners Officers' Schools in Peking: Manchu, Chinese, astronomy (*tianwen*), and mathematics (*suanxue*), with frequent and rigorous testing in riding and shooting. The charters were embedded in the Qianlong emperor's continuing demands that written Manchu be revived among the bannermen. "Every single man has a responsibility to study written Manchu," the emperor had con-

---

language education see also Crossley, *Orphan Warriors*, and Rawski, *The Last Emperors*, 37–38.
47. See Crossley, "Manzhou yuanliu kao," 779–81, and *Orphan Warriors*, 19–30.
48. *QSG* 106:3111–12.
49. *QSG* 108:3170.

tinued his endless and largely unheeded sermon. "This is the root of his mission!"[50]

The reform of higher education within the garrisons was, however, quickly seen to be useless without a corresponding emphasis upon the cultivation of boys. The perceived cultural and social condition of the garrison populations is revealed in the edict, in 1800 (after the Qianlong emperor's death), demanding that garrison officers identify talented boys, on the order of about one out of every five or six, to receive intensive instruction from their company corporals in Manchu, *qishe*, and a very small number of administrative arts. At the same time, the state affirmed its intentions never to return to the unfocused, comprehensive education policies of earlier times. "Of the Manchus' roots, *qishe* is the first. If the Eight Banner dependents concentrate on and are allowed to be successfully examined on [the Four Books], they will despise the bow and the horse, and that will not fortify our military preparedness; on the contrary they will contravene the very purpose for which the nation established the garrisons. Hereafter the officers of each provincial garrison will select dependents who will be dedicated to the task of preparing for the examinations, and they will thus advance our fundamental interests."[51] The abandonment of the Shunzhi-Kangxi idea of bannermen as universal functionaries as well adapted to the Hanlin Academy as to the command of an elite cavalry corps, in favor of a rigid regime of cultural purification, physical reinvigoration, and spiritual reintegration, had implications far beyond what the Qianlong and Jiaqing courts foresaw. What later emperors were advocating, in essence, was a vocational, even professional, course of study for the bannermen, in which expertise in Manchu—as the language of the military sector—was fundamental, and in which the more liberal, more obviously civil educational elements had little or no place. The significance of this did not emerge until the military and educational reforms of the period after the Opium War. Courses on armaments, both Qing and foreign, were added to the garrison officers' schools, and this inevitably led to limited technical studies by midcentury. Particularization of banner identity thereafter led to the banner schools becoming a source for the specialized military academies, language schools, and technical institutes of the later nineteenth century.[52]

50. Lei, "Jingzhou qixue de shimo ji qi tedian," 57–59.
51. *QSG* 106:3117.
52. On banner schools and their relationships to the modern institutions superseding them see Nancy Evans, "The Banner-School Background of the Canton

The history of the Qing court and its relation to the Manchus may be viewed as the aggregate of the processes by which the court attempted to resolve this conflict through formalization of the old culture. In its political aspects this meant progressive bureaucratization, regulation, and depersonalization of the state in displacement of the personal, diffused authority that had once been vested by tradition in the lineages and confederations. In its cultural and ideological facets, it meant the systematic documentation of descent, myth, lineage history, and shamanic practice; what had once been various and mystically obscure was now made visible, manageable, standard, and, by virtue of its literary form, classical. The many mechanisms of Qing formalization were mutually reinforcing, each contributing to the concentration of authority and legitimacy in the institution of the emperorship. In actuality neither political practice nor the dynastic culture was fully formalized; to the end of the Qing period, archaic elements were in evidence and in conflict with formal institutions, whether political or ritual. Nevertheless the direction of most of these efforts was toward ossification or obviation of those elements of the Manchu heritage that threatened to impede the centralization and codification of the state. The process proceeded in mutual interaction not only with centralization in the emperorship but with consolidation of putative "Chinese" and putative "Mongol" identities.

FOLLOWING CHINGGIS

The right to absolute rule inherent in the Mahākāla cult—which Lighdan claimed but which other regional leaders rejected—was connected to some of the few generalized criteria of Mongol affiliation that existed in Lighdan's time. One was devotion to Chinggis Khaghan as a spirit who still ruled over all Mongols. A second was deference to the descendants of Chinggis, who were exclusively entitled to function as *jinong,* or prince-priests of the Chinggis cult. Beyond these two fundamental characteristics, there was little that consistently distinguished "Mongols" from other inhabitants of Inner Asia and the Northeast. For the early Qing rulers, the Chinggis complex, patronage of Buddhism, and the Mahākāla cult were enough to be getting on with in claiming the right to rule Mongolia, whether by defeat-

T'ung-wen Kuan," *Papers on China,* 22A (May 1969): 89–103; Lei, " Jingzhou qixue de shimo ji qi tedian"; Tan, "Wan Qing Tongwen guan yu jindai xuexiao jiaoyu."

ing its present leaders in war or persuading them to join the forces of conquest. By the Qianlong period, however, the impulse to historicize and taxonomize had been applied to "Mongols" as to the "Manchus" and to "Chinese." The combined effect of the documentary literature, regulations for language learning, and banner assignments was to generate a "Mongol" constituency of the emperorship. Its languages were Mongolian and Tibetan, iconographic dialects of Buddhism, and a representation of shamanic fundamentals—particularly the worship of Chinggis Khaghan. Its constituency were the putative venerators of Chinggis, descendants of the imperial Mongols, hardy nomadic archers and riders, shock troops of the Eight Banner cavalry, and guardians of the emperor, his family, residence, and shrines. The constituency corresponded only awkwardly to basic historical features of the populations signified under this "Mongol" identity. They inhabited, very generally speaking, two large and well-differentiated zones. One, which may be associated with Inner Mongolia, Qinghai (Kokonor), and Tibet, was Buddhist in orientation and closely linked to the Qing court by the end of the seventeenth century. The other, for purposes of simplification associated with Outer Mongolia and Central Asia, was characterized by a diversity of religious associations (mainly with Buddhist sects or with Islam), a diversity of languages, and a tenuous—in many instances hostile—relationship to the Qing court. Politically it is not surprising that the court attempted to hide one in the glare of the other.

The Mongol Eight Banner aristocracy, drawn mostly from the leading lineages of the Khorchins, Kharachins (Yüngsiyebü), Chakhars, and other early followers of Nurgaci and Hung Taiji from eastern Mongolia, were by the later seventeenth century in close intimacy with the Qing court—frequent marriage partners, participants in the various cults of the Aisin Gioro lineage, provincial governors, in some cases leading bureaucrats. They were the Qing link to the Northern Yuan and its continuation of the imputed imperial rights of the Chinggis-Khubilai line. The Mongol Eight Banner leadership was also prominent in representation of the Mongolian cultural legacy to the Qing court. Manchu princes learned Mongolian from Mongol tutors in the palace school (*Shangshu fang*). In addition, the court did not neglect the education of Mongol bannermen, even as it attempted to co-opt or decapitate the traditional leadership hierarchies of the steppe.[53] Indeed, the Qing effort to educate bannermen in Mongolian at the banner schools and to disseminate Mongolian translations of important works in

---

53. For an introduction to education in Mongolian during the Qing see Leung, "Mongolian Language Education and Examinations."

other languages stimulated the production, from the eighteenth century on, of Mongolian grammars and dictionaries that were critical to the standardization of the Mongolian language.[54]

In the Hung Taiji and Shunzhi years the functions of the Imperial Colonial Office were extended; it continued to manage matters associated with Mongol livelihoods but increasingly oversaw the affairs of other regions as well. After the conquest of northern China, the Imperial Colonial Office was brought under the jurisdiction of the Board of Rites (*libu*—the umbrella organ for foreign relations). It now assumed responsibility for governing other absorbed societies and managing the interface between their semi-autonomous leaders and the Qing court. By the middle eighteenth century these included the local headmen (*tusi*) of the populations of Sichuan, Yunnan, Guizhou, and parts of Burma, and the *khōja*s of Turkestan. These regions were governed through the Imperial Colonial Office as military provinces outside the civil, bureaucratic government—a model based upon the early Qing rule over the "Mongols," particularly the Khalkha khans of eastern Mongolia. From the Shunzhi period, the Imperial Colonial Office also became the locus for early communication with Tibet. After the Qing conquest of north China in 1644, the court entered into direct communications with the Dalai Lama. From the time of his visit to Peking in 1651, the Imperial Colonial Office became the Dalai Lama's bureaucratic arm as judge and arbitrator among the populations of eastern Mongolia and, after 1698, Qinghai. As the Dalai Lama was given delegated authority for the mediation of Mongol life, however, the Dalai Lamas themselves were brought increasingly under the observation and regulation of the Qing court, so that by the end of the Shunzhi era in 1661 the Imperial Colonial Office was overseeing the selection of the Dalai Lamas. It was one of many expressions of the complex intermingling of culture and politics of Mongolia and Tibet, which worked sometimes to Qing advantage and sometimes not.

The earliest Mongol Eight Banner populations were joined by a number of Khalkha commoners and noblemen even before the conquest of China. Members of the Khalkha federations had had contact with Nurgaci in the very late sixteenth century, before conclusion of the wars against the

---

54. As examples one might cite the Manchu-Mongol primer, *Menggu huaben* (1761), the *Menggu wenjian* (redacted from the *Qingwenjian* of 1708), and, to demonstrate the persistence of this concern, the *Manju monggo nikan ilan acangga su-i tacibure hacin-i bithe*, compiled by Jiang Weiqiao, Zhuang Yu, and Rongde and published with a preface by Xiliang in 1909. See also Lu, "Qingdai beifang ge minzu yu zhongyuan hanzu de wenhua jiaoliu ji qi gongxian."

Hūluns. In ensuing years the relationship with the Khalkhas became much more complex, as the Jin came to open war with Lighdan. The Khalkha were Lighdan's primary resisters in the vicinity, and as Hung Taiji in particular pressed his campaigns against Lighdan, his patronage and formal incorporation of the Khalkha khans into his regime proceeded apace. The Khalkha leaders' relationship to the Qing court remained tenuous, however. They more than any other federation realized that the Qing campaigns in Mongolia were older than those in China and that with the defeat of Lighdan the Qing had actually achieved their Mongolian ambitions in part. Though by the eighteenth century the Khalkhas had become the numerical if not the historical center of Qing rule over "Mongolia," they were also the first major federation to be wary of the burgeoning of Qing ambitions and to experiment with ways to play other powers off against the aggression of the new empire. For their part, the Qing feared that Khalkha leaders or Oyirods[55] (particularly the powerful Oyirod subgroup, the Dzunghars) would attempt to enlist Russian aid in their power struggles and bring Romanov military presence into Mongolia permanently. But in the early 1660s, Khalkha leaders—fearing a recrudescence of Oyirod power—decided to ally with the Qing against Romanov Russia after intervention of the Grand Lama Cheptsundampta, leader of the Reformed Sect (Yellow Hat) in Mongolia.

55. Manchu Urūt. The name is unstable both in original citations and in transliteration. It apparently derives from the plural of a medieval Mongolian word meaning "a congregation, people who remain near each other" and became the dialect word for a federation. Transliteration of the name can be a proprietary issue among specialists. There are several attested variants of the name in "Mongolian" records, including those in Oyirod dialect (which the *lifan yuan* considered a distinct language), which after the early seventeenth century was written in the amended script created by Zaya Pandita. Including the Oyirod texts, one finds at a minimum the name written as Oyirad, Oyirod, and Oyirid. This would permit any of these as transliterations (Joseph Fletcher preferred Oyirod), as well as the frequently found "Oirat." It would not, however, permit Olot or Ölöt, which seem to be ersatz back-constructions from Chinese *elete*. Nevertheless, in the eighteenth century the Chinese phonology was borrowed into Manchu, and forms such as "Olot" and "Ulet" are found. General histories often identify the Oyirods with the Kalmyks or Kalmuks (Mongolian *khalimakh*), which may be slightly lacking in precision. "Kalmyk" is most often associated with that group, primarily Torghuuds, who were forced into their tragic flight across the Volga in 1771. They had distinguished themselves from the majority of Oyirods by seeking, under their leader Ayuuki, to make peace with the Romanov empire. Thus, though all Kalmyks in the eighteenth century were Oyirod-speakers and had Oyirod antecedents, not all Oyirods were Kalmyks.

Tensions between the Khalkhas in the east and the Oyirods in the west did indeed ensue, for nearly two decades. The Kangxi court was absorbed in stabilizing its rule in China (and suppressing the Three Feudatories) and so chose not to actively interfere. But as soon as the war against the Three Feudatories was concluded in 1683, the Qing informed Khalkha khans, and the Oyirod leader Galdan, that it would now turn its attention to military affairs in Mongolia. The Kangxi emperor proposed a conference of Galdan, the Dalai Lama, and Khalkha leaders. The first attempt in 1686 was unsuccessful, and Galdan invaded Khalkha territory soon after. By the tens of thousands the Khalkhas poured into Qing territory. In 1689 the political balance of Inner Asia was dramatically altered with the accomplishment of a border and trade agreement between the Qing and Romanov empires in the Treaty of Nerchinsck. This considerably lessened the strategic options of all leaders in Mongolia, including Galdan. The Kangxi emperor offered amnesty to Galdan, and rewards if the Oyirod leader would surrender. At the same time, the Qing began outfitting a new military expedition, arming the vanguard with muskets and cannon for a renewed assault on Galdan's bases.

The Khalkha khans formally accepted the Kangxi emperor as Great Khan (*khaghan*) and successor to Chinggis at Dolonnor in 1691. By 1694 the Khalkhas had their legal affairs removed to a special section of the Imperial Colonial Office, and their nobles, clerics, and merchants were permitted to reside in Peking (roughly 10,000 were doing so within a year of the change). They also joined the cultic catalog of the Qing court: The Cheptsundampta *khutukhtu*s (the reincarnated spiritual leaders of Mongolia) were permitted to perform the ceremony of presenting the "nine white" sacrificial animals to the emperor personally. The khans of Qinghai (Kokonor) followed the Khalkhas into submission (to Chinggis Khaghan, after all) in 1698. The Qing organized the Khalkha territories into "banners"— *ghōšun* (*khōšighun*) divided into "armies" (*jalan*, adopted directly from the Eight Banners) and "companies" (*sumun*)—but these were in reality territorial rather than demographic units. "Banners" were in this case a way of disrupting existing hierarchies by imposition of new administrative lines whose divisions mimicked those of the Eight Banners. The restructuring of Khalkha Mongolia demanded not only the creation of new jurisdictions but also the integration of the noble class of the steppe, through the usual means of marriage alliances and incorporation of the steppe leaders into the imperial aristocracy. Thus the three great khans of the Khalkha region were allowed to remain as administrative entities after their surrender to the Kangxi emperor, and all were incorporated into the imperial lineage through marriage alliances.

In 1706 a new khanship, the Sayin Noyon, was created and at the same stroke married into the imperial lineage. Tsereng, the first Sayin Noyon Khan, became in fact the symbol of steppe submission to the empire, and enjoyed the peculiar honor of having his tablet worshiped in the imperial lineage temple (the only other Mongol to be so honored being Sengger-inchin, the hero of the Taiping War who was assassinated in 1865). The newly legalized trade between China and the Khalkha territories grew rapidly in the 1720s. Soon the Khalkha leaders were protesting that they were on the short end of the exchange, and in the 1750s the Qianlong court attempted to permit the khans to limit and regulate the trade.[56] They appear to have created no impediments, however, and by 1800 Urga had become a thriving commercial center. From that point, Khalkha leaders began to complain more sharply of economic sufferings from interpretations of laws relating to land ownership and grazing rights, currency regulations, and especially the increasing indebtedness of Khalkha nobles and commoners to Chinese bankers. But by the time an economic crisis had welled up in Khalkha (now termed Inner Mongolia, meaning on China's side of the Gobi), the Qing court was beset by a series of internal and external crises that would have made a way of solving these problems—had there been a will—from Peking all but impossible. Over the course of a century, the Khalkhas had been enfolded into the Qing empire by a combination of circumstances: The enmity with Lighdan, which had caused them to become allies of Hung Taiji; the collapse of hopes of playing the Romanov empire off against the Qing; and the growing threat of a continuing war with Galdan. Of the three, the last was surely decisive. The submission of Khalkha and Qinghai to the Qing empire did not solve the Galdan problem, however. The Qing empire remained at war, in one form or another, in the territories of the Oyirods (Dzungharia, Turkestan, and part of Tibet) until virtually the end of the empire. Though the Qing could not be said to have utterly conquered the Oyirod groups, they can be said to have utterly transformed them—into Mongols, which even Chinggis himself had not been able to do.

The Oyirods were both a strategic and an ideological problem for the Qing. They had not been incorporated into the Chinggisid empires, and since the middle ages had been comparatively independent, both politically

56. Chia, "The Li-fan Yüan," 30, 41, 177ff., 318, 330.

and culturally, in Central Asia. In post-Yuan times, the "Four Oyirods" (*dörbön oyirad*) apparently included the Oyirods proper, the Torghuuds (Manchu Turgūt), the Khoshuuds, and the Dzunghars (that is, *jegünghar,* or "left wing"). Though ambitious leaders of the Oyirod federations in the fourteenth and fifteenth centuries sometimes aspired to gain associations, either through marriage or political alliance, with the Chinggisid lineages of the east (where the "Northern Yuan" was based, later to be the Chakhar federation), they were not devotees of the Chinggis cult; they respected the cult's political prestige in Mongolia but did not define themselves as those who were ruled over by his spirit. On the contrary, because of their geographical location they maintained strong connections with a variety of re- *Oyireds* ligious establishments in Tibet, including not only Buddhist but also openly shamanist sects. It was probably Oyirod missionaries who brought popular lamaism to Mongolia, before a political recentralization among the eastern Mongols fostered recognition of the Dalai Lamas, and it may well have been Oyirod missionaries who first took lamaism to northern Liaodong and Jilin. But the Oyirods were also thrown increasingly into contact and rivalry with the Muslim rulers of the oasis towns of Turkestan. On those occasions when peace could be concluded between Oyirod and Muslim potentates, the result was sometimes marital alliance, with or without conversion, by one or another of the parties. Finally, increasing contacts with Russians made Oyirods familiar to a slight degree with Orthodox Christianity. Through their religious and trade connections, leaders of the Oyirod confederacies functioned within an extremely wide geographical range, including all Mongolia and Tibet, large parts of Central Asia, and the western portion of the Northeast. Certainly there were a small number of Oyirods among the first bureaucrats and examiners of Hung Taiji's bureaucracy at Mukden, and it was most likely their influence that caused the Imperial Colonial Office to classify Oyirod (which from about 1600 had a script slightly different from classical Mongolian) as a separate language. For their part, the Oyirods of the early Qing period understood "Mongols" (*mong-gholi*) to be the Chakhars, and other eastern populations. They referred to themselves as the "Four Oyirods" (*dörbön oyirad*). By the eighteenth century, the influence of the early Oyirod advisors of Hung Taiji had been forgotten, and there was no delicacy at the Imperial Colonial Office regarding whether they were or were not Mongols—they were *moxi elete menggu,* "the Oyirod Mongols west of the Gobi."

So long as the Oyirods remained hostile to the Qing this terminology was of little importance to them. And in Shunzhi and early Kangxi years, the Oyirods, under the Dzunghar leader Khung Tayiji (d. 1655?), were very hostile. Khung Tayiji frequently appealed to the Romanov officials, requesting firearms, cash, and advisors. Like the Mongol unifier Altan Khaghan a hundred years before, Khung Tayiji also used Tibetan religion to consolidate his authority, even sending his talented son Galdan to Tibet to be educated for service as a *lama*. Galdan (1632 or 1644–97) returned to Mongolia in the late 1670s. In the ensuing years he prosecuted a war of unification among neighboring groups that strongly resembled Nurgaci's early career as a putative avenger among the Jurchens. Some of the groups Galdan battled were based not in Mongolia but in Turkestan, and Galdan invaded the westward region in 1678. He conquered several of the major caravan cities, including Kashgar, Yarkand, Hami, Yili, and Turfan, and brought the Muslim populations there under his control.[57] Galdan's leverage against the rising wave of Qing expansion was dramatically diminished by the Kangxi emperor's conclusion of the Treaty of Nerchinsk and the alliance of the Qing and the Khalkha khans in the 1680s. In 1690 Qing troops defeated him at Ulanbutung (only about a dozen miles north of the imperial hunting grounds at Mulan in Inner Mongolia), though Tong Guogang was killed in the battle while he commanded the cannoneers, as his grandfather had done for Nurgaci. Local legend commemorates the imperial uncle in the name of a small lake that is usually (but not always) at the foot of the rock outcrop there, since it is said that his cannon sank into the ground and the lake sprang from the depression.

On the heels of this defeat, Galdan was met with a surprise challenge from within. His nephew Tsewan Araptan (Ts'ewang Rabten) drove him out of the Khalkha territories in 1690. Desperate to regain influence and decent grazing lands, Galdan's decimated forces again attempted an invasion of Khalkha, but this time Qing troops stationed there repelled him. In 1694 a drought in Dzungaria and Turkestan forced Galdan to attempt a final incursion into Khalkha lands. A force of 80,000 men under the emperor's command turned him away and pursued him into Turkestan. Galdan's supporters, including his wife and many of his children, died; survivors defected to Tsewan Araptan. Galdan himself escaped and for a time lingered in the vicinity of Hami in Turkestan, where his fourteen-year-old son was being held captive by the Muslim ruler. The Kangxi emperor, realizing that Galdan was all but finished, did not relent. In 1697 Galdan received news that the Qing were organizing a new campaign against him. Betrayed, surrounded, and hopeless, he poisoned himself. His nephew

57. See also Millward, *Beyond the Pass.*

Danjira had his body cremated and took the ashes to Tibet. Tsewan Araptan subsequently controlled Siberia and as far west as (but not including)
Hami, and Danjira, shortly after returning from Tibet to inter his uncle's
ashes, himself took up service as Qing governor (*jasak*) of the Oyirods—
a post the Kangxi emperor had offered to Galdan, who had turned it down.

The defeat of Galdan did not mean an end to Oyirod power in western
Mongolia and Turkestan. Tsewan Araptan was himself ambitious. He defeated the Kirghiz and dominated them as far as Lake Balkash, defeated and
absorbed the Torghuuds (once a branch of the Oyirods who had had a mis-
erable sojourn in the vicinity of the Volga before returning to Mongolia to
become victims of Tsewan Araptan's expanding regime),[58] renewed campaigns by Russia aimed at taking territory in Turkestan, and in the early
eighteenth century was successful in controlling part of Tibetan territory
and deposing the last secular king of the country. His expansion stalled in
Tibet, where the Qing fought ferociously to establish a military outpost after 1718 and where Tsewan Araptan was opposed by some Tibetan factions.
He died in 1727 with the Tibetan situation unresolved, but his son Galdan
Tseren and other members of his family held out so tenaciously against
further Qing expansion that the Qianlong emperor, still new to the throne
in 1738, agreed to a truce, drawing a line at the Altai mountains between
the Qing empire and the territories of "Dzungaria."

This line held until Galdan Tseren's death in 1745 sparked a dispute over
the succession. The Qing moved immediately to intervene, and though the
Dzunghars were not subjugated outright, they suffered severe privations
from the renewed warfare. A minor Dzunghar prince, Amursana, defected
to the Qing in 1755 and in the characteristic Mongol-against-Mongol practice of the Qing was dispatched by the Qianlong court back to Dzungaria

---

58. The late Kangxi-era saga of the Torghuuds was the background to the embassy and resulting travel record of Tulišen, who in 1712 was sent to confer with
the Torghuud khan Ayuuki (then aged eighty-three) on the lower Volga. The Qing
court was evidently attempting to confirm that Ayuuki would, if pressed, actively
try to engage Tsewan Araptan in battle. Tulišen's misadventures (including waiting
three months for the Angara River at Irkutsk to warm up), indirect routing, and obscure daily goals contributed to stretching the mission over two years, culminating
in a brief and rather vague consultation with the elusive Ayuuki. Tulišen's record of
his travels, *Lakcaha jecen de takōraha babe ejehe bithei*, the facsimile Manchu text
of which has been published by Chuang Chi-fa, is one of the best-known Manchu
texts and, though clearly not a reclamation narrative of the sort provided by Umuna
(nor providing language for the court's epical self-presentation), is an entertaining
travel narrative like those published by many of his eighteenth-century contemporaries from Russia and Europe who were also exploring the climatic, mineral, cultural, political, and other landscapes of Siberia.

to finish off the last resistance.[59] His forces easily took Ili, in Turkestan, and Amursana then decided to rebel.[60] He had learned of and spread the news that the empire desired to break the Dzunghars into four small, weak khanates, and declared that a better outcome would be a single strong khanate, with himself as khan. Amursana's rebellion ignited support, to be considered below, from nobles in various parts of Mongolia and Turkestan—including the Qing stronghold of Khalkha. The political outcry on his behalf, however, was slightly greater than the ability of his supporters to gather and move troops. The Qing cornered him in Turkestan, and as the Turkic, Islamic (mostly Kazakh) communities there were captured by or sheltered him, they too were set upon by the forces of the empire. In 1757 Amursana was killed, but turmoil in Turkestan continued. Rebellions by the loosely organized Muslim leaders of the oasis towns were serially suppressed, and by the later eighteenth century virtually all of Turkestan was under Qing military occupation.

The Qianlong emperor was convinced that military suppression of the Dzunghars, who since Galdan had had a century of military strife (which meant glory, whether winning or losing) behind them, was insufficient; their name had to be literally destroyed, their peoples dispersed, and any possibility of a new leader finding legitimation for himself obliterated. The current name (but not the historical reference) Dzunghar was banned absolutely; only "Oyirod" or "Oyirod Mongol" was permitted. Some former Dzunghars fled to Siberia and to the Khalkha territories, others were deported to the mines of Heilongjiang. Those who remained in Turkestan came under the harsh rule of the Manchu occupier, Joohoi (Zhaohui, 1708–64), who also oversaw continued suppression of Muslim revolts. And the latent enthusiasm in other parts of Mongolia for Amursana's rebellion was not forgotten. For good measure, the discovery of Cheptsundampta *khutu-khtu* among the populations of Mongolia was banned; reincarnations would in future have to limit their appearances to Tibet, which Tsewan Araptan had fought to dominate but which the Qing now controlled through their installation at Lhasa. All "Mongols," the court asserted, would be happy to

59. Amursana's reception at the Mulan hunting grounds, where leaders of the Kharachins and other peoples of eastern Mongolia who had already joined the Qing had special ritual roles and were the emperor's ostensible hosts, was the subject of a series of paintings by the Castiglione group (see Hou and Pirazzoli, "Les Chasses").

60. The following account is a very economical treatment of a very detailed saga. For a narrative see Bawden, *The Modern History of Mongolia*, 110–34, and for more details (as given in Russian sources primarily) see Bergholz, *The Partition of the Steppe*, 387–419.

see the Qing patronizing the reformed Yellow Hat sect from there. The overwriting of Dzunghar identity with a Mongol label was very literally enacted in the ensuing history of Turkestan, where Amursana had made his last stand. Qing pacification of Turkestan was in one aspect not different from the quelling of Chakhar or Khalkha rebellions against the early empire: Eight Banner Mongols—now Bandi (d. 1755), Changling (1758–1838), and others, following in the path of Minggadari (d. 1669) a century before—were sent in to suppress resisting "Mongols" of the frontier. For the remainder of the empire, Mongol aristocrats (all still loyal to Chinggis Khaghan in his new incarnation as the Qing emperor) were in the forefront of the military occupation of Turkestan, which became the Qing province of Xinjiang in 1880.[61]

The Qing ideological policy of symbolic co-optation of Mongol rulership (through the Chakhar khanate) was accompanied by an administrative policy of strict and progressive fragmentation of groups with Mongol lineage references. Mongols incorporated after the conquest of China, however, were taxonomized and administered very differently from those who had joined before. The majority who populated Mongolia were known by their individual federation and lineage designations. Their noblemen were in most cases allowed to retain nomenclature and were frequently enfeoffed by the Qing court as a sign of imperial favor and recognition. The region was, however, stripped of all real autonomy, partly because of the continuing strategic concern over Russian incursions into this northern border territory. Moreover, the tendency over the course of the Qing was to further fragment and rename the existing confederations, so that the Mongolian-speakers were eventually reduced to lineage groups under historical federation rubrics. For the peoples of Mongolia, the Qianlong emperor was frank about his plan to keep them divided and weak. His devotion to the ideals of Mongol sources for Qing virtue was on one side; on the other was the fact that he was a very astute tactician when it came to deepening Qing dominion in Mongolia itself. In communications with his military planning council, he pointed out in 1756—when the empire was in the process of quashing the last of the great rebellions among the Oyirod or Khalkha princes—that the reason the Oyirods must be fragmented into four khanates was "in order to keep their forces divided. Each has to be concerned

61. On the background to the history of Qing occupation of Turkestan, see Lattimore, *The Pivot of Asia: Sinkiang and the Inner Asian Frontiers of China and Russia;* Fletcher, "China and Central Asia," 219–24; Waley-Cohen, *Exile in Mid-Qing China,* 12–32; Millward, *Beyond the Pass.*

about his own welfare, and submit to the empire for protection from the others." As a corollary of the Qing policy of fragmenting Mongol federations into progressively smaller portions, the names and divisions multiplied. Before the final suppression of Oyirod/Dzunghar power, the Imperial Colonial Office of the Qing listed eighty-six Mongol "banners" in four khanates (*bu*) of Khalkha. The addition of Ningxia, Gansu, and Qinghai increased this by twenty-nine banners in five khanates. After suppression of the Dzunghars, the regions of Hami, Turfan, and the rest of Xinjiang were described as having thirty-four banners in ten khanates. Thus, by about the middle of the eighteenth century, the political decentralization of Mongolia, Turkestan, and Qinghai was posited on a total of 149 banners, under nineteen khans. The trend continued to the end of the imperial period; "Draft History of the Qing" (*Qingshi gao*) lists peoples of parts of Mongolia and Xinjiang under thirty-eight khanates (*fanbu*).[62]

Given the history of Mongolia and Turkestan before the coming of the Qing, and the complex story of why the Qing called certain peoples "Mongols," it is not very surprising that one finds few informative statements of Mongol sentiments in the Qing period. Chakhar nobles were best known as early dissenters from Qing intentions of standardizing and centralizing control over their territories. Though Lighdan's son had become a Qing follower, and married a daughter of Hung Taiji, Lighdan's grandson Burni attempted an armed uprising against the Kangxi emperor in 1675 (taking advantage of the Three Feudatories War). The Kangxi emperor had Burni (his cousin, as both were grandsons of Hung Taiji) executed. The remaining native command structures of the Chakhars were dismantled, and Chakhar affairs were thereafter overseen by commissioners (*amban*) of the Imperial Colonial Office. Chakhar commoners were incorporated into the Eight Banners. But apart from the Chakhars, the populations of eastern Mongolia who formed the early elites of the Mongol Eight Banners or the Khalkha khanates may have been inclined to see the Qing court as it wished to be seen. From the Kangxi period, certainly, the court worked hard to patronize the considerable Mongol literate stratum it had inherited from Lighdan (printing Saghang Sechen's "Precious History" [*Erdeni-yin tobchi*]—which the Qing court normally cataloged as "Origins of the Mongols" [*Menggu yuanliu*]—in 1662 and in 1716 producing a special edition of the Geser epic), while scrupulously placing itself at the center of the Chinggis cult and working the Mahākāla spell on those who credited

---

62. *Qingshi gao* 7:14319–528.

it.[63] Thus Lomi, the mid-eighteenth-century poet and Kharachin nobleman who was himself a descendant of Chinggis, wrote in his history of his family, "Can we say that it is not a great good fortune for us descendants of Chinggis that we have continued to have the grace of the Holy Lord Chinggis constantly bestowed on us? In my opinion, the fact that our Mongol nation, when about to collapse, was restored again, and when on the point of falling apart was reborn, is in truth entirely due to the amazing mercy of the Holy Emperors [of the Qing]."[64] On the other hand Galdan Tseren, a near-contemporary of Lomi, speaking from the perspective not of the Kharachin nobles and the imperial court but of the Oyirods, used the Chinggisid principle against the Qing court: "Considering that you [nobles] are the heirs of Chinggis Khaghan, and not wanting you to be the subjects of anyone else, I have spoken with the emperor of China about restoring Khalkha [i.e., Inner Mongolia] and Kokonor [i.e., Qinghai] as they were before. But now the emperor of China wants to organize us, too, like Khalkha and Kokonor, into banners and companies, and give us titles, and because of this I am going to oppose him by force of arms." Indeed this pronouncement was an inspiration to the rebel—and sometime Qing agent—Chingunjab, who in 1756–57 led an uprising that spread quickly through a Mongolia chafing under heavy Qing taxation, expropriative mining rights for Chinese entrepreneurs, corvée and "tribute" (a kind of official cattle rustling), finding its imposed "banners" under increasingly heavy debt to immigrated usurers, and losing some of its best pastureland to the Qing-sponsored "aristocracy" of the region. The rebellion was a vivid demonstration of the disaffection of populations throughout the Khalkha region. Nevertheless, it was badly organized, received inconstant support from the religious authorities (primarily the Cheptsundampta Khutukhtu), and was brutally suppressed by the Khalkha governor (*jasak*) Choijab. Chingunjab and his brothers were publicly executed at Peking. His male adult followers throughout the Khalkha region were executed,

63. The history of the publication of the *Erdeni-yin tobchi* is treated in the introduction to Fletcher, "Erdeni-yin tobči"; Ulaghan Ulan discusses the *Erdeni-yin tobchi* in relation to other Mongol origin histories sponsored by the Qing court, particularly *Menggu chao yuan shi* (*Mongghol ughsaghatan-u ugh ijaghur-un bichigh*) and *Menggu qiyuan shi* (*Mongghol-un ijaghur-un teüke*). I. J. Schmidt translated *Erdeni-yin tobchi* into German as *Geschichte der Ost-Mongolen und ihres Fürstenhauses, verfasst von Ssanang Ssetsen Chungtaidschi der Ordus* (St. Petersburg: Imperial Academy of Sciences, 1829). See also Chapter 5, n 30.

64. Letter to Lhamjab, from *Monghol Borjigid Oboghu teüke*. Translated and cited by Bawden, *The Modern History of Mongolia*, 114.

and adolescent rebels—of whom there were many—were enslaved. A political inquisition continued for a year, in which noblemen were generally pressed into confessions of rebellious sentiments, or professions of loyalty.[65]

Galdan Tseren's objections to Qing reorganization of Mongolia were without major effect. The two-vector plan of extreme political fragmentation combined with extreme taxonomic unity worked: At the end of the Qing period, "Mongolia" and "Mongols" were found to be credible identities, and continue today, among peoples who once fought rather determinedly not to have the names, religion, or even standardized language that the Qing prescribed for them applied. A comparison of the twentieth-century persuasiveness of "Mongols" and "Mongolian" to the historical situation before the Qing is instructive. During the Yuan and Ming periods, language could not be used to identify any people as "Mongol" with absolute accuracy. In Chinggis' own time and shortly after, many Turkic-speaking groups had been subsumed under the Mongol political alliance, and under the Mongol empires Turkic speakers such as Kipchaks and Kazakhs dominated the Golden Horde regime of the Mongols in Russia and its successor, the White Horde. Mongol rulers of the Ilkhan territories in Persia had adopted Arabic and Persian as their preferences, and the Moghuls of northern India used Persian as their court language. The learned language of Mongolia during the Qing period was Tibetan, and Chinese was very widely used in preference to Mongolian. Only at the end of the Qianlong prescriptive process was the Mongolian language an issue connected with identity.

Religion, too, was historically problematic. Islam was the religion of the Kipchaks (Golden Horde) in southern Russia, of the Jagadai khanate that so vexed the Yuan empire of Khubilai, and the Ilkhans eventually converted. During the fourteenth century Islamic adherence became a definitive trait of putative Mongol descendants of Central Asia, who, like the Seljuks before them, adopted the *ghazi* role as part of the new political identity. However, it was not the case that Islam invariably divided Mongol groups from each other. The Kazakhs—whose rulers were, like Tamerlane, Turkic speakers, Islamic, but of putative Chinggisid descent—were affiliated with eastern federations until their legal alienization by the Qing, who while recognizing their residence within the empire taxonomized them as foreign-

---

65. For details see Bawden, *The Modern History of Mongolia*, 188–129; Bergholz, *The Partition of the Steppe*, 392–94.

ers and communicated with them through the tribute system.[66] In Mongolia, religion became an icon in Mongol divisions and Mongol power struggles in the sixteenth century. The imperial line among the Chakhars continued to claim dominion, at least over the Mongols east of Karakorum. They were, however, challenged by the Tumets under the leadership of Altan Khaghan (d. 1582), who brought the third Dalai Lama to Mongolia and used "lamaism" as a unifying element to challenge the Chakhar rulers. It was an effective strategy for the time; though the power Altan Khaghan accrued was lost in later generations, the consolidating effects of lamaism on the populations of Mongolia continued to grow. A century later, the institution of the Dalai Lamas provided a focal point at which the Qing could control the political climate of both Mongolia and Tibet. In vivid contrast to the cultural history of the Mongols before the Qing, modern writers can even argue that ancestors registered as Muslim cannot be considered Mongol, nor can their descendants.[67] And there is an additional, vivid reminder of the effects of Qing policy upon modern perceptions: the Dalai Lama is now a political icon associated intimately and exclusively with Tibet, the centuries during which the Dalai Lamas had been critically influential in Mongolia being virtually ignored.

The policies used among the Manchus for standardization of the language were all used among the Mongols, too: translation of the histories of the Liao, Jin, and Yuan into Mongolian;[68] composition and distribution of grammars and examination preparation books; display of the language on monuments, edicts, and ceremonial scrolls; and a requirement that the language be taught to Mongol bannermen and aristocrats in a standard form (a pointed demand, when the protectiveness of the Oyirods toward their seventeenth-century language and script is remembered). The Qianlong emperor was convinced that there was an authentic Mongolian (as there was an authentic Manchu) that would be revealed through an ostensible reuniting of the Mongols (as Ašoka's Jambudvīpa would be uncovered by the

---

66. Hence, unlike the vast majority of groups called "Mongol" by the eighteenth-century court, they are among the collected peoples of the *Huang Qing zhigong tu* (see below; Chuang, *Xiesui Zhigongtu Manwen tushuo jiaozhu*, 136). Today they are recognized again as affiliated "Mongols" by the cultural bureaucracy of Mongolia, though not in the People's Republic of China.

67. See the impassioned note by a descendant of the Yuan poet Saduri, arguing that descendants cannot claim Mongol "nationality" on the basis of descent from him (Sa Zhaowei, "Wei Menggu zu hua de simu shiren Sadouri").

68. The process has been recently reviewed in A Guanhu, "Qianlong chao chongxin Liao, Jin, Yuan san guo peixi."

conquests of the new *cakravartin*): "Since the time of Nurgaci and Hung Taiji, the Mongol federations bordering us have been our hereditary subordinates (*shichen*). Moreover, at present the Kharachins, the Qinghai, and the Four Oyirods have successively submitted to us (*guishun*), so that now there is no Mongol who is not our subordinate. Among the languages of the federations there are some differences in sound, but in principle, all are the same."[69] Despite the imperial enthusiasm for standardizing, displaying, and demanding the mastery of languages assigned to certain identities, the Qing period seems to have resulted in an overall decline in Mongolian speakers (as was also the case with Manchu). Though Qing territory expanded to include greater areas of Mongol cultural affiliation, this was at significant cost to the size of those populations; in the eighteenth-century campaigns to finally quash the Dzunghars, Qing records claim a million dead on the Dzunghar side, with survivors totaling only in the tens of thousands.[70] Whether more or less precise, the general ratio of slaughter to survival was probably an authentic representation of the scale of bloodshed in the most intense campaigns in Mongolia and Turkestan. The result was not only fewer potential resistors, but access to newly ownerless lands for horse breeding and grazing, mining, and farming. By 1800 there may altogether have been fewer than four million Mongolian speakers within the Qing territories and half that number at the end of the empire.[71] Of these, the overwhelming concentration was in the Eight Banner aristocracy (many residing in Peking) and the Khalkha territories, which together may have had as many people as Dzungharia, Turkestan, Qinghai, Tibet, and the Northeast combined.[72] There is little wonder in this, since the same forces effecting language change among Manchus were clearly working on major portions of the Mongolian-speaking populations. What is remarkable is that the daily markers of local identity, place, and function were not, at the end of the empire, found more persuasive than the abstract, remote, and imperially imposed standards of Mongol identity: worship of Chinggis

69. From the imperial preface to *Manzhu Menggu Han zi san he qieyin Qing-wen jian* (*xu: juan* 170), quoted in A Guanhu, "Qianlong chao chongxin Liao, Jin, Yuan san guo peixi."

70. Figures cited and briefly discussed in Borei, "Economic Implications of Empire Building," 28; 36.

71. The figures have been given thus: 700,000 in Outer Mongolia, 2.6 million in Inner Mongolia, 200,000 in Xinjiang and Qinghai combined. See Fletcher, "Ch'ing Inner Asia," 48.

72. See also recent estimates of population change over the Qing period in Wang Longyi and Shen, "Menggu zu lishi renkou chucao."

Khaghan who "rules over absolutely all Mongols,"[73] the Mongolian lan- *the all mode*
guage, and lamaism. In combination, they have served to mark an "Inner
Mongolia" complex in the twentieth century and to maintain the cultural
connections with Tibet that were so central to the ideological, as well as the
strategic, integrity of the Qing empire. As for the western Mongolian world
of which the Oyirod and the Kazakhs had been commingled if often hostile
components,[74] Qing representation rigorously set it apart. Oyirod descen- *Uigur*
dants living in the "new frontier" of Turkestan were part of the newly constructed Muslim—"Hui" or "Uigur"—constituency; it was dimly represented through the introduction of the Arabic-derived Uigur script in some
monuments of the Qianlong era, through the admission of a very small
number of Hui to the Eight Banners (there were a total of four students
registered at the Peking officer's academy in the later Qianlong era), and a
small glamour business built on the legends of the Fragrant Concubine sent
to the Qianlong court from the newly subject Muslim regions.[75] The historicization of the constituency was extraordinarily thin and its markings
two-dimensional. This is not surprising, when it is considered that the
Uigur constituency was created partly to obscure the complexity and range
of Mongolian affiliations in the real world of the sixteenth and seventeenth
centuries, that it papered over a violent and strategically perilous situation
that was not resolved in Qianlong times, and that even the Qianlong emperor could find no graceful way of containing Islam among the infinite—
but rigidly delimited—worlds within his universe.[76]

THE EMPTY CONSTITUENCY

Much of Qianlong universalism was founded on a complex of religious and
political ideals that bound together Tibet, Mongolia, and ultimately Chinese Turkestan. During the Qianlong era, Tibet in particular functioned as
an ideological resource, while at the same time being subject to the strate-

73. Serruys, "Two Complaints from Wang Banner, Ordos, Regarding Banner
Administration and Chinese Colonization (1905)," *Monumenta Serica* 34 (1979–
80): 471–511.
74. The history of the struggle between Kazakhs and Oyirods for local dominance is outside the discussion here, but see Bergholz, *The Partition of the Steppe*,
355–78.
75. Millward, "A Uyghur Muslim in Qianlong's Court."
76. See also Lipman, *Familiar Strangers*, 58–102, particularly on Qianlong of
Muslim violence and its interaction with law and frontier policy.

early
Q. -
not so
close.
but
Q/L

gic interventions of imperial forces.[77] Earlier Qing emperors had generally satisfied themselves with hosting the *lamas*, engaging in the appropriate ritual relationship, and presenting themselves as the earthly successors of Chinggis and Khubilai. For the Qianlong emperor, this was insufficient. He intended to make his imperial capital at Peking the spiritual capital of the lamaist realm. He initiated a massive project that not only rendered the Tibetan Tripitaka into Mongolian and Manchu but also produced original commentaries on Tibetan scriptures by Mongol and Manchu scholars. Tibetan Buddhisms were enshrined in various temples closely linked with the imperial family, the most prominent being the great palace of "Eternal Harmony" (Yonghe gong)—the Qianlong emperor's birthplace—which during the late eighteenth and early nineteenth centuries housed several hundred Tibetan, Mongol, and Manchu monks and served as a teaching center of the Yellow Hat sect. At Peking, the supreme religious leaders of the Mongolian territories were appointed, Dalai Lamas were selected, and later maintained their administrative offices. Even the Potala residence of the Dalai Lamas at Lhasa was replicated at the summer palace at Rehe.

Tibet was an odd constituency among the Qing collection, in that it appeared primarily as an idea, a set of cultic practices, and a language. There was, however, virtually no history. The near reason is that there were no Tibetan bannermen (unless they were found among those registered as Mongol), but closely related, too, is the fact that the political and military turmoil of Dzungharia and Turkestan that continued to rage in the Qianlong era was intimately connected to Tibet. The conquest history of Turkestan (Xinjiang) would be commissioned in the Qianlong era, but no project narrating the "pacification" of Tibet seems to have been welcomed by the court. The facts of Qing military occupation of Tibet in this period were, for the Qianlong court, footnotes to the greater story of the subjugation of Turkestan, Qinghai, and western Mongolia narrated above. What was important to the Qianlong emperor was what had occurred to Nurgaci in encountering his first Tibetan *lamas:* Tibet was the source of supernatural aid to the ruler and the source of an established code of dominion over the "Mongols." To the Qianlong emperor particularly, it was also the avenue to personal enlightenment and a heightened sense of the universal ruler's mission in the world. This does not mean that in its strategic considerations the Qing court had ever been able to ignore the extraordinary range of po-

---

77. For background on Qing-Tibet relations see, most recently, Rawski, *The Last Emperors*, 249–55.

litical influences of the Tibetan aristocracy or the Tibetan clerics. Nor does it mean that the Qing court ever piously separated its religious and ideological interests in "Tibet" from the political uses to which that religious influence could be put in Mongolia, Qinghai, and Dzungharia. By the later seventeenth century, Qing awareness of these possibilities had been strengthened by the hope that Tibetan ideology would provide license for military intervention that would protect Qing interests against the development of independent power centers in south China, against a recrudescence of Mongolian power, and against Russian intervention in Mongolia and Central Asia.

The relationship of the Shunzhi emperor to the Dalai Lama was formalized face to face during the much-celebrated visit of the Fifth Dalai Lama to Peking in 1652,[78] and the Imperial Colonial Office was thereafter the bureaucratic organ of the Dalai Lama in his role of spiritual leader and temporal adjudicator of selected affairs among the populations of eastern Mongolia and Qinghai. The Dalai Lamas themselves were brought increasingly under the observation and regulation of the Qing court, so that by the end of the Shunzhi era in 1661 the Imperial Colonial Office was overseeing their selection. But Lhasa and Peking were far apart, and the political situations in China, let alone Mongolia and Central Asia, were far from stable at this time. The young Kangxi emperor was reminded of this when Wu Sangui declared independence and initiated war against the empire. Wu immediately attempted to cultivate Tibetan favor by creating regular trade with Lhasa along the Kham-Yunnan road and appealed for help to the Dalai Lama. When the Dalai Lama responded by appearing not to endorse Qing suppression of Wu's independence, the Qing court experienced some difficulty in persuading its Chakhar subjects and Khalkha allies to aid in the Qing side of the war.[79]

Though relations with Tibetan clerics were repaired after suppression of the Three Feudatories, the Kangxi emperor remained wary of strategic combinations between Tibet and the Dzunghar or other Oyirod groups. In the early 1660s, Khalkha Mongols had decided to ally with the Qing against Romanov Russia after intervention of the Grand Lama Cheptsundampta, leader of the Yellow Hat sect in Mongolia. But Qing attempts to make peace between the Khalkhas and the Oyirods in the 1680s were impeded by the actions of the Tibetan regent Sangye Gyatso, who had secretly entered into

78. Hevia, "Lamas, Emperors and Rituals."
79. Lee, "Frontier Politics," 34–37.

alliance with Galdan and was concealing the death of the Dalai Lama (from whom the Khalkha khans were awaiting guidance). The result was that when the Kangxi emperor had destroyed Galdan, he turned to Lhasa as his next target. With the backing of the Qing, Tibetan nobles deposed Sangye Gyatso in 1705 and restored political power to Lhabzang khan, who as it happened would be the last secular king of Tibet. Tsewan Araptan, who had succeeded Galdan to leadership of the Oyirods, invaded Lhasa in 1717 and *[Kangxi]* deposed Lhabzang. The Qing intervened, and in 1718 occupied Lhasa, after which they installed the Seventh Dalai Lama. This first Qing attempt at military occupation of Tibet was not a success; Tsewan Araptan destroyed the Qing regiment left in place at Lhasa. In 1720 Qing regiments of Qinghai and Sichuan retook Lhasa. A permanent Eight Banners garrison was established and as in the case of the Chakhars noble administration was displaced by the commissioners of the Imperial Colonial Office (*amban*), who were basically political informants to the emperor. The kingship was abolished, and Tibet was thus stripped of claims to secular political independence. When, in 1757, the Dzunghars were finally defeated in Mongolia, the strategic emergency in Tibet abated. Qing control of the symbolic significance of Tibet was enhanced through elevation and magnification of the Panchen Lama. The Fifth Dalai Lama, who had taken steps to secure good relations with the rising Qing power by dispatching his emissaries to Mukden and Peking, and finally visited Peking himself in 1651, had been the first to recognize the Panchen Lama incarnations as teachers of the Dalai Lamas. After the beginning of prolonged turmoil in Tibet after 1700, few of the Dalai Lamas outlived their tutors; only one between the Fifth and the Twelfth lived past the age of twenty-three, and the death of the Eleventh Dalai Lama is regarded as suspicious. In time, the Panchen Lamas became effective regents to the Dalai Lamas and were recognized by the Qianlong court as the worldly rulers of most of Tibet and the spiritual rulers of the Buddhist world, outranking the Dalai Lama.

Behind the strategic centrality of the country and the mystique of the Tibetan clerical connection with the Qing court was the actual social entity of Tibet, which in the Qing records is virtually nonexistent apart from the "Illustrations of Tributaries of the Qing Empire" (discussed below) and the Imperial Colonial Office. The agriculturally based Tibetan nobility dominated the civil service, the reincarnations of the Dalai Lamas (before Qing domination of the country in the eighteenth century), and the local clergy (which constituted about a fifth of the population). Their ability to monopolize local land rights and commercial privileges was not impeded by the Qing military governors. The one Qing attempt to alienate an important noble privilege—the "golden urn" method of choosing Dalai Lamas by lot—was ignored by the nobility until they considered it in their interest to use it. Moreover, after the abolishment of the kingship, the Dalai Lama was acknowledged as the temporal as well as spiritual ruler of most of Tibet (with the exception of the Panchen Lama's domain in Ladakh) and was permitted to collect his own taxes in Tibet and Qinghai—indeed the Dalai Lama continued to collect revenues even as the Qing garrison in Lhasa went bankrupt in the early nineteenth century and had to go into debt to the Dalai and Panchen Lamas in order to be able to supply the troops. The Tibetan aristocracy also maintained its own foreign policy and welcomed trade with Nepal up to the military conflicts of the 1850s. Thereafter the entrenched economic and political powers in Lhasa were wary of the aggressiveness of the British East India Company. They primarily feared that—as Dzunghar incursions in 1717 had led to Qing occupation of the capital in 1718 and Gurkha aggression in the 1790s had led to the largest Qing invasion of Tibet and acceptance of the "golden urn"—British intrusiveness would provoke another massive military occupation by the Qing. This happened, in fact, in 1905. The Qing response was surprising both to Tibetans and to the British in its effectiveness and speed but was meaningless in the overall context of the approaching Qing demise.

The difficulty of extracting a satisfactory narrative of the regions of Tibet—the place—on the basis of Qing records is frustrating to historians and a baffle to those who would like to reconstruct the nature of relations between the Qing empire and "Western Tsang" (Xizang, Wargi Dzang)—or, as it is often put, "China" and "Tibet." The intense and ubiquitous presence of Tibetan rituals, cult objects, teachers, and, no doubt, beliefs among the Qing ruling lineage from the time of Nurgaci suggests a proximity between the court and the Tibetan land that does not accord with the thin and sporadic military involvements, the superficial political presence, or the daily independence of Tibetan nobles in managing local affairs. There are voluminous Qing publications, particularly of the Qianlong era, on Tibetan Buddhist sects, liturgies, and poetry, and there were huge expenditures on monastic institutions. But there is no conventional conquest narrative of Tibet and no formal compilations of administrative documents. It is probably best to think of the facts of Qing domination of Tibet as resembling those of the "local headman" (*tusi*) systems of rule (virtually all coordinated through the Imperial Colonial Office) that the early Qing had instituted among the same peoples in Gansu, Qinghai, southwest China, and parts of Burma and Thailand, many of whom had strong trade or cultural ties with Tibet.[80] Certainly the Qing interfered no more in local governance than they did in the regions governed under the "local headman" system, and the records resemble these systems more than they do the military occupation zones of Turkestan (Xinjiang), Gansu, and Sichuan. But the "Tibetan" constituency to which the Qing court addressed itself was in fact empty of people—as it was ideally empty of all other differentiations in the Qianlong emperor's beliefs.

The problem of documentation of "Tibet" in the later eighteenth century is at the verge of, and underscores the usefulness of understanding, the distinction between what are called here "constituencies" and what might otherwise be called "peoples"—the latter being normally the objects of ethnographers, whether eighteenth century or modern. Though a Tibetan people were not a constituency of the Qing emperorship, the Qing empire was fully aware of peoples living in Tibet, and acknowledged them outside the narrative literature through which the imperial constituencies had been historicized. One of the most important vehicles for this was the collection usually known as "Illustrations of Tributaries of the Qing Empire" (*Huang Qing zhigongtu*), produced in several forms between 1790 and 1805. There, a variety of peoples are identified as living in "Tibet" (Xizang, Wargi Dzang), but none are called "Tibetan," even though the Qing court identified the Tibetan written language (in standardized form) as one of its constituent expressive media, Tanggūt. But the half dozen peoples identified as living in "Western Tsang"—including the Minyaks, whose ancestors had founded the Tangut empire of Xi Xia—are not acknowledged as speaking any form of this imperial dialect. This characteristic of the "Illustrations" is an important sign of the genre it represents within court publications of the eighteenth century. The imperial constituencies were given narrative histories of their origins, which highlighted their cultural integrity, the ancient charisma of their ruling institutions, and their generative role in the development of the Qing emperorship primarily (the generation of the empire being important but derivative of the emperorship itself). But the peoples of the "Illustrations" are present fun-

80. This system of local rule is normally associated with southwest China and the history of the Yi people in particular but over a long (though not continuous) history from Yuan to Qing times was employed in several variations over a wide expanse of the Qing western regions. Among more recent scholarship see Yang Minghong, "Lun Qingdai Lengshan Yi qu de tusi zhidu yu gaitu guiliu," 92–95, as well as forthcoming work by John Herman and Donald Sutton.

damentally as elements in the catalog of peoples trading with the Qing empire, and expressing that subordinate trade relationship through the rituals of the tributary courts—whether the Honglu and Taichang courts, where rituals derived from earlier Ming practices continued, or the Imperial Colonial Office, where the Qing additions to the communications systems tended to be managed. In form the "Illustrations" clearly evinces a debt to the catalogs and historical geographies that from time to time had been composed on the basis of materials from the "Translators Bureaux" (*siyi guan*).[81] The "Illustrations'" guiding principles of organization are historical preeminence among the tributaries, and geographical proximity (thus the Dutch are included among the many local peoples of Taiwan). The peoples normally administered through the Imperial Colonial Office are intermixed with traditional tributaries, which suggests that with relation to trade and gifting the Imperial Colonial Office was seen as having many functions analogous to the Honglu and Taichang courts—though, significantly, that analogy did not compel amalgamation. Koreans are first, followed by the Liuchiu kings[82] and the peoples (including English, French, Swedish, Portuguese, Hungarians, and other Europeans) whose contact with the empire came through the southern coasts. This was an updating but not a fundamental alteration of the structure of the tributary calendar in Ming times, and indicative of the Qing understanding that the Ming tribute system had been enfolded and preserved as a Qing imperial function. A striking aspect of the Qing updating was the precise terminological template for identifying groups. Unlike the nomenclature of Translators Bureaux' archives, in which peoples are flatly nominalized as being of this or that "nation" (*guo*), the Manchu entries are consistent in identifying groups as being "of" a district, region, or traditional territory. This is like the terminology used in the Yongzheng emperor's "Great Righteousness," in which the Manchu genitive or possessive case is reflected in Chinese (for example, *Zhongguo zhi ren*), and works consistently to qualify, indeed to unreify, the terminology normally used in Chinese documents. In relation to this, group identifications almost invariably have "people, persons" (*niyalma*) as the nominative, which reduces the regional or genealogical characterization to a subordinate clause. In total these uses might be fairly characterized as a mid-Qing style of denomination that was grammatically and conceptually a departure from the standards established under the Ming and earlier em-

81. Crossley, "Structure and Symbol."
82. On use of Manchu by Liuchiu kings participating in tributary ritual, see Crossley and Rawski, "A Profile."

pires from whom the Qing inherited centuries of historical, linguistic, economic, and in a few instances cultural commentary.[83]

The entries in the "Illustrations," though tempting modern readers to use them as ethnographic documents, are rather precisely crafted to fit the interests of trade officials. Histories are absent, with the exception of dates and a few eighteenth-century document fragments indicating the time at which each individual people began to trade with, or conduct embassies to, an empire based in China. Nor do the entries pretend to supply an understanding of the customs or beliefs of these peoples except as they relate to the concrete concerns of the trade and communication officials. In many cases the precise rank of the hereditary headman in the administrative system is the leading information, and in the few cases where there is an administratively (and sartorially) significant difference between "officials" and commoners, the two groups have separate entries (reminiscent of the early Nurgaci tendency to make a categorical distinction between "officials" and "commoners" among the Nikans). The stuff of which clothing is made is noted, the use of snuff by some Europeans is remarked, the role of livestock and animal husbandry described, and information on literacy or illiteracy among groups at the borders is provided. The most vivid significance of the "Illustrations" for the discussion here of universalism, constituencies, and emperorship is the careful excision from the catalog of any reference to the imperial constituencies as groups. "Manchus," "Mongols," "Chinese," "Uigurs," and "Tibetans" are all conspicuously absent. This is the more remarkable when it is noted that some groups with obvious cultural relationships but disallowed political relationships to the conquest elites are listed with no indication of such a relationship. The Torghuuds, for instance, were that unfortunate group among the early Oyirods who attempted to save themselves from Qing absorption by allying with the Romanov empire, only to be betrayed later by Russian governors on the Volga and forced to flee to Qing territory to escape annihilation by the Cossacks. Of the many absorbed groups whom by this time the Qing court was naming as "Mongols," the Torghuuds were excluded, and in the "Illustrations" no mention of any "Mongol" connection is made; indeed the word "Mongol" appears nowhere in the "Illustrations."[84] The lack is nearly as conspicuous for the Kazakhs, who are given no connection with either the Mongols or with Islam.[85] Strangest is the treatment of the remnant Northeastern

Torghuuds

83. See also Introduction, n 94.
84. An Oyirod ancestry is as far as it gets (Chuang, *Xiesui Zhigongtu*, 165).
85. Chuang, *Xiesui Zhigongtu*, 137.

peoples who had not been forcibly incorporated into the Eight Banners and whose cultural connections with the Manchus had been celebrated as late as the time of the Kangxi emperor. The Oronchon, Kilen, Kuye, Fiyaka, Kiyakara, Nadan hala (Qixing), and Hezhe are briefly described as illiterate hunters and gatherers of Jilin and Heilongjiang, some riding horses and some not, some more water oriented and some limited to the forests. As with all literature of Qianlong times, the omission is more than half the story. Here, the important omission is of the Evenks, the most populous, most linguistically intimate, and best assimilated into the Banners of the Northeastern peoples. The Evenks and the Manchus were in court ideas so identified (to the point of court encouragement of use of the Evenk language to correct glossaries of some dynastic histories) that including the Evenks would have given the game away. The "Illustrations" is a document of objectification and alienation; certainly it catalogs the provinces of Qing imperial reach, but it does not identify constituencies indispensable to imperial personification, expression, or legitimation.

Qianlong representations of the imperial constituencies had an obvious influence over the tendency to associate language, in particular, with identity. This was to some extent a self-fulfilling prophecy, since a major element in court-sponsored scholarship was philologically oriented (including the exhaustive discovery and reconstitution of "original" words from the Liao, Jin, and Yuan histories through application of "evidentiary" techniques),[86] and since a large part of the state printing in the eighteenth century was given over to the primers and dictionaries ("mirrors," *jian/buleku*) in Manchu, Mongolian, and—in the later eighteenth century—Tibetan and Uigur. These languages had tremendous monumental uses, not only when carved on stelae and gates, or stitched into commemorative scrolls, or blessing imperial burial shrouds, but also when displayed running simultaneously across literary monuments such as the "Imperially Commissioned Five-Language Lexicon." What was being represented, however, was the emperor's capacities for simultaneous expression. And it was no requirement of the Qianlong emperor's ability to encompass worlds that the represented worlds be large in number or historically coherent. Those who were being addressed—his constituencies—in his simultaneous languages were formally instructed in their abilities to hear in the banner academies or the civil academies where aspiring officials toiled. They were fully apprised of the distinction between formal, abstract language use and the

86. See also Crossley, "The Formalization of the Manchu Heritage," and Wu Che-fu, *Siku quanshu xuanxiu zhi yanjiu,* 172–73.

daily business of communication. The same distinction existed between the constituencies and real peoples: No vernacular identities were of much interest in the imperial ideology. The peoples of south and southwest China, who had never been anything but objects of the conquest, whose languages (when they could be written) did nothing to expand the moral realm of the emperor, were not constituencies addressed by the imperial voice(s). Their representations would be limited to the curiosity industries in which circulated copies of the Qing catalog of tribute peoples, or the "Miao albums" [87] that provided entertainment for the literati in the eighteenth century. Nor was there room in the universal iconography for the ambiguous: As the Chinese-martial had been revised as "Chinese," the Oyirods were revised as "Mongols."

The distance between the idealized constituencies and life as it was lived was, however, no major impediment to the final persuasiveness of the identity documentation of the eighteenth century. Nineteenth- and twentieth-century writers have accepted the ideologically framed documentation of the eighteenth century as sources for social and political history and for our own enterprises of "ethnic" and "cultural" studies. Every lie is a truth, of course, if seen from the right angle. But what is more surprising about Qing imperial ideologies of identity was their ability to define and, indeed, to ossify the language and the concepts of their avowed enemies—the nationalists who dealt the death blow to the empire in the early twentieth century.

87. See forthcoming work by Laura Hostetler.

Race and Revolution at the End of the Empire

Between 1895 and 1912, nationalists in China had reversed the position they considered the Chinese population had historically endured under emperors. There was a reclamation, as it was seen, of some words: *Guoyu,* "national language," which had meant Manchu under the Qing, would now mean standard Chinese. *Hanjian,* "Han traitors," would no longer mean, as it had under the Qing, Chinese who pretended to work for the empire but actually betrayed it; "Chinese traitors" were now Chinese who really had worked for the Qing, primarily the Chinese-martial bannermen or their descendants. The great emblematic episode in this reversion, as suggested in the Introduction to this book, was the case of Duanfang, who, when set upon by a murderous crowd for being a bannerman, tried unsuccessfully to argue for his life by claiming he was "really" Chinese. The referential legacy of the eighteenth century allowed such a statement to be sensible, but it could hardly save one from a clubbing: Anybody who was really a Chinese and really a bannerman was really a traitor, and the brand of "race traitor" has been applied to Chinese-martial descendants consistently by nationalists in the twentieth century. This was not the only notion nationalists adapted from the middle Qing. The revolutionaries intended to, and in 1923–24 managed to in fact, nationalize the property of the imperial household. More important, they claimed the emperors themselves. The former proprietors became property, as their narrative of conquest and occupation was used to press territorial claims against Japan and Russia on behalf of some yet undefined "China" (later, a better but not perfectly defined "China" would use the same appropriation in border disputes with the Soviet Union and India, as a legitimation for the military occupation of Tibet and ongoing militant rhetoric respecting Taiwan). As part of that larger appropriation, the concepts and in many cases the terms used by the emperorship to generate and sustain its constituencies were adapted to the definition of a "Chinese" majority within the successor state(s), and identification of "minority nationalities" apart. The result was a new tension between roots and branches, at least as complex as the Qianlong transitions just examined.

In the nineteenth century the importance of the Qianlong legitimation of genealogical thinking and idealization of cultural knowledge became immediate. The government was repeatedly hampered in its ability to deal with the West by a rigid approach to information that was the recognizable child of the Qianlong preference for authority—the emperorship's ability to taxonomize the universal empire—over science. Chinese nationalists called for destruction of the dynasty and eradication of the Manchu presence in China (for most, these were two sides of the same coin), while peoples identifying themselves with the imperial constituencies moved, in the last years of the Qing, between loyalism to the moribund dynasty and secessionism from a state dominated by the Chinese. The extent to which the imperial ideology informed the emergence of "nationalist" and "ethnic" movements in the last years of the empire is suggested by the fact that peoples accorded no status as constituencies under the empire had weak secessionist, nationalist, or ethnic movements. Those who claimed correspondence between themselves and Qing imperial constituencies recognized in Central and Inner Asia were able to generate ethnic movements of varying degrees of coherence and efficacy. And the Chinese, the subordinate majority of the empire, defined themselves by a process of mutual differentiation from the others, particularly the Manchus (an inversion of the processes of the seventeenth century). Indeed the rhetorics of radical Chinese nationalism— those of Lu Haodong, Zou Rong, Zhang Binglin, and, at one time, Sun Yatsen—were profoundly dependent upon a stereotyped historical characterization of the Manchus for the internal coherence of their characterization of the Chinese.[1] In developing their rhetoric, the nationalistic scholars and polemicists of the late nineteenth and early twentieth centuries drew both upon the dissident tradition of the seventeenth century and upon the eighteenth-century Qianlong ideology of genealogical and archetypical identity.

Treatments of the origins of nationalist discourse in late-nineteenth-century China often emphasize the role of imported words, concepts, texts,

---

1. On this see Crossley, *Orphan Warriors*, 187–228, and forthcoming work of Edward J. M. Rhoads.

and sometimes a "modernity" framework to explain the stimulus and the form of Chinese nationalism.[2] Foreign influence is incontrovertible, but many other scholars have, particularly with reference to Liang Qichao (1873–1929) and Zhang Binglin (1869–1936), placed those influences in the context of traditional ideas.[3] It is not necessary to belabor the point that a choice between "foreign" or "traditional" sources for Chinese nationalism is not required.[4] As Frank Dikötter and others have demonstrated, "racial taxonomies were being formed well before the intrusion of Europeans in China."[5] Liang Qichao made a conscious effort to stress the significance of literacy in foreign concepts, and the result has been a supposition that foreign concepts were of decisive importance in his own thinking. A nice example was his treatment of Zhang Binglin in his *Intellectual Trends of the Ch'ing Period* (*Qingdai xueshu gailun*). Without noting that Zhang represented at the time of writing (1920) an alienated wing of the nationalist movement (like himself, at the other extreme), Liang compliments Zhang on his sometime role as a protagonist of the "Orthodox" (Wang Niansun) school[6] and notes what appears to be a youthful infatuation with

2. See, for instance, Tang Xiaobing, *Global Space and the Nationalist Discourse of Modernity*. For the most comprehensive general background on nationalist thought, see Gasster, *Chinese Intellectuals and the Revolution of 1911*. See also Laitinen, *Chinese Nationalism in the Late Qing Dynasty*, esp. 38–54, and Pusey, *China and Charles Darwin*.

3. For general background on Liang, see Levenson, *Liang Ch'i-ch'ao and the Mind of Modern China*; Chang hao, *Liang Ch'i-ch'ao and Intellectual Transition in China*; Huang, *Liang Ch'i-ch'ao and Modern Chinese Liberalism*; and these studies focused more on specific aspects of Liang's thought: Judge, *Print and Politics*; Tang, *Global Space and Nationalist Discourse*; Pusey, *China and Charles Darwin*; Kwong, *A Mosaic of the Hundred Days*; Nathan, *Chinese Democracy*, 45–66; Huang Kun, "Liang Qichao duo bian lun." For general background on Zhang see, for the most comprehensive recent treatment, Weber, *Revolution und Tradition*; also Shimada Kenji, *Pioneer of the Chinese Revolution*; Laitinen, *Chinese Nationalism in the Late Qing Dynasty*; Wong, *Search for Modern Nationalism*; Gasster, *Chinese Intellectuals and the Revolution of 1911*, 190–227; Fogel, "Race and Class in Chinese Historiography"; Furth, "The Sage as Rebel"; Zhang Kaiyuan, "'Jufen jinhua lun' de youhuan yizhu"; Warren Sun, "Chang Ping-lin and His Political Thought." The two are very fruitfully compared in terms of "racial" thinking in Dikötter, *The Discourse of Race in Modern China*, 97–136.

4. Benedict Anderson and Ernest Gellner's exaggeration of the disjuncture between nationalist and prenationalist "consciousness" has been itself exaggerated and questioned by Prasenjit Duara (see *Rescuing History from the Nation*). But for a necessary exploration of a specific aspect of global communications and their impact on Chinese political ideology, see Lydia Liu, *Translingual Practice*.

5. Dikötter, *The Discourse of Race in Modern China*, 34.

6. Wang Niansun (1744–1832), a *kaozheng* (evidentialism) and *xiaoxue* (philology) expert who with his son Wang Yinzhi (1766–1834) was seen as progenitor of

"early political tracts intentionally limited to a single 'doctrine of racial revolution,'" then goes on to examine the more mature—presumably more acute—Zhang's interest in interpreting Daoism through the conceptual medium of Buddhism. He also notes with approval that Zhang became "more erudite" after reading Western works.[7] Liang's strong suggestion that cosmopolitanism is preferable to culturalism in the narrow sense is characteristic, and undoubtedly a genuine projection of his hopes for the Chinese intellectual elite. But it seriously distorts both Zhang's intellectual sources and Liang's own. What is at issue in this Postscript is an examination of the particular reflections of eighteenth-century ideological dispositions in the more prominent theoretical debates of the transition from imperial to republican China.

Whether at Liang Qichao's end of the spectrum, or at Zhang Binglin's, Wang Fuzhi, Huang Zongxi, and Gu Yanwu[8] in particular proved indispensable as intellectual "ancestors" of the nationalist movement. The documentary chain linking the later nineteenth century to the seventeenth and eighteenth centuries was in place. Selected writings of Wang Fuzhi[9] and Huang Zongxi had been either included in the "Four Treasuries" libraries, or had been recognized in the codices. Even suppressed work, as in the case of Wang Fuzhi, was likely to remain well known if it had attracted enough critical writing and comment from the Qianlong emperor. In the years after the Taiping War, the civil governors were in charge of reconstituting the local libraries, and in the process of commissioning new printing blocks of-

---

a major Jiangnan legacy. As I have noted elsewhere, Zhang shared with his Manchu antagonist, Jinliang, a claim to inheritance of the Wang intellectual mantle (see *Orphan Warriors*, 162–63; 181–86). On the Wangs see also Huang Aiping, "Qian Jia xuezhe Wang Niansun, Wang Yinzhi fu zi xueshu yanjiu"; Elman, *From Philosophy to Philology*, 112–29. Liang, of course, specifically meant by calling Zhang "orthodox" to place him in the greater line of descent, via Wang, to Gu Yanwu, whom for his breadth Liang considered one of the three great progenitors (with Yan Roju and Hu Wei) of Qing thought.

7. Liang, *Intellectual Trends in the Ch'ing Period*, 111.

8. Zhang's response to the debate over emperorship is the more striking when his youthful infatuation with Gu Yanwu is remembered. He adopted a literary name (Taiyan) invoking Gu's own name and once had the ambition of completing Gu's *Xingshi lun*, his compendium of the constitution of the Chinese people on the basis of the great lineages.

9. An incomplete collection of his works was brought into print by Zou Hanxun between 1840 and 1842. In 1871 Zeng Guofan's printing office at Nanking remade blocks of Wang's collection, *Chuanshan yishu*, which had been destroyed in the Taiping War. What remained unprinted of Wang's surviving works were published by Liu Renxi between 1897 and 1917.

ten restored to public access works that the "Four Treasuries" suppressed or neglected. Liang Qichao and his contemporaries were at pains to direct their sympathizers' attention to these works, including the writings of Lü Liuliang preserved in the Yongzheng emperor's "Great Righteousness Resolving Confusion," and to bring out new editions of works neglected or banned in the eighteenth century. Liang was most self-congratulatory for republishing Huang Zongxi's indictment of imperial despotism, "Advice to the Prince" (*Mingyi daifang lu*), which contrary to Liang's claim had not been suppressed by the "Four Treasuries," which included all Huang's work in its codices.[10] What is striking is not the reclamation often envisioned for this period of "loyalist," "nationalist," "racist," or "anti-Manchu" works suppressed by the Qing but the careful selection of the seventeenth-century cosmologists of difference, such as Wang, Huang, Gu, and Lü, over the more descriptive and politically critical ethnographers of the same period, such as Xiao Daheng, Mao Ruizheng, or Ye Xianggao.

The historical resources for the nationalists did not in fact lie outside imperially generated documents of the seventeenth and eighteenth centuries, but their boldest immediate appropriation from the empire was the notion of where the boundaries of a national "China" should be. The nationalists ultimately—certainly by 1911—demanded that the future republic should assume the geographical contours of the entire Qing empire. The irony is underscored by the meticulousness with which Qing imperial ideology had objectified China as a province of the empire. Late consensus among nationalists on what geographical China was had grave ideological and considerable strategic implications. To the extent that a discrete cause for the desired transferal of the "Qing" corpus to "China" can be found, it may be said to rest in the sociology of nationalisms in late-nineteenth- and early-twentieth-century Qing domains. Their interaction placed an inexorable governor on the ability of exclusivist philosophy to gain political ground after the turn of the century and led to the isolation of Zhang Binglin, Liu Shipei, and others from the development of national political rhetoric. In broadest terms, a sociology of nationalisms in the period from about 1850 to 1911 would recognize a nationalizing center and several ethnicizing margins. In various ways, both trace their origins to the Taiping War era (1850–65), when state bankruptcy precluded continuation of the eighteenth-century policies of official culture, when the ideological position of the emperorship was newly dedicated to a two-dimensional "Confucian" pre-

10. Sun Hui-wen, *Liang Qichao de minquan yu junxian sixiang*, 15.

sentation, and when the social dynamics of civil war heightened the opportunities and the pitch of racial invective and intercommunity strife.

There is at this time little persuasive evidence that China before the Taiping War was beset by deep or intractable racial animosities. This is not to say that individual Chinese or Manchus did not have a dislike for people on the other side, or that Chinese generally did not resent the advantages the Manchus as a group were assumed to enjoy. It is rather to suggest that ethnic conflicts were not a primary cause of political or social unrest and that racial invective was typically appended to the rhetoric of troubles that had decipherable proximate causes. Even the Taipings did not unequivocally hypothesize irremediable hostilities between Chinese and Manchus on the basis of hypostatic racial qualities. But it is hard to deny that something significant did change with the establishment of a Taiping order and the dissemination of Taiping propaganda. Because of their ability to create an independent rhetoric, to promulgate it, and to sustain it over a period of time, the Taipings ascended to a level of explicitness and to a theory of racial divisions that had not previously been evident in the empire. Their religion provided them with the theory: The Manchus were the personal representatives of Satan, and the Taipings the representatives of God. Playing upon the status of the bannermen as military slaves of the court, Taiping propagandists were able to portray China as being in a condition of enslavement by slaves, a conceit that would become a fairly ubiquitous feature of nationalist rhetoric at the turn of the century.[11] The war saw episodes of massive slaughter of garrison populations whose majorities were noncombatant old people, women, and children, so that Manchus, Mongols, and those still retaining Chinese-martial status were conscious of the fact that they were, for their ethnic qualities, being sought out and killed, or starved to death in their own homes. And the mechanisms of population registration under the Taipings demanded a vocabulary of ethnic identification that was wholly unlike that of the empire, resulting in the introduction of terms such as *hanzu, mengzu,* and *manzu,* which would be willingly assumed as self-identification in the last decade of the Qing.[12]

The greatest significance of the Taiping War may be its aftermath. Many garrison compounds in Jiangnan were destroyed or gravely damaged during the war, and most installations had experienced a sharp worsening of their normally precarious economic circumstances. The Qing government

11. Crossley, *Orphan Warriors,* 127.
12. See also Crossley, "Thinking about Ethnicity."

did not have and would never secure the resources for rebuilding these physical plants or sustaining the garrison populations. Nationalist propagandists such as Zou Rong and Chen Tianhua who later depicted the Manchus as battening off the famous "three taels" of monthly allowance knew very well that few bannermen in the post-Taiping era received any regular pay and that what was received was frequently months late, reduced by the graft of officers, or counterfeit. Because of the official policy of impoverishment (which was accompanied by other policies of alienation), the fortunes of the garrisons were determined by their ability to define themselves as communities. Some were unsuccessful at this and were within a short time neither functioning nor identifiable. Others were successful and not only organized well to meet their economic and educational needs, but appear to have experienced a sharpening of their consciousness of being "peoples"—now not a leveled mass of banner servants of the Qing, but "Manchus," "Mongols," "Sibos," and other peoples, with histories (which had been richly attested by the Qing court in the eighteenth century) and with futures.[13] There is ample evidence that until the last decades of the empire these peoples—the post-garrison bannermen—continued to see themselves as having an intimate and indelible connection to the Qing court. After the Boxer Uprising, however, there was a discernible alteration in the orientation of some of these "ethnic" groups, who now came closer to being nationalistic. As the end of the empire came to appear inevitable, secessionist movements in Manchuria and in Mongolia began to take form. They augmented a set of local separatist movements already in train, particularly in parts of Xinjiang, in Gansu, and in Tibet.[14] Modern scholarship in the People's Republic has tended to interpret these movements as bourgeois revolutionary movements, because they appear to be "anti-Qing." In fact the movements generally were anti-Chinese, in the sense that they were based upon the expectation that the demise of the empire would be followed by attempts to impose direct Chinese control over these former imperial territories. By the early years of the twentieth century—perhaps by the time of the Hundred Days' Reform movement, because of its rejection of the moderate, progressive Manchu faction—these other nationalist movements were taking both indignation and inspiration from Chinese nationalism. Manchus, Mongols, and Sibos tended to continue to define themselves as "loyalists," and Manchus in particular could justify Northeastern

13. Compare to the Muslim process described by Gladney, *Muslim Chinese,* 79–93, and Lipman, *Familiar Strangers,* 190–223.
14. Grunfeld, *The Making of Modern Tibet,* 53–69.

secessionism on the grounds that the Qing could return to their homeland after the retreat from Peking. Yet the connections of these movements to the empire and the Qing imperial lineage were complex, and it seems clear that at least some portion of Mongol and Manchu leaders were in the strictest sense nationalist, hoping to establish independent states for their peoples in what they construed to be their historical territories.[15]

Awareness of the evolving self-identities of non-Chinese in the domain of what was supposed to be "China" presented a conceptual crisis to the Chinese nationalists, regardless of their own varieties of ideological commitment. Those who by the turn of the century had identified themselves with the movement for constitutional monarchy, foremost Kang Youwei and Liang Qichao, could hardly assent to Zhang Binglin's exclusivist position with respect to non-Chinese in the future Chinese state. And though Sun Yatsen seems to have been sympathetic to exclusivist views in his own early days as a nationalist leader, geopolitical factors ultimately led him to an accommodation of the sort Zhang abhorred. By the time the expiration of the Qing empire was imminent, Tibet had been subverted by Britain, Russia was a power in Central Asia, and inchoate secessionist movements in Mongolia and Manchuria were being underwritten by Japan. Notions of peaceful coexistence between a purified China and its alien borderlands, though already old among the Chinese nationalists, were proving with the dawn of an era of real political responsibility to be unrealizable.[16] Sun Yatsen's rhetoric changed dramatically after 1905, positing a China of the "Five Races" (*wu zu*), which was faintly reflected in the Manchu-Mongol-Tibetan-Muslim Treaty of Favorable Treatment in 1912.[17] The political intention was to avert the dilemma of a weak, though "pure" and independent, China surrounded on three sides by equally weak and easily subverted alien states. The chaos of the early years of the Republic may be partly at-

15. A particularly complex case is that of the bannerman Zhang Yong, who was, probably on account of his separatism, murdered by operatives of Zhao Erxun in 1912. See Crossley, *Orphan Warriors*, 200–201; also McCormack, *Chang Tso-lin in Northeast China*, 26.

16. Gasster, one of the few writers to have dealt with this problem, referred to it as the Scylla or Charybdis offered the exclusivist Wang Jingwei: a new China absorbing its hated aliens or allowing them to split off and form new, possibly hostile states of their own (see *Chinese Intellectuals and the Revolution of 1911*, 82).

17. This was one of two "articles of favorable treatment" (*youdai tiaojian*) promulgated by the new government in 1912. One guaranteed the private property and some of the public privileges of the imperial family, the other promised protection of the property and civil rights of the minorities mentioned (and only those). See also Crossley, *Orphan Warriors*, 198.

tributable to this, since Manchu and Mongol separatists turned repeatedly to the cause of restoration to attempt to realize their nationalistic hopes and were systematically encouraged by the Japanese to do so. The Mongolian movement under Babojab and the uprising of Shanqi (Prince Su) in 1916, as well as the "restoration" by Zhang Xun of Puyi in 1917 were only the best known of the incidents growing out of these dislocations and occasionally puncturing public awareness. The ideological result was nil—the eleventh-hour detour to an insincere and philosophically empty pluralism left the Republic with no conceptual currency of cultural diversity and political openness.

The relationship of the emperorship to the Chinese polity in general and to cultural identity in particular was an issue of which nationalists were aware, and on which they felt there were decisions to be made. Before the Guangxu emperor's death in 1909 there was the pressing question of whether or not to support a constitutional monarchy, usually implied to be modeled on that of Meiji Japan. But even those rejecting constitutional monarchy had to deal with the issue of how centralized rule was to be constructed in a profoundly fragmented, regionalized, and economically and culturally differentiated republic. The particulars of the positions taken by Liang Qichao and Zhang Binglin will be discussed below, but it is first of all important to establish that the constructed position of emperorship with respect to "tradition" carried some assumptions about the character of the imperial institution that were generally shared by those who were familiar with the philosophical writing of the Ming and early Qing periods. What was manifest to Chinese nationalists of the late Qing was that this promise of unchallenged and unbroken control by a single individual had proved intoxicating to many border chieftains who had been bound by their own native traditions of corporate rule (some of which were codified as early as the *Zhenguan zhengyao* of the Tang period, a work that intrigued the Qianlong emperor from a young age) and who played critical roles in the repeated revitalizations and refinements of the emperorship in China. According to the *Shujing* (which some of these scholars regarded as authoritative), "law" (*fa*), which Liang Qichao associated with the depredations of emperorship, was not itself native to the Chinese but had been invented by the Miao, who unlike the Chinese were incapable of being swayed by moral considerations. It appeared also, as Liang was careful to point out later, that the first Minister of Punishments in ancient China was in fact the first officer for pacification of the barbarians, who particularly used his punishments to bend barbarians and aborigines to the will of the state; the Chinese were to be subjected, in contrast, to moral suasion. These powers generated by the early monarchy to deal with the barbarian problem were later corruptly applied to the general population, and the long road to despotism was opened.

In this paradigm, the Manchu, Mongol, and other peoples brought to China by the Qing regime were subsumed under the emperorship itself, which was a perversely authoritarian institution that forced the Chinese to live under the rule of and at constant risk of depredation by alien peoples. Indeed the history of emperorship in China was itself a product of alien intrusion. The rejection of the Qing order and the rejection of aliens in China became identical, which was a logical extension of the "dissident" discourse of the seventeenth century. Ideologically, the Qing emperorship was seen to have terminated itself, and the history of emperors in China, at the moment of its own birth. As nationalists elsewhere in the world had before them (and would after them), the nationalists of the very late nineteenth and early twentieth centuries in China were now able to portray the entirety of the country as a community, one that as a body had suffered under barbarian depredation and its instrument, the emperorship. Thanks in part to developments in eighteenth-century court ideology that have been detailed in this book, they could use terms taken from the lexicon of kinship (*zu*) to mediate this concept. A republic would mean the end to the inimical relationship between the state and communities that had been part of imperial history. In its early stages, the revolutionaries by identifying the Manchus with the state could give the emperorship the face of a hated enemy (instead of the "Confucian" rectitude in which it had lately tried to cloak itself) and destroy it under the blows of national unity and outrage. Democracy, particularly for Liang, would be the long-term result of the ability of governors to articulate and realize (perhaps even to intuit) the wishes of the majority of the governed. In fact, it appears that possibilities for political participation by communities may have been profoundly impeded by the identification of the state with the community— or the creation of a false congruence between the two—at least as late as the Mao era. In contrast to Russia, where the Romanovs had been expected to be the archetypical Russians and nationalistic discourse had to consciously differentiate (or over-differentiate) between the state and the people, in China nationalistic discourse was a priori posited upon an over-differentiation of the "Manchus" from the "Chinese" and thus idealized the organic relationship between any "Chinese" state and the "Chinese" people.[18]

18. Cherniavsky, *Tsar and People*, 229–30, suggests that nationalism was more rapidly achieved in Germany and Italy, for instance, which were first unified in the

This rhetorical approach was smoothed by the fact that the post-Taiping emperorship in China, though not in fact centralized, sanctioned an overtly China-oriented, "orthodox" (in the sense discussed earlier) Confucian state rhetoric that was easily opposed by ideas generated by the seventeenth-century cosmologists mentioned above, by the Qing court, and by the New Text movement associated with Kang Youwei and his student Liang Qichao at the end of the nineteenth century. In most cases, a post-Taiping court rhetoric stressing hierarchy, conformity, harmony, and cultural uniformity was opposed by text-based philosophies of change, equality, and—most damaging to the imperial cause—particularistic identities through which justice ("for the Chinese") was interpreted. In order to stress the distinction between the state (which was ephemeral and not in origin necessarily legitimate) and society (which was eternal, and "natural"), many writers were attracted to the "Legalists," whom emperors had insisted their spokesmen should vilify. The problem with the Legalists was not, Zhang Binglin insisted, that they had posed society against the state, but that their techniques of governing had been selectively applied for despotic purposes. Liang Qichao, like Zhang Binglin, was also a defender of Mo Di, who had been repeatedly excoriated by Mencius and Mencian interpreters of Confucius. Liang criticized what he called Confucian "patriarchism," which he considered an artifact of Mencianism (though he stated that democratization, not Legalism, was the remedy).[19] He criticized Mencius for failing to recognize the issue of "rights" in familial relationships, by extension condemning the traditional parallel of the father-son and sovereign-minister relationship.[20] He also disliked the uses to which Mencius' thought had been put by Gu Yanwu, who had cited it to construct moral hostilities between Chinese and non-Chinese, and Liang evidently disapproved so much of Lü Liuliang (for which he would have received merits from the Yongzheng emperor) that he replaced him as a seventeenth-century "ancestor" with the materialist scholar (and go-between with Japan) Zhu Shunshui.

Liang agreed with other nationalist scholars that Xunzi had been the most dynamic thinker of late Zhou times and the one who had best presaged the political conditions of modernity; he did not, however, relinquish

---

nineteenth century and could develop national myths without "obstruction" from the imperial myth. But I read his comment as suggesting that nationalist idiom in Russia at the end of the imperial period expressed highly problematic relationships between the identity of the nation and the character of the sovereign.

19. Liang, *History of Chinese Political Thought*, 48.
20. Liang, *History of Chinese Political Thought*, 57.

his respect for Mencius' moral ideals, nor did he absolve Xunzi of the ancient charges that he attempted to imbue Confucianism with an excessive authoritarianism. He saw Xunzi as having defined human beings through their ability to conceive of and to participate in a political process, believing that from this, and not from an inherent moral nature, the concept of morality had sprung. *Qun*, "grouping," the word that Xunzi had used to describe the uniquely human practice of initiating and sustaining volitional communities, was for Liang the basic intelligence behind political life. Liang was, however, unhappy with Xunzi's insistence that the legitimation of the community and the legitimation of rulership should be the same and took the opportunity to blame Xunzi and the quasi-Legalist tradition for having justified tyranny in China over the ages.[21] As important as Xunzi was to Liang, Wang Fuzhi was more important. Xunzi, after all, had explained only why humans form communities. Wang had explained something far more important to the nationalists, which was why people must form communities with specific other people. Like Xunzi, Wang adapted the word *qun* to his explication of how cosmology was, to use Alison Black's term, "expressed" in human social history—how like attracts like, and communities connect themselves to history. Extending Xunzi and Wang Fuzhi, Liang reasoned that since humans are by nature inclined to group, the extent to which normal individuals can define their interests in contrast to or distinct from those of the group is limited. Thus for an educated and well-nourished society, there will always be hope of an orderly and just political life. Liang stated, in "On Constitutional Law" (*Lixian fa lun*), that regardless of status ("whether sovereign, minister or commoner") all were motivated by the national interest, and so no law or its implementation could conflict with native imperatives. Thus, after 1898 Liang was able to open his model of political development to the possibilities of constitutional monarchy, a move that demanded a conciliatory posture toward the Manchus and split him and Kang Youwei from Zhang, Liu Shipei, Wang Jingwei, and others. As an initiate of the New Text school that had lately been most dramatically espoused by Kang, Liang was a believer in progressive, if not epochal, political revelation. In the age to come China would be a democracy, or perhaps have superseded democracy in the beauty of its political system. In the near term, however, a central authority with the prestige of the emperorship behind it would be necessary to lead the people along the path of enlightenment.

21. Chang Hao, *Liang Ch'i-ch'ao and Intellectual Transition*, 100–102.

The last point is a key to Liang's profound rootedness in Qing construc- ✓✓
tions of the emperorship. He considered the late Zhou and Qin periods to
have been a most instructive demonstration of the relationship between
emperorship and cultural survival. Thanks in part to the wisdom of Guan
Zhong and others, the emergence of strong centralized rule, realized in the
emperorship in the state of Qin in 221 BCE, had allowed the Qin to survive
when all other states had evaporated. Liang did not consider it to be the case
that the other Zhou states were destroyed by Qin. They were, on the contrary, weakened by the progressive decline of their aristocracies, leading to
the rise in the power of barbarous tribal peoples. Only Qin, which had no
aristocracy, was unaffected by this epochal change and was able to perpet-
uate Chinese culture. Liang did not think that the Qin order had been perfect. But it had generalized a respect for literacy and civilization, and with
the coming Han age the "democratic" influences of Confucius and Mencius
were established.[22]

But Liang went beyond pronouncements calculated to incite the latent
resentments of Chinese against Manchus and together with Tan Sitong secretly reprinted and distributed tens of thousands of copies of Wang Xiuchou's "Ten Days at Yangzhou" (*Yangzhou shiri ji*), the most famous memoir of the most famous massacre during the conquest of China in the middle
seventeenth century. Later, Liang approvingly quoted from Huang Zongxi's
"Advice to the Prince" regarding the lasting hatred of the people for emperors, the cynical attempts by emperors and obsequious scholars to use
philosophy as propaganda ("applying such abstract terms as 'father' and
'heaven' in order to inhibit men from action"), exploitation of laws in order to maintain despotism, and the manipulation of Mencian idealism to
justify the inconsistent and self-serving attitude of sovereigns toward the
law. "People say," Liang quoted Huang from "Primordialism" (*Yuanfa*),
"that when one has the rule of good men, one does not need law, but I say
that until there is the rule of law, there is no rule of man." His revival of
Huang's writings, Liang later commented, "contributed powerfully to the
sudden alteration of thought in the late Ch'ing."[23] Liang understood
Huang to say that law, emperorship, and authoritarianism were necessary
evils. A superior society would, as the Mencians had always insisted, be
ruled by moral feeling, elite example, and unselfishness. Substituting the
rule of law for such qualities would make society hollow or make it liable
to collapse from within. For this reason the emperorship (or dictatorship)

22. Liang, *History of Chinese Political Thought*, 28–31.
23. Liang, *Intellectual Trends in the Ch'ing Period*, 37–38.

must be tutelary or "enlightened" (*kaiming*), itself respectful of law and reason, but also aggressively instruct and improve its citizens, until the necessity for its own existence has been obviated (and national imperialism has sprouted). Under pressure to find political solutions and justify them, Liang had only succeeded in making the logic of imperial Confucianism explicit.

As on many other issues, Zhang Binglin was at the opposite end of the spectrum from Liang in his interpretation of imperial morality in China. Liang Qichao had accorded respect to Xunzi, who had in any event become a central figure in orthodox criticism from the eighteenth century on, and he had worked to reopen study of other early thinkers, too. But Zhang Binglin was the true uncompromising advocate of what would come to be called the study of the "various schools" (*zhuzi*), of the pre-imperial and early imperial era. He strongly rejected the dominance of Mencius and had none of Liang's scruples about the abstract value of Mencius' moralism. Zhang was open to the claim by the New Text school that there was in the "genuine" Confucian canon some kernel of relevant political wisdom, but as an adherent of the Old Text school he would admit to no special insights of Confucius or Mencius; they had as much to offer the serious reader as any other historical work. The New Text idea that there might be revelations in the ancient documents, or that Confucius might on the basis of his prophetic qualities be venerated as a religious figure, Zhang resisted with a ferocious energy.

Zhang was never an adamant advocate of democracy, though he also never absolutely denied that the potential for democratic theory had been present in the Chinese tradition. Emperorship in China, he felt, had not been corrupted by legalism. It had been the other way around: Confucianism had perverted the history of centralized, orderly rule in the country. Mencian pieties about the morality of the monarch, the aristocracy, and the bureaucracy had been used to justify a system in which the sovereign virtually owned the country and commanded reverence from those he had reduced to the status of slaves. Most specifically and most damagingly, Mencian monarchy had not only tolerated but encouraged the growth of a selfish, bloated aristocracy, to the point that the Qing now (in the first decade of the twentieth century) governed China virtually by aristocracy alone. The emperorship had become, by means of its reduction to a few Confucian slogans, the means for repeated alien domination of China. Inefficiency, irrationality, and injustice had been the unceasing result. Zhang praised the First Emperor of the Qin, who had been the icon of political sins for the imperial Confucianists for centuries. The First Emperor had tolerated no aristocracy, no regionalisms, no selfishness. His standardizations of roads, currency, and time would have been a foundation for modernization, and his just, if harsh, legal codes would have prevented the dispossession of the Chinese majority by alien minorities. Mencians were to be doubly condemned for having not only eradicated the First Emperor from China's legitimate political history, but for having discredited the contributions of Mo Di, Xunzi, Yang Zhu, Shang Yang, Dong Zhongshu, and others who had seen the need to define government apart from society and to conduct the state in the most rational manner possible. It was the history of alliance between Confucians and emperors, in his view, that had crippled Chinese development for centuries and left the country vulnerable to usurpation by crafty barbarians who could learn to patronize the Mencians and mouth a few "Confucian" axioms. Zhang did not advocate an emperorship for China, a constitutional monarchy, a tutelary dictatorship, or a centralized authority of any kind. He urged his readers to take a cue from Gu Yanwu and to divide China into small "kingdoms" (*wangguo*), each to be ruled independently and further divided into circuits (*dao*). The total effect would be to dismantle the provincial system of administration, which had been imposed by the Mongols anyway, and to return China to its pre-imperial pattern. Unlike Liang, who saw China moving toward a new form of imperialism and thus as envisaged a geographical entity that was a perpetuation of the present empire, Zhang wished to see China completely purged of the imperial process, even at the sacrifice of a grand territorial sway. In this way, he escaped the strategic dilemma out of which Sun Yatsen and Wang Jingwei had found no graceful exit. He had no wish to prevent the alien peoples from splitting off and forming their own countries. He foresaw these as buffer states, protecting the Chinese from hostile encroachment by whites (Russians from the north or west and British from the west or southwest). The Manchus, he noted, had already bungled their way into the loss of Manchuria, so they could not be required to go "home." Instead, he would grant them lands north of the Yellow River and let them prevent further Russian expansion toward the south.

Zhang was intensely aware of and more resentful than Liang at the extraordinary relationship in the Qing empire between the emperorship and the written word. All emperorships had, of course, been dependent upon the written word for communications, instruction, and edicts, and many had sponsored the writing of the histories of their predecessors. But the Ming, with the "Yongle Encyclopedia" (*Yongle dadian*), their continuation of the polylingual monumentalism of the Yuan before them, and their sophisticated censorial system, set an example that the Qing adopted and in their own turn elaborated. The literary inquisitions of the Yongzheng and Qianlong periods, the "Four Treasuries" projects, their obsession with the codifications of the historical and literary records, and frequent interferences in the examinations brought literature inescapably within the functions of the emperorship. Liang Qichao's later insistence that a people must, by definition, have a documented history was a direct adaptation of imperial ideology. Zhang Binglin's insistence that of all empires the Qing was the most obnoxious because of its unprecedented determination to control history would have been accepted by the Qianlong emperor as high praise.

Prior to 1898 there is little evidence that Liang Qichao sought what Joseph Levenson would have called a "cosmopolitan" politics or a cosmopolitan nationalism.[24] Liang's adherence to "New Text" Confucianism caused him to take a rather more expansive view of possibilities of Confucian applications in the modern context, but it did not prevent him from engaging in the narrow racist invective for which he later condescended to Zhang Binglin. Indeed Liang was as great a youthful enthusiast of "the doctrine of racial revolution" (*zhongzu geming zhi lun*) as was Zhang. In 1897 he was instrumental in organizing the Academy for Contemporary Affairs (*Shiwu xuetang*) in Hunan, which in its short one year of existence distinguished itself for vivid racial polemic, all of which was strictly subversive (though protected by local elites). A passage from his lecture notes gives the flavor of the daily (and nightly) fare at the Academy for Practical Affairs: "[The Manchus] butchered the cities and the countryside, and for generations afterward have retained the demeanor of common thieves. Reading of the accounts of the rape of Yangzhou leaves one tearing the hair and blind with tears. With due knowledge of this atrocity the world would not shrink from holding them to account, and there would be great benefits in that for mankind."[25] Unlike Zhang (or Lu Haodong or Zou Rong), Liang never advocated race war against the Manchus. On the contrary he repeatedly warned against the strategic disadvantages of such a war. He later characterized his incendiary bigotry of 1897 and 1898 as an attempt to exploit the racist passions of the common people in order to foment a revolutionary movement. Nationalism, in his view, was still a subtlety somewhat beyond the comprehension of the population at large; racial hatred was handier, and bountiful. In his later writings he encapsulated this strategy in his phrases "expel the Manchus in order to facilitate a republic" (*paiman yi xing*

24. See also Levenson, *Liang Qichao and the Mind of Modern China*.
25. Quoted in Sun Hui-wen, *Liang Qichao*, 14, from notes of Liang's lectures at the academy. The author also cites a similar passage in *Yijiao congbian, juan 5, ye 8*.

gonghe). This had a parallel manifestation in "Destructionism" (*pohuai zhuyi*), with its slogan, "Destroy in order to build the civil state" (*pohuai yi jian minguo*).[26] Liang was, at the time, convinced that years of barbarian imperialism had caused not only the material deprivation of the Chinese, but a deprivation of their right to political advancement as well. He followed not only the official Qing construct of Manchu political origins but also the anti-imperial critique when he lamented that the "sons of the Yellow Emperor" (*huangdi zisun*) had had their political consciousness crippled in the south for 300 years under the Manchus but in the north for 700 years (that is, under the Liao, Jin, and Yuan empires successively).[27] It did not need to be said, though it was said by Tang Caichang and others of Liang's associates, that Southerners were consequently better adapted to political leadership than Northerners.

In 1898, following the collapse of the Hundred Days' Reform movement, Liang abandoned his program of "racial revolution" for a new program to "protect the emperor" (*baohuang*) and create a constitutional monarchy. The impulses behind this transformation must have been complex. Liang had known the Guangxu emperor, Zaitian, personally and may even have felt some responsibility for the emperor's fate. But it is also clear that his time in Japan directly following the purge and execution of some of the reformers had impressed upon him that republicanism was no end in itself. From the people's power (*minchuan*) would grow the power of the nation (*guochuan*). From national power would grow a national imperialism (*minzu diguo zhuyi*), which Liang felt the Chinese would achieve at what, in comparison to the history of the West, was an accelerated pace. Liang's own geographical conception of China, then, had an inner logic that explains its resemblance to the Qing empire: His ultimate aim was not a Chinese republic, but a Chinese national empire—an imperial order in which not an emperor but the Chinese as a class would rule over others.[28] How, in such a paradigm, civil rights were to be grounded was never clearly explained. The argument was more by analogy: Britain, France, Germany, the United States of America, and Japan had civil democracies in which the people's powers were directly manifested in their abilities to secure resources

26. Sun Hui-wen, *Liang Qichao*, 18, from "Pohuai zhuyi" chapter of the work *Ziyou shu*. Gasster, *Chinese Intellectuals and the Revolution of 1911*, 69–71, shows the issue complicated by the Qing offer of constitutional monarchy. See also Zhang Kaiyuan, "Xinhai geming shi yanjiu zhong de jige wenti."

27. Sun Hui-wen, *Liang Qichao*, 15, from both "Lun shangwu," *Xinmin cong-bao* 28, and also *Xinmin shuo* (1959 Zhonghua edition), 111.

28. Sun Hui-wen, *Liang Qichao*, 20–26; 77–85.

from other peoples beyond their borders (or to extend their borders to where the resources were). Empire building was not only necessary to secure wealth and freedom for citizens; it was a definitive element in the criteria of being an identifiable people. Liang carefully distinguished between two heuristic groups, those who "had" a history (*you lishi de zhongzu*) and those who did "not have" (*fei you lishi de zhongzu*) a history. He did not include among those who had histories peoples who were merely documented, for after all the empire had documented many peoples with no orderly lineages, no civilization, no nations. To "have" a history meant to have been instrumental in the building of empires, which is to say, in the process of creating the history of others. The Qing had made exactly this distinction in their recognition of the special status of Manchus, Mongols, Chinese, Tibetans, and Uigur constituencies. Not very curiously, Liang's grouping of peoples was, in its particulars, a reiteration of the Qing scheme: Of those peoples in China who "had" history he included the Chinese, the Mongols, the Manchus, the Tibetans, the Turks, and the Muslims.

As it happened, Liang had a historical model—more properly, an interpretive construct—for his notion of national imperialism. It was a modern manifestation of the cultural imperialism that had greatly improved the world during China's "feudal" period, particularly the later Zhou. In his short essay "Feudalism and Its Effects," Liang explained that the two great phenomena of the later Zhou had been "The dissemination of civilizing influence, and assimilation of aliens." There should be no question of the reader imagining that this process was now part of China's past. It was ongoing, and Liang Qichao was part of it. "The rulers of Chow undertook the tremendous task of colonization by dispersing civilized groups among the aboriginal semi-barbarous tribes. There was great opposition to this by the aborigines. It took several hundred years of persevering struggle to civilize the region between the Tai Hsing mountains on the north and the Yangtze River on the south. This cultural expansion is one of the greatest and most difficult undertakings recorded in the history of China. Even now it is an unfinished task. But its first effective advance was due to feudalism." [29] Its next greatest advance would be due to national imperialism. The echoes here of Wang Fuzhi, who after all was not among the more extreme of the seventeenth-century "dissidents" on the barbarian issue, are strong. The Chinese represent the future of those around them, and the destruction of tribal cultures is essentially humane. In the expansion process, ge-

29. Liang, *History of Chinese Political Thought*, 157.

nealogies and genealogical metaphors would stabilize Chinese identity—anchor the expanding tendrils of civilization. The ruthlessness of official Qing policy toward indigenous, peripheral or otherwise nonimperial cultures is also suggested. The idea is perceptibly reinforced by the influence of Japanese imperialism, "pan-Asianism," and the particular interpretations of social Darwinism to which Liang was exposed. A powerful addition was the biological racism that in his maturity convinced Liang that only whites and Asians were capable of generating cultural advancement.[30] But the first inspiration was straight from Qing discourses on identity. In fact, Liang's position on moral transformation follows the logic of no one else quite as consistently as it does that of the Yongzheng emperor in "Great Righteousness Resolving Confusion."

Liang believed that national differences were not, as many in the past and in the present claimed, immutable. The "Spring and Autumn Annals," he felt, was explicit in its assertion that barbarians could be changed and that changing them was a central process of civilization. In a work for general distribution to the West, he compared what he regarded as the genuine teachings of Confucius, to whit, that one should not do to others what one would not wish done to oneself, to what he regarded as the narrow contentiousness of "what the West calls nationalism," to the cold indifference of capitalists to their laborers, to the vindictiveness of Marxists. "In the eyes of those who study Confucian teachings, the nonalienation of mankind must be the minimum basis of the social ethic." Liang never pretended to speak outside his strong and persisting New Text assumptions, and so the statement, though extraordinarily dismissive of whole ages of self-styled "Confucian" thought, was the logical extension of the Yongzheng ideology of Confucian-sanctioned alien rule and of the "nationalist" movement that had taken as its central concepts constitutional monarchy, imperial dominion over non-Chinese territories, and transformation of moral identities (as well as exclusion of Lü Liuliang from Liang's ideological sources).

Zhang Binglin was, once again, at the polar opposite of Liang on this question. Chinese and barbarians could not and should not be amalgamated, and the empire should be broken up in order to accommodate the separate destinies of its peoples. Chinese were not only different from barbarians but were hostile and inferior. He went far beyond Tan Sitong's visceral characterization of the Manchus and Mongols as "debased" races and developed

Zhang

---

30. Dikötter, *The Discourse of Race in Modern China.*

a scholarship of Chinese identity that depended heavily upon a series of intellectual premises related to the identity of aliens. He was clearly aware of Darwinian notions of transformation through the historical process,[31] but Zhang was an environmentalist, and parallels could be found between his thinking and that of contemporaries—George Kennan the elder, Theodore Roosevelt, George T. Ladd, Nitobe Inazo—who concluded that a people's natural history, food, climate, and topography determined their national characteristics. His profoundest referents were the essentialists of the seventeenth century, whose idealistic notions of identity had been legitimated by the Qianlong court. Though Zhang Binglin was an enemy of the campaign to apotheosize Confucius, there was a body of literature that he regarded with something like reverence. He believed, as had Lü Liuliang before him, that there existed in the philosophical and historical literature a subliminal anti-barbarian message, the supposed "secret counsel" to support the Chinese sovereign in order to expel barbarians. It informed, in his view, the "Annals of Zuo," the "Spring and Autumn Annals," many writings of the Song period, the early Qing, and more modern literature, too. He contended, for instance, that Dai Zhen's "Comments on the Mencius" (*Mengzi yi shu*) was a covert diatribe against the Manchus. The essence of this message, to Zhang, was eternal: Loyalty to one's own kind, tenderness for one's own kind, self-sacrifice for one's own kind. From this would spring justice and the advancement of civilization. But Zhang was, like Lü Liuliang and Gu Yanwu, scornful of those who would observe only "respect the monarch" (*zunwang*) and neglect its goal, "expel the barbarians" (*rangyi*); indeed he used Gu Yanwu's condemnation of early medieval scholars to repudiate his own teacher, Yu Yue.[32] In this respect Zhang shared some rhetoric with his seventeenth-century heroes. But his essential reasoning was quite different from theirs. Zhang's obsessive hatred of the Manchus was so unrelenting, so obstructive of his logic, and so unnecessary to his racialist politics that it is very difficult to explain. Unlike Liang and others, Zhang never claimed that his anti-Manchu proselytizing had

31. See also Zhang Kaiyuan, "'Jufen jinhua lun,'" 114. On the particularly strong influence of Terrain de Lacouperie, whose diffusionist ideas were later adapted by the National Essence scholars, see Bernal, "Liu Shih-p'ei and National Essence," 96–99.

32. Gu had cited as offenders Liu Yin, who had served the Earlier Zhao dynasty, and Cui Hao, the renowned minister of the Northern Wei. See also Man-Kam Leung, "The Political Thought of Chang Ping-lin," 36. Yu had scolded Zhang for his secret revolution activity, his residence in Japan, and his racial invective; see Crossley, *Orphan Warriors*, 182–83.

been merely a "strategy." It is true that in his later life he concentrated rather more on the problem of European, American, and ultimately Japanese imperialism than he had before 1911, but Zhang was an anti-Manchu bigot from a very young age, and even Manchus who knew and liked him knew this about him.[33] For Zhang, even the general Chinese/barbarian distinction was secondary to the contradiction between Chinese and Manchus specifically. In most ways Zhang was a strong pan-Asianist and believed that for strategic reasons China and Japan should form a cooperative sphere. But the reasons were not merely strategic. Japanese and Koreans, in contrast to Manchus (and Mongols), were not "aliens" but were the "same people" (*tongzu*) as the Chinese. The fundamental contradiction, for Zhang, was historical. The ancestors of the Manchus could be identified continuously from the "Annals of Zuo"—now made especially convenient thanks to the literary programs of the Qianlong emperor—through all the empires, finally emerging under the pseudonym of "Manchus" in the late Ming. Their nature was constant, always blood-thirsty, always lusting for power, gold, women, and the goods of the Chinese. They would never cease to scheme to subvert and control the society of the Chinese. Liang Qichao and Kang Youwei had not been willing to admit in 1898 that there were Manchus who were educated, judicious, and humane. Zhang was willing to admit it, and to name them in print (specifically [Aisin Gioro] Shoufu, and [Gūwalgiya] Jinliang), but with a stern warning: These men may be good, but they are a dangerous obstacle to universal rejection of the Qing empire, which is evil. Zhang reminded his readers not to forget the admonition of "The Annals of Zuo": "He who is not of my kind has a heart unlike mine."[34] Similarly, Zhang was infuriated by the promises of the court, after 1904, to establish a constitution. Whether they establish a constitution or not, Zhang fulminated, they will be exterminated. Whether they do good for the people or not, they will be exterminated. Whether they are just or not, whether they save the people or not, they will be exterminated.

More insidious to Zhang than the promises of a constitution were the frequently made assertions that the Manchus had somehow been transformed, assimilated, civilized. On this question, Zhang stuck resolutely to the Gu/Lü side of the seventeenth-century debate—the side actually championed by the Qianlong court. Peoples do not change their natures. To Zhang, this was the genius of Xunzi's insight into the distinction between

33. See also Crossley, *Orphan Warriors*, 162–86.
34. See Luo Baoshan, "Guanyu Zhang Binglin zhengzhi lichang zhuanbian de jipian tiaowen."

society and government: Unlike Mencius, who believed that human nature can be perfected and that the state would ultimately find its greatest goodness in the full expression of human character, Xunzi had more accurately perceived that human nature is flawed and can never be significantly improved and that the state existed to prevent humans from the full expression of their nature. Similarly, the characters of individual peoples do not change. The language they speak, the manner of their dress, their religion, even their social forms, are all secondary to who they really are. Natures were formed in the distant past, over the duration of epochs. Zhang was willing, on the basis of his cosmological materialism, to admit that change, in the abstract sense, was perceptible. What it represented, however, was not the gradual improvement of barbarians who were converging with the civilization of the Chinese. In fact all that happened was that "good" and "evil" advanced in equal measure, in their separate directions. The good become slightly better, the evil become slightly more evil. The contradiction between the Manchus and the Chinese was profound and could not be cured by a policy of absorbing Manchus or Mongols into the nationalist movement or into a new state.[35] Zhang departed from his seventeenth-century ancestors in his understanding of the substance of difference. Even those like Gu and Lü who had posited immutable differences between Chinese and barbarians had understood the difference to be a moral one. Zhang insisted that Manchus and Chinese were inimical to one another and that historically the Manchus had shown themselves to be grasping and ruthless. Beyond that, the Chinese were not defined by moral essence. For Zhang, Chinese owed loyalty to themselves because they were themselves. They were an agnatic entity, all descendants of the Yellow Emperor, and all shared the traits that his offspring had absorbed from their environment. What those traits were could only be ascertained on the basis of "national studies" (guoxue, inspired by the kokugaku of the Tokugawa era), a series of researches in philology, historical geography, and archeology. From these researches would emerge an understanding of the "national essence" (guocui, i.e., kokusui) that would illuminate the appropriate "national polity" (guoti) for the Chinese.[36] In finding a "race" for China, Zhang believed he had found a future, too.

35. See also Zhang Kaiyuan's comments on the possible derivation of this thesis from the eighteenth-century work of Nakae Chōmin: "'Jufen jinhua lun,'" esp. 117–18.

36. On "national essence" see Bernal, "Liu Shih-p'ei and National Essence," and Schneider, "National Essence and the New Intelligentsia."

Neither Zhang nor Liang, as heirs of the Qing literary environment, had any difficulty discerning what a people was: It had to be distinguished by identifiable and continuing lineages, and it had to have a history. Both Liang and Zhang adapted the Japanese term *minzoku* (*minzu*) to capture their no- ✓ tion of a "people," specifically the Chinese people, upon whom a new state was to be founded. The exact intentions of the Japanese adaptation from German have been explored elsewhere, and what is important here is that both Liang and Zhang undoubtedly read the word as *min* plus *zu*. The word *zu* was, of course, the one great signifier of heritable identity, one that was energetically institutionalized by the court in the eighteenth century. *Min* had also a particular meaning in Qing official parlance, for it specifically indicated a civilian.[37] This is important to note with respect to the term *guomin*, used both by Liang and by Zhang to indicate a people in a condition of civic participation. But *guo* ("nation," "people," "territory," "polity") remained a great difficulty that faced Liang and before which he made many twists and turns in his political temper and his terminology.[38] Zhang Binglin had found an intellectually pleasing solution to the problem of what to do with the Qing empire once there was no longer an emperor. For Zhang, the best solution was to let the Qing constituencies (for he seems never to have doubted the reality of these imperial constructions) to the way they would have gone without the transcendent, universalist, coercive integrationism of the Qianlong period: Let them all be pure and independent societies. Liang was skeptical on several grounds. First, it was a strategic improbability that a "China" would survive in such an environment. Liang's exposure to social Darwinism, history, and journalism convinced him of the ruthlessness and predatoriness of Europe, America, and Japan; small, happy, self-absorbed China would not thrive. Second, Liang as a transformationalist did not actually believe in unchanging national essences, whether or not they corresponded to the Qing constituencies. The transformational process was ongoing in all the imperial territories and in their border territories; there were no objective grounds, as Zhang seemed to argue, for believing that distinct and fixed nations existed, let alone that they should all be politically independent, each enwrapped in its familial sympathies.

37. That is, one who was not *zongshi* (nobility), *wanggong* (aristocracy), *qiren* (bannerman). These groups were all liable, under various circumstances, to *bianmin*, "become a civilian."
38. Huang Kun, "Liang Qichao duo bian lun," 165–67.

But without an emperor, the cultural simultaneities, the coexistence of historicized constituencies, had little chance of being coherent. Liang hoped that in the long term a republic would mean political participation by "all." For "all" to participate, there must be a minimum number of universally accepted political beliefs and standards of behavior. In a republic, all should minimally believe that a republic is good. Liang would also have liked them to believe that Mencian values (as he interpreted them) were good and that people left to their own devices would follow them in their political as well as their personal behaviors. For marginal diversities there would always be room. But on fundamental issues, there must surely be sufficient uniformity to constitute a political culture. The Qianlong emperor may have been able to create the sensation of being all-in-one. But a republic would demand one-in-all. Liang hoped that "one" would be a culture in which Chinese identity and loyalties, Mencian values, democracy, humane competition, and forceful education of subject peoples in these ideas would not merely dominate but absolutely unify. He saw, otherwise, no hope of a large, powerful, wealthy, influential China.

The precision or wisdom of Liang's ideas could be debated,[39] but when seen in light of the reflections they contain of the conflicting elements of Qing imperial ideology, Liang's republic dilemma vividly underscores a drama widespread in the world of Liang's time: How, when, and to what extent to appropriate imperial elements in the national republics emerging from the empires' remains. The successors of the Romanovs and the Qing made one kind of choice: To continue imperial geopolitical entities without the integrating mechanism of emperorship (which had in any event deteriorated beyond revival). Turkey made another choice: To carve a distinct national entity from the imperial wreckage and set the bits adrift. In either scenario, sources had to be found for new rhetorics of legitimacy, of loyalty, of unity, of privilege, and of disenfranchisement. Joseph Levenson suggested, in his *Confucian China and Its Modern Fate*, that the loss of universalism was intolerable to the first Chinese republic; that, to oversimplify his very complex thesis, the loss of a unifying political culture, which Confucianism had provided, was not compensated by nationalism alone and ultimately had to be found in the new universalism of communism. But

---

39. Compare Liang's response to Zhang Binglin's criticism of his inconsistency, "I really am quite a flighty and changeable person," (cited in Huang Kun, "Liang Qichao duo bian lun") to his preface to *Intellectual Trends in the Ch'ing Period:* "Today my fundamental views do not differ significantly from those of eighteen years ago."

that Confucianistic (and very New Text) "universalism" that Levenson saw as lamented in the early twentieth century was not in fact an "orthodoxy" of very long standing in China; indeed the period when Levenson saw it breaking down, in the years after the Taiping War, appears to be the period in which it was being constructed, after the disintegration of the universalist imperialism of the Qianlong era. Nationalism (Chinese or otherwise) was indeed no sufficient replacement for the ideology that had sustained the empire. That ideology until the nineteenth century had not been one of Confucian universalism, but the narrative, ethical, and ideological self-containment of early modern emperorship. Its succession by a nationalistic political culture was not peculiar to China, nor are the deficiencies of nationalism alone to be found only in comparison to some more powerful and ubiquitous "universalistic" political culture of the past. Extensive, geopolitically contiguous but culturally discontinuous spaces under the dominion of a monolithic rulership—whether civil or despotic—entails an overwhelming historical contradiction. The tensions are likely to bedevil all polities that persist in sustaining dead empires long after circumstances have extinguished the transcendentally integrating possibilities of simultaneous emperorship.

Bibliography

A Guanhu. "Qianlong chao chongxin Liao, Jin, Yuan san guo peixi." *Nei Menggu daxue xuebao* 2 (1977): 26–34.

Abe Takeo. "Shinchō to ka i shishō." *Jimbun kagaku* 1, no. 3 (December 1946): 150–54.

———. *Shindai shi no kenkyū.* Tokyo: Sobunsha, 1971.

Agui et al. *Qinding manzhou yuanliu kao.* Taipei: Wenhai, 1966 (photo reprint of 1783 original).

———. *Qing kaiguo fanglue.* Taipei: Wenhai, 1966 (photo reprint of QL bingwu original).

Ahmad, Zairuddin. *Sino-Tibetan Relations in the Seventeenth Century.* Rome: Instituto italiano peril Medio ed Estremo Oriente, 1970.

Allsen, Thomas T. *Mongol Imperialism.* Berkeley: University of California Press, 1987.

Ames, Roger. *The Art of Rulership.* Honolulu: University of Hawaii Press, 1985.

Amiot [Amyôt], Jean-Joseph-Marie. *Éloge de la ville de Moukden, poème composé par Kien-Long, empereur de la Chine et de la Tartarie, actuellement regnant.* Paris, 1770.

An Shuangcheng. "Shun Kang Yong sanchao baqi ding'e qianxi." *Lishi dang'an* 2 (1983): 100–103.

Anderson, Benedict. *Imagined Communities: Reflections on the Origins and Spread of Nationalism.* London: Verso, 1983.

Anderson, Perry. *Lineages of the Absolutist State.* London: Verso, 1974.

Arlington, L. C., and William Lewisohn. *In Search of Old Peking.* Oxford: Oxford University Press, 1987 (originally published Peking: Henri Vetch, 1935).

Atwell, William. "From Education to Politics: The Fu-she." In William Theodore de Bary, ed., *The Unfolding of Neo-Confucianism.* New York: Columbia University Press, 1975.

Bai Shouyi, ed. *Qingshi guoji xueshu taolun hui.* Shenyang: Liaoning renmin, 1990.

Banton, Michael. *The Idea of Race.* London: Tavistock, 1977.

———. "The Idiom of Race: A Critique of Presentism." In Cora Bagley Marrett and Cheryl Leggon, eds., *Research in Race and Ethnic Relations,* vol. 2. Greenwich, Conn.: Jai Press, 1980, pp. 21–42.

Barlow, Tani E. "Colonialism's Career in Postwar China Studies." In Tani E. Barlow, ed., *Formations of Colonial Modernity in East Asia.* Durham, N.C.: Duke University Press, 1997 (originally published in *positions* 1, no. 1 [Spring 1993]).

Bartlett, Beatrice S. *Monarchs and Ministers: The Grand Council in Mid-Ch'ing China, 1723–1820.* Berkeley: University of California Press, 1991.

Bastide, Marianne. "Official Conceptions of Imperial Authority at the End of the Qing Dynasty." In Stuart R. Schram, ed., *Foundations and Limits of State Power in China.* London/Hong Kong: School of Oriental and African Studies/Chinese University Press, 1987.

Bawden, Charles R. *The Modern History of Mongolia.* New York: Praeger, 1968.

Bayly, Susan. "Saints' Cults and Warrior Kingdoms in South India." In Nicholas Thomas and Caroline Humphrey, eds., *Shamanism, History and the State.* Ann Arbor: University of Michigan Press, 1996, pp. 117–32.

———. *Saints, Goddesses, and Kings: Muslims and Christians in South Indian Society, 1700–1900.* Cambridge: Cambridge University Press, 1989.

Bendix, Reinhard. *Kings or People: Power and the Mandate to Rule.* Berkeley: University of California Press, 1978.

Bergholz, Fred W. *The Partition of the Steppe: The Struggle of the Russians, Manchus, and the Zunghar Mongols for Empire in Central Asia, 1619–1758: A Study in Power Politics.* New York: Peter Lang, 1993.

Bermingham, Ann. *Landscape and Ideology.* Berkeley: University of California Press, 1986.

Bernal, Martin. "Liu Shih-p'ei and National Essence." In Charlotte Furth, ed., *The Limits of Change: Essays on Conservative Alternatives in Republican China.* Cambridge, Mass.: Harvard University Press, 1976.

Beurdeley, Ceciley, and Michel Beurdeley. *Castiglione: A Jesuit Painter at the Chinese Court.* Trans. Michael Bullock. Rutland, Vt.: Tuttle, 1972 (originally published Paris, 1971).

Beyer, Stephan. *The Cult of Tārā.* Berkeley: University of California Press, 1973.

Black, Alison Harley. *Man and Nature in the Thought of Wang Fu-chih.* Seattle: University of Washington Press, 1989.

Bol, Peter K. *"This Culture of Ours": Intellectual Transitions in T'ang and Sung China.* Stanford: Stanford University Press, 1992.

Borei, Dorothy. "Economic Implications of Empire Building: The Case of Xinjiang." *Center and Inner Asian Studies* 5 (1991): 22–37.

Borokh, L. N. "Anti-Manzhou Ideas of the First Chinese Bourgeois Revolutionaries (Lu Huadong Confession)." In S. L. Tikhvinsky, ed., *Manzhou Rule in China* (Manchzhurskoe vladichestvo v Kitae), trans. D. Skvirsky. Moscow: Progress, 1983, pp. 297–311.

Bouvet, Joachim. *L'Histoire de l'empereur de la Chine.* The Hague: Mendert Uytwerf, 1699.

Bredon, Juliet. *Peking: A Historical and Intimate Description of Its Chief Places of Interest.* Shanghai: Kelly and Walsh, 1922.

Brown, Melissa J. "On Becoming Chinese." In Melissa J. Brown, ed., *Negotiating Ethnicities in China and Taiwan.* Berkeley: Institute of East Asian Studies, 1996.

Brunnert, H. S., and V. V. Hagelstrom. *Present-Day Political Organization of China.* Trans. Beltchenko and Moran. Shanghai, 1911.

Burke, Peter. *The Fabrication of Louis XIV.* New Haven: Yale University Press, 1992.

Burov, V. G. *Mirovozzrenie kitaiskogo mysliteliya XVII veka Van Chuanshaniya.* Moscow: Nauka, 1976.

Cai Yurong. *Nanping jilue.* Reprinted in Zhongguo shehui kexueyuan lishi yanjiu suo Zhingshi yanjiushi, ed., *Qingshi ciliao,* vol. 3. Peking: Zhonghua shuju, 1982.

Ch'en Chieh-hsien [Chen Jiexian]. "Introduction to the Manchu Text Version of the Ch'ing Emperors' Ch'i-chu-chü." *Central Asiatic Journal* 17, nos. 2– 4 (1973): 111–27.

———. "Lun Baqi tongzhi." In Tielang et al. *[Qinding] Baqi tongzhi.* Taipei, 1966.

———. *Manzhou congkan.* Taipei: Guoli Taiwan daxue, 1963.

———. "The Value of *The Early Manchu Archives.*" In Ch'en Chieh-hsien [Chen Jiexian] and Sechin Jagchid, eds., *Proceedings of the Third East Asian Altaistic Conference.* Taipei, 1969, pp. 58–77.

Ch'en Chieh-hsien [Chen Jiexian] and Sechin Jagchid, eds. *Proceedings of the Third East Asian Altaistic Conference.* Taipei, 1969.

Ch'en Ching-fang [Chen Jingfang]. *Qingmo Man Han zhengzhi quanli xiaozhang zhi yanjiu.* Taipei: Wenhua, 1961.

Ch'en Wen-shih [Chen Wenshi]. "The Creation of the Manchu Niru," trans. P. K. Crossley. *Chinese Studies in History* 14, no. 4 (1981). Originally published as "Manzhou baqi niulu de goucheng," *Dalu zazhi* 31, nos. 9–10 (1965).

———. "Qingdai Manren zhengzhi canyu." *Zhongyang yanjiuyuan lishi yuyan yenjiusuo jikan* 48, no. 4 (1977): 529–94.

Ch'oe Ha-kyun. *Kugyok Mongmun Manju sillok.* 2 vols. Seoul: Pogyong Munhwasa, 1992.

Chai Yü-shu [Zhai Yushu]. *Qingdai Xinjiang zhufang bingzhi de yanjiu.* Taipei, 1969.

Chan Hok-lam. *Legitimation in Imperial China: Discussions under the Jurchen Chin Dynasty (1115–1234).* Seattle: University of Washington Press, 1984.

Chan, Wing-tsit. *A Source Book in Chinese Philosophy.* Princeton: Princeton University Press, 1969.

Chang, Chun-shu. "Emperorship in Eighteenth-Century China." *Journal of the Institute of Chinese Studies of the Chinese University of Hong Kong* 7 (December 1974): 551–72.

Chang Chung-ju [Zhang Zhongru] et al. *Qingdai kaoshi zhidu ciliao.* Photo reprint, Taipei: Wenhai, 1968.

Chang Hao. *Liang Ch'i-ch'ao and Intellectual Transition in China, 1890–1907.* Cambridge, Mass.: Harvard University Press, 1971.

Chang Te-ch'ang. "The Economic Role of the Imperial Household (Nei-wu-fu) in the Ch'ing Dynasty." *Journal of Asian Studies* 31, no. 2 (February 1972): 243–73.

Chao Ch'i-na [Zhao Qina], "Qingchu baqi hanjun yanjiu." *Gugong wenxian;* 4: 2:55–56.

Chen Chi-yun. "Orthodoxy as a Mode of Statecraft: The Ancient Concent of Cheng." In Kwang-ching Liu, ed., *Orthodoxy in Late Imperial China.* Berkeley: University of California Press, 1990.

Chen Jiahua. "Qingchu baishen ren xi." *Minzu yanjiu* 5 (1985): 63–71.

———. "Qingdai yibu guanliao shi zu de jiapu." *Minzu yanjiu* 5 (1983): 39–45.

Chen Wan. "Shi Tingzhu shiyi yu jiapu jikao." *Qingshi yanjiu tongxun* 2 (1986): 33–36.

Cherniavsky, Michael. "Khan or Basileus: An Aspect of Medieval Political Theory." *Journal of the History of Ideas* 20 (1959): 459–76.

———. *Tsar and People: Studies in Russian Myths.* New York: Random House, 1969.

Chia Ning. "The Li-fan Yüan in the Early Ch'ing Dynasty." Ph.D. diss., Johns Hopkins University, 1991.

Choirolzab. "Guanyu 'Gesir' zhong chuxian de 'Menggu' yici." *Nei Menggu daxue xuebao* 2 (1997): 50–52.

Chow, Kai-wing. *The Rise of Confucian Ritualism in Late Imperial China: Ethics, Classics, and Lineage Discourse.* Stanford: Stanford University Press, 1994.

Chow, Rey. *Woman and Chinese Modernity: The Politics of Reading between West and East.* Minneapolis: University of Minnesota Press, 1991.

Chu, Raymond, and William G. Saywell. *Career Patterns in the Ch'ing Dynasty.* Ann Arbor: University of Michigan Center for Chinese Studies, 1984.

Chu Wen-djang. *The Moslem Rebellion in North China: A Study of Government Minority Policy.* The Hague: Mouton, 1966.

Chuang Chi-fa [Zhuang Jifa], annotator. *Xiesui Zhigongtu Manwen tushuo jiaozhu.* Taipei: Guoli gugong bowu yuan, 1989.

Cleaves, Francis Woodman. "A Mongolian Rescript of the Fifth Year of Degedü Erdem-tü (1640)." *Harvard Journal of Asiatic Studies* 46, no. 1 (June 1986): 181–200.

———. "The Sino-Mongolian Edict of 1453." *Harvard Journal of Asiatic Studies* 13 (1950): 431–46.

Crossley, Pamela Kyle. "Chaos and Civilization: Imperial Sources of Post-imperial Models of the Polity." *Ssu yü yen* 36, no. 1 (March 1998): 119–90.

———. "*Manzhou yuanliu kao* and the Formalization of the Manchu Heritage." *Journal of Asian Studies* 46, no. 4 (November 1987): 761–90.

———." 'Historical and Magic Unity': The Real and Ideal Clan in Manchu Identity." Ph.D. diss., Yale University, 1983.

———. "An Introduction to the Qing Foundation Myth." *Late Imperial China* 6, no. 1 (December 1985): 3–24.

———. "Making Mongols." In Pamela Kyle Crossley, Helen Siu, and Donald Sutton, eds., *Empire and Ethnicity in Early Modern China*, forthcoming.

———. "Manchu Education." In Benjamin A. Elman and Alexander Woodside, eds., *Education and Society in Late Imperial China, 1600–1900*. Berkeley: University of California Press, 1994.

———. *The Manchus*. Oxford: Basil Blackwell, 1997.

———. *Orphan Warriors: Three Manchu Generations and the End of the Qing World*. Princeton: Princeton University Press, 1990.

———. "The Qianlong Retrospect on the Chinese-martial (*hanjun*) Banners." *Late Imperial China* 10, no. 1 (June 1989): 63–107.

———. "The Rulerships of China: A Review Article." *American Historical Review* 97, no. 5 (December 1992): 1468–83.

———. "The Sian Garrison." Unpublished, 1979.

———. "Structure and Symbol in the Role of the Ming-Qing Foreign Translation Bureaus." *Central and Inner Asian Studies* 5 (1991): 38–67.

———. "Thinking about Ethnicity in Early Modern China." *Late Imperial China* 11, no. 1 (June 1990): 1–35.

———. "The Tong in Two Worlds: Cultural Identity in Liaodong and Nurgan during the Thirteenth through the Seventeenth Centuries." *Ch'ing-shih wen-t'i*, 4, no. 9 (June 1983): 21–46.

Crossley, Pamela, and Evelyn S. Rawski. "A Profile of the Manchu Language in Ch'ing History." *Harvard Journal of Asiatic Studies* 53, no. 1 (June 1993): 63–102.

Curwen, Charles A. *Taiping Rebel: The Deposition of Li Xiucheng*. Cambridge: Cambridge University Press, 1977.

de Bary, William Theodore. "Chinese Despotism and the Confucian Ideal: A Seventeenth-Century View." In John King Fairbank, ed., *Chinese Thought and Institutions*. Chicago: University of Chicago Press, 1957.

———, ed. *The Unfolding of Neo-Confucianism*. New York: Columbia University Press, 1975.

de Bary, William Theodore, Wing-tsit Chan, and Barton Watson, comp. *Sources of Chinese Tradition*. New York: Columbia University Press, 1960.

Deng Shaohan. *Nurhachi ping zhuan*. Shenyang: Liaoning renmin, 1985.

———. *Qingdai baqi zidi*. Tianjin: Zhongguo huaqiao, 1989.

———. "Shilun Ming yu Hou Jin zhanzheng de yuanyin ji qi xingzhi." *Minzu yanjiu* 5 (1980).

Dennerline, Jerry. *The Chia-ting Loyalists: Confucian Leadership and Change in Seventeenth-Century China*. New Haven: Yale University Press, 1981.

Dent, Anthony A., and Daphne Machin Goodall. *A History of British Native Ponies*. London: J. S. Allen, 1988.

di Cosmo, Nicola. "Nuove fonti sulla formazione dello stato mancese, I Parte: Il rapporto di Yi Minhwan." *Catai* 2–3 (1982–83): 139–65.

Dikötter, Frank. *The Discourse of Race in Modern China*. Stanford: Stanford University Press, 1992.

———. "Group Definition and the Idea of 'Race' in Modern China (1793–1949)." *Ethnic and Racial Studies* 13 (1990): 420–32.

———. *Sex, Culture, and Modernity in China: Medical Science and the Construction of Sexual Identities in the Early Republican Period*. London: Hurst, 1995.

Diyi lishi dang'an guan, Guan Xiaolian, and Guo Meilan, trans. and eds. "Manwen guoshi dang xuanyi." *Lishi dang'an* 4 (1982): 15–25.

Du Jiaji. "Qingdai baqi lingshu wenti kaocha." *Minzu yanjiu* 5 (1987): 91.

Duara, Prasenjit. "Knowledge and Power in the Discourse of Modernity: The Campaigns against Popular Religion in Early Twentieth-Century China." *Journal of Asian Studies* 50, no. 1 (February 1990): 67–83.

———. *Rescuing History from the Nation: Questioning Narratives of Modern China*. Chicago: University of Chicago Press, 1995.

———. "Superscribing Symbols: The Myth of Guandi, Chinese God of War." *Journal of Asian Studies* 47, no. 4 (1988): 778–95.

Dumont, Louis. *Essays on Individualism: Modern Ideology in Anthopological Perspective*. Chicago: University of Chicago Press, 1986.

Dunnell, Ruth W. *The Great State of White and High: Buddhism and State Formation in Eleventh-Century Xia*. Honolulu: University of Hawaii Press, 1996.

Durrant, Stephen. "Manchu Translations of Chou Dynasty Texts." *Early China* 3 (1977): 51–55.

———. "Sino-Manchu Translations at the Mukden Court." *Journal of the American Oriental Society* 99 (1979): 653–61.

Eberhard, Wolfram. *Conquerors and Rulers*. Leiden: E. J. Brill, 1965.

Elliott, Mark. "Bannerman and Townsman: Ethnic Tension in Nineteenth-Century Jiangnan." *Late Imperial China* 11, no. 1 (June 1990): 36–74.

———. "Resident Aliens: The Manchu Experience in China, 1644–1760." Ph.D. diss., University of California, Berkeley, 1993.

Elman, Benjamin A. *Classicism, Politics, and Kinship: The Ch'ang-chou School of New Text Confucianism in Late Imperial China*. Berkeley: University of California Press, 1990.

———. *A Cultural History of Civil Examinations in Late Imperial China*. Berkeley: University of California Press, 2000.

———. *From Philosophy to Philology: The Evidential Scholarship Movement in Eighteenth-Century China*. Cambridge, Mass.: Harvard University Press, 1984.

Elman, Benjamin A., and Alexander Woodside, eds. *Education and Society in*

Late Imperial China, 1600–1900. Berkeley: University of California Press, 1994.

Elunchun zu minjian gushi xun. Shanghai: Wenyi, 1989.

Etō Toshio. *Dattan* (Tatars). Tokyo, 1956.

———. *Manshū bunka shi jo no ichi shinw*a. Tokyo, 1934.

Fairbank, John K., ed. *The Cambridge History of China*. Vol. 11, *Late Ch'ing, 1800–1911, Part I*. Cambridge: Cambridge University Press, 1978.

———. *The Cambridge History of China*. Vol. 11, *Late Ch'ing, 1800–1911, Part II*. Cambridge: Cambridge University Press, 1980.

———. *The Chinese World Order: Traditional China's Foreign Relations*. Cambridge, Mass.: Harvard University Press, 1968.

Fang Chao-ying. "A Technique for Estimating the Numerical Strength of the Early Manchu Military Forces." *Harvard Journal of Asiatic Studies* 13, no. 1 (1950).

Fang Hao. *Zhongguo tianzhujiao shi renwu zhuan*. 3 vols. Hong Kong: Zhonghua shuju, 1970.

Farquhar, David. "Emperor as Boddhisattva in the Governance of the Ch'ing Empire." *Harvard Journal of Asiatic Studies* 38, no. 1 (1978): 5–34.

———. "Mongolian versus Chinese Elements in the Early Manchu State." *Ch'ing-shih wen-t'i* 2, no. 6 (June 1971): 11–23.

———. "The Origins of the Manchus' Mongolian Policy." In J. K. Fairbank, ed., *The Chinese World Order: Traditional China's Foreign Relations*. Cambridge, Mass.: Harvard University Press, 1968.

Feng Erkang. *Yongzheng zhuan*. Peking: Renmin, 1985.

Feng Guozhe and Yang Naiji. "You guan Heshen chushen, qiji wenti de kaocha." *Qingshi luncong* 4 (1982): 141–51.

Feng Junshi. "Oulunchun zu caiyuan." *Jilin shifen daxue bao* 2 (1979): 77–86.

Feng Qiyong. *Cao Xueqin jia shi, Honglou meng wenwu tulu*. Hong Kong: Joint Publishing, 1983.

Fincher, J. "China as a Race, Culture, and Nation: Notes on Fang Hsiao-ju." In D. Buxbaum and Frederick W. Mote, eds., *Transition and Permanence: Chinese History and Culture (Festschrift in Honor of Dr. Hsiao Kung-ch'üan)*. Hong Kong: Cathay Press, 1972, pp. 59–69.

Fisher, Thomas Stephen. "Lü Liu-liang (1629–1683) and the Tseng Ching Case (1728–1733)." Ph.D. diss., Princeton University, 1974.

Fletcher, Joseph Francis, Jr. "Ch'ing Inner Asia, c. 1800." In John K. Fairbank, ed., *The Cambridge History of China*, vol. 10, part 1. Cambridge: Cambridge University Press, 1978.

———. "China and Central Asia, 1368–1884." In John K. Fairbank, ed., *The Chinese World Order: Traditional China's Foreign Relations*. Cambridge, Mass.: Harvard University Press, 1968, pp. 206–24.

———. "Manchu Sources." In Donald D. Leslie et al., *Essays on the Sources for Chinese History*. Canberra: Australian National University Press, 1973, pp. 141–46.

————. "The Mongols: Ecological and Social Perspectives." *Harvard Journal of Asiatic Studies* 46 (1986): 11–50.

————. "Turco-Mongolian Tradition in the Ottoman Empire." In Ihor Sevcenko and Frank E. Sysyn, eds., *Eurcharisterion* I. Cambridge, Mass.: Ukrainian Research Institute, 1978, pp. 240–41.

Fogel, Joshua A. "Race and Class in Chinese Historiography: Divergent Interpretations of Zhang Bing-lin and Anti-Manchuism in the 1911 Revolution." *Modern China* 3, no. 3 (July 1977): 346–75.

Forêt, Philippe C. "Making an Imperial Landscape in Chengde, Jehol: The Manchu Landscape Enterprise." Ph.D. diss., University of Chicago, 1992.

Foucault, Michel. *The Archeology of Knowledge.* New York: Pantheon, 1972.

Franke, Herbert. "Chinese Texts on the Jurchen: A Translation of the Jurchen Monograph in the San-ch'ao hui-pien." *Zentralasiatische Studien* 9 (1975): 119–86.

————. "Etymologische Bemerkungen zu den Vokabularen der Jürcen-Sprache." In Michael Weiers and Giovanni Stary, eds., *Florilegia Manjurica in Memoriam Walter Fuchs.* Wiesbaden: Otto Harrassowitz, 1982.

————. "Some Folkloristic Data in the Dynastic History of the Chin (1115–1234)." Sarah Allan and Alvin Cohen, eds., *Legend, Lore, and Religion in China.* San Francisco: Chinese Materials Center, 1979.

Fu Guijiu. "Donghua lu zuozhe xinzheng." *Lishi yanjiu* 5 (1984): 168–70.

Fu Kedong. "Baqi huji zhidu chucao." *Minzu yanjiu* 6 (1983): 34–43.

Fu Tsung-mou [Fu Zongmou]. "Qingchu yizheng tizhi zhi yanjiu." *Guoli Zhengzhi Daxue xuebao* 11 (May 1965): 245–95.

Fu Yuguang and Meng Huiying. *Manzu samanjiao yanjiu.* Peking: Beijing Daxue, 1990.

Furth, Charlotte. "The Sage as Rebel: The Inner World of Chang Ping-lin." In Charlotte Furth, ed., *The Limits of Change: Essays on Conservative Alternatives in Republican China.* Cambridge, Mass.: Harvard University Press, 1976.

————, ed. *The Limits of Change: Essays on Conservative Alternatives in Republican China.* Cambridge, Mass.: Harvard University Press, 1976.

Garthwaite, Gene R. *Khans and Shahs: A Documentary Analysis of the Bakhtiyari in Iran.* Cambridge: Cambridge University Press, 1983.

————. *The Persians.* Oxford: Basil Blackwell, forthcoming.

Gasster, Michael. *Chinese Intellectuals and the Revolution of 1911: The Birth of Chinese Radicalism.* Seattle: University of Washington Press, 1969.

Gellner, Ernest. *Nations and Nationalism.* Ithaca, N.Y.: Cornell University Press, 1983.

Gibb, Hamilton, and Howard Bowen. *Islamic Society and the West.* Vol. 1, *Islamic Society in the Eighteenth Century,* part 1. Oxford: Oxford University Press, 1950.

Gladney, Dru. *Muslim Chinese: Ethnic Nationalism in the People's Republic.* Cambridge, Mass.: Council on East Asian Studies, Harvard University Press, 1991.

————. "Relational Alterity: Constructing Dungan (Hui), Uygur, and Kazakh Identities across China, Central Asia, and Turkey." *History and Anthropology* 9, no. 4 (1996): 445–77.

Gluck, Carol. *Japan's Modern Myths: Ideology in the Late Meiji Period.* Princeton: Princeton University Press, 1985.

Goldberg, David Theo. *Racist Culture: Philosophy and the Politics of Meaning.* Oxford: Basil Blackwell, 1993.

Goodrich, Luther Carrington. *The Literary Inquisition of Ch'ien-lung.* Baltimore: Waverly Press, 1935.

Goodrich, Luther Carrington, and Chao-ying Fang. *Dictionary of Ming Biography.* 2 vols. New York: Columbia University Press, 1976.

Grousset, René. *The Empire of the Steppes: A History of Central Asia.* Trans. Naomi Walford. New Bruswick, N.J.: Rutgers University Press, 1970.

Grube, Wilhelm. *Die Sprache und Schriften der Jucen.* Leipzig: Otto Harrassowitz, 1896.

Grunfeld, A. Tom. *The Making of Modern Tibet.* Armonk: M. E. Sharpe, 1996.

Grupper, Samuel Martin. "A Handlist of Manchu Epigraphical Monuments: I. The Reigns of T'ai-tsu, T'ai-tsung and the Shun-chih Emperor." *Manchu Studies Newsletter* 1 (1977–78): 75–90.

————. "The Manchu Imperial Cult of the Early Ch'ing Dynasty: Texts and Studies on the Tantric Sanctuary of Mahakala at Mukden." Ph.D. diss., Indiana University, 1980.

————. "Manchu Patronate and Tibetan Buddhism during the First Half of the Ch'ing Dynasty: A Review Article." *Journal of the Tibet Society* 4 (1984): 47–75.

————. "Review of Klaus Sagaster, *Die Weisse Geschichte.*" *Mongolian Studies* 7 (1981–82): 127–33.

Guan Tianting. "Qingdai huangshi shizu ji xuexi." In *Caizheng ji.* Peking: Zhonghua shuju, 1980.

Guan Xiaolian. "Manwen laodang de xiufu yu chongchao." *Lishi dang'an* 3 (1987): 125–29.

Guang Dong. "Jiufuquan de chansheng, fuzhan he xiaowang chu cao." *Minzu yanjiu* 2 (1985): 19–28.

Guo Chengkang. "Qianlong chao fenghan wenzi yu caixi." *Qingshi yanjiu tongxun* 2 (1988): 18–23.

————. "Qingchu niulu de shumu." *Qingshi yanjiu tongshun* 1 (1987): 31–35.

————. "Shixi Qing wangchao ruguan qian dui hanzu de zhengce." *Minzu yanjiu* 3: 15–22.

Guo Songyi. "Qingdai de renkou zengzhang he renkou liuqian." *Qingshi luncong* 5: 103–39.

Guy, R. Kent. *The Emperor's Four Treasuries: Scholars and the State in the Late Ch'ien-lung Era.* Cambridge, Mass.: Harvard University Council on East Asian Studies, 1987.

Halkovic, Stephen A., Jr. *The Mongols of the West.* Indiana University Uralic and Altaic Series, no. 148. Bloomington: Research Institute for Inner Asian Studies, 1985.

Han Jinchun and Li Yifu. "Hanwen 'minzu' yici de chuxian chuqi shiyong qingkuang." *Minzu yanjiu* 2 (1984): 36–43.

Harrell, Stevan, Susan Naquin, and Ju Deyuan. "Lineage Genealogy: The Genealogical Records of the Qing Imperial Lineage." *Late Imperial China*, 6, no. 2 (December 1985): 37–47.

Harvey, L. P. *Islamic Spain, 1250–1500*. Chicago: University of Chicago Press, 1990.

Hay, Jonathan. "The Suspension of Dynastic Time." In Jonathan Hay, ed., *Boundaries in China*. London: Reaktion, 1994.

——, ed. *Boundaries in China*. London: Reaktion, 1994.

Heissig, Walther. *The Religions of Mongolia*. Trans. G. Samuel. London: Routledge and Kegan Paul, 1980.

Henderson, John. *The Development and Decline of Chinese Cosmology*. New York: Columbia University Press, 1984.

Herman, John E. "Empire in the Southwest: Early Qing Reforms to the Native Chieftain System." *Journal of Asian Studies* 56, no. 1 (February 1997): 47–74.

Hess, Laura. "The Manchu Exegesis of the *Lünyü*." *Journal of the American Oriental Society* 111, no. 3 (1993): 402–17.

Hevia, James. *Cherishing Men from Afar: Qing Guest Ritual and the Macartney Embassy of 1793*. Durham, N.C.: Duke University Press, 1995.

——. "Lamas, Emperors and Rituals: Political Implications in Qing Imperial Ceremonies." *Journal of the International Association of Buddhist Studies* 16, no. 2 (Winter 1993): 243–78.

✓ Heywood, Colin. "'Turco-Mongolian Kingship'?: The Fletcher Thesis Reconsidered." Paper delivered to Royal Asiatic Society/Wellcome Institute symposium, London, 1997.

Hiu Lie. *Die Manschu-Sprachkunde in Korea*. Bloomington: Indiana University Uralic and Altaic Studies Program, 1972.

Ho Ping-ti. "The Chinese Civilization: A Search for the Roots of Its Longevity." *Journal of Asian Studies* 35, no. 4 (1976): 547–54.

——. "In Defense of Sinicization: A Rebuttal of Evelyn Rawski's 'Reenvisioning the Qing.'" *Journal of Asian Studies* 37, no. 1 (February 1998): 123–55.

Hongli [Qing Gaozong Shun Huangdi]. *Han i araha Mukden i fujurun bithe*. Wuying dian edition, 1748.

——. *Yuzhi Shengjing fu*. Wuying dian edition, 1748.

Hou Ching-lang and Michèle Pirazzoli. "Les Chasses d'automne de l'empereur Qianlong à Mulan." *T'oung Pao* 45, no. 1–3 (1979): 13–50.

Hou Shouchang. "Kangxi muxi kao." *Lishi dang'an* 4 (1982): 100–106.

——. "Qianlun Tong Yangxing." *Lishi dang'an* 2 (1986): 105–10.

Howland, D. R. *Borders of Chinese Civilization: Geography and History at Empire's End*. Durham, N.C.: Duke University Press, 1996.

Hsiung Ping-chen [Xiong Bingzhen]. "Shiqi shiji Zhongguo zhengzhi sixiang zhong fei chuantong chengfen de fenxi." *Jindai shi yanjiu suo jikan* 15, no. 1 (June 1986): 1–31.

Hsü Dau-lin. "The Myth of the 'Five Human Relations' of Confucius." *Monumenta Serica* 39 (1970–1971): 27–37.

Hua Li. "Qingdai de Man Meng lianyin." *Minzu yanjiu* 2 (1983): 45–54.

Huang Kun. "Liang Qichao duo bian lun." *Lishi yanjiu* 4 (1987): 164–77.

Huang, Pei. *Autocracy at Work: A Study of the Yung-cheng Period, 1723–1735*. Bloomington: Indiana University Press, 1974.

Huang, Philip C. *Liang Ch'i-ch'ao and Modern Chinese Liberalism*. Seattle: University of Washington Press, 1972.

Huang Tianji. *Nalan Xingde he ta de ci*. Canton: Guangdong sheng xinhua shudian, 1983.

Huang Weihan. *Heishui xianmin zhuan*. Shenyang, 1924.

Hume, David. *An Inquiry Concerning Human Understanding*. Ed. Charles W. Hendl. Upper Saddle River, N.J.: Prentice Hall, 1995.

———. *A Treatise of Human Nature*. Ed. L. A. Selby-Bigge. Oxford: Clarendon Press, 1888.

Hummel, Arthur W., et al. *Eminent Chinese of the Ch'ing Period*. Washington, D.C.: U.S. Government Printing Office, 1943.

Humphrey, Caroline. "Shamanic Practices and the State in Northern Asia: Views from the Center and Periphery." In Nicholas Thomas and Caroline Humphrey, eds., *Shamanism, History, and the State*. Ann Arbor: University of Michigan Press, 1996, pp. 191–229.

Hyer, Paul, and Sechin Jagchid, trans. and annotators. *Menggu youmu ji*, by Zhang Mu [Chang Mu]. Unpublished.

Ikeuchi Hiroshi, *Man Son shi kenkyū*. Tokyo, 1949.

Im, Kaye Soon. *The Rise and Decline of the Eight-Banner Garrisons in the Ch'ing Period (1644–1911): A Study of the Kuang-chou, Hang-chou, and Ching-chou Garrisons*. Ann Arbor, Mich.: University Microfilms, 1981.

Ishibashi Takao. "The Formation of the Power of Early Ch'ing Emperors." *Memoirs of the Research Department of the Toyō Bunkō* 48 (1990): 1–15.

Ishida Mikinosuke. "Joshin-go kenkyū no shin shiryū." In *Tō a bunkashi sō kō*. Tokyo, 1973 (originally published in 1940).

Jagchid, Sechin, and Paul Hyer. *Mongolia's Culture and Society*. Boulder, Colo.: Westview Press, 1979.

Ji Dachun. "Lun Songyun." *Minzu yanjiu* 3 (1988): 71–79.

Ji Wenfu. *Wang Chuanshan xueshu luncong*. Peking: Zhonghua shuju, 1962.

Jiang Xiusong. "Qingchu de Hurha bu." *Shehui kexue zhanxian* 1 (1981).

Jin Guangping and Jin Qizong. *Nuzhen yuyan wenzi yanjiu*. Peking: Wenwu, 1980.

Jin Qizong. *Nuzhen wen cidian*. Peking: Wenwu, 1984.

Jinliang. *Manzhou bidang*. Peiping, 1934. Reprinted in Shen Yunlong [Shen Yün-lung], ed., *Jindai Zhongguo shiliao congkan*. Taipei: Wenhai, 1966.

———. *Manzhou laodong bilu*. Peiping, 1929. Reprinted in Shen Yunlong

[Shen Yün-lung], ed., *Jindai Zhongguo shiliao congkan*. Taipei: Wenhai, 1966.

Judge, Joan. *Print and Politics: "Shibao" and the Culture of Reform in Qing China*. Stanford: Stanford University Press, 1996.

Kahn, Harold L. "A Matter of Taste: The Monumental and Exotic in the Qianlong Reign." In Chen Ru-hsi and Claudia Brown, eds., *The Elegant Brush: Chinese Painting and the Qianlong Emperor 1735–1795*. Phoenix: Phoenix Art Museum, 1985, pp. 288–300.

———. *Monarchy in the Emperor's Eyes: Image and Reality in the Ch'ienlung Reign*. Cambridge, Mass.: Harvard University Press, 1971.

Kanda Nobuo. "Remarks on *Emu tanggū orin sakda-i gisun sarkiyan*." In Sungyun, *Emu tanggū orin sakda-i gisun sarkiyan*. Taipei: Chinese Material Center, 1982, pp. iii–ix.

———. "Shinshō no *beile* ni tsuite." *Tō yō gakuhō* 40, no. 4 (March 1958): 349–71.

———. "Shinshō no *yizheng daren* ni tsuite." In *Wada Hakushi kenreki kinen tō yō shi ronsō*. Tokyo: Dai Nihon Yū benkai Kō dansha, 1951.

Kanda Nobuo and Matsumura Jun. *Hakki tsushi retsuden sakuin*. Tokyo: Toyo Bunko, 1964.

Kanda Nobuo et al., trans. and annotators. *Tongki fuka sindaha hergen i dangse*. Vols. 1–7. Tokyo: Toyo Bunko, 1956.

Kanda Shinobu. "Qingchao de *Guoshi liezhuan* he *Erchen zhuan*" (trans. Wang Ling). *Qingshi yanjiu tongshun* 3 (1986): 57–60.

Kang Le. "Zhuanlun wang guannian yu Zhongguo gudai de fojiao zhengzhi." *Bulletin of the Institute of History and Philology, Academia Sinica* 67, no. 1 (1996): 109–43.

Kessler, Lawrence. "Ethnic Composition of Provincial Leadership during the Ch'ing Dynasty." *Journal of Asian Studies* 28, no. 2–3 (May 1969): 179–200, 489–511.

———. *K'ang-hsi and the Consolidation of Ch'ing Rule, 1661–1684*. Chicago: University of Chicago Press, 1976.

King, J. R. P. "The Korean Elements in the Manchu Script Reform of 1632." *Central Asiatic Journal* 31, no. 3–4 (1987): 252–86.

Kiyose, Gisaburo N. *A Study of the Jurchen Language and Script: Reconstruction and Decipherment*. Kyoto: Horitsubunka, 1977.

Klaproth, Jules. *Chrestomathie Mandchou, ou recueil de textes Mandchou*. Paris, 1828.

Krader, Lawrence. "Qan-Qaγan and the Beginnings of Mongol Kingship." *Central Asiatic Journal* 1 (1955): 17–35.

Kuhn, Philip. *Soulstealers: The Chinese Sorcery Scare of 1748*. Cambridge, Mass.: Harvard University Press, 1990.

Kwong, Luke S. K. *A Mosaic of the Hundred Days: Personalities, Politics, and Ideas of 1898*. Cambridge, Mass.: Harvard University Council on East Asian Studies, 1984.

———. "On 'The 1898 Reforms Revisited': A Rejoinder." *Late Imperial China* 8, no. 1 (June 1987): 214–19.

Lai Hui-min [Lai Huimin]. *Tiang huang gui zhou, Zhongyang yanjiu yuan, jindai shi yanjiu suo* [Chung-yang yen-chiu yuan, chin-tai shih yen-chiu so]. Nankang, 1997.

Laitinen, Kauko. *Chinese Nationalism in the Late Qing Dynasty: Zhang Binglin as an Anti-Manchu Propagandist*. London: Curzon Press, 1990.

Langlois, John. "Chinese Culturalism and the Yuan Analogy: Seventeenth-Century Perspectives." *Harvard Journal of Asiatic Studies* 40, no. 2: 355–98.

Lattimore, Owen. *The Pivot of Asia: Siankiang and the Inner Asian Frontiers of China and Russia*. Boston: Little, Brown, 1950.

Lee, James Z., and Cameron Campbell. *Fate and Fortune in Rural China: Social organization and Population Behavior in Liaoning, 1774–1873*. Cambridge: Cambridge University Press, 1997.

Lee, Ki-Baik. *A New History of Korea*. Trans. E. Wagner. Cambridge, Mass.: Harvard University Press, 1984.

Lee, Peter H. *Songs of Flying Dragons: A Critical Reading*. Cambridge, Mass.: Harvard University Press, 1975.

Lee, Robert H. G. "Frontier Politics in the Southwestern Sino-Tibetan Borderlands during the Ch'ing Dynasty." In Joshua A. Fogel, ed., *Perspectives on a Changing China*. Boulder, Colo.: Westview Press, 1979.

———. *The Manchurian Frontier in Ch'ing History*. Cambridge, Mass.: Harvard University Press, 1970.

Legge, James, trans. *The Works of Mencius*. Oxford: Clarendon Press, 1895.

Le Glay, Marcel, Jean-Louis Voisin, and Yann Le Bohec. *A History of Rome*. Trans. Antonia Nevill. Oxford: Basil Blackwell, 1996. Originally published as *Histoire romaines*. Paris: Presses universitaires de France, 1991.

Lei Fangsheng. "Jingzhou qixue de shimo ji qi tedian." *Minzu yanjiu* 3 (1984): 57–59.

Leung, Irene. "Conflicts of Loyalty in Twelfth-Century China: The Multiple Narratives of Cai Wenji." Paper presented at the annual meeting of the Association for Asian Studies, 1997.

Leung, Man-Kam. "Mongolian Language Education and Examinations in Peking and Other Metropolitan Areas during the Manchu Dynasty in China (1644–1911)." *Revue Canada-Mongolie* 1, no. 1 (1975): 29–44.

———. "The Political Thought of Chang Ping-lin (1876–1936)." M.A. thesis, University of Hawaii, 1967.

Levenson, Joseph R. *Confucian China and Its Modern Fate: A Trilogy*. Berkeley: University of California Press, 1968.

———. *Liang Ch'i-ch'ao and the Mind of Modern China*. Cambridge, Mass.: Harvard University Press, 1953, 1959; reissued New York: Harper and Row, 1966.

———. *Modern China and Its Confucian Past: The Problem of Intellectual Continuity*. New York: Anchor Books, 1964.

―――. *Revolution and Cosmopolitanism: The Western Stage and the Chinese Stages.* Berkeley: University of California Press, 1971.

Li Chien-nung. *The Political History of China, 1840–1923.* Trans. S. Y. Teng and J. Ingalls, Stanford: Stanford University Press, 1956.

Li Hsüeh-chih [Li Xuezhi]. "An Analysis of the Problem in the Selection of an Heir during the Reign of Nurhaci of Emperor Taitzu of the Ch'ing Dynasty." In Ch'en Chieh-hsien [Chen Jiexian] and Sechin Jagchid, eds., *Proceedings of the Third East Asian Altaistic Conference.* Taipei, 1969.

―――. *Cong jige manwen mingci tantao manzhou (nuzhen) minzu de shehui zuzhi.* Taipei: Academia Sinica, 1981.

Li Qiao. "Baqi shengji wenti shulue." *Lishi dang'an* 1 (1981): 91–97.

Li Xinda. "Ru Guan qian de baqi bingshu wenti." *Qingshi luncong* 3 (1982):155–63.

Li Yaohua. "Guanyu 'minzu' yici de shiyong he yiming wenti" (Problems on the Usage and Meaning of the Word *minzu*). *Lishi yanjiu* 2 (1963): 175.

Li Zhiting. "Ming Qing zhanzheng yu Qingchu lishi fazhan shi." *Qingshi yanjiu tongshun* 1 (1988): 7–12.

Liang Ch'i-ch'ao. *History of Chinese Political Thought during the Early Tsin Period.* Trans. L. T. Chen. New York: Harcourt, Brace, 1930.

―――. *Intellectual Trends in the Ch'ing Period.* Trans. Immanuel C. Y. Hsü. Cambridge, Mass.: Harvard University Press, 1959.

―――. *Zhongguo jin sanbainian xueshu shi.* Peking: Beijing shi shudian, 1985.

Ling Chunsheng. *Songhuajiang xiayou de hezhe zu.* 2 vols. Nanking: Zhongyuanyan, 1934.

Lipman, Jonathan N. *Familiar Strangers: A History of Muslims in Northwest China.* Seattle: University of Washington Press, 1997.

Liu Chia-chü [Liu Jiaju]. "The Creation of the Chinese Banners in the Early Ch'ing," trans. P. K. Crossley. *Chinese Studies in History* 14, no. 4 (1981). Originally published as "Qingchu hanjun baqi de zhaojian," in *Dalu zazhi* 34, nos. 11–12 (1967).

Liu Danian. "Lun Kangxi." *Zhongguo jindaishi zhu wenti.* Peking: Renmin Chubanshe, 1965.

Liu Guang'an. "A Short Treatise on the Ethnic Legislation of the Qing Dynasty." *Social Sciences in China* 4 (Winter 1990): 97–117 (from *Zhongguo shehui kesue* 6 [1989]).

Liu Housheng. *Jianming Man Han cidian.* Kaifeng: Henan daxue, 1988.

Liu, Kwang-ching. "Socioethics as Orthodoxy: A Perspective." In Kwang-ching Liu, ed., *Orthodoxy in Late Imperial China.* Berkeley: University of California Press, 1990.

Liu, Kwang-ching, ed. *Orthodoxy in Late Imperial China.* Berkeley: University of California Press, 1990.

Liu Lu. "Qingdai huanghou cili yu baqi da xing shi zu." *Gugong bowuyuan yuankan* 1 (1977): 52–65.

Liu, Lydia. *Translingual Practice: Literature, National Culture, and Modernity — China, 1900–1937.* Stanford: Stanford University Press, 1995.

Liu Qinghua. "Manzu xingshi shulue." *Minzu yanjiu* 1 (1983): 64–71.

Liu Xiamin. "Qing kaiguo chu zhengfu zhu bu jiangyu kao." *Yanjing xuebao* 23, no. 6 (1936). Reprinted in *Qingshi luncong* 1 (1977): 107–46.

Liu Zhongpo. *Hezhe ren.* Peking: Minzu, 1981.

Loh Wai-fong. Review of Preston M. Torbert, *The Ch'ing Imperial Household Department. Harvard Journal of Asiatic Studies* 38, no. 2 (1978): 492–501.

Lü Guangtian. *Ewenke zu.* Peking: Minzu, 1983.

———. "Qingdai buteha daxing Ewenke ren de Baqi jiegou." *Minzu yanjiu* 3 (1983): 23–31.

Lu Minghui. "Qingdai beifang ge minzu yu Zhongyuan hanzu de wenhua jiaoliu ji qi gongxian." *Qingshi yanjiu ji* 6 (1988): 125.

Lui, Adam Yuen-chung. "Censor, Regent, and Emperor in the Early Manchu Period (1644–1660)." *Papers on Far Eastern History* 17 (1978): 81–102.

———. "The Ch'ing Civil Service: Promotions, Demotions, Transfers, Leaves, Dismissals, and Retirements." *Journal of Oriental Studies* 8, no. 2 (1970): 333–56.

———. "The Education of the Manchus: China's Ruling Race (1644–1911)." *Journal of Asian and African Studies* 6, no. 2 (1971): 125–33.

———. "The Imperial College (*Kuo-tzu-chien*) in the Early Ch'ing (1644–1795)." *Papers on Far Eastern History* 10 (1974): 147–66.

———. "Manchu-Chinese Relations and the Imperial 'Equal Treatment' Policy, 1651–1660." *Journal of Asian History* 19, no. 2 (1985): 143–65.

———. "Syllabus of the Provincial Examination (*hsiang-shih*) under the Early Ch'ing (1644–1795)." *Modern Asian Studies* 8, no. 3 (1974): 391–96.

Lundbaek, Knud. "Imaginary Chinese Characters." *China Mission Studies* 5 (1983): 5–23.

Lundbaek, Knud, trans. *A Traditional History of the Chinese Script — from a Seventeenth Century Jesuit Manuscript.* Aarhus: Aarhus University Press, 1988.

Luo Baoshan. "Guanyu Zhang Binglin zhengzhi lichang zhuanbian de jipian tiaowen." *Lishi yanjiu* 5 (1982): 56–62.

Luo Ergang. *Luying bingzhi.* Peking: Zhonghua Shuju, 1984.

Ma Wensheng. "Fu'an Dong Yi kao." From Wanli period. Reprinted in Shen Xu et al., *Qing ru guan qian shiliao xunji* 1. Peking: Zhongguo renmin daxue, 1984.

Mair, Victor H. "Perso-Turkic *Bakshi*-Mandarin *Po-shih:* Learned Doctor." *Journal of Turkish Studies* 16 (1992): 117–27.

Mancall, Mark. *Russia and China: Their Diplomatic Relations to 1728.* Cambridge, Mass.: Harvard University Press, 1971.

Mango, Cyril. *Byzantium: The Empire of the New Rome.* London: Weidenfield and Nicholson, 1980; London: Phoenix, 1994.

Manzu jianshi. Peking: Zhonghua, 1979.

Mao Ruizheng. *Huang Ming xiangxu lu,* ed. Wang Yu-li [Wang Youli]. Taipei: Wenhua, n.d. (photo reprint of Chongzhen period original; published with Ye Xianggao, *Siyi Kao;* Wang Yu-li [Wang Youli], ed.).

Maruyama, Masao. *Studies in the Intellectual History of Tokugawa Japan.* Princeton: Princeton University Press, 1974, 1989.

McCormack, Gavan. *Chang Tso-lin in Northeast China, 1911–1928.* Stanford: Stanford University Press, 1977.

McMorran, Ian. *The Passionate Realist: An Introduction to the Life and Political Thought of Wang Fuzhi.* Hong Kong: Sunshine, 1992.

———. "The Patriot and the Partisan." In Jonathan D. Spence and John E. Wills, Jr., eds., *From Ming to Ch'ing.* New Haven: Yale University Press, 1979.

McNeill, William H., and Marilyn Robinson Waldman, eds. *The Islamic World.* London: Oxford University Press, 1973.

Meadows, Thomas T. *Translations from the Manchu with the Original Texts.* Canton: S. Wells Williams, 1849.

Melikhov Georgii Vasil'evich. *Man'chzhury na Severo-Vostoke, XVII v.* Moscow: Nauka, 1974.

Menegon, Eugenio. "A Different Country, the Same Heaven: A Preliminary Biography of Giulio Aleni S.J. (1582–1649)." *Sino-Western Cultural Relations Journal* 15 (1993): 27–51.

———. "Jesuits, Franciscans, and Dominicans in Fujian: The Anti-Christian Incidents of 1636–37." In T. Lipiello and R. Malek, eds., *Proceedings of the International Symposium "Giulio Aleni S.J. (1582–1649), Missionary in China."* Monumenta Serica Monograph Series, forthcoming.

Meng Huiying. "Man—Tunggusi yuzu minzu shenhua." *Manzu yanjiu* 3 (1996): 56–61.

Meng Sen. "Baqi zhidu kao." *Guoli zhongyang yanjiu yuan, Lishi yuyan yanjiusuo jikan* (Academia Sinica, Bulletin of the Institute for History and Philology) 6, no. 3 (1936): 343–412.

———. *Ming Qing shilun zhu jikan.* Taipei: Shijie, 1961.

———. *Qing chu san da yi'an kaoshi,* ed. Shen Yün-lung [Shen Yunlong] Taipei: Wenhai, 1966.

———. *Qingshi qianji.* Taipei: Tailian guofeng, n.d.

Millward, James A. *Beyond the Pass: Economy, Ethnicity, and Empire in Qing Central Asia, 1759–1864.* Stanford: Stanford University Press, 1998.

———. "A Uyghur Muslim in Qianlong's Court: The Meanings of the Fragrant Concubine." *Journal of Asian Studies* 53, no. 2 (May 1994): 427–58.

Mitamura Taisuke. "Manshu shizoku seiritsu no kenkyū." *Shinchō zenshi no kenkyū.* Kyoto: Toyoshi kenkyūkai, 1965.

Miyake Shunjo. *Tohoku Ajia kokugaku no kenkyū.* Tokyo: 1949.

Mo Dongyin, *Manzu shi luncong.* Peking: Sanlian, 1979 (reprint of 1958 original).

Morgan, David. *The Mongols.* Oxford: Blackwell, 1988.

Mori, Masao. "The T'u-chüeh Concept of Sovereign." *Central Asiatic Journal* 41 (1981): 47–75.

Moses, Larry W. *The Political Role of Mongol Buddhism.* Indiana University

Uralic Altaic Series, no. 133. Bloomington: Research Institute for Inner Asian Studies, 1977.

Moses, Larry W., and Stephen A. Halkovic Jr. *Introduction to Mongolian History and Culture.* Indiana University Uralic and Altaic Series, no. 149. Bloomington: Research Institute for Inner Asian Studies, 1985.

Mou Ranxun. "Mingmo xiyang dapao you Ming ru Hou Jin kaolue, II." *Mingbao yuekan* (October 1982).

Najita, Tetsuo, and Irwin Scheiner, eds. *Japanese Thought in the Tokugawa Period, 1600–1800: Methods and Metaphors.* Chicago: University of Chicago Press, 1978.

Naquin, Susan. "The Peking Pilgrimage to Miao-feng Shan: Religious Organizations and Sacred Site." In Susan Naquin and Chün-fang Yü, eds., *Pilgrims and Sacred Sites in China.* Berkeley: University of California Press, 1992, pp. 333–77.

Naquin, Susan, and Chün-fang Yü, eds. *Pilgrims and Sacred Sites in China.* Berkeley: University of California Press, 1992.

Naquin, Susan, and Evelyn S. Rawski. *Chinese Society in the Eighteenth Century.* New Haven: Yale University Press, 1987.

Nathan, Andrew J. *Chinese Democracy.* New York: Knopf, 1985.

Necipoglu, Gulru. *Architecture, Ceremonial, and Power: The Topkapi Palace in the Fifteenth and Sixteenth Centuries.* Cambridge, Mass.: MIT Press, 1991.

Netanyahu, Benzion. *The Origins of the Inquisition in Fifteenth-Century Spain.* New York: Random House, 1995.

Ng, Vivien W. "Ideology and Sexuality: Rape Laws in Qing China." *Journal of Asian Studies* 46, no. 1 (February 1987): 57–70.

Niida Noboru. *Chū goku hō seishi kenkyū.* In *Keihō.* Tokyo, 1959.

Nivison, David S. "Ho-shen and His Accusers: Ideology and Political Behavior in the Eighteenth Century." In David S. Nivison and Arthur R. Wright, eds., *Confucianism in Action.* Stanford: Stanford University Press, 1959.

Norman, Jerry. *A Concise Manchu–English Lexicon.* Seattle: University of Washington Press, 1978.

Nosco, Peter, ed. *Confucianism and Tokugawa Culture.* Princeton: Princeton University Press, 1984.

Nowak, Margaret, and Stephen Current. *The Tale of the Nisan Shamaness.* Seattle: University of Washington Press, 1977.

Okada Hidehiro. "How Hong Taiji Came to the Throne." *Central Asiatic Journal* 23, no. 3–4 (1979): 250–59.

———. "Mandarin, a Language of the Manchus: How Altaic?" In Martin Gimm, Giovanni Stary, and Michael Weiers, eds., *Historische und bibliographische Studien zur Mandschuforschung.* Aetas Manjurica, vol. 3. Wiesbaden: Otto Harrassowitz, 1992.

———. "Yōsei tei to Taigi kakumeiroku." *Tō yō shi kenkyū* 18, no. 3 (1959): 99–123.

Onogawa Hidemi. *Shimmatsu seiji shisō kenkyū.* Kyoto: Toashi kenkyūkai, 1960.

Ooms, Herman. *Tokugawa Ideology: Early Constructs, 1570–1680.* Princeton: Princeton University Press, 1985.

Ortai et al. *Baqi tongzhi* [chuji]. Original edition, 1739.

Ostrogorsky, G. "The Byzantine Emperor and the Hierarch World Order." *Slavonic and East European Review* 35 (1956–57): 1–14.

Oxnam, Robert B. *Ruling from Horseback: Manchu Politics in the Oboi Regency, 1661–1669.* Chicago: University of Chicago Press, 1970.

Pao Tso-p'eng (Bao Zuopeng) et al. *Zhongguo jindai shi luncong,* vol. 1. Taipei: Zhengzhong, 1966.

Pelliot, Paul. "Le Sseu-yi-kouan et le Houei-t'ong-kouan." In "Le Hôja et le Sayyid Husain de l'Histoire des Ming." *T'oung Pao* 38 (1948): 2–5, Appendix 3: 207–90.

Peng Bo. *Manzu* (The Manchu Nationality). Peking: Minzu, 1985.

Peng Guodong. *Qing shi kaiguo qian ji.* Taipei, 1969.

Petech, Luciano. *China and Tibet in the Early Eighteenth Century: History of the Establishment of Chinese Protectorate in Tibet.* Leiden: E. J. Brill, 1972.

Peterson, Willard J. "The Life of Ku-Yen-wu (1613–1682)." *Harvard Journal of Asiatic Studies* 28 (1968): 114–56; 29 (1969): 201–47.

Pirazzoli-t'Serstevens. "The Emperor Qianlong's European Palaces." *Orientations* 3 (November 1988): 61–71.

Polachek, James. *The Inner Opium War.* Cambridge, Mass.: Harvard University Press, 1992.

Pulleyblank, E. G. "The Chinese and Their Neighbors in Prehistoric and Early Historic Times." In David N. Keightley, ed., *The Origins of Chinese Civilization.* Berkeley: University of California Press, 1983.

Pusey, James Reeve. *China and Charles Darwin.* Cambridge, Mass.: Council on East Asian Studies, Harvard University, 1983.

Qian Qinsheng and Qian Shaoyun. *Shengjing huang gong.* Peking: Zijincheng, 1987.

Qian Shipu, ed. *Qing ji xin she zhi guan nianbiao.* Peking: Zhonghua, 1961.

———. *Qing ji zhongyao zhi guan nianbiao.* Peking: Zhonghua, 1959.

Qiang Xiangshun and Tong Tuo. *Shengjing huanggong.* Peking: Zijincheng, 1987.

Qingchao yeshi daguan. 1936. Reprint, Shanghai: Shanghai shuju, 1986.

Qingdai dang'an shiliao congbian. Vol. 11. Peking: Zhonghua, 1982.

Rawski, Evelyn S. *The Last Emperors: A Social History of Qing Imperial Institutions.* Berkeley: University of California Press, 1998.

Rockhill, W. W. "The Dalai Lamas of Lhasa and Their Relations with the Manchu Emperors of China." *T'oung Pao* 11 (1910): 1–104.

Rosen, Sydney. "In Search of the Historical Kuan Chung." *Journal of Asian Studies* 35, no. 3 (May 1976): 431–40.

Rossabi, Morris. *The Jurchens in the Yüan and Ming.* Ithaca: Cornell University, China-Japan Program, 1982.

———. "Muslim and Central Asian Revolts." In J. D. Spence and J. E. Wills Jr., eds., *From Ming to Ch'ing: Conquest, Region, and Continuity in Seventeenth-Century China*. New Haven: Yale University Press, 1979.

Roth [Li], Gertraude. "The Manchu-Chinese Relationship." In J. D. Spence and J. E. Wills Jr., eds., *From Ming to Ch'ing: Conquest, Region, and Continuity in Seventeenth-Century China*. New Haven: Yale University Press, 1979.

———. "The Rise of the Early Manchu State: A Portrait Drawn from Manchu Sources to 1636." Ph.D. diss., Harvard University, 1975.

Rozycki, William. *Mongol Elements in Manchu*. Bloomington: Indiana University Research Institute for Inner Asian Studies, 1994.

Rule, Paul. "Traditional Kingship in China." In Ian Mabbett, ed., *Patterns of Kingship and Authority in Traditional Asia*, London: Croom Helm, 1985.

Sa Zhaowei. "Wei Menggu zu hua de semu shiren Sadouri." *Beijing shehui kexue* 1 (1997): 86–91.

Sagaster, Klaus. *Die Weisse Geschichte: Eine mongolische Quelle zur Lehre von den beiden Ordnungen Religion und Staat in Tibet und der Mongolei*. Wiesbaden: Otto Harrassowitz, 1976.

Samuel, Geoffrey. *Civilized Shamans: Buddhism in Tibetan Societies*. Washington, D.C.: Smithsonian Institution Press, 1993.

Santangelo, Paolo. "'Chinese and Barbarians' in Gu Yanwu's Thought." In *Collected Papers of the Thirty-ninth Congress of Chinese Studies*. Tübingen, 1988, pp. 183–99.

Sayingge. "Jilin waiji." In Li Shutian, ed., *Changbai congshu*, Vol. 1. Jilin: Jilin shifan xueyuan, guji yanjiu suo, 1986.

Schneider, Laurence A. "National Essence and the New Intelligentsia." In Charlotte Furth, ed., *The Limits of Change: Essays on Conservative Alternatives in Republican China*. Cambridge, Mass.: Harvard University Press, 1976.

Serruys, Henry. *The Mongols and Ming China: Customs and History*. Ed. Françoise Aubin. London: Variorum Reprints, 1987.

———. "A Note on Arrows and Oaths among the Mongols." *Journal of the American Oriental Society* 78 (1958): 279–94. Also in Serruys, *The Mongols and Ming China*.

———. "Remains of Mongol Customs in China during the Early Ming." *Monumenta Serica* 16 (1957): 137–90. Also in Serruys, *The Mongols and Ming China*.

———. "Pei-lou Fong-sou: Les Coutumes des Esclaves Septentrionaux de Siao Ta-heng." *Monumenta serica* 19 (1945): 117–64. Also in Serruys, *The Mongols and Ming China*.

———. *Sino-Jürched Relations in the Yung-lo Period (1403–1424)*. Wiesbaden, 1955.

———. "Yellow Hairs and Red Hats in Mongolia." *Central Asiatic Journal* 15, no. 2 (1971): 131–55.

Shavkunov, Ernst Vladimirovich. *Gosudarstvo Bokhai i pamyatniki ego kulturi v primor'e*. Moscow: Nauka, 1968.

Shen Xu et al. *Qing ru guan qian shiliao xunji* 1. Peking: Zhongguo renmin daxue, 1984.

Shepherd, John R. *Statecraft and Political Economy on the Taiwan Frontier, 1600–1800*. Stanford: Stanford University Press, 1993.

Shimada Kenji. *Daigaku • Chū yō*. 2 vols. Tokyo: Asahi shimbun, 1978.

———. *Pioneer of the Chinese Revolution: Zhang Binglin and Confucianism*. Trans. Joshua A. Fogel. Stanford: Stanford University Press, 1990.

Shin Chung-il [Shen Zhongyi]. *Kōnju jichōng dorok*. Taipei: Tailian guofeng, 1971 (photo reprint of 1597 original).

———. *Kōnju jichōng dorok xiaozhu*. Ed. Xu Huanpu. Shenyang: Liaoning daxue lishi xi, 1979.

Shin, Tim Sung Wook. "The Concepts of State (*kuo-chia*) and People (*min*) in the Late Ch'ing, 1890–1907: The Case of Liang Ch'i-ch'ao, T'an Ssu-tu'ung, and Huang Tsun-hsien." Ph.D. diss., University of California, Berkeley, 1980.

Shirokogoroff, Sergei Mikhailovitch. *Social Organization of the Manchus: A Study of the Manchu Clan Organization*. Shanghai: Royal Asiatic Society, North China Branch, 1924.

Siikala, Anna-Leena, and Hoppál, Mihály. Studies on Shamanism. Helskinki: Finnish Anthropological Society; Budapest: Akadémiai Kiadō, 1992.

Sinor, Denis. "The Inner Asian Warriors." *Journal of the American Oriental Society*, 101, no. 2 (April–June 1981): 133–44.

Smith, Anthony D. *The Ethnic Revival*. Cambridge: Cambridge University Press, 1981.

Snellgrove, D. A. "The Notion of Divine Kingship in Tantric Buddhism." In *The Sacral Kingship*. Leiden, 1959.

Snellgrove, D. A., and Hugh Richardson. *A Cultural History of Tibet*. 2d Ed. Boston: Shambala, 1995 (originally published London: Weidenfeld and Nicholson, 1968).

Sollors, Werner. *Beyond Ethnicity: Consent and Descent in American Culture*. New York: Oxford University Press, 1986.

Spence, Jonathan D. *Emperor of China: Self-Portrait of K'ang-hsi*. New York: Knopf, 1974.

———. *Ts'ao Yin and the K'ang-hsi Emperor: Bondservant and Master*. New Haven: Yale University Press, 1966.

Spence, Jonathan D., and John E. Wills, Jr., eds. *From Ming to Ch'ing*. New Haven: Yale University Press, 1979.

Stanford's Geographical Establishment. *Stanford's Map of China and Japan*. London: Edward Stanford, 1911.

Stary, Giovanni. *China's ërste Gesandte in Rußland*. Wiesbaden, 1976.

———. "The Manchu Emperor 'Abahai': Analysis of an Historiographic Mistake." *Central Asiatic Journal* 28, no. 3–4 (1984): 296–99 (originally published in *Cina* [China] 18 [1982]: 157–62).

———. "Mandschurische Miszellen." In Michael Weiers and Giovanni Stary, eds., *Asiatische Forschungen, Band 80, Florilegia Manjurica.* Wiesbaden: Otto Harrassowitz, 1982.

———. "A New Subdivision of Manchu Literature: Some Proposals." *Central Asiatic Journal* 31, no. 3–4 (1987): 287–96.

———. "'L'Ode di Mukden' dell'imperator Ch'ien-lung: Nuovi spunti per un analisi della tecnica versificatoria mancese." *Cina* 17 (1981): 235–51.

———. "Die Struktur der Ersten Residenz des Mandschukans Nurgaci." *Central Asiatic Journal* 25 (1985): 103–9.

Struve, Lynn. "Huang Zongxi in Context: A Reappraisal of His Major Writings." *Journal of Asian Studies* 47, no. 3 (1988): 474–502.

———. *The Southern Ming, 1644–1662.* New Haven: Yale University Press, 1984.

Sudō Yoshiyuki. "Shinchō ni okeru Manshū chūbō no toku shusei ni kansuru ichi kō satsu." *Tōhoku gakuhō* 11, no. 1 (1959): 176–203.

Sun Hui-wen [Sun Huiwen]. *Liang Qichao de minquan yu junxing sixiang.* Taiwan: National Taiwan University (Guoli Taiwan Daxue, Wenxue yuan), 1966.

Sun, Warren. "Chang Ping-lin and His Political Thought." *Papers on Far Eastern History* 32 (1985): 57–69.

Sun Wenliang. *Nurhachi pingzhuan.* Shenyang: Liaoning daxue, 1985.

Sun Wenliang and Li Zhiting. *Qing Taizong quanzhuan.* Changchun: Jilin wenshi Chubanshe, 1983.

Sun Zhentao et al. *Erchen zhuan* [undated colophon]. Guoshi guan shanben, 1785.

Sungyun. *Emu tanggū orin sakda-i gisun sarkiyan, Bai er lao ren yulu.* Taipei: Chinese Materials Center, 1982 (reprint of 1791? original).

Tambiah, Stanley J. *Culture, Thought, and Social Action.* Cambridge Mass.: Harvard University Press, 1985.

Tamura Jitsuzo et al. *Kotai Shimbun kan yakukai.* Kyoto: Kyoto University, 1966.

Tan Yi. "Wan Qing Tongwen guan yu jindai xuexiao jiaoyu." *Qingshi yanjiu ji* 5 (1984): 344–61.

Tang Xiaobing. *Global Space and the Nationalist Discourse of Modernity.* Stanford: Stanford University Press, 1996.

Tang Zhiyun, ed. *Zhang Taiyan nianpu changbian.* 2 vols. Peking: Zhonghua, 1979.

Tang Zhiyun and Benjamin Elman. "The 1898 Reforms Revisited." *Late Imperial China* 8, no. 1 (June 1987): 205–13.

Tao Jingshen. *The Jurchens in Twelfth-Century China.* Seattle: University of Washington Press, 1976.

Taylor, Romeyn. "Rulership in Late Imperial Chinese Orthodoxy." Paper presented at Absolutism and Despotism Conference, University of Minnesota, Minneapolis, October 27, 1989.

Teng, Ssu-yü. *Historiography of the Taiping Rebellion.* Cambridge, Mass.: Harvard University East Asian Research Center, 1972.

Thapar, Romila. *A History of India.* Vol. 1. London: Pelican, 1966.

Thomas, Nicholas, and Caroline Humphrey, eds. *Shamanism, History, and the State.* Ann Arbor: University of Michigan Press, 1996.

Tieliang et al. *[Qinding] Baqi tongzhi.* 1799 (reprinted Taipei, 1966).

Tikhvinsky, S. L., ed. *Chapters from the History of Russo-Chinese Relations, Seventeenth–Nineteenth Centuries.* Trans. V. Schneierson. Moscow: Progress, 1985.

———. *Manzhou Rule in China.* Trans. V. Schneierson. Moscow: Progress, 1983.

Tillman, Hoyt. "One Significant Rise in Chu-ko Liang's Popularity: An Impact of the 1127 Jurchen Conquest." *Hanxue yanjiu* 14, no. 2 (December 1996): 1–38.

Togan, Isenbike. *Flexibility and Limitations in Steppe Formations: The Kerait Khanate and Chinggis Khan.* Leiden: E. J. Brill, 1998.

Torbert, Preston M. *The Ch'ing Imperial Household Department: A Study of Its Organization and Principal Functions, 1662–1796.* Cambridge, Mass.: Harvard University East Asian Monographs, 1977.

Tu, Wei-ming. *Centrality and Commonality: An Essay on Confucian Religiousness.* Albany: State University of New York Press, 1989.

Tucci, Giuseppe. *The Religions of Tibet.* Trans. Geoffrey Samuel. Berkeley: University of California Press, 1988. Originally published as *Die Religionen Tibets und der Mongolei* by Giuseppe Tucci and Walther Heisseg. Stuttgart: W. Kohlhammer, 1970.

Tulišen. *Lakcaha jecen de takōraha babe ejehe bithei, Man Han Yi yü lu jiaozhu.* Trans. Chuang Chi-fa. Taipei: Wen Shi Zhe, 1983.

Turan, Osman. "The Ideal of World Domination among the Ancient Turks." *Studia Islamica* 4 (1955): 77–90.

Turner, Jane, ed. *The Dictionary of Art.* London: Macmillan/Grove, 1996.

Ubingga, Li Wengang, Yu Zhixian, and Jin Tianyi. *Manzu minjian gushi xuan.* Shanghai: Wenyi chubanshe, 1982–83.

Ulaghan Ulan. "'Menggu yuanliu' de liu chuan ji qi yanjiu." *Menggu xue xinxi* 1 (1997): 20–25.

van der Sprenkel, Sybille. *Legal Institutions in Manchu China.* London: Athlone Press, 1962.

Vorob'ev, M. V. *Chzhurchzheni i gosudarstvo Czin' (X v.–1234 g.). Istoricheskii Ocherk.* Moscow, 1975.

Wagner, Edward Willett. *The Literati Purges: Political Conflict in Early Yi Korea.* Cambridge, Mass.: East Asian Research Center, 1974.

Wakeman, Frederic, Jr. *The Great Enterprise: The Manchu Reconstruction of Imperial Order in Seventeenth-Century China.* Berkeley: University of California Press, 1985.

———. "Localism and Loyalism during the Ch'ing Conquest of Kiangnan: The Tragedy of Chiang-yin." In Frederic Wakeman, Jr., and Carolyn Grant, eds., *Conflict and Control in Late Imperial China.* Berkeley: University of California Press, 1975.

Waley-Cohen, Joanna. "Commemorating War in Eighteenth-Century China." *Modern Asian Studies* 30, no. 4 (1996): 869–99.

———. *Exile in Mid-Qing China: Banishment to Xinjiang, 1758–1820.* New Haven: Yale University Press, 1991.

Wang, Chen-main. "Historical Revisionism in Ch'ing Times: The Case of Hung Ch'eng-ch'ou (1593–1665)." *Bulletin of the Chinese Historical Association* 17 (1985): 1–27.

Wang Dezhao. "Qingdai keju rushi yu zhengfu." *Xianggang Zhongwen daxue Zhongguo wenhua yanjiusuo xuebao* 12 (1981): 1–21.

Wang Longyi and Shen Binhua. "Menggu zu lishi renkou chucao (shiqi shiji zhongye—ershi shiji zhong ye)" *Nei Menggu daxue xuebao* 2 (1997): 30–41.

Wang Tiangen and Li Guoliang. *Sishu baihua jujie.* Taipei: Wenhua shuju, 1944.

Wang Xiuchou [Wang Hsiu-ch'u]. "A Memoir of a Ten Day's Massacre in Yangzhow." Trans. L. Mao. *T'ien-hsia Monthly* 4, no. 5 (1936): 515–37.

Wang, Y. C. "The Su-pao Case: A Study of Foreign Pressure, Intellectual Fermentation, and Dynastic Decline." *Monumenta Serica* 24 (1965): 84–129.

Wang Zhonghan, ed. *Chaoxian Lichao shilu zhong de nüzhen shiliao xuanpian.* Shenyang: Liaoning Renmin daxue, 1979.

———. *Manzu shi yanjiu ji.* Peking: Zhongguo shehui kexue, 1988.

Wang Zongyan. *Du Qingshi gao za ji.* Hong Kong: Zhonghua, 1977.

Weber, Jürgen. *Revolution und Tradition: Politik in Leben des Gelehrten Chang Ping-lin (1865–1936) bis zum Jahre 1906.* Hamburg, 1986.

Wechsler, Howard J. *Mirror to the Son of Heaven: Wei Cheng at the Court of T'ang T'ai-ts'ung.* New Haven: Yale University Press, 1974.

Wei Qingyuan, Wu Qiheng, and Lu Su. *Qingdai nupei zhidu.* Peking: Zhongguo renmin daxue, 1982.

Weiers, Michael, ed. *Die Mongolen Beiträge zu ihrer Geschichte und Kultur.* Darmstadt: Wissenschaftliche Buchgesellschaft, 1986.

Weiers, Michael, and Giovanni Stary, eds. *Florilegia Manjurica in memoriam Walter Fuchs.* Weisbaden: Otto Harrassowitz, 1982.

Wiens, Mi-chu. "Anti-Manchu Thought during the Ch'ing." *Papers on China* 22A (1969): 1–24.

Wilhelm, Hellmut. "A Note on the Migration of the Uriangkhai." *Studia Altaica* 1957: 172–76.

———. "On Ming Orthodoxy." *Monumenta Serica* 29 (1970–71): 1–26.

Wills, John E., Jr. "Maritime China from Wang Chih to Shih Lang: Themes in Peripheral History." In Jonathan D. Spence and J. E. Wills Jr., eds., *From Ming to Ch'ing.* New Haven: Yale University Press, 1979.

———. *Pepper, Guns, and Parleys: The Dutch East India Company and China, 1662–1690.* Cambridge, Mass.: Harvard University Press, 1974.

Wilson, Thomas A. *Genealogy of the Way: The Construction and Uses of the Confucian Tradition in Late Imperial China.* Stanford: Stanford University Press, 1995.

Wittfogel, Karl A., and Feng Chia-shêng. *History of Chinese Society: Liao.* Philadelphia: American Philosophical Society, 1949.

Wong, Young-tsu. "Chang Ping-lin and the Rising Chinese Revolutionary Movement, 1900–1905." *Bulletin of the Institute of Modern History, Academia Sinica* 12 (1983): 219–47.

———. *Search for Modern Nationalism: Zhang Binglin and Revolutionary China, 1869–1936.* Hong Kong: Oxford University Press, 1989.

Woodruff, Phillip H. "Foreign Policy and Frontier Affairs along the Northeastern Frontier of the Ming Dynasty, 1350–1618: Tripartite Relations of the Ming Chinese, Korean Koryo, and Jurchen-Manchu Tribesmen." Ph.D. diss., University of Chicago, 1996.

Woodside, Alexander. "Emperors and the Chinese Political System." Paper presented at the Four Anniversaries China Conference, Annapolis, Md., September 1989.

———. "Some Mid-Qing Theorists of Popular Schools: Their Innovations, Inhibitions, and Attitudes toward the Poor." *Modern China* 9, no. 1 (1983): 3–35.

Wright, Mary Clabaugh. *The Last Stand of Chinese Conservatism: The T'ung-chih Restoration, 1862–1874.* Stanford: Stanford University Press, 1957.

Wright, Mary Clabaugh., ed. *China in Revolution: The First Phase, 1900–1913.* New Haven: Yale University Press, 1968.

Wu Che-fu [Wu Zhefu]. *Siku quanshu xuanxiu zhi yanjiu.* Taipei: Wensheng ciye, 1990.

Wu Han. "Guanyu Dongbei shi shang yiwei guaijie xin shiliao." *Yanjing xuebao* 10, no. 7 (June 1935): 59–87.

Wu Hung. "Emperor's Masquerade—'Costume Portraits' of Yongzheng and Qianlong." *Orientations* 26, no. 7 (1993): 24–41.

———. *Monumentality in Early Chinese Art and Architecture.* Stanford: Stanford University Press, 1995.

Wu, Silas. *Passage to Power: K'ang-hsi and His Heir Apparent, 1661–1722.* Harvard University East Asian Series, no. 91. Cambridge, Mass.: Harvard University Press, 1979.

Wu ti Qingwen jian. Peking: Minzu, 1957 (photo reprint of Qianlong-period original).

Wu Yuanfeng and Zhao Zhiqiang. "Xibo zu you Kharqin Menggu qi bianru Manzhou baqi shimo." *Minzu yanjiu* 5 (1984): 60–55.

Wylie, Alexander. *Translation of the Ts'ing Wan K'e Mung.* Shanghai: London Mission Press, 1855.

Xu Duanmen. "Dongyuan jilin Xiyuan yin." *Lishi dang'an* 2 (1987): 80–85.

Xu Zengzhong. "Zeng Jing fan Qing an yu Qing Shizong Yizheng tongzhe quanguo de da zheng fangzhen." *Qingshi luncong* 5 (1984): 158–78.

Xu Zhongshu [Hsü Chung-shu]. "Mingchu Jianzhou nuzhen ju di qian tu kao." *Academia Sinica, Bulletin of the Institute of History and Philology* 6, no. 2 (1936): 163–92.

Yan Chongnian. *Nurhachi zhuan.* Peking: Beijing chubanshi, 1983.

Yanai Watari. *Wulianghai ji dadan kao.* Translation of 1914 original, *Orankai sanei meisho kō.*

Yang Boda. "Castiglione and the Qing Court—An Important Artistic Contribution." *Orientations* 3 (November 1988): 44–60.

Yang Buxi et al. *Yilanxian zhi.* Yilan, 1920.

Yang Li-ch'eng [Yang Licheng]. *Siku mulue.* Taipei: Zhonghua shuju, 1969.

Yang Lien-sheng. "The Organization of Chinese Offical Historiography." In W. G. Beasley and E. G. Pulleyblank, eds., *Historians of China and Japan.* London: Oxford University Press, 1961.

Yang Minghong. "Lun Qingdai Lengshan Yi qu de tusi zhidu yu gaitu guiliu." *Minzu yanjiu* 1 (1997): 88–95.

Yang Qijiao. *Yongzheng di ji qi mizhe zhidu yanjiu.* Hong Kong: Sanlian, 1981.

Yang Xuechen and Zhou Yuanlian. *Qingdai baqi wanggong guizu xingxhuai shi.* Shenyang: Liaoning renmin, 1986.

Yang Yang, Sun Yuchang, and Zhang Ke. "Mingdai liuren zai Dongbei." *Lishi yanjiu* 4 (1985): 54–88.

Yang Yang, Yuan Lukun, Fu Langyun. *Mingdai Nurgan dusi ji qi weisuo yanjiu.* Zhumazhen (Henan): Zhongzhou shuhuashe, 1981.

Yang Yulian. "Mingdai houqi de Liaodong mashi yu Nuzhen zu de xingqi." *Minzu yanjiu* 5 (1980): 27–32.

Yang Zhen. *Kangxi huangdi yijia.* Peking: Xueyuan, 1994.

Ye Xianggao. *Siyi kao.* Taipei: Wenhua, n.d. (photo reprint of Chongzhen-period original; published with Mao Ruizheng, *Huang Ming xiangxu lu;* ed. Wang Yu-li [Wang Youli]).

Yinzhen [Qing Shizong]. *Dayi juemi lu.* Photo reprint in Jindai Zhongguo shiao congkan series, ed. Shen Yün-lung [Shen Yunlong]. Taipei: Wenhai, 1966.

Young, Robert C. *Colonial Desire: Hybridity in Theory, Culture, and Race.* London: Routledge, 1995.

———. *White Mythologies: Writing History and the West.* London: Routledge, 1990.

Yu Yue. "Du Wang shi pai shu." In *Yu lou ji juan.* Box 6, *ce* 46, *juan* 28.

Zelin, Madeleine. *The Magistrate's Tael: Rationalizing Fiscal Reform in Eighteenth-Century China.* Berkeley: University of California Press, 1984.

Zhang Binglin. "Qin zheng ji." In Liu Zongyuan et al., *Lun Qin shihuang.* Shanghai: Renmin, 1974.

Zhang Binglin and Tang Zhiyun, eds. *Zhang Taiyan nianpu changbian (1868–1918); (1919–1936).* 2 vols. Peking: Zhonghua shuju, 1979.

Zhang Bofeng. *Qingdai gedi jiangjun dutong dachen deng nianbiao, 1796–1911.* Peking: Zhonghua shuju, 1977.

Zhang Jinfan and Guo Chengkang. *Qing ru guan qian guojia falu zhidu shi.* Shenyang: Liaoning renmin, 1988.

Zhang Kaiyuan. "'Jufen jinhua lun' de youhuan yizhi." *Lishi yanjiu* (Historical Studies) 5 (1989): 113–22.

———. "Xinhai geming shi yanjiu zhong de jige wenti." *Lishi yanjiu* 4 (1981): 53–58.

Zhang Shucai. "Zai tan Cao Fu zui zhi yuanyin ji Cao jia zhi qi jie." *Lishi dang'an* 2-80–88.

Zhang Yuxing. "Fan Wencheng gui Qing kaobian." In *Qingshi luncong* 6. Peking: Zhonghua.

Zhang Zhongru et al. *Qingdai kaoshi zhidu ciliao.* N.d. (photo reprint, Taipei: Wenhai, 1968).

Zhao Erxun. *Manzhou mingchen zhuan.* 1928 (reprint, Taipei: Tailian Guofang, n.d.).

Zhao Erxun et al. *Qingshi gao.* 1928 (punctuated reprint, Peking: Zhonghua shuju, 1977).

Zhao Yuntian. *Qingdai Menggu zhengzhi zhidu.* Peking: Zhonghua shuju, 1989.

Zhou Yuanlian. "Guanyu baqi zhidu de jige wenti." *Qingshi luncong* 3 (1982): 140–54.

———. *Qingchao kaiguo shi yanjiu.* Shenyang: Liaoning renmin, 1981.

Zhu Chengru. "Qing ru guan qian hou Liao Shen diqu de Man (Nuzhen) Han renkou jiaoliu." In Bai Shouyi, ed., *Qingshi guoji xueshu taolun hui.* Shenyang: Liaoning renmin, 1990, pp. 74–86.

Zhu Jiajin. "Castiglione's *Tieluo* Paintings." *Orientations* 3 (November 1988): 80–83.

Zhu Xizu. *Hou Jin guohan xingshi kao.* 1932.

Zito, Angela Rose. *Of Body and Brush: Grand Sacrifice as Text / Performance.* Chicago: University of Chicago Press, 1997.

Zürcher, E. *The Buddhist Conquest of China: The Spread and Adaptation of Buddhism in Medieval China.* Leiden: E. J. Brill, 1959.

Abbreviations

BMST	*Baqi manzhou shizu tongpu*
DJL	*Dayi juemi lu*
DMB	Goodrich and Fang, *Dictionary of Ming Biography*
ECCP	Hummel et al., *Eminent Chinese of the Ch'ing Period*
KF	*[Huang Qing] Kaiguo fanglue*
KJD	Shin, *Kŏnju jichŏng dorok*
JMD	*Jiu manzhou dang*
JS	*Jin shi*
MR	*Mambun rōtō*
MSOS	*Mitteilungen des Seminars für Orientalische Sprachen*
MY	*Minzu Yanjiu*
MYK	*Manzhou yuanliu kao*
QKZC	Zhang Zhongru et al., *Qingdai kaoshi zhidu ciliao*
QSG	*Qingshi gao*
TC	Tiancong reign
TM	*Tianming*
XZ	*Xiaoting zalu*

Index

Design:	Margery Cantor
Text:	10/13 Aldus
Display:	Strayhorn and Aldus
Composition:	G & S Typesetters, Inc.
Printing and binding:	Thomson-Shore, Inc.